BORDERS AND CONFLICT

The potential for peace among established, stable democracies is evident in this map, as are the ravages of colonialism. The dominance of democracy is also clear, though Russia alone is enough to remind us to consider that "trend" with some caution. We can also see how tenuous and conflict-prone transitional governments can be, as well as how contentious borders remain.

MAIN MAP KEY

Types of government

- Multiparty democracy for more than 10 yrs
- Multiparty democracy within last 10 yrs
- Single-party government
- Military regime
- Theocracy
- Monarchy
- Non-party system
- Transitional regime

Conflicts and international disputes

- Major active territorial or border disputes
- Countries involved in internal conflict
- Active territorial or border disputes and internal conflict

▲ Dates from which current boundaries have existed

- 1990–present
- 1966–1989
- 1946–1965
- 1915–1945
- 1850–1914
- 1800–1849
- Pre-1800

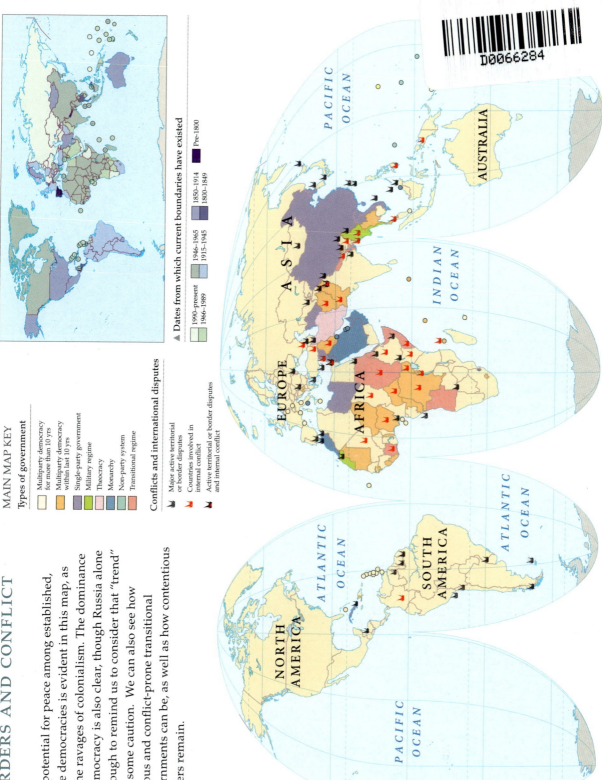

NORTH AMERICA

SOUTH AMERICA

EUROPE

ASIA

AFRICA

AUSTRALIA

PACIFIC OCEAN

ATLANTIC OCEAN

ATLANTIC OCEAN

INDIAN OCEAN

PACIFIC OCEAN

ATLANTIC OCEAN

ECONOMIC SYSTEMS

As evident as globalization and interdependence are in this map, so too are the discrepancies in wealth and international financial relationships. Note the disparities in GDP and the sources and endpoints of the various arrows representing foreign direct investment (see Chapters 9 and 10).

Gross Domestic Product (GDP*)
(nominal per capita US$)

- 40,001–90,000
- 10,001–40,000
- 6251–10,000
- 2501–6250
- 1501–2500
- 501–1500
- 251–500
- 0–250
- data unavailable

*Gross Domestic Product (GDP) is defined as the total market value of all final goods and services produced in a country.

Direct Investment

- from USA
- from Europe
- from Japan

- major stock exchange
- stock exchange

SOUTH AMERICA

NORTH AMERICA

New York

AFRICA

EUROPE

London

ASIA

Tokyo

AUSTRALIA

HEALTH

This map illustrates that people living in the developed world have a higher life expectancy on average than those in the developing world. At almost every stage of life, people in developing countries are more susceptible to health problems than those in richer ones, because poverty, limited access to health care and medication, malnutrition, and poor sanitation contribute to the spread of infectious disease (see Chapter 11).

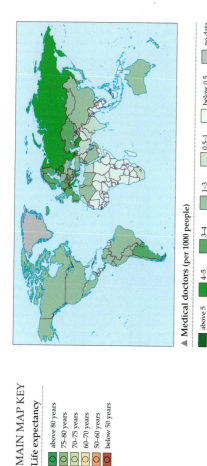

MAIN MAP KEY

Life expectancy

- above 80 years
- 75–80 years
- 70–75 years
- 60–70 years
- 50–60 years
- below 50 years

▲ Medical doctors (per 1000 people)

- above 5
- 4–5
- 3–4
- 1–3
- 0.5–1
- below 0.5
- no data

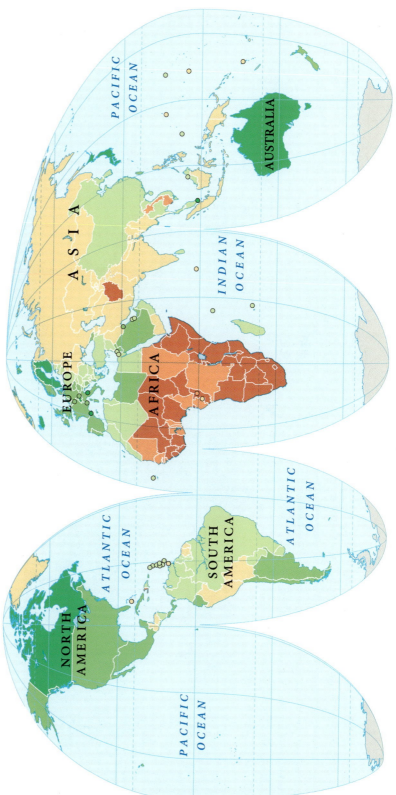

PACIFIC OCEAN

ASIA

EUROPE

AFRICA

INDIAN OCEAN

AUSTRALIA

ATLANTIC OCEAN

NORTH AMERICA

SOUTH AMERICA

ATLANTIC OCEAN

PACIFIC OCEAN

TRAVEL AND COMMUNICATIONS

In an era of globalization, more people are on the move, able to travel and communicate across long distances. As this map shows, however, the patterns of travel and communication vary in different parts of the world. People in the industrialized world travel for business and vacation; people in the developing world usually migrate in search of jobs.

Global transportation

- ········· major road
- ——— major rail

Airline passenger volume
passengers per year

- more than 2 million
- 1.5–2 million
- 1–1.5 million
- 0.75–1 million
- 0.5–0.75 million
- ● major airport

AFRICA

EUROPE

ASIA

AUSTRALIA

NORTH AMERICA

SOUTH AMERICA

Madrid
Paris
London
Frankfurt
Amsterdam

New York
Philadelphia
Miami
Toronto
Detroit
Chicago
Atlanta
Orlando
Minneapolis
Dallas
Houston
Denver
Las Vegas
Phoenix
Seattle
San Francisco
Los Angeles

Beijing
Bangkok
Hong Kong
Tokyo
Singapore

POPULATION

By 2050, the current world population of more than 6.7 billion people is projected to increase to 9.2 billion.

96 percent of the projected growth will occur in the developing states, where medical advances such as vaccinations have reduced death rates, even as birth rates remain high. Concurrent with this trend is the "graying" of industrialized countries where birth rates have fallen dramatically, leading to older populations (see Chapter 11).

MAIN MAP KEY

Population density
(persons per sq mile)

- 77–390
- 39–77
- 19–39
- 7–19
- 4–7
- 2–4
- 0.5–2
- 0–0.5

▲ Population growth rate (annual % change)

- above 4%
- 3 to 4%
- 2 to 3%
- 1 to 2%
- 0 to 1%
- -1 to 0%

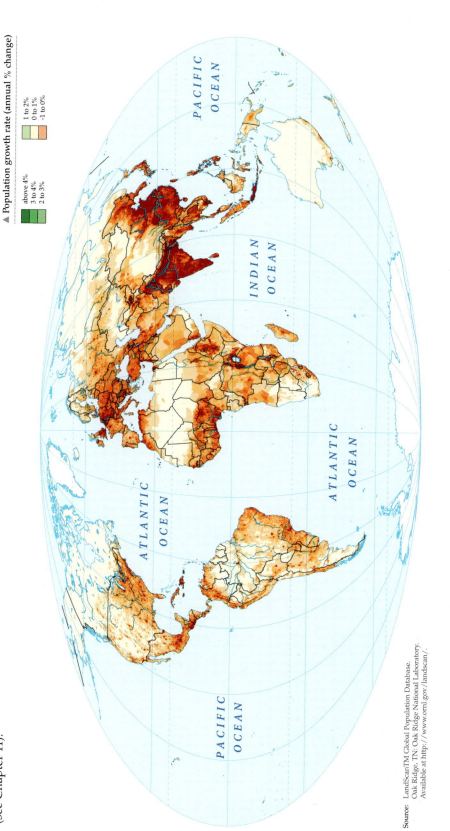

Source: LandScan™ Global Population Database.
Oak Ridge, TN: Oak Ridge National Laboratory.
Available at http://www.ornl.gov/landscan/.

WATER RESOURCES

Today, over a billion people lack clean water, and approximately 2.5 billion live without adequate sanitation (see Chapter 12). Access to safe water is related to a population's health—nearly 80 percent of all cases of disease have been linked to contaminated water. Moreover, the depletion of water has already begun to lead to conflict within and between states.

MAIN MAP KEY

Availability of fresh water
total renewable
(cubic yards/capita/per year)

- less than 1300 (water scarcity)
- 1300–2222 (water stress)
- 2222–3922 (insufficient water)
- 3922–13,078 (relatively sufficient)
- 13,078 or more (plentiful supplies)

major drainage basin

▼ over 50% of water resource originating from outside country

▲ Access to safe drinking water source
(percentage of population)

- 91%–100%
- 76%–90%
- 50%–75%
- below 50%
- no data

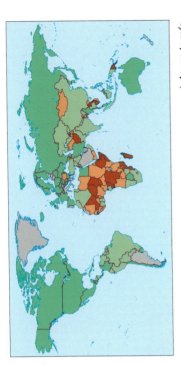

PEOPLE AND THE ENVIRONMENT

The human causes of environmental degradation are usually local, but global in effect, such as deforestation in the Amazon (the conversion of forested land for other uses, such as cropland, or urban and industrial use) and the burning of fossil fuels in Chinese factories and on American highways. For the global public good, solutions must be found, but local politics may stymie such efforts (see Chapter 12).

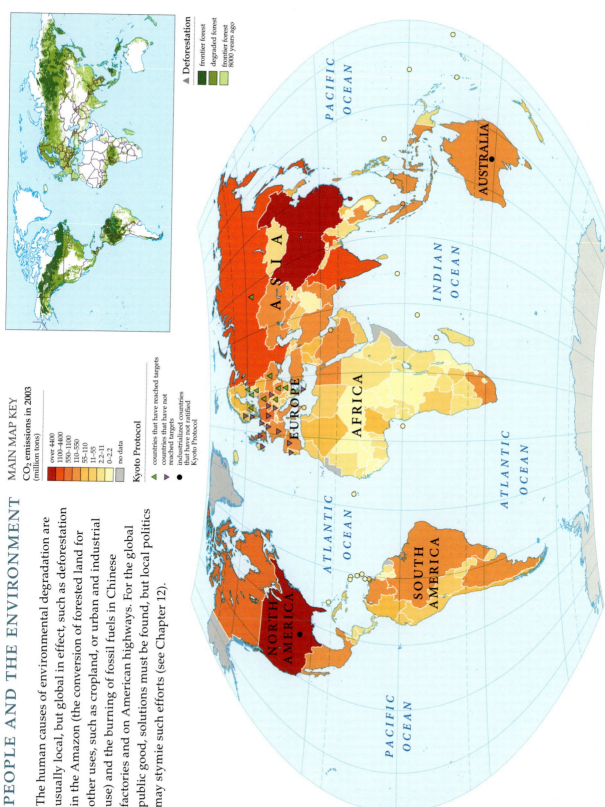

MAIN MAP KEY

CO₂ emissions in 2003 (million tons)

- over 4400
- 1100–4400
- 550–1100
- 110–550
- 55–110
- 11–55
- 2.2–11
- 0–2.2
- no data

Kyoto Protocol

- ◢ countries that have reached targets
- ◢ countries that have not reached targets
- ● industrialized countries that have not ratified Kyoto Protocol

▲ Deforestation

- frontier forest
- degraded forest
- frontier forest 8000 years ago

ASIA

EUROPE

AFRICA

AUSTRALIA

NORTH AMERICA

SOUTH AMERICA

PACIFIC OCEAN

INDIAN OCEAN

ATLANTIC OCEAN

ATLANTIC OCEAN

PACIFIC OCEAN

LANGUAGE

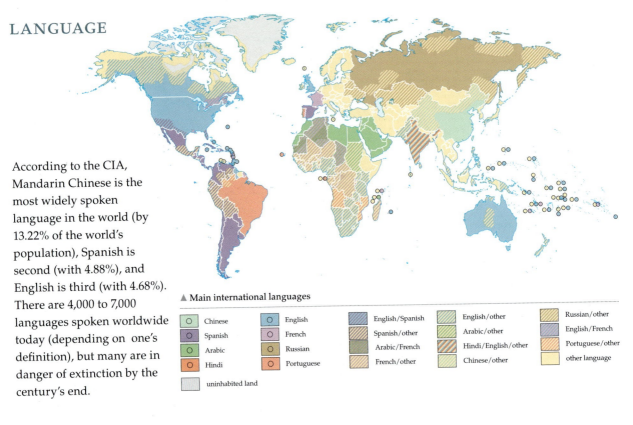

According to the CIA, Mandarin Chinese is the most widely spoken language in the world (by 13.22% of the world's population), Spanish is second (with 4.88%), and English is third (with 4.68%). There are 4,000 to 7,000 languages spoken worldwide today (depending on one's definition), but many are in danger of extinction by the century's end.

▲ Main international languages

○ Chinese	○ English
○ Spanish	○ French
○ Arabic	○ Russian
○ Hindi	○ Portuguese
uninhabited land	

English/Spanish · Spanish/other · Arabic/French · French/other · English/other · Arabic/other · Hindi/English/other · Chinese/other · Russian/other · English/French · Portuguese/other · other language

RELIGION

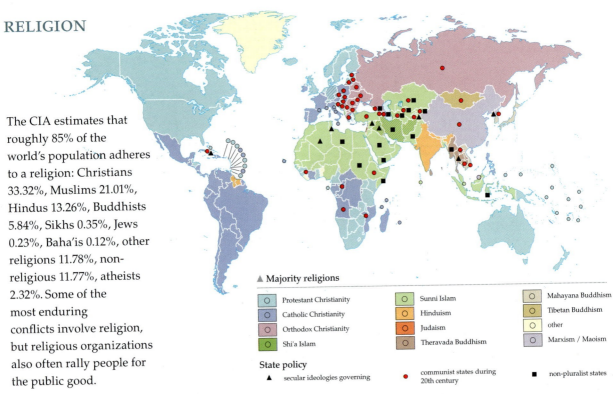

The CIA estimates that roughly 85% of the world's population adheres to a religion: Christians 33.32%, Muslims 21.01%, Hindus 13.26%, Buddhists 5.84%, Sikhs 0.35%, Jews 0.23%, Baha'is 0.12%, other religions 11.78%, non-religious 11.77%, atheists 2.32%. Some of the most enduring conflicts involve religion, but religious organizations also often rally people for the public good.

▲ Majority religions

○ Protestant Christianity	○ Sunni Islam	○ Mahayana Buddhism
○ Catholic Christianity	○ Hinduism	○ Tibetan Buddhism
○ Orthodox Christianity	○ Judaism	○ other
○ Shi'a Islam	○ Theravada Buddhism	○ Marxism / Maoism

State policy

▲ secular ideologies governing　　● communist states during 20th century　　■ non-pluralist states

WORLD POLITICS
IN A NEW ERA

WORLD POLITICS
IN A NEW ERA

■ **FIFTH EDITION** ■

Steven L. Spiegel
University of California, Los Angeles

Elizabeth G. Matthews
California State University San Marcos

Jennifer M. Taw
Claremont McKenna College

Kristen P. Williams
Clark University

Oxford   New York

OXFORD UNIVERSITY PRESS

Oxford University Press, Inc., publishes works that further Oxford University's
objective of excellence in research, scholarship, and education.

Oxford New York
Auckland Cape Town Dar es Salaam Hong Kong Karachi
Kuala Lumpur Madrid Melbourne Mexico City Nairobi
New Delhi Shanghai Taipei Toronto

With offices in
Argentina Austria Brazil Chile Czech Republic France Greece
Guatemala Hungary Italy Japan Poland Portugal Singapore
South Korea Switzerland Thailand Turkey Ukraine Vietnam

For titles covered by Section 112 of the U.S. Higher Education Opportunity Act,
please visit www.oup.com/us/he for the latest information about pricing
and alternate formats.

Published by Oxford University Press, Inc.
198 Madison Avenue, New York, New York 10016
http://www.oup.com

Oxford is a registered trademark of Oxford University Press

Library of Congress Cataloging-in-Publication Data

World politics in a new era/Steven L. Spiegel ... [et al.].—5th ed.
     p. cm.
Includes bibliographical references and index.
ISBN 978-0-19-976627-7
1. World politics. 2. Economic history. I. Spiegel, Steven L.
D217.S75 2009
327—dc22   2010045451

Printing number: 9 8 7 6 5 4 3 2

Printed in the United States of America
on acid-free paper

To my wife, Fredi, and our children,
Mira, Nina, and Avi
—SLS

To my mother and father
—EGM

To my husband, Steve, and our children,
Emily, Max, and Keenan
—JMT

To my husband, James, and our children,
Anne and Matthew
—KPW

Brief Contents

Contents

Chapter 4   **World Politics and Economics: The Cold War**   111

Chapter 6

Globalization and Fragmentation in a New World Order: 1991 to the Present

201

PART II   **THE MAJOR ISSUES IN WORLD POLITICS**   **237**

Chapter 11   **Human Issues: Demographic Trends**   427

Maps

Special Features

WHAT WOULD YOU DO?

AT A GLANCE

SPOTLIGHT

Preface

What Is the Nature of World Politics Now?

Students today live in an era of fragmentation in which the interests of individual nation-states have been challenged by the competing ideals of globalization. Essentially, globalization encourages greater movement and cooperation between countries. This global phenomenon blurs the line between domestic and international concerns—driving nations economically, socially, and politically towards integration and interdependence.

Globalization has both advantages and disadvantages. Take, for example, the 2008 recession in the United States, which quickly spread throughout Europe and became a global economic crisis. Most countries are beginning to experience a fragile recovery from the recession, but the consequences have been devastating and will be long-lasting. Issues of national security have also arisen, with European countries adjusting domestic policies to respond to the threats being posed by disaffected young Muslim immigrants. The resurgence of the Taliban in Afghanistan and rising civil strife in Pakistan present huge challenges in that region, compounded by a burgeoning narcotics trade. Al Qaeda continues its efforts to network with, fund, and mobilize terrorists around the globe.

The fifth edition of this book aims to reflect the changes for good and for ill that have occurred since the collapse of the Berlin Wall—a poignant example of globalization. Seeking to distinguish the time period by what it is rather than by what it is not, we have teased out the competing threads of globalization and fragmentation, examining how they tangle and weave through studies of global politics, economics, and culture, with their significance and effects boosted over the 1990s and 2000s by technological advances. By introducing these studies with theory and then supporting them with history, we have created a book that should serve as a comprehensive, contemporary, and thought-provoking text for introductory courses on world politics.

Organization

This volume is designed to provide students with the basic knowledge and skills needed to appreciate the full range of international politics in contemporary affairs.

This edition is divided into two parts. In the first half of the book, "Foundations of World Politics," we present the fundamental building blocks for comprehending international relations. We begin with an illustration of the complexity of international relations, specifically with an eye to the distinctions between cooperation and conflict, globalization and fragmentation, and order and anarchy. In Chapter 2 we review the theories of international relations and explain how they attempt to identify patterns amid the chaos of world politics. The remaining chapters in this first part cover political and economic history since the founding of the current international system in the Peace of Westphalia in 1648. We focus on historical eras from 1648 to the present, but reserve a chapter to consider, in particular, imperialism and its legacy (Chapter 5). When we move into the modern era, we look at the world since the end of the Cold War, the ramifications of 9/11, and the effect on international relations of a dominant United States.

In the second part of the book, "The Major Issues in World Politics," we break international relations into their components, focusing on security, economics, demography and resources, and international institutions. Chapters 7 and 8 present, respectively, security theories and the contemporary security issues that are at work in international politics, from nuclear deterrence to the extent and significance of terrorism. The next two chapters contend with economic issues at work in contemporary politics. Chapter 9, in addressing matters of trade and investment, handles issues that concern primarily the more developed countries and the established arenas of globalization in the international system. Chapter 10 introduces theories of development and discusses them in light of current practices and progress in the international system.

Chapters 11 and 12 deal with the broad cross-country issues that are affecting worldwide trends, such as population and migration on the one hand and energy and environment on the other.

Although this part begins in the security chapters with an emphasis on conflict, it moves in Chapter 13 to the study of international cooperation as represented by international law and organizations. Though a far cry from global governance, these international institutions both represent and facilitate cooperative relationships, communication, and mutual understanding

Finally, in Chapter 14 we close by highlighting the role of ethics in studies of international relations, placing the study of world politics into the broader context of political science, and then—coming full circle—positing the different futures that realists, liberals, and constructivists might anticipate, given their assumptions and beliefs.

New to This Edition

This fifth edition of *World Politics in a New Era* has been thoroughly updated. We have further integrated the discussion of theory across all of the chapters. We have raised constructivism's profile throughout the book as a paradigm on par with realism and liberalism. We have paid more attention to terrorism, counter-narcotics, and other contemporary security challenges and have also discussed the 2008–2009 recession and its effects on the global economy.

The introductory (Chapter 1) and concluding (Chapter 14) chapters continue to offer a context for the book as a whole, placing the examination of international relations and world politics within the larger realm of political science and global studies.

The theoretical chapter (2) examines the major theories studied in international relations. Whereas the last edition used DR-CAFTA as the illustration of each theoretical paradigm and level of analysis, this edition focuses instead on climate change, a more topical and global subject. The chapter now includes a more detailed discussion of political culture.

The historical chapters (3–5) provide a more focused framing of the chosen events. Each chapter includes a section explaining why the events in the chapter are important or how they relate to events in the new era. As such, it will be much clearer to students why studying history is important. Maps have been added to enhance student understanding of the geographical orientation of international relations. Contemporary research and analysis have been added in select sections to bring the discussions up-to-date with the most recent findings concerning historical events. Chapter 6 has been completely updated to include the most recent events in the Middle East, South Asia, and the Korean Peninsula. Updates have also been included on Darfur, the wars in Iraq and Afghanistan, and global terrorist incidents.

The two security chapters (7 and 8) are thoroughly updated. Both chapters now contain discussions of human security, and Chapter 7 discusses the constructivist concept of "securitization." Military figures, such as weapons and defense spending, are updated, as is the discussion of defensive weapon systems and arms control treaties. Chapter 8 contains a full update of the nuclear programs of North Korea and Iran, active terrorist organizations, and the violence in Mexico caused by drug cartels.

Chapters 9 and 10, on trade and economic development, respectively, both now have references throughout to the effects of the global economic crisis. Each also has updated and additional data, including changes over time in trade balances, GDPs, internet usage, and top multinational corporations. Substantively, the discussion of constructivism, and of John Ruggie's work, in particular, is now more thorough. Overall, with their discussions of economic theorists from Adam Smith to Immanuel Wallerstein, and their coverage of issues pertaining across the board from advanced postindustrial states to the world's least-developed countries, these chapters continue to offer a solid foundation for understanding the role economics play in international relations as a whole.

The human demographics and resource issues chapters (11 and 12) are thoroughly updated. For example, the most recent data on refugees and internally displaced peoples, global health, global carbon emissions, world oil producers, and consumers is provided. In addition, both chapters include new material that reflects the Obama administration's positions on these issues, such as immigration and climate change (particularly the UN Climate Change Conference held in Copenhagen in December 2009).

Chapter 13, international law and organizations, has been updated (i.e., current peacekeeping operations; IMF's response to the economic crisis in Greece in mid-2010) and also includes new material, such as women's rights as human rights (i.e., UN Security Council Resolution 1325's call for more women in the peace negotiations); Responsibility to Protect and peacekeeping after conflict ends; and the UN Human Rights Council (which replaced the UN Human Rights Commission). The sections have been updated to include information reflecting the new Obama administration (i.e., International Criminal Court).

Features

The text includes a number of features designed to reinforce the main themes of the text and to encourage a better understanding of world politics, including:

- **Coverage of Globalization versus Fragmentation** explains when and how globalization influences world politics
- **Theoretical material**—realism, liberalism, constructivism, and a few select alternative theories—is presented in Chapter 2, giving students a basic primer on IR theory, following which theory is discussed in the narrative of every chapter and summarized in the At A Glance feature.
- **At A Glance feature** addresses these theories and how they explain the topic under discussion, but also shows how the "Levels of Analysis" interact with the theories to provide students with the deepest level of understanding.

AT A GLANCE

The Prisoner's Dilemma Game

The Prisoner's Dilemma game is usually described in terms of two prisoners who have been picked up by the police and placed in separate rooms for interrogation. The game is set up so that each prisoner will give up the goods on the other to receive a reduction in sentence. Ultimately, it is clear that if each stayed mum, they would both be better off, but the game's payoff structure ensures that each will rat out the other, leading to a worse (but not the worst possible) outcome for each prisoner. Let us state the game in terms of an international agreement and work through it that way. Say India and Pakistan have negotiated an arms control agreement. If they both cooperate (see the top left quadrant in the accompanying chart), they both do well. If they both defect from the agreement (see the bottom right quadrant), they have made no progress. If one country defects (fails to destroy a certain number of warheads, for example) and the other cooperates, then the defector gains an advantage. There is therefore an incentive for each state to defect. But what is the rational thing to do? Each state must consider what the other is likely to do.

it is also clearly in Pakistan's interest to defect (see the lower right quadrant), because to cooperate in the face of the Indians' defection would leave Pakistan at a strategic disadvantage. So, either way, the Pakistanis, being rational actors, would defect. The same is true for the Indians. The game is set up in such a way that two rational actors are guaranteed an "irrational" outcome because the payoffs and logic demand defection over cooperation.

Prisoner's Dilemma: Cooperation vs. Defection

		India	
		Cooperate	Defect
Pakistan	Cooperate	2,2	0,3

What Would You Do?

North Korea's Nuclear Test

You are a political scientist. North Korea is threatening to test another nuclear device. You must provide policy advice on the potential for international conflict and cooperation. You have also been asked to explain the fragmentary impulses North Korea's move both represents and could stimulate worldwide. Finally, you need to explain how globalization has led to this crisis, how it exacerbates it, and how it might also help mitigate and even resolve it.

What Would You Do?

- **Historical material** is covered in four chapters, beginning with the treaty of Westphalia and the start of the nation-state system, and proceeding to the present, giving students an international relations perspective on historical events.
- **Historical maps** help students grasp the ebb and flow of geopolitics over the centuries; thematic maps reinforce key points visually; and graphs, charts, and tables summarize statistical information.

- **What Would You Do?** These features ask students to step into the role of decision/policy maker to address a contemporary or historical issue in World Politics.
- **Spotlight features** provide students with an in-depth look at people, places, and situations as extended examples of the chapter topic(s), showcasing important international events and colorful personalities in greater depth, or focusing on specific aspects of complex conflicts or theories.
- Each chapter ends with a list of **key terms** and **discussion questions**

■ SPOTLIGHT ■

The Operational Code

The concept of the operational code was originally developed by a political scientist named Nathan Leites.[i] He conceived of the code as a kind of cognitive map that would take into account the fact that decision makers respond not to the external world but to their own perceptions and impressions of the external world. Alexander George adopted and then refined the concept of the operational code, turning it into a sophisticated analytical tool.[ii] He stated that decision makers' belief systems serve as filters that influence leaders' understanding of and response to any given political circumstance or issue.

George developed the following questions for identifying philosophical beliefs ("assumptions and premises...[made]...regarding the fundamental nature of politics, the nature of political conflict, the role of the individual in history, etc."[iii])

Supplements

- **Companion Website at www.oup.com/us/spiegel**
  Written by text author Elizabeth Matthews, this student study and review site offers learning objectives, key concepts, chapter summaries, multiple-choice quizzes, chapter exams, short-answer essay quizzes, case studies, flashcards, and web links. These resources are located at www.oup.com/us/spiegel
- **Instructor's Resource Manual with Test Bank**
  Written by text author Elizabeth Matthews, each chapter of the Instructor's Resource Manual includes Learning Objectives, a Chapter Summary, Lecture Suggestions, Video Suggestions, and a section discussing how the themes introduced in the book are woven into each chapter. Each chapter of the Test Item File includes up to 150 questions in multiple-choice,

short-answer, or essay formats. The Test Item File is available as a Microsoft Word file for download from the companion website that accompanies the text.

- **PowerPoint-based slides**
  For each chapter of the text, succinct chapter outlines are available in PowerPoint format. These slides are available for download from the website listed above.
- **Instructor's Resource CD**
  This resource puts all of your teaching tools in one place. The CD includes the Instructor's Resource Manual with Tests, the Computerized Test Bank, the PowerPoint-based slides, and the graphics from thetext.

Packaging Options from Oxford University Press

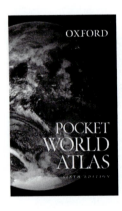

Adopters of *Introduction to Global Politics*, First Edition, can package *ANY* Oxford University Press book with the text for a 20 percent savings off the total package price. See our many trade and scholarly offerings at www.oup.com, then contact your local OUP sales representative to request a package ISBN. In addition, the following items can be packaged with the text for free: *Oxford Pocket World Atlas, Sixth Edition*: This full color atlas is a handy reference for International Relations/Global Politics students.

Very Short Introduction Series: These very brief texts offer succinct introductions to a variety of topics. Titles include *Terrorism* by Townshend, *Globalization, Second Edition,* by Steger, and *Global Warming* by Maslin, among others.

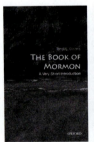  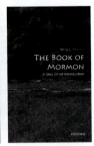

Not For Profit. *All* for Education

For more than five hundred years, Oxford University Press, the world's largest University Press, has published work that furthers Oxford's objective of excellence in research, scholarship, and education. At Oxford, we do not publish in order to generate revenue, we generate revenue in order to publish...and to support the University's wider educational mission. Unlike a for-profit publisher, we do not need to inflate our prices to please a group of shareholders on Wall Street. For-profit publishers are under pressure to reach a certain profit margin; our aim isn't to maximize profits but to fulfill our mission.

We are in a unique position to offer high quality textbooks at a much more reasonable price than many of our competitors. On average, in the United States, an Oxford University Press textbook is 20 percent less expensive than competing books in the same market. Over the years, Oxford University Press has funded hundreds of yearly scholarships that make a University of Oxford education possible for students who could not otherwise afford it. Thanks to these scholarships, hundreds of world-class scholars from more than forty countries have studied at Oxford University, including many from the United States. In addition, surplus generated by Oxford University Press in the United States funds educational publishing, including academic monographs, reference books, and many other important scholarly works, such as the *Oxford English Dictionary*.

We know you can't put a price on a great education. But we *can* put a price on a textbook. We are determined to bring you high-quality educational resources at a reasonable price.

Acknowledgments

We thank Jennifer Carpenter (Politics Editor) for her enthusiasm and encouragement of this new edition, providing us with excellent advice as we proceeded through production. We appreciate the assistance of Maegan Sherlock (Editorial Assistant) as we moved through the copyediting process and for obtaining permissions for the photos, cartoons, and so forth, and Barbara Mathieu (Senior Production Editor) for working with us seamlessly at the copyediting stage. And we are grateful to the research assistants who helped gather the material for the most recent updates, including, at Claremont McKenna College, Kathryn Leonnig, at California State University San Marcos, Ricardo Morones Torres and Holly Gerrity, and at Clark University, Liisa Locurto, Lindsay Labrecque, and Rachel Maimon. Finally, we thank the following reviewers for their extremely useful feedback that helped us to improve this edition: John Barkdull, Texas Tech University; Distinguished Visiting Professor at U.S. Air Force Academy 2008–2010; Michael T. Corgan, Boston University; Mark Haas, Duquesne University; Robert P. Hager, Jr., UCLA; Kathleen Hancock, University of Texas, San Antonio; Aref N. Hassan, St. Cloud State University; Valerie M. Hudson, Brigham Young University; Ardeth Thawnghmung, University of Massachusetts Lowell; Hiroshi Nakazato, Boston College; Robert L. Ostergard, Jr., University of Nevada, Reno; Houman A. Sadri, University of Central Florida; Noha Shawki, Illinois State University; Liubomir K. Topaloff, Northeastern University; and Patricia Weitsman, Ohio University.

About the Authors

Steven L. Spiegel, Professor of Political Science at UCLA and Director of the Center for Middle East Development there, specializes in the analysis of world politics, American foreign policy, and American foreign policy in the Middle East. In addition to *World Politics in a New Era,* he is now working on a volume about American strategies in the Middle East. He also serves as the chair of the Middle East Regional Security Program for the statewide Institute on Global Conflict and Cooperation of the University of California. Through the innovative and informal negotiation techniques he has developed in these capacities, Dr. Spiegel helps produce cutting-edge ideas for promoting Middle East regional security and cooperation. For this work, he received the Karpf Peace Prize in 1995, awarded to the UCLA professor considered to have done the most of any faculty member for the cause of world peace in the previous two years. He has authored or coauthored over 100 books, articles, and papers. Specifically, his other books include *The Other Arab-Israeli Conflict: Making America's Middle East Policy from Truman to Reagan* (University of Chicago Press, 1986); *The International Politics of Regions: A Comparative Approach* with Louis Cantori (Prentice Hall, 1970); and *The Dynamics of Middle East Proliferation,* edited with Jennifer Kibbe and Elizabeth Matthews (Edwin Mellen Press, 2002). He is also the editor of a book series on Middle East issues published by Routledge Press.

Elizabeth G. Matthews is an Assistant Professor in the Department of Political Science at California State University San Marcos. Dr. Matthews lectures and writes on American foreign policy, international negotiations, the Middle East peace process, U.S.–Russian relations, decision making, and human rights. She is the coauthor of *Strategic U.S. Foreign Assistance: The Battle Between Human Rights and National Security* with Rhonda L. Callaway (Ashgate, 2008) and the editor of *The Israel-Palestine Conflict: Parallel Discourses,* with the assistance of David Newman and Mohammed Dajani (Routledge Press, 2011). She also serves as the academic coordinator for a book series to be published by Routledge Press on Middle East security issues.

Jennifer M. Taw is an Assistant Professor of Government in the International Relations Program at Claremont McKenna College. She teaches courses on international relations, U.S. foreign policy, and security. She spent ten years as a RAND policy analyst and has also served as assistant editor and contributing editor for *Studies in Conflict and Terrorism* and on the editorial board of *Small Wars and Insurgencies.* Professor Taw has published journal articles, monographs, reports, book reviews, and chapters in edited books, including "A Strategic Framework for Countering Terrorism," with Bruce Hoffman, in Fernando Reinares, ed., *European Democracies Against Terrorism* (Dartmouth Press, 2000).

Kristen P. Williams is Associate Professor of Political Science at Clark University. She teaches courses on international relations, including world order and globalization, women and war, U.S. national security, U.S. foreign policy, and peace and war. Professor Williams has published journal articles, books, and chapters in edited books, including *Despite Nationalist Conflicts: Theory and Practice of Maintaining World Peace* (Praeger, 2001); *Identity and Institutions: Conflict Reduction in Divided Societies* with Neal G. Jesse (SUNY, 2005); *Ethnic Conflict* with Neal G. Jesse (CQ Press, 2011); and *Women, the State and War* with Joyce P. Kaufman (Lexington, 2007).

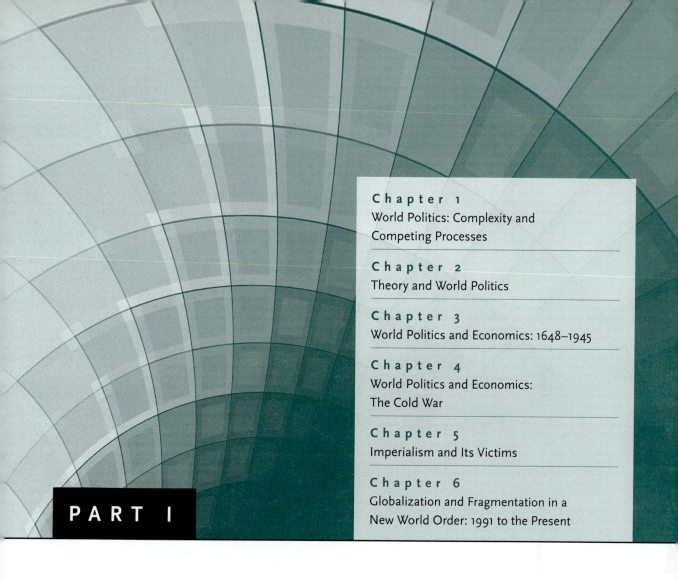

PART I

Foundations of World Politics

CHAPTER 1

World Politics: Complexity and Competing Processes

Conflict and Cooperation

In the fall of 2006, when North Korea first tested a nuclear device, the international community scrambled to come up with an appropriate response. The fundamental question was whether the countries of the world should escalate the situation into an active **conflict** with harsh responses, sanctions, and threats or whether they should attempt **cooperation** with the rogue state, bringing North Korean leader Kim Jong-Il back to the bargaining table with his neighbors and the United States. This kind of tension between conflict and cooperation lies at the heart of world politics. Indeed, one could even see it in the process states undertook to determine the best response to the nuclear test. To avoid becoming mired in divisions and disagreements among themselves (conflict), members of the **United Nations Security Council (UNSC)** relied on that body's formal structure for debate and decision making to maintain their focus on North Korea's intransigence (cooperation).

■ **Conflict**
A state of disharmony or opposition.

■ **Cooperation**
Joint operation or action.

Cooperation and conflict epitomize the complex and often contradictory nature of political interactions. At the international level, cooperation refers to political actors proactively working together, whether that involves operating within existing structures, like the UN, the African Union (AU), the European Union (EU), or the North American Free Trade Agreement (NAFTA); starting new ones like the Kyoto Protocol dealing with the environment; responding multilaterally to global or regional issues, as signatories to the International Criminal Court (ICC) did in response to genocide in Sudan; or holding bilateral talks to mitigate conflict and find common ground, as India and Pakistan did in their series of talks in 2004 and 2005 over the serious disputes between them.[1] Note that cooperation is a broader concept than peace: Peace merely signifies the absence of war, whereas cooperation is inherently active, requiring interaction and communication to achieve mutually agreeable outcomes.

Cooperative efforts in world politics can take place even without any governmental involvement. For instance, **international organizations (IOs)** can work directly with local **nongovernmental organizations (NGOs),** and NGOs from one country can develop associations with NGOs in another country. The World Wildlife Fund, Greenpeace, and other environmental groups all have worked with local environmental NGOs around the world, and similar associations have taken place on many other issues.

> In the past ten years, China's nongovernmental organizations (NGOs) have been playing an increasingly important role in the delivery of social services. Horizontal linkages among NGOs, as well as between NGOs and other sectors, in China and abroad have enhanced the advocacy capacity of NGOs. In Guangdong, linkages among Chinese and foreign NGOs, multinational corporations, and scholars are quietly forming. Joint activities in this region include the provision of services and assistance to migrant labor.[2]

Conflict likewise takes many forms, whether as deliberate withdrawals of diplomatic relations, open disagreements, economic or rhetorical attacks, limited military actions (blockades or massing of troops, for example), or full-blown warfare. International conflict usually garners far more attention than does cooperation. Although cooperation is constant and ongoing, most people think of conflicts—indeed, of wars—when they think about world politics. Americans, for example, measure recent history in terms of the prewar era, World War I, the interwar period, World War II, the Cold War (and, within it, the Korean War and the Vietnam War), the post–Cold War, and the post-9/11 era (with the Iraq War, the war in Afghanistan, and the War on Terror predominating).

Like cooperation, conflict can involve the full range of international actors. Conflict between governments is common and, as mentioned earlier, ranges from critical public statements through warfare. Conflict can also take place between governments and subnational actors. Terrorism comes to mind, of course, but tensions are also common between national governments and foreign NGOs (some of which actually are funded by governments and are therefore suspected of being agents of back-door foreign policy). Uzbekistan cracked

■ **United Nations Security Council (UNSC)** The fifteen-member council that makes binding decisions for the United Nations as a whole; it is composed of five permanent veto-holding members (the United States, China, Russia, France, the United Kingdom) and ten nonpermanent members who have staggered two-year terms; for a resolution to pass, it must receive nine affirmative votes and not be vetoed by any of the five permanent members (see Chapter 13).

■ **International organization (IO)** An international institution involving many different countries (e.g., the United Nations).

■ **Nongovernmental organization (NGO)** An association that is not affiliated with any local, state, or national government.

down on foreign NGOs and foreign-funded NGOs in 2004, shutting several down entirely.[3] Sri Lanka's government has expressed frustration with foreign NGOs and is attempting to monitor them more effectively.[4] Similar concerns have arisen between governments and foreign NGOs in Ghana, Zimbabwe, China, and the United States.

Conflicts don't even have to begin with global actors to have global effects, however. Internal wars—within a country's borders—can have regional and even worldwide consequences and can develop into international conflicts. The wars in Sudan—both the country's long-standing north–south conflict and the more recent Darfur emergency—created international tension as the United Nations, national governments, NGOs, **multinational corporations (MNCs)**, and individuals around the world became involved. Sudan's racial and religious violence and the local economic competition to control the country's vast oil resources were reproduced in the international community's involvement. Saudi Arabia and Egypt came out in support of the Sudanese government at the same time that the United States accused it of genocide; African government representatives on the UNSC opposed UN action against Sudan's government on the basis that it would constitute interference in a state's internal affairs; China, which pumps oil through a pipeline out of Darfur and whose operations are protected by Sudanese government troops, opposed sanctions against Sudan, as did Russia, which sells arms to the Sudanese government. The United States was accused of crying genocide as an excuse to get its hands on Sudanese oil and was also accused of crying genocide too quietly as a palliative for the Russians and Chinese, with whom it had bigger fish to fry. In this case, as in countless others worldwide, many different kinds of relationships are entangled, occurring simultaneously among many different international and domestic actors and involving complex combinations of political, ethical, economic, and security interests.

Although they are often depicted as dichotomous, conflict and cooperation should not be treated as mutually exclusive. Often the same global actors have cooperative relationships on some issues and conflictual interactions with regard to others. A good example of this is the volatile but increasingly fruitful relationship between China and Taiwan. The two countries have become ever more interdependent in terms of trade, with bilateral trade between them reaching $102 billion in 2007, compared to just $8 billion in 1991.[5] Despite this productive economic relationship, however, the political and security tension between China and Taiwan continues, especially after China's spring 2005 "anti-**secession**" law, in which China reasserted its right to retain Taiwan (which it believes to be part of its own country) through "nonpeaceful means" if necessary. Both countries continue to arm themselves and to seek strategic advantages in the strait (see Map 1.1).

The relationship between China and Taiwan is **bilateral,** but complex cooperative and conflictual relations can be **multilateral** as well. For example, participants in the six-party talks (China, North Korea, South Korea, Japan, Russia,

---

▪ **Multinational corporation (MNC)** A large corporation with branches in many countries, most often headquartered in the developed world, and with huge investments throughout the world. Examples include General Motors, PepsiCo, Sony, and Shell Oil.

▪ **Secession** A group's, territory's, or other subnational entity's withdrawal from political association with a country; breaking away.

▪ **Bilateral** Between two countries; two-sided.

▪ **Multilateral** Among three or more countries; many-sided; more than two-sided.

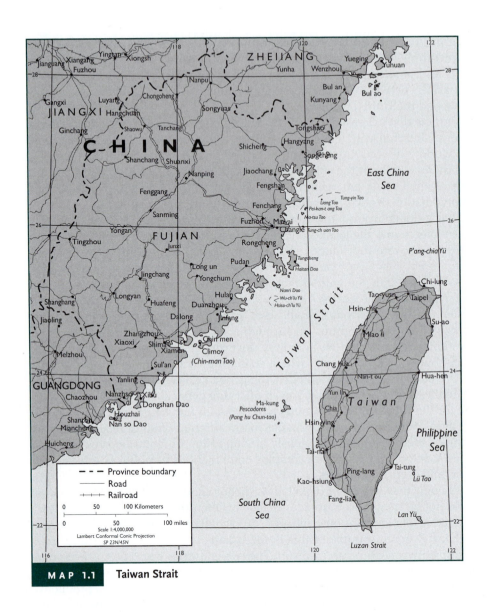

MAP 1.1   Taiwan Strait

■ **Subnational groups**
Usually interest groups, often nongovernmental organizations, sometimes based on identity (ethnicity, religion, nationality, etc.), and always within a state.

and the United States) have been seeking an agreement by which North Korea would give up production of nuclear material in exchange for some kind of concessions by the other states. This is true despite the fact that Japan and South Korea, Japan and China, the United States and China, and the United States and Russia have some very serious disagreements on other issues. Such complex relations can take place among many combinations of actors as well, including not only states but also IOs, NGOs, MNCs, **subnational groups,** and individuals.

Globalization Versus Fragmentation

Just as world politics are typified by the tension between conflict and cooperation, so are they exemplified by the competing processes of **globalization** and **fragmentation.** The first drives the world economically, socially, and politically toward greater integration and interdependence. It is facilitated by more open borders and the concomitant flow of capital and goods as well as human migration. In addition to more fluid trade and travel, there is a freer flow of ideas and culture. Because of the global pervasiveness of Western culture, particularly American culture—through television, movies, music, and consumer items—globalization is often equated with Westernization and even Americanization. The proliferation of Starbucks in London alone could lead to this conclusion. But globalization is a bigger concept, referring more generally to what Thomas L. Friedman has so famously alluded to as a "flatter" world, with unprecedented connectivity, interaction, and opportunity. In its most cautious form, globalization is greater movement and cooperation between countries; at its most ideal, globalization is the creation of a worldwide society of people, a communitarian planet. In stark contrast, fragmentation pulls regions, subregions, states, and even subnational actors back to focus on their own specific and unique interests and concerns. Fragmentation is retrenchment, identity politics, a rejection of outside agendas, meddling, interference, or influence. It is reflexive, defensive, and reactionary, and it is often a response to threats against cultural norms, local industries, domestic distributions of power, traditional ways of life, and autonomy and independence.

Some argue that globalization has begun to marginalize nation-states. As **international regimes,** regional and subregional **trading blocs**, NGOs, and MNCs promote and take advantage of relaxed constraints on the movement of goods, capital, and labor, states necessarily cede some of their authority to these other groups. Fragmentation, on the other hand, is driven precisely by local, domestic, and regional social, environmental, political, and economic considerations, thus impeding globalization by forcing government attention back home to constituents, interest groups, and local imperatives.

Neither globalization nor fragmentation is particularly new. In fact, the notion of global thinking goes back 500 years and even before. The spread of religion—whether through **diasporas, crusades,** conquest, or missionaries—predates modern globalization. Writers in the fourteenth century, such as Dante, proposed a governing system that would include all of Christendom. The emergence of international law in the sixteenth century meant that some leading advocates were arguing that there should be a uniform set of rules for the entire "civilized" globe. **The Enlightenment** of the eighteenth century focused on the "social unification of the world." With the development of capitalism (transcontinental trade of coffee began as early as the thirteenth century), more people saw themselves as part of a larger world. For example, in the eighteenth century, several transatlantic traders in London saw themselves as "citizens of the world."[6]

▪ **Globalization**
Used here to mean increasing general connectivity and interdependence globally (culturally, technologically, politically, militarily, economically, etc.); often used in purely economic terms in reference to the increased mobility of goods, services, labor, technology, and capital throughout the world.

▪ **Fragmentation**
Used here to mean adherence to or embracing of regional and even local political authority, economic development, social and cultural associations, ethnic or national divisions, and so on; more generally, the act, process, or result of breaking something into smaller pieces.

▪ **International regimes**
International laws or norms that set the rules for cooperation.

▪ **Trading blocs**
Groups of states that set trade rules cooperatively, usually involving the reduction or elimination of trade restrictions within the bloc (perhaps the most famous example is the European Union; NAFTA is another).

▪ **Diaspora**
The dispersion of people throughout the world from their original homeland.

▪ **Crusade**
A holy war sanctioned by the Pope; a Christian military expedition to recover the Holy Land from the Muslims.

Yet globalization's progress has been slowed, time and again, precisely by resistance to it, by peoples and states refocusing on regional, national, or local issues as they reject involvement in the broader world. The spread of religion was rarely a peaceful or uncontested process and often involved fragmentation within the religious organizations themselves (consider, for example, the split within Christianity between Catholics and Eastern Orthodox Christians). Dante's proposed governing system was never successfully implemented. International law to this day is eclipsed by national laws. The Enlightenment was followed in the nineteenth century by **Romanticism,** particularly **Romantic nationalism.** Indeed, this tendency toward fragmentation has been a constant companion to globalization.

More recently, in the years preceding World War I, the international system underwent tremendous geographical expansion through imperialism. Economic interactions, integration, and interdependence among countries grew exponentially, aided by new technologies such as the telegraph and by lower priced, more efficient transportation. As one analyst described the period:

> [T]he European and the world economies were quite open to the movement of goods and people by 1910. Low rail and steam-ship transport costs, and economic policies that, in historical perspective, were still liberal, underlay these highly internationalised economic relations.... [B]y 1913 Europe's trade/gross national product ratio, at a peak not achieved again until the 1960s and 1970s, indicated that the late nineteenth century nationalist/liberal international order supported markets at least as free as those created by the post 1945 institutions of **GATT** and the **IMF.**[7]

It is no coincidence that this period led directly into the fragmentation represented by World Wars I and II, inspired as they were by rampant **nationalism.** The tug between globalization and fragmentation has been evident in each period since. During the Cold War, globalization was fed by the creation of the United Nations and its related organizations, the World Bank and the International Monetary Fund (IMF; see Chapter 4). At the same time, of course, the United States and the Soviet Union were splitting the world in two between them, as much as they could, with the **Third World** alternately asserting itself against, and taking advantage of, the increasing bipolarity.

At the end of the Cold War, the world went through another round of fragmentation as the Soviet Union dissolved, Yugoslavia broke up, and several African states were rent by internecine warfare. Between 1990 and 2000 there were fifty-six different major armed conflicts in forty-four different locations. All but three of the major armed conflicts during that period were internal struggles for control over the government or territory of a specific state.[8] In the absence of the superpower competition, many of these conflicts garnered worldwide attention. From the violence involving indigenous farmers of Chiapas, Mexico, to the violence involving white ranchers in Zimbabwe, it looked like fragmentation had the upper hand. At the all-too-common extreme, nationalism and ethnic association sparked **genocide**—the ultimate assertion of one people over another—as well as other forms of violent conflict, from war to terrorism. From Bosnia to

Rwanda and Palestine to Northern Ireland, these have proven to be powerful motivating forces that are among the most difficult to moderate.

Even amid all that, however, globalization proceeded apace as the number of NGOs burgeoned, the United Nations took on a more proactive role internationally, the Internet linked people as never before, the global economy continued to grow, and flow of people, goods, and capital across borders increased at unprecedented rates. The media, too, was crossing national boundaries as never before (CNN International, BBC World Service, and Al Jazeera, to name just a few). Globalization made it possible for terrorists to move about the world with greater ease, too, sharing ideologies, techniques of violence, and means of destruction. The same Internet that permitted hitherto unimagined global cooperation also permitted the fomenting of previously inconceivable violence. Perhaps most significant, however, was the globalization of crises and the international reactions to them: universal outcry in response to photos of Somali babies' distended bellies; the ripple effects of internal conflicts in Europe, Central Asia, and the Middle East; the worldwide consequences of the Southeast Asian economic collapse and the major role global institutions (the World Bank, the IMF) played in responding to them; and the global charitable response to devastating natural disasters in Southeast Asia, China, Haiti, and Latin America.

Of course, each of the competing trends has cultural elements, as well. To assess these, one can simply look at the international spread of consumer goods. Although one immediately thinks of the predominance of American popular culture since the 1950s, from jeans and tennis shoes to blockbuster movies and television shows (all with implied values, from equal rights to disposability), the exchange has gone both ways. Americans' daily lives have become increasingly permeated by foreign goods: Americans watch foreign films, decorate their homes with housewares imported from Africa and Asia, eat authentic Chinese and Ethiopian and Mexican food, and drink European beer and French sparkling water.

Yet the world has not become homogenized as many have feared and seems to be well removed from a universal culture. Language remains a huge cultural signifier, despite the use of English on the Internet and the disappearance of some languages. People worldwide still associate themselves with a specific country, typically eat traditional foods, and preserve their cultural heritage through songs, stories, theater, literature, poetry, film, and even commerce. Interestingly, even the epitome of Americanization, McDonald's, adapts its menu to the local culture. For example, in Singapore, the restaurant offers the Chicken SingaPorridge as well as the Curry Pie, and McDonald's in India (home to nearly 200 restaurants, up from 34 in 2006) responded to religious sentiments opposing beef and pork products by offering the Maharaja Mac (mutton) and Chicken Maharaja Mac.[9] Despite the global proliferation of American fast food, Levi's jeans, and Nike basketball shoes, homogeneity remains a long way off.

One of the questions students of world politics ask is to what extent globalization and fragmentation are natural, immutable processes and to what extent

▪ **Third World**
During the Cold War, terminology evolved in which the world was divided between the First World (the United States and its friends and allies), the Second World (the Soviet Union and its sphere of influence), and the Third World, unaligned states that sought to use their neutrality to insulate themselves from the U.S.–Soviet competition or to manipulate the two superpowers.

▪ **Genocide**
The systematic and deliberate extermination of a specific group of people, usually an ethnic, racial, religious, national, or political group.

PHOTO 1.1   **Children during the 1992 crisis in Somalia.**

they can be controlled, manipulated, mitigated, or even reversed. Many countries have deliberately sought the benefits of globalization, whereas others, conversely, have rejected it aggressively and retreated into nationalism. An advertisement that Straldja, Bulgaria, put on the Internet epitomizes the first approach. The ad asks (in English), "Why Straldja?" and goes on to emphasize the town's low costs, abundant labor pool, rail connections, political stability, and available plant locations. Here globalization is being courted, with the understanding that foreign investors will bring a much-needed infusion of cash and jobs into the town. The French region of Lorraine has a similar website (also in English) promoting the 67,000 jobs created by the region's 421 foreign companies from twenty different countries. Comparable advertisements can be found on the Internet for the South Korean island of Jeju, the Bahamas, and many other places seeking to attract foreign investment.

In contrast, consider the fear of foreign cultural influence expressed in a January 30, 2002, speech by Khayriddin Sultonov, state advisor to the Uzbek president:

> [I]t is a major problem, the president said, that we still fail to grasp the extent of the huge negative influence on our young people from abroad. The negative influence from abroad includes various underground and harmful sects of a religious, terrorist, extremist and destructive nature, channels for supplying them with funds, people who secretly publish and distribute leaflets, their underground publishing houses, the forces which are behind them, the inflow of dollars for supporting subversive activities and so on. We are underestimating all these threats and we have not drawn up clear-cut measures to counter them. It is a big shortcoming of ours.[10]

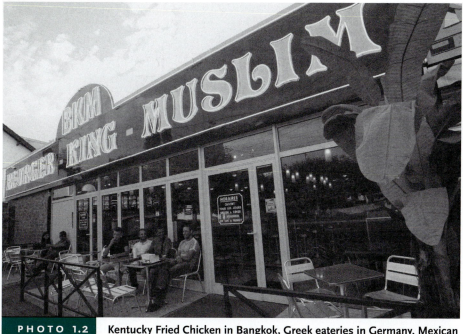

PHOTO 1.2 Kentucky Fried Chicken in Bangkok, Greek eateries in Germany, Mexican chorizo on British breakfast plates, and Ethiopian restaurants in Los Angeles may seem remarkable, but food has been globalizing since the earliest explorations of the world.

The prevention of foreign influence is written right into Iran's constitution, and it is a key motivating principle for the foreign policies of North Korea and Burma (Myanmar). Likewise, legislation in Singapore prevents more than 3 percent foreign ownership of any local newspaper, for fear that foreign interests will gain control over the presentation of information. Xenophobia is not the sole source of fragmentation, nor is fragmentation an issue only in developing countries. In 2001, the United States created enormous tensions worldwide with its decision to withdraw from the Anti-Ballistic Missile (ABM) Treaty. The decision—justified by the U.S. government as necessary given its pursuit of National Missile Defense (NMD)—combined with the unilateral withdrawal of the United States from the Kyoto Greenhouse Gas Emission Protocol that same year, was received as an indication that the country was willing to put potentially divisive national interests before collective concerns.

Ultimately, the pendulum between globalization and fragmentation swings because there are so many different factors that influence governments' and groups' decisions. Concerns about preservation of language and culture struggle with the pressure to liberalize economically and provide jobs and growth opportunities. Social rejection of immigrants competes with the need for more, and cheaper, labor. Pressures for expanded security regimes are mitigated by

PHOTO 1.3   Sign at Irish Medium School in Newry, Northern Ireland.

historical animosities and tensions. Secessionist movements fighting for the worthy causes of human rights and self-rule create political instability and threaten economic development. As economic **liberalization** progresses, many countries' short-term interests are sacrificed for long-term gains, or, if they are not, long-term gains are threatened.

Clearly, the dilemmas are serious, but they are not altogether devoid of humor. One example of the tension between globalization and fragmentation has to do with matches. Australian entrepreneur, adventurer, and philanthropist Dick Smith produced matches in protest of foreign takeovers of Australian companies. On the matchbooks was printed:

> We would have to be complete [expletive based on the founder's name] to let most of our famous Australian brands be taken over by foreign companies. Brands such as Vegemite, Aeroplane Jelly, Arnott's, Speedo and Redhead matches are in overseas hands. This means the profit and wealth created goes overseas and robs our children and grandchildren of a future.[11]

Ironically, the *"Australian Made"* campaign protested the entrepreneur's matches despite his message. Although the matchboxes and striker plates were made in Australia, the matchsticks came from Russia and the match heads were from Japan.

Anarchy Versus Order

These sets of tensions—between cooperation and conflict and between globalization and fragmentation—lie at the crux of studies of world politics. Embedded within them are all the complexities of the international system. Notably, they are

▪ **Liberalization**
In general, the reduction of government involvement, interference, or oversight; in economic terms, the reduction of government rules and regulations with regard to the **private sector.**

▪ **Private sector**
The realm of nongovernmental economic activity; business.

in part a function of the lack of order and certainty in the international system. States must function and interact without enforceable legal **norms** or even a universal code of ethics. There is no international police force or global system of justice. In other words, international politics are **anarchic,** and the basic tensions in global relations stem from this. North Korea's virulent nationalism (fragmentation), the ripple effects of its actions throughout the international system (globalization), its paranoia-fueled aggression (conflict), and the multinational response to it (cooperation) can all trace their roots to the absence of a comprehensive global regime or set of rules.

That brings us back to where we began, with North Korea's nuclear test and the international response. In this single example, we can see conflict and cooperation, the effects of globalization and fragmentation, and the impact of states functioning in an anarchic environment. North Korea knew, when it tested its nuclear device, that the international community would stand up and take notice, especially because North Korea's geographic location guarantees that its aggressive behavior will get attention. This was as true in 1950 as it is now. Back then, when the Soviet Union and China championed the North in its invasion of the U.S.-dominated South, the United Nations authorized international defense of South Korea. Foreign governments and, indeed, the international community believed they had a stake in the outcome of the conflict for control over the Korean peninsula. Today, the peninsula remains strategically important and the stakes have been raised. South Korea is deeply tied into the international economy, primarily because of its relations with the United States, Japan, China, and Russia. South Korea and the United States have a unique security relationship as well, with thousands of American soldiers stationed in South Korea to help provide for its defense. North Korea, for its part, despite its isolation from the rest of the world and its grinding poverty, manages to extend its influence through the development, sale, and testing of missiles, biological and chemical weapons, and nuclear devices. Moreover, North Korea's population is poised on the borders of South Korea and China. A war involving North Korea, therefore, would have enormously costly global ramifications. Although the United States and South Korea could probably decisively win a war against North Korea, enough to extract favorable terms of peace, the war would nonetheless be incredibly expensive. For example, even if North Korea's long-range missiles were to fail or its nuclear weapons turned out to be more show than substance, the country could inflict tremendous damage on South Korea, the American forces fighting there, and, if it wished, Japan (see Map 1.2). Were North Korea to use its chemical and biological weapons, immediate mortality and health effects, not to mention long-term environmental costs, could be astronomical. Either way, damage to the infrastructures of South Korea and, most likely, Japan would have ripple effects throughout the global economy. Furthermore, it is predicted that North Korean refugees would flow into both South Korea and China, creating further (and long-term) pressures on the economies in those countries and, therefore, on the economies of those countries' many trading partners. Although a relatively united international community today is committed to diplomacy with Kim Jong-Il, in

▪ **Norm**
A generally accepted rule or standard.

▪ **Anarchic**
Lacking a legitimate, hierarchical structure. Under anarchy, there is no higher authority to whom to appeal; there is no arbiter; there are no universal, enforceable rules. This distinguishes the international system from its components, states with hierarchical internal structures. States only become anarchic when they fail.

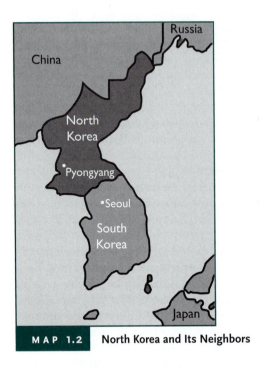

MAP 1.2   **North Korea and Its Neighbors**

the event of an actual war, China would be torn between its security commitments to North Korea and its broader economic and political interests. Russia's stance is not immediately predictable. Tensions would undoubtedly arise within the international community more generally as to how best to respond. Indeed, even assuming the best-case scenario—North Korea does not deploy **weapons of mass destruction (WMD)** and the war is quick and decisive against it—world relations, the global economy, and international security would suffer the ramifications for years, if not decades.

All of this to say that it is indeed a small (and complex) world after all, and not only because a relatively small, poor country like North Korea can make powerful shock waves resonate throughout the globe. In more ways than we realize, our lives have been internationalized, for both good and ill. Benefits of greater globalization include a much larger marketplace for jobs, goods, and services; access to different cultures, foods, music, art, literature, and lifestyles; and faster, more reliable means of communication, creating improved international transparency. On the downside, there are tensions created by migration, fears of growing cultural homogeneity, and impossible-to-control product flows, including illegal narcotics and nuclear technologies.

As globalization proceeds exponentially with the assistance of technological developments, tying the world together with information and mutual economic interests, its opposing process, deeply rooted in history, works against it. Nationalism, regionalism, racism, cultural differences, religious affiliations

▪ **Weapons of mass destruction (WMD)** Chemical, biological, radiological, or nuclear weapons.

and religious conflicts, economic competition, and perceptions of insecurity all contribute to continued, even increased, fragmentation as regions, states, and individuals pursue their desires to maintain their autonomy and identities. From the dissolution of the Soviet Union and Yugoslavia into their component states to the ongoing struggles for homeland of the Kosovars, Basques, Palestinians, Chechens, and Kurds, fragmentary pressures ensure that we will not be one world and one people any time soon.

Conclusion

Keep the fundamental elements and processes of world politics in mind as you work your way through the following chapters. Cooperation and conflict remain the primary components of world politics, and all international studies directly or indirectly examine one, the other, or both. Globalization and fragmentation are likewise defining features of international relations. We see these processes but still do not know much about how they drive and are driven by various global actors, whether individual decision makers, subnational organizations, states, or regional groups. We know they occur within and across economic, security, political, and cultural relations, but we don't know when which will take precedence.

Chapter 2 helps us begin to address these questions by introducing analytical tools and describing how some of the best-known theories deal with these issues. Chapters 3–6 provide historical context for studies of world politics, first bringing us back to the creation of the state system, then through the Cold War, then shifting gears to look at the worldwide effects of imperialism and the development of the non-European world, and finally moving us into the present with a discussion of global affairs since 1991. Chapters 7 and 8 focus on security, first providing some insights into the most prominent theories and then delving into contemporary security issues. Chapters 9 and 10, in turn, focus on economics;

What Would You Do?

North Korea's Nuclear Test

You are a political scientist. North Korea is threatening to test another nuclear device. You must provide policy advice on the potential for international conflict and cooperation. You have also been asked to explain the fragmentary impulses North Korea's move both represents and could stimulate worldwide. Finally, you need to explain how globalization has led to this crisis, how it exacerbates it, and how it might also help mitigate and even resolve it.

What Would You Do?

Chapter 9 examines trade and investment, and Chapter 10 looks at development. Chapter 11 explores demographic trends and their effects on world politics. Chapter 12 surveys contemporary resource issues: declining oil reserves, diminished supplies of fresh water, shifting international demand, and so forth. Chapter 13 is focused on global governance and the respective influence of international law and international organizations. Finally, the book concludes with Chapter 14, which peers a bit into the future, offering analyses based on the three major theoretical paradigms in political science that we are about to explore.

The tensions in world politics are obvious throughout. That the relationship between conflict and cooperation has always been complicated, for example, is demonstrated by the Peace of Westphalia at the end of the bloody Thirty Years War in Europe and by the nineteenth-century Concert of Europe in which relative peace was a by-product of ruling elites' mutual interests in preserving the status-based social structure. The tensions between globalization and fragmentation are equally obvious, for example, between World Wars I and II, as states sought to draw together politically in the League of Nations even as, economically, they acted—destructively—in their own self-interests. The following chapters illuminate and illustrate these complex dynamics across the full spectrum of world politics.

Discussion and Review Questions

1. How significant are nongovernmental actors in world politics? Are states the most important units of analysis when examining international relations?
2. What would need to happen internationally to eliminate anarchy?
3. Why does globalization appear to be met so often with fragmentation? What is the relationship between the two tendencies, if any? Is either tendency ascendant?
4. Violent conflict dominates the news. Is violent conflict the most significant, or the most important, form of international conflict?
5. What success, partial success, or failure of international cooperation has the media been covering recently? What do you think is responsible for the outcome to date? What might be done to create better chances for success?

Key Terms

Anarchic 13
Bilateral 5
Conflict 3
Cooperation 3
Crusade 7
Diaspora 7
The Enlightenment 8
Fragmentation 7
GATT 8
Genocide 9
Globalization 7
IMF 8

International
  organization 4
International regimes 7
Liberalization 12
Multilateral 5
Multinational
  corporation 5
Nation 8
Nationalism 8
Nongovernmental
  organization 4
Norm 13

Private sector 12
Romantic nationalism 8
Romanticism 8
Secession 5
Subnational groups 6
Third World 9
Trading blocs 7
United Nations Security
  Council 4
Weapons of mass
  destruction 14

CHAPTER 2

Theory and World Politics

Students of world politics are faced with a challenge: They must come up with an explanation for, or an explication of, relations between international actors. However, given the tremendous complexity of global interactions, the range and interrelatedness of the issues on which they touch, the huge number of international players involved, and the constant shifts and adjustments as international actors respond to each other over time, identifying causal relationships or clarifying key dynamics may seem nearly impossible. Faced with this profusion of ever-changing, constantly accumulating information, political scientists have developed ways of dipping into the stream of relations, pulling out samples, and probing them for useful clues as to how international affairs work. In other words, they select certain aspects of international relations to study and then further narrow their exploration by choosing specific analytical tools with which to conduct their investigation. This chapter is about that process. Using the international response to climate change as an example, we introduce and discuss some of the typical analytical tools scholars of world affairs use to parse the confusion.

Climate Change

Climate change has been an incredibly controversial topic, debated internationally and nationally. It has mobilized individuals, nongovernmental organizations, corporations, governments, and regional and international organizations to come into the public realm forcefully, seeking to protect their interests. People have become activists both in favor of addressing global warming and as skeptics that there is anything to address. The issue has generated extremely weak international agreements [like the Kyoto Greenhouse Gas Emission Protocol (hereafter called the Kyoto Protocol) and the Copenhagen Accord—see Chapter 12], and it has raised serious questions regarding the nexus of politics, science, and commerce.

Scientists have been warning about climate change and its effects on health, food and water supplies, industry, and the environment since the beginning of the twentieth century. Reports about the climate effects of carbon dioxide surfaced as early as the 1920s. Concerns about human contributions to climate change have been media fodder for the better part of a century, with headlines blaring the fearful effects of, alternately, cooling and warming. Every aspect of climate change has been vigorously debated, with the arguments falling into unsurprising patterns. Those who would bear the immediate costs of mitigating or addressing climate change are the most vocal in making the following arguments: There is no climate change; if there is, humans do not contribute to it; if there is, it is beyond human control to address; if there is, it can be beneficial. Those who see climate change as a medium or long-term threat make the opposite arguments: There is climate change; it is dangerous; humans are contributing to it; humans can mitigate it and its effects. (See Figure 2.1)

We might think that this question is easily resolved by simply looking at the evidence, but, as Copernicus and later Galileo learned when faced with adamant rejection of their supposition that the earth revolves around the sun and not vice versa, science is readily politicized. The preponderance of climatologists worldwide appear to agree that climate change is occurring and that the infusion of greenhouse gases into the atmosphere, along with other human behaviors such as deforestation, are contributing to it. These scientists argue that the consequences of climate change will be dire and are already obvious in the melting of the polar ice caps, the rising seas, and harsher weather, to include more (and more intense) heat waves and cold snaps and storms. Yet naysayers are quick to point to flaws in analysis, to question the climatologists' methodologies, to produce scientists with competing research, and to argue that the process of climate science itself is a function of politics and that the generally accepted findings are therefore misleading, exaggerated, and hyperbolic. This debate will be discussed again later in the chapter.

Despite challenges to claims of climate change, the trend internationally has been to recognize it as a potentially serious problem and to begin to take steps to address it. In 1988, the Intergovernmental Panel on Climate Change (IPCC) was

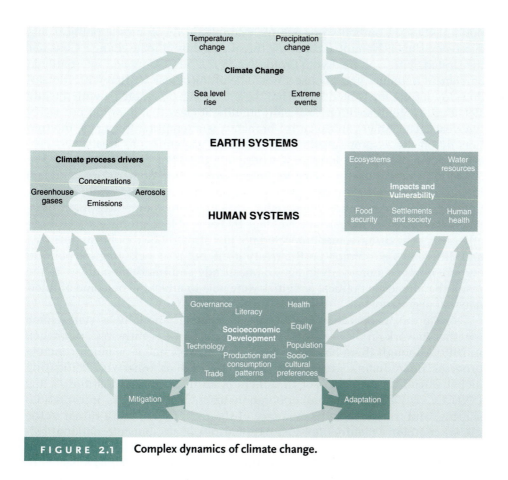

FIGURE 2.1 **Complex dynamics of climate change.**

established for reviewing and sharing scientific research and for disseminating guidance to governments regarding reducing global warming and mitigating its effects. Four years later, 154 countries signed the United Nations Framework Convention on Climate Change (UNFCCC). That treaty represented a willingness to study the effects of greenhouse gas emissions on global warming, but it set no legally binding restrictions on such emissions, nor did it require any actions from signatories. By 2009, 192 countries had become parties to the treaty. Members meet annually in the Conference of Parties (COP) to assess progress. Climate change concerns have also driven policy by the European Union and by many individual states. In most cases, however, there has been far more talk than action and far more debate than policy.

Using the various tools of analysis most prominent in the study of international relations, we can begin to understand the dynamics underpinning the international politics of climate change. For example, in this one story we have conflict and cooperation, globalization and fragmentation, and a plethora of political actors. Conflict is present, for example, in the domestic political disagreements in each country about the threat posed by climate change. Consider the United States and the Kyoto Protocol, a 1997 UNFCCC-related international agreement to reduce greenhouse gases. The protocol was written with tremendous input from the United States, but the U.S. Senate preempted it with the July 1997 Byrd-Hagel resolution—basically making it clear that it would not **ratify** the treaty. The American executive branch was attempting to engage internationally on the assumption that a greenhouse gas emissions treaty was necessary for reducing the long-term worldwide threat of global warming. The Senate, however, was attempting to protect shorter-term domestic and national interests, using legislation to express its concern that Americans would bear an unfair burden in greenhouse gas reduction relative to competitors like China, who would have an industrial advantage by being able to produce at lower relative cost. –The disagreement reflected not just strongly held political positions and differences of opinion on the treaty itself, but also jockeying for political authority and economic advantages domestically and internationally, with the result that domestic political activities were able to affect the outcome of international negotiations.

Despite this, cooperation has been evident internationally as states come together to work on the issue of climate change, most recently in Copenhagen in 2010. Although there has yet to be a binding agreement or much concrete progress on reducing greenhouse gas emissions or otherwise mitigating global warming, the very fact that there is an international institution (the UNFCCC) in place to promote cooperation, technology transfers, information-sharing, and transparency is evidence of the recognition that a threat to the **global commons** requires not just national responses, but international **collective action.**

As for globalization and fragmentation, climate change politics reflect both tendencies. On the one hand, climate change is itself a form of globalization: National-level industrial and agricultural practices and policies have a global effect, whether it is agribusinesses cutting down the Amazon rainforest to make way for cattle, villagers felling trees for firewood, industry burning coal to fuel economic growth, or commuters clogging the streets in overpopulated cities. Decisions made locally are having global effects that require global responses that will, in turn, affect local practices. But climate change reflects fragmentation as well, the differentiation of interests by state and by region. For example, the lesser-developed countries (LDCs) argue that they should be able to pollute as a process of industrialization just as the developed countries did and, moreover, that if the developed countries want to mitigate global warming, then they should underwrite the green technology LDCs need. Countries, and within them competing interest groups, each measure the relative costs of global warming and the means of addressing it very differently, depending on their own agendas, capacities, and priorities. In this sense, the problem of climate change serves to inflame tensions between various international actors.

▪ **Ratification**
A country's legislative approval of a treaty signed by the executive.

▪ **Global commons**
Ungoverned areas shared by all countries, such as the seas, space, and the atmosphere.

▪ **Collective action**
Efforts undertaken by a group in its members' mutual interests.

PHOTO 2.1   One of the effects of climate change is increased desertification.

The story of climate change is just one of the many ongoing narratives that accumulate, combine, and intertwine to make up the complexity of world politics, but it aptly illustrates the themes underlying the study of international affairs. We study these international relations to find patterns, reasons, and signposts within the global system's profusion of actors, dynamics, agendas, and interests. We need to know how to winnow out simpler, more basic stories from the confusion; we need to know how to identify what is really important, where explanations lie, and how we can begin to describe accurately the processes that make up world affairs. Examining the dynamics that underpin the international politics of climate change can give us insight into this process. If we consider the relative significance of different actors; identify various assumptions related to analysis of the treaty; contemplate the relevance of economics, security, ethics, and so on; and attempt to explain it in light of the key countervailing forces of modern international affairs, we can use this case to explore the study of world politics itself.

Levels of Analysis

When we look at the story of climate change, we see relevant political interactions taking place across the levels of analysis. The levels of analysis are nothing more than a way of methodically sorting the complexity of world affairs. They are typically broken down into the systemic level of analysis, the domestic level of analysis, and the individual level of analysis, although different terms may be substituted or additional levels added. These three levels, however, are the most commonly used and suit our examination of climate change well.[1]

Before describing the levels of analysis, it is important to explain their purpose, which is very simple. Using the levels of analysis is one way to divide the huge, complex, confusing picture of world politics into manageable, analyzable pieces. We know that countless factors and variables contribute to any snapshot we take of international affairs. If we choose to look, as we are doing, at climate change in the first decade of the twenty-first century, it is clear that this is interrelated with the rest of world affairs and that all of history has contributed to bringing us to this place and this point and that it will rush on to move us from it, too. There are factors clearly beyond the control of policymakers that set the constraints and opportunities for the treaty. However, we also know that climate change and international responses to it were not predestined; people conceived of and promoted the Kyoto Protocol, for example, as others raised their voices in opposition. Deliberate decisions helped to influence the form the pact took, helped determine which countries would ratify it when, and will explain, in part, how the treaty ultimately is implemented. The levels of analysis help us segment and sort the flow and flux of world politics into more controllable, digestible pieces. They help us untangle the various threads that led to and will lead on from contemporary responses to climate change. In so doing, they help us achieve improved understanding, provide us with some explanations, and ideally give us some insights into what we can and cannot control.

Systemic Level of Analysis

The systemic level of analysis provides the biggest picture; it is like looking at the forest, not the trees. Using a slightly different metaphor, we are looking at the roads, not at the cars on them. This level of analysis encompasses the others because it is focused on the system as a whole.

We treat states as **unitary actors** at this level of analysis and we assume that states' relations and sometimes behaviors can be explained by the nature of the international system. Of the plethora of international actors, the only ones we care about at this level are states and sometimes international organizations. When we use this level, we are assuming that states' internal functions do not matter and that their structures and institutions are irrelevant. In terms of our metaphors, we do not care about the functions or types of trees or who is in what kind of car. We assume that states' interactions are driven by the nature of the international system itself rather than by any domestic political processes, decisions, or behaviors.

Probably the most distinguishing feature of the international system is that it is anarchic. As discussed in Chapter 1, the international system is distinguished from most domestic systems by its lack of legitimate governmental authority. There is no final arbiter, no agency with a monopoly on the legitimate use of force, and no accepted regime that can set standards, rules, and laws to which its components—states—can be held accountable. Systemic-level analyses are based on the assumption that this anarchic **structure** is largely responsible for how international affairs play out.

■ **Unitary actor**
Within the study of international relations (IR), a simplifying assumption is one in which states are treated as if they are unified entities rather than composites of many domestic actors.

■ **Structure**
The ordering of units (usually states) within the system.

The systemic level of analysis is not appropriate for explaining specific policies, decisions, or actions. Rather, it is used to describe how the stage is set for international actors; it sets the context within which they act. Using international responses to climate change as an example, a systemic-level analysis would focus on how the anarchic international system creates incentives or disincentives for this particular kind of cooperation among states. Using the systemic level of analysis, we can ask the following types of questions: Will states that opt to cooperate be rewarded or punished for subsuming state authority to regional or supranational authority? Can an institution such as the UNFCCC reflect participating states' mutual interests, or will it simply mask the exploitation of weaker states by the **hegemon** (the United States, in this case)? Can the creation of such an institution, in and of itself, change the nature of the international system to promote future cooperation?

Clearly, we are not trying to get into the specifics of international responses to climate change with this level of analysis. We are simply examining how the system itself will affect the nature of the treaty and likelihood of its success. It all comes down to what we think anarchy entails. Here there is a debate. Some argue that anarchy leads to a brutal world of constant competition in which might makes right. Others argue that anarchy could lead to such a world but that people can overcome it by developing institutions and agreements that protect them. Still others argue that anarchy is what we make of it. So, if we believe that because the international system, by dint of being anarchic, is a dog-eat-dog, **zero-sum** world, or a **self-help** system, then we are likely to doubt that something like the Kyoto Protocol or a subsequent climate change agreement will have the teeth to force signatories to assume costs they would rather not bear. We are more likely to focus on the fact that the United States, the most powerful country in the world today, ultimately refused to participate in the Kyoto Protocol and was resistant during recent negotiations in Copenhagen on the grounds that it feared international accords would create advantages for America's economic competitors. If we believe, in contrast, that the international system is anarchic but nonetheless allows for the pursuit of mutual interests—particularly when institutions are built to enhance cooperation—then we might look at international responses to climate change in a different light, as a necessary or deliberate means of overcoming the international system's pressure for ruthless competition through the creation of institutions that allow for discussion, negotiation, and cooperation. These different assumptions are important and are discussed in much more detail in a later section, "Theoretical Paradigms/Worldviews."

In addition to assuming that states are unitary actors, it is common when using the systemic level of analysis to assume that they are **rational actors** as well. Nobel Prize–winning economist Thomas C. Schelling wrote of the utility of this device:

> [T]he assumption of rational behavior is a productive one. It gives a grip on the subject that is peculiarly conducive to the development of theory. It permits us to identify our own analytical processes with those of the hypothetical participants in a conflict; and by demanding certain kinds of consistency in the behavior of our hypothetical participants, we can examine alternative courses of behavior

- **Hegemon**
Predominant world power.

- **Zero-sum**
One entity's loss is another's gain, and vice versa.

- **Self-help**
When there is no higher authority to which to appeal.

- **Rational actor**
An IR simplifying assumption in which states are presumed to make the best possible decision based on their set priorities.

according to whether or not they meet those standards of consistency. The premise of "rational behavior" is a potent one for the production of theory. Whether the resulting theory provides good or poor insight into actual behavior is, I repeat, a matter for subsequent judgment.[2]

The assumption of rationality is taken to the limit in game theory, which involves mathematical analyses of interdependent decisions and is often used by structural theorists. Using game theory, structural theorists attempt to predict the cumulative effect of states' rational responses to systemic stimuli. The simplest game theoretic construct is the Prisoner's Dilemma (see At a Glance, "The Prisoner's Dilemma Game").

AT A GLANCE

The Prisoner's Dilemma Game

The Prisoner's Dilemma game is usually described in terms of two prisoners who have been picked up by the police and placed in separate rooms for interrogation. The game is set up so that each prisoner will give up the goods on the other to receive a reduction in sentence. Ultimately, it is clear that if each stayed mum, they would both be better off, but the game's payoff structure ensures that each will rat out the other, leading to a worse (but not the worst possible) outcome for each prisoner. Let us state the game in terms of an international agreement and work through it that way. Say India and Pakistan have negotiated an arms control agreement. If they both cooperate (see the top left quadrant in the accompanying chart), they both do well. If they both defect from the agreement (see the bottom right quadrant), they have made no progress. If one country defects (fails to destroy a certain number of warheads, for example) and the other cooperates, then the defector gains an advantage. There is therefore an incentive for each state to defect. But what is the rational thing to do? Each state must consider what the other is likely to do. So, Pakistan will consider its options. If India cooperates, it is clearly in Pakistan's interest to defect (see the lower left quadrant), because then Pakistan will gain a strategic advantage; if India defects, then

it is also clearly in Pakistan's interest to defect (see the lower right quadrant), because to cooperate in the face of the Indians' defection would leave Pakistan at a strategic disadvantage. So, either way, the Pakistanis, being rational actors, would defect. The same is true for the Indians. The game is set up in such a way that two rational actors are guaranteed an "irrational" outcome because the payoffs and logic demand defection over cooperation.

Prisoner's Dilemma: Cooperation vs. Defection

		India	
		Cooperate	*Defect*
Pakistan	*Cooperate*	2,2	0,3
	Defect	3,0	1,1

Some analysts offer the Prisoner's Dilemma as a metaphor for the difficulty of achieving international cooperation in an anarchic system. Others note that the game's simplifying assumptions—there are only two players, there is no communication between them regarding cooperation versus defection, it is a one-shot deal rather than part of an iterative (repeated) process, and there is no **linkage** to other issues—go far toward demonstrating the value, in the context of cooperation, of multiple players, communication, iteration, and linkage.

Game theory can help clarify some of the issues related to the international response to climate change. The assumption of rationality allows researchers to overlook the often tumultuous internal politics of each of the signatories and instead to consider the states' interests in general terms of whether a country should sign a climate change agreement if other states all might do so. This question is not unlike the dilemma posed by the Stag Hunt game. In that game, several hunters join together to hunt for a deer. If they work together, they can catch the deer and each take home a good chunk of venison. However, they all know that if even one person leaves the group to go hunt a rabbit (which would yield that hunter much less food), the rest of them will be unable to catch the deer and will go home hungry. What would a rational actor do? Defect and get the bit of rabbit meat, as that would be a guaranteed meal? Or stay with the group, but risk having no meal at all in the event that someone else defects? This game is focused on the role of trust in cooperative endeavors. It highlights the kinds of decisions any rational actor must make when considering the risks and benefits of cooperation. As with the Prisoner's Dilemma, the state's best choice will depend on what other states do. Just as the Prisoner's Dilemma highlights the need for communication, iteration, and linkage, the Stag Hunt suggests the additional need for **confidence-building measures** in any cooperative arrangement, whether a peace treaty or a free trade agreement.

■ **Linkage**
Negotiating more than one issue concurrently, so that concessions on one might be made up by gains on another.

■ **Confidence-building measures**
Stipulations built into treaties or agreements to reduce the likelihood of defection and to enhance communication.

Domestic Level of Analysis

Whereas the systemic level of analysis gives us a tool for exploring the effects of the structure of the international system on world politics, the domestic level of analysis allows us to examine the effects of domestic structures, institutions, and cultures. We are shifting our focus from the forest to the trees, or, to continue with our alternative conceptualization, we are no longer looking at the roads, we are now looking at the cars on the road to see why each is driving as it is.

When we use the domestic level of analysis, we are trying to find predictable patterns of world affairs based on countries' internal mechanisms. Moreover, whereas the systemic level of analysis really just allows us to consider the context within which international relations take place, by using the domestic level of analysis we can seek explanations for specific behaviors and actions. So, for example, we might expect democracies to behave differently, internationally, than do dictatorships. We might expect **secular** states to behave differently than **theocracies.** We would ask questions like these: Do more traditional cultures function differently in world politics than more modern ones? Do capitalist countries function differently internationally than communist states? Are there demographic, environmental, or geographic factors that influence how a state acts in international affairs?

At this level of analysis we look more closely at how states' internal processes and guiding principles affect their political behavior at the international level. Do, for example, states develop foreign policy as a function of the balance of power within their bureaucracies (e.g., in the United States, whether the State Department or the Department of Defense has more influence)? Do states develop foreign policies on the basis of standard operating procedures in each of their governmental agencies? Do states develop foreign policies as a result of how their institutions reward certain aspects of leadership, whether it is charisma and confidence or proven track records and substantive achievements? Do states' foreign policies stem from the role, structure, organization, or relative strength of their civil societies? Do particular interest groups (economic, ethnic, or ideological) influence policy? All of these represent the kinds of questions an analyst might ask when using the domestic level of analysis.[3]

If we consider the international politics of climate change from the domestic level of analysis, we might analyze participating countries' willingness to ratify a climate change treaty based on their relative economic stability, growth, power, or potential. Or we might try to find a **correlation** between how democratic the countries are in practice and how quickly they ratified the Kyoto Protocol. Alternatively, we might consider their political stability and evaluate its effects on their interests in addressing climate change. Or we might want to see what agencies within each government were favorable and which were opposed or which groups (unions, manufacturers, environmental groups, etc.) favored or opposed cooperation. We could also approach the question somewhat differently, comparing each participating country's interests internationally against its ability (as measured using domestic factors like industrial

▪ **Secular**
Nonreligious.

▪ **Theocracy**
A government ruled by or subject to religious authority.

▪ **Correlation**
A relationship between two variables.

output, type of economy, political stability, etc.) to project its agenda regionally and internationally.

In any event, at this level of analysis, we are looking for a domestic explanation for why and how each state has responded at the international level to the threat of climate change. We are trying to identify what **factors** or **variables** within all the countries account for their individual foreign policies and the combined outcome that they create. The key international actors can include any combination of governments (including their component departments, institutions, and agencies), NGOs, interest groups, business groups, lobbies, unions, and so forth. Clearly, at this level, we are looking beyond the state as unitary actor to consider each state's mechanisms and functions—as well as nongovernmental political actors within each state—and their effects on world affairs. We are considering how each tree affects the forest; we are looking at how each car, given its model, year, efficiency, capacity, passengers, and so forth, affects the road conditions.

One prominent school of thought at the domestic level of analysis focuses on the role political culture plays. Political culture is defined as how citizens in different groups, societies, and countries perceive, respond to, and involve themselves in government and politics as well as how they define their interests and priorities. The underlying assumptions are that political values and beliefs represent a social framework independent of institutions, economics, or other factors and explain political behavior at a group, rather than individual, level. Political culture is most commonly used by **comparativists** to assess how different countries' constituents' political culture or cultures influence their political behaviors and expectations. For example, do the constituents feel disassociated from government, or do they believe government is accountable to them? What issues do the constituents believe the government should control, and which do they believe should be beyond government intervention? Studies of political culture also have to consider uniformity versus heterogeneity. Within a state, is there a single dominant political culture, or are there competing political cultures?

Although the concept of political culture usually falls within the realm of comparative studies, it is a useful idea at the domestic level of analysis in the field of international relations. As will be discussed later in the chapter, Randall Schweller is a prominent international relations theorist who uses political culture to explain states' behavior internationally. The concept can also be used to combine the two fields, for example, to determine under what domestic conditions a country will be most receptive to international democratization efforts or to assess how a country will respond to negotiations on a particular issue. Other well-known applications of political culture to the study of international relations include Samuel Huntington's idea of a "clash of civilizations" and Amy Chua's concerns about a "world on fire." In the former, Huntington posits that there will be a future of worldwide fragmentation and discord rooted in conflicts between "civilizations," the "highest cultural grouping of people and the broadest level of cultural identity people have short of that which distinguishes human

▪ **Factor**
Variable; a contributor to an outcome.

▪ **Variable**
Factor.

▪ **Comparativists**
Those who work within the field of comparative politics, a subfield of political science.

beings from other species. It is defined by both common objective elements such as language, history, religion, customs, institutions, and by the subjective self-identification of people." It was in this context that Huntington reiterated Kishore Mahbubani's concern about "the West versus the rest."[4] In Chua's book, she argues that "market dominant minorities," usually established immigrant groups or colonists' progeny with both political clout and economic success, are often at odds with larger disenfranchised local majorities.[5] The simmering tensions between these two very different political cultures can erupt into violence or even attempted genocide when free-market democracy is introduced into a country with this domestic political situation. In this case, there is a feedback loop wherein tensions created by one form of globalization (immigration or colonization) are exacerbated by another form of globalization (the export of market-based democracy), and these can then have spillover effects into the region or the world more generally.

The concept of political culture can be applied to the international politics of climate change, too. Political culture would definitely seem to be at play in the western European embrace of emissions control; these postindustrial states have a notably "green" mentality and both a national-level and a regional-level emphasis on sustainability. It was in western Europe that Green parties first took root more than thirty years ago and raised ecological issues to top priorities, linking them to everything from health care to disarmament.[6] And it is in western Europe today that countries are voluntarily reducing their greenhouse gas emissions and seeking other means to control climate change and its effects. In contrast, the issue of global warming resonates less in the political cultures in China, the United States, and Russia. A 2009 Pew public opinion poll found that "concern about global warming is low among the publics of some big polluters—including the U.S., Russia and China. Only about four-in-ten in the U.S. (44%) and Russia (44%) say that global warming is a very serious problem. The Chinese express the least concern—only 30% say it is a very serious problem, up slightly from last year (24%)."[7]

Political culture as a form of analysis is intuitively appealing, but not without its critics. The biggest problem for political culture is the question of **causality**. That is, is political culture a dependent or an **independent variable**? For example, does civic culture lead to democracy, or does democracy lead to civic culture? Do environmental concerns lead to a political culture amenable to green solutions, or does political culture lead to awareness of environmental threats? Or is there perhaps correlation and no causality in either direction? Might there be another variable that can explain both concerns about climate change and a political openness to government attention to them? An independent variable such as an actual heightened threat could explain the simultaneous existence of both. Other challenges raised for political culture include charges that it is too easy to adjust or relax assumptions about culture to make them explanatory, arguments that the concept is too vague and facile, critiques that the idea is hard to prove and impossible to measure, and assessments that political culture as a concept is prone to stereotyping.

▪ **Causality**
The relationship of cause and effect.

▪ **Independent variable**
A causal factor; that which acts on something else, rather than being acted upon. The dependent variable is that which is acted upon.

Despite these criticisms, political culture can be a useful tool of international relations analysis, as long as attention is paid to correlation and causation and it is cautiously applied. Using political culture as an explanation is intuitively appealing precisely because of culture's durability and flexibility. Centuries of migration, interaction, conquest, and trade have not eliminated each European state's identity, for example; globalization has led to cultural dissemination without the loss of cultural integrity. Even in places beaten down by colonialism, culture has often emerged defiantly: Korean culture in the face of Japanese acculturation, Indian culture in the face of British rule, Georgian and Ukrainian culture despite decades of Soviet domination. And across Africa, many contemporary problems are a result of clashes of cultures—nomadic versus sedentary, Muslim versus Christian or animist, and tribal—created by colonialism, by the forcing together of peoples within arbitrary borders and under culturally unappealing or alien forms of governance.

Individual Level of Analysis

It is difficult to carry the forest–trees metaphor any further to describe the individual level of analysis. Using the roads and cars metaphor, though, we might say that at the individual level, we would care about each car's driver. Whereas the roads set the constraints and opportunities and the types of cars and their passengers create their own options and imperatives, the ultimate responsibility for how the car drives among all the others on the road lies with the driver. So it is in world politics. Individual leaders may be constrained by the international system as well as by their own countries' political systems, resources, structures, cultures, and traditions, but ultimately, decision making lies with them. Although there are elements of international affairs that seem immutable to individuals' influence, there are innumerable ways in which individuals shape and drive international politics.

As with systemic-level and domestic-level analyses, individual-level analyses usually seek to find specific factors or variables that can account for, and perhaps even help predict, individuals' behaviors. There are many different approaches to individual-level analysis. Some researchers prefer to create **typologies,** wherein specific personal traits are measured and compared to decision-making patterns. Does how positive or negative a person is affect decision making? Does how passive or active a person is affect his or her ability to influence politics? Can knowing how religious, educated, old, or wealthy a person is help us predict his or her behavior? Other researchers prefer to examine how individuals' beliefs about things like their own political efficacy affect their decision making. To this end, Alexander George, a leading scholar in political science, adopted and refined the concept of the **operational code,** a kind of cognitive (information-processing) map of individuals' political beliefs and priorities (see Spotlight, "The Operational Code").

■ **Typology**
Method of classification.

■ **Operational code**
Cognitive roadmap; complex tracking of belief system.

▪ S P O T L I G H T ▪

The Operational Code

The concept of the operational code was originally developed by a political scientist named Nathan Leites.[i] He conceived of the code as a kind of cognitive map that would take into account the fact that decision makers respond not to the external world but to their own perceptions and impressions of the external world. Alexander George adopted and then refined the concept of the operational code, turning it into a sophisticated analytical tool.[ii] He stated that decision makers' belief systems serve as filters that influence leaders' understanding of and response to any given political circumstance or issue.

George developed the following questions for identifying philosophical beliefs ("assumptions and premises...[made]...regarding the fundamental nature of politics, the nature of political conflict, the role of the individual in history, etc."[iii]) and instrumental beliefs (regarding political ends–means relationships).

- ▪ *Philosophical*
  - What is the essential nature of political life? Is the political universe one of harmony or conflict?
  - What are the prospects for the eventual realization of one's fundamental political value and aspirations?
  - Is the political future predictable? In what sense and to what extent?
  - How much "control" or "mastery" can one have over historical developments? What is one's role in moving and shaping history in the desired direction?
  - What is the role of chance in human affairs and historical developments?

For example, a political scientist considering these questions with reference to former U.S. president George W. Bush might observe that Bush had a strong belief in the essential nature of conflict in international affairs but was optimistic that his objectives could be fulfilled and events predicted, that he believed strongly in the possibility of shaping history in ways that he desired, and that he was not deeply affected by failures.

- ▪ *Instrumental*
  - What is the best approach for selecting goals or objectives for political action?
  - How are the goals of action pursued more effectively?
  - How are the risks of political action being calculated, controlled, and accepted?

- What is the best timing for action to advance one's interests?
- What is the utility and role of different means or tactics for advancing one's interests?

Again, with reference to Bush, we might answer the instrumental questions with observations like: Bush believed in the use of the military as a normal and frequent option, he often relied on his intuitive "gut" feelings by his own testimony, he did not calculate risks carefully because he was confident he could prevail, and he tended to think that if his tools of diplomacy, such as unilateral action, declaring a war on terrorism, or seeking to spread democracy, were well-intentioned, they ultimately would prevail.

These two sets of questions are intended to help a researcher both predict an individual's behavior and compare that individual with others for whom the same questions have been answered. Since George introduced this refined approach to the operational code, it has been applied scores of times by political scientists, including in studies of most of the U.S. presidents, Russian Prime Minister (and former president) Vladimir Putin,[iv] former U.S. Secretary of State Dean Acheson,[v] former chairman of the Chinese Communist party Mao Zedong,[vi] and even the entire Egyptian military elite of the late 1970s.[vii]

PHOTO 2.2 One study of Chairman Mao's operational code shows that his complex strategic beliefs were a product of the times and his own personality.

The concept of the operational code continues to be revised and refined as well.[viii] One of the modifications involves distinguishing between general and targeted operational codes, the latter offering insights into distinctions leaders make between issues. In other words, how leaders might answer the questions just listed could differ from one issue to the next; their perceptions of their ability to control and predict on one issue might not be consistent with their impressions of their abilities to do so regarding others.

Overall, the appeal of the psychological, individual-level approach to political analysis is clear. It addresses the problems related to analyzing the effects on decision making of perception, miscommunication, bias, assumptions, and personal interpretation. It has the potential to be predictive. It also brings the focus of the analysis to "where the buck stops": the decision maker, the final authority, the last word. The limitations of such an approach are also clear, however. It does not take into account the bigger picture, the historical imperatives and political constraints and opportunities with which a decision maker is presented. We do not see the broader context; we only see the final product. Using this approach, we are looking very specifically at the result of a leader's interpretation of and response to the external world.

Ultimately, although it does not afford us a broad view, the value of focusing on this piece of the global politics puzzle should not be underestimated. George wrote of the operational code:

> [K]nowledge of this belief system provides one of the important inputs needed for behavioral analyses of political decision-making and leadership styles. The "operational code" construct does this insofar as it encompasses that aspect of the political actor's perception and structuring of the political world to which he relates, and within which he attempts to operate to advance the interests with which he is identified.[ix]

---

i. Nathan Leites, *The Operational Code of the Politburo* (New York: McGraw-Hill, 1951).

ii. Alexander George, "The 'Operational Code': A Neglected Approach to the Study of Political Leaders and Decision-Making," *International Studies Quarterly* 23 (1969): 190–222.

iii. Ibid., 199.

iv. Stephen Benedict Dyson, "Drawing Policy Implications from the 'Operational Code' of a 'New' Political Actor: Russian President Vladimir Putin," *Policy Sciences* 34 (2001): 329–346.

v. David S. McLellan, "The 'Operational Code' Approach to the Study of Political Leaders: Dean Acheson's Philosophical and Instrumental Beliefs," *Canadian Journal of Political Science* 4 (1971): 52–75.

vi. Huiyun Feng, "The Operational Code of Mao Zedong: Defensive or Offensive Realist?," *Security Studies* 14 (2005): 637–662.

vii. David Bullard Smith, "The Egyptian Military Elite: An Operational Code" (Master's thesis, Naval Postgraduate School, 1977).

viii. Stephen G. Walker, "The Evolution of Operational Code Analysis," *Political Psychology* 11 (1990): 403–418.

ix. George, "The 'Operational Code,'" 220.

An individual-level analysis of the international politics of climate change thus could focus on something as apparently minor as the skills of a particular diplomat over the course of negotiations, or it could take into account the personal experiences of individual legislators as they decided whether to vote for or against ratification of a climate change treaty. An individual-level analysis of the international responses to climate change could also look at and compare the personalities of the various world leaders, considering their motivations and capabilities vis-à-vis international cooperation on climate change. One could consider, for example, why Australia changed its position on the Kyoto Protocol when it changed leadership in 2007. Systemic level factors would not be useful for explaining such a shift, since nothing had changed at the international level. Domestic-level factors might have been able to explain a shift in Australia's policy toward the Kyoto Protocol, but certainly the country's political system was unchanged, its structure was intact, and the same political players were involved. Really, the only significant change was that Kevin Rudd, a supporter of international efforts to combat global warming, took over as prime minister from John Howard, an avid opponent of the international agreement. Indeed, Prime Minister Rudd's first act in office was to sign the instrument of ratification of the Kyoto Protocol. Rudd stated, "This is the first official act of the new Australian Government, demonstrating my Government's commitment to tackling climate change."[8] In this instance, the best explanation for a change in international level behavior is at the individual level of analysis (see Table 2.1).

Levels of Analysis: Analytical Tools

The three levels of analysis are not mutually exclusive. The levels of analysis are only tools that we can use to help us simplify the process of evaluating what we see in world politics. Whatever problem or question we have set for ourselves, the levels of analysis provide one means by which to sift and sort possible explanations. That is not to say, however, that one cannot look at any given international relations issue and explain it using every level of analysis. In general, we expect that the system will set the stage, provide opportunities, and constrain certain actions. The domestic level will determine what interests are affected by the system, what tools are available for response or action (and how powerful those tools are), and who will make decisions. Then the individual level will determine how the international system's constraints and opportunities are perceived, the style of the response, and which tools are wielded in what way to achieve the desired outcome. For any given action, behavior, decision, undertaking, or trend in world affairs, we probably can piece together and tell a relatively complete story by using all the levels of analysis together. The problem is that the more that we add back into our analysis—the more factors we require and combine in unique ways—the more we shift from a **generalizable** explanation to a singular description. We lose **parsimony.**

Imagine a scale that has full and detailed descriptions of unique events on one end and simple, generalizable, parsimonious explanations on the other. Political

■ **Generalizable**
Applicable to other situations, issues, and cases.

■ **Parsimony**
Simplicity.

TABLE 2.1	The International Politics of Climate Change and Potential Explanations Based on the Levels of Analysis
Systemic	1. Cooperation at the international level is possible when states have mutual interests and can overcome the security dilemma through the establishment of institutions that allow for increased communication, transparency, oversight, and confidence. The establishment of the UNFCCC and the signing and ratification of the Kyoto Protocol by 187 states reflect this dynamic.
	2. The anarchic international system prohibits substantive cooperation that could lead to relative gains. The failure of states to conclude a binding agreement to reduce greenhouse gas emissions is a function of each state's concerns that assuming the costs of such mitigation would reduce their industrial products' price competitiveness relative to other states in the system.
Domestic	The international response to climate change is influenced in large part by domestic considerations, including countries' dependence on greenhouse gas–producing industries. It is no coincidence that the last two efforts to develop climate change agreements—the Kyoto Protocol and the Copenhagen Accord—were scuttled by the United States and China, each, respectively, the world's largest greenhouse gas producer at the time of the negotiations.
Individual	Global warming as an issue has been personified by former U.S. vice president Al Gore. With his book and movie *An Inconvenient Truth* and his very public activism for a greater international response to climate change, Gore has been both a leader and a lightning rod. Proponents of climate change legislation cite Gore's sources and statements. Texas A&M climatologist Steven Quiring observed that: "whether scientists like it or not, *An Inconvenient Truth* has had a much greater impact on public opinion and public awareness of global climate change than any scientific paper or report."[a] Opponents attempt to smear climate change as an issue by ridiculing Gore himself. In an opinion piece in the *New York Post* entitled "Al Gore's Latest Whopper," for example, columnist Alan Reynolds wrote: "Al Gore's defense of global-warming hysteria in Sunday's New York Times has many flaws, but I'll focus on just one whopper—where the 'Inconvenient Truth' man states the *opposite* of scientific fact."[b]

[a]Steven M. Quiring, "Science and Hollywood: A Discussion of the Scientific Accuracy of *An Inconvenient Truth*," *GeoJournal* 70.1 (September 2007): 1–3, http://www.springerlink.com/content/e135182138xl0412/?p=4be8836dc4ad49ca92083a09356fa72b&pi=0.

[b]Alan Reynolds, "Al's Latest Global Warming Whopper," *New York Post*, 2 March 2010, http://www.nypost.com/p/news/opinion/opedcolumnists/al_latest_global_warming_whopper_TolFbG2ccT5XPtKtXoOxoL.

scientist Kenneth Waltz wrote strongly in favor of the explanatory option over the descriptive. Referencing the opportunity to increase the number of factors in an analysis to bring it closer to reality, he wrote:

> But that would be to move away from a theory claiming explanatory power to a less theoretical system promising greater descriptive accuracy. One who wishes to explain rather than to describe should resist moving in that direction if resistance is reasonable.... [It is because one] gains clarity and economy of concepts.[9]

Waltz's recommended standard is rigorous and most applicable to the systemic level of analysis, where the focus is on the system itself as an explanatory variable. As we move into the domestic and individual levels of analysis, more factors tend to come into play and there is a necessary increase in the complexity of explanations; systemic-level analyses thus tend to be the most parsimonious and individual-level analyses the most descriptive. Also, and relatedly, systemic-level analyses tend to provide explanations for the most general aspects of world politics, domestic-level analyses can explain more specific events and actions, and individual-level analyses can offer insights into particular behaviors and decisions. Nonetheless, as a general rule, regardless of the level of analysis we choose to apply, when we analyze international relations, we do wish to eliminate from our consideration as many of the peripheral variables as possible so that we can identify and study the one factor or very few key factors that explain whatever we are examining. In that way, we can hope to anticipate, re-create, or avoid the same political circumstances in the future. In other words, we are trying to be as **scientific** as possible, looking for the independent variables on which the outcome in question hinges.

It is worth noting that although most political scientists are, indeed, trying to be as scientific as possible in their approach to examining world politics, there are a couple of schools of thought that reject this positivist approach. Postmodernists, for example, argue that our language and perceptions inevitably color our analysis, making it impossible for us to assess international relations objectively. That is, our abilities to read and then convey our understandings of world affairs are both skewed, so that trying to be scientific is naive. Critical theorists likewise argue that we cannot assess international relations **objectively,** but they lay the blame on our **subjective** beliefs and preferences. In contrast to the postmodernists, who argue that we cannot see or communicate neutrally, the critical theorists maintain that we bias our findings both by how we choose and frame our subject matter and by how we then interpret our findings.

These criticisms are discerning and valuable; they remind us, as we study politics, that we are working with clumsy tools and are too often guided by preconceptions. In our efforts to simplify (find the smallest number of **necessary and sufficient variables**) we may veer too far from the messy complexities of the real world. Nonetheless, the scientific approach has its benefits as well, allowing us to sort the chaff from the grain, to consider the relative impact on world politics of specific variables, and to examine the components of international relations individually before we try to understand the larger, more confusing whole. If

■ **Scientific**
Systematic and logical; replicable; positivist.

■ **Objective**
Unbiased, neutral, independent, dispassionate.

■ **Subjective**
Prejudiced, skewed, biased.

■ **Necessary and sufficient variables**
Factors that are adequate for determining—and that must be present to achieve—a specific outcome.

we keep in mind the critiques of the postmodernists and critical theorists, we might be able to avoid some of the more egregious bias built into the analytical process.

Theoretical Paradigms/Worldviews

Several times thus far, we have mentioned how our own beliefs, preconceptions, and assumptions might color our understanding of international relations. In Table 2.1, for example, the two alternative systemic-level explanations for the international response to climate change represent two very different understandings of how international affairs function. Likewise, we posited earlier how differently analysts perceive the significance of the anarchic nature of the international system, some seeing it as a dog-eat-dog world, others as more ripe for cooperation, and yet others as a product of our own interpretation and actions. In this section we discuss the **theoretical paradigms** or **worldviews** that infuse studies of global politics. The three main paradigms are realism, liberalism, and constructivism.

Realism

Political realism does not require, nor does it condone, indifference to political ideals and moral principles, but it requires indeed a sharp distinction between the desirable and the possible—between what is desirable everywhere and at all times and what is possible under the concrete circumstances of time and place.

—*Hans J. Morgenthau*[10]

▪ **Theoretical paradigm**
Worldview;
Weltanschauung; set of theories based on shared assumptions.

▪ **Worldview**
Weltanschauung;
perspective on human nature.

▪ **Idealism**
Belief that people can and should work towards achieving a just and peaceful world order.

▪ **Realpolitik**
Interest-based (rather than ethics-based or ideals-based) foreign policy.

The school of thought known as realism is the most venerable paradigm in international relations theory. Its roots can be traced back hundreds of years to the Greek historian Thucydides and his *History of the Peloponnesian Wars* (431–404 B.C.); to Kautilya (around 300 B.C.), a Hindu statesman and philosopher; and to Sun Tzu (500 B.C.), author of the Chinese classic *The Art of War.* At the core of the realist paradigm is an emphasis on the study of war and peace (high politics) over trade and domestic issues (low politics), combined with a belief that people are inherently and primarily motivated by self-interest and the quest for security from, if not power over, their peers.

Realism today borrows from political theorists such as Niccolò Machiavelli (1469–1527) and Thomas Hobbes (1588–1679) and developed after World War II as a response to the failure of the interwar period's (1919–1939) **idealism.** In rejecting the naive and utopian orientation of idealism, many scholars and policy makers, such as Hans Morgenthau, E. H. Carr, Reinhold Niebuhr, George Kennan, Henry Kissinger, and John Foster Dulles, emphasized the logic of **realpolitik** (literally, the "politics of realism"), power politics, and the treacherous—amoral and selfish—nature of humans in shaping interstate relations.[11] These realists viewed the world as governed only by the "law of the jungle," wherein each state's leaders must protect the state's vital interests, political independence, and territorial **sovereignty** at any cost. In such a dog-eat-dog environment, military power is often necessary for national survival. If a state becomes militarily weaker vis-à-vis other states, its survival might be jeopardized. The realists' international system consequently resembles Charles Darwin's theory of natural selection, in which only the fittest survive.

Contemporary realists share a set of related core assumptions:

- Anarchy is the foundation of international politics and leads to power politics (realpolitik) as states try at least to ensure their security and often to enhance their power.
- Because of anarchy, states are prone to conflict, not cooperation.
- Stability in the international system is better preserved by conflict than by cooperation.
- States that prioritize cooperation or economic gain over security will not fare as well in the international system.
- States are the key political actors in the international system, and it is relations among them that matter most in the study of world politics.

There are many variants of realism. The types of realism coincide, roughly, with the levels of analysis. At the systemic level, for example, there is neorealism, also known as structural realism. Structural realism borrows from academic disciplines such as microeconomics and biology. In contrast to classical realists, who emphasize the fearful and conflictual nature of humankind, adherents of structural realism such as Kenneth Waltz and Joseph Grieco argue that the structure of the international system accounts for the behavior of states.[12] Structural realists share a set of fundamental assumptions:

1. The international system is anarchic.
2. All states within the system are unitary, rational actors.
3. The primary concern of all states is survival.

The unique assumption among these, defining this as neorealism, is that the state is a unitary and rational actor. In a deliberate effort to simplify world politics, structural realists deemphasize the role of actors within the state and give precedence to the international system itself as the causal variable shaping the state's actions. This conception of states often likens them to billiard balls on a pool table. Just as players do not care what is inside the balls, neorealists have little concern for what goes on within states. It is the external pressure exerted on them that determines their behavior.

Positing that all states seek survival above all else also serves to streamline the neorealists' analysis and signals the set of assumptions underpinning it. Neorealists argue that, because the international system is an anarchic, self-help system, each state is left alone to guarantee its own survival because no other

■ **Sovereignty**
Exclusive political authority over a defined territory and the people within it.

▪ **Absolute power**
Total amount of power.

▪ **Relative power**
Amount of power compared to other entities.

▪ **Security dilemma**
When distrust runs so high between states that when each seeks to increase its defensive capabilities, the other perceives that as a threat and increases its own, creating an arms race.

▪ **Unipolar**
An international structure dominated by a single power.

▪ **Bipolar**
An international structure dominated by two major powers.

▪ **Multipolar**
An international structure dominated by several great powers.

▪ **Balancing**
When states seek to prevent another state's or other states' domination of the international system either by ensuring through domestic development that they are equally powerful or by creating alliances that are equal to a state's or another alliance's power.

▪ **Great powers**
The few states in the international system whose outstanding economic and military power set them qualitatively apart from the next tier of states.

▪ **Superpowers**
One or two states whose powers are so great that they cannot be effectively challenged for domination of the international system.

state will do so.[13] States are therefore assumed to place security at the top of their list of priorities, to see power as the means to security, and therefore to maximize their own power. Moreover, a state's **absolute power** is not considered as important as a state's **relative power** or position with regard to other states. The inherent danger of this situation, of course, is that the heavy emphasis on security compels each state to increase its own safeguards, thus decreasing other states' relative security, leading them, in turn, to increase their own safeguards, creating a vicious cycle referred to as the **security dilemma**.[14]

Although the international system encompasses all states in the world, structural realists are primarily concerned with the most powerful states, or great powers. For these theorists, the structure of the international system is defined by the distribution of power among the great powers—in other words, the number of great powers in the system and their relative capabilities. Neorealists therefore typically describe the structure of the international system in terms of polarity, with each major power representing a "pole" of the system. A **unipolar** system is one in which a single dominant power (a hegemon) exists (e.g., post–Cold War, arguably, with the demise of the Soviet Union and the United States as the preeminent world power), a **bipolar** system is one with two great powers (e.g., during the Cold War), and a **multipolar** system (e.g., in the early nineteenth century, at the time of the Concert of Europe) has three or more great powers. (See Chapter 3 for more on the various historical structures of the international system.)

Structural realists are interested in the shifts in power among the major states and the impact these will have on the stability of the international system. Stability as it is used here refers to the absence of large wars or other political actions with the potential to significantly shift power in the international system. Part of maintaining stability is maintaining balance in the international system. Neorealists depict the international system as zero-sum; that is, one state's relative gain in power and influence can take place only at a cost to other states. As these shifts occur, there is a potential for destabilization. Structural realists argue that states therefore keep each other in check—and maintain the system's integrity—by **balancing,** making and breaking alliances as needed to ensure that no state or group of states gains ascendancy. This appears to describe well how **great powers** behaved between 1815 and the start of the twentieth century, as well as the behavior of the **superpowers** during the Cold War (1945–1989) (see Chapters 3 and 4).

An alternative to balancing is **bandwagoning,** in which states, rather than allying themselves against a rising power, ally themselves with it. Neorealists argue that this behavior is most likely to take place when weaker states calculate that the costs of resisting a rising power are higher than the benefits of joining it.

Structural realism as an analytical approach was dealt a blow with the collapse of the Soviet empire. The only way to explain the collapse, in the absence of any substantive systemic changes, was by looking into the USSR itself. This real-world event highlighted weaknesses of neorealism that analysts had long acknowledged. Because its adherents, for the benefits of simplicity and parsimony, resist **reductivism,** they cannot acknowledge or anticipate the effects of changes within states—this despite the fact that the long bipolar peace of the Cold War was due as much to U.S. and Soviet internal efforts to balance (by mobilizing their domestic economic and industrial resources and converting them to military power) as to each country's alliance building. Although neorealism gained tremendous buy-in in the analytical community throughout the Cold War, its influence has since declined as researchers and scholars rely increasingly on other forms of realism and on other theoretical paradigms.

Some realists, for example, have embraced the complex dynamics between national and international politics. Among these are the neoclassical realists,[15] who argue that the relative power each state has as measured by its resources and capabilities determines its position on the world stage, but only insofar as its political structures allow effective employment of the resources. For these scholars,[16] states' internal dimensions—in terms of both resources (material or national power) and political organization and culture (state power)—serve as filters for the international system. Neoclassical realists still consider the international system the independent variable, but in contrast to neorealists' concerns about reductivism, they hold domestic-level factors to be important **intervening variables.** When looking at the international politics of climate change, this would suggest that domestic politics in each member country would influence that state's interpretation of how cooperation would affect its economic competitiveness and thus relative power.

Neoclassical realists have breathed life back into realists' use of domestic-level variables. Realists in the past did try to correlate national character and war. They believed that the cause of war lay in culture and in some states' proclivities toward violence. Scores of studies were done to find correlations between war and various national factors, such as population density, level of economic development, political structure, religious affiliation, and internal conflict. Most of these, however, found weak or no correlations.[17] Today, neoclassical realist Randall Schweller's contemporary concept of a **revisionist state**[18] hearkens back to this body of work, insofar as it is rooted in the concept of a state's identity. Schweller argues that states will become revisionist—they will attempt to overthrow the current international system—when they are so dissatisfied with the system and their position within it that they are willing to risk everything to force change. Schweller characterizes states as lions (contented with the status quo because they rule it), lambs (weak and hoping only to avoid being caught up by more active states), jackals (risk averse but opportunistic), and revisionist wolves (predatory and desperate enough to take huge risks to better their relative positions). Whether states ally to prevent the ascension of a hegemon (balance) or hitch their fortunes to the rising power (bandwagon) depends, according to Schweller, on which kind of state they are.

Finally, classical realists (in comparison with neorealists and neoclassical realists) tend to rely on the individual level of analysis, in which human nature and biology are the explanatory factors. As mentioned earlier, such political science icons as Morgenthau and Carr subscribed to the view that humans are inherently

▪ **Bandwagoning**
When (usually weak) states seek to ally themselves with rising powers to take advantage of their strength.

▪ **Reductivism**
Using domestic- or individual-level variables in an analysis of world politics; looking beyond systemic level factors for explanations.

▪ **Intervening variables**
Factors that influence but do not determine an outcome; factors that filter the effects of an independent variable.

▪ **Revisionist state**
A state that is dissatisfied with its position in the international system and therefore intent on changing the system itself.

power-seeking and that international affairs are simply an extension of human nature. Classical realists reject both idealism (in favor of prudence) and political science (which at the time was based on the assumption that, as rational beings, people could identify that which led to war and conflict and overcome it using reason and will). These scholars, looking at the international responses to climate change, would reject any idealistic claims of its progenitors and look, instead, for who stood to gain what from the process and the outcome. Indeed, Morgenthau quoted George Washington as saying:

> A small knowledge of human nature will convince us, that, with far the greatest part of mankind, interest is the governing principle; and that almost every man is more or less, under its influence. Motives of public virtue may for a time, or in particular instances, actuate men to the observance of a conduct purely disinterested; but they are not of themselves sufficient to produce persevering conformity to the refined dictates and obligations of social duty. Few men are capable of making a continual sacrifice of all views of private interest, or advantage, to the common good. It is vain to exclaim against the depravity of human nature on this account; the fact is so, the experience of every age and nation has proved it and we must in a great measure, change the constitution of man, before we can make it otherwise. No institution, not built on the presumptive truth of these maxims can succeed.[19]

Liberalism

The tensions between globalization and fragmentation and between conflict and cooperation are mirrored in the tensions between realists and liberals. Like realism, liberalism has venerable and centuries-old roots. Hugo Grotius (1583–1645) wrote extensively about **Just War, natural law,** and the concept of an international society in the seventeenth century, breaking down for the leaders of the time the conditions under which wars legitimately could be fought, the standards to which soldiers and their masters should be held accountable on the battlefield, our fundamental rights to protect our lives and property regardless of states' laws, and the potential advantages of a world community. In his writings against unnecessary or unjustified wars, Grotius also emphasized the value of negotiations and compromise in efforts to settle disputes. Finally, Grotius introduced the concept of the **State of Nature,** a metaphor for the anarchic world with no government or authorities. John Locke (1632–1704) borrowed the idea of the State of Nature and put it to use in his *Second Treatise on Government,*[20] in which he laid out the value of **social contracts** in protecting life, liberty, and property. Although Locke was talking about domestic institutions, his observations pertain at the international level as well. Immanuel Kant (1724–1804), in his 1795 *Perpetual Peace: A Philosophical Sketch,*[21] outlined the conditions for peace in the international community. In that book he called for sovereignty, the peaceful resolution of differences, abjuration of devious tactics during war that could undermine future confidence in negotiations (poisoning, assassination, etc.), and, most famously, **republican** constitutions (democracies).

▪ **Just War**
A specific set of criteria about when resorting to the use of force is acceptable (*jus ad bello*) and a set of criteria about how combatants should behave (*jus in bello*).

▪ **Natural law**
Universal law that transcends man-made rules and regulations.

▪ **State of Nature**
A metaphor for a world in which there is no higher authority to which to turn and in which each individual can depend only on himself or herself.

▪ **Social contracts**
Agreements between people, groups, or states, in which the parties defer some autonomy to an authority they form to act on behalf of the group as a whole.

▪ **Republican**
Based on popular consent and representation.

All of these philosophers shared the basic tenets of liberalism:

- Cooperation is not only possible despite anarchy and human nature, but beneficial.
  - There is more cooperation than conflict in the world.
  - People can learn and adapt.
- International politics is a **variable-sum**, not a zero-sum, game.
- Cooperation can be facilitated by:
  - Interdependence.
  - Institutions.
  - Democracy.
- States that focus on cooperation and mutual interests will do better in the international system than those that focus exclusively on security.
  - Stability in the international system is better preserved by cooperation than by conflict.

As with realism, there are many variants of liberalism and, again, we can describe them in rough correspondence with the levels of analysis. Relying on the systemic level are the neoliberals who argue that **institutions, regimes,** and other forms of coordination can overcome the challenges anarchy poses. Tied into this discussion, too, is the concept of **interdependence** as a means of raising the costs of conflict and promoting the benefits of cooperation. Neoliberals share with neorealists the assumptions that the international system is anarchic and that the players within it are unitary, rational actors. However, they challenge structural realists' claims that the primary concern of all states is survival, that states are the only relevant actors in international politics, that the world is zero-sum, that states benefit more from prioritizing security than from promoting economic well-being, and that international stability is better preserved by military competition than by cooperation.

Neoliberals instead argue that because politics is a variable-sum game, rather than zero-sum, and because states and other international actors (MNCs, NGOs, IOs) have varied and complex interests, many of which are interrelated and even interdependent, cooperation is key to ensuring that international actors' interests are protected and furthered. These scholars acknowledge that cooperation is difficult in an anarchic environment, but posit that it is nonetheless possible when institutions are created to temper international actors' concerns and enhance their confidence that none of the states or groups with which they are working will take unfair advantage of cooperative agreements. Such institutions can run the gamut from international norms to international laws to actual brick-and-mortar organizations like the UN, the World Trade Organization, and the International Criminal Court.

Regime theory,[22] or institutionalism, involves the proposition that states and other international actors develop—deliberately or serendipitously—rules, norms, laws, or organizations to enhance and protect cooperation. Oran Young, a well-known political scientist, defines institutions as "social practices consisting

▪ **Variable-sum**
Potential for expanding, and mutual, benefits; opposite of zero-sum.

▪ **Institution**
An international norm, law, agreement, treaty, group, or organization formed around a common interest or region; synonymous with regime.

▪ **Regime**
An international norm, law, agreement, treaty, group, or organization formed around a common interest or region; synonymous with institution.

▪ **Interdependence**
Symbiosis; a relationship of mutual dependence between two or more entities in which changes in one entity affect the other entities.

of easily recognized roles coupled with clusters of rules or conventions governing relations among the occupants of these roles."[23] Institutions might emerge around geographical areas, specific activities, or some other aspect of world affairs involving a subset of the world community. The concept of institutions includes all the possible means of promoting cooperation, from commonly accepted but informal rules of behavior (like opposition to genocide) to international regulations (such as the Laws of War) to international organizations (e.g., the United Nations).[24] The assumption is that when a need arises for mediated cooperation (when states had interests to protect and not all that much trust of each other), institutions form. The Organization of the Petroleum Oil Exporting Countries (OPEC) is often used as support for institutionalism: The members joined the organization to ensure their mutual interests while setting in place means of preventing any one member from taking advantage of the others' willingness to cooperate. They could stabilize oil prices and ensure steady incomes by agreeing among themselves when and under what circumstances they would increase or decrease oil production.

Institutionalism arose in part as a denial of some neorealists' claims that international cooperation could only take place if a hegemon were in place and chose to promote, underwrite, and enforce cooperative efforts. Some institutionalists, in fact, claim that institutionalism subsumes realism entirely.[25] This debate between neorealists and neoliberals is a modern version of the long-standing difference of worldviews reflected in the writings of Thomas Hobbes (1588–1679) and John Locke (1632–1704). Whereas the former argued that it would take a **Leviathan**[26] to overcome the "war of all against all" in the State of Nature, Locke wrote that man could conquer the same challenges through social contracts, in which each participant would give up some autonomy for the benefits of a legitimate authority.[27]

Accepting the basic precepts that rational, unitary actors interact under anarchic conditions, institutionalists seek to define under what circumstances international actors will choose cooperation over conflict. Institutionalists argue that institutions achieve results by reducing **transaction costs,** creating confidence, serving as forums for communication, setting clear expectations, and providing information. In other words, by increasing trust, reducing the possibility of a state's defection from an agreement, and providing an opportunity for regular communication, institutions promote cooperation.

Institutionalists can make their argument in part because they reject the neorealists' presumption that states strive only for **relative gains** instead of **absolute gains.** Neorealists have trouble with the concept of cooperation because they believe that states are more concerned with their position vis-à-vis other states in the system than they are with their position in general. In other words, realists believe that states would sacrifice absolute gains if they could instead reap relative gains. By rejecting this premise, institutionalists can posit that states will cooperate not only when they each believe they are gaining more than the rest of the states, but even when they understand that they all will benefit from the cooperation.

▪ **Leviathan**
Per Hobbes, an absolute sovereign; a benevolent dictator.

▪ **Transaction costs**
The costs of doing business.

▪ **Relative gains**
Increases in wealth or strength relative to others.

▪ **Absolute gains**
Absolute increases in wealth or strength, regardless of others' increases.

Thomas Hobbes proposed a strong, centralized government to overcome the "war of all against all" in the State of Nature.

With respect to the international responses to climate change, an institutionalist approach might involve arguing that any response will depend the facilitating structure of the UNFCCC and any agreements that can be produced through the annual COP. An institutionalist would point to the structure of the institution itself to demonstrate where confidence-building measures have been included, standard means of communication have been delineated, and costs for defection have been established. The UNFCCC is an example of a new institution being developed to create rules for cooperation among the states signing the agreement so that they can all benefit. In this sense it fits the institutionalist approach perfectly.

Interdependence is another concept on which many neoliberals rely. Although institutions can lower the costs of cooperation, interdependence can raise the costs of conflict. If countries' economies are intertwined, for example, the costs of going to war will be borne not only in terms of military outlays, lives lost, infrastructural damage, and so forth, but also in terms of the economic costs of diminished or terminated trade and investment: lost jobs, lost income, bankruptcies, and so forth. Many studies have been done on this relationship between economic ties and conflict, the most sophisticated of which have found that the **inverse correlation** is true under specific circumstances, but not universally. Moreover, interdependence itself might sometimes cause tensions that can escalate into overt hostilities.[28] Understanding interdependence and its relationship to conflict can help policymakers design agreements and promote interdependence in the most constructive and positive ways while side-stepping potential hazards of such close involvement.

Not all liberal analyses use the systemic level of analysis. Indeed, one of the best known and most hotly debated liberal theories relies on one key domestic-level factor: democracy. Since the 1980s, Democratic Peace theory has relied on a simple contention: **Liberal democracies** are extremely unlikely to go to war against each other. They may go to war against nondemocracies, but not against each other. The argument predates the modern debate; Immanuel Kant wrote in his aforementioned 1795 essay *Perpetual Peace* that there were several requirements for the elimination of international war, one of which was that states must be constitutional republics. His logic was that in a democracy, it would be impossible to get a majority of the public to vote for war, except in self-defense, thus eliminating the possibility for war. Nearly 200 years later, debate over the concept of a Democratic Peace erupted in the field of political science.[29] Whereas some observed that democracies do not go to war against each other, others argued that such a finding could not possibly be statistically significant because there are only so many democracies in the world. In addition, other scholars noted that democracies may not go to war with each other, but they do engage in policies short of war, such as covert operations, against other democracies. Still others sought to demonstrate the logic of a Democratic Peace. This domestic-level liberal theory has reverberated in academic and policy circles ever since.

Indeed in part because many political scientists came to believe in the 1980s and 1990s that there was ample evidence that democracies do not go to war against each other or at least almost never do, the Bush administration concluded after 9/11 that if it could increase the number of democracies in the Middle East, war and support for terrorism would be reduced. The problem was that the administration tended to equate democracy with elections, forgetting that democracy also requires institution building and a supportive culture of civil society developed over many years, if not decades. As a consequence, in many cases, such as Iraq, Afghanistan, and Palestine, the American push for democracy failed to achieve the anticipated reforms, development, and subsequent stability.

▪ **Inverse correlation**
A relationship in which an increase in one factor corresponds to a decrease in another.

▪ **Liberal democracy**
A representative democracy moderated by a constitution, protecting the freedom and rights of individuals and the minority, guided by the will of the majority, and with an accountable government.

PHOTO 2.4   **U.S. President Barack Obama at the UNFCCC's COP 15.**

Finally, liberals applying the individual level of analysis are likely to seek answers to questions like these: What personal characteristics determine whether political leaders will promote the public good? What personality traits do the best negotiators have? What views of politics must political leaders hold if they are going to pursue international cooperation? What kind of operational codes did the most famous liberal politicians have? Those studying international responses to climate change and using this paradigm and level of analysis might consider how participating leaders' personal views and political acumen could help predict or explain their progress toward or resistance to an international accord.

Constructivism[30]

Many of constructivism's proponents conceive of it as an evolutionary step in political science. Constructivists define their own approach by its differences from realism and liberalism. For example, those two paradigms, at the systemic level of analysis, share the assumptions that states are self-interested rational actors, that their identities and interests are **exogenously given,** that their behaviors generate outcomes, and that they are the dominant actors in the international system. In contrast, constructivists argue that states are far from rational, that they develop their identities and interests internally, and that their assumptions, beliefs, and behaviors determine the effect of the international system.

▪ **Exogenously given**
Determined externally; imposed, rather than derived from within.

It is important to understand that whereas structural realists and liberals rely on science and economics as the templates for their theories, constructivists instead turn to other fields, like psychology and sociology. Thus, although structural realists and liberals focus on the effects of the system (in particular, its anarchic nature) on international actors, constructivists argue that it is the actors' interpretations and responses to the structure of international relations that determine the international system.

For example, a constructivist will point out that although the international system is anarchic, it is not necessarily a self-help system, as realists and even liberals assume. Rather, imagine that the very first states dealing with each other in the international system chose to trust each other and act decently toward each other. This behavior, in turn, would have led to more such behavior as each state realized that it could trust its neighbors and work confidently with them as long as it demonstrated its own honesty and good intentions. Had this taken place, the anarchy of the international system would have been irrelevant because states would have created for themselves—by their behavior, assumptions, and reciprocity—a system in which the paranoia and fear of self-help were not necessary.

It is with this kind of scenario (although this is much simplified) in mind that constructivists argue that international actors make their own reality. They are not driven by the system; the system does not predetermine their behaviors; they have choices and those choices will be reflected back at them as other states respond. Moreover, it is from their actions and interactions—from **process**—that states' identities will be created, both for themselves and for each other. It is from their identities that their interests will devolve. If they identify as competitors, their primary interest might well be security. If they identify as partners, on the other hand, their primary interest could be something like economic growth, sustainability, or the promotion of good health. For constructivists, therefore, the international cooperation to date on climate change represents a shift in the perception of climate change, a recognition of it as a threat, and the beginning of a global conversation that will, in turn, shape the potential next steps. Indeed, constructivists can readily accommodate the evolution of international thinking about global warming and potential means by which to address it. As understanding of the science of climate change has become more nuanced, and both the media and policymakers have brought their perceptions of climate change more in line with mainstream scientists' views, the appreciation of the potential threat has increased, as has the diversity of potentially politically acceptable responses. Whereas at the time of the Kyoto Protocol the emphasis was on reducing greenhouse gas emissions, views as to what might be possible have expanded to include expanding **carbon sinks, emissions trading** schemes, **reforestation,** and even more radical solutions, such as "geo-engineering," which involves drastic efforts like placing giant lenses between the earth and the sun, infusing the earth's atmosphere with reflective sulfur, or dumping iron dust into the oceans to grow carbon-sucking algae blooms.[31] In fact, many constructivists argue that there is an element of **securitization** in what is taking place with reference to

▪ **Process**
Series of interactions over time.

▪ **Carbon sinks**
Forests, oceans, and other reservoirs that absorb and store carbon.

▪ **Emissions trading**
Also known as "cap and trade," emissions trading involves setting a limit on greenhouse gas emissions that, if exceeded, will lead to fines or sanctions. The trading can take place when an entity knows it will not reach its emission limit and trades, for a price, its allowance to an entity likely to exceed its own emissions limit.

▪ **Reforestation**
The opposite of deforestation; the planting of trees to act as carbon sinks.

▪ **Securitization**
Most simply, securitization is the act of naming something a security concern so that it becomes an elevated priority justifying greater national attention and resources.

climate change. Global warming is increasingly being cast as a security concern and therefore both as more worthy of attention and as falling more within the purview of executive branches than legislatures.[32] This focus on how thinking about an issue and acting on it can in turn affect the next possible steps is a hallmark of constructivism clearly illustrated by the evolution of thinking on climate change, its effects, and potential responses.

Constructivist theories do not break down neatly within the levels of analysis. They tend to emphasize the big picture at the systemic level of analysis. Nonetheless, constructivist theories are, ultimately, calls to action that can reverberate down to the domestic and individual levels of analysis. Indeed, by pointing out that systems are **self-reinforcing** (e.g., in a self-help system, competition is rewarded and altruism is punished), constructivists are warning political leaders and decision makers against **reification** and encouraging them to recognize the effects of their own decisions and assumptions.

Critics of constructivism argue that it is not a theory: There is no independent variable, no single factor like the system's structure or a government's organization that can explain whether cooperation will or will not occur. Others suggest that constructivism is a throwback in some ways to idealism, steeped as it is in the assumption that states can make the world work better simply by choosing to behave better themselves. Still others argue that constructivism is a confusing rehashing of the more theoretical tit-for-tat game theory outlined by Robert Axelrod. Axelrod used game theory to demonstrate that, within an iterated (repetitive) game, states will respond well when other states behave well toward them and will respond punitively when other states behave badly toward them, thus slowly moving toward cooperation as **complex learning** takes place.[33]

Despite these criticisms, constructivists have created an important new discussion among political scientists, raising significant questions about structural theorists' assumptions and suggesting interesting and valuable new ways of introducing the concepts of perception, behavior, and consequences back into discussions of world affairs.

Blurring the Lines

Just as there are gray areas between the levels of analysis, so do the various worldviews sometimes blur. As noted earlier, for example, constructivists point out the similarities between weak realists and weak liberals, both of which explain cooperation and institutions in terms of self-interests. Perhaps the best example of the permeable lines between the paradigms is regime theory:

> Different theoretical schools of international relations put forward their own explanations for the origins of regimes and their relative influence....Realism directs our attention to the role of power in creating and sustaining regimes, as well as what consequences regimes may have for the distribution of power in the international system. Neoliberal insights center on viewing regimes as mechanisms that facilitate achieving optimal outcomes by reducing uncertainty. Cognitivists draw

▪ **Self-reinforcing**
Initial perceptions or assumptions lead to preferences that will satisfy those perceptions or assumptions.

▪ **Reification**
Fallacy of treating something man-made (an object or idea) as if it were naturally occurring.

▪ **Complex learning**
Learning from experience; learning by imitation.

our attention to the fact that regimes are fundamentally social entities. Therefore, norms, identities and discourse are important in shaping regimes and are, in turn, themselves influenced by regimes.[34]

Other Theoretical Paradigms/Worldviews

Realism, liberalism, and constructivism are far from the only theoretical paradigms, although they tend to dominate most of the current discussion. Two other prominent worldviews are feminism (arguably on the rise) and world systems theories (arguably on the decline since the collapse of the Soviet Union).

Building on constructivist theories, in recent decades **feminist** scholars have challenged traditional concepts of international relations, contending that gender-biased theories and analysis offer an incomplete and distorted picture of international affairs. They argue that because the overwhelming majority of actors in international conflict, politics, and economics have been men, the study of world affairs has been biased toward the high politics of war, adversarial bargaining, and realpolitik, which grow out of men's experience. Conversely, roles and concerns traditionally ascribed to women, such as health, education, child care, and home and community economics, have been considered irrelevant to the workings of the international system. As a result, both the theory and practice of international relations have overemphasized security, power, hierarchy, and domination, in keeping with the privileged status of values that society ascribes to men and defines as primarily male pursuits.

Feminist theorists of international relations seek to change all this. In the 1990s, scholars such as J. Ann Tickner, V. Spike Peterson, Anne Sisson Runyan, Rebecca Grant, and Kathleen Newland began to develop an approach to world politics that takes the perspectives, values, and concerns of women explicitly into consideration. For such scholars, gender is the category of analysis (gender refers to the socially constructed notions of masculinity and femininity).[35] Feminist perspectives can particularly deepen our knowledge of the world economy, as women are typically affected first and most strongly in times of economic hardship. Feminist scholars also seek to challenge or redefine core concepts of international relations such as security, power, and sovereignty, claiming that these ideas are based in values traditionally associated with masculinity and constructed to exclude women from full participation in international relations (in this way, male/masculinity is valued more highly than female/femininity). For example, many feminist critics contend that realist theories, which conclude that states must be self-reliant and seek military power to preserve their security, are generalizations from male values and experience that do not reflect the perceptions and concerns of women.

As more women take leading roles in governments, economic enterprises, and international institutions, the systems and structures of world politics may take on more gender-inclusive forms. However, the extent to which women will

▪ **Feminist**
One who believes in equality of the sexes.

change international affairs, or will be changed by it, is not yet clear, as female policymakers are socialized into the same institutions and confront the same problems as their male colleagues. In any event, by analyzing world events through a "gender-sensitive lens," feminist scholars offer an alternative view of the world that can bring the needs and experiences that lead to cooperation and conflict into sharper focus.

With regard to the international responses to climate change, some feminists have expressed concern that the means of measuring the potential threat, as well as proposed solutions, fail to take into account that women are disproportionately affected by global climate change because of, among other things, their roles as gatherers of food, fuel, and water.[36] These analysts argue for rethinking both the dangers of climate change and solutions, taking into account issues such as disparate effects, sustainability, and environmental justice.

In contrast to realists, liberals, and constructivists, all of whom are focused on questions of conflict and cooperation, world systems theorists, with their roots in Marxism, focus on uneven economic development and the exploitation of "peripheral" states by those in the "core." In this view, the best-known proponent of which is Immanuel Wallerstein, the international system is the "capitalist world economy" in which the underdeveloped states on the **periphery** provide inexpensive natural resources and wide open markets for manufactured goods to the industrialized, wealthy states in the **core.**[37] The system is self-perpetuating, meaning that it is very difficult for a country on the periphery to break into the core because the structure is stacked against such advancement. As in more traditional Marxist analyses, world systems theorists hold that the elite oppresses the masses by denying them access to the means of production; in this case, countries that produce industrial inputs (basic resources) find it difficult, within the constraints of the international economy, to diversify, their products rarely garner adequate profits, industrialization is a costly process, and often their own governments are in collusion with the industrialized countries' elites. World systems theorists could argue that the international politics of climate change are dominated by capitalist elites seeking to reap immediate wealth despite the likely medium- and long-term costs to the poorest people, regions, and countries who will be least able to mitigate the effects of global warming. Indeed, those most vulnerable to global warming can do little to reduce it. They are entirely dependent on the producers of greenhouse gases, those who profit from the means of production, to address climate change in any meaningful, substantial way. Yet the global industrial elite and the political leaders with whom they collude, in this Marxist vision, have shown no interest in sacrificing profits for sustainability; despite all the rhetoric about the threat of global warming, greenhouse gas emissions have continued to increase since 1990.[38] Along these lines, some analysts speak in terms of "climate debt" and argue for reparations for those facing the most dire consequences of greenhouse gas emissions.[39]

■ **Periphery**
A Marxist term for the developing world; the global proletariat; states that are economically reliant on the sale of their natural resources.

■ **Core**
A Marxist term for the developed, industrialized world; the great powers; the global bourgeoisie; countries that exploit the international economy in their own interests regardless of costs to others.

World systems theories bridge systemic-level and domestic-level analyses. They describe the world system as a replication of states' domestic class systems, seeing individual states' elites working together at the international level to oppress workers globally. Ostensibly, this means that there is also an opportunity for oppressed laborers to unite across states to overthrow the international capitalist structure.

Critics of world systems theory tend to point out that, in ignoring the role of states to focus, instead, on classes, the theory is overlooking the big elephant in the room. Whether or not there is a class system, and whether or not it is perpetuated at the international level, to assume that classes act independently of the state structure is problematic. Critics also point out that nationalism throws a bit of a wrench in the world systems theories because it inhibits efforts to unify across states. Finally, critics point out that countries from the periphery have successfully made the leap to the industrialized core, including Taiwan, South Korea, and, now, China and India. Moreover, dividing the world into core and periphery could be misleading, as so many states are at different points in their development and because development itself can be measured along so many different parameters. Finally, in terms of the international response to climate change, it is often developing countries that demand the right to pollute in the process of industrialization, perceiving greenhouse gas emissions as a necessary evil in the creation of a strong local economy.[40]

World systems theorists highlight economic exploitation, an issue that is overlooked by other systemic-level theories but is important as globalization and global governance continue to evolve. Their analyses can be drawn in interesting parallel to realist studies, since both highlight the effects of imbalances of power. In the first instance, the imbalance is class based and transnational and power is strictly economic; in the latter, states are the unit of analysis and power is equivalent to the ability to coerce. In both forms of analysis, however, developing countries and the people within them are too weak to resist exploitation and the effects of others' self-interested actions.

Summary and Preview

This chapter is intended as an introduction to the analytical tools available to students of international politics. The levels of analysis and theoretical paradigms are nothing more than ways of deliberately slicing up the convoluted, big picture of world politics into smaller, more manageable pieces (see At a Glance, "Levels of Analysis and Paradigms in Review").

Levels of Analysis and Paradigms in Review: International Responses to Climate Change

	Realism	Liberalism	Constructivism
Individual	In 2007, Sheila Watt-Cloutier, an Inuit political leader, won the UN award for activism against climate change. A realist would interpret Ms. Watt-Cloutier's efforts as rooted in self-interest and power-seeking. She has established herself as a politician and won support by expressing views that will resonate with her constituency. She has won numerous awards and gained international attention. And she has increased her personal influence by establishing her authority on the issue of global warming.	Liberals would point out that Ms. Watt-Cloutier has used international legal mechanisms and institutions to draw attention to the plight of Arctic communities.[i] She has committed herself to improving the condition of her constituents through communication and cooperation at the global level. And she has explained how her own people's challenges are a harbinger of what the world more generally is likely to face if the issue of climate change is not addressed.	A constructivist might focus not on Ms. Watt-Cloutier's personal motivations, but on her effort to change how people consider the effects of global warming by recasting them as violations of the Inuit people's cultural and environmental human rights. By making climate change a legal and human rights issue, Ms. Watt-Cloutier is changing perceptions of the problem.
Domestic	There are balances of power within states as well as among them. Within states, policies that reduce immediate costs for highly organized and active interest groups while producing potential long-term negative effects for diffuse populations will yield far more political capital than will the reverse. In the United States, China, and many European nations, climate change legislation threatens well-organized, deep-pocket industries while producing hard-to-measure long-term benefits for the population at large.	Institutions promote cooperation by reducing the security dilemma, enhancing transparency, and creating a forum and structure for negotiations. It is therefore unsurprising that the EU's member states have been among the most successful reducers of greenhouse gas emissions. Moreover, EU membership has created a political fallback for politicians who might have faced domestic opposition; they can point to their obligations as EU members to justify politically unpopular programs.	A conducive political culture can create the political conditions for states to actively reduce greenhouse gas emissions and participate in cooperative efforts internationally. Norway is a prime example of a state in which the population is willing to assume short-term costs to protect the environment, thus giving political leaders the leeway necessary to pass ambitious and comprehensive climate legislation.

(continued)

	Realism	*Liberalism*	*Constructivism*
Systemic	In the absence of great-power buy-in, climate change reduction cannot take place. But great-power buy-in is precluded by great-power competition and the fear that the costs of reducing greenhouse gas emissions and undertaking other mitigation efforts will be unequally born, thus creating unacceptable relative losses. China and the U.S, the world's two largest greenhouse gas producers, are in direct competition and do not trust each other. While those conditions exist, no substantive steps toward influencing climate change can be taken.	When it is in their mutual interests, states will find ways to cooperate. Because climate change affects the global commons, it is too big for any one state to effectively address and cooperation will be necessary. The seeds of cooperation have been sown via the IPCC and the UNFCCC, as well as through the initial steps represented by the Kyoto Protocol and the Copenhagen Accord.	There is an ongoing process of defining the relationship between climate and international relations. As perceptions of the nature of the threat and of the potential means of resolving or mitigating it change, so will the steps countries are willing to take. As the world grapples with ideas such as "sustainability," "climate debt," and "geo-engineering," worldwide behavior will reflect the evolving concepts, as will the nature and distribution of actors and influence.

[i.] "Inuit Leader Wins UN Award for Activism Against Climate Change," UN News Centre, 20 June 2007, http://www.un.org/apps/news/story.asp?NewsID=22973&Cr=climate&Cr1=change.

TABLE 2.2 **Theoretical Paradigms**			
	Neorealism	*Neoliberalism*	*Constructivism*
Central Variable	Power	Interests	Knowledge
Orientation	Rationalist	Rationalist	Sociological
Behavioral Model	Relative gains- seeker	Absolute gains-maximizer	Role player
Institutionalism	Weak	Medium	Strong

Source: Slightly amended from Andreas Hasenclever, Peter Mayer, and Volker Rittberger, *Theories of International Regimes* (New York: Cambridge University Press, 1997), 6.

We can use different filters, as well, but they are all interrelated: We can focus on relative military strength or on economic growth and development, we can consider ethics, we can look at political culture, we can examine demographic trends or even the role of geography or weather in politics. Ultimately, however, all of those can be addressed using the ideas introduced in this chapter. It is important, moreover, not only to be able to use these tools, but to recognize them as well. We should be able to read journal articles or books in the field and identify on which theoretical paradigm (see Table 2.2) the author is pinning his or her argument or from which level of analysis he or she is proceeding. Understanding this allows us to recognize what is being left out of the argument as much as it lets us interpret what is being included.

The following chapters bring you through the history of international relations and into in-depth discussions of contemporary issues in world politics. Throughout, however, we will return to the analytical tools introduced here, showing their relevance along the way and, hopefully, demonstrating the value and charm of theory.

What Would You Do?

Drilling for Oil

You are the leader of a small country that has been very isolated from the rest of the world. Recently, explorers from foreign oil companies have asked for permission to do exploratory drilling in your country. You know that the explorers will bring with them money, information, jobs, opportunities, and modernization, things that many of your people will appreciate and from which they will benefit. However, the newcomers will also bring pollution, economic change, new sources of competition, an infusion of new ideas, and an introduction to other cultures and languages likely to eventually subsume your own. What might influence whether or not you give the foreign explorers permission to drill?

What Would You Do?

Discussion and Review Questions

1. Which level of analysis is most descriptive? Which is most predictive?
2. What assumptions do realists and liberals share? Where do the paradigms diverge?
3. Constructivism is about the roles of ideas, assumptions, perceptions, and practices in world politics. Can you think of an assumption underpinning current international relations practices that, if relaxed or eliminated, would change world politics?
4. How might you use the levels of analysis to provide insights into the conflict between Israel and the Palestinians? What different practical information could each level of analysis yield?
5. How does each of the major paradigms deal with nonstate actors? What are the analytical costs and benefits of each approach?

Key Terms

Absolute gains 44	Factor 29	Multipolar 40
Absolute power 40	Feminist 50	Natural law 42
Balancing 40	Generalizable 35	Necessary and sufficient
Bandwagoning 41	Global commons 22	variables 37
Bipolar 40	Great powers 40	Objective 37
Carbon sinks 48	Hegemon 25	Operational code 31
Causality 30	Idealism 38	Parsimony 35
Collective action 22	Independent variable 30	Periphery 51
Comparativists 29	Institution 43	Process 48
Complex learning 49	Interdependence 43	Ratification 22
Confidence-building	Intervening variables 41	Rational actor 25
measures 27	Inverse correlation 46	Realpolitik 38
Core 51	Just War 42	Reductivism 41
Correlation 28	Leviathan 44	Reforestation 48
Emissions trading 48	Liberal democracy 46	Regime 43
Exogenously given 47	Linkage 27	Reification 49

CHAPTER 3

World Politics and Economics: 1648–1945

As discussed in Chapter 1, conflict and cooperation—as well as globalization and fragmentation—epitomize the nature of international interaction. The following four chapters will provide the historical narrative of these processes from 1648 to the present. Although conflict garners much more attention than cooperation, these chapters will demonstrate the simultaneous occurrence of all four processes. There will indeed be extensive discussion of conflict and fragmentation, as with the World Wars, numerous conflicts during the Cold War, and the dissolution of Yugoslavia to name a few, but there are also a plethora of examples of cooperation and globalization, such as the Concert of Europe, the formation of the United Nations, and the establishment of the Bretton Woods system. The worldviews discussed in Chapter 2 are also highlighted by the historical narrative. You will see the realist approach present in the numerous balance-of-power systems and states' attempts to gain and maintain their own power. Liberalism will be evident in the many examples of international organizations and economic cooperation. Finally, the constructivist approach will be demonstrated in the different understanding states have of the international system and the role they perceive themselves as playing in it. Thus, you should pay attention to the themes presented in Chapters 1 and 2 as they appear repeatedly throughout the four history chapters. These chapters should help you apply the theories and trends you learned about in the previous chapters.

You may be asking yourself, "Why study history?" Most people have heard the old adage, "Those who fail to learn from history are doomed to repeat it." You may or may not accept this as truth, but it is undeniable that there is a wealth of information to learn from the past that can be applied to the present and future state of international relations. If we are to understand where we are and where we are headed, we need to understand where we have been.

To truly comprehend the complex tapestry of world politics, to analyze the causes and consequences of international relations, we all must know the history of interstate relations in the modern period. Thus, what follows in the historical chapters are the major historical events that shaped international relations from 1648 to the present. While these represent the events most often focused on by scholars, it is important to remember that we are always learning new things about the past and applying new analytical tools to the facts. For example, the worldviews discussed in Chapter 1 are constantly evolving, and hence their application provides us different lenses through which to view the same event.

Further, to understand contemporary events, historical analysis provides a valuable explanatory tool. For example, later in this chapter we discuss the Munich Analogy. Prior to the outbreak of World War II, Great Britain and France appeased Hitler by handing over the Sudetenland, believing that this would prevent a conflict with Germany (see Spotlight, "The Munich Analogy," later in this chapter). This hope proved to be false and World War II ensued. As a consequence, policymakers have repeatedly invoked the Munich Analogy to highlight why aggressive behavior should not be appeased. In the United States, for example, the specter of World War II and the "evil" of Hitler have been used by policymakers time and time again to justify state actions. Truman used it in explaining why North Korea must be confronted after its invasion of South Korea in 1950, the Executive Committee of the National Security Council (Excom) repeatedly cited the Munich Analogy in its meetings during the Cuban Missile Crisis (see Chapter 4), George H. W. Bush compared Saddam Hussein to Hitler following the Iraqi invasion of Kuwait in 1990 (see Chapter 6), and the George W. Bush administration used the analogy to justify elements of the War on Terror after the 9/11 attacks. While all the decisions made in applying the lessons of history may not have been successful, that does not undermine the importance of the historical lesson. Knowledge of history is critical in analyzing international relations, as demonstrated by the fact that understanding an event that transpired in the 1940s can help explain events happening in 2010.

In keeping with the spirit of "learning from history," this chapter outlines the development of the nation-state from its beginnings in seventeenth-century Europe through its expansion throughout the world in the eighteenth and nineteenth centuries and ends with a discussion of the two World Wars. The central term in the expression *international relations* is *nation*, but the nation-state has not always been the central focus of world politics. In fact, before the seventeenth century, the nation-state as we know it did not exist. The change in the nature of world politics from relations between rulers to relations between nations was a historical development of tremendous importance. It had a powerful impact not only on politics, security, and commerce, but also on every field of human endeavor. As such, the time and place where the system of nation-states originated is the logical point from which to begin our study of world politics.

The sovereign nation-state originated in Europe and subsequently spread to other parts of the globe, making the European nation-state system the blueprint for the rest of the world. This fact requires the initial historical chapter of this book to concentrate heavily on Europe. The European focus of this chapter should not be construed to mean that nothing important was happening outside Europe during this period; far from it. Chapter 4 will show how Europe was eclipsed after 1945 as the center of world politics and will demonstrate how developments outside of Europe created the economically globalized but politically fragmented world of the late twentieth century. In addition, Chapter 5 will be entirely focused on the process and effects of imperialism on the non-European world. For better or worse, however, Europe set the pattern for the organization of and interaction among nation-states that persists to the present day. Any examination of how world politics came to attain its present form must therefore begin in Europe.

Thirty Years' War and the Peace of Westphalia

The expansion of seagoing trade in the fifteenth and sixteenth centuries began to convince many Europeans that the confusing and fragmented **feudal** order was stifling commerce and economic development.[1] A major political and social upheaval would be required, however, before a more stable system could be established. That upheaval was the Reformation, the Protestant revolt against the religious authority of the Roman Catholic Church, which began in the early sixteenth century. A popular backlash against widespread corruption in the Church added fuel to the doctrinal fire, and, as realists would predict, political leaders exploited this religious schism to further their own ambitions. The claims of authority over most of Europe asserted by the popes and the Holy Roman emperors became more burdensome to European kings as these monarchs expanded their realms of authority. Worried that religious fragmentation and growing autonomy of secular European leaders were undermining their spiritual and political authority, popes and emperors sought to crush these challenges, and the challenges and repressions culminated in the Thirty Years' War (1618–1648).

This war was a catastrophic conflict that wiped out more than a third of Europe's population; nearly eight million people died from the devastation it caused. Originally sparked by the religious conflict between Catholics and Protestants within the German lands of the Holy Roman Empire and the revolt

▪ **Feudal**
Rulers of smaller political units, such as city-states, counties, or duchies, often owed allegiance to the rulers of larger principalities or kingdoms and were granted title over their lands in exchange for promises of money or military service.

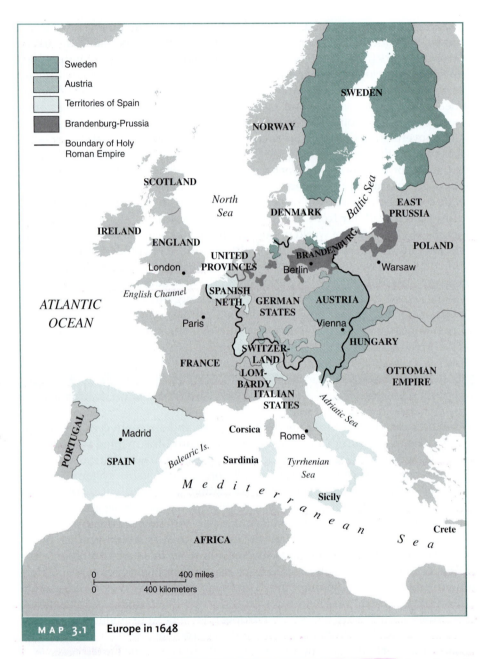

MAP 3.1   **Europe in 1648**

of the Protestant estates of Bohemia against Prussia's Ferdinand II (then Catholic king of Bohemia), the war came to involve the military forces of Austria, England, France, the Netherlands, Spain, and Sweden. Religion did not provide the major motivation for most of these combatants, who were far more interested in preserving their own political power.

After many bloody battles, horrendous massacres, and sudden shifts in alliances, the Thirty Years' War finally ended with the signing of the **Peace of Westphalia** in 1648 (see Map 3.1). This treaty established the important principle of **sovereignty** that remains the foundation of contemporary international politics. In an obvious blow to the Church, this meant that kings could decide domestic policy, such as the official religion within their domains, free from outside interference. The principle of sovereignty recognized in the Peace of Westphalia represents an essential element in the creation of the modern nation-state. The idea that political legitimacy could derive from secular legal authority rather than from divine sanction paved the way for the development of constitutional government.

Eighteenth-Century Europe

The emerging nation-state system did not, however, lead to stability in Europe. Much as they do today, the opposing forces of globalization and fragmentation contributed to conflict in the eighteenth century. Whereas trade and **colonialism** were strong forces for globalization in Asia, Africa, and the Americas (see Chapter 5), fragmentation was occurring in the political center of the newly emerging European system. In Central and Eastern Europe, the disintegration of the Holy Roman Empire and the weakening of the Ottoman Empire after 1700 meant that new actors, mainly Prussia and Russia, emerged to challenge Austria, which had been the dominant power in the region (see Map 3.2). European states became less isolated from one another and from the rest of the world, and more and more, European politics became an integrated system in which developments in one area affected events in other nations.

Great Powers

Although the status of individual states fluctuated constantly during the eighteenth century, at no point did fewer than four **great powers** compete against one another. The number of great powers in the system and their relative capabilities are the focus of structural realists (see Chapter 2). The international system during this period was therefore multipolar (containing more than two major actors). Not dependent on other states for security, and militarily and economically stronger than other countries, the great powers played a major role in the security calculations of other countries. Only a great power could threaten another great power militarily or challenge it politically, and most great powers could exert considerable influence beyond their own borders. In modern parlance, they possessed capabilities for **power projection** that less powerful countries could not match.

▪ **Peace of Westphalia**
The 1648 treaty that ended the Thirty Years' War and marked the beginning of the modern international system by legitimizing the state as the ultimate sovereign authority over people and geographic territory.

▪ **Sovereignty**
Exclusive political authority over a defined territory and the people within it.

▪ **Colonialism**
A policy by which a nation maintains or extends its control over foreign dependencies. The two main types of colonialism are movement of people from the mother country to form a new political institution in the designated distant land and external powers' rule over indigenous peoples.

▪ **Great power**
A state that possesses, exercises, and defends interests throughout the world. Great-power status may be quantitative, such as a certain level of gross national product or the size of its armed forces. It may also be qualitative, demonstrated by a high level of industrialization or the capability to make and use nuclear weapons. Great powers may also be distinguished by institutional recognition, such as that accorded by the League of Nations or the UN.

▪ **Power projection**
Influence, often by force, beyond one's borders.

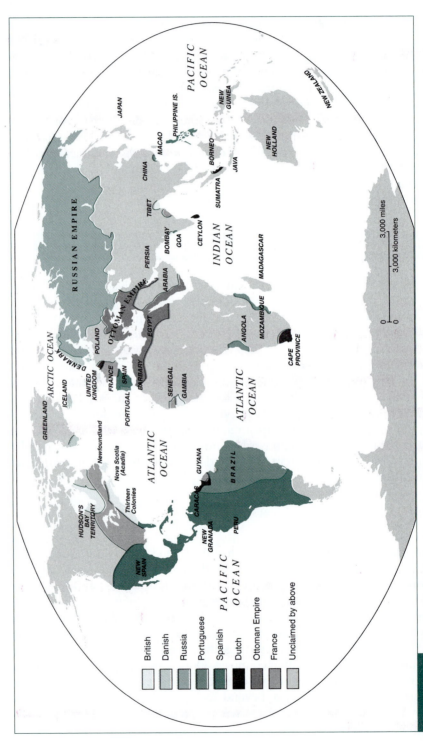

MAP 3.2   European Empires, Seventeenth and Eighteenth Centuries

Legend:
- British
- Danish
- Russia
- Portuguese
- Spanish
- Dutch
- Ottoman Empire
- France
- Unclaimed by above

The exact qualifications for great-power status have always been imprecisely defined, but it is generally agreed that to be a great power, a state needs a relatively large territory and population, a well-organized military, and a strong economy. To have only one of these attributes without the others generally means that the state cannot sustain its influence in the international system for very long. For example, seventeenth-century Holland, in spite of its prosperous economy, had the misfortune of being located next to much larger France and having to compete with England for overseas trade. States possessing all of the necessary factors of power, on the other hand, could exercise political influence for long periods. Russia, although isolated and undeveloped at the start of the eighteenth century, became a great power as the century progressed, largely because of its huge population and vast natural resources. Japan, on the other hand, has used its strong economy as a way to maintain influence even without a large military.

The influence of each great power on the others linked their fates together. The elimination of any one power by another could threaten the interests, and possibly even the survival, of others. Therefore, most major powers sought to prevent the domination of the Continent by any single state. In other words, the great powers tried to preserve a balance of power by allying with weaker powers against stronger states to protect themselves from present and future threats. This is a prime example of a realist approach to international relations. A balance of power is pursued in order to protect each state's interests. Furthermore, the multipolar nature of the eighteenth century meant that alliances shifted often and wars were frequent, although limited in scope. The great powers involved themselves in three major wars during the course of the eighteenth century.[2] As one might expect from monarchs, two of these were provoked by dynastic struggles (see At a Glance, "'World Wars' of the Eighteenth Century").

Aftermath of War and Two Revolutions

Following the Seven Years' War (see again At a Glance, "'World Wars' of the Eighteenth Century"), France had no realistic means of directly challenging England's gains in North America because of British control of the seas. Meanwhile, the American colonists grew resentful of Britain's efforts to retire its war debt by increasing tax levies on its colonies. Much of the "taxation without representation" decried by Americans in the 1760s and 1770s was levied to pay for the Seven Years' War, and so helped to make the resulting British supremacy in North America short-lived. With the start of the American War of Independence in 1776, France saw a golden opportunity to weaken England. By assisting the rebels, France sought to shift the balance of power in its favor. France assisted the colonists by providing them money and arms and by engaging in active military support. This forced England to divert resources to other fronts and made the resupply of its forces in North America more difficult.

AT A GLANCE

"World Wars" of the Eighteenth Century

War of the Spanish Succession (1701–1714)

Cause

Controversy over who would inherit the Spanish throne when King Charles II of Spain died without an heir. King Louis XIV of France, with Spanish support, attempted to crown his grandson Philip king of Spain.

Alliances

France and Spain versus the Grand Alliance of Austria, Britain, and the Netherlands, which was later joined by Portugal and other states.

Outcome

Although neither side could decisively defeat the other, the terms of the treaties that concluded the fighting favored the Grand Alliance, and thus both France and Spain made territorial and trade concessions to Britain and Austria.

War of the Austrian Succession (1740–1748)

Cause

The death of the Austrian King Charles VI, who was also the Holy Roman emperor, severely weakened Vienna's power. The ensuing confusion provided the opportunity for King Frederick II of Prussia, better known as Frederick the Great, to seize the prosperous territory of Silesia from Austria, alarming the other great powers because Frederick had violated a treaty that pledged to uphold the integrity of Austrian possessions.[i]

Alliances

Prussia, France, and Spain versus England and Austria.

Outcome

Stalemate. The Treaty of Aix-la-Chapelle in 1748 called for a general return to the status quo ante bellum (literally "the situation before the war"), but Prussia retained control of Silesia. The fact that upstart Prussia had successfully challenged Austria's dominant position in Germany, however, put the stability of Central Europe under a cloud.

Seven Years' War (1756–1763)

Cause

Prussia was surrounded by enemies, who took advantage of the situation to launch the war known in North America as the French and Indian War.

Alliances

Austria, France, and Russia versus Prussia and Britain.

Outcome

England was established as the dominant power in India and North America, where it was awarded all of Canada. England, France, and Russia had important interests both within and outside Europe, but Prussia and Austria were solely European powers.

[i.] Gordon A. Craig and Alexander George, *Force and Statecraft* (New York: Oxford University Press, 1983), 19–20.

The Treaty of Versailles in 1783, which recognized an independent United States of America, forced Britain to concede several other overseas possessions to France. These losses demonstrated the process of fragmentation and weakened Britain's position in North America, which was even more precarious because the new United States now represented a threat to Britain's remaining colony, Canada. This Peace of Versailles might thus have represented a major victory for Paris, but France's triumph would prove Pyrrhic. Throughout the eighteenth century, France was the most powerful state in Europe and by the end of the century the tremendous costs of maintaining the state's military and international political power caused a severe social and economic crisis that culminated in the French Revolution of 1789. One of the most momentous events in world history, the revolution and the conflicts that followed represented a radical departure from the rule of autocratic monarchy (the *ancien régime*) and from the balance of power that defined eighteenth-century European politics.

The immediate causes of the French Revolution were the debilitating debt accumulated by France during the American War of Independence and the losses incurred in the Seven Years' War. As a consequence of this debt, in May 1789, the nobility and clergy in France began challenging the king's authority and set in motion forces beyond their control, as the politically and economically disenfranchised middle and lower classes seized the opportunity to assert their own demands. Riots and protests swept through Paris, and on July 14, 1789, a mob stormed the Bastille, a prison where many political prisoners were held. Rioting spread throughout the country, and an attempt to set up a constitutional monarchy failed to quiet protests and restore order. France was proclaimed a republic in 1792, and King Louis XVI and his queen, Marie Antoinette, were guillotined in 1793.

The revolution was inspired by two political ideologies. One of them, liberalism, held that the power of government should reside in the people and that government should, to the greatest extent possible, allow individuals responsibility for controlling their own actions. The second ideology, nationalism, called for popular loyalty to focus on the nation rather than on the monarch. This was a radical departure from previous ideas of the state and government. It was a concept of political order that, for the first time, defined a country in terms of its people rather than in terms of its rulers.[3]

Napoleonic Era

Warfare convulsed Europe for more than two decades after the French Revolution. The turmoil of revolution and war brought many opportunities to the daring and ambitious, and at the end of the eighteenth century no one in Europe was bolder or more ambitious than Napoleon Bonaparte.[4] In the wake of France's military setbacks and increased domestic disorder, Napoleon led a successful coup in 1799 and quickly seized dictatorial power. The revolution

PHOTO 3.1   Napoleon Bonaparte looks benign in this period painting. At the height of his power, however, Napoleon turned the idealistic principles of the French Revolution (Liberté, Égalité, Fraternité) into a battle cry threatening all of Europe.

had laid strong military foundations for France, and now the nation would be led by a brilliant strategist and capable administrator with a vision of a Europe united under French domination. Napoleon represents a prime example of the individual level of analysis discussed in Chapter 2.

Once Napoleon completely consolidated his control of France in 1802, he began to wage the Napoleonic Wars (1803–1815), campaigns that abandoned the eighteenth-century norms of limited war. In a deliberate return to the practices of the Roman Empire, Napoleon accepted only the complete submission and occupation of a defeated country. He often installed members of his own family as nominal rulers of conquered territories; for example, one of his brothers ruled Spain, and his brother-in-law became king of Naples. Formally ratifying a status Napoleon had achieved in fact, in May 1804, the French Senate proclaimed him Emperor Napoleon I.

His control of Europe almost complete, Napoleon banned the importation of British goods to the Continent in 1806, creating the Continental System, a means of expanding French economic control of Europe and weakening the British. By 1810, at the height of his power, Napoleon's empire controlled Spain, western and southern Germany, most of Italy, the Netherlands, Switzerland, and the Grand Duchy of Warsaw (the Polish state that he reestablished) and maintained alliances with Austria, Denmark, Norway, and Prussia (see Map 3.3). Although Britain retained its naval supremacy after decisively defeating the combined French and Spanish fleets at the Battle of Trafalgar in 1805, France dominated continental Europe.

Napoleon's power was eventually undermined by his own ambition. In addition to his inability to defeat Spain and Portugal in the long and bloody Peninsular War (a conflict that drained French resources substantially), his boundless ambition led him to make a disastrous strategic blunder: In June 1812 Napoleon invaded Russia with an army of more than 500,000 troops. At first, his forces drove the Russians farther and farther east, and by September the French occupied Moscow. In retreat, however, Russian troops destroyed and burned anything that might have been useful to the conquerors in the policy of scorched earth, and even the fall of Moscow did not cause them to submit. Overextended, far from its bases of supply, and unable to decisively defeat the Russians, Napoleon's army was forced to withdraw. As they stumbled back toward Poland, the emperor's forces were decimated by Cossack cavalry and the severe Russian winter. By the end of 1812, only 40,000 men, less than one out of ten of those who had originally invaded, crossed back into Poland.

Exhausted by the fighting on two fronts (Russia and the Iberian Peninsula), the French forces began to collapse. Then, France's allies and satellites turned against Napoleon. Although exhausted and reluctant to pursue Napoleon through Central Europe, Russian, Austrian, Prussian, and Swedish forces, with financial and material assistance from Britain, continued the fight. By 1814 Napoleon's armies in both the east and south retreated. In March the anti-French allies occupied Paris, and on April 6 Napoleon abdicated. The First Peace of Paris, signed on May 30, forced France to give up most of the territory it had taken since 1792 and restored Louis XVIII to the French throne.

However, the Napoleonic era was not quite over. With divisions among the victorious allies and domestic instability in France, Napoleon escaped from exile on the island of Elba and returned to power in March 1815. Quickly rallying the tattered remnants of the French army, he again threatened the peace of Europe. This time, however, the allies quickly sent their armies against him. On June 18 Napoleon's final Hundred Days came to an end when British, Prussian, and Dutch forces led by Generals Wellington and Blücher defeated him at Waterloo.

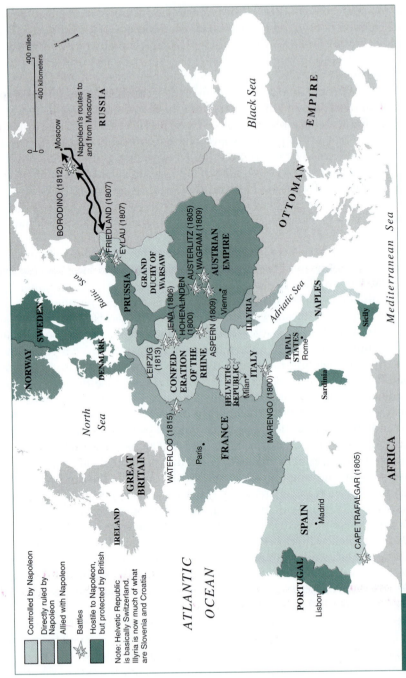

MAP 3.3   Napoleonic Europe

Controlled by Napoleon

Directly ruled by Napoleon

Allied with Napoleon

Battles

Hostile to Napoleon, but protected by British

Note: Helvetic Republic is basically Switzerland. Illyria is now much of what are Slovenia and Croatia.

RUSSIA

Moscow

Napoleon's routes to and from Moscow

BORODINO (1812)

FRIEDLAND (1807)

EYLAU (1807)

PRUSSIA

GRAND DUCHY OF WARSAW

AUSTERLITZ (1805)

WAGRAM (1809)

AUSTRIAN EMPIRE

OTTOMAN EMPIRE

Black Sea

Baltic Sea

SWEDEN

NORWAY

DENMARK

North Sea

GREAT BRITAIN

IRELAND

ATLANTIC OCEAN

LEIPZIG (1813)

JENA (1806)

HOHENLINDEN (1800)

CONFED-ERATION OF THE RHINE

ASPERN (1809)

Vienna

ILLYRIA

Adriatic Sea

NAPLES

Sicily

Mediterranean Sea

HELVETIC REPUBLIC

Milan

ITALY

MARENGO (1800)

PAPAL STATES

Rome

Sardinia

WATERLOO (1815)

Paris

FRANCE

AFRICA

CAPE TRAFALGAR (1805)

SPAIN

Madrid

PORTUGAL

Lisbon

400 miles

400 kilometers

The victorious allies then exiled him to the South Atlantic island of St. Helena, where he died in 1821.

Concert of Europe

After Napoleon's defeat in 1814, the great powers of Europe (Austria, Prussia, Russia, Britain, and France) gathered in a critical meeting in Vienna to chart the future of the Continent. The conference sought first and foremost to restore Europe to what it considered to be "normalcy," meaning a return to the old monarchical system. Ideological consensus, revulsion at the horrors of war, and economic exhaustion fostered cooperation among the states in forming a new international system. The Treaty of Vienna of 1815 was an attempt to incorporate the lessons of twenty-two years of nearly constant warfare against France by Britain, Russia, Prussia, and Austria, and it reflected the leading role of Russia and Britain in the alliance that defeated Napoleon. The great powers were to contain France by establishing and guaranteeing the neutrality of buffer states between France and the other great powers (See Map 3.4). Britain's demands for restoring the independence of the Netherlands and Belgium (which France had absorbed) as a unified state reinforced France's confinement. The victors also forced France to pay an indemnity, further eroding its gains from the war.

These realpolitik steps did not fully satisfy the various states that had attempted to defeat France over the years, however. Many leaders believed there would have to be cooperation among the great powers to prevent another recurrence of any such threat. They agreed to meet periodically to review developments in Europe to pursue their common interests and the peace of the Continent. Thus the Vienna settlement established the **Concert of Europe**, in which the great powers sought to cooperate in maintaining peace and order on the Continent. The Quadruple Alliance—Britain, Russia, Prussia, and Austria—agreed that a French attack on one constituted an attack on all, thus creating a collective security arrangement.

They had also learned a valuable lesson from years of war: that because domestic developments had international repercussions, they had to be contained. Therefore, they agreed that the great powers could regulate domestic disturbances. In other words, they reserved the right to intervene in countries where liberalism appeared to be emerging as a threat. The Concert of Europe thus became the world's first international security organization. As such, it was a major step toward the globalization of world politics. From the start, however, the Concert contained more discord than harmony. Despite the apparent unity among the great powers, dissension roiled just beneath the surface. Specifically, Russia and Austria had demanded that the great powers agree to intervene in the domestic affairs of others should revolution threaten; Britain disagreed. In spite of Britain's opposition, the states reached a settlement.

▪ **Concert of Europe**
A special system of consultation used by the great powers of Europe after the Napoleonic Wars. A great power could initiate international conferences when it believed that the security and peace of Europe were compromised.

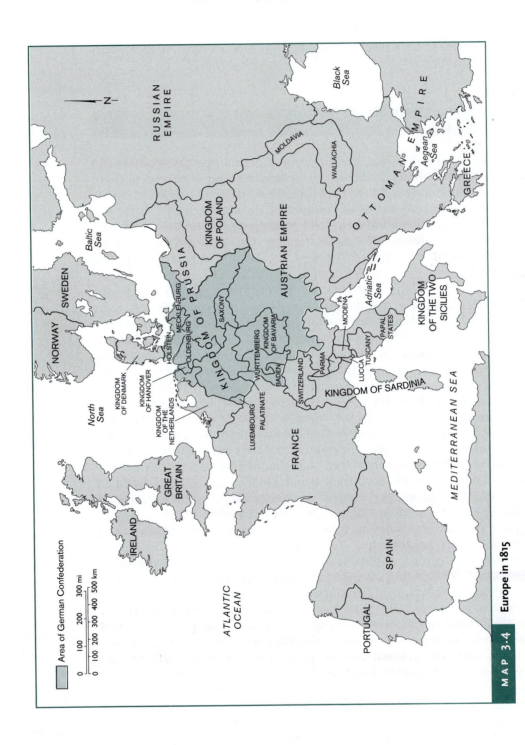

Europe in 1815

MAP 3.4

Area of German Confederation

0   100   200   300 mi
0 100 200 300 400 500 km

NORWAY

SWEDEN

RUSSIAN EMPIRE

Baltic Sea

KINGDOM OF PRUSSIA

KINGDOM OF POLAND

MOLDAVIA

WALLACHIA

OTTOMAN EMPIRE

Black Sea

Aegean Sea

GREECE

AUSTRIAN EMPIRE

MECKLENBURG

OLDENBURG

HOLSTEIN

SAXONY

KINGDOM OF BAVARIA

WÜRTTEMBERG

BADEN

SWITZERLAND

MODENA

PARMA

LUCCA

TUSCANY

PAPAL STATES

Adriatic Sea

KINGDOM OF THE TWO SICILIES

KINGDOM OF SARDINIA

KINGDOM OF DENMARK

KINGDOM OF HANOVER

KINGDOM OF THE NETHERLANDS

LUXEMBOURG

PALATINATE

FRANCE

North Sea

GREAT BRITAIN

IRELAND

ATLANTIC OCEAN

SPAIN

PORTUGAL

MEDITERRANEAN SEA

N

Unification of Italy and Germany

The Vienna settlement marked a restoration of the old order on two levels. First, many dethroned monarchies came back into power (most important, in France). Second, the dispensation of territory again was used to reward victors and punish losers. The settlement also changed past practice in that it explicitly sought to institutionalize the supremacy of particular great powers through the Concert of Europe. The restoration of the old order was illusionary however, for the French Revolution had unleashed new forces of nationalism and liberalism that could not be ignored.

In the first half of the nineteenth century, rulers feared nationalism because it threatened a revision of the territorial status quo and it was tied to liberalism. Notwithstanding the early association between liberalism and nationalism, the relative degree of fear of nationalism greatly depended on the previous history of the various parts of Europe. In western Europe, the state and the nation were essentially contiguous by the mid-nineteenth century, so ruling elites had little reason to fear that the extension of political rights to the working class would lead to the dissolution of the state. Germany and Italy profited from the growing force of nationalism, using it to unify their nations into single states.

Italian Unification

Napoleon III of France moved quickly to assist the movement for unity among the Italian city-states, or *Risorgimento*, as the Count di Cavour of Piedmont-Sardinia assumed leadership of the Italian unification movement. In July 1858 Cavour and Napoleon agreed that France would support Piedmont's cause in return for French acquisition of Nice and Savoy. In 1859 French forces intervened to push Austrian troops out of northern Italy. Nationalist troops led by Giuseppe Garibaldi won control of Sicily and Naples in 1860, paving the way for their union with Piedmont, which dominated northern Italy. An Italian parliament proclaimed a unified kingdom of Italy in 1861.

The unification of Italy produced a profound revision of the territorial settlement of 1815. It also removed a significant source of friction between Paris and Vienna, which had previously competed for influence among the republics, principalities, and city-states of the peninsula. The new state at first was too weak to pose a major threat to either France or Austria, and it provided a useful buffer between these two powers. Italy had achieved territorial unity but remained politically divided and economically underdeveloped, so it never attained the great-power status to which its leaders aspired.

German Unification

Italy's unification left one major European nation, the Germans, still divided. In 1862 King William I of Prussia appointed Otto von Bismarck as his chancellor. The

PHOTO 3.2 Otto von Bismarck created a unified Germany through three quick, carefully calculated wars in the 1860s and 1870s. The "Iron Chancellor" dominated European politics for the next twenty years.

dominant personality of Europe during the second half of the nineteenth century, Bismarck sought to protect and improve the position of the monarchy at the expense of a liberal parliament that had limited powers. Bismarck had no particular interest in German unity initially, but he gradually realized that nationalism could become the means of assuaging the masses while preserving most of the aristocracy's prerogatives and expanding Prussia's international power and prestige.

Bismarck was committed to realpolitik in foreign policy. He was concerned only with advancing the state interest by whatever means: diplomacy if possible, war if necessary. Bismarck had no qualms about resorting to military means if that would provide an opportunity to strengthen the domestic position of conservatives, the monarchy, and the army. He agreed with the German military theorist Clausewitz that "war is nothing but the continuation of politics by other means."[5] Thus, Bismarck was known as the Iron Chancellor for his determination to unite Germany under Prussian domination and for his statement that "it is not by speeches and resolutions that the great crises of the times are decided, but by iron and blood."[6] He used this determination to win three quick and decisive wars to unite Germany (see At a Glance, "Wars of German Unification").

The declaration the formation of the new German Empire on January 18, 1871, heralding the unification of Germany under the Prussian Crown, profoundly affected European politics and radically shifted the balance of power. Through these short wars based on rapid mobilization and decisive battles, the process of German unification influenced strategy and military organization in virtually all of the European states. The new German Empire was now the strongest country in continental Europe. Resentment smoldered in France, but that nation was too weak to act alone and could find no allies.

AT A GLANCE

The Wars of German Unification

1864

Opponent

Denmark

Outcome

Bismarck signed an alliance with Austria, and Austrian and Prussian forces won a quick victory and gained control of the largely German-speaking areas of Schleswig and Holstein.

1866

Opponent

Austria

Outcome

With superior organization, and by clever use of the emerging technologies of the railroad and telegraph, Prussia could mobilize and concentrate its forces more rapidly. This advantage proved decisive, and Prussia soundly defeated Austria within two months.

In the peace settlement, Austria gave up its authority in German and Italian affairs (the Italian city of Venice, at various times part of the Austrian Empire, was finally transferred to the kingdom of Italy), and the northern German states were incorporated into the Prussian-dominated North German Confederation.

1870–1871

Opponent

France

Outcome

Again making good use of new technology and its army's superior organization, Prussia rapidly defeated the French forces within a matter of weeks. The Prussians captured Napoleon III, and after a four-month siege, took Paris as well. France was forced to pay a huge indemnity and cede to Prussia the provinces of Alsace and Lorraine, which had long been part of France. The loss of both troubled the French for decades thereafter.

Thus, the achievement under Bismarck's leadership of a unified German nation was secure for the time being.

The Industrial Revolution

In addition to ideological and political change, the late eighteenth and nineteenth century also witnessed rapid economic change. The French Revolution was paralleled by the Industrial Revolution, which began in Britain in the late eighteenth century. The Industrial Revolution moved manufacturing out of the home and into factories, where it became more efficient through the use of mass production and interchangeable parts. In addition to radically changing the organization of industrial production, the Industrial Revolution harnessed new sources of energy, especially steam power, which enabled manufacturing to be increasingly mechanized. Beginning with textiles and food processing and expanding into the iron and steel, machine-building, transportation, and communication industries, the Industrial Revolution made it possible for more people to make more things faster and better than ever before.

The Industrial Revolution changed everything. Populations exploded as new farming techniques produced more food, railroads reliably transported it to where it was needed, and improvements in sanitation and medicine lowered infant mortality and raised life expectancy. Cities grew rapidly as workers flooded in from the countryside in search of better-paying jobs. Successful investors in industry made huge sums of money, amassing fortunes that rivaled and ultimately dwarfed those of the traditional aristocracy, whose wealth was usually obtained from farming on large estates. Technology improved at a pace unsettling to many, as railroads and the telegraph allowed goods and information to move faster than had ever been dreamed possible. Families were transformed from the extended family group suited to a sedentary, agricultural way of life into what was later called the nuclear family of one couple and its children, which moved frequently as one or both parents sought jobs. Growing shortages of skilled workers encouraged women to enter the labor force for the first time in substantial numbers (although the radical idea of women being able to earn their own money was often slow to catch on in traditional societies). The rich enjoyed the opportunity to make unprecedented profits, although often at considerable risk. A new urban middle class of small investors, technicians, and managers flourished. Workers earned higher wages and could buy more consumer goods but faced the possibility of unemployment if businesses lost money or failed.

The benefits of the increase in material wealth during the Industrial Revolution were numerous and widespread but unevenly distributed, as factory owners became wealthy even as many of the jobless and the working poor continued to eke out a bare existence. The rich got richer faster than ever before, and the middle classes prospered, but the living conditions of the poor were slower to improve. In time, rich and poor alike would suffer from another legacy of the Industrial Revolution—deforestation and pollution (see Chapter 12).[7]

The spread of the Industrial Revolution slowly but inexorably changed the European system. With its origins in Britain, the Industrial Revolution was a major source of that country's strength. Industrialization spread very unevenly, depending on social and political conditions within particular countries. France industrialized slowly, Austria even more so, and Russia had barely begun the process of industrial development by the end of the nineteenth century. Prussia, on the other hand, industrialized rapidly. With increased production came increased opportunities for trade, and the Industrial Revolution increased British support for a liberal trade regime under which goods could be freely bought and sold between countries. Seagoing commerce expanded rapidly, and trade forged economic and political links among nations all over the globe. Britain sought to maintain the system of free trade with its financial, industrial, and naval strength. Innovations in manufacturing, communications, and finance promoted international borrowing and investment throughout nineteenth-century Europe. The Industrial Revolution was thus a major impetus for the globalization of the world economy.

British Economic Hegemony and Its Challenges

As the first industrialized nation, Britain enjoyed the advantages of economic and technological leadership, achieving what many analysts consider to be hegemonic status. In Britain, already a highly commercialized economy with the largest market in Europe by the late eighteenth century, population growth and rising agricultural productivity laid the groundwork for rapid industrialization.[8] Britain's long and successful experience with international trade, a relatively unrestricted labor market (facilitating the internal migration of workers from rural to urban areas), and availability of capital paved the way for the development of industry, wool spinning (later textile weaving), and iron making in particular. Within this context, British entrepreneurs developed different techniques of production (such as the use of fertilizer in agriculture and the steam engine and coal in manufacturing) to drastically reduce the costs of production. As a result, the country enjoyed an explosion of exports.

In the wake of the Napoleonic Wars, Britain moved away from a protectionist foreign economic policy and promoted a more open international economy. Convinced that trade and exchange were "a source of peaceful relations among nations because the mutual benefits of trade and expanding interdependence among national economies tended to foster cooperative relations,"[9] British policymakers turned toward free trade. The movement toward free trade in Britain, however, was not without political difficulty. After the initial burst of free trade following the Congress of Vienna, Britain began to experience a growing urban population and falling export prices, necessitating the search for a means to counter growing unemployment and economic troubles at home while reestablishing competitiveness abroad. Exports no longer acted as "the engine of growth," falling from 18 percent of the national income in 1801 to 11 percent in 1841.[10] The loss of export markets for agricultural products, mainly wheat, threatened politically powerful landed interests. In the late eighteenth and early nineteenth centuries, British landowners were accustomed to trade protection through the set of tariffs and other restrictions on agricultural imports collectively known as the Corn Laws. Along with the growing working class, British manufacturing and financial interests came to regard these agricultural restraints as barriers to solving Britain's problems. Proponents of freer trade hoped that a unilateral reduction in British tariffs would induce other countries to adopt freer trade policies as well, leading to an international division of labor. This division would lead those countries with abundant labor to exploit their comparative advantage in agriculture while other countries (Britain in particular) would specialize in the production of capital-intensive manufactured goods (for an explanation of comparative advantage, see Chapter 9). Britain's landed elites ultimately recognized that they could not defend the Corn Laws any longer. By 1846 these laws were repealed, facilitating a boom in international trade. As one scholar recounted, "For a decade or so, in the 1860s and 1870s, Europe came as close as ever to complete free trade until after World War II."[11]

As many economic realists would predict, Britain's hegemonic dedication to free trade following the abolition of the Corn Laws worked to its advantage in the short term, giving it markets for its goods and promoting cooperation with its European neighbors. In the long term, however, it worked to its competitors' advantage because they could free-ride on Britain's benevolence and grow relatively faster, ultimately eclipsing Britain's industrial and agricultural capabilities. British trade on the Continent, particularly in manufactured goods, facilitated continental industrialization because these exports were necessary for economic development, and they reduced the capabilities gap between Britain and other European powers.[12] The United States, meanwhile, was experiencing unprecedented industrial development of its own (see Table 3.1). Although quantitative indicators of economic power do not capture the whole picture, it is clear that Britain's relative economic standing among the great powers suffered. The United States and Germany began to emerge as significant economic and potential military rivals.

British hegemony thus brought the first taste of free trade to the international economy; spurred tremendous economic, technical, and technological developments in agriculture and industry; and demonstrated the advantages—in terms of growth and stability—that accrued from trade cooperation. However, by assuming the costs of maintaining free trade and by sharing its own advancements, Britain inevitably allowed competing, free-riding states to surpass its rate of development.

▪ **Corn Laws**
A set of tariffs and other restrictions on agricultural imports that protected British landowners in the late 1700s and early 1800s. Repeal of these laws in 1846 helped facilitate a boom in international trade.

TABLE 3.1   Distribution of World Industrial Production, 1820–1913

Country	Percentage of Global Industrial Production, Year(s)					
	1820	1840	1860	1881–1885	1896–1900	1913
Britain	24	21	21	27	20	14
France	20	18	16	9	7	6
Germany	15	17	15	17	17	16
Russia	—	—	—	3	5	6
Italy	—	—	—	2	3	3
United States	4	5	14	29	30	36

Source: Walt W. Rostow, *The World Economy: History & Prospect* (Austin: University of Texas Press, 1978), 52–53.

Bismarckian System

As economies were expanding, relations on the European continent were controlled in the last decades of the nineteenth century by a succession of alliances known collectively as the **Bismarckian system**. Germany used these defensive alliances to moderate the demands of its allies, prevent the formation of coalitions of opponents that could seriously threaten its vital interests, and forestall the escalation of local conflicts into general war. A delicate balancing act performed by a master political acrobat, Bismarck's system worked splendidly for a time, but it could not resolve the domestic and international conflicts that ultimately led to his downfall and his system's collapse.

The strategic objective of Bismarck's alliance system was to keep Germany, Austria-Hungary, and Russia together while isolating France. This was no easy task because the goals of Bismarck's two major allies, Austria-Hungary and Russia, were opposed. Bismarck had been able to ally with both of these adversaries—first with Austria-Hungary in the Dual Alliance in 1879, then with both in the Three Emperors' Alliance in 1881—but this balancing act was threatened by political developments, particularly in the Balkans. Independence movements challenged Turkish control of the Balkans, and the weakening Ottoman Empire could neither suppress nor satisfy nationalist demands. As a result, Austria-Hungary and Russia increasingly supported various Balkan nationalist movements in a competition for territory and influence in the region. Agreements brokered by Bismarck at the Congress of Berlin in 1878 temporarily stabilized the Balkans, but issues of Austro-Hungarian and Russian competition had still failed to resolve themselves. Further, seeking to reduce the tensions caused by territorial disputes between Rome and Vienna, Bismarck brought Italy into his

■ **Bismarckian system**
A succession of alliances sought by Otto von Bismarck in the twenty years after the unification of Germany in 1871; these were pursued to moderate the demands of Germany's allies, prevent the formation of opposing coalitions, and prevent local conflicts from escalating into general war.

alliance system in 1882 with the Triple Alliance between Germany, Austria-Hungary, and Italy.

By 1888, however, Bismarck's system was struggling to hold itself together. Russia became increasingly distrustful of German diplomacy, which effectively prevented Russia from actively pursuing its goals in the Balkans. In its competition with Russia, Austria-Hungary grew increasingly dependent on Germany as a protector. Bismarck tried to juggle Russian and Austrian interests, but none of the great powers could control events in the Balkans, which were driven largely by the ambitions and antagonisms of the local peoples fighting for greater autonomy from Ottoman suzerainty. This mixture of independent action on the part of the Balkan states and the irreconcilable interests of Austria-Hungary and Russia in this region played a major role in the decline of Bismarck's system.[13] German domestic politics (including the growing power of groups seeking protective tariffs and favoring aggressive colonialism) eventually undermined Bismarck's position, and he was removed from office in 1890. By the time of his dismissal, most of Europe had enjoyed almost two decades of peace, but the seeds of a great-power war had been sown.

The Eve of War: Protectionism and Discord

The international economy continued to expand in the years from 1873 to 1914. Industrialization even spread to a limited extent to less developed states. The continuing expansion of production promoted a greater degree of interdependence among national economies. At the same time, however, this growing interdependence led to an intensified call for protectionism, beginning in the 1880s. Capital owners and laborers who relied on uncompetitive industries for their livelihood lobbied their respective governments for protection from cheaper foreign imports.

Nationalism's revival, particularly in Germany and Italy, but in the United States and elsewhere as well, was a major factor driving the late nineteenth century's increased protectionism. All states were sensitive in this period to the promotion of their industries as a matter of national honor. In some sense, economic power was seen as an achievement worthy of national pride. Further, rising security concerns stemming from the fears of military aggression that accompanied the changing balance of power in Europe prompted states to employ tariffs (the direct income tax was not yet known) as a means to raise funds to pay for military expenditures. Taken together, as one scholar argued, "nationalism and the lag in industrialization made protection inevitable."[14]

Through it all, Britain remained the center of world trade and finance, commanding 31 percent of world trade in manufactured goods, with Germany at 27.5 percent and the United States at 13 percent, even as late as 1913.[15] Britain also remained the dominant financial power of the time, possessing 44 percent of the great powers' overseas investment, compared to France's 19.9 percent and Germany's 12.8 percent in 1914. Yet the great powers' ability to manage the increasingly interdependent world economy proved more and more difficult after 1870, beginning with two unforeseen economic developments: the huge influx of cheap U.S. and Russian grain into European markets and the depression of 1873–1879.

By the 1870s, the growth of railroads enabled the United States to export its surplus wheat more rapidly from the fields of the Great Plains states to markets in Europe. As more wheat entered the world market, the price of wheat began to fall. As other commodity producers began to sell their goods internationally, this pattern repeated itself. Regional commodity markets broke down and developed into international markets, increasing world supply and reducing prices. Although this was good for consumers, it was bad for many countries that relied on commodity sales for national wealth. In combination with an economic depression between 1873 and 1879, falling commodity prices resulted in a shuffling of traditional political and economic alignments throughout Europe and the world, especially on the tariff issue, and an intense lobbying effort for protection by those industrial and agricultural producers whose livelihoods were threatened by cheaper imports.

By the close of the 1880s, much of the free trade system had begun to collapse. However, these events manifested themselves slowly over time. One reason relative stability prevailed as long as it did before World War I was the existence of a strong international monetary (exchange rate) system. The **gold standard** lasted between 1870 and 1914 (and was reintroduced again after World War I). Traders therefore did not have to worry that changes in exchange rates might destroy their profits or that the currency of the countries they hoped to trade with was not convertible on the international market (for more on exchange rates, see Chapter 9).

As World War I approached, Britain remained staunchly committed to an open international economy, but the failure of France and Germany to follow suit undermined its efforts. Protectionism became more popular as domestic groups who had opposed the gold standard, like labor and import competitors, increased their political power. In many ways, the growing tide of protectionism, fed by nationalistic fervor, helped to create the spiral of insecurity that led to World War I. The European powers' economic interdependence failed to prevent the four bitter years of military struggle that disrupted the world economy and redistributed international economic power. The international coalition that had functioned to preserve Britain's hegemony broke down, leaving few vestiges of either hegemony or multilateral cooperation.

The World Wars

At the start of the twentieth century, through military power, economic strength, and colonial empires, the European great powers dominated the world's political and economic system. By the middle of the century, however, Europe was

▪ **Gold standard**
A fixed exchange-rate system in which each nation's currency value is set to gold.

struggling to recover from catastrophic devastation, and political and economic leadership had passed from London, Paris, and Berlin to capitals thousands of miles away from Europe's center of gravity. This radical change in the structure of world politics was brought about by two horrific wars, unequaled before or since in scope or destructiveness. World War I (1914–1918) and World War II (1939–1945) were the means by which the Eurocentric world order self-destructed and was replaced by a globalized economic and political system. We will examine the causes and consequences of the world wars and their impact on world politics. Our discussion of these complex conflicts will not go into great detail on how they were fought but will instead concentrate on why they occurred and what the fighting and the peace settlements that followed did to change the nature and structure of world politics.

Causes of World War I

The devastation wrought by the four years of World War I led to a continuing debate as to its causes. Although opinions differ, it is clear in hindsight that the complex relations among the European states prior to 1914 created the context for the crisis that arose in July 1914. The decisions made by European leaders during that crisis led to a war that none of them wanted and that would destroy the world as they knew it. Amid all the controversy over the origins of World War I, six factors are recognized as playing an important role in European politics and diplomacy in the years leading up to the outbreak of war in 1914: the rise of Germany, the system of alliances, the changing balance of economic power, nationalism, imperialism, and the cult of the offensive. (See At a Glance, "World War I and the Levels of Analysis," to apply the levels of analysis to the causes of World War I.)

Rise of Germany

With the stunning defeat of France in 1871 and Germany's subsequent unification, Germany took center stage in European international relations. Being at the center of Europe had both advantages and disadvantages for German diplomacy. The advantages were that Germany was well situated to expand trade, investment, and political contacts with the whole of Europe and could concentrate its military forces rapidly to meet a threat from any direction. The disadvantage was that Germany's central location meant that it had more points of potential conflict with other states than any other great power, and thus it feared encirclement by hostile neighbors. At the same time, Germany's neighbors became alarmed by Germany's growing economic and military strength—particularly France, which sought the return of Alsace and Lorraine, annexed by Germany as

AT A GLANCE

World War I and the Levels of Analysis

Systemic

The distribution of power led to the creation of a rigid alliance system; industrialization led to the creation of imperial rivalries; the cult of the offensive led to the desire to strike first in an attempt to secure victory.

Domestic

Germany: There was an important role for the army in decision making leading to the formation of the Schlieffen Plan; public support for naval and imperial expansion.

Austria-Hungary: Multinational society with different nationalities looking for independence.

France: Revival of popular nationalism against Germany through the loss of Alsace and Lorraine in the war of German unification.

Individual

Germany: Kaiser Wilhelm II possessed a desire to turn Germany into a world power, and expected to do so through the building of a large navy.

Austria: Franz Joseph was concerned about nationalist uprisings in the empire and wanted to punish Serbia as it was seen as the main threat to the empire.

---

a result of the Franco–Prussian War (1870–1871). France, Russia, and Britain saw Germany as a potential hegemon and recognized the need to balance power on the European continent.[16]

Kaiser Wilhelm II, who came to the throne in 1888, felt that Germany's natural affinity was with other Germans and thus began to tie Germany closer to Austria-Hungary, and Russo–German relations consequently deteriorated. The kaiser also believed that Germany required a powerful navy to maintain its status as a great power, and Admiral Tirpitz and many other officials in Berlin concurred. Thus, in 1898 Germany initiated a rapid expansion of its fleet.

News of the ambitious German naval construction program was received with great apprehension in London. From the British perspective, there was no logical reason for Germany to construct a large fleet unless it planned to challenge the dominant position of the Royal Navy. Britain regarded its naval supremacy as absolutely necessary to protect the island nation from invasion and to guard its extensive overseas empire. The kaiser's policies thus heightened the security dilemma in Europe on both land and sea. By 1914 Germany was engaged in a naval arms race with Britain and, together with its ally Austria-Hungary, in a ground-forces arms race with Russia and France.[17]

Alliance System

France, tired of diplomatic isolation and intent on replacing Bismarck's system of alliances with one that better protected its interests, seized the opportunity to court Russia when antagonism between Berlin and St. Petersburg began to increase. Although reluctant at first to make an alliance, Russia agreed in 1894 to a defensive treaty with France that explicitly sought to counter the increased power of Germany.[18] This treaty marked the beginning of an alliance system locking the great powers into commitments to intervene if their alliance partners were threatened. The agreement was designed to make Russia and France feel more secure, but to the Germans it represented the first step in a hostile encirclement.

Germany hoped to counter the Franco–Russian alliance with closer ties to Britain but played its diplomatic hand poorly. Ill-conceived attempts to convince Britain that it needed German support to protect its colonial empire backfired. Germany's heavy-handed policy worsened relations by arousing public opinion in both countries against an Anglo-German alliance.

One up-and-coming nation with which Britain did share strategic interests, however, was Japan. Both Britain and Japan were concerned about Russian expansion in Asia, and in 1902, the two nations signed a treaty in which they agreed to remain neutral if either country fought one other major power and to support each other should either be at war with two other powers. This Anglo–Japanese alliance presented France with a dilemma. If Japan and Russia went to war, French failure to support Russia would antagonize an ally crucial for the balance of power in Europe. If France actively assisted Russia, it would, at minimum, alienate Britain and, at most, lose a naval war to it. As France had plans for colonial expansion in North Africa, it could ill afford to antagonize Britain, so it had to take steps to improve Anglo-French relations.

Therefore, in April 1904 the two countries signed an entente (diplomatic French for an agreement or understanding) in which France recognized British supremacy in Egypt and Britain recognized France's predominant role in Morocco. The entente bound Britain into an alliance with the nation that had been its perennial enemy, France, and drew Britain closer to another ancient foe, Russia. Britain had several conflicts with Russia, especially over the Turkish Straits and Persia, but events in Europe would continue to bring the two together.

The Bismarckian system of flexible alliances that was set up to prevent a major war in Europe was thus followed by a rigid system ensuring that if two of the great powers went to war, the rest would quickly follow. None of the countries wanted a general European war, but each had its own designs and fears. Some, such as Germany, wanted to increase their influence, whereas others, like Austria-Hungary and Russia, sought to recapture their failing great-power status. Russia, Austria-Hungary, and the Ottoman Empire were the last of the antiquated autocratic monarchies of Europe and were rapidly being eclipsed by the other great powers in terms of economic development, military strength, and political and social organization.[19] As the Russian, Ottoman, and Austrian situations became increasingly desperate, their leaders became prepared to risk anything, up to and including war, to hold on to their internal cohesion and international stature. In the end, Italy had joined the Entente Powers—France, Russia, Britain, and Serbia (collectively referred to as the Allies)—in 1915, and by 1917 Montenegro, Romania, Greece, Portugal, and Japan had joined the Allies. Germany and Austria-Hungary (the Central Powers) were joined by the Ottoman Empire in October 1914 and Bulgaria in 1915.

Economic Change and Competition

The foreign and domestic political problems confronting the European powers in the late nineteenth and early twentieth centuries were compounded by the wrenching changes brought about by industrialization. Among its many other effects, the Industrial Revolution led to massive growth in Europe's population. In the first years of the new century the population of Europe was 50 million; in 1870 it was roughly 200 million, and by the eve of war in 1914 the population had soared to 300 million.[20] This population explosion generated great pressures on the economic systems of states, which had to reconcile competing demands for civilian consumption, capital investment, and military spending. Particularly in the economically and politically backward Austro-Hungarian, Russian, and Ottoman empires, it became increasingly difficult to simultaneously satisfy the resource requirements for foreign, domestic, and security policy.

The only thing that outstripped the population growth was the growth in industrial production. This growth was not evenly spread either among countries or within them. Italy, Russia, and Austria-Hungary lagged behind Britain, France, and Germany in industrial development. As the twentieth century opened, Britain, as the first state to industrialize, was declining relative to late-developing states such as Germany and the United States. In 1850, Britain was the undisputed world industrial leader and France the continental powerhouse. In that year, Britain alone accounted for over one-third of the combined manufacturing output of the great powers. During the Bismarckian period, however, Germany emerged as the most powerful continental state, and by the end of the century Germany was encroaching on Britain's lead as well, surpassing the United Kingdom in steel production and overall manufacturing.[21] During the same period, another up-and-coming power, the United States, was beginning its takeoff, and by 1914 it would evolve into an industrial giant. Table 3.1 gives a rough indication of how the European powers and the United States stacked up against one another in terms of economic power as European conflicts intensified.

As the industrial capacity of states grew, their ability to challenge the other great powers for political leadership grew correspondingly. As Germany's economic strength approached and then surpassed Britain's, the main objective of European alliances changed from containment of France and Russia (as had been the case in the eighteenth and early nineteenth centuries) to containment of

Germany. Meanwhile, increased industrial output was intensifying competition for resources and markets. Industrialization thus heightened the potential for conflict among the great powers at the same time that it enhanced their capacity to make war.[22] On both sides of the Atlantic, leaders were slow to recognize how changes in the global economic system created new dangers and opportunities and made the collective security system originally envisioned in the Concert of Europe increasingly difficult to manage.

Nationalism

The most powerful political doctrine of the nineteenth and early twentieth centuries was nationalism. The French Revolution solidified the nation-state as the supreme focus of allegiance. Those who clung the tightest to the ideas of nationalism in the early twentieth century, however, were people whose nations did not have independent states, namely those in eastern Europe and the Balkans. These regions were dominated by competing powers, the Russian, Austro-Hungarian, and Ottoman empires, which were convinced that suppressing nationalism within their borders was necessary for their survival as political entities. As a result, campaigns of persecution were launched against minorities who did not seem to belong to the national image. Russia forced the Poles in its empire to conform, the Jews in eastern and central Europe were persecuted, and all over Europe attempts were made to crush nationalist forces.

One of the greatest victories for nationalism was the unification of Germany, but its effect was not limited to the creation of the German Empire. The nationalism of the various ethnic groups within the many empires of Europe became a pressing issue in the twentieth century. The empires of eastern Europe were threatened by groups demanding separation and independence. These included Poles in Prussia and the French in Alsace and Lorraine who desired freedom from the German Empire; Serbs, Czechs, Romanians, and many others from the Austro-Hungarian Empire; Finns, Poles, and Balts from the Russian Empire; and Bulgarians, Greeks, Serbs, and Arabs from the Ottoman Empire.

The empire that felt most threatened by nationalist movements was Austria-Hungary. Here was the only country in Europe that was held together not by national identity, but by the principle of personal dynastic rule. Emperor Franz Josef I had ruled over the numerous nationalities within the empire since 1848. The Hungarians and the Austrians were actually minorities in a patchwork of Slavic groups, including Poles, Czechs, Slovaks, Slovenes, Croats, and Serbs. Austria was opposed to Russian encroachment in the area and was even more concerned about further independence in the Balkans. Vienna was afraid that the independent Balkan states, especially Serbia, would stir up trouble within the empire. The various nationalities under Austrian rule longed for independence and needed little encouragement from their kin, but many independent Balkan states supported nationalist agitation in hopes of unifying all people of their respective nationalities. In particular, the domestic problem presented by

MAP 3.5   The Balkans Before World War I

Slavic nationalism was exacerbated by the desire of Serbia, aided and abetted by Russia, to expand at Austria-Hungary's expense (see Map 3.5).

In general, empires tended to suppress nationalists within their own borders while encouraging those in neighboring empires, hoping to make political gains at the expense of their imperial rivals. This created an explosive situation in the ethnically diverse and politically fragmented Balkans, where the assassination of Archduke Franz Ferdinand, heir to Austria-Hungary's crown, in Sarajevo on June 28, 1914, sparked World War I.

Imperialism

Empires were not confined to Europe. By 1900 most of the world outside Europe (except the Americas) was under the domination of some European power (see

Chapter 5 for more on imperialism). Nearly all of Africa had been partitioned without regard to national or ethnic boundaries, and most of Asia was also under de facto if not de jure control by European colonial regimes.[23] Because power and security depended on controlling resources, acquisition of colonies for their resources and markets was considered essential by many European leaders. However, with most of the world already divided among the colonial empires, there was nowhere left to colonize. The states that felt left out of the colonial race, especially Germany, thought they deserved more and worried that without colonies they would not be able to obtain enough raw materials or have sufficient trading partners to remain competitive with the other great powers. The breakup of the "sick man of Europe," the faltering Ottoman Empire, presented an opportunity to acquire more territory (especially in the Middle East) that some states found irresistible.[24]

Many conflicts over colonial interests in Africa and Asia heightened tensions among the great powers in Europe. Britain and France frequently clashed over colonies and **spheres of influence,** as did Britain and Russia, but these great powers avoided war with each other over colonial disputes in the nineteenth century. As the twentieth century approached, however, colonial problems intensified the mutual antagonism between Britain and Germany.

Cult of the Offensive

With the advent of new technology, it appeared that the side that could swiftly mount an effective offensive would win. In the late nineteenth and early twentieth centuries, most European strategists subscribed to this belief in what modern strategic analysts refer to as the cult of the offensive.[25] There were two main reasons this became the primary strategic doctrine for European military planners. The first, as mentioned, had to do with technology. The expansion of railroads, among other technological improvements, enabled states to rapidly deploy troops to the front, and the telegraph allowed generals to receive reports and transmit orders faster, enabling them to control larger armies more effectively. Also, the breech-loading rifle and the machine gun were widely thought to increase the ability of attacking troops to concentrate their firepower at the point of assault. (For some reason, the ability of defending troops against this was downplayed.)

Second, recent experience with wars in Europe seemed to indicate that the side that landed the first blow would win. Prussia defeated its adversaries in 1864, 1866, and 1870–1871 quickly and with relatively few **casualties.** Most European generals expected the next great-power war to resemble the last and, accordingly, based their strategies on rapid mobilization and offensives. The same leaders chose to ignore differing experiences, including the American Civil War (1861–1865), which was a protracted struggle and produced a frightening number of casualties.

The inherent dangers of the cult of the offensive were not fully realized at the time. When political and military leaders believe that war will bring great gains at little cost, war becomes more likely. States act more aggressively by

▪ **Sphere of influence**
A region influenced by one great power. In a sphere of influence, the dominant power does not have sovereignty but imposes its will over several neighboring states, restricting the maneuverability of local territorial leaders.

▪ **Casualties**
Members of the armed forces who have been killed, wounded, or captured or are interned, sick, or missing and, therefore, are no longer a part of active duty.

increasingly challenging their neighbors through military buildups and coercive threats of war. As these neighbors grow more fearful, they, too, build up their forces and seek stronger alliances to better secure themselves in the event of war. Even if none of the states actually seek war, this spiral of tension makes conflicts of interest more severe and likely to lead to violence. The cult of the offensive thus enhances the security dilemma and encourages preemptive attacks because when crises threaten to escalate into war, states have great incentives to strike first and defeat their enemies before their enemies can defeat them.

The cult of the offensive influenced the military plans of most of the European great powers. Beginning in 1892, German Chief of Staff Alfred von Schlieffen changed Germany's strategy. Previously, in the event of a two-front war with Russia and France, Germany planned to attack Russia first while German forces stood on the defensive against France. The new **Schlieffen Plan** called for Germany to knock out France with a fast-moving offensive, just as Prussia had done in the Franco–Prussian War, and then shift its troops by rail to the eastern front to fight the slower moving Russian forces. Pursuing this strategy helped Germany because war would be initiated before Russia achieved full military capacity.[26] Russia and France, however, had similar plans for rapid mobilization and offensive in the event of a war with Germany. The cult of the offensive thus put the massive military machines of the great powers on a hair trigger.

Consequences of World War I

As the preceding section outlined, there are plenty of possible explanations for why World War I occurred. Taken together, they offer more than enough reasons why Europe was pushed over the brink of war in 1914. Instead of the quick war of maneuver that European strategists had counted on, however, the conflict became a war of attrition in which thousands of men would die fighting for advances measured in yards rather than miles.[27] Attempting to break through defensive lines, both sides used poison gas, a new weapon that caused agonizing deaths and crippling injuries but did not alter the stalemate. Tanks and aircraft were introduced in further attempts to generate offensive momentum, but these military machines were still in early stages of development and had only a marginal effect on the fighting. At sea, the fleets of British and German dreadnoughts fought only one major battle (the Battle of Jutland in 1916), which proved indecisive. Most of the naval war was fought between German U-boats (submarines, another new tool of warfare) and British convoy escorts.

Most wars in Europe since 1648 had been limited wars that did not cause widespread devastation or huge numbers of military and civilian casualties. World War I, however, which ended with the armistice signed on November 11, 1918, was a total war, in which the whole of each involved nation's human and

▪ **Schlieffen Plan**
Developed by German Chief of Staff Alfred von Schlieffen and put into operation at the beginning of World War I, this strategic plan directed German forces to knock out France with a fast-moving offensive, then shift by rail to the eastern front to fight Russia.

PHOTO 3.3   European leaders and their followers expected a quick, easy war when hostilities broke out in August 1914. Instead, troops were forced to dig elaborate trenches and erect barbed wire fortifications as the battlefront became static. Horrendous casualties resulted.

material resources was devoted to the conflict, and defeat threatened national survival. The destruction caused by the war was overwhelming. An estimated 8 million soldiers were killed during the war, with another 7 million permanently disabled. In addition, more than 5 million civilians were killed in Europe outside Russia, and the number of Russian civilian casualties is probably much higher.[28] An entire generation of young Europeans was all but destroyed. The world sighed with relief when the Great War ended in 1918, but winning the peace would prove to be a struggle in itself, as there were numerous profound consequences of World War I.

Russian Revolution

The war with Germany and Austria created additional pressures on the decrepit tsarist regime in Russia. By the end of 1916, the Russian army had suffered many defeats and more than 3.6 million casualties, with another 2.1 million Russian soldiers taken prisoner. These losses prompted St. Petersburg to drastically increase draft calls, which in turn increased unrest among peasants and urban workers. Additionally, food supplies were not getting to the cities due to an inadequate transportation system, and inflation had skyrocketed. Finally, insufficient supplies of weapons, ammunition, and food were reaching soldiers at the front. Strikes, mutinies, and rioting culminated in the overthrow of Nicholas II in March 1917. The new provisional government, a coalition of Democratic, Socialist, and Communist parties headed by Alexander Kerensky, continued the war, a decision that increasingly incurred the wrath of soldiers and the civilian population. In November the Bolshevik (Communist) party seized power, and the revolutionary leader Vladimir Lenin assumed leadership on a platform of "land, bread, and peace." The Bolsheviks delivered on one plank of their platform; they signed an armistice with Germany in December, and in the March 1918 Treaty of Brest-Litovsk, the Bolshevik government signed a separate peace with Germany, relinquishing Russian claims to the Baltic states of Latvia, Lithuania, and Estonia, as well as Finland, Poland, and other territories in eastern Europe. German forces remained in occupation of the western portions of Ukraine and Russia.

Versailles Settlement

The treaty that ended World War I unleashed unforeseen consequences on the international system. With the destruction caused by the Great War fresh in their minds, the victorious Allies took upon themselves the responsibility for bringing order and stability to Europe and the rest of the world. In January 1919 the United States, Britain, France, and Italy convened the Paris Peace Conference at the palace of Versailles. The conference was attended by a number of smaller states, but neither Germany nor Austria-Hungary was invited. Because France had suffered the most during the war, it played a leading role at the conference, as did the United States, in recognition of its military and economic clout. French goals were relatively straightforward: Punish Germany and take revenge not only for the losses incurred between 1914 and 1918 but also for the humiliation of 1871. Prime Minister David Lloyd George of Britain was also bent on exacting punishment to a lesser degree, but Britain and Italy, along with the smaller Balkan states, were mainly there to gain territory from the division of the fallen empires. The goals of the European conferees were thus in line with old-fashioned realpolitik as it had been practiced at the Congress of Vienna.

What Would You Do?

Russia and the Path to War

You are the tsar of Russia in early August 1914. You are backing the Serbians, your Orthodox Christian brethren, whom Austria and, by extension, Germany have threatened over the assassination of the heir to the Austrian throne on his visit to Bosnia, an Austrian province that Serbia covets.

You are trying to decide whether to order full mobilization of your forces against Austria. You are aware that mobilization may precipitate the next war. You have suggested to your military commanders that the country partially mobilize, thereby keeping its options open. If the crisis abates, you can easily demobilize; if the crisis leads to war, you will at least be partially ready. However, your generals tell you that this is not possible: No one ever devised a scheme for partial mobilization; it is either all or nothing. Mobilization will threaten Germany and will likely lead to war. If you wait a few years until you are stronger industrially, you may be in a better position to fight and win.

Although you have made great strides in bringing your country into the industrial age in the last twenty years (such as building more munitions factories, steel mills, and kilometers of railroads), you have also heightened expectations on the part of the working classes for greater economic and political reform. The Japanese defeat of your armies in 1905 revealed your country's lack of military and economic preparation, and it incited a domestic revolt. You do not want to risk a repeat of this event.

On the other hand, you want to maintain your alliance with France, which opposes Germany. Your military experts tell you that if you do not mobilize your forces to thwart a possible Austrian attack against Serbia, the Austrians and their patrons, the Germans, could easily win a war. Your military officers keep saying that the first country to mobilize will win the next war. Six years ago during a similar crisis in the Balkans, you caved in and your position, and that of your clients, the Serbs, only deteriorated. If you wait too long to decide, you might appear weak and indecisive to both client and foes.

You face a dilemma. The war could be lost if you decide not to mobilize, but mobilization could lead to war. If it leads to a war that you lose, it could mean your downfall.

What Would You Do?

The goals of the United States were distinctly different. President Woodrow Wilson argued that America had entered the war (which occurred in April 1917, three months after Germany's decision to launch unrestricted submarine warfare) not out of a narrow self-interest but to make the world "safe for democracy." Basically, Wilson hoped to use the conference to create a new world order based on mutual respect and cooperation between nations (see Spotlight, "An Idealist at Versailles").

▪ SPOTLIGHT ▪

An Idealist at Versailles

President Woodrow Wilson provides an illuminating example of the individual level of analysis and the impact individuals can have on world political events. Wilson's leadership style contained an intriguing mix of traits that paradoxically prevented him from achieving his major foreign-policy objectives. Idealistic, moralistic, and self-righteous, Wilson was also an activist, a genuine product of the Progressive era in America. The influence infused him with a desire to take part energetically in various problem areas of policy to come up with the best possible remedy. Unfortunately, this essentially optimistic desire to fix problems was counterbalanced by a negative inflexibility—a lack of willingness to reach a bargain or compromise solution with one's political opponents. A political scientist by profession and former president of Princeton University, Wilson was elected president of the United States in 1912 on a platform emphasizing the reform of American domestic politics. Shortly after his election, he remarked to a close friend, "It would be an irony of fate if my administration had to deal chiefly with foreign affairs." Fate wasted little time in handing him an irony. After campaigning for reelection in 1916 with the slogan "He kept us out of war," Wilson reluctantly decided to take the United States into World War I within a few months of the start of his second term.

After the war, President Wilson took a leading position at the Paris Peace Conference. "To make the world safe for democracy," he proposed a new world system in which states "all act in the common interest and are free to live their own lives under a common protection."[i] Wilson's vision of a collective security community was the League of Nations, intended to maintain peace by ensuring justice and self-determination for all peoples as envisioned in his Fourteen Points.

The peace conference became, in effect, a battle between Wilson and representatives of the other Allied powers, led by French Premier Georges Clemenceau, who favored the maintenance of a balance-of-power system. Wilson, considered by his fellow peacemakers to be an upstart American with little practical experience in world affairs, was never able to convince his colleagues to agree to a system of collective security. When he returned to the United States in February 1919, he remained confident that he would be able to secure Senate support for the Versailles Treaty. Yet Republicans in the Senate, led by Henry Cabot Lodge, argued that the League would lead the United States back into war, give Britain too much influence, and, most importantly, threaten the nation's isolationist tradition. They would not accept the treaty without an overhaul of the League of Nations Covenant, which Wilson had just helped write.

In an effort to gain Republican support, Wilson returned to Paris in March 1919 and secured amendments to the League's Covenant, but Republican opposition remained steadfast and public sentiment grew increasingly negative. Failing to garner public support for the treaty on his return to the United States, Wilson refused to compromise with the Republicans and asked Senate Democrats to vote against the Senate's proposed version of an amended League of Nations Covenant because it did not incorporate the strong provisions for collective action against aggression on which he insisted. His lack of flexibility, no doubt tied to his strong sense of self-righteousness, prevented the United States from signing the treaty and joining the League, which became ineffective without U.S. involvement. As a result, the United States retreated into its prewar isolationist mode and played a relatively minor role in world politics during the tumultuous 1920s and 1930s. Wilson also refused to recognize the American public's weariness with its involvement in Europe's affairs and lack of enthusiasm for any role as global policeman.

---

i. Quoted in Gordon A. Craig and Alexander L. George, *Force and Statecraft* (New York: Oxford University Press, 1983), 52.

The delegates to the conference spent months arguing amongst themselves.[29] Finally, after resolving their many differences, the Allies presented Germany with a treaty. This document took Wilson's idealistic proposals and Clemenceau's vengeful demands and combined them to form a compromise that satisfied no one. The treaty called for Germany to return Alsace-Lorraine to France, cede some of its eastern territory to the re-created state of Poland, permit French and British occupation of the economically vital Saar region, and demilitarize the Rhineland (the portion of Germany bordering France). In addition, the treaty required Germany to adhere to strict disarmament provisions that limited the size of its army; forbade it to possess submarines, tanks, or an air force; and outlawed conscription.

Consistent with the principle of national self-determination, and an example of fragmentation, the Austro-Hungarian Empire was divided into a number of successor states: Austria, Hungary, Czechoslovakia, and Yugoslavia (which united Serbs, Croats, Slovenes, Montenegrins, and Muslim Slavs among others in an artificial kingdom). Poland, which had been partitioned out of existence in 1795, was reunited and joined Italy and Romania in claiming other parts of the former Hapsburg Empire. Austria, most of whose population was Germanic, was forbidden from joining with Germany, and a large German population was incorporated into Czechoslovakia in an area known as the Sudetenland.

PHOTO 3.4 Woodrow Wilson making a whistle-stop speech.

Despite all the talk about self-determination of nations, the treaty granted self-determination to some nationalities but not to others; in particular, the doctrine was not applied to the Germans. Much to the dismay of the Arabs and the European colonies, the principle was not applied at all outside Europe. The British had promised the Arabs independence if they aided in the fight against the Ottoman Turks, but this turned out to be an empty promise, as Britain, France, and Russia made plans to carve up the Ottoman Empire among themselves before the war had even finished (see again Map 3.4).[30]

Finally, Germany was held responsible for the war and was forced to pay extensive reparations to the Allies, particularly France. Germany objected to many parts of the treaty, but no clause did more to create a lasting sense of betrayal and resentment than Article 231. This article was the "war guilt" clause, which held Germany and its allies wholly responsible for the war and all the damage it caused. The clause would foster rage and resentment among the German people that nationalist extremists were quick to exploit. Germany had little choice but to accept the treaty, as the Allies continued to blockade German ports and maintained large forces in position to strike at German territory until the treaty was signed. The onus of accepting the punitive treaty fell to the new Weimar Republic, which had replaced the German monarchy after the kaiser's November

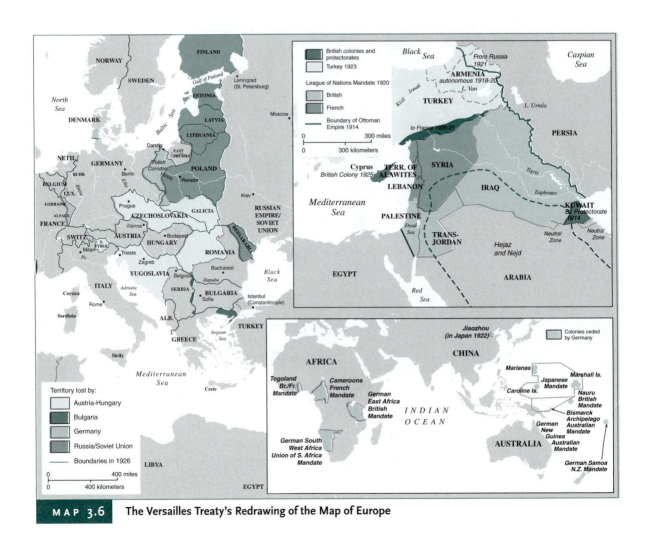

MAP 3.6   The Versailles Treaty's Redrawing of the Map of Europe

1918 abdication. The signing of the peace agreement discredited the infant democratic regime in the minds of many Germans. The treaty was signed in the Hall of Mirrors at the Palace of Versailles, where in 1871 Bismarck had proclaimed the German Empire that was now no more. The Great War was officially over, but the peace settlement was soon to create almost as many problems as it had solved (see Map 3.6).

A Weak League and the Road to Another World War

The hope of establishing peace and stability through the League of Nations (see again Spotlight, "An Idealist at Versailles") was thwarted by the decision of the United States not to join. The U.S. Senate refused to ratify the Treaty of Versailles. Aside from the Senate's fear of "entangling alliances," some senators demanded an amendment asserting the primacy of the U.S. Constitution, which would protect Congress's prerogative to declare war. Wilson refused to compromise, the Senate refused to ratify the treaty, and the United States remained outside the League. The absence of the United States, which had proposed and been a driving spirit behind the League, left it a body without substance. Without the world's largest industrial power, the League of Nations was weakened to the point that many doubted its capability to satisfactorily resolve the many challenges to the new political order established at Versailles. The global security system Wilson envisioned thus never got off the ground.

In sum, the potential for an upsurge in German resentment, the American return to isolationism, the revolution and civil war in Russia (renamed the Union of Soviet Socialist Republics by the Bolshevik government in 1922), and the splintering of eastern Europe made the European balance of power inherently unstable. Europe became more fragmented in political, economic, and security terms than it had been before 1914.

In response to the uncertain situation, European diplomats scrambled to set up new security agreements. France established a network of defense pacts with Poland, Czechoslovakia, Romania, and Yugoslavia in an attempt to contain Germany should the need arise. (Because the reliability of these alliances was questionable however, France began in 1930 to build an extensive system of defensive fortifications, called the **Maginot Line,** on its border with Germany.) Britain, Italy, France, Belgium, and Germany addressed security concerns in western Europe in the Locarno Treaties of 1925, and in 1926 Germany was allowed into the League of Nations.

These international security arrangements, however, would soon be undermined by domestic developments in the various European great powers. Hoping to avoid a recurrence of the devastation that the Great War had brought to all of Europe, postwar public opinion in Britain and France was strongly against spending money on defense. The desire to avoid war at any cost was fed by a growing belief that weapons and arms races lead to war, by disgust with "merchants of death" who reaped huge profits from manufacturing weapons and war material, and by reassessments of the war's origins that did not heap all of the blame on Germany. (As the earlier sections on the causes of World War I recount, there was plenty of blame to go around.) Antiwar sentiments would later guide the proponents of the policy of **appeasement,** a policy dissuading aggressors from attacking by conceding part of their demands to satisfy their appetite for expansion (see Spotlight, "The Munich Analogy").

In contrast to the growth of pacifism in the West, many Italians and Germans, feeling cheated (for different reasons) by the outcome of World War I, increasingly turned to radical forms of nationalism as their social and economic situation led to disillusionment with democracy. In Italy, social upheaval nearly led

■ **Maginot Line**
An extensive system of defensive fortifications built by France in 1930 along its border with Germany.

■ **Appeasement**
One-sided concessions to a potential opponent.

▪ SPOTLIGHT ▪

The Munich Analogy

The frequency with which historical analogies are used to make inferences about current problems underscores the importance of historical knowledge. Whether they know it or not or admit it or not, policymakers actually use history in their decision-making processes.[i] History, of course, is a double-edged sword. We can learn from the mistakes of the past and better understand our future with a focus on history. An overuse of historical analogies, however, can be dangerous. No two events are exactly the same, and attempting to force the facts of a "new" event into an "old" one can have disastrous results. The Munich Analogy is a case in point.

Munich was an experience seared into the memory of all who witnessed the promises made and broken in 1938. The Munich Conference became synonymous with the discredited appeasement policy of British Prime Minister Neville Chamberlain. Adolf Hitler, Chamberlain, French Prime Minister Edouard Daladier, and Italian Prime Minister Benito Mussolini met in Munich on September 29, 1938, to resolve the crisis over the Sudetenland of Czechoslovakia. Hitler was threatening to go to war to annex the Czech territory, where 3 million ethnic Germans lived. Germans, and Hitler in particular, despised the Treaty of Versailles and wanted to incorporate all German-speaking peoples into the German state. Chamberlain and the others sought to appease Hitler by agreeing to cede the Sudetenland to Germany, on the basis of Hitler's guarantee not to attack the remaining portion of Czechoslovakia. Chamberlain was greeted as a hero when he returned to Britain, for it was believed that war had been averted.

At the time, appeasement was a popular policy, credited with keeping Europe out of another ruinous war. Within six months, however, Chamberlain and his appeasement policy were thoroughly discredited when Hitler invaded the rest of Czechoslovakia. Hitler viewed the concessions made as a sign of weakness, and the Western powers failed to understand Hitler's motivations, goals, and lack of limits.[ii] Appeasement became a dirty word, and Munich became a metaphor for encouraging aggression by giving in to an aggressor.

In later years, leaders have referred to Munich in attempts to win support for standing firm against an opponent's challenges. During the Cold War, many U.S. policies designed to contain the Soviet Union were justified by citing the Munich Analogy, most notably the decisions to send forces to counter communist threats in Korea in 1950 and Vietnam in 1965. U.S. President George H. Bush invoked the Munich analogy to convince Congress to authorize the use of force against Iraq in 1991 and called Iraqi president Saddam Hussein a "new Hitler." His son, President George W. Bush, used similar language to justify military action against Hussein's regime in 2003. Ever since Munich, it appears, politicians have consistently painted their enemies as Hitlers, doing as much as they are able to avoid being remembered as Chamberlains.

---

i. For an in-depth discussion of the use of history by policymakers, see Richard E. Neustadt and Ernest R. May, *Thinking in Time: The Use of History for Decision-Makers* (New York: The Free Press, 1986).

ii. For an in-depth discussion of the role of ideological beliefs in the outbreak of World War II, see Mark L. Hass, *The Ideological Origins of Great Power Politics, 1789–1989* (Ithaca, NY: Cornell University Press, 2005).

---

to civil war. Fearing the possibility of a communist-inspired revolution, King Victor Emmanuel III appointed Benito Mussolini, head of the ultraconservative and nationalist Fascist party, prime minister in 1922. Mussolini, called *Il Duce* (the leader), soon established a dictatorial regime promising to end the social and economic chaos.[31]

Economic Collapse and the Great Depression

By collapsing trade within Europe and forcing economies onto a war footing, World War I disrupted the international economy, which had been dominated by Europe's great powers. The war was a boon to producers and exporters outside of Europe, however. The United States, in particular, quickly emerged as the chief supplier of war-related matériel to the Allied powers. By war's end, Britain and France had accumulated more than $10 billion in war debts to the United States, which therefore became the world's largest creditor. Other states benefited from the war's disruption of traditional export markets and created significant export sectors of their own. Japan, for example, experienced dramatic industrial improvements in the course of meeting the various needs of markets in Europe and Asia.[32]

The Europeans came out of the war with huge war debts, a devastated production base (Britain and France, in particular, lost almost an entire generation of young men), inflation, and the loss of traditional export markets. As the vanquished power, Germany faced punitive demands for reparations, which Britain and France forced on that country to pay off their debts to the United States. This produced a precarious situation for the world economy, a situation exacerbated by the inability of the world's leading industrial economies to cooperate to manage the ensuing economic turmoil.

Tellingly, the most important diplomatic negotiations throughout the 1920s centered on the issue of war debts and reparations.[33] Two things proved constant over the decade—the United States insisted on being paid back for its war loans to France and England, and these Allies were determined to extract reparations from Germany, both for punitive reasons and to pay back their war debts. By 1924, it became apparent that Germany would be unable to meet its obligations. It was forced to print money to pay its debts. Printing money, however, led to the condition known as **hyperinflation,** which made German prices rise as much as 500 percent or more each month. In addition, German currency became almost worthless (the U.S.–German exchange rate exceeded 1 million marks to the dollar). In response, the Allies, Germany, and the United States signed the 1924 **Dawes Plan.** Under the agreement, the United States (primarily American private investors) would lend money to Germany, which it could use to pay its reparations to the Allies. These reparations payments could then be transferred to the U.S. government from the Allies to service war loans.

Why would the United States lend money to Germany only to have it return as Allied debt repayment? It is important to note that the American private sector, not the U.S. government, was primarily investing in Germany. The German government was willing to pay an attractive interest rate, much like a bank pays interest on a savings account, so American investment in Germany was out of self-interest, not for humanitarian reasons. When this money was recycled to the U.S. government as debt service, all parties, including the U.S. government and investors, seemed to benefit. The Dawes Plan thus stabilized the international economy for the next few years, allowing many countries' economies, including that of the United States, to grow rapidly.

The already shaky global economy was dealt a crushing blow when the American stock market crashed in 1929. The crash hurled first the United States and then Europe into the Great Depression, the worst economic disaster in modern times. Banks failed, the supply of capital dried up, investments and savings vanished, and millions of workers lost their jobs. Almost overnight, international trade broke down as nations erected trade barriers to protect jobs and domestic markets. The 1930 Smoot-Hawley Tariff dramatically increased American import duties and aggravated the situation by closing off the U.S. market from industrial imports. The closing of world markets spread, further exacerbating Germany's inability to pay its war debts.[34] Unable to get new loans from America, Germany renounced payment of war reparations, which in turn led France and Britain to default on their debts.

The Great Depression exacerbated political and economic conflicts all over the world. The German economy, in particular, was devastated, and its political system was paralyzed. Many Germans looked for a strong hand to lead them out of the crisis, and the National Socialist (Nazi) party, led by Adolf Hitler, offered one. In elections held from 1930 to 1933, the Nazis continuously gained seats in the Reichstag (parliament) until they controlled more seats than any other party, thus clearing the way for Hitler to become chancellor in January 1933. The man who would become the world's most infamous dictator thus came to power through the democratic process.

▪ **Hyperinflation**
An extreme, rapid, and uncontrolled rise in prices and concomitant decline in a currency's value.

▪ **Dawes Plan**
A plan to alleviate the economic pressure on Germany caused by reparations imposed after World War I. Under this agreement, American banks would lend money to Germany for its reparations payments to the Allies. These payments could then be transferred to the U.S. government from the Allies to service war loans.

Causes of World War II

Global instability, both economically and politically, paved the way for the most destructive war in human history. The reasons for the outbreak of World War II have not been debated as extensively or enthusiastically as the causes of World War I. It is almost universally accepted that if Germany, Italy, and Japan had not pursued expansionist policies in the mid- to late 1930s, World War II might well have never occurred or at least would not have become such a massive conflict. Nevertheless, five factors may be identified as candidates for the prime cause of World War II. Some of these factors, particularly the aforementioned expansionism on the part of Germany, Italy, and Japan and the rise of **fascism** in Europe, may have had greater influence than others, and each factor when taken individually may not have been necessary or sufficient to cause a global war. All, however, are likely to have exerted some influence on the rapid collapse of the fragile

■ **Fascism**
A doctrine promoted by the far right seeking an authoritarian society built around the rule of an elite led by a dictator or supreme leader.

AT A GLANCE

World War II and the Levels of Analysis

Systemic

Germany, Japan, and Italy were rising powers who were seeking a change in the balance of power. Failure of the League of Nations marked a failure of collective security due to the self-interest of states.

Domestic

Germany: People demanding improved situation after Treaty of Versailles; popularization of *Lebensraum*, the idea of the German people needing more space.

Japan: Government was becoming increasingly militaristic and engaging in an expansionist foreign policy.

Great Britain and France: Public support for the appeasement policy.

Individual

Germany: Hitler's desire for power and the supremacy of the so-called Aryan race led to German

aggression against its neighbors, and ultimately World War II with the German invasion of Poland on September 1, 1939.

Great Britain: Prime Minister Neville Chamberlain's commitment to avoiding war with Hitler prompted the appeasement policy and the Munich Pact in 1938. This policy paved the way for Hitler's consumption of Czechoslovakia and the eventual invasion of Poland.

Italy: Dictator Benito Mussolini's desire to restore the greatness of Italy and his imperialistic designs led to an alliance with Hitler, but he did not enter Italy into World War II until 1940.

Japan: Prime Minister and General Hideki Tojo led the military faction that supported war with the United States; he approved the attack on Pearl Harbor and advocated the war being fought to the bitter end.

peace of the 1920s and 1930s. (See At a Glance, "World War II and the Levels of Analysis," to apply the levels of analysis to the outbreak of World War II.)

The first possible reason for the outbreak of another world war was that the terms of the Versailles Treaty were too harsh. As discussed earlier, the self-determination granted to many of Europe's nationalities was not extended to the German people, many of the treaty's provisions infringed on German sovereignty, and many Germans came to support a revision of the terms of the peace, by force if necessary (See again Spotlight, "The Munich Analogy"). On the other hand, it has been argued that a second major war occurred because the terms of the Versailles Treaty were not enforced. The European powers were reluctant to use force to compel Germany to adhere to the treaty's provisions, which may have encouraged progressively greater violations of the peace treaty. One of the biggest mistakes made by the Allies was failure to understand the scope of, and subsequently respond to, the rearmament of Germany in the 1930s.[35] This was in part because Britain, France, and Russia failed to make an effective alliance and instead chose to "pass the buck" in terms of confronting Germany.[36] Because France and Britain were not interested in making an alliance with Russia, the Soviet state found a willing participant in Germany (see the discussion of the Nazi-Soviet Non-aggression Pact later in this chapter). Additionally, the League of Nations never functioned as it was designed to and was severely weakened by the nonparticipation of the United States; thus it was unable to deter aggression or maintain collective security in Europe and elsewhere.

Third, the changing balance of power may have played an important role in the outbreak of a new world war. In particular, Japan, Germany, and the Soviet Union became markedly stronger during the 1930s, which may have made conflict with the other great powers inevitable as the rising stars on the world scene challenged Britain, France, and the United States for world leadership. In addition, there was fear amongst the rising powers of each other—in particular, Germany was concerned about the growing power of Russia and needed to eliminate the Russian threat. Originally this was done through alliance, but that was followed by betrayal and invasion. In 1939, Soviet leader Joseph Stalin and German leader Adolf Hitler shocked the world by signing the Nazi-Soviet Non-aggression Pact. The treaty stipulated that if either Germany or the Soviet Union became embroiled in a conflict with a third country, the other would practice neutrality. Beyond this, however, the treaty defined the boundaries of each side's sphere of influence and facilitated Soviet occupation of their assigned portion of Poland almost immediately after the German invasion in 1939. Hitler eventually disregarded this treaty when he turned on Stalin and invaded the Soviet Union in Operation Barbarossa in 1941.[37]

However, changes in the balance of power do not always lead to war. This has led some analysts to contend that German, Italian, and Japanese expansionism was the deciding factor in the eruption of a global conflict. These states, according to this argument, decided to expand their territory and global reach to resolve or avoid a variety of domestic and international political problems. If leaders in Berlin, Rome, and Tokyo had chosen different solutions for their internal difficulties, war might not have resulted.

Finally, many of the same pressures that prompted the Axis powers to expand before the war prompted the rise of fascism in a number of European states and in Japan. The authoritarian and militaristic ideology of fascism was anathema to the Western democracies (as was the totalitarian communism practiced in the Soviet Union under Stalin). Perhaps if Hitler and Mussolini had not come to power, or if the Nazi party had not stamped out democracy and human rights so brutally, the great powers would have been able to resolve their differences without resorting to war.

Consequences of World War II

The beginnings of both the world wars stunned strategic planners. In 1914, Germany hoped to achieve a quick victory over France as it had in 1871, but its forces soon bogged down in immobile trench warfare. In 1940, the Allies expected trench warfare and thought France would be safe behind the formidable Maginot Line, but German armies circumvented French defenses and smashed through to Paris much as they had in 1871. Confident that France was done for, Italy joined the war on Germany's side in June. (Germany and its allies were thereafter referred to as the Axis, after the Rome-Berlin Axis signed in May 1939.) The Allied powers included France, Britain, and eventually the USSR (after Hitler broke an agreement with Stalin and launched **Operation Barbarossa**) and the United States (after the Japanese attack on Pearl Harbor).

World War II was even more destructive than the first. It is estimated that the war killed at least 40 million to 50 million people. The USSR alone suffered 7.5 million to 11.5 million soldiers killed and 6 million to 8 million direct civilian deaths, although the total of all Soviet war-related deaths is probably between 20 million and 25 million.[38] Entire cities in Europe and Asia were destroyed by aerial bombing, by ground combat, or by occupying forces as reprisals for resistance activity. Most of the combat and devastation occurred in central and eastern Europe, but the war was fought everywhere, from the frozen tundra of Lapland to the sweltering jungle of Burma, from the Aleutian Islands in the North Pacific to the estuary of the Río de la Plata in the South Atlantic. Only nine sovereign states remained neutral by the end of the war, although many nations that declared war on the Axis committed few troops to combat. World War II was truly a global war.

Uneasy Alliance

World War II in Europe came to an end on May 8, 1945, when, eight days after Hitler committed suicide in his Berlin bunker, Germany unconditionally surrendered, and the Allies declared victory in Europe. Hitler's Thousand-Year Reich

▪ **Operation Barbarossa**
The invasion of the Soviet Union ordered by Hitler on June 22, 1941.

had collapsed within twelve years. The end of the war in Europe created new political problems for the Allies. Not the least of these was resolving the question of what to do with the defeated Germany. Throughout the war the major Allied powers held a series of summit conferences to discuss strategy and other war concerns. Until the conflict's final stages, little thought was given to what Europe would look like after the defeat of the Axis Powers, as the immediate goal was to win the war. On this score the Allies were united. However, once the common enemy was eliminated, the wartime consensus began to break down. This became evident in the two main conferences held in 1945 at Yalta and Potsdam.[39]

Churchill, Roosevelt, and Stalin, the "Big Three" leaders, met for the final time at Yalta in the Soviet Crimea in February 1945 to address some important issues regarding postwar Europe. The most significant of these was the fate of the liberated nations of eastern Europe. It was important to the Allies, and especially to the Americans, that the countries liberated by the Soviets be granted self-determination and that they be able to choose their own (preferably democratic) governments.

Stalin agreed to elections in the eastern European countries, but he did not take the issue seriously. He was more concerned with Soviet security and German reparations. In both world wars Russia had been invaded through eastern Europe, and hence Stalin sought to maintain effective control over these countries so that they could never again support Germany against Russia. The Big Three also differed on the issue of war reparations, with sharp disagreement occurring between the Soviets, who demanded huge reparations, and the United States and Britain, who did not want to permanently cripple Germany. In the end, the decision was postponed until the next meeting. As will be seen in the next chapter, these hurried decisions had a fateful impact on post-World War II relations that the three leaders could not foresee.

In July 1945, shortly after the end of the war in Europe, the Allies met again to discuss the postwar settlement, this time in Potsdam, a Soviet-occupied German town near Berlin. Of the former Big Three, however, only Stalin remained. Roosevelt had suddenly died of a cerebral hemorrhage in April, leaving Vice President Harry Truman as the new president. Churchill's Conservative party was voted out of office during the proceedings, so the new prime minister, Clement Atlee, replaced him in mid-conference. At this meeting it was confirmed that Germany was to be disarmed and that British, American, and Soviet troops would each occupy part of Germany. Berlin, located within the area to be occupied by the USSR, would also be divided among the three nations. Under pressure from Paris, Britain and the United States added France as a participant in the occupation, so Germany was divided into four zones of occupation, as was Berlin (see Map 3.7). Once again the issue of war reparations was discussed, and it was agreed that the Soviets would be able to take reparations and booty out of their own German zone of occupation and would receive a quarter of any reparations assessed in the American, British, and French zones.

The distrust brewing among the Allies was all the more apparent by the time of the Potsdam meeting. In particular, the Allies were concerned about the Soviet occupation of eastern Europe. Despite glossing over their animosity toward the

MAP 3.7   **A Divided Germany, Post-World War II**

Soviets during the war (to the extent that Stalin was portrayed as "Uncle Joe" to the American people), the British, French, and Americans were wary of Moscow. Fresh on their minds were Stalin's brutal political purges and his forced collectivization of Soviet agriculture in the 1930s, which killed millions. The strains between the wartime allies were exacerbated, however, by the change in personnel at the top. Truman, Atlee, and Stalin did not have the same history of communication and cooperation that Roosevelt, Churchill, and Stalin had enjoyed.

The Holocaust

One of the most profound consequences of World War II was the genocide of 6 million European Jews committed by the Third Reich, known as the Holocaust. It was the official policy of the Nazis, who made the Jewish people the scapegoat for most of Germany's post-World War I hardships. They considered Jews, Gypsies, and homosexuals "inhuman" and likened their murder to the extermination of pests. Millions of Jews and other victims were captured, transported, enslaved, and put to death in concentration camps such as Auschwitz, Buchenwald, Dachau, and Bergen-Belsen.

The concentration and extermination camps had one aim: the murder of those who entered. Either one faced outright gassing, was worked to death in slave labor, or died of starvation or disease. The killings occurred on a scale unseen before in human history, using the organized and methodical techniques of mass production for murder.

Accompanying the undeniable horror of the "Final Solution," Hannah Arendt has described the banality of the evil that took place.[40] The German railroads were paid full fare for transporting victims to the camps, and large corporations located factories near the camps to take advantage of the free forced labor. Gruesome as well were notorious medical experiments attempting to prove twisted genetic theories and the making of soap, candles, and even lampshades out of the remains of human beings. The gold retrieved from victims' teeth also was a ghastly booty. Bodies were either buried in mass graves or cremated in huge ovens, spreading a pall of ash over the surrounding area.

The Holocaust ended with the end of the war. None of the Allied troops who liberated the camps were prepared for what greeted them: the sight of skeleton-like prisoners and their accounts of grisly horror. The Nazi leaders responsible for this crime against humanity (with the exception of those who escaped or committed suicide) were tried and convicted after the war at a special war-crimes tribunal at Nuremberg, and all the world's nations vowed that such horrors should never be allowed to happen again. As we will see in later chapters, however, other genocides have occurred in the twentieth and twenty-first centuries.

Atomic Bomb

A consequence of World War II that changed the political and military landscape forever was the American use of the A-bomb. At Potsdam, Truman was eager to gain Soviet engagement in the fight against Japan. The United States had been fighting essentially alone against an implacable enemy in the Pacific throughout the war. Eventually, the United States gained the upper hand and secured bases from which bombing raids could be launched against the Japanese home islands. In an attempt to undermine the Japanese people's will to fight, most of Japan's major cities were extensively bombed; the firebombing of Tokyo alone killed about 200,000 people in only one week in 1945. However, as in Germany and in England, the bombing of civilians did not break the will of the Japanese, and they continued to resist.

This left the United States with a fearsome prospect: the invasion of Japan itself, which some U.S. military leaders calculated would result in more than 1 million American casualties. Although the Soviets would be likely to exact concessions and try to establish lasting control over whatever territory they occupied, as they had done in Europe, Truman still considered their participation in the war essential if American casualties were to be contained. At this point, however, another option became available. Fearing that Nazi scientists were working to develop a nuclear weapon, the United States started the top-secret Manhattan Project in 1942 to produce an atomic bomb before the Germans did. This project

PHOTO 3.5   Nazi war criminals listen at the Nuremberg Trials. Each was prosecuted for crimes against humanity committed during World War II.

was so secret that not even the vice president knew about it—Truman learned of the work on the atomic bomb only when he assumed the office of president on Roosevelt's death. The German atomic bomb project never got off the ground, but on July 16, 1945, while Truman was in Potsdam, Manhattan Project scientists detonated the first atomic bomb near Alamogordo, New Mexico.[41]

The development of the new weapon made Truman's dilemma much easier. If Japan were to surrender once it had seen the devastating potential of the atomic bomb, American lives would be spared. Other benefits included the saving of Japanese lives (compared with the staggering death toll that an invasion would have caused) and being relieved of the disadvantages of Soviet participation in the war. For Truman, however, sparing American casualties was the essential point. He therefore decided to use the new weapon.[42] On August 6, 1945, an American B-29 bomber, the *Enola Gay,* dropped the "Little Boy" atomic bomb on the Japanese city of Hiroshima. In the blinding flash and subsequent firestorm, 80,000 to 100,000 Japanese were killed. The explosive force of the atomic bomb was equivalent to 14,000 tons of TNT, ten times more powerful than had been predicted. In the absence of an immediate Japanese surrender, the Soviets declared war on Japan on August 8, and a second atomic bomb (the "Fat Man") was dropped on the city of Nagasaki on August 9. The following day, the Japanese government decided to sue for peace, and Japan formally surrendered on September 2. Humankind's most terrible weapon had ended its most terrible war.

Conclusion

Together, World Wars I and II combined to fundamentally alter world politics. Except for the Soviet Union, the old empires were gone, replaced by a growing number of states claiming to represent a particular nation. Moreover, the European powers no longer had the ability (whether they recognized it or not)

AT A GLANCE

Levels of Analysis and Paradigms in Review: Examples from 1648 to 1945

	Realism	*Liberalism*	*Constructivism*
Individual	Otto von Bismarck was committed to realpolitik and was concerned with advancing the interests of the state by whatever means necessary: diplomacy if possible, war if necessary.	After World War I, Woodrow Wilson promoted a system in which all states would act in the common interest for common protection. His collective security dream was the League of Nations.	Napoleon succeeded in consolidating power and becoming a legend in his own time by framing his political innovations and conquests in France's best interest.
Domestic	To begin the American Revolution, colonists revolted against Britain out of resentment over tax increases needed to pay the debt from the Seven Years' War. Thus, public outcry drove the attainment of power and the creation of the United States.	The desire of the American public to invest in Germany after World War I prompted the U.S. government to sign the Dawes Plan, which allowed Germany to pay its reparations to the Allies and the Allies to service their war loans to the United States.	In 1789, the nobility and clergy in France began challenging the king's authority, causing the politically and economically disenfranchised middle and lower classes to assert power. These actions overturned the cultural understanding of government and led to the establishment of a republic in France. This marked a radical departure from long-standing ideas of the state and government.
Systemic	As a cause of the War of the Austrian succession, King Frederick II of Prussia alarmed the other great Continental powers in the system by attempting to disturb the balance of power, causing the powers to ally against Austria.	Ideological consensus, war weariness, and economic exhaustion fostered cooperation among states in creating the Concert of Europe, in which the great powers sought to maintain peace and order on the European continent.	After the Napoleonic Wars, Britain promoted a more open international economy out of the belief that the benefits of trade and exchange foster peace and interdependence. Thus, there was a belief that cooperation among states was achievable through economic opportunities.

to maintain their colonial holdings. The age of European political and economic domination was thus over, as the combat begun in 1914 had resulted in an astonishing process of self-destruction. One of the most important results of World War II was a much higher degree of globalization of world politics. The European powers and Japan suffered staggering human and material losses from which they would need decades to recover.

At the end of the war, only the United States and the Soviet Union had the resources to contend for global leadership. It was not immediately clear, however, that the two massive powers would be adversaries. On the one hand, both states (as well as Britain, France, and China) had seats on the newly formed Security Council of the United Nations, which was designed to facilitate cooperation among the great powers in resolving conflicts. Washington and Moscow thus recognized each other as partners in maintaining world peace just as they had been partners in victory during the world war. On the other hand, the United States and the USSR had very different political and economic systems, and their leaders espoused beliefs and values that were diametrically opposed. These political differences created a climate of mistrust that had already prompted the two countries to view each other's actions with suspicion. The world wars had decisively destroyed the old world order, but they built the foundations of a new system for resolving global issues. Whether the new order would be cooperative or conflictual, however, remained to be seen.

Discussion and Review Questions

1. Which "revolution" had the most impact on world politics: the American Revolution, the French Revolution, or the Industrial Revolution?
2. Could World War I have been prevented? Discuss the competing explanations for the war and what alternative actions could have been taken.
3. Was the Treaty of Versailles a victory of realism over idealism or idealism over realism?
4. Explain the factors and calculations involved in the Italian and Japanese decisions to enter World War II and America's policy of neutrality from September 1939 to December 1941.
5. Discuss the examples of globalization and fragmentation, and conflict and cooperation, evident in this chapter. Provide examples of each trend.

Key Terms

Appeasement 97	Fascism 101	Peace of Westphalia 63
Bismarckian system 79	Feudal 61	Power projection 63
Casualties 88	Gold standard 81	Schlieffen Plan 89
Colonialism 63	Great power 63	Sovereignty 63
Concert of Europe 71	Hyperinflation 100	Sphere of influence 88
Corn Laws 78	Maginot Line 97	
Dawes Plan 100	Operation Barbarossa 103	

CHAPTER 4

World Politics and Economics: The Cold War

As you read in Chapter 3, the themes of conflict and cooperation, and globalization and fragmentation, are evident throughout history. International politics during the post–World War II period were no different, dominated as they were by the struggle for power between the United States and the Soviet Union: the Cold War. The term describes a situation in which the two super-powers were locked in an apparently intractable conflict, punctuated by crises and haunted by the danger of nuclear war, but nevertheless managed to avoid direct combat. Despite the intense competition between the two superpowers, the Cold War period, which extended roughly from 1945 to 1990, was relatively stable compared to the shifting alliances and frequent wars of earlier years. As mentioned in Chapter 2, this period was dominated by balancing between the two superpowers. Despite this competition, there were numerous successes at cooperation between the two superpowers specifically and the global commu-nity generally, including the establishment of the United Nations and efforts toward arms control.

As explained in Chapter 3, history provides us with clues to our future and lays the foundation for the world we live in today. The period of the Cold War is a prime example of a time, although faded into memory, that dramatically impacts the interstate and intrastate state relations, institutions, monetary policy, and technological advancements we experience today. Current U.S.–Russian relations, for example, bear the burden of the forty-plus years of hostility experienced during the Cold War, and as relations between the two have been tenuous in the new era, many have been prompted to conjure up images of a new Cold War. Further, the U.S. hostility toward communist countries during the Cold War helps illuminate the continuing tension with North Korea, Cuba, and even China today. The creation of the United Nations, International Monetary Fund, and World Bank; the evolution of European economic integration (now known as the European Union); research and development on more and more powerful and technologically advanced weapons; and the creation of Israel and the subsequent process to create a homeland for the Palestinian people are among the major developments during the Cold War that have a dramatic impact on the world in which we live today. Thus, this period of history is vital in understanding relations in the new era.

For more than four decades, the Cold War was characterized by periods of rising tension followed by waves of relaxation. The pattern was shaped by various factors, including the personalities and beliefs of Soviet and American leaders (the individual level of analysis), domestic politics and economics (the domestic level of analysis), and unanticipated events on the world stage (the systemic level of analysis). As realists would predict, often these events prompted each of the superpowers to take actions benefiting its own interests at its adversary's expense. This chapter begins by advancing six explanations for why the Cold War began, discusses the major events and particular trouble spots of the Cold War, and ends with possible explanations for why the Cold War ended.

Who or What Caused the Cold War?

In the aftermath of World War II, the world became divided into two camps, the U.S.-led Western democracies and the communist regimes, led by the Soviet Union. Right or wrong, conflicts throughout the world came to be viewed in the context of the relations between the two superpowers. As explained in Chapter 2, the bipolar structure of the international system meant the system was dominated by two major powers. The question of whether or not bipolarity was inescapable, creating a situation in which the superpowers were predestined to be hostile to each other, will occupy students of world politics long after the Cold War itself has faded from living memory. The various explanations that have been advanced for why the Cold War began can be summarized in six main lines of argument. (See At a Glance, "The Origins of the Cold War and the Levels of Analysis," to apply the levels of analysis to the causes of the Cold War.)

AT A GLANCE

The Origins of the Cold War and the Levels of Analysis

Systemic Level

Bipolarity

The United States and Soviet Union were the only states to emerge after World War II as dominant powers. They were the only two states left who could challenge each other; thus the conflict was inevitable. Bipolar competition created a zero-sum game, in which a gain for one state was viewed as a loss by the other. This condition enhanced the security dilemma as each perceived the other's actions as hostile, resulting in a spiral of conflict.

Domestic Level

Soviet Union

The inherent aggressiveness and expansionist character of the Soviet system prompted them to expand their influence in eastern Europe. The United States was forced to respond with the containment policy to thwart communist expansion across the globe.

United States

The capitalist system required the United States to attempt to expand into other markets, threatening Soviet control of eastern Europe. The United States failed to understand the Soviets' legitimate security concerns in creating a buffer zone in eastern Europe (to prevent another invasion via Poland).

Ideological Conflict

Conflict was driven by the insurmountable differences between capitalism and communism. For the West, communism was perceived as monolithic, antidemocratic, and totalitarian and as a direct threat to capitalism's need for markets and international stability. For the Soviets, capitalism was viewed as the cause of war, and peace would come only with the worldwide overthrow of the capitalist system.

Individual Level

Harry Truman

Truman replaced Franklin Roosevelt after Roosevelt's death in April 1945 and had little experience in foreign affairs. He was more suspicious than Roosevelt of Soviet intentions. His mistrust resulted in unnecessarily harsh policies that strained the relationship with the Soviet Union.

Joseph Stalin

His brutal, increasingly paranoid behavior raised fears among the Western powers that they might be dealing with another Hitler (a vicious autocrat bent on territorial acquisition). His main concern may have been the preservation of Soviet security, but his suspicious nature was enhanced by Western actions after World War II, reinforcing his paranoia.

It Was Moscow's Fault

First, the conventional American view is that the Soviet Union was primarily responsible for the Cold War. From this perspective, if the Soviets had not been bent on territorial acquisition, especially their subjugation of eastern Europe, the United States would have retreated into its prewar position of isolationism. This explanation paints the USSR as an "evil empire" that, without American efforts, would have taken advantage of western Europe's war-torn and desolate conditions to conquer it. According to this interpretation of the Cold War's origins, the United States was correct to adopt the policy of containing Soviet attempts to expand. Without an activist American **containment** policy, the Soviets would have continued to expand in Europe, the Middle East, and Asia. Note that this is a domestic-level argument, as it contends that the USSR was inherently aggressive and expansionist.

No, It Was Washington's Fault

A second interpretation of the origins of the Cold War takes the opposite position. Here the United States is to blame for the outbreak of the Cold War because it insisted on trying to expand its overseas export markets in eastern Europe after World War II and failed to comprehend the security problems facing the Soviet Union at the end of the war. After all, because the USSR suffered about 20 million deaths in the war, amounting to almost 10 percent of its population, it was understandable that the Soviets would want to protect their territory by controlling countries such as Poland, which twice within half a century had been the invasion route for Germany against Russia. Stalin thus demanded that the USSR possessed the right to have "friendly" nations on its borders. Note that this explanation is also a domestic-level analysis. This perspective therefore contends that the United States mistook legitimate security precautions as aggressive designs and thereby initiated the Cold War, to which the Soviets were forced to react.

A variant position maintains that American use of the atomic bomb at the end of World War II caused the USSR to look to its own security. It has been argued that the United States used the atomic bomb on Japan not to quickly end the war, which was already nearing its conclusion, but as a warning to the USSR not to encroach further into Asia and as a demonstration of the destructive power of the new American weapon. Although he would never admit it publicly, Stalin was very concerned by the fact that the war ended with the United States in sole possession of atomic weapons. When President Harry Truman mentioned to him at the Potsdam summit that the United States had developed a powerful new weapon (of which he had already been informed by Soviet intelligence), Stalin replied only that he hoped the United States would make good use of it. On his return to Moscow, however, he told Soviet military industrial officials, "You know that Hiroshima has shaken the whole world. The balance has been destroyed. Provide the bomb—it will remove a great danger from us."[1] Until Soviet science was able to fulfill Stalin's order, the American nuclear monopoly could only have exacerbated Soviet security concerns.

▪ **Containment**
U.S. foreign policy during the Cold War aimed at halting Soviet expansion through American military and economic power.

Ideological Conflict

A third explanation for the origins of the Cold War claims that the difference in ideologies and ways of life that the Soviet and American political systems represented was the primary cause for the conflict between these nations. According to this domestic-level explanation, it would have been impossible for two potential competitors to avoid conflict when one represented an open democracy and the other a closed totalitarian system. For each, the other presented a threat of immense proportions; each saw the other as expansionist and bent on ideologically converting the world. This argument portrays the Cold War as a clash of political ideas and forms of government.

This explanation views the conflict as driven by the vast differences between capitalism and communism. Capitalism is a system based on markets, competition, and individual choice. To function properly, it requires trading partners, open world markets, and international stability. Its essence is the private ownership of the means of production and the existence of a mobile labor force. Western democracy is anchored in the protection of individual rights and freedom. From the West, communism was perceived as monolithic, antidemocratic, and totalitarian. The communist system rejected private property, required a centralized system of production and distribution of resources, and enforced narrow limits on individual rights such as freedom of religion, assembly, and speech.

Soviet ideologues supported the explanation of ideological incompatibility, though they naturally portrayed capitalism as reprehensible. Marxist–Leninist ideology shaped Soviet perceptions of world politics. According to socialist ideology, capitalism was the cause of war and conflict, and peace would come only with the worldwide overthrow of the capitalist system. Many communists also sought to spread their ideology to other countries throughout the world, advocating a global communist revolution, and viewed any Western resistance to this idea as evidence of the intent of Western governments to destroy Soviet communism.

Leadership or the Lack Thereof

A fourth explanation for the Cold War focuses on individual leaders in both the United States and the Soviet Union. In both states, according to this argument, foreign policy is ultimately the responsibility of one person, the leader. In the United States, for example, the president has considerably more leeway in foreign affairs than in domestic politics, where he competes with Congress, the Supreme Court, and special-interest groups. Consequently, his personality, beliefs, and image can significantly affect foreign policy and the nature of interstate relations. Harry Truman, who replaced Roosevelt on his death in April 1945, had little experience in foreign affairs and was suspicious of Soviet intentions. Truman, according to this line of reasoning, relied heavily on the many Roosevelt aides who were similarly suspicious of the Soviet leadership—more so than Roosevelt had been. This resulted in unnecessarily harsh policies that strained Soviet–American relations. Examples include strict Marshall Plan regulations that made it impossible and even insulting for the USSR to accept American aid and the withholding of economic assistance.

Stalin also plays a role in this explanation. This brutal, increasingly paranoid dictator had already been responsible for the deaths of millions of his own citizens even before World War II started. His totalitarian rule and brutal practices at home and abroad were likely to raise fears among democracies that had just fought the most horrible war in history, which had been caused in part by their failure to respond in time to actions of a vicious autocrat. Although Stalin framed his actions in a Marxist–Leninist context, his primary concern may have been the maintenance of his own power and strength and the security of the Soviet state. However, his suspicious nature, which undoubtedly magnified his perceptions of the threats to the USSR posed by Western actions immediately after World War II, led to responses by the Western powers that only reinforced his paranoia.

The argument that the Cold War was primarily the fault of individual leaders therefore does not necessarily portray United States or Soviet leaders as heroes or villains; rather, it emphasizes that they were fallible human beings. Of course, consistent with this explanation, one could (and many did) blame either Truman or Stalin as responsible for starting the Cold War.

One World Divided by Two Superpowers Equals Conflict

A fifth explanation for the origins of the Cold War concentrates on the fact that the United States and the Soviet Union emerged after World War II as the two dominant powers in the world. They were the only two capable of projecting influence and challenging each other for global leadership; ultimately, they were the only states that could threaten the other's survival. As such, they were destined to be natural adversaries. Note that this is a systemic-level argument, fitting into the realpolitik, or "everybody wants to rule the world," view of world politics, in which states by their very nature seek power in the international system. Accordingly, this argument holds that had Britain emerged more powerful than the USSR at the end of World War II, the Cold War would still have occurred, with London and not Moscow perceived as the main threat to American security.

As Chapter 3 demonstrated, great powers have always rivaled one another throughout the history of world politics. At the end of World War II, only two superpowers remained, and it would have been unprecedented if their relations had been purely amicable. Bipolarity promotes a zero-sum view of world politics. Each superpower saw a gain for the other side, no matter how small, as a loss for itself, and vice versa. Some form of conflict between the United States and the USSR was therefore inevitable, as neither side could afford to let the other attain a decisive advantage in the bipolar competition.

The position that the Cold War started because of the great-power conflict based on the bipolar structure that emerged after World War II is also in keeping with the security dilemma. The action–reaction spiral of the bipolar security dilemma encouraged intensive competition between the two superpowers. For example, when the United States first tested and then used atomic weapons in 1945, the USSR stepped up its program to develop an atomic bomb, which culminated in a Soviet nuclear test in 1949; the Soviet test prompted U.S. efforts in the early 1950s to develop the even more powerful thermonuclear bomb. As we will see in this chapter, a similar action–reaction dynamic would often drive the superpowers to engage in a strategic arms race.

From this systemic perspective, there is no point in assigning blame, as the two powers became locked in conflict as a consequence of their circumstances and the structure of the postwar international system. As in a Western film, the superpowers both knew that "this town ain't big enough fer the both of us," and it didn't matter who was wearing the black or the white hat.

It Was All a Misunderstanding

The sixth explanation for the origins of the Cold War, also fitting into the systemic-level framework, suggests that each side misperceived the intentions of the other. On the one hand, the United States misunderstood that Soviet actions were designed to guarantee the USSR's security after the trauma inflicted by Hitler's surprise attack and the devastation the Soviet people suffered. On the other hand, according to this argument, the Soviets also misunderstood American interests and concerns, seeing U.S. efforts to aid its allies and trading partners as an attempt to encircle and challenge the USSR. Each superpower assumed the worst about its adversary and acted accordingly. This process led to a series of events that eventually solidified into a worldwide competition. Although theories of bipolarity conclude that superpower rivalry and conflict were inevitable, the misperception thesis argues that it could have been avoided through better communication and mutual understanding. As liberalism contends, conflict can be minimized and cooperation promoted if states can communicate clearly and have complete information. The Cold War thus developed out of a vicious circle of mutually reinforcing misperceptions. If only both powers had comprehended the basic defensive nature of the policies of the other, the Cold War would never have occurred, or at least the competition between the superpowers would have been defused. Because the information on which each group of leaders had to base its policies was often very limited, however, particularly with respect to its adversaries' intentions, it is not easy to see exactly how Soviet and American leaders could have broken the circle of misperception.

The reasons for the Cold War have been debated from the outset, and, even with the new information available to historians with declassification of archival materials in Moscow and Washington, the question of the origins of the Cold War is likely to remain an open debate for many years. The reader is invited to draw his or her own conclusions from the events and personalities involved in the conflict, to which this chapter now turns.[2]

Heating Up the Cold War

World War II ended with increasing tensions between the Soviet Union and the Western allies, especially over the future of eastern Europe and Germany, but the wartime allies did not immediately become bitter enemies. The prospect of impending conflict between the United States and the USSR, let alone the shape that conflict would take, was not yet apparent. Postwar events, however, soon propelled the two emerging superpowers into confrontation.

Initial Confrontation: Iran

During World War II, both the USSR and Britain feared the expansion of Nazi influence in the Middle East. In 1941 the Soviets and British agreed to jointly occupy Iran—the Soviets in the north and the British in the south—with the intent of protecting Iran from Nazi influence and securing supply lines to Russia during the war. The agreement specified that both Soviet and British troops were to be removed after the war. When the war ended in May 1945, the British pulled out, but Stalin refused to withdraw the Soviet troops. President Truman resolved to confront Soviet obstinacy with a "get tough" stance: A warning was dispatched to Moscow, and an aircraft carrier was sent to the eastern Mediterranean to maintain an American presence. The crisis was defused in April 1946, when the Soviets pledged to leave Iran after Tehran agreed to set up a joint Iranian–Soviet oil company. Truman and his advisors determined from the incident that the best way to check Soviet expansion and the possibility of Soviet control of western Europe was to counter Stalin's actions directly and stand firm against Soviet demands.

The Iron Curtain Descends and Conflict Intensifies

By the end of 1945 it was clear that the USSR had firmly established itself as the dominant power in eastern Europe. Many Western leaders, alarmed by Soviet efforts to expand into the Middle East and Mediterranean and by the presence of massive Soviet forces in eastern and central Europe, began to perceive a growing Soviet threat. In 1946, Winston Churchill warned Americans that "from Stettin in the Baltic to Trieste in the Adriatic, an iron curtain has descended across the Continent."[3] Using the example of Munich, he pleaded for an alliance of Western democracies to exert influence over Russia and thwart further Soviet expansion.

In early 1947 the British government informed the United States that it would no longer be able to maintain its presence in Greece and Turkey due to economic concerns and the unwillingness of the Labour government to risk British troops in foreign civil wars. The British concluded that they could not be responsible for countering Soviet advances in the region and feared that unless the United

States stepped in, a power vacuum would develop and lead to dangerous consequences.

This was a dramatic change in the international system. At the end of World War II, it was widely believed that there would be three superpowers in the postwar world: the United States, the Soviet Union, and Great Britain.[4] Britain, however, had been devastated and exhausted by the effort needed to withstand the Nazi onslaught and consequently began to relinquish political control and withdraw its forces from India, Palestine, Iraq, Jordan, and other former colonies. The British now concluded that it was necessary to reduce their role in areas that were independent, such as Greece and Turkey, but in which Britain still had important interests.

To the Truman administration, the British decision came as a shock, especially because the president believed that Greece and Turkey were still threatened by the possibility of Soviet encroachment. American officials decided that the Soviet Union had to be blocked and that the United States would have to replace the British power vacuum in the region. Many in Washington felt that Moscow was trying to pull an "end run" around Europe, and as Undersecretary of State Dean Acheson put it, "We and we alone are in a position to break up the play."[5] The Truman administration's willingness to assume greater responsibilities in world affairs marked a major turning point in the foreign policy of the traditionally isolationist United States. In accordance with this new role, the administration put forth a set of interlocking policies that, taken together, created the political, economic, military, and strategic doctrine of the United States in the Cold War.

Truman Doctrine

In essence, the Truman administration had decided it would have to deny the Soviets any possibility of expansion, especially in Europe. This aim would necessitate an unprecedented engagement of the United States abroad in peacetime, as it would require abandonment of its traditional isolationist stance. Yet as Truman and his aides soon found when they began to brief Congress, to place this issue in purely realpolitik terms would not satisfy the American people. There was a strong movement in the United States to return to its prewar position of isolation. Republican Senator Arthur Vandenberg, chairman of the Senate Foreign Relations Committee, advised Truman that he would have to "scare the hell out of the American people" to make them receptive to his plans.[6] Therefore, the president rose before Congress on March 12, 1947, and introduced the **Truman Doctrine,** which some regard as an American "declaration of the Cold War." Truman's speech concentrated on the ideological conflict between freedom and totalitarianism.

To gain domestic support, the president couched his appeal for economic and financial aid to Greece and Turkey in terms of global and moral responsibility. The United States would now be called on to help the nations of the free world gain and keep their freedom. Critics were concerned about the manner in which the Truman Doctrine was to be defined. Did this mean that the United States

▪ **Truman Doctrine**
Pledged U.S. military and economic aid to countries (initially Greece and Turkey) to resist communism.

would intervene anywhere at any time? The president's aides had to admit that the United States would not be able to involve itself in every situation worldwide, but they were unable to clarify the limits of commitment. Despite these uncertainties, Congress overwhelmingly approved the Truman Doctrine and authorized a $400 million program of assistance for Greece and Turkey.

Marshall Plan

In 1947, the Truman administration was also confronting economic decline in Europe. Social and economic institutions had been demolished by the war; an unusually severe winter and meager harvest compounded the crisis. France and Italy were internally besieged by communist parties, and economically exhausted Britain was retreating from its empire abroad. Winston Churchill described Europe as "a rubble heap, a charnel house, a breeding ground of pestilence and hate."[7] There was widespread fear in Washington that communist agents would topple the governments of western Europe in preparation for a Soviet invasion, and the war-ravaged countries would be unable to purchase American goods, which would threaten the American economy and perhaps return the world to its prewar state of depression.

The response to this potential catastrophe was the Marshall Plan, named after Secretary of State George C. Marshall, who announced the plan in an address at Harvard University's commencement exercises as a way to "help start the European world on its way to recovery."[8] Because the United States emerged from World War II an economic superpower and escaped the destruction of war at home, it was in a strong position to take this action.

The Marshall Plan, perhaps the most successful U.S. foreign-policy program in history, offered American economic and military assistance to promote free-market economies within Europe. The plan was originally offered to the Soviet Union and its satellites, but in July 1948 Soviet Foreign Minister Molotov declared that the program would infringe on the sovereignty of the participating states, and thus Moscow would not participate. Various reports and documents declassified years later reveal that Stalin's true concerns were that American revitalization of Great Britain, France, and Germany would restore their great-power status and return the world to the pre-1939 political system.[9] Stalin believed that this would be detrimental to Soviet vital interests, especially in eastern Europe; it represented, he thought, a threat to the security of the USSR. As a result, Marshall Plan aid, which was administered through the Economic Cooperation Act of 1948 and comprised 2.75 percent of America's gross national product, was transferred only to the democracies of the West.[10]

The Marshall Plan had three main effects. First, it revitalized European economies and restored Britain, France, and eventually Germany to major-power status (although not to the level of the United States or USSR). Second, it thwarted communist control within the western European countries as it helped end the economic hardships that served as a breeding ground for discontent and increased the influence of communist parties, particularly in France and Italy. Finally, it helped to create the basis for a movement toward

European economic integration we now know as the European Union, and it facilitated the eventual integration of West Germany into the European economy.

Berlin Blockade

West Germany's integration was a bumpy road, however. As noted in Chapter 3, Germany was divided into four zones of military occupation after World War II, one each for France, the United States, Great Britain, and the USSR. An oddity of the arrangement was that Berlin, the capital of prewar Germany, was also divided among the four powers but was entirely surrounded by the Soviet zone (see Map 3.7 for occupation zones). All means of transportation and communication to the western sectors of the former capital thus had to go through Soviet-occupied territory. In June 1948, ostensibly in response to a currency reform in the western sectors of Berlin, Stalin ordered the closure of all land access routes between Berlin and the western occupation zones. West Berlin was isolated and surrounded by Soviet forces.

The Berlin blockade was a fateful event. Stalin would not allow the transport of food, fuel, or other basic necessities to the western sectors; if no way could be found to supply West Berlin, the population would soon starve. Truman appeared to be forced to decide between two unpalatable alternatives: The United States could go to war against the huge Soviet army in eastern Germany to reestablish Western rights of access to Berlin, or it could allow the Soviets to control the entire city, with horrendous results for West Berliners and a major defeat for the West. Truman and his advisors, however, came up with a third option: initiating a dramatic airlift of supplies to West Berlin. "Operation Vittles," as it was called, was a colossal undertaking to supply the 2.5 million West Berliners. At the height of the airlift, 4,500 tons of supplies were flown in each day. At the same time, Truman moved B-29 bombers, the same type of aircraft that had dropped the two atomic bombs on Japan in 1945, to bases in England. Stalin could have challenged the airlift, but that would have meant war with the Western allies, and he was not prepared to go so far. He halted the blockade in May 1949, although the airlift continued until September.

Stalin's attempt to use military force to gain political concessions failed. A serious crisis had passed without escalating to war. Many in the West believed that the failure of the Berlin blockade verified a prediction by George Kennan (see Spotlight, "The Telegrams: Mr. X and Containment and the Novikov Telegram") that the Soviets would retreat when their efforts were resolutely resisted. Meanwhile, each side proceeded with the consolidation of its parts of occupied Germany. The West backed the formation of the Federal Republic of Germany, with its capital at Bonn, and the USSR formed the Democratic German Republic, with East Berlin as its capital. Each superpower had wanted a single German state on its own terms, but both sides realized after the Berlin blockade that neither could concede all of Germany to the other. Neither side could attain its first preference, so both settled for a divided Germany as their second choice, and the division of Germany thus resulted by default.

▪ S P O T L I G H T ▪

The Telegrams: Mr. X and Containment and the Novikov Telegram

The Truman Doctrine and the Marshall Plan were based on the doctrine of containment, which was developed by George Kennan, a Soviet specialist based in the American Embassy in Moscow. His "Long Telegram" of February 1946 alerted American officials to the threat they faced from Soviet insecurities and expansion and suggested possible solutions.

In July 1947 Kennan published an article in *Foreign Affairs* under the pseudonym "X," which delineated the policy of containment, the basis for future American actions in the Cold War.[i] He argued that the Soviets threatened free institutions throughout the Western world and were determined to fulfill the Marxist–Leninist desire for worldwide revolution. "X" claimed that Soviet actions could be contained by the "joint and vigilant application of counterforce at a constantly shifting series of geographical and political points around the world." Kennan later regretted using the term *counterforce* because he advocated economic and political, rather than military, instruments for dealing with the Soviets. This distinction would become a major controversy in the conduct of American foreign policy.

In essence, Kennan argued that the Soviets would seek to expand until counteraction from the United States forced them to retreat. Ultimately, he believed that the containment approach would cause the Soviet Union to collapse internally and force it to negotiate, a prediction that would prove accurate forty years later. Kennan's containment theory provided American decision makers with a critical vision for organizing U.S. foreign policy and remained the centerpiece of American grand strategy for the next four decades.

The Soviet perspective in the early stages of the Cold War is illuminated by a cable sent to Foreign Minister Molotov by Soviet Ambassador to the United States Nikolai Novikov on September 27, 1946. In his cable, Novikov declares, "The foreign policy of the United States, which reflects the imperialist tendencies of American monopolistic capital, is characterized in the postwar period by a striving for world supremacy."[ii] Similar to Kennan's warning concerning Soviet motives, Novikov warns Soviet officials that the Truman administration is bent on dominating the world politically, economically, and militarily. This document clearly lays out why the Soviet Union perceived the United States as a threat in the late 1940s, including U.S. diplomacy to further expansionist aims, naval and air bases across the globe, the arms race, and research on and development of weapons systems. Novikov also did something in his cable that Kennan did not. He explains why the United States might perceive the Soviet Union as threatening, recognizing that growing Soviet political influence and "established regimes that have undertaken to strengthen and maintain friendly relations with the Soviet Union" in eastern Europe would be issues of concern to the United States. The cable ends with an ominous warning: "Careful note should be taken of the fact that the preparation by the United States for a future war is being conducted with the prospect of war against the Soviet Union, which in the eyes of American imperialists is the main obstacle in the path of the United States to world domination."

Taken together, these two documents help explain the attitudes of the two superpowers toward one another during the Cold War. Clearly, there was a lack of trust and a determination of the motives of the opponent that was negative at best. It was these attitudes that permeated the Cold War and helped prolong the tension for more than four decades.

---

i. "X" [George F. Kennan], "The Sources of Soviet Conduct," *Foreign Affairs* 20 (1947): 556–582.

ii. The text of the Novikov telegram (translated into English) is available in Kenneth M. Jensen, ed., *Origins of the Cold War: The Novikov, Kennan, and Roberts "Long Telegrams" of 1946* (Washington, DC: United States Institute of Peace, 1993).

NATO and the Warsaw Pact

The Berlin blockade was intended in part to thwart a Western alliance but actually helped to speed plans for a formal security agreement to counter what the Western countries perceived as Soviet aggression. In April 1949 the North Atlantic Treaty Organization (NATO) was established. The nations of western Europe banded together with the United States and Canada to commit themselves to resisting Soviet aggression. In joining NATO, the United States effectively renounced isolationism and accepted membership in a peacetime "entangling alliance" for the first time in its history. The Soviet Union responded to the creation of NATO and the admission of West Germany into the alliance in 1954 (and its rearmament) by organizing its client states in eastern Europe into a rival alliance formed in 1955, the **Warsaw Pact** (see Map 4.1). Both alliances were collective security organizations: An attack on one would be viewed as an attack on all.

▪ **Warsaw Pact**
An alliance between the Soviet Union and its client states in eastern Europe formed in 1954 in response to the 1949 creation of NATO.

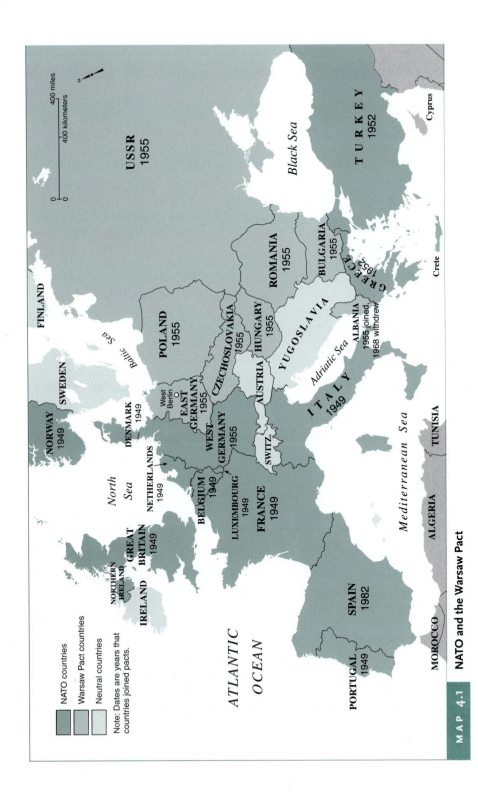

MAP 4.1 NATO and the Warsaw Pact

NATO countries
Warsaw Pact countries
Neutral countries

Note: Dates are years that countries joined pacts.

Transformation of the World Economy

Although the competition between the United States and the Soviet Union was the central feature of the Cold War, economic changes and developments were equally important. While conflict was brewing between the United States and Soviet Union, the world economy was undergoing dramatic changes. Foremost among these changes was the emergence of U.S. hegemony. The events of 1939 to 1945 both revealed and underscored the dominance of the U.S. economy. The United States dominated the world in terms of production. The supply of war matériel and finance, largely through the lend-lease program to the Allies during the war, and the vast destruction of European physical and capital stock, ensured a prominent role for U.S. finance following the war. By war's end, the United States was producing 40 percent of the world's armaments, and its productivity (output per unit of input, usually labor) far surpassed that of its nearest competitors. The result was a massive increase in U.S. **gross national product** (GNP), from $88.6 billion in 1939 to $135 billion in 1944.[11]

This rise of American hegemony coincided with a rapid resumption of growth in the world economy. Bolstered by the Cold War and the desire to preserve economic stability and peace, international trade and investment grew within the American sphere of influence. Living standards rose rapidly in the 1950s and 1960s throughout much of the industrial world. From 1950 to 1973, Europe's major industrial countries' production rose at an average rate of 4.8 percent, and the rate of productivity increased dramatically as well.[12] Economic growth, fueled by newly accessible Middle Eastern oil, a relatively cheap source of energy, solidified the recovery of western Europe and Japan.

The Bretton Woods System

Unlike the disarray characteristic of the international economy during the interwar period, the growth of the world economy after 1945 took place within the context of an institutionalized economic system known as the Bretton Woods system. The foundations for the postwar liberal economic system, one designed to avert economic nationalism and the mistakes of the interwar period by fostering free trade and a high level of interdependence, were laid at a 1944 conference held at Bretton Woods, New Hampshire. Here policymakers attempted to tackle the difficult tasks of creating an international monetary system, a prerequisite for the smooth operation of international economic transactions, and an international lending mechanism to help nations get back on a secure economic footing. To realize these ends, the conferees at Bretton Woods established the **International Monetary Fund** (IMF) and the **International Bank for Reconstruction and Development** (IBRD, more commonly known as the World Bank) to assist in the recovery effort.[13]

The IMF coordinated national currencies by establishing fixed exchange rates and helping to settle international accounts by advancing credit to countries

▪ **Gross national product** The total sum of all goods and services produced by a nation.

▪ **International Monetary Fund (IMF)** Established as part of the Bretton Woods system, the IMF is a global lending agency that originally was to aid industrialized nations in stabilizing their economies after the shocks of the Great Depression and World War II. Its goals today are promotion of market economies, free trade, and high growth rates.

▪ **International Bank for Reconstruction and Development (IBRD, or World Bank)** Established as part of the Bretton Woods system, the World Bank was initially created to help finance reconstruction after World War II. Since the 1950s and 1960s, it has lent money to developing countries to finance development projects and humanitarian needs.

with balance-of-payments deficits. On the basis of rosy recollections of how the nineteenth-century gold standard worked, the IMF established fixed exchange rates in the belief that they would best promote economic stability. The Bretton Woods monetary system fixed the dollar's value in gold at $35 per ounce and pegged the value of other currencies to that of the dollar (that is, governments were committed to intervene in the currency exchange market to keep the value of their currencies within the permissible bounds of the fixed rate). As the largest holder of the world's gold at the time and the primary contributor of funds to the IMF, the United States exercised a preponderant influence in the institution.

One of the primary purposes of the IMF was to provide short-term loans so that countries could rebuild their war-torn economies (the Marshall Plan, discussed earlier, was one such vehicle for doing this) and rectify balance-of-payment deficits. In the case of very serious imbalances, the IMF permitted countries to devalue their currency relative to the value of other currencies, with the intention of increasing export revenue and reducing international debts.

Also established at Bretton Woods was the World Bank. Created to help finance reconstruction after the war, the World Bank played only a marginal role to that end. As interest grew in developing newly independent nations following the collapse of imperialism in the 1950s and 1960s, however, the bank found a new purpose, lending billions of dollars annually to these lesser developed countries. Creating institutions designed to manage international trade proved to be somewhat more complicated.[14] The **General Agreement on Tariffs and Trade** (GATT) was an interim set of rules adopted by twenty-three countries in 1947 pending the creation of an international trade organization. GATT survived for nearly fifty years, providing a framework within which international negotiations to reduce tariffs and other obstacles to trade could take place.

The Cold War in Asia

Our account of the early Cold War years so far has focused on the centers of conflict in Europe, but conflict was also occurring in Asia. Here, in the early days of the Cold War, the centerpiece of the new competition was China. America's China policy became difficult after the war's end, when communist forces led by Mao Zedong and the Nationalist government of Chiang Kai-shek resumed their civil war. Chiang's Nationalist party, the Kuomintang (KMT), had sunk in popularity because of rampant internal corruption and dictatorial practices. In a predicament that would recur throughout the Cold War, the United States found itself caught between the possibility of a future communist regime viewed as a natural ally to the Soviet Union on the one hand and an unpopular and repressive right-wing government on the other. Predictably, U.S. policy took a middle position: The United States offered just enough economic aid and military assistance to further alienate the Chinese communists but not enough to have a real

▪ **General Agreement on Tariffs and Trade (GATT)** An agreement established in 1947 to encourage freer trade. Several rounds of GATT rules negotiations since its founding progressively lowered tariffs and nontariff barriers to trade among member states.

chance of saving the KMT. Just as predictably, this strategy failed. In October 1949 the communists finally won the civil war and established the People's Republic of China, and the Nationalists were driven offshore to the island of Taiwan.

The American government assumed that the victory of the Chinese Communist party would mean automatic alliance with their comrades in the USSR. The Soviets did offer guidance and assistance to Mao's Communist party. However, it is now known that even during the civil war, Stalin had qualms about a Chinese communist victory and was not averse to doing business with the Nationalists. A strong China under united communist control might represent more of a threat to Soviet interests than a weakly divided China under the Nationalists. When presented with a conflict between communist objectives and Soviet national interests, Stalin chose the latter, establishing a pattern that his successors in the Kremlin would often follow throughout the Cold War. The inherent tensions between Soviet and Chinese interests would eventually lead to hostilities between the two communist giants.

It has often been argued that accommodation between the Chinese Communist party and the United States would have been possible in the 1940s if not for the anticommunist position of the United States. Undoubtedly, the United States was anticommunist and supportive of the KMT, but Mao's U.S. policy was not simply a reaction to U.S. behavior; it was based on a patent unwillingness to pursue diplomatic relations with Western countries.[15] Mao's main focus was maintaining and enhancing the momentum of the revolution in China, and his use of anti-American discourse was a "means of mobilizing the masses for his continuous revolution" and a part of his "grand plans for transforming China's state, society, and international outlook."[16] At the same time, despite the disagreements between Mao and Stalin (and Chinese and Soviet communists) that were just mentioned, there was a spirit of cooperation between Chinese Communist party and the Soviet Union in 1949.[17] Thus, despite claims to the contrary, there was very little opportunity for reconciliation between the Chinese communists and the United States at this time.

NSC-68

America enjoyed a monopoly on nuclear weapons until September 1949, when the USSR tested its first atomic bomb. The rapid development of the Soviet bomb (which can be attributed partially to espionage but also to a massive "crash" program in the USSR) changed the nature of the conflict. Many officials were beginning to think more in military terms rather than concentrating on the political and economic instruments that had been the focus of Kennan's approach as adopted in the Truman Doctrine and the Marshall Plan. A document, **NSC-68,** was prepared by the National Security Council (NSC) to address the question of what was to be done to counter the spread of international communism.

NSC-68 called for a major expansion of America's armed forces, adding military instruments to the political and economic means of containment. This

■ **NSC-68**
A document prepared by the U.S. National Security Council in early 1950 to counter the spread of international communism. NSC-68 called for expansion of America's armed forces, adding an important military dimension to the economic and political means of containment.

approach would significantly alter the form and content of U.S. foreign policy and would eventually lead to direct American military involvement in conflicts in Korea and Vietnam. President Truman, although he agreed with the concept and principles of NSC-68, was not prepared in early 1950 to accept a major escalation in defense spending. He feared that the United States could not afford any such increase and that high military spending would ruin the economy. Unexpected developments in Asia, however, soon changed Truman's mind.

Korea: The Turning Point

The escalating pressures on both the international and domestic scenes came to a head in Korea in 1950. After the Japanese surrender that ended World War II, Korea was divided by the victorious Allies along the thirty-eighth parallel, with the north occupied by the Soviets and the south occupied by the United States. Despite the desire for union in both halves of Korea, the United States and the USSR were unable to agree to a formula for holding elections under the auspices of the United Nations (UN). The Soviets, in particular, objected to a national poll and instead held Soviet-style elections in the north, where only the Communist party had any chance of winning. At the head of the new communist government was Kim Il-Sung, a youthful Korean communist who had spent many years in the USSR and served as an officer in the Soviet army. (He remained in power until his death in 1994.) Confident in the loyalty of Kim's government, the USSR withdrew its occupation forces by January 1949. The United States was then under pressure to similarly withdraw from the south, which it did by the middle of that year.

An event then occurred that pushed the Cold War past the point of no return. On June 25, 1950, North Korea launched a massive surprise attack against South Korea (see Map 4.2). Stalin originally failed to endorse Kim Il-Sung's plan to unite his country by force, fearing a direct U.S.-Soviet military confrontation. He was convinced otherwise, however, by the exclusion of Korea from America's Pacific defense perimeter (in January 1950) and by Mao's assertion of his belief that United States would not involve itself in a civil war in East Asia. Hence, Stalin sent large amounts of military aid and Mao sent soldiers to North Korea.[18] In the end, this was a gross miscalculation of the American reaction. This attack immediately brought to mind the lesson the West had learned at Munich: Aggression had to be checked, or aggressors would become bolder and more ambitious. American leaders saw the North Korean offensive as a major test of U.S. leadership and credibility.

Because Moscow refused to participate in the United Nations Security Council debate on Korea, the Soviets were unable to veto a U.S.-framed initiative to send UN troops to Korea. (As we explain in Chapter 13, one veto by a permanent member is sufficient to reject a UN Security Council initiative. At the time of the debate on Korea, the USSR was boycotting the Security Council to protest the assignment of China's seat on the council to Chiang's KMT government in

PHOTO 4.1 U.S. infantrymen make their way through a village to the Northern Korean front in 1950.

Taiwan rather than Mao's communist People's Republic of China.) The Security Council authorized a military response to the invasion, and a U.S.-led coalition sent forces to oppose the North Korean offensive.

There is no doubt that the intervention of the United States and its allies saved South Korea. Despite the engagement of the Chinese (or perhaps because of it), UN and communist forces fought to a stalemate near the original division between North and South Korea. Throughout the conflict, Stalin was determined to avoid the direct military confrontation with the United States that had made him hesitant to support Kim Il-Sung's military ambitions at the outset. When Dwight D. Eisenhower became the U.S. president in January 1953, he immediately advised the communists that in the event that the conflict in Korea could not be resolved, the United States "intended to move decisively without inhibition in our use of [nuclear] weapons, and would no longer be responsible for confining hostilities to the Korean Peninsula."[19] This warning, part of the Eisenhower strategy of **massive retaliation,** and growing success on the ground by Allied forces encouraged the communists to agree to a cease-fire in July 1953.

▪ **Massive retaliation** The Eisenhower administration's strategic doctrine that Soviet-sponsored aggression would be countered with large-scale nuclear retaliation.

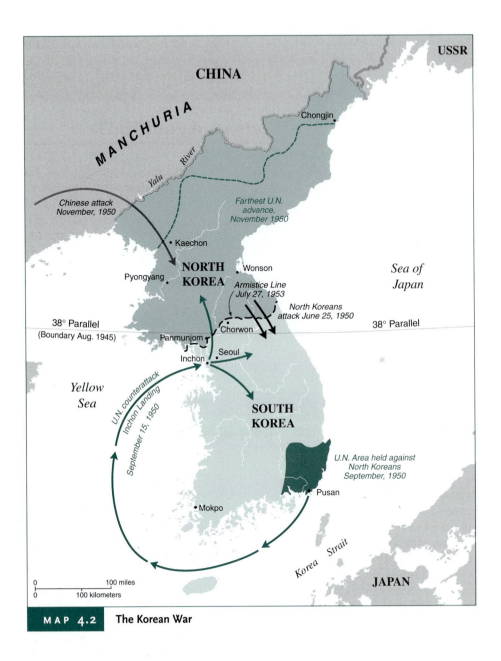

MAP 4.2   The Korean War

Korea was a turning point in the Cold War for several reasons. First, the war prompted the expansion of American military forces called for in NSC-68 and a similar buildup of NATO forces in Europe. Second, it stimulated American involvement in Asia and therefore heightened the confrontation with the Soviet Union and China. Third, the Korean War solidified the bipolar competition between the United States and the Soviet Union for clients around the globe, as the United States began to view communist actions in every part of the world as a threat to its own interests. Finally, although both the United States and USSR possessed them, nuclear weapons were not used in the war and fighting was restricted to Korean territory. The conflict was thus referred to as a **limited war,** fought for limited goals by limited means, which set a pattern for restricted actions throughout the Cold War period. The Korean War thus irrevocably moved the containment effort of the West to the military sphere without escalating into actual military conflict between the superpowers. As the destructive potential of nuclear weapons made total war unthinkable, the superpowers would have to carry on their global conflict by more subtle means.

The Cold War and the Third World

The reach of the Cold War extended beyond Europe and Asia. By the early twentieth century, the spread of nationalism throughout Europe led to calls for independence in the colonial world (see Chapter 5). In the aftermath of war, native cultures everywhere were emboldened to seek independence, and one by one the weakened imperial powers concluded that these territories were not worth keeping at the military, political, and economic costs they would take to maintain. This conclusion was not an easy one to reach; in some areas, such as Algeria and Vietnam, the decision to retreat from empire was made only after bitter and protracted war between nationalist movements and the colonial power. Ultimately, history had imposed a harsh irony on the imperial powers. From Vietnam to Algeria to India to Palestine to Kenya, European ideas of nationalism and political sovereignty served to undermine the colonial powers' legitimacy. The age of empire was over.

Yet in the wake of imperialism, power vacuums began to emerge as the European powers withdrew their forces and political control. In the zero-sum political environment of the Cold War, the superpowers viewed each newly independent country in what became known as the Third World (now referred to as developing countries) as a potential ally or an opportunity for the other side to expand its power and influence. Thus, under Nikita Khrushchev's aggressive leadership in the 1950s, Moscow began to expand its influence by establishing political ties with countries that previously had been controlled by European colonial empires, such as India, Egypt, Syria, and Indonesia. Many of these Third World countries emerged on the international scene with serious internal problems. Many were politically unstable and militarily and economically weak. This combination of factors created strategic uncertainties that the superpowers believed they could ignore only at peril to themselves. As a result, Third World countries were drawn into the bipolar conflict of the Cold War, which further globalized the superpower rivalry and multiplied the number of locations where Soviet and American interests collided.

▪ **Limited war**
A conflict in which states with nuclear weapons choose to limit combat to conventional means.

In the early phases of the Cold War in the Third World, U.S. policy focused on intervening in countries where local nationalists, many of whom were agents of the global Soviet communist regime, were implementing change in their countries. In 1953 the Central Intelligence Agency (CIA) engineered a coup that overthrew Iranian Premier Mohammed Mossadegh, who sought to nationalize British-controlled oil fields in Iran, and restored the Shah, Mohammad Reza Pahlavi, to power. The following year, another CIA-backed coup ousted Guatemalan President Jacobo Arbenz, who was heavily influenced and supported by communists, and replaced him with the staunchly anticommunist Castillo Armas.

In other parts of the developing world, the superpowers became involved in conflicts arising from decolonization. In 1956, Egypt's President Gamal Abdel Nasser nationalized the Suez Canal, which had been owned by an Anglo–French consortium. The American government believed that the matter could be settled by negotiations, but Britain and France saw Nasser's action as directly challenging their continued influence in the Middle East. Without America's knowledge, Britain, France, and Israel secretly colluded to attack and topple Nasser's regime. Israeli forces overran the Sinai, but to keep up the pretense that no collusion had occurred, the British and French had to wait to move their forces into place until Egypt had refused their ultimatum. By the time they "intervened" in the conflict, a furious Eisenhower was exerting economic and diplomatic pressure on them to stop. The Soviets backed Egypt with blustering threats against Britain, France, and Israel when the crisis was abating. In the end, Nasser remained in power, the Suez Canal was blocked for many months, Britain and France were humiliated, and the United States replaced them as the major Western influence in the Middle East.

Moscow and Washington were not always able to gain influence over newly independent Third World states, as their governments often found it beneficial to play one superpower against the other. As a result, the **Nonaligned Movement** emerged in international politics in the mid-1950s, with India's Jawaharlal Nehru, Egyptian President Nasser, and Yugoslavia's Tito at the forefront of its leadership. By playing the United States against the Soviet Union, these countries attempted to gain aid from the competing superpowers. Soviet technological advances impressed many newly independent regimes, and the Soviet model of centralized, state-controlled economic and political development was initially quite attractive to developing countries. In addition to providing an example (for a time) of a successful alternative to capitalism, the Soviets established close relations with a wide variety of developing states, including Indonesia, Ghana, India, Egypt, Syria, Iraq, and Algeria. Moscow provided aid in the form of weapons, agricultural and industrial machinery, and military and technical advisors. During the Cold War, educational exchange programs allowed an estimated 72,000 students from Third World countries to attend learning institutions in the USSR.

The United States, however, was wary of the Nonaligned Movement, believing that it facilitated the growth of Soviet influence in the developing world.

▪ **Nonaligned Movement** Refers to those state leaders who, during the Cold War, chose not to align their countries with either superpower, instead playing one off against the other in the pursuit of their own interests.

In response, Washington stepped up military and economic assistance to states it considered more reliable as U.S. allies, such as Nicaragua, Iran, and South Vietnam, before anti-U.S. governments came to power in those nations. As a result, a considerable amount of aid flowed from both superpowers to the developing world, but not in the manner the originators of the Nonaligned Movement had intended.

Trouble Spots: Berlin and Cuba

The late 1950s and early 1960s marked a period of increased tensions between the two superpowers. Fear of the possibility of nuclear war between the United States and Soviet Union intensified when the Soviets launched the world's first artificial satellite, Sputnik, which orbited the earth in October 1957. This accomplishment caused many in the West to fear that the Soviets had gained a major technological advantage over the United States that could be exploited for military purposes. Khrushchev deliberately fed those fears, never missing an opportunity to mention the USSR's arsenal of rocket weapons, although the Soviets would not actually deploy missiles capable of striking the United States until 1960.[20]

As the political sting of recent Soviet gains spread throughout the West, Khrushchev felt strong enough to press the USSR's advantage. In November 1958 he suddenly announced that the Soviet Union had decided to renounce the remnants of the joint Allied occupation regime in Berlin. In subsequent notes to the United States, Britain, and France, he demanded that they withdraw their occupation forces from West Berlin, declare it a demilitarized "free city," and negotiate directly with the German Democratic Republic (East Germany) on terms of access to the city. He threatened that if the Western powers did not make an agreement with the East Germans within six months, the Soviet Union would give the German Democratic Republic control of western military supply routes to Berlin. This action was tantamount to renouncing the post–World War II arrangements for Germany, and it revived memories of the darkest days of the Berlin blockade. With the backing of its NATO allies, the United States refused to accede to Khrushchev's demands, and John Foster Dulles replied that NATO would oppose any attempt to change the status of Berlin "if need be by military force."[21]

At the same time, a new arena of East–West conflict was emerging closer to American shores. A revolution brought Fidel Castro to power in Cuba in January 1959. Castro's forces had overthrown a much-hated dictator, Fulgencio Batista, who had maintained close ties to the United States. Washington reacted strongly to Castro's ascension to power, especially when his procommunist leanings became apparent. When the United States levied sanctions on Cuba, Castro turned to the USSR for aid. The existence of a Soviet-supported regime just ninety miles off the coast of Florida inflamed U.S. leaders and fomented fears that other countries in Latin America would follow Cuba into the Soviet camp.

JFK, Cold Warrior

Eisenhower's vice president, Richard Nixon, narrowly lost the 1960 presidential election, and in 1961 John F. Kennedy took office committed to a more activist American foreign policy. He developed the strategy of **flexible response.** The first challenge Kennedy faced involved redressing the supposed missile gap. Rapid U.S. production of bombers, **intercontinental ballistic missiles (ICBMs),** and **submarine-launched ballistic missiles (SLBMs)** provided a balanced strategic triad of land-, sea-, and air-based weapons. In a classic example of the security dilemma in action, Khrushchev's bluff that the USSR could outproduce the United States in missiles had been called; the Soviet Union had actually developed only a minimal missile capability by the early 1960s, and the strategic balance remained in America's favor throughout his tenure in the Kremlin.

Although the missile gap proved to be a hoax, the United States nevertheless appeared weak. In March 1961, the CIA orchestrated an invasion by Cuban exiles at the Bay of Pigs intended to provoke a general rebellion against Castro and topple his government. The invasion, poorly planned and executed, ended in disaster when Castro's forces easily defeated the invaders. This ham-handed attempt to unseat Castro only reinforced the image of declining American power. This view of Kennedy contributed to his choices during the conflict that brought the United States and Soviet Union closer to nuclear war than any other time prior or since: the Cuban Missile Crisis.

Berlin Wall

Meanwhile, back in Europe, tensions in Germany increased steadily. East German refugees, a high proportion of whom were professionals, intellectuals, and skilled workers, continued to flee to the West, creating a serious "brain drain" for East Germany. To stem the flow of refugees, the East German government suggested the creation of a barrier around West Berlin, and Khrushchev agreed. Without warning, on August 13, 1961, barbed-wire barricades were thrown up all around the city and were soon replaced with concrete. The western sectors were surrounded by the Berlin Wall. The Western Allies would have had to resort to force to remove the wall, but they were unwilling to take that risk, although at one point during the crisis, U.S. and Soviet tanks confronted each other at the Brandenburg Gate on the dividing line between East and West Berlin. The U.S. government portrayed the outcome of this new Berlin crisis as a win for the West, as West Berlin remained in Allied hands, but it was never Khrushchev's intention to take over the western sectors. Both sides could therefore claim victory, but the fact remained that Kennedy had been unable to respond effectively to a Soviet challenge.

▪ **Flexible response**
The Kennedy administration's military doctrine that replaced massive retaliation and focused on countering the Soviet threat across the entire spectrum, from operations other than war to conventional warfare to nuclear exchange.

▪ **Intercontinental ballistic missile (ICBM)**
A land-based missile able to deliver a nuclear payload to a target more than 3,400 miles away (in practical terms, capable of going directly from the United States to Russia or vice versa).

▪ **Submarine-launched ballistic missile (SLBM)**
A long-range ballistic missile carried in and launched from a submarine.

Cuban Missile Crisis

By 1962 the United States was far ahead of the USSR in long-range missile capability, but Khrushchev may still have believed that JFK lacked the resolve necessary to prevail in a direct confrontation. In 1962 the Soviet leader ordered offensive missiles to be placed secretly in Cuba. His motives for doing so remain unclear. He may have been trying to exploit a perceived American political weakness, to partially redress the U.S.–Soviet strategic balance, to forestall another attempt to overthrow Castro, or all of these. Khrushchev's gamble failed, however, when U.S. intelligence discovered the missiles in October 1962. The resulting confrontation was the most acute crisis of the Cold War. Kennedy had publicly warned Khrushchev that he could never allow the Soviet Union to station offensive weapons on Cuba. The young president could not allow the Soviets to achieve a major political victory by stationing nuclear weapons so close to American shores.

To compel Khrushchev to withdraw the missiles from Cuba, Kennedy and his advisors decided to impose a blockade on all shipments of weapons to the island. When he revealed the missiles' existence to the world and announced the blockade on Cuba, Kennedy demanded the removal of the missiles, warning that their use against any country in the Western Hemisphere would be regarded as an attack by the USSR against the United States. The possibility of nuclear war seemed closer during the Cuban Missile Crisis than at any other time before or since. If the USSR did not back down, the United States clearly intended to remove the missile sites by military action, which would have involved combat between Soviet and American forces and potentially nuclear war. Unknown to the Americans at the time, but since revealed by Soviet officials, there were forty-two intermediate-range missiles with warheads in place as well as nine short-range nuclear missiles operational in preparation for an American invasion.[22]

Because the United States possessed conventional military superiority in the Caribbean region and held an indisputable advantage in strategic nuclear forces, once Khrushchev's bluff was called, he had no real choice but to back down. In exchange for the removal of the missiles, the United States promised not to invade Cuba again and to withdraw its own short-range Jupiter missiles from Turkey (a withdrawal Kennedy had previously ordered but that had not been implemented). Despite these gestures intended to avoid the humiliation of its adversary, the crisis ended with an embarrassing defeat for Moscow.[23]

The Cuban Missile Crisis had a number of important consequences. First, and paradoxically, one of the initial results of the crisis was a sudden abatement in Cold War tensions. Having confronted each other at the brink of war, both Kennedy and Khrushchev enjoyed the opportunity to reduce hostilities through a series of U.S.–Soviet agreements, including a limited nuclear test ban treaty and the establishment of a "hotline" that enabled Moscow and Washington to communicate with each other instantly in case of a crisis anywhere in the world. Second, however, Soviet leaders set about challenging America's strategic

PHOTO 4.2	A provision of the agreement that ended the Cuban Missile Crisis was that the Soviets had to remove all missiles from Cuba. This photo, taken on November 5, 1962, shows Soviet missile equipment being loaded at the Mariel naval port.

nuclear superiority with renewed urgency. The Kremlin attempted to catch up with the United States, determined that it would never again be caught in as weak a position as it had been in the Cuban Missile Crisis. The USSR achieved strategic parity with the United States by the late 1960s, but only at tremendous cost. Moscow's strategic programs diverted vast human and material resources away from development of industry, technology, and social welfare, creating hardships and distortions that would eventually lead to the collapse of the Soviet economy and political system. Finally, after Washington demonstrated its resolve and military strength in the missile crisis, many Americans became overconfident, believing that the United States could accomplish any task in foreign policy to which it was fully committed. Whereas in the period leading up to the Cuban Missile Crisis the United States had overestimated Soviet power, it now underestimated the difficulties of containing communism in the Third World.

What Would You Do?

Soviet Missiles in Cuba

You are the leader of the Soviet Union in 1962. Someone in the Politburo has presented you with a risky, yet possibly golden, opportunity to extend your global influence. It involves the secret installation of missiles—capable of striking the United States—in Cuba.

If successful, the ploy could accomplish several important foreign- and domestic-policy objectives simultaneously. First, it could redress the strategic imbalance with the American capitalist ruling class and offer you a bargaining chip by which you could gain the removal of U.S. Jupiter missiles in Turkey. Second, it offers a potential means of deterring another imperialist invasion against Castro; after all, having failed miserably to oust Castro in the Bay of Pigs fiasco, the United States is even less likely to repeat this action against a nuclearized Cuba. Third, it provides a chance to convince the Chinese that "peaceful coexistence" with the U.S. imperialists does not mean you are unwilling to seize opportunities to extend communist influence in the Third World, thereby pulling China back into your camp. Finally, it could boost your popularity at home.

On the other hand, if the ploy is unsuccessful, it could be prohibitively expensive. First, instead of treating the move as a fait accompli, as it did with the construction of the Berlin Wall, the U.S. imperialists could call your bluff and demand removal of the missiles. You are aware from intelligence reports that the U.S. president is still under tremendous pressure from the opposition Republican party to "get tough" with Castro. The United States might actually remove the missiles and Castro through a full-scale invasion or air strike. Second, it could further alienate the leadership of the People's Republic of China and possibly increase communist China's influence in the Third World. Finally, it could provoke a military or party coup against you.

This is a risky decision.

What Would You Do?

Vietnam and Its Consequences

Once again, another promising turn in the Cold War was quickly reversed. The assassination of Kennedy in November 1963 and the overthrow of Khrushchev the following year brought new teams of leaders to both capitals. Hostile tendencies that Kennedy and Khrushchev had endeavored to overcome were gradually reinforced. The new Soviet leaders, Leonid Brezhnev and Alexei Kosygin, increased military spending, sustained repressive regimes in eastern Europe, and found themselves in an intensified competition with China.

The new U.S. president, Lyndon B. Johnson, had little experience and, initially, not much interest in foreign policy, but he was nevertheless committed to a strong anticommunist position worldwide. His administration saw both China and the USSR as dangerous threats, and these fears were reinforced by China's test of an atomic bomb in October 1964. The Cold War had now reached a point of tragic irony. The period after the Cuban Missile Crisis boiled over with U.S. self-confidence and zeal. Rushing about from one trouble spot to another, America almost seemed destined to trip over its own power. It stumbled and fell over Vietnam.

In 1960 a guerrilla movement officially known as the National Liberation Front but commonly referred to as the Vietcong began to attack the American-backed government of South Vietnamese President Ngo Dinh Diem with strong support from North Vietnam (Vietnam had been divided in 1954 after the defeat of the colonial power in the region, France, at the hands of communist-led Vietminh rebels). Diem's policies had alienated various sectors of the South Vietnamese population, especially in the countryside, providing opportunities for communist influence. Kennedy had attempted to use Vietnam to show that it was possible to defeat communist-backed wars of national liberation, and he increased American military and economic aid to the South. Building on the several hundred advisors sent by Eisenhower, Kennedy increased U.S. military personnel to 16,000 by 1963. Nevertheless, Diem's position continued to deteriorate, and he was killed in 1963 (two weeks before JFK was assassinated) in a military coup to which the United States acquiesced. A succession of generals followed as president, each ousted by a new military figure hoping to pursue the war more effectively and gain the spoils of power for himself.

It became clear by 1965 that stronger American intervention would be required to prevent a Vietcong victory in the South. President Johnson was forced to choose between withdrawal, an intermediate level of escalation, or full-scale war. Johnson initially chose the middle option for U.S. intervention, which meant an immediate bombing campaign of the North and deployment of ground forces to protect air bases. As the war progressed, however, the administration repeatedly determined that more troops were required and continued to send more, only to conclude that still more forces were needed.

By mid-1968, 500,000 American troops were fighting in Vietnam, but the United States was no closer than before to achieving the military or political breakthrough necessary to salvage the South Vietnamese regime and permit U.S. withdrawal. American casualties mounted, eventually numbering 58,000 deaths. The seemingly endless and fruitless intervention in Vietnam turned the American public against the war, diminished the public's enthusiasm for the competition with the USSR, and compromised U.S. credibility with many of its allies, especially in Europe. Meanwhile, Moscow sought to capitalize on America's diminished prestige and weakened political will to resist Soviet expansion. To compete with China for influence in North Vietnam, Moscow provided Hanoi with military and economic assistance. Thus, the Vietnam War enabled the Soviet Union to increase its standing throughout the developing world while the United States was vilified for conducting an ineffective campaign that resulted in more than 2.5 million military and civilian deaths.[24]

PHOTO 4.3 Soldiers of the U.S. 1st Infantry wade through swampy South Vietnamese territory in October 1965. By the late 1960s, more than 500,000 U.S. troops were engaged in the Vietnam conflict.

The Apparent Decline of U.S. Economic Hegemony

Juxtaposed against the backdrop of U.S. involvement in Vietnam was the superpower's decline in economic status. The Bretton Woods system ultimately fostered two concurrent outcomes: the rise of western European and Japanese economic power and the development of U.S. trade imbalances. These conditions, along with greater fluidity in international financial markets, destabilized the international economic order. To understand its eventual demise, however, one must focus on the actual decline of U.S. hegemony. Although the United States was still the dominant player in the international economy, other industrialized nations became increasingly important. Although U.S. export volume increased throughout the 1960s, West German, French, and Japanese exports increased much more rapidly. Moreover, these countries, in contrast to the United States, captured an increasingly greater share of the world export market throughout the decade. By 1972, West Germany nearly rivaled the United States in terms of volume and percentage of world exports.

Associated with these divergent export growth paths were adverse trends in the U.S. economy. A glance at some data reveals an inflating trade deficit by the early 1970s. In 1960, the United States had a current-account surplus equal to $1.8 billion. By 1972, the balance spiraled into a deficit of more than $8.4 billion.[25] In addition to the deteriorating U.S. trade balance, budget deficits were increasing rapidly and the economy was slowing down at home. Fueled in large part by domestic expenditures on new antipoverty and social welfare programs, the rising costs of financing the Vietnam War, and the refusal to either raise taxes or cut spending, budget deficits and inflation on the home front contributed to a crisis in the international economic arena.

In 1971, after several years of seeing its share of the world export market decline, the United States began to register a persistent trade deficit. This deficit added to the costs of the war effort and shortfalls in domestic revenue, ultimately proving detrimental to the international monetary system. Continued "benign neglect" in the area of monetary policy proved untenable in the face of rising foreign pressure. As the U.S. ability to maintain the system faltered, disagreements arose between the United States and its now powerful allies. The French and the Japanese governments most strenuously resisted U.S. pressure to share the burden, with France insisting that the United States honor its commitment to convert dollars into gold and Japan demanding that the United States fix its domestic economic problems. Finally, on August 15, 1971, President Richard Nixon announced that the United States would no longer bear a disproportionate share of the burden of maintaining the international monetary system. The United States suspended its commitment to convert dollars to gold, imposed domestic wage and price controls, demanded dollar depreciation, and imposed a 10 percent tariff on imports. Collectively, these actions amounted to a rejection of the basic rules of international monetary relations and a demand for greater "burden-sharing" by U.S. military and economic allies.

Following the U.S. decision, negotiations continued for thirteen months over how to salvage the Bretton Woods regime. Ultimately they failed, and the leading industrial powers agreed to eliminate the fixed exchange-rate system. By March 1973, most major currencies floated in financial markets. Thus, the U.S. role shifted significantly. Whereas the United States had been the preeminent state in the world economy, forging a united front with its allies against the Soviets and serving as a necessary stabilizer for the international economy, by the 1970s, efforts to restore order in international economic relations took on a decidedly more multilateral cast. Just as the United States and Western industrial powers began the arduous task of restoring international monetary order, however, unexpected crises further complicated an already difficult endeavor.

Détente

The period that began in the early 1960s with joint Soviet and American moves to limit conflict ended with escalated military activity by both superpowers. Throughout the 1960s the USSR built an arsenal of nuclear weapons and missiles roughly equal to that of the United States. This round of the action–reaction spiral of the nuclear arms race resulted in a situation in which neither superpower could claim military superiority over the other, but both were vulnerable to nuclear attack. Paradoxically, both the United States and USSR liked it that way. American strategists, guided by a doctrine known as **mutual assured destruction** (appropriately shortened to MAD), believed that if both sides knew that they had no chance of prevailing in a nuclear war and would be virtually annihilated in a nuclear holocaust, neither would launch a nuclear attack. Soviet leaders, on the other hand, expected that the achievement of strategic parity would finally force the United States to regard the USSR as a political equal and accept its brand of communism as a legitimate force in world politics. Although some believed the time was ripe for mutual disarmament, both sides planned further increases in their nuclear capabilities to prevent the other side from achieving superiority.

The only major breakthrough of the period came in 1968, with the signing of the Nuclear Nonproliferation Treaty. Three of the five nuclear powers, the United States, the USSR, and Britain (China and France initially refused to join), pledged not to employ nuclear weapons against or share nuclear weapons technology with nonnuclear states that signed the treaty. In return, the nonnuclear nations pledged not to develop nuclear weapons. This treaty was a major achievement and certainly slowed the spread of nuclear weapons, but it could not prevent countries such as Israel, India, Pakistan, Iraq, South Africa, and North Korea from proceeding with their nuclear programs (for more on nuclear weapons, see Chapter 7).

The Opening of China, the Moscow Summit, and SALT

Although the United States had squandered a portion of its military and political advantages by assisting South Vietnam, the Soviet Union remained vulnerable to American pressure because of its conflict with China and its weak economy. After Johnson declined to run for reelection in 1968, the new administration of Richard Nixon, who had been a staunch anticommunist during the 1940s and

▪ **Mutual assured destruction (MAD)** A condition that exists when nuclear states can survive a first strike with sufficient nuclear forces to retaliate in a second strike and inflict unacceptable damage on their opponent. Because any nuclear strike would result in both opponents' destruction, there is no incentive to initiate a nuclear war.

PHOTO 4.4 President Richard Nixon's historic February 1972 visit to Beijing improved relations after more than thirty years of Chinese–American hostility. Here Nixon and Chinese Premier Zhou Enlai toast each other at a banquet hosted by the visiting Americans.

1950s, recognized the depths of the Sino–Soviet dispute and the opportunities it represented for American diplomacy. When border clashes broke out between the USSR and China in April 1969, the Nixon administration used the conflict to gradually improve relations with China. This opening culminated in Nixon's dramatic visit to Beijing in February 1972.

At the same time, the Nixon team attempted to transform the Soviet Union from a revisionist power to one comfortable with the status quo. In some ways, this was an unexpected course for Nixon to take, as he had begun his political career as a hard-line anticommunist. In particular, Nixon and his chief foreign-policy advisor, Henry Kissinger, sought to pursue three policies vis-à-vis the Soviet Union to augment cooperation.[26] First, they acknowledged that the USSR was a coequal with the United States, a superpower. By doing so, the United States recognized that the Soviets had achieved nuclear parity and would no longer be treated like a younger sibling. Second, they set out to create a number of institutions in the area of arms control and crisis management that would restrain the security dilemma and define acceptable behavior. Third, they sought to pursue a strategy of linkage politics, intended to prevent the Soviets from seeking cooperation in one area while trying to gain unilateral advantages elsewhere. Instead, they encouraged cooperation and discouraged aggression through a combination of "carrots and sticks," especially economic inducements that could be extended as rewards and withdrawn as punishments.

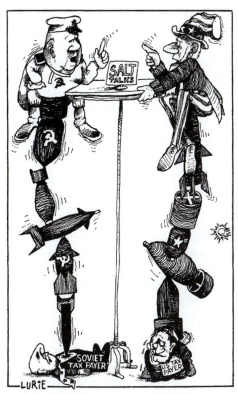

Many commentators criticized the SALT negotiations for not going far enough in capping the number of weapons each country could build.

After the opening to China and increased diplomatic pressure on the Kremlin, a U.S.–Soviet summit was convened in Moscow in May 1972. Washington was interested in using this opportunity to create a number of mutually supporting relationships with the Soviet Union. Nixon sought not only agreements for controlling the escalating arms race but also Soviet assistance in ending the Vietnam War. The interests of the two superpowers dovetailed because Brezhnev sought access to Western technology and goods. The Kremlin's defense spending was an increasing burden on the Soviet economy, which was proving increasingly unable to simultaneously maintain the USSR's massive military power and produce enough consumer goods for the population's basic needs.

The Moscow Summit, therefore, set the stage for an unprecedented series of agreements. First, Nixon and Brezhnev signed the first Strategic Arms Limitation Treaty (SALT I). The two powers agreed to restrict the deployment of **antiballistic missiles** (ABMs; missiles designed to shoot down incoming missiles) and to cap the growth of strategic offensive missiles. Designed to stabilize the arms race, these agreements allowed both countries to continue developing nuclear

■ **Antiballistic missile (ABM)**
A missile designed to destroy incoming missiles or their warheads before they hit the designated targets.

arms but placed temporary limitations on the number of weapons they could build. Most important, the agreements demonstrated that both sides finally understood that neither would gain from an ever-accelerating arms race. In addition to SALT I, a series of economic agreements were reached that would open the door to expanded trade, including large American grain sales to the USSR. An agreement on the "basic principles of mutual relations" was intended to spell out a "code of conduct" for the superpowers' interactions with each other and their respective allies. This phase of the Cold War, which seemed again to promise a more cordial superpower relationship, became known as **détente,** after the French word for "relaxation of tensions."

Tensions in Détente

As détente progressed, however, it became increasingly apparent that both sides' expectations for the new superpower relationship varied significantly and that neither side fully understood the other's perspective. In the United States, détente was intended to transform the nature of superpower relations from one of mortal confrontation to one of limited rivalry by giving the USSR a "stake in the system," which would create incentives for both powers to avoid challenging each other's interests. To the Soviet Union, however, détente meant that Cold War competition would continue, but by new rules. From the Soviet viewpoint, there was no contradiction between détente and support for socialist or communist "national liberation movements" throughout the Third World. Although the Soviet leaders promised to halt future aggressive actions, they still sought to make gains without directly challenging the United States, as would soon be seen clearly in the Middle East, Southeast Asia, and Africa.

American domestic politics were entering a turbulent period as the Vietnam War and the Watergate scandal eroded America's confidence in its leaders. The Vietnam experience made many in the United States wary of getting involved in faraway conflicts. Thus, when South Vietnam was overrun by North Vietnamese forces in the spring of 1975, the United States did not intervene. Halting communist aggression became a secondary issue, and stopping any further disastrous foreign escapades attained primary importance. "No More Vietnams" became the slogan of the day in the 1970s. This was quite ironic, as the resolve to have "No More Koreas" in the 1950s had led to early U.S. involvement in Vietnam.

Any Soviets who anticipated a variety of gains in Southeast Asia, however, were probably disappointed by the emerging conflicts between communist states. In 1975, the year of communist victory in Vietnam, a civil war in Cambodia ended with a Chinese-backed communist insurgency, the Khmer Rouge, in control of the country. The Khmer Rouge regime, led by Pol Pot, proved to be unspeakably brutal. It turned the country into "killing fields," carrying out a program of genocide that killed as many as 2 million people. This tyrannical regime was not ousted by the West but was overthrown in 1978 by an

▪ **Détente**
French for "relaxation of tensions." During the Cold War, détente between the United States and Soviet Union referred to cooperation on areas such as arms control, trade, and technology.

invasion by the neighboring communists in Vietnam, who promptly installed a puppet regime. This action and other conflicts led to a border war between China and Vietnam in 1979.

Escalation of conflict in the Middle East further undermined détente. In October 1973 the Soviet Union did not explicitly warn the United States of an impending attack by Syria and Egypt against Israel. Issuing a clear warning would have entailed significant political costs for the USSR, and an order from Moscow to evacuate the dependents of Soviet personnel in Egypt and Syria just before the attack may have been intended as a tacit warning, but the United States did not perceive it as such. The result was the Yom Kippur War (known also as the October War), in which both the United States and USSR resupplied their clients with massive airlifts of arms. Washington was further antagonized when the USSR encouraged additional Arab states both to join the fray and to impose an oil embargo against the United States. In an effort to pressure the United States to end its support for Israel, Arab members of OPEC joined together to reduce total oil production and institute a ban on shipments to the United States and the Netherlands. By January 1974, crude oil prices had risen from $3.01 a barrel at the outset of the crisis to $11.65, a near fourfold increase, and prices for gasoline and heating oil more than doubled. In the face of unprecedented oil prices, the developed countries experienced severe economic dislocations, including reduced purchases of many goods, long lines at the gas pumps, and inflation. Indeed, throughout 1974 and 1975, many countries in the developed world experienced **stagflation,** a combination of low, or stagnant, economic growth and a high rate of inflation. The OPEC embargo caused a major energy crisis, but U.S. aid to Israel continued. U.S. and Soviet efforts to bring about a cease-fire eventually succeeded, but only after the United States placed its nuclear forces on alert in response to hints that Moscow might send troops to support Egypt.

From Dialogue to Discord

The tensions in détente ultimately brought the period of improved relations to an end, but Jimmy Carter took office in 1977 committed to improving the U.S.–Soviet relationship. Although Carter's policies achieved notable advances in the field of human rights (a focus of Carter's own philosophy), his less confrontational stance toward the USSR in the early years of his administration may have led some Soviets to believe that the United States would not oppose the further expansion of Moscow's influence, especially in the Third World. Cuban forces intervened in conflicts in Ethiopia and Angola to help solidify Soviet positions in those African countries. Cuban actions could not have been taken without Soviet approval because the USSR was heavily subsidizing Cuba's international military actions (as well as its domestic economy).

Soviet actions and American reactions in the Third World heightened mutual suspicions and thereby threatened progress on arms control. Despite

▪ **Stagflation**
A combination of low or stagnant economic growth coupled with high rates of inflation.

mutual agreement on the need for another arms-control accord, the United States and USSR squabbled endlessly over the details of a new treaty. An initial agreement between Brezhnev and Gerald Ford had been reached in the Soviet city of Vladivostok in 1974, but the talks dragged on, complicated by criticism from American conservatives and Soviet deployments of new nuclear missiles. In 1979 Carter and Brezhnev finally signed the SALT II treaty, which set a cap on all offensive strategic weapons. Critics argued, however, that the new treaty left American land-based ICBMs vulnerable to destruction by a Soviet surprise attack, reservations that delayed ratification of the new treaty. (The U.S. Senate must approve all treaties signed by the United States before they can come into force.)

The Invasion of Afghanistan

Any chance of ratification was lost when, in December 1979, the USSR sent 80,000 troops into Afghanistan to overthrow an unstable fledgling Marxist government and replace it with a stronger pro-Soviet regime. The invasion marked the first time the USSR had deployed a large number of troops outside of the Warsaw Pact states of eastern Europe. The reasons Soviet leaders felt they could take such a blatantly forceful step without serious international political consequences remain unclear. Perhaps they had become accustomed to the Carter administration's lack of strong resistance to Soviet-sponsored activities in the Third World. Perhaps Moscow believed that the invasion would be quickly successful and forgotten just as rapidly. Perhaps Brezhnev and other Soviet communist leaders were hopelessly out of touch with domestic and international political realities and consequently confident that Afghanistan would accept communism without a fight.

The invasion was denounced in the West and much of the Third World as an act of naked aggression. In actuality, the invasion proved disastrous both for Soviet domestic politics and for the morale of Soviet troops. Soviet military resources were seriously depleted when an alliance of Islamic groups established a guerrilla campaign based in neighboring Pakistan, supported by the United States.

In an effort to coerce the Soviet Union to withdraw, Carter suspended grain sales to the USSR, withdrew the SALT II agreements from consideration by the Senate, increased defense spending, and refused to allow the U.S. Olympic Team to participate in the 1980 Summer Olympics in Moscow. These steps failed to convince Moscow to withdraw its forces, however, and Soviet troops soon became bogged down in a quagmire in Afghanistan just as American troops had become mired in Vietnam fifteen years earlier.

The Reagan Doctrine

The war in Afghanistan pushed America toward a revival of Cold War perceptions. The rise of a renewed Cold War in turn contributed to the election of Ronald

Reagan as U.S. president in 1980. Although Carter had increased defense spending during the latter part of his term, Reagan expanded defense budgets still further. Through both direct U.S. intervention and indirect support for insurgencies, Reagan abandoned the policy of détente and returned to an assertive form of containment. Like Truman at the outset of the Cold War, Reagan couched his arguments for opposition to Soviet expansion in terms of moral duty, labeling the Soviet Union "the focus of evil in the modern world."[27]

Supporting indigenous anticommunist insurgencies came to be the Reagan administration's specialty. The resulting so-called **Reagan Doctrine** was played out in a variety of locations around the world. Anticommunist insurgents were encouraged in Angola, Cambodia, and, most controversially, in Nicaragua, where assistance was provided to the Contra rebels even after Congress prohibited direct military aid. Governments threatened by Soviet- or Cuban-supported insurgencies also received substantial assistance, especially those in Central America such as El Salvador and Guatemala. The United States unsuccessfully intervened in Lebanon in 1982 in an attempt to restore the unity of the country after a long civil war. In 1983 Reagan sent U.S. forces to Grenada to defeat a newly imposed Marxist government supported by Cuban advisors and construction troops. Afghan rebels were supplied with highly effective Stinger missiles that brought down Soviet aircraft in great numbers. The growing successes of the rebels confounded Soviet forces, and the USSR finally abandoned its war effort and withdrew its troops in 1989.

Reagan's policies in the 1980s helped reverse what many had viewed as a decline in U.S. power and influence in the 1970s, but this turnabout didn't come cheaply. During his presidency, Reagan authorized more than $2 trillion in defense spending, increasing the size and quality of American nuclear and conventional forces. Critics claimed these defense expenditures wasted American resources that were needed to address domestic problems, especially during a severe recession in 1981 and 1982. Reagan's political popularity, however, enabled him to continue his defense policy. Despite protests from peace activists in the United States and Europe, he carried out the deployment of intermediate-range nuclear missiles to Europe, which NATO had agreed on during the Carter administration to counter a Soviet buildup of missiles designed for use against European targets.

Why Did the Cold War End?

While the Cold War was being fought with renewed vehemence in the international arena in the early 1980s, the Soviet Union began experiencing a series of domestic political upheavals. Due to rapid changes in Soviet leadership, Soviet policy entered a period of inertia as the Reagan Doctrine applied pressure to the USSR and its allies. In 1985, when Mikhail Gorbachev assumed leadership of the Soviet Union, Soviet–American relations had reached a low ebb, recalling the

▪ **Reagan Doctrine**
The Reagan administration's abandonment of détente and return to an assertive form of containment. This was characterized by direct U.S. intervention and indirect support of anticommunist insurgencies.

tense early days of the Cold War, and the Soviet political and economic system was in need of a massive overhaul. Several important changes occurred within the Soviet Union itself as Gorbachev's policies of **glasnost** ("political openness") and **perestroika** ("economic restructuring") promoted democratization and free markets. However, on the whole, the economic reforms did not go far enough to reinvigorate the USSR's economy, while political changes swept forward at a pace that was exhilarating to some and threatening to others. As the 1990s began, the entire communist system was being challenged and was failing to overcome the obstacles it faced.

The liberalization that began in Soviet society spread to eastern Europe, culminating in a series of mostly peaceful revolutions in 1989. Regimes that had taken decades to establish were overthrown within months or weeks and even, in Czechoslovakia and Romania, in a matter of days. The deterioration of living standards and the perceived illegitimacy of the governments of these eastern European countries led to mass uprisings that erupted as soon as the Soviet Union declined to use its forces to keep communist governments in power. Popular movements, such as **Solidarity** in Poland, that had been in perilous existence for years were finally able to assume power in their countries. In an ironic domino effect, the governments of eastern Europe fell one by one, first Poland, followed by Hungary, East Germany, Czechoslovakia, and Romania. What had seemed impossible for more than a generation finally occurred when the Berlin Wall was dismantled in November 1989 and Germany was reunited in 1990. Thus, appropriately, the Cold War ended where it had begun, in eastern Europe. An abortive coup in Moscow by hard-line communists attempting to resurrect the old order in August 1991 resulted in the final discrediting of the old regime and the disintegration of the Soviet Union. This example of fragmentation brought the era of U.S.–Soviet antagonism to a close.

The Cold War between the United States and the Soviet Union lasted for more than four decades and at times took on the appearance of a permanent fixture in international politics. It had arisen gradually and predictably, but it ended abruptly and in a manner that caught the entire world by surprise. As with the Cold War's origins, a variety of possible explanations have been advanced for its end, each corresponding to one of the images of world politics and levels of analysis discussed in Chapter 2. (See At a Glance, "The End of the Cold War and the Levels of Analysis," to apply the levels of analysis to the end of the Cold War.)

The Gorbachev Factor

Many analysts who adopt the "great-man" theory of world politics point to Mikhail Gorbachev and argue that the end of the Cold War could have come about only with someone of his character and stature at the helm. Just as an individual like Stalin or Truman might have been a necessary ingredient in causing the Cold War or influencing its nature, this argument contends that it took someone like Gorbachev to bring it to a close.

▪ Glasnost
Russian for "openness," referring to the political policies that followed Mikhail Gorbachev's 1985 rise to power in the USSR.

▪ Perestroika
Mikhail Gorbachev's policy for restructuring the economy of the Soviet Union; it promoted democratization, privatization of the economy, and free markets.

▪ Solidarity
A popular labor union begun in the 1970s in Poland led by Lech Walesa. Solidarity made political and economic demands on the communist government for many years before winning elections and assuming power under a new constitution in 1989.

The End of the Cold War and the Levels of Analysis

Systemic Level

Decline of Bipolarity

The bipolar struggle, manifested in the arms race, took a toll on both the United States and the Soviet Union. Massive military spending exhausted the Soviet Union and allowed countries like Japan and Germany to rise in economic power because the United States provided for their security while they invested in their domestic industry. The result was that the world was no longer bipolar, but economically multipolar.

Domestic Level

Glasnost and Perestroika

To overcome internal stagnation, the USSR determined that it had to liberalize its political and economic system, adopt a less confrontational posture toward the West, cut back on military expenditures, and stop attempting to maintain exclusive spheres of influence in eastern Europe and parts of the developing world.

Failure of Communism

The ideology of communism had demonstrably failed, causing any state attempting to remain competitive in the international system to adopt Western ideas of democracy and market economics or fall irretrievably behind.

Individual Level

Gorbachev

The "great-man" theory would suggest that Mikhail Gorbachev's ascension to power in the Soviet Union in 1985 was the ultimate factor in ending the Cold War. He adopted glasnost and perestroika (political and economic openness), signed the Intermediate-Range Nuclear Forces (INF) Treaty (1987) and Strategic Arms Reduction Treaty (START) (1991), and withdrew Soviet forces from Afghanistan. His efforts to reverse the downward trend in superpower relations ended the Cold War.

Reagan

The U.S. defense buildup in the 1980s, including the deployment of INF missiles in Europe, conventional and nuclear force modernizations, and research on the Strategic Defense Initiative, caused the end of the Cold War by convincing the Soviets that they could no longer compete. Reagan's belief that the United States could spend the Soviet Union into ruin coupled with his unwavering vision of U.S. victory forced the concessions made by Gorbachev.

With initial hesitancy but growing energy, Gorbachev worked to reverse the downward trend in superpower relations. Under Gorbachev's leadership, major agreements were reached in the arms-control arena, beginning with an agreement on the elimination of intermediate-range nuclear forces (the INF Treaty) in 1987; continuing on to START I of 1991, by which Soviet and American strategic forces were to be reduced by approximately one-third; and progressing with further unilateral cuts on both sides announced later in 1991. Gorbachev also ended the USSR's Afghan debacle by ordering the withdrawal of Soviet forces in 1989. Had Soviet leaders with attitudes similar to those of Brezhnev or Stalin been in power during the late 1980s, the Soviet policies that contributed to the reduction of U.S.–Soviet tensions would probably never have been adopted.

Failure of Communism

A second explanation deemphasizes the role of individual leaders and instead claims that the failures of communism and the spread of democratic ideas to the Eastern bloc account for the waning of the Cold War. According to this domestic-level argument, internal changes within the USSR precipitated a new foreign policy. The most important changes were Gorbachev's policies of glasnost and perestroika, which encouraged a gradual process of democratization and the attempt to open the country to free markets and foreign investment. Through these reforms, Soviets sought to embrace private property and individual rights such as freedom of religion, assembly, and speech. In fact, the Soviets sought American and Western help and sought out Western advisors to assist in making the transition from a planned to a market economy. The outcome was that in the West, the talk of reform led many to believe that Soviet society would shortly mirror its own and would no longer be foreign or threatening.

The End of the Evil Empire

A third explanation for the close of the Cold War holds that it ended because the Soviet Union collapsed. The decline of the Soviet Union demonstrated that the communist system had failed. The Soviet economy was fraught with inherent inefficiencies and outdated technology, particularly after computers and information technology transformed the world economy in the 1980s. The prolonged fiasco tarnished the reputation of Communist party elites. Additionally, with Gorbachev, a new generation came to power in the USSR that had experienced the economic deprivation and political stagnation of the communist system but had not endured the immense suffering of World War II, which had so often been used as an excuse for continued demands for sacrifice to defend the (increasingly dubious) achievements of communism and to control eastern Europe. With the USSR no longer able to compete, the superpower competition ended. To this way of thinking, George Kennan's original containment doctrine was proven correct, as the American political and economic "counterforce" had prevailed without the need for direct military confrontation.

A variant of this explanation holds that competition with the West was the deciding factor in the political, social, and economic decline of the Soviet system. In part, the laggard nature of the Soviet economy was a result of the huge military expenditures necessary to compete with the United States. It is argued by

PHOTO 4.5 Friendly meetings between U.S. President Ronald Reagan and Soviet Premier Mikhail Gorbachev symbolized the improvement of Soviet-American relations as the Cold War came to a close.

some that the U.S. defense buildup undertaken during President Reagan's tenure in the 1980s, including the deployment of INF missiles in Europe, conventional and nuclear force modernizations, and research into space-based missile defenses (the **Strategic Defense Initiative,** or SDI), convinced many in the Soviet elite that the USSR could no longer compete. The United States thereby won the Cold War through economic and military strength as well as the inherent superiority of capitalism and democracy. From this perspective, Reagan's policies and his unwavering vision of U.S. victory in the Cold War both forced and facilitated Gorbachev's concessions.

The End of Bipolarity

A fourth explanation cites the changes in the international system in the decades since World War II and concludes that U.S.–Soviet antagonism was bound to lessen because of the decline of bipolarity. As noted in the discussion of the origins of the Cold War, one explanation for the rise of U.S.–Soviet enmity was the advent of a bipolar distribution of power. To be sure, massive military spending exhausted the Soviet Union, but it also seemed apparent

■ **Strategic Defense Initiative (SDI)**
A 1980s U.S. program that proposed the creation of a highly ambitious ballistic missile defense system that would provide a total defense against strategic nuclear weapons and missile systems. Also known as "Star Wars," SDI threatened to upset the nuclear balance of power by giving the United States an ability to launch a first strike without fear of a Soviet counterattack. Its potential effectiveness was controversial.

that the arms race took its toll on the United States. The consequence, from this viewpoint, was that in fact the real "winners" of the Cold War were countries like Japan and Germany, which rode on American coattails, allowing the United States to provide for their security while they invested in their domestic industry. The decline of the Soviet Union therefore meant that Moscow was no longer the greatest threat to American security and that the world was moving in the direction of either unipolarity, with the United States as the sole superpower, or multipolarity, with Japan and Germany (or perhaps a unified Europe) as the new economic superpowers confronting the United States.

From this systemic perspective, the Soviet Union posed only a minimal threat even before its final collapse, and a decline in U.S.–Soviet tensions could have been expected even in the absence of ideological change or a reformist leader such as Gorbachev. Many people would dispute this conclusion, but just as the reasons why the Cold War began were argued while U.S.–Soviet competition raged, the reasons why that competition ended are likely to be debated for many years.[28]

Conclusion

A comparison of this chapter with the previous historical chapter reveals that the Cold War era was a relatively stable one. This is not to say that there was no bloodshed during this period (conflict), but that in contrast to previous periods, there was no war among the great powers. Indeed, for most of the Cold War a total war between the United States and Soviet Union was unthinkable, as it would have meant the nuclear destruction of global civilization. As dangerous as it was, the fact that the two superpowers did not go to war despite their many differences and periodic sharp confrontations, and the numerous examples of global cooperation during the period, makes the Cold War a comparatively peaceful interval in the long and bloody annals of international politics.

Perhaps more than any previous period, the Cold War saw the complete globalization of political conflict. In its wake, political fragmentation coexisted with economic globalization, but the peaceful end to the once seemingly intractable U.S.–Soviet rivalry offered hope that local disputes could be kept from escalating into global confrontations and that global conflicts need not be resolved by global war. Despite the present dangers of ethnic conflict, terrorism, and the proliferation of weapons of mass destruction, the same hope animated the new era. As will be seen in Chapter 6, conflict and cooperation, and globalization and fragmentation, continued to coexist in the new world order.

Levels of Analysis and Paradigms in Review: Examples from the Cold War

	Realism	Liberalism	Constructivism
Individual	After Stalin refused to withdraw Soviet troops from Iran in 1945, Truman determined that he must confront Stalin with a "get tough" stance. Truman concluded that the best way to check Soviet expansion was to directly counter their actions and stand firm against their demands.	After coming to power in 1985, Mikhail Gorbachev worked to reverse the downward trend in superpower relations. He believed that the best way to achieve the goals of the Soviet Union (both domestic and international) was to create a calm international environment, and that required improved relations with the United States.	Truman's willingness to have the United States assume a greater role in the world after World War II marked a major shift in thinking about U.S. global responsibilities. This demonstrated a new understanding of the role of the traditionally isolationist United States. As a consequence, to gain domestic support, Truman couched his appeal for economic and financial aid to Greece and Turkey in terms of global and moral responsibility.
Domestic	In 1947, the British government informed the United States that it could no longer maintain its traditional role in the Mediterranean. Their inability to continue this role was due to significant economic problems as a result of World War II and the unwillingness of the Labour government to risk British lives in foreign civil wars.	After World War II, the economies of Europe were in shambles. There was widespread fear in the U.S. government that communist agents would topple the governments of western Europe in preparation for a Soviet invasion, and the war-ravaged countries would be unable to purchase American goods. The concern over the threat to the American economy prompted the United States to adopt the Marshall Plan, which offered American economic and military assistance to promote free-market economies within Europe.	Many countries of the Nonaligned Movement were impressed by Soviet technological advances and the model of centralized, state-controlled economic and political development. Thus, a wide variety of states felt it was in their best interest to establish close relationships with Moscow.

(continued)

	Realism	Liberalism	Constructivism
Systemic	Concern in the Soviet Union over the U.S. development and use of the atomic bomb was rooted in the belief that the balance of power had been upset between the two states. The American nuclear monopoly served to exacerbate Soviet security concerns.	The growth of the world economy after 1945 took place within the context of an institutionalized economic system, known as the Bretton Woods system. In laying the foundations for the postwar liberal economic order, policymakers succeeded in creating an international monetary system (the IMF) and an international lending mechanism (the World Bank).	During the period of détente, both the United States and Soviet Union had different expectations for the new superpower relationship. For the United States, détente was intended to transform the nature of superpower relations from one of mortal confrontation to one of limited rivalry. To the Soviet Union, détente meant that the competition would continue but by new rules.

Discussion and Review Questions

1. Which explanation for the start of the Cold War do you find most persuasive? Think through the strengths and weaknesses of the explanation and discuss the level of analysis the explanation represents.
2. Discuss the significance of the Cuban Missile Crisis. Why did this confrontation occur, and why was it resolved in the way that it was? Which level of analysis best explains it beginning and resolution?
3. Discuss the significance of Nixon's trip to China, détente, and the Reagan Doctrine.
4. Discuss examples of realism, liberalism, and constructivism evident during the Cold War.
5. Discuss the effects of bipolarity during the Cold War. Define the concept, and provide examples from the Cold War of how bipolarity affected states' behavior.

Key Terms

Antiballistic missile (ABM) 143
Containment 114
Détente 144
Flexible response 134
General Agreement on Tariffs and Trade (GATT) 126
Glasnost 148
Gross national product 125
Intercontinental ballistic missile (ICBM) 134

International Bank for Reconstruction and Development (IBRD, or World Bank) 125
International Monetary Fund (IMF) 125
Limited war 131
Massive retaliation 129
Mutual assured destruction (MAD) 141
Nonaligned Movement 132

NSC-68 127
Perestroika 148
Reagan Doctrine 147
Solidarity 148
Stagflation 145
Strategic Defense Initiative (SDI) 151
Submarine-launched ballistic missile (SLBM) 134
Truman Doctrine 119
Warsaw Pact 123

CHAPTER 5

Imperialism and Its Victims

Although it was necessary to begin our historical coverage in Europe, as explained in Chapter 3, Europe's development did not take place in a vacuum; the states of that region evolved as they did because of their competition over, and associations with, the rest of the world. What we see worldwide today in terms of globalization and fragmentation and conflict and cooperation is rooted in the international dynamics, relationships, and structures that resulted not only from European empire building (including Spanish, Dutch, Portuguese, Italian, and British) but also from empire building in general (including, notably, Ottoman, as well as Japanese, Russian, and Mongol).

Imperialism is the process of extending a nation's authority by territorial acquisition or by the establishment of political and economic hegemony over other nations. Throughout history, empires have risen and fallen. The Egyptians, Persians, Romans, Chinese, Aztecs, and Incas all established extensive empires dominating their local regions of the world. However, these empires were isolated from one another by what probably seemed to be insurmountable geographical barriers, vast mountain ranges, oceans, and deserts. By the 1400s, however, European and Chinese explorers were discovering what the Vikings before them

■ Imperialism
A superior-inferior relationship in which one state controls the people and territory of another area.

knew: The world was a bigger, but more navigable, place than most of its inhabitants imagined. The voyages of these early explorers were the first major steps toward the political and economic globalization of the modern world.

Regardless of their time or place, whether they were continental or extended over water, empires served the same basic functions: They represented the extension of one people's control over another, the extension of one state's hegemony over others' territory, the opportunity to extract goods cheaply without concern for local costs, and the chance to extend values (religious, moral, cultural, and social) to other people. Empires reflected the same beliefs in national or cultural or racial superiority, in other peoples' subhumanity, in a god's or gods' preference for, and privileging of, one group of people over others. Every empire influenced the development of world politics, for good or ill. Empires changed the course of history by influencing regional and sometimes worldwide power dynamics for generations; they spread goods, ideas, religion, peoples, illnesses, plants, and animals over the face of the globe; they forced the early demise of some cultures and extended the reach of the others; they caused peace and led to war.

Many of the conflicts we see in the new era can be traced back to the lasting impact of imperialism. We will discuss the genocide in Rwanda (1994) in Chapter 6, but the roots of that tragedy can be traced back to the domination of the area by Belgium in the first half of the twentieth century. The Belgians intensified the ethnic divisions that ultimately erupted in unspeakable violence. Similarly, when one looks at the conflict between the Israelis and Palestinians (also discussed in Chapter 6), British domination of the territory of Palestine between the World Wars clearly impacted the conflict we see today. Further, in considering the current conflict in Afghanistan (led by the United States), the failed imperialistic efforts of the Soviet Union in Afghanistan during the Cold War (see Chapter 4) cannot be ignored. It is also important to remember that in parts of the world colonial powers drew arbitrary borders—some of which divided peoples who wished to be together and others that united peoples who wished to be apart (the creation of arbitrary borders, for example, has caused a plethora of problems on the African continent). Last, it is important to note that discussion of imperialism is not a thing of the past. When the United States (and the coalition of the willing) invaded Iraq in 2003 and deposed Saddam Hussein (we will discuss this further in Chapter 6), there was much global discussion of possible U.S. imperialist motives, most notably the desire to control Iraq's oil supply. The United States has been accused repeatedly (and not just over the invasion of Iraq) of pursuing a new imperialism for the twenty-first century. Thus, awareness of the origins and consequences of imperialism is necessary for an understanding of contemporary international relations.

With this in mind, the first half of this chapter will focus on the causes of imperialism, with a particular focus on European empires and their competition for global predominance. The different economic and political strategies that each empire employed as well as the various decolonization processes are also surveyed. The chapter's second half considers the effects of imperialism on the areas of the world that were subjected to or influenced by it. The collapse of empires, and imperialists' lasting impact on their subjects, illustrate fragmentation and globalization, respectively. The legacy of imperialism is likely to remain a matter of debate for a very long time, but it is evident that throughout the world many people suffered from it, some greatly gained because of it, and it has left a deep and lasting imprint on global civilization.

Origins of Imperialism

At the beginning of the sixteenth century, regions of the world were so isolated from one another that most had little or no knowledge of other peoples and civilizations. For example, when Hernán Cortés led his band of mercenaries into the Aztec Empire in 1519, many Aztecs believed that Cortés and his men were gods. This isolation would soon end. Within three centuries, European states ruled the Americas and large parts of Africa and Asia, controlled all significant world trade from spices to slaves, and increasingly competed against one another for international predominance. In short, European expansion gradually but inexorably globalized world politics. No longer could any country or empire isolate itself from events and processes in the rest of the world, although a few countries, such as Japan, did resist such influences until the mid-nineteenth century.

The expansion of European political and economic dominance, which reached its peak in the first half of the twentieth century, was built on three foundations: first, the search for trade routes to Asia, the source of high-value commodities like spices; second, the expectation that controlling this trade or exploiting resources found in other areas would strengthen the European home country, the **metropole,** in its competition with other European countries; and third, a growing and rapidly accelerating European superiority in technology, including shipbuilding, communications, weaponry, and medicine.

One critical key to European expansion was the result of both a social necessity and a technological revolution in seafaring. By the fifteenth century, western Europe was one of the most densely populated regions of the globe, land was scarce, and natural resources were being exhausted. When population begins to outstrip resources, deep crises can result. For example, this contributed to the collapse of the Mayan Empire in Central America and the cycles of China's dynasties. Yet, instead of turning inward, some European countries directed their endeavors outward to the seas.

Long before the sixteenth century, Europeans came into contact with Asia. For centuries, the European demand for spices and other valuable commodities from Asia was supplied via a land route across Asia and the Middle East and then transported through the Mediterranean by Italian, primarily Venetian, merchants. In the mid-fourteenth century, Prince Henry, the Navigator of Portugal, formed a special center to focus the efforts of expert navigators, shipbuilders, and seamen on expanding Portuguese trade and dominion overseas. One

■ **Metropole**
A home country in relation to its colonies.

advance in navigation, the sextant, enabled sailors to plot direction by use of the stars. This invention allowed explorers to travel farther, to heretofore unknown waters, while still being able to return home with some degree of certainty. Long-distance navigation became feasible.

In an effort to break into the Asian spice trade, both Spain and Portugal commissioned sailors to use the new technology to find alternative routes to Asia. The most famous of these explorers was Christopher Columbus. Columbus did not find an alternative route to Asia, but he stumbled onto the Americas, two continents rich in natural resources and fertile land but lacking the spices that first generated interest in exploration.[1] The Portuguese explorers Bartholomeu Dias and Vasco da Gama made equally important contributions to the global-ization of trade. From 1487 to 1498 they led the first European expeditions to round the Cape of Good Hope at the southern tip of Africa, thereby opening up a new route to India and China through the Indian Ocean. The need for fresh water and food led the Portuguese to establish supply stations along the west-ern and eastern coasts of Africa, as well as on the Indian subcontinent and in Southeast Asia.

For the next three centuries, the competition for trade routes to East and South Asia was dominated by the Portuguese, then the Dutch, and finally the British. Controlling extensive tracts of territory was not the prime motive. Rather, it was sufficient to control a port and to provide support to local leaders to ensure the provision of commodities. Local leaders gained in the exchange as well, as the European supply of weapons and other goods strengthened their positions relative to regional opponents. The competition among various local elites eased the ability of the Europeans to make inroads, especially in India and other parts of Asia. This allowed Europeans to bypass the Arab monopoly on trade with Asia.

In the Americas, European competition was equally intense, although it took a different form. The vast land and natural resources of the New World enabled Spain, France, and Britain to acquire important raw materials and ease their pop-ulation pressures. These attractions increased the rivalry among the contending empires. In short, one of the most fundamental distinctions among European empires was that some emphasized territorial conquest, whereas others concen-trated on control of trade routes. Territorial empires, such as the Spanish and Russian, tended to concentrate on the conquest of interior regions where nat-ural resources could be exploited and immigrants settled. By contrast, trading empires like the Dutch and Portuguese were typically interested in strategic ports from which the exchange of goods could be carried out in a predictable and secure manner. Both imperial strategies could be used to increase the power of the metropole, and the strategy chosen was often a result of the particular needs at a particular time in the metropole.[2]

Without the application of the advanced seafaring technologies, without the political and economic competition engendered by the fragmented European state system, and without the belief that rich lands and salvageable souls lay just over the horizon, European countries could have turned inward as did China and

Japan at the time. Instead, European explorers, conquerors, and settlers ventured out to chart unknown waters and far-off lands. The following sections present a brief history of European imperialism, offering an overview of the rise, decline, extent, and global impact of each major empire. Included in this discussion is a review of several non-European empires: the United States, the Ottomans, and the Japanese. Thus, we present here an overview of the major empires from the fourteenth to the twentieth centuries.

The First Transoceanic Empires: Spain and Portugal

The year 1492 was pivotal in Spanish history. The country was becoming a unified, cohesive entity. The two major Spanish kingdoms had been unified through the marriage of Isabella I of Castile and Ferdinand II of Aragon in 1469. These two monarchs consolidated their power in 1492 to defeat and evict the last of the Moors (North African Muslims) from southern Spain. In the same year, the ardently Catholic king and queen attempted to "ethnically cleanse" their kingdom by decreeing that all Jews were either to convert to Christianity or leave the country. Having completed its military, political, and religious reconquest and unification of its own territory, Spain was ready and eager to focus its energies on the conquest of the new lands that Christopher Columbus encountered in 1492 and claimed in the name of Spain.

Meanwhile, by the end of the fifteenth century, the Portuguese had already been extremely active in oceanic exploration. The area that is now Portugal was wrested from the Moors about 200 years before the final Moorish stronghold, Granada, fell to Spain. Subsequently, the Portuguese worked to maintain their independence from neighboring Spanish kingdoms. However, because of their small landmass, the Portuguese turned to the seas as a means of conquest and survival. At around the same time Columbus was attempting to go west toward the Indies, the Portuguese were heading east toward the same goal.

Colonial Collusion: Dividing the World

To avoid conflict over their competing expansion, representatives of Spain and Portugal established in 1494 an imaginary line that ran north to south approximately 300 miles west of the Azores Islands, a Portuguese possession in the Atlantic Ocean. The **Treaty of Tordesillas** thus purported to divide up the world: Spain was granted possession of all lands to the west of this line, and Portugal was granted the lands to the east. The treaty thus established the authority of Spain in the New World except for what is now Brazil, which was on the Portuguese side of the line drawn up at Tordesillas (although Europeans would not land in

■ **Treaty of Tordesillas**
A 1494 treaty between Spain and Portugal that purported to divide up the world. It drew an imaginary line that ran north to south approximately 300 miles west of the Azores Islands. Spain was granted possession of all lands to the west of this line, Portugal the lands to the east.

Brazil until 1500). The Portuguese, in turn, gained supremacy over Africa and the Indian Ocean, indeed a lucrative trade route.

At first, it seemed that Spain was left with a less appealing territory, but the vast wealth of what Europeans came to call the New World soon became apparent: First gold and then silver enriched the coffers of the Spanish Crown. In particular, the discovery of a major silver vein in Bolivia in 1545 meant riches that would finance Spain's many military endeavors back in Europe as well as further exploration.[3]

Spanish Colonial Administration

The Spanish Empire in the New World emphasized the acquisition of territory, and Spain's expansion into the New World took a relatively short time. Conquistadors like Hernán Cortés, who defeated the Aztecs in Mexico, and Francisco Pizarro, who vanquished the Incas of Peru, were aided by a number of factors. European use of gunpowder and muskets vastly outclassed the weapons of the Aztecs and Incas. Native Americans had less immunity to the diseases that had ravaged Europe and Asia, so the maladies the Europeans carried to the New World devastated the indigenous population. Moreover, the political systems of the Aztecs and Incas were so tyrannical that foreign intervention was often welcomed by many subjects over continued rule by the established elites.

The Spanish Crown quickly moved to consolidate its control over the territory subdued by the conquistadors. The Crown was the ultimate authority on matters in the New World, though a large bureaucracy actually did most of the direct work of governing. The main characteristics of this colonial administration reflected the idea that the role of Spanish possessions was to enrich the mother country. For instance, the Crown monopolized the mining of gold and silver and, at the same time, restricted trade in other goods. Spanish possessions were to trade only with Spain, and the formation of industries in the New World was thwarted. Over the centuries, these restrictions would eventually lead to dissatisfaction and then rebellion among many colonial subjects.[4]

Portuguese Colonialism

The colonial situation in Portuguese lands was different than in the Spanish territories. Most of the Portuguese Empire was based on trade. Rather than subduing and occupying territory on a grand scale, the Portuguese were content to establish trading ports.[5] The far-flung but strategically placed Portuguese colonies reflect this approach: Outposts included Guinea-Bissau, the Cape Verde Islands, Sao Tome and Principe, Angola, and Mozambique along the coast of Africa; Goa in India; and Macao on the coast of China.

Even in South America, the Portuguese did not colonize with the same vigor as the Spanish. What was to become modern-day Brazil was sparsely populated and devoid of gold and silver. The Portuguese turned to growing sugar cane in large plantations, primarily on the northeastern coast. African slaves were imported to compensate for the lack of indigenous labor. These slaves were readily available because a large slave trade already existed off the coast of Africa. In southern Brazil, the climate was quite temperate, similar to that of Europe, and many Europeans were attracted to the open land for cattle ranching and farming. The wide influx of various groups into Brazil contributed to its rich ethnic diversity.

Spanish-American Independence

The Spanish monarchy attempted to keep close tabs on its far-flung possessions, prohibiting trade with countries other than Spain and reserving for itself control of the lucrative mines. The proscription on free trade, especially with other colonies and with England, irritated many of the elites in the colonies. Despite festering discontent within the colonies, rebellion did not break out until events in Europe created an opening during the Napoleonic Wars. In 1808 Napoleon continued his quest to dominate Europe by invading Spain (see Chapter 3). The Spanish king was forced to abdicate, and Napoleon's brother, Joseph, was placed on the throne. This move sparked protest and rebellion within Spain itself, and also made refusal to obey Napoleonic rule a patriotic endeavor in the colonies. Elites in the colonies took advantage of the situation to press for independence, even after Napoleon was defeated in 1815 and Ferdinand regained the crown of Spain.

The struggle for independence was encouraged by Great Britain, which was often alone in carrying on the struggle against Napoleon in Europe and therefore welcomed the opportunity to harm Spain, now a French ally, by removing a critical source of its wealth. In addition, England was eager to trade freely with the colonies, and thus preferred to have them be independent countries. Spain was not willing to relinquish its possessions blithely, and the fight for independence lasted roughly from 1810 to 1825. Most of Spain's American colonies (excluding the islands of Puerto Rico and Cuba) achieved political independence under the leadership of the legendary Simon Bolivar, the "Great Liberator" of South America. Bolivar attempted to unify the continent in a United States of South America, but the divisions among the Latin American peoples were too great to overcome.

Independence from Portugal

Portugal's empire was more enduring than Spain's, in part because it was never as extensive. For instance, by the sixteenth century Portugal's trading empire had already been usurped, mainly by the Dutch. Portugal's American colony, Brazil, gained its independence rather painlessly. The catalyst for independence came, as it had with the rest of Latin America, with the Napoleonic Wars in Europe. However, when Portugal was invaded, the Portuguese monarchy was whisked

PHOTO 5.1   Simon Bolivar is revered as a hero
throughout much of Latin America for
leading the fight for independence in
what are now the countries of Venezuela,
Colombia, Ecuador, Peru, Panama, and
Bolivia.

away by British ships to Brazil. Throughout the French occupation, the center of the
Portuguese Empire resided in its colony, and the Portuguese king, Joao IV, allowed
Brazilians to trade freely with other countries, particularly England. When Dom
Joao returned to Portugal, he left his son Dom Pedro in charge, but the Brazilians
chafed at the new trade restrictions the Portuguese wished to impose. In 1822 Dom
Pedro bowed to domestic social pressure and peacefully announced the formation
of the independent Brazilian Empire. Thus, with relatively little conflict, and certainly without the enormous bloodshed that the rest of the continent experienced,
Brazil became an independent country. However, the independence of Portugal's
colonies in Africa, Mozambique, Angola, and Guinea-Bissau would wait until the
1970s, occurring only after decades of bitter colonial and civil war.

Dutch Empire

The Dutch Empire began with the founding of the Dutch East India Company
in 1602. Like the Portuguese, the Dutch were not particularly concerned with
controlling extensive continental territory, but rather key strategic trading ports,
straits, and coasts (see Map 5.1). In the Indian Ocean, the Dutch established trading stations at the Cape of Good Hope in southern Africa and at Batavia on the

island of Java (now part of Indonesia), effectively giving them control over both ends of Indian Ocean trading. Soon thereafter, the Dutch ruled all of Java, the key island of Ceylon (now Sri Lanka) off the southern coast of India, and most of the coast of South Africa, displacing the Portuguese by the mid-1600s as the naval hegemon in Asian waters. In the New World, the Dutch picked up the Caribbean Islands of Curacao and St. Eustatius, the South American territory of Guyana, and the North American island of Manhattan, establishing the settlement of New Amsterdam. The Anglo–Dutch Wars of 1652–1674 forced them to cede New Amsterdam to England, and the village was renamed New York. Overall, the Dutch Empire never became a major factor in the colonial struggle in the Americas.

The real wealth of the Dutch colonial empire came from the spices of the Dutch East Indies and from tea plantations on the island of Ceylon. These precious commodities brought very high profits in European markets. The Dutch were well situated in Europe to take advantage of this trade because, unlike the Spanish and Portuguese, the Dutch had extensive trading networks into Prussia and the other German states, France, the British Isles, Scandinavia, and even Russia. Their navy was large enough to protect the trade from the Indian Ocean, but, perhaps of greatest importance, the Dutch cities of Amsterdam, the Hague, and Rotterdam were the financial centers of European trade. Thus, the Dutch bankrolled much of the emerging global trade in the sixteenth and seventeenth centuries. The colonial empire was in essence just one appendage of growing Dutch participation in global commodities and financial markets, and, as a result, the colonies' impact in spurring high levels of international trade was far greater than their size, population, or longevity would indicate.

Dutch power waned in the 1700s, but the key event for the Dutch Empire was the Napoleonic Wars. The Netherlands was conquered by Napoleon, and the British responded by seizing Ceylon in 1796 and the Cape Colony in South Africa in 1806, effectively ending major Dutch colonial presence in the Indian Ocean. However, the British did allow the Netherlands to retain Java and the other East Indies islands in the 1815 settlement at the Congress of Vienna. Thereafter, the Dutch East Indies were ruled by the Netherlands until the Japanese invaded and conquered the islands during World War II. After the war, a growing nationalist movement fought for and achieved independence in 1949 as Indonesia, leaving the Netherlands with only a few Caribbean islands as the last vestige of a once impressive trading empire.

Anglo–French Rivalry

After the 1588 defeat of the Spanish Armada by the British, Spanish power rapidly declined. Portugal and Holland did not have the population or resources to defend, let alone extend, their colonial outposts. This left the principal colonial competition to Britain and France for most of the eighteenth and nineteenth

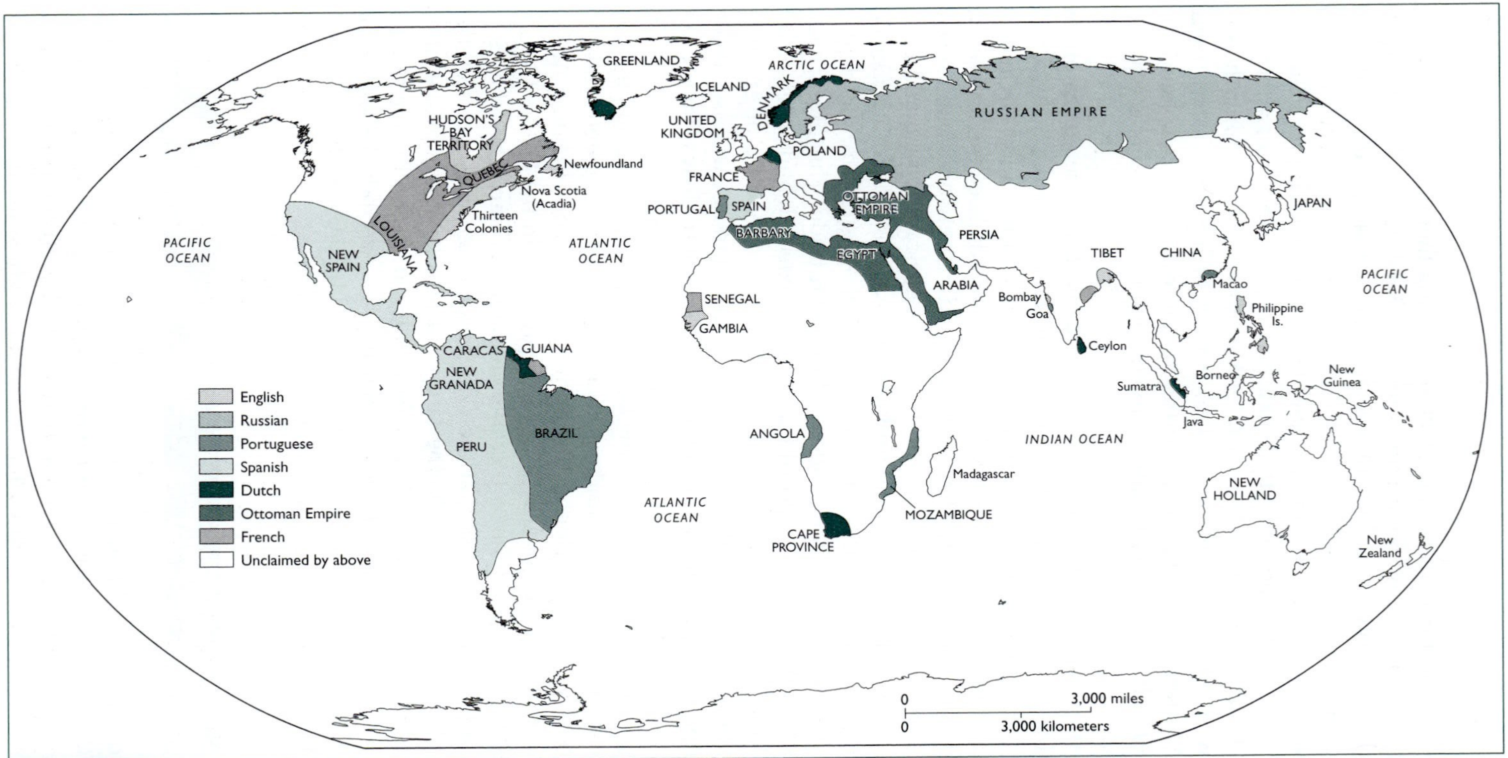

MAP 5.1 Worldwide Empires, Seventeenth and Eighteenth Centuries

Legend:
- English
- Russian
- Portuguese
- Spanish
- Dutch
- Ottoman Empire
- French
- Unclaimed by above

3,000 miles

3,000 kilometers

centuries. The Anglo–French rivalry for colonies was one of the most enduring political contests of modern history, taking place throughout the world and, as we saw in Chapter 3, frequently leading to war.

Britain and France brought different strengths and weaknesses to their struggle. Because the British Isles made foreign invasion unlikely, Britain could focus its energies on the Royal Navy and neglect creating a large standing army. Moreover, although Britain had coal, it had to trade for many raw materials and a significant portion of its food. By contrast, France was a continental power with vulnerable borders and therefore had to devote large amounts of its resources to a standing army. As a result, the French navy was never able to overcome British oceanic hegemony. In addition, French self-sufficiency in food meant that France was consistently more inward-looking in economic matters, whereas British population pressure encouraged emigration to overseas colonies. The combination of these factors gave Britain consistent advantages over France in their colonial competition. In the eighteenth century, the British–French struggle took place in North America and India, with Britain emerging victorious. In the nineteenth century, Britain and France vied for colonies in Africa, the Middle East, Southeast Asia, and the Pacific, yet after the Napoleonic era the two countries were able to resolve their colonial differences without going to war.[6]

France's Bid for Empire

The first area of overseas colonization by French explorers was along the St. Lawrence River in North America. The French soon established the cities of Québec and Montréal in New France (today the Canadian province of Québec), and thereafter established a series of forts along the Great Lakes and down the Mississippi River, including New Orleans. They also seized the western half of Hispaniola (now Haiti) as well as a few other smaller Caribbean islands such as Martinique and Guadeloupe. In the Indian Ocean, they established a number of trading outposts on Mauritius, Madagascar, and the Seychelles, as well as in the Indian coastal cities of Mahe and Pondicherry. These French overseas possessions, however, never attracted great numbers of French settlers. Thus, although the French typically emphasized control of territory, they never fully succeeded in achieving lasting dominion.

This early French Empire collapsed as a result of the Seven Years' War (1756–1763) between Britain and France (see Chapter 3). Initially, the French utilized their inland fort system along the Appalachian Mountains and Mississippi and Ohio Rivers in alliance with a number of Native Americans to capture some critical British outposts on the North American frontier. However, the British navy decisively defeated its French counterpart in 1759, and thereafter French overseas forces wilted for lack of reinforcements and supplies. In 1762–1763 France was forced to cede Québec to England and Louisiana to Spain, effectively removing the French presence in North America. France regained Louisiana in 1803 as a result of the Napoleonic Wars, only to sell it to the United

States the following year. In India, French influence was limited to a few small coastal cities.

After the Napoleonic Wars, France again began to build an overseas empire, this time in Africa, Southeast Asia, and the Pacific. In 1830, motivated in part by the need to stop raids by the Barbary pirates, France conquered Algeria in North Africa. Elsewhere, in West Africa, the French extended their influence inland, coming to dominate a vast region of little economic value because of the arid climate and sparse population. In Asia they were able to colonize Indochina and a number of Pacific islands such as Tahiti. The French saw their role as bringing culture and civilization to backward peoples and thus attempted to assimilate and colonize them to the French way of life. This French Empire was extensive in its territory, covering large areas of Africa. Moreover, in light of France's protectionism, virtually all trade involving French colonies was conducted with France.[7] After World War I, the French also expanded to the Middle East, adding the territories now known as Syria and Lebanon.

Given the high level of French political commitment to and control of their colonies, decolonization was a particularly difficult ordeal for the French Empire, demonstrating the potential bloody path of fragmentation. The end of the French Empire was precipitated by the disastrous results for France in World War II. German victories in North Africa and Japanese advances in Asia demonstrated the inherent weakness of the colonial powers. In Indochina, for instance, insurgents led by Vietnam's Ho Chi Minh immediately began to fight for independence at the end of World War II. The decisive battle in a long struggle came at Dien Bien Phu in 1954, when a portion of the French Foreign Legion was defeated and captured. No sooner had France withdrawn from Indochina when rebellion began in Algeria. That war dragged on for many years as well, until Charles de Gaulle became president, and by 1962 completed the process of granting independence to most of the African colonies. Today, only a few Caribbean and Pacific islands remain "overseas departments" of the French Republic.[8]

British Empire

It is difficult to overstate the importance of the impact of the British Empire on the peoples of the Americas, Africa, Asia, and the Pacific. Today some fifty nations, including Canada, Australia, and New Zealand are members of the Commonwealth of Nations, and for many, the British monarch remains their official head of state (Australia, for example, held a referendum in 1999 on its status as a constitutional monarchy but voted to continue having the British monarch as its head of state). By 1914 the British Empire had more than 500 million inhabitants; today more than 2 billion people live in areas that were once British colonies. In short, the British Empire was one of the most important political entities in the history of humanity, and England probably contributed more to the globalization

What Would You Do?

The Costs of Imperialism

You are the leader of France in early 1954. Your country has spent nearly 150 years building your second overseas empire. Colonies have long been considered a source of pride and a demonstration of a state's power and influence in the international system. In addition, your country has expended great effort in spreading the French way of life and bringing culture to backward people in Africa, Southeast Asia, and the Pacific.

World War II, however, took a great toll on your country. The German blitzkrieg allowed for only five weeks of survival before France fell, leaving a path of death and destruction in its wake. Your financial situation is precarious, and reconstruction is expensive. To compound your difficulties, communist insurgents in Vietnam, led by Ho Chi Minh, have begun fighting for their independence from your colonial control. Continuing to fight to maintain control of your colony has significant costs, both financially and politically. The war is draining your coffers at a time you need to allocate the money to domestic endeavors.

You are not alone in this fight, however, and exiting Vietnam also presents costs. The United States has been funding your war efforts (paying 80 percent of the war costs at this point) and would like you to continue to fight the Vietminh. This war is being perceived in Washington as a Soviet-funded battle between communism and democracy. Further, if you leave Vietnam, both the regional balance of power in Asia and the global balance of power will be affected. Your great power status could be aversely affected by withdrawal, as you have seen happen with Great Britain since the end of World War II. Your decision to continue to suppress the rebellion in Vietnam is crucial and complex.

What Would You Do?

---

of the modern world than any other country, as evidenced by the primacy of the English language in international trade, diplomacy, and entertainment.

In reality, there were several British empires that can be delineated both by era and by the type of colonialism. In the seventeenth and eighteenth centuries, British colonialism was mostly composed of settler colonies in North America, the Caribbean, and later in the South Pacific; these colonies emphasized territorial expansion and control. In the eighteenth and nineteenth centuries, the British Empire increasingly added territories in Africa and Asia, where British colonial officials ruled over masses of indigenous people, but where there existed relatively few European settlers. In these colonies, the British were content to increase trade and investment (see again Map 5.1).

Seventeenth and Eighteenth Centuries

The very first area of English overseas colonization was at Jamestown, Virginia, in 1607. Soon thereafter, other colonies with numerous English settlers were established on the North American coast: Massachusetts, New Hampshire, Connecticut, Pennsylvania, Maryland, the Carolinas, and Georgia. Dutch and Swedish settlements in New York, New Jersey, and Delaware were seized by the British in 1664. Elsewhere in North America, colonies were established in Hudson Bay, Newfoundland, and Nova Scotia; and in the Caribbean, the British seized Jamaica from Spain. The British victory in the Seven Years' War (1756–1763) added large amounts of North American territory to the British Empire, including Québec from France and Florida from Spain. This English hegemony in North America lasted only a few years. The American Revolution left England with only Canada, where many loyalists from the thirteen colonies had fled.[9]

The British Empire in Asia lasted longer. In India the British gained footholds in Bengal, Bombay, and Madras in the eighteenth century (see Spotlight, "British India"). Decisive military victories over the French and the Mughal Empire (the Muslim Empire that ruled central India) during the Seven Years' War paved the way for British domination of the subcontinent. The capture of South Africa, Ceylon, and other Indian Ocean islands during the Napoleonic Wars ensured that the Indian Ocean would become a "British Lake."[10]

Nineteenth and Twentieth Centuries

During the nineteenth century, the British added Burma (Myanmar) and Malaya to their Asian empire and attempted but failed to conquer Afghanistan. Moreover, Australia and New Zealand were colonized by the British as their indigenous peoples, the Aborigines in Australia and the Maoris in New Zealand, were ruthlessly repressed and their land was converted to sheep and dairy farming.

During the nineteenth century, the British government in London, fearing a repeat of the American Revolution, moved to grant self-government (so-called dominion status) to the white settler colonies of Canada, Australia, and New Zealand. With Latin America independent and open to British trade and South Asia under British hegemony, the British generally refrained from adding new territories to their empire. However, the rise of Germany and the renewed push by France for colonies in the early 1880s posed a difficult problem for Britain. If Germany and France gained colonies, Britain would have been essentially locked out of those areas because of the high protectionism that characterized German and French foreign economic policies. Therefore, as the so-called scramble for Africa of the 1880s got under way, Britain again became a very active imperialist power.

When the competition for colonies reached a fever pitch in the late 1880s, Britain used its superior naval and strategic resources to secure the proverbial "lion's share," especially in eastern and southern Africa. The most ambitious "man on the spot" in Africa was Cecil Rhodes, an English chauvinist and white supremacist who began his colonial career as an impoverished diamond prospector in South Africa. Rhodes founded the DeBeers company (which still controls most of the world's supply of diamonds), became prime minister of Cape

▪ SPOTLIGHT ▪

British India

It is a mistake to believe that European imperialism was a precisely executed plan for global domination controlled and ordered directly from Madrid, Lisbon, Paris, or London. Instead, many explorers and conquerors, such as Da Gama, Columbus, Magellan, Cortés, Pizarro, Hudson, Cartier, Cook, and even Lewis and Clark, had only the vaguest notion of what lands and civilizations they might find. Much of European expansion resulted from a combination of initiative by the explorers and collaboration by natives who often detested their native rulers. Some have referred to this kind of expansion as the "turbulent frontier," where new lands were added to empires in the monarchs' names but without their orders and sometimes even without their knowledge. Nowhere was this more evident than in the extension of the British rule in India.

The first British citizens to go to India did so under the auspices of the English East India Company, a semiprivate company given a monopoly to trade with India. The company set up trading ports on the Indian coast, but by the mid-eighteenth century, it had gained effective political control over much of eastern India. The East India Company achieved political supremacy mostly through economic superiority, which allowed the company to hire many native collaborators to fight for them. In 1757 these troops won the Battle of Plassey in the Bengal region of India, which ensured the company's control of the critical Ganges River valley. Over the next few decades, one kingdom or region of India after another fell under rule of the company until virtually all of the subcontinent was effectively subordinated, whether under direct administration or indirectly through "princely states." Typically these kingdoms or princely states were conquered by Indian mercenary troops under the command of ambitious British officials who only ex post facto informed their superiors in Calcutta, Bombay, or London of the latest addition to the empire.

In 1857, however, many of the native troops mutinied, exposing the thin grip of the East India Company. The British government then intervened, put down the rebellion, and instituted a series of reforms, including replacing the East India Company with a colonial regime that became known as the British Raj. Thereafter, the British built an extensive network of railroads and roads throughout the subcontinent that increased trade, helped to unify a huge region, and ensured British economic and political dominance. By the late nineteenth century, India had become the "brightest jewel in the crown" of the British Empire, and Queen Victoria was crowned Empress of India. However, few British citizens were even remotely associated with India. The day-to-day administration of India was actually carried out by newly trained Indian civil servants, and the vast majority of the police and the army were Indian as well. Thus, British rule in India was based on the massive collaboration of the indigenous population.

World Wars I and II dramatically weakened British authority in South Asia. Limited self-government was extended to India, including some economic policymaking powers after World War I. By the 1930s British rule in India was clearly waning, and the Indian National Congress under Mahatma Gandhi led numerous campaigns and demonstrations demanding that Britain "quit India."

After World War II, with British resources depleted and spread precariously thin around the world and a new Labour government in London, the former Raj was split into two independent states, India and Pakistan. British rule in India and Pakistan, which had so haphazardly assembled, was thus quickly removed. The British colonial elite that had conquered and ruled India for almost two centuries was replaced by an emerging Indian elite—many of whom (such as Gandhi and Jawaharlal Nehru) had been educated in England. Waves of ethnic and religious fighting broke out immediately, however, and the threat of communal violence haunts India to the present day. The legacy of British rule in India is therefore a mixed one. Although British colonialism fostered economic development and brought India squarely into the global economy, it did little to alleviate the subcontinent's potentially dangerous political fragmentation.

Colony, and dreamed of "painting the map red" (establishing British dominion) from the mouth of the Nile River to the Cape of Good Hope. Rhodes gained most of central Africa for British influence by establishing Northern and Southern Rhodesia, which today are Zambia and Zimbabwe, respectively.[11] Although his career ended in scandal and disgrace, many of his dreams for British control of Africa were fulfilled, as Britain dominated the whole of the Nile Valley, including Egypt, the Sudan, Uganda, and Kenya.

Britain's most important and costly colonial war, the Boer War, took place in South Africa. Disputes between the Dutch Afrikaners and British in South Africa increased after huge deposits of gold were found in the nominally independent Dutch Boer republic of the Transvaal. Rhodes tried to engineer British control over the Transvaal with a raid in 1895; his attempt to foster a coup failed disastrously and increased the antagonism between Britain and Germany. Anglo–Boer tensions finally broke into warfare in 1899. By mid-1900, Britain occupied the capitals of both Boer republics, the Orange Free State and the Transvaal; the war then became a guerrilla conflict in which the British rounded up Boer families into what were essentially concentration camps. As the war became increasingly unpopular and expensive, Britain reached a compromise peace with the

Boers in 1902. Eight years later, the Boer republics were absorbed into the newly created Union of South Africa, which was granted self-governing dominion status (although only whites enjoyed full civil and political rights).

Britain was also able to reserve for itself some of the most fertile areas of the West African coast in the colonies of Nigeria, the Gold Coast (modern Ghana), and Sierra Leone. By the eve of World War I, the "sun never set" on an empire that extended from the South Pacific islands to the hinterlands of Africa to the British Isles and through Canada. With victory in World War I, Britain added the mandates of Palestine, Trans-Jordan, and Iraq from the Ottoman Empire in the Middle East and Tanganyika (now Tanzania) and Southwest Africa (now Namibia) from Germany in Africa. It was at this apex of expansion and influence that the empire began to unravel.

Twilight of Empire

The first country to break free of the British Empire since the American Revolution was Ireland. In 1922, after eight centuries of British rule, decades of agitation, and six years of civil war, Britain granted home rule to most of Ireland. (Northern Ireland remains a part of the United Kingdom.) In the Middle East, in the period between World Wars I and II, the Arab states began to gain their independence. By this time, Mahatma Gandhi was leading the Indian National Congress in noncooperation campaigns to get Britain to "quit India" (see Spotlight, "The Mahatma"). World War II sealed the fate of London's Asian empire, as an exhausted Britain simply no longer had the resources to hold on to territories halfway around the world. India was granted independence and partitioned into India and Pakistan in 1947. Burma (Myanmar), Ceylon, and Israel gained independence in 1948. In Africa, most colonies were also granted independence between the mid-1950s and the early 1960s, followed by most of the Caribbean and South Pacific island territories over the next decade. Of enormous significance for later developments, Britain left the Persian Gulf in 1971, where its navy had held sway for a century and a half. This created a power vacuum, and the region has been embroiled in conflict ever since, including the Persian Gulf War of 1991 (see Chapter 6).

Perhaps the most remarkable aspect of the decolonization of the British Empire was how generally peaceful it was. When the British saw the sun finally setting on their empire, they got out before they were sucked into any quagmires, a lesson learned from both the American Revolution and the Boer War. Even the violent Mau Mau opposition in Kenya and the communist rebellion in Malaya in the 1950s caused very few British casualties, but often the local population suffered grievously from internal conflicts, as in Kenya and Malaya. Similarly, war among the former colonial subjects often followed British departures, as in India and Palestine. British policies were very effective in ruling with little cost, but the withdrawal of British power often left nothing to contain indigenous conflicts. On the whole, however, Britain's assembly and relatively peaceful divestment of its vast empire were both remarkable accomplishments.[12]

▪ **S P O T L I G H T** ▪

The Mahatma

One of the greatest heroes in the annals of the human spirit is Mohandas Karamchand Gandhi. Born to a Hindu family in Bombay in 1869, Gandhi initially pursued a career in law, studying for the bar in London and practicing in India and South Africa. As a young barrister, he affected the dress and mannerisms of an affluent English gentleman, working within the colonial legal system to fight discrimination against Indians. As his struggle for political and civil rights continued, however, he set his sights higher and devoted himself to the abolition of the colonial system in his home country. He returned to India in 1915, renounced all material possessions and adopted a life of voluntary poverty, vegetarianism, celibacy, and nonviolent opposition to colonial oppression. (After his vow of poverty, Gandhi always dressed in simple homespun clothes, usually only a loincloth. When someone commented on his scanty attire during a meeting with King George V at Buckingham Palace in 1931, he replied, "The King was wearing enough for us both.")

Campaigning tirelessly against British rule, Gandhi developed the resistance strategy of *satyagraha*, or "holding to the truth," which sought to expose the immorality of oppression through peaceful civil disobedience. He used personal fasts and hunger strikes as nonviolent weapons against the colonial authorities and was repeatedly jailed for his protests against the British. Realizing that philosophy alone could not effect political change, he proved to be a brilliant political tactician, organizing strikes, boycotts, and, in 1930, a 200-mile march from Ahmadabad to the sea to gather salt crystals in defiance of the government monopoly on the sale of that basic necessity of life. This demonstration electrified India and precipitated a wave of peaceful protests throughout the subcontinent. Gandhi was arrested, as he had been many times before, but he knew that his movement had scored a major victory. As he put it, "The honor of India has been symbolized by a fistful of salt in the hand of a man of nonviolence."

Gandhi's methods and infinite patience got results. His "Quit India" campaign persuaded London that British control of India could not be maintained, and in 1947 the colonial Raj was dismantled. The two new nations of India and Pakistan were immediately wracked by bloody fighting between Hindus and Muslims, and in 1948 the aged, frail philosopher fasted until Hindu and Muslim leaders signed a peace agreement. He was not able to enjoy the fruits of his lifelong struggle for independence, however; he was fatally shot by a Hindu extremist that same year.

Throughout his long fight against colonialism, Gandhi displayed a rare combination of enlightened spirituality and political canniness. The most fitting tribute to Gandhi is the sobriquet he was granted by his followers and by which he will be remembered throughout the world as an example of nonviolent resistance: Mahatma, or Great Soul.

PHOTO 5.2 Mohandas Karamchand Gandhi's nonviolent approach to battling colonialism earned him the nickname "the Mahatma," or Great Soul.

Two Great Continental Empires: Russia and the United States

All empires examined thus far have been transoceanic empires of the major states of Western Europe. However, most empires throughout history have been continental in scope, with expansion based on extending control by land from already conquered territories. During the era of Portuguese, Spanish, Dutch, French, and British overseas colonialism, other empires were pursuing the strategy of contiguous imperialism. Two of these empires, Russia and the United States, deserve particular attention because of their critical role in modern history, especially for their impact on the peoples of Asia, the Middle East, and the Americas. Both political entities were extremely successful in coming to dominate vast areas that spanned continents.

The Russians

The Russian Empire was the most territorially vast of the European empires and the longest lived (see Map 5.2). Although Russia relentlessly pursued a policy of territorial expansion for more than a millennium, it deliberately remained economically and culturally isolated. As a result, Russia remained the least advanced of the major European powers in terms of technology and economic and political organization, and this backwardness ultimately was the root cause of its collapse. The history of the Russian Empire may be roughly divided into three periods. From its earliest days until the late seventeenth century, Russia was essentially a feudal or absolutist monarchy. Between the late seventeenth and early twentieth centuries, the political and social system of Imperial Russia was dominated by the struggle between absolutism and Western political ideas. The victory of one of those ideas, communism, led twentieth-century Soviet Russia to the zenith of its global power and then to the stagnation and collapse of its empire.

Ninth Through Eighteenth Centuries

The origins of the Russian Empire lie in Kievan Rus, a feudal state founded in the tenth century that united the Slavic peoples of what is now Ukraine, Belarus, and western Russia. Political and cultural links with Europe were strengthened at the end of the tenth century when Grand Duke Vladimir adopted Greek Orthodox Christianity as the state religion. Russia was drawn away from the European orbit in the thirteenth century, however, when the Mongol Empire under Genghis Khan and his sons destroyed the Kievan state and conquered most of the territory between the Black Sea and the Pacific Ocean.

After the decline of Mongol power, Ivan the Terrible, who ruled from 1533 to 1584, used terror and violence unsparingly to construct a centralized absolute monarchy. Based in Moscow, he simultaneously tried to expand the empire in all directions. Throughout the sixteenth and seventeenth centuries, the Russian Empire expanded relentlessly to the east across Siberia and toward the Baltic Sea. Trade and contact with Europe nevertheless remained limited, and thus Russia was little affected by advances in modern science, capitalism, and democratic government.

After Peter the Great ascended to the throne in 1689, Russia's territorial expansion continued unabated, most notably in east-central Europe in the eighteenth century and in the Caucasus, central Asia, and North America in the nineteenth

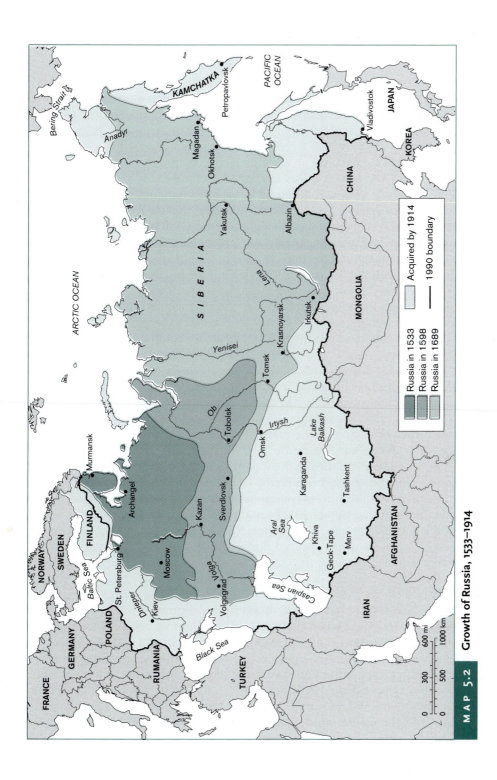

MAP 5.2 Growth of Russia, 1533–1914

century. Russian armies conquered most of Poland and made subsequent gains against the Ottoman Empire and Persia.

Nineteenth and Twentieth Centuries

Russia became firmly established as a European power during the reign of Alexander I (1801–1825), when Russian forces were instrumental in the defeat of Napoleon and the establishment of the Concert of Europe in 1814 and 1815 (see Chapter 3). Westernizing forces were strengthened by active participation in European politics, but after an attempted coup by progressive officers in 1825 (the Decembrist Revolt) failed, Russia aligned itself for many years with the conservative European powers that sought to suppress nationalism.

It was clear to even the most conservative leaders that the Industrial Revolution was reforging the economic and strategic environment, but industrialization in nineteenth-century Russia began late and progressed slowly. At the same time, Russian expansionism led to conflicts with other European empires and Japan, and Russian defeats in the Crimean War (1853–1856) and the Russo–Japanese War (1904–1905) spurred economic and political reforms. However, these reforms did not go far enough to enable the Russian regime to meet its internal and external challenges, and although a revolution in 1905 failed to topple the tsar, it demonstrated that the Russian Empire's political structure could not meet the needs of a modern society.[13]

By 1917, under the strains of world war, Russia, which had missed or attempted to suppress the major intellectual and socioeconomic revolutions of its European neighbors, finally had one of its own, led by the visionary communist Vladimir Lenin. The Bolshevik Revolution and the civil war that followed destroyed the centralized, bureaucratic, and repressive Russian Empire and replaced it with the equally centralized, bureaucratic, and repressive Union of Soviet Socialist Republics. After Lenin's death, Joseph Stalin quickly and ruthlessly consolidated his leadership of the Communist party. Tremendous material and human resources were poured into the Soviet military, especially after the German invasion of 1941 brought the USSR into World War II. By the end of the war, Soviet forces had repulsed the invasion, defeated the German army on the eastern front, captured Berlin, and established Moscow's domination over eastern Europe, at the cost of about 20 million military and civilian deaths.[14]

As discussed in Chapter 4, Russian influence over world politics peaked during the Cold War that followed, as the superpower rivalry between the Soviet Union and the United States was played out in political conflicts and "proxy" wars in Europe, Asia, the Middle East, Africa, and Latin America. The Soviet–American conflict never erupted into a direct military confrontation, but massive military spending and continued inability to compete with Western technology exhausted the USSR nonetheless. By the time Mikhail Gorbachev came to power in 1985, many Soviets regarded their country as economically stagnant and the Communist party as politically and morally bankrupt. The USSR might have been able to sustain either its status as a superpower or its communist system, one or the other. Gorbachev tried to preserve both and failed, but in so doing he stimulated the growth of nationalist and democratic forces throughout the Soviet Empire. By 1992 the collapse of the empire was complete, the USSR was broken up into its constituent republics, Russia was governed by a fledgling democratic regime, and Moscow controlled less territory than it did in 1689.

Considering the vast territories the Russian Empire once controlled and its role as a major power in world politics for centuries, its bequest to the contemporary world is remarkably small. Russia's lack of natural defenses and the difficulty of communications with far-flung provinces made it vulnerable to invasion, which heightened security consciousness and prompted political repression at home and "defensive expansion" abroad. Both these policies made Russia's neighbors and other great powers distrustful throughout its history. The collapse of the Russian Empire was rapid and disorderly, though accompanied by little large-scale violence. Russia continues in the twenty-first century to struggle to maintain democracy, rebuild a functioning economy, and reclaim its status as a major world power.

The Americans

Just as Russia expanded eastward through Asia, the United States expanded westward through North America in the nineteenth century. Like Russia, the United States first concentrated on contiguous expansion and territorial absorption. In 1803 it bought the Louisiana Territory from Napoleon and in 1819 acquired Florida from Spain in exchange for $5 million. The admission of the republic of Texas (which had broken away from Mexico) to the United States in 1845 set the stage for the Mexican–American War of 1846–1848, in which the United States seized what is now the American Southwest and California. These conquests made the United States a transcontinental country and raised the question of whether slavery would be permitted in the new territories, setting off the Civil War. After the war, the United States bought Alaska from Russia. The social, economic, and political organization in these territories was transformed to conform to the established American patterns from the eastern seaboard. Thus, the United States ensured its hegemony over North America.

Until the end of the nineteenth century, Americans resisted overseas expansion and instead focused on developing the western frontier. In 1898, like a coiled spring unleashed, the United States entered the ranks of the overseas imperialist powers. In a brief but decisive war with Spain, the United States obtained Puerto Rico and the Philippines, the remnants of the Spanish Empire. Elsewhere, it seized Hawaii, Guam, and other Pacific islands, making it a major power in the Pacific. Taken together, these acquisitions transformed the United States into a global power. In contrast to the American West, these overseas territories were acquired primarily to expand American economic and political influence and were not used as new realms for settlement, with the partial exception of Hawaii.

The United States did not take official possession of all overseas territories. Like the British in the nineteenth century, it also created an "informal empire," where it controlled political and economic development de facto without direct colonial rule. After the turn of the century, for instance, Washington increasingly dominated the Caribbean region. In 1903 the United States backed a rebellion that detached Panama from Colombia and then proceeded to build the Panama Canal. In Nicaragua and Haiti, the United States "sent in the Marines" in numerous interventions, making it the effective ruler of these countries. In 1917 it bought the Virgin Islands from Denmark. American political and economic influence in Cuba, Guatemala, Honduras, and El Salvador was also considerable. This empire allowed the United States to project naval power throughout the world and thus protect and promote American foreign trade, especially in the Caribbean, South America, and the Pacific.

Because the United States generally avoided direct colonial rule, certain aspects of decolonization never presented the difficult political problems faced by Britain and France. For instance, the Philippines was granted independence after World War II on July 4, 1946, and Puerto Rico was granted commonwealth status, internal self-governance, in 1952. (The possibility of statehood or independence remains a major issue in Puerto Rico.) Nevertheless, American attempts to keep "friendly" governments in power in some Third World (developing) countries often led to disaster. Probably the furthest outpost of American influence in the post–World War II era was South Vietnam, the best case of the "overextension" of American power in the 1960s (see Chapter 4). Regimes bent on reducing previous American influence occurred after violent revolutions in China, Cuba, Iran, and Nicaragua. Only in Nicaragua was this process reversed, when pro-American Violeta Chamorro defeated the Sandinista revolutionary Daniel Ortega in an election in 1989.

In many ways, however, American expansionism was successful. The territorial strategy of the nineteenth century brought about the total and unquestioned absorption of the western half of North America and Alaska. Compared to the dissolution of the Soviet Union or even the decolonization of the British and French Empires, the American assimilation of most territories and peoples into its existing political framework provides a model that few other political units have ever achieved.

The overseas record of the American trading empire is less formidable and more spotty. Hawaii did achieve statehood; other Pacific islands, like Guam and American Samoa, have remained territories of the United States; and the Philippines has remained friendly. However, although the frequency of U.S. intervention in Latin America has been declining in recent decades, there remains a latent (sometimes even blatant) anti-Americanism in the region that is typical of anticolonial movements elsewhere in the developing world. This "Yankee Go Home" attitude reflects the ambiguity of American expansionism, which at times has been extremely territorial and in other periods was concentrated merely on expanding and controlling trade. Overall, though, compared to the Russians, the

Americans adjusted to their imperial decline with relatively minimal domestic political upheaval.[15]

Ottoman Empire

The one successful non-Christian empire since 1500, the Muslim Empire of the Ottoman Turks was a major force in world politics for more than 500 years. Many of the violent conflicts in the world today, including the fighting in the former Yugoslavia, the Arab–Israeli conflict, the Greek–Turkish dispute over Cyprus, and the various troubles in the Persian Gulf, are located in former Ottoman territory and are influenced by developments that occurred during the centuries of Ottoman rule. From the early fourteenth to the beginning of the twentieth century, the Ottoman Empire grew from a small and weak principality in western Turkey to, at its height in the seventeenth century, a mighty empire that controlled the Balkans, the Middle East, North Africa, and parts of what are now southern Russia and Ukraine (see Map 5.3). The empire slowly declined until after World War I, when it ceased to exist and was replaced by the Turkish Republic in 1923. How did this important Islamic entity compete in a period when the great Christian empires were emerging? To understand the evolution of the Ottoman Empire, we must look to its origins.[16]

Fourteenth Through Eighteenth Centuries

The source of this empire, which would become the most important Islamic political unit in world politics for centuries, hardly seemed auspicious: a small and relatively weak principality in western Turkey, bordered to the east and west by more powerful neighbors. Around 1300, however, Osman, the empire's founder (from whose name "Ottoman" comes) launched successful raids against areas controlled by one of those neighbors. From the very beginning, the Ottomans encountered the fundamental problem of facing foes both to the west and to the east. Their expansion into the Balkans, however, was facilitated by social disorganization and fragmentation there. Eventually this expansion met opposition, led by the Serbs, in an ironic precursor that would have an impact on conflicts within the former Yugoslavia in the 1990s. In 1389 the Ottomans defeated the Serbs, who were joined by Bosnian and Bulgarian contingents, at the Battle of Kosovo. The contemporary hostility between the Serbs and the Muslims in Bosnia dates back to this period.

The Ottoman victories generated more serious threats. The Hungarians organized a crusade, joined by the French and Venetians, which the Ottomans defeated in 1392. From the east came the Mongol hordes, who defeated the Ottoman army in the Battle of Ankara in 1402. Later, though, the Ottomans gradually regained power and eventually resumed their conquests. By the end of the fifteenth century, they had conquered Constantinople, the rest of Turkey, Greece,

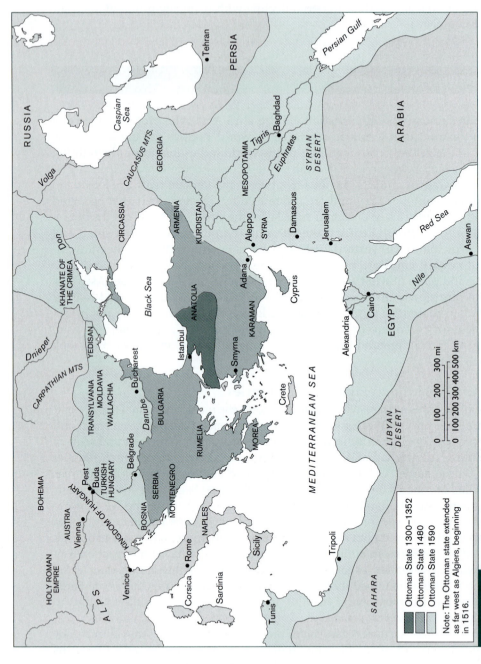

MAP 5.3 Growth of Ottoman Empire, 1300–1566

Ottoman State 1300–1352
Ottoman State 1480
Ottoman State 1590

Note: The Ottoman state extended as far west as Algiers, beginning in 1516.

and parts of Albania after defeating the Venetians, and the Balkans after again defeating the Serbs.

By the beginning of the sixteenth century, Ottoman control of the Balkans was secured, but a new struggle developed with the Hapsburg Empire. The Ottomans took Hungary, and in 1529 unsuccessfully besieged Vienna, the fall of which would have left open central Europe. Their advance in the west had been stopped. To the east, the Ottomans neutralized Persia and proceeded to conquer most of what we now know as the Middle East. This included Egypt and the western littoral of the Arabian peninsula, as well as Mecca and Medina, the two holiest cities in Islam, thus consolidating the Ottoman claim to be the protector and benefactor of Islam.

The conquest of the Middle East also brought economic gains, namely, control of the important land routes connecting Asia and Europe. Ironically, however, the opening of sea routes between Europe and Asia cut into and eventually eliminated profits from the land routes. In fact, the increasing economic, political, and military strength of European states prevented further Ottoman development. No longer able to expand, and with the profits from the land routes dwindling, the Ottoman government was forced to rely solely on internal sources of revenue, such as agriculture. At home, peasants resented the Ottoman tax demands and political control. They often fled or formed rebel bands that created streams of lawlessness. These conflicts were compounded by the constant problems generated by the frequent changes of Ottoman rulers and their occasional incompetence.

Nineteenth and Twentieth Centuries

In the nineteenth century, the weakened Ottoman Empire increasingly came under attack from Russia and Austria, both of which vied for control over the former Ottoman territories. As the century proceeded, the Ottoman decline accelerated, notwithstanding internal attempts at reform and the efforts of different European countries, especially Britain, to prevent a total collapse. The British saw the Ottoman Empire as a critical counterweight to Russian expansion. The increasingly obvious weakness of the empire only encouraged external intervention on the part of European powers anxious for some of the spoils left by the crumbling Ottoman authority. Yet because each of the European great powers had interests to protect in Ottoman-controlled areas, all sought to ensure that none would gain the upper hand. They thus tended to counterbalance each other, and all the while the "sick man of Europe" gradually continued to deteriorate.

In 1829 Russia defeated the Ottomans and received parts of what is today Romania. A rebellion broke out in Serbia in 1804, and it gained autonomy in 1830 and independence in 1878. The French invasion of Egypt of 1789–1801 by Napoleon undermined Ottoman control there. The Greeks rebelled in 1821, and when the combined forces of Russia, France, and Britain defeated the Ottoman attempt to subdue Greece, Greek independence, achieved in 1830, was a foregone conclusion.

Although the Ottoman Empire progressively sought to adopt Western military technologies, its fate was no longer in its own hands. It had fallen too far behind, and the social, educational, and technical obstructions to modernization were too difficult to overcome. The intensification of nationalism in the Balkans naturally led to rebellions, which the Ottomans attempted to repress violently. Russia, which claimed to be the protector of fellow Slavs, responded with force in 1877, only to be restrained by other great powers. In the four decades before World War I, the Ottomans gradually lost control of the area to either Austria and Russia or to newly independent states.

As we saw in Chapter 3, the resulting chaos eventually created the spark that triggered World War I. In that war, the Ottoman Empire joined on the side of Germany and Austria-Hungary, in part because of the influence of German military advisors on the Ottoman army, in part because of the favorable impression the early German successes made, and in part in the hope that revenge could be exacted on Russia for many past defeats. By joining what was to be the losing side, the Ottoman Empire signed its death warrant; at the end of the war it was stripped of its Middle Eastern territories.[17] In 1923 Turkey was declared a republic, and in 1924 the caliphate was abolished and all members of the Ottoman dynasty were expelled.

Although the Ottoman Empire, like its Austro-Hungarian counterpart, dissolved in World War I, its legacy continues to be felt. The territorial claims of successor states remain a bone of contention. Many Arab–Israeli disputes (see Chapter 6) are in part conflicts over the rights to former Ottoman lands. Moreover, Iraq's long-standing claim that Kuwait was part of Iraq when Iraq was in the Ottoman Empire is part of the background to its invasion and occupation of Kuwait in 1990 and 1991. (Because Iraq itself had no independent existence prior to 1914, this claim is difficult to justify as well as historically inaccurate in that Kuwait was declared autonomous by the Ottoman sultan in the 1890s.) Similarly, the intermingling of Muslims, Serbs, Croats, and other ethnic groups forms the backdrop of the breakup of Yugoslavia and the subsequent fighting that wracked the Balkans in the early 1990s.

Too Little, Too Late: German and Japanese Empires

Not every country that pursued imperialism succeeded as well as those discussed in the previous sections. Some empires, such as the Chinese, were simply too stagnant to compete with European imperialism and even struggled just to maintain their independence. Others, such as Austria-Hungary and Italy, were too weak and internally divided to extend their domain overseas with any lasting conviction. Two additional countries attempted to create empires and deserve attention, not because they were very successful in the long term but also because their aspirations and failures had global implications. Those countries are Germany and Japan.

The bids by Berlin and Tokyo for empire produced numerous bloody wars between 1860 and 1945. In terms of territory actually ruled, neither the Germans nor the Japanese were effective in creating permanent structures, largely because of their defeat by other powers. At the end of the nineteenth century, Berlin was able to secure only a few areas of Africa (present-day Togo; Cameroon; Tanzania, including Zanzibar; and Namibia) and a few islands in the South Pacific. The Japanese conquered Taiwan in 1895 and annexed Korea in 1910. However, for both countries, attempts to seize much larger areas provoked immense opposition, particularly from Britain and the United States. These free-trade democracies opposed both Germany and Japan in part because they both were protectionist and authoritarian. Moreover, by the end of the nineteenth century, new colonies would have to be established only by subjugation of previously independent territory or by acquisition of territory previously held by another great power. There were no new, easily gained "open spaces" like those other Europeans had found in Africa in the late nineteenth century. Indeed, after World War I, Germany was stripped of its overseas colonies, which became League of Nations' mandates but were administered by Britain and France. German bitterness over the loss of these territories helped to undermine support for the ill-fated Weimar Republic. In the 1930s the Japanese bid for empire started in China and eventually resulted in war with the United States, which Japan decisively lost (see Chapter 3).

Decline of Imperialism

As the preceding sections describe, the empires expanded prodigiously in the eighteenth and nineteenth centuries. The conflicts among them in the first half of the twentieth century, however, undermined their respective holds over their colonies. Under costly, fragmentary pressure from the peoples subjected to their rule, unable to bear the costs of long-distance administration, and facing competition from each of the other imperial powers, the empires—with the exception of the United States and the Soviet Union—were unable to survive the two world wars of the twentieth century.

The Ottoman Empire fell first, during World War I. In the aftermath of World War II, local peoples were emboldened to seek independence from the economically strapped imperial powers, most of which eventually concluded that the territories were not worth fighting for at the military, political, and economic costs they would take to maintain. Over the course of the 1950s and 1960s the last remnants of the European empires gained independence, and new sovereign states arose throughout Asia and Africa.

Ultimately, history imposed a harsh irony on the imperial powers. From Vietnam to Algeria to India to Palestine to Nicaragua to Kenya, European ideas of nationalism and political sovereignty served to undermine the colonial powers' legitimacy. The age of empire is over. Today, few countries even acknowledge overseas territories as being part of an empire. France calls its South Pacific islands, such as Tahiti, "overseas departments" of the republic of France; Britain no longer has an empire but rather a Commonwealth of Nations; and the United States has "territories" such as Guam and the Virgin Islands, but meticulously avoids any reference to "empire." Empire has become politically incorrect, as the subjugation of foreign lands is no longer justifiable in terms of "civilizing missions" or "white man's burdens."

The empires might have fallen, but their impact is evident on the map: New borders were drawn, new countries were created, peoples were brought together, and others were separated by often arbitrary lines of control. They profoundly altered the economic, political, and social organization of the peoples of the Americas, Africa, Asia, and the Pacific. Moreover, although the empires had lost their political hegemony, they had in large part maintained their economic control over foreign resources, their hold over new countries' mines, forests, fields, and wells often reinforced by advantageous relationships with brand new—and often very corrupt—national governments.

Imperialism also created global links that would otherwise have hardly been possible and established the basis for ethnic fragmentation in many former colonies. In many ways the impact of empire was more important on the colonies than the metropole, and this is where we now turn our attention, beginning with the changes wrought on the societies subject to varying degrees of colonial domination.

Social Impact of Imperialism

Today virtually all countries that comprise the developing world are direct descendants of European empires and colonialism. There were two forms of colonialism that most significantly affected the social organization of the colony: **settler colonialism,** where immigrants seized land from the indigenous population and became the dominant population, and **elite colonialism,** where the indigenous rulers were replaced by a European political and economic elite but the native population remained essentially in place and thus much of the culture remained intact.

Probably the most important factor determining whether a territory would be subjected to settler or elite colonialism was geography—more specifically, climate. Settler colonies tended to be located in regions with a temperate climate, such as North America, the southern cone of Latin America (Argentina), and Australia and New Zealand. Because western Europe has a temperate climate, this offered European settlers the least difficult environmental transition in a process that was otherwise very hazardous. By contrast, tropical colonies were far less hospitable for European settlers because of endemic diseases, particularly malaria and yellow fever, against which most Europeans had very little

▪ **Settler colonialism** Immigrants seize land from the indigenous population and become the dominant population.

▪ **Elite colonialism** Indigenous rulers are replaced by a European political and economic elite but the native population remains essentially in place; much of the culture thus remains intact.

immunity. Therefore, virtually all large-scale European settlement in tropical areas took place in highland regions (such as the Andes and central Mexico) where tropical pests and ailments were less numerous. As a result, most tropical colonies were characterized by elite colonialism, where Europeans ruled (often ruthlessly) but did not oust the native population. A brief review of the European impact on the Americas, Asia, Africa, and the Pacific shows how the two types of colonialism led to different social consequences.

North America

European conquest of North America is one of the best cases of settler colonialism. Starting in the early seventeenth century on the Atlantic seacoast, settlers, often fleeing religious persecution in Europe, quickly overwhelmed the native population and in essence transplanted their cultural traditions onto North American soil. Typically, the new European settlers established their own family farms, something that was almost impossible to do in most areas of northwest Europe, where the landed aristocracy dominated politics and monopolized control of land. These settlements initiated a centuries-long process of driving Native Americans into smaller and smaller enclaves while replacing them with mostly European immigrants.

The Caribbean

The Caribbean region also experienced large-scale settler colonialism, but most "settlers" were Africans imported as slaves to work on sugar plantations. The indigenous peoples often fell victim to European diseases (especially smallpox and various venereal diseases) and escaped from servile labor on tropical plantations. Because Europeans could not survive tropical diseases, there was an acute labor shortage. The colonial powers needed a labor force for plantation agriculture, and they found it in Africa. On the western coast of Africa, a multitude of mutually hostile ethnic groups often battled with one another, abducting and selling the defeated or defenseless into slavery as the booty of war. These unfortunates were then transported as slave labor to European colonies in the New World. The net result for most Caribbean countries was a type of settler colonialism where a European elite ruled over African slave laborers. Today most Caribbean countries are either overwhelmingly African in ancestry, as in Jamaica and Haiti, or heavily mulatto (mixed African-European ancestry), as in Cuba.

Latin America

In the early sixteenth century, Spanish conquistadors toppled the despotic Aztec and Inca Empires and proceeded to establish an equally tyrannical system of *haciendas,* where natives were turned into servile laborers and forced to convert

PHOTO 5.3   Sugar plantations in Brazil and the Caribbean operated only with the use of slave labor.

to Catholicism and to adopt the Spanish language. Yet relatively few Spaniards and even fewer Spanish women emigrated to Spain's vast empire in the New World. Instead, many Spanish colonialists took indigenous wives and concubines, resulting in a three-tiered social structure: (1) a small white political and economic elite; (2) a significant population of *mestizos* (mixed European–Native American ancestry), who played an intermediate role in towns and villages; and (3) a countryside of indigenous workers and peasants.

Thus, Latin America experienced a hybrid mixture of settler and elite colonialism. In some colonies, such as Guatemala, Peru, Ecuador, and Bolivia, Native American ethnic groups survived Spanish forced-assimilation attempts. In other colonies, such as Mexico, Colombia, and Venezuela, the Spanish language replaced native languages, even though a large mestizo population ensured the perpetuation of cultural symbols and practices predating the arrival of Columbus. Yet in the most temperate of Spanish colonies, Argentina, European settlers pushed the natives to the social, economic, political, and geographic fringes of the country.

Africa

Most of Africa was spared European colonization until the late nineteenth century, when medicines for such diseases as malaria and yellow fever permitted Europeans to survive in the tropical parts of the continent for extended lengths of time. Virtually all of European imperialism in Africa was elite colonialism; examples include Nigeria, Ghana, Senegal, Cameroon, Uganda, and Tanzania. Although there was some missionary activity that did convert some Africans to Christianity, European colonialism did not result in the wholesale destruction of native cultures or languages. For many Africans who lived far from cities or trade routes, European colonialism only marginally affected their daily existence.

There were, however, a few African colonies that did experience some settler colonialism, most notably South Africa, Kenya, Rhodesia (now Zimbabwe), Angola, and Algeria. In the latter four cases, European settlers in the late nineteenth and early twentieth centuries confiscated some of the best agricultural land in the territories but did not achieve a large enough population base to sustain their political and economic supremacy once Africans began to mobilize politically after World War II. After bitter anticolonial struggles, the European settlers in Algeria, Kenya, Angola, and Rhodesia surrendered political power to Africans during the 1960s and 1970s and in many cases emigrated elsewhere.

In South Africa, however, European settlers became far more deeply entrenched. Cape Town was established by the Dutch as a strategic trading port in 1652. At first many Boers took native wives and concubines, as few European women immigrated to the then-distant supply and trading outpost. In 1806 Britain seized the Dutch enclave for its own strategic trading reasons and brought English settlers and political administrators to the colony. After bitter struggles throughout the nineteenth century, including the Great Trek inland by the Boers in the 1830s and the Boer War (1899–1902), the English and Boers agreed to a white dominion government (1910) within the British Empire that attempted to secure white political and economic supremacy. In 1948 the Afrikaner Nationalist Party won an election and soon created a legal system of even more rigid racial hierarchy, eventually known as *apartheid* ("separateness").

For most of the twentieth century, the minority whites ruled over and thus excluded majority black Africans from any meaningful political participation. In South Africa, this hybrid system of elite and settler colonialism persisted even after other African colonies achieved independence in the 1960s. However, by the 1980s, white domination was slowly but surely unraveling as blacks gained in economic power domestically and the white government became ever more isolated internationally. Apartheid began to unravel and difficult steps taken by the principal white and black organizations to create a new political system that can accommodate the very diverse mix of ethnicities, languages, and cultures. A major step along this path occurred when Nelson Mandela took office as the first black president in May 1994. Despite these positive steps, many South Africans

PHOTO 5.4   Nelson Mandela casts his vote in the first democratic election in South Africa.

continue to live in poverty and the country suffers other social woes (including the AIDS pandemic; see Chapter 11), many of which can be traced back to the era of apartheid.

Asia

The northern half of Asia, Siberia, is one of the most sparsely populated regions in the world. This condition allowed Russian settlers and internal exiles of the tsarist regime to range ever eastward in the seventeenth and eighteenth centuries until reaching the Pacific, creating the world's largest country. Siberia thus experienced settler colonialism; it remains part of Russia, and most inhabitants of that region are ethnically Russian. By contrast, the southern half of Asia is among the most densely populated regions of the planet. Yet nowhere in South Asia did Europeans settle in any significant numbers.

Thus, South Asia is one of the most obvious cases of elite colonialism. The British may have claimed their objective in India was to turn Indians into "brown Englishmen," but the Indian political elite that took control after Britain granted independence in 1948 appealed to India's rural masses using traditional cultural symbols. In fact, the reliance of Europeans on indigenous collaborators in Asia was so great that one might say that Europeans reigned but did not really rule.[18] The French colonization of Indochina was also elite colonialism, but it was a particularly intense form of direct rule. Although very few French actually settled in Indochina and little of the land was alienated, the French sent as many administrators to Indochina as the British sent to India. As a result, the French administration was extremely intrusive into and disruptive of the traditional Vietnamese society.[19] On the other hand, a high level of colonial taxation allowed the French authorities to build a relatively elaborate system of modern transportation and communications. These improvements in time reduced the incidence of famine and disease and thus allowed for high population growth rates. Overall, the French introduced radical changes in the social and economic structure of Vietnamese life but did little to encourage the formation of a native elite with the skills necessary to govern a modern society. Indeed, the contradictions of French rule set the stage for the twentieth century's longest anticolonial revolution.

The Pacific

In the island nations of Indonesia and the Philippines, a European elite ruled from the sixteenth century onward, concentrating on directing the export of tropical spices, but the tropical climate never attracted significant numbers of permanent European settlers. In contrast, British colonialism in Australia led to the near genocide of the Aborigines by British settlers. On the island of Tasmania, south of Australia, Europeans actually hunted the Aborigines virtually into extinction. Similarly, on the mainland, Aborigines survived the European onslaught only in the wilds of the Australian outback. Today Australia is overwhelmingly white in ancestry and thus is one of the most extreme cases of settler colonialism. The Aborigines now constitute only 1 percent of the Australian population. Even though they have received legal and civil rights since the 1960s, their communities remain tiny, poor, and isolated. In New Zealand the British overwhelmed the Maoris, but their culture survived. They still represent 9 percent of the population and play a meaningful role in society.

China and Japan

East Asia was the only part of the world (save for inaccessible mountainous countries like Ethiopia and Nepal) that avoided direct colonial rule by European powers. By the nineteenth century, however, after sustained attempts to remain insulated from Western influence, both China and Japan were in severe economic crises. Meanwhile, European powers were growing ever more powerful and threatening. Large parts of China rebelled against Manchu rule from Beijing in the mid-nineteenth century, including the massive Taiping Rebellion (1850–1864), which left tens of millions dead from war and starvation. In Japan, Western pressure, especially from the United States via Commodore Matthew Perry in 1853 and 1854, ended Japan's isolation, leading to the Meiji Restoration (1868), in which the young emperor Mutsuhito decided that his country should modernize and begin to adopt Western ways. In neither case did European powers ever impose foreign colonial rule, but China was forced to sign "unequal treaties" that gave Western powers control over foreign trade and granted Europeans special legal privileges (for example, areas such as parks reserved for Europeans in Shanghai had signs that read, "No dogs or Chinese allowed").

China was divided into spheres of influence among the great powers in the late nineteenth century only to regain genuine independence in 1949 with the rise of Mao Zedong's communist regime. By contrast, Japan quickly adopted many Western reforms in government, education, industry, and finance, and thus reestablished its political independence by the late nineteenth century.[20] Japanese emulation of the West included turning to imperialism and expansion. Japan annexed Taiwan (1895) and Korea (1910), placing Tokyo on a collision course with the United States.

Two important factors allowed China and Japan to avoid direct colonial rule. First, East Asia is on the other side of the globe from Europe, and the sheer magnitude of the distance served to insulate both countries from European imperialism until the nineteenth century, when ships were invented that depended on steam, not wind, to travel. However, other countries in the region such as Indonesia and the Philippines were colonized earlier, so the second point is particularly significant. Both China and Japan's dense populations and centralized governments made them uniquely capable of resisting and eventually adapting to foreign political pressures without capitulating formal political independence. To summarize, although both China and Japan attempted to isolate themselves from European influences, Japan's isolation was ended by Commodore Perry, and China was coerced into unequal treaties before adapting politically and economically to Western pressures in the late nineteenth and early twentieth centuries.

Economic Consequences of Colonialism

The economic effects of European colonialism are, generally speaking, more uniform than the social repercussions. Colonies, almost by definition, are subordinate economic units to the metropole. Almost invariably, European metropoles initiated economic trading policies that constrained their colonies to be little more than producers of raw materials for export to the mother country and captive markets for manufactured goods from the metropole.

Latin America, Africa, and the Pacific

The North American colonies of Québec and the thirteen English colonies, for example, initially sent furs, timber, fish, and tobacco back to France and Britain, respectively. In fact, a major impetus for the American Revolution stemmed from the restrictions that Britain placed on American exports (they could be transported only on British ships to British ports) that severely limited the colonists' economic options. From American independence through the mid-nineteenth century, the export of cotton from the American South helped to spur Britain's textile industry and at home created a regional economic and political schism that resulted in the American Civil War.

In South America the Spanish plundered and mined large quantities of gold and silver. They also transplanted two high-quality food sources to Europe from the New World: corn and the potato. After independence in the 1810s and 1820s, many South American countries in the nineteenth century exported coffee, grains, copper, and other minerals to Britain.

The major export from Africa in the sixteenth, seventeenth, and eighteenth centuries was coerced labor in the form of slaves. However, Britain abolished most trans-Atlantic slave trade in the 1830s, and by the late nineteenth century, African colonies turned to such raw material exports as cocoa, coffee, palm oil, tea, cotton, ivory, tropical hardwoods, copper, and gold.

In the Pacific, Britain turned Australia and New Zealand into huge sheep and dairy farms in the late nineteenth century, supplying Britain with wool and food. Thus throughout Latin America, Africa, and the Pacific in this period, natural resource-poor Britain traded for raw materials in return for railroads, textiles, capital goods, and foreign investment. This has led some observers to characterize the nineteenth century as *Pax Britannica,* in which Britain created a far-flung informal trading empire based on the import of raw materials and the export of manufactured goods and finance capital.[21]

Asia

Trade among India, China, the Dutch East Indies (now Indonesia), and Europe was actually complicated by the era of European domination. Britain, for one, did not gain control of overseas trade routes primarily to seize natural resources but rather to gain control over Asian trade. In 1840, for example, China attempted to shut off the import of opium because of the social problem of high rates of drug addiction and the gold drain on the faltering Chinese economy. However, the British navy in the Opium War of 1839–1842 forced China to cede Hong Kong and keep China open to opium and other imports. Only in the rubber plantations of Malaya (now Malaysia) did Britain impose an export crop on its Asian colonies. Yet Britain did use its hegemonic position to ensure that British-manufactured goods received de facto preferential treatment in these captive markets. For instance, British textile exports to India undermined India's labor-intensive native weavers in the nineteenth century. The Indian National Congress under Mahatma Gandhi in the first half of the twentieth century used the spinning wheel as a powerful symbol of its opposition to British rule in India.

Economic Consequences: An Assessment

Whatever economic difficulties colonialism may have introduced, there can be no denying that colonialism did create a degree of political and economic predictability that allowed for increased trading opportunities, higher levels of foreign investment, and thus economic growth for the colonies as well as for the metropole. This is particularly true of physical infrastructure. Most of the railroads that now run throughout Asia and Africa were built under European tutelage during the colonial era. European colonialism also created predictable conditions in which ports, electric power plants, roads, schools, hospitals, and water systems could be built. Of course, the principal beneficiaries of such infrastructure improvements during the colonial era were mostly European colonial officials. For instance, railroads in the colonial era were typically segregated by race, with the Europeans riding first class, complete with dining cars, whereas natives had to ride in (or on top of) overcrowded third-class cars.

Colonial rule also significantly increased the building of such "public goods" as roads and extended modern education and health care to areas previously unexposed to the advanced technologies available in Europe. Moreover, the colonial system provided for economic predictability—for instance, by introducing stable currencies, codified laws, and access to the home markets of the metropole. Such stability may seem trivial compared to the excesses of colonialism, but as many developing countries have discovered since independence, economic development is impossible without political stability and economic predictability.[22]

Cultural and Ideological Impact of Colonialism

In the cultural and ideological legacies of European domination, the distinction between settler and elite colonialism again becomes meaningful. Where settler colonialism took root, the transplantation of European political, legal, cultural, and ideological traditions was relatively easy. By contrast, where elite colonialism took root, there were many more difficulties. To explain why, it is necessary to consider several examples of colonialism and their impact on culture and ideology in the former colonies.

Colonialism and Culture

For countries that were settled by European immigrants, their colonial era is typically viewed as a necessary step in the development of the nation, like childhood in the growth of a human being. In the United States, Canada, Australia, and New Zealand (the clearest cases of settler colonialism) the legacy of Anglo-Saxon traditions of rules of law, private property, and individual rights has never been seriously questioned as the basis for a legitimate political order. Most debates in these countries have concerned the pace and scope of the extension of political rights to excluded groups, principally ethnic minorities and women. Moreover, because of the compatibility of political interests with Britain in particular, these countries have maintained relatively high levels of trade and foreign investment with Europe, which in turn has helped to secure long-term economic growth and prosperity. With such significant economic resources available, these countries have achieved a high degree of political cohesion and stability.

Where settler colonialism did not take root, where European administrators governed an indigenous population, postcolonial political cohesion and stability has been much more difficult to achieve, for numerous reasons. One element typical of elite colonialism was the strategy of "divide and conquer," coined by the Romans and perfected by the British. European colonial officials often attempted to accentuate ethnic and cultural differences among their colonial subjects to make rebellion and resistance to colonial rule more difficult to organize and sustain. For example, in India, Britain used Muslim mercenary troops against Hindus and vice versa, thus contributing to the maintenance of indigenous ethnic conflicts that eventually resulted in the bloody partition of the subcontinent at independence in 1947 into India and Pakistan.

In many other places, colonialism similarly contributed to contemporary political fragmentation. In Africa, European colonial officials often established ethnically based police and army forces that had little in common with other ethnic groups in the colony. After independence, these forces, some of which were little more than mafia cliques, frequently staged military coups d'etat, intensifying political instability. In Uganda, for example, the British established a very tall height standard for enlistment into the colonial army that effectively excluded most Ugandans and created an army of uneducated "Nubians" (southern Sudanese) who had precious little in common with other Ugandans. A few years after independence, the army led by "Field Marshall" Idi Amin seized power and ruthlessly pillaged the country. Similar military coups have occurred in other formerly British territories such as Sudan, Nigeria, and Ghana, as well as in the colonies of other Western powers such as the Belgian Congo (now the Democratic Republic of the Congo) and the former French territories of Guinea and the Central African Republic. In these cases, this type of military rule only contributed to economic collapse and social chaos.

Beyond the inheritance of European divide-and-conquer tactics, European colonialism also created countries in Africa and parts of Asia that made little if any political sense. It often threw together peoples that had little in common and divided ethnic groups across borders for no better reason than to satisfy European diplomats quarreling over which European country should control a given port, river, or mountain. Somalis in the Horn of Africa were divided among Italian, British, French, and Ethiopian imperialists and are today still fighting among one another as well as with their neighbors over the definition of Greater Somalia. Elsewhere, Nigeria, Africa's most populous country, has three major and dozens of minor ethnic groups all struggling for their share of political power and economic development. In 1966 the Ibo tribe revolted and tried to create the country of Biafra until it was defeated by the central Nigerian government. Most other African states were afraid to back Biafra—despite the relative legitimacy of its claim for independence and its suffering at the hands of the Nigerian armies— for fear a dangerous precedent would be set for their own countries. Indeed, the first successful secession in Africa occurred only in 1993 with the independence of Eritrea from Ethiopia after a thirty-one-year war. In the Middle East, the Kurds are a stateless and restless minority in Iraq, Iran, Turkey, and Syria.

Clearly, most African and Asian countries have numerous ethnic and religious divisions in their societies. If every African ethnic group had its own country, there would be literally thousands of African countries, so it is impossible in practical terms to make every African country a nation-state. Thus, for many developing countries, the lack of a common culture, language, or religion has meant that there is no consensus on the fundamental political values of the country.[23] This fragmentation in turn has made the governance of these societies problematic. It is often very difficult to secure stability in institutions and policy, and disaffected groups can and do resort to violence in an attempt to redress their grievances and achieve their aims.

Colonialism and Ideology

The ideological impact of colonialism on political ideals has been a double-edged sword. On the one hand, European notions of liberty and democracy were to some degree diffused over the past two centuries. For instance, some former colonial territories have maintained democratic government in the postcolonial era, especially formerly British-ruled countries such as India, Botswana, Malaysia, and Jamaica. Other former British colonies have often vacillated between democracy and dictatorship, such as Nigeria, Zambia, the Sudan, and Pakistan. In general, the longer the British ruled, the greater the likelihood that democracy would be sustained in the postcolonial era. The world's largest democracy is India, and it is inconceivable that contemporary India would be democratic without some two centuries of British colonial rule. In contrast, there are many countries where Britain ruled for a relatively short period (such as Kuwait, Sudan, Uganda, and Malawi) where democracy has not taken root.

Generally speaking, democracy in formerly French colonies such as Vietnam, Cambodia, Syria, Algeria, Madagascar, Guinea, and Gabon has been more difficult to achieve and is often absent. In such cases, democratic characteristics such as a free press, elections, and truly representative legislatures typically were only granted as the last step prior to independence, too little and too late for creating stable democratic rule in the postcolonial era. Thus, dictatorships often prevail in many parts of the contemporary developing world, especially the Middle East, Africa, and Asia. In others, the lasting impact of the communist movement, led by the USSR throughout most of the twentieth century, can be seen today, most notably in Vietnam and North Korea.

Finally, there is one ideological movement that virtually all developing countries have agreed on: anticolonialism. One major legacy of elite colonialism in particular has been to make the postcolonial countries exceptionally resentful of foreign domination. Unlike settler colonies, there is no romanticization of the colonial period. Rather, the former elite colonies often look on colonialism as an era of profound humiliation in their long and proud cultural history; this in turn can create a backlash in the form of rejection of "Western" influence. Many leaders of newly independent countries in the 1950s and 1960s achieved power by being more anticolonial than any other rival political leaders. Gamal Abdel Nasser in Egypt, Patrice Lumumba in the Belgian Congo, Ho Chi Minh in Vietnam, Kwame Nkrumah in Ghana, and Jomo Kenyatta in Kenya all appealed to the masses by denouncing colonialism and Western foreign domination.

This anticolonialism is easily understandable. European colonial rulers often arrogantly denigrated and offended native cultures and beliefs while claiming that European imperialism was the "white man's burden" to spread civilization. Not surprisingly, colonial subjects often protested against and sometimes violently resisted having their cultural traditions insulted and being ruled by foreigners. When colonial subjects began to organize politically, the "masses" almost spontaneously supported anticolonial nationalist movements for political independence. However, the problem with anticolonialism in its postcolonial form of an anti-Western bias is that it often serves to rationalize economic policies that have very high costs. This tends to hinder the accelerated economic development that independence is expected to bring.

Conclusion

We have seen in this chapter how empires served to globalize international relations over the last several centuries and how, in modern history, they also contributed to fragmentation, especially in the developing world. The indignity, cruelty, and brutality inflicted by European imperialism on many people in the developing world is undeniable. At the same time, imperialism integrated Asia, Africa, Latin America, and the Pacific into the world economy in a way that benefited many in developing areas and set the stage for possible further economic and social progress after the achievement of independence. The legacy of imperialism is thus a mixed one. The era of imperialism is past, but its effects on the world economy and global politics remain, as we will see in many of the chapters to follow.

For now we can conclude that it is clear that contemporary world political dynamics are rooted in the expansion and then collapse of multiple empires across oceans, continents, and time. This history of expansion and contraction, with its implications for political, economic, and social structures, set the stage for contemporary globalization and fragmentation. The frustration of Middle Eastern states steeped in memories of the greatness of the Ottoman Empire, the long-standing corruption of many African states left predisposed by European colonial structures to avaricious leadership, and the tendency in many former colonies to turn to military leadership in the face of incompetent civilian control are all consequences of imperialism. So, too, however, are India's strong democracy, the powerful international economy, and the recognition by most people on earth that they are part of a larger, global society with shared interests, needs, and even aspirations.

AT A GLANCE

Levels of Analysis and Paradigms in Review: Examples from Imperialism

	Realism	*Liberalism*	*Constructivism*
Individual	In an effort to increase the reach of Portugal, Prince Henry the Navigator formed a special center to focus the efforts of expert navigators, shipbuilders, and seamen on expanding Portuguese trade and dominion overseas.	Japan's young Emperor Mutsuhito led the Meiji Restoration in 1868, in which he decided that his country should modernize and begin to adopt Western ways. The Meiji Restoration was the catalyst for industrialization and helped create Japan as a military power by the twentieth century.	Christopher Columbus and other explorers operated on the assumption that they were superior to native peoples; this allowed them to behave in ways that today would be perceived as unconscionable.
Domestic	The competition for trade routes dominated by the Portuguese, Dutch, and British over the centuries benefited the local leaders as well. They would use the European supply of weapons and other goods to strengthen their positions relative to regional opponents.	Apartheid began to unravel in the 1980s, and difficult steps have been taken by both white and black organizations in the country to create a new political system that can accommodate the very diverse mix of ethnicities, languages, and cultures in South Africa.	Governments that were kept in place by social, cultural, and religious beliefs in God's chosen people (as most royalty were believed to be) were unsurprisingly quick to transpose such beliefs onto their interactions with foreign peoples, over whom they naturally considered themselves to have God-given dominion; that the imperial powers sent missionaries and sought to spread their culture and religions to local peoples is therefore entirely consistent with their understandings of their role, obligations, and rights.

	Realism	Liberalism	Constructivism
Systemic	One of the most fundamental distinctions between empires was that some emphasized territorial conquest (such as the Spanish and Russians, who sought conquest of interior regions where natural resources could be exploited and immigrants settled), whereas others concentrated on control of trade routes (such as the Dutch and Portuguese, who were typically interested in strategic ports). Both strategies could be used to increase the power of the metropole.	Spain and Portugal entered into the Treaty of Tordesillas in 1494 in an effort to avoid conflict over their competing expansion. That treaty purported to divide up the world with an imaginary line that ran north and south approximately 300 miles west of the Azores Islands. Spain was granted possession of all lands to the west of this line, Portugal the lands to the east.	Seeing the world as a zero-sum competition over limited resources led imperial powers to compete viciously for control of the seas and newly discovered territories, which they quickly claimed as their own and over which they felt free—entitled—to impose complete control in whatever ways they wished as they extracted resources, subjugated (or ignored) local peoples, and otherwise enriched themselves and enhanced their own power. Today, states' influence abroad is much less direct and often more focused on reciprocal gains. Also, states today decline to refer to their possessions abroad as colonies, and instead call them overseas departments or territories.

Discussion and Review Questions

1. Discuss the "What Would You Do?" scenario in this chapter. Discuss the costs you would be willing to incur as the leader of a colonial power to keep control of colonial possessions.
2. Discuss the life of British citizens who would have chosen to go to India under the auspices of the East India Company. Then discuss the lives of the native Indians living under the control of the British.
3. Discuss how colonies earned their independence. Identify former colonies, and discuss the path they took to independence.
4. Identify cultural, economic, and social aspects of current societies derived from colonialism.
5. Was colonialism a positive or negative phenomenon? Provide examples of the pros and cons of colonialism.

Key Terms

Elite colonialism 186
Imperialism 157

Metropole 159
Settler colonialism 186

Treaty of Tordesillas 161

CHAPTER 6

Globalization and Fragmentation in a New World Order: 1991 to the Present

When the Cold War abruptly ended, completely surprising spies, analysts, policymakers, and the world in general, no one knew what to expect. It was a "new era" with all kinds of possibilities. U.S. President George H. W. Bush termed it a "New World Order," UN Secretary-General Boutros Boutros Ghali foresaw a world in which countries would rally in support of humanitarian values and peace, U.S. citizens hopefully anticipated a peace dividend and a scaling back of military capacity, and there was a sense, worldwide, of possibilities and new options. What actually happened in the 1990s, however, was as surprising as the end of the Cold War itself and far more disturbing. In this chapter, we examine this complex period and how it contributed to today's political, economic, security, and environmental concerns. Many of the events that transpired in the post–Cold War period have their roots in the issues discussed in the previous historical chapters, and many are ongoing today or impact current events. The chapter thus serves as a bridge from the theory and history of the book's first half to the second half's emphasis on contemporary events and issues.

In the 1990s, the international system was characterized by a paradox. On one hand, the end of the Cold War laid to rest the specter of nuclear holocaust that haunted relations between the superpowers. On the other hand, regional and ethnic conflicts, the violent collapse of governments, and threats of nuclear proliferation and terrorists armed with weapons of mass destruction led many to believe that the world was more dangerous than ever. Overall, the historic processes of globalization and fragmentation, and cooperation and conflict, all seemed to be running faster than ever, on parallel tracks to an unknown destination.

Globalization and Fragmentation

The end of the Cold War came as a great shock to most policymakers, academics, and citizens around the globe. Most believed that the struggle between the United States and the Soviet Union for global domination was intractable and that it would last for the foreseeable future. Many others feared it would end in war, a nuclear holocaust that would end civilization as we knew it. The changes underway in the Soviet Union prior to 1989 were viewed as simply another alteration along the course of more than forty years of post–World War II relations between the two superpowers (and actually viewed as tricks by those highly suspicious of the Soviets). No one anticipated (most certainly not Gorbachev) that these changes would end not only the Cold War but also the existence of the Soviet Union (see Chapter 4).

Despite the surprise (or perhaps in part because of it), optimism was the prevailing sentiment beginning in 1989 (with the freeing of the Soviet satellite states) and continuing into the early 1990s. Globalization and cooperation were evident in NATO's expansion, in the signing of NAFTA and the EU's monetary union, and in the UN's efforts to become an effective force for peace and stability. The optimism of this period is perhaps best illustrated by the 1989 work of social scientist Francis Fukuyama, **"The End of History."** Fukuyama's work is idealistic and upbeat (albeit over the very long term). His central point is that the end of history is "the universalization of Western liberal democracy as the final form of human government." In other words, Fukuyama sees humankind in the Hegelian sense, evolving politically and socially not interminably, but with an end point in sight. That end point is the kind of democratic, liberal, capitalist system and society that the western European powers are closest to achieving. For Fukuyama, the Western liberal democracies are the first evidence that Hegel was right when he claimed in 1806 that humankind had reached the end of history, at least ideologically.[1]

▪ **End of History**
A theory that posits that the apex of human political and social development is reached by successfully democratizing, guaranteeing human rights, achieving stability, and implementing economic liberalization.

Western democracies' existence is not Fukuyama's only evidence of how the end of history will look. He posits that economic liberalization worldwide; the failures of monarchy, fascism, and then communism; and the spread of Western ideals and culture are other important indicators. He argues that despite the rise of various ideologies, there is no system other than liberal democracy that will give people what they want: security and recognition. Because of that, even if we have not reached it, we can see how it will all end.

Many assumed that the terrorist attacks of September 11 debunked Fukuyama's theory, but Fukuyama leaves plenty of room for the kind of attack Al Qaeda made on the United States. In fact, he leaves room for wars, continued slavery in Africa, and authoritarianism in North Korea and Burma (Myanmar). What he suggests is that most countries are still mired in history, far from reaching the end, with serious obstacles in their way. Following 9/11, Fukuyama responded to critics by restating his point: The end of history is a long way off, though there are adequate indicators to tell what it will look like. In the meantime, there are cultures and civilizations that may not even know that such a democracy is in their future. Fukuyama also states that Islam is a particularly hard case because, more than any other civilization or culture, it resists modernization. Nonetheless, Fukuyama believes that liberalism will prevail even in the Muslim world and that this is the case because no other ideology, including Islam, could ultimately dominate world politics.

Fukuyama eventually came to the conclusion that his theory was incomplete, but not for the reasons stated by his critics. Fukuyama became concerned by humankind's control of its own evolution. Scientific and technological advances were allowing humans to exercise unnatural control over evolution that could have profound and devastating effects on liberal democracy.[2] Regardless, his arguments concerning liberal democracy being the final form of human government illustrate the optimistic mood of the post–Cold War world.

Despite the prevalence of this rosy view, globalization walked hand in hand with fragmentation following the end of the Cold War: The North American Free Trade Agreement (NAFTA) was signed, in part, as a regional response to the threat posed by the EU's economic successes, and NATO expanded as a response to the Soviet Union's collapse (and caused conflict in the new relationship between the United States and Russia) and the violent breakup of Yugoslavia. Likewise, the global coalition that came together to coordinate a worldwide war against terrorism in late 2001 was a response to the terrorist attacks in New York and Washington, DC, the express purpose of which was to drive the U.S. military, and American economic and cultural influence, out of the Middle East.

These events seemed to confirm the most prominent view arising from the end of the Cold War from the fragmentationist camp: that of Samuel P. Huntington. Huntington's premise in his thought-provoking yet highly controversial 1993 *Foreign Affairs* article (which later became a book) **"The Clash of Civilizations?"** is that future conflict will not be economic or ideological, but cultural. Conflict between civilizations will increase precisely because of globalization. As globalization shrinks the world, bringing disparate people ever more into contact, people will increasingly identify themselves and each other by civilization, or culture, a much less mutable attribute than class (someone rich can become poor, and vice versa) and political association (a labor party affiliate can switch to the opposition). Someone who is Japanese cannot become Chinese; someone who is Russian cannot become an Azeri; someone with a strong affiliation to Judaism will not likely shift to Islam or identify with Hindus.

■ **Clash of Civilizations**
A theory that suggests that the future of international politics will be characterized not by the state-against-state or ideological conflicts of the past but, rather, by clashes of civilizations as they seek to defend their traditions, beliefs, territory, and general interests against competing cultures.

Although one can take issue with Huntington's assumptions about cultural immutability (which appears to decline with development), his point remains compelling that some historically antagonistic cultures remain at odds and are unlikely to fuse in the global melting pot. Although it would be nice if we could all just get along, people from vastly different cultures can still be motivated by completely opposing worldviews, ethical beliefs, and behavioral standards. Equalizing economic opportunities and greater communication and exposure to each other's cultures might reduce some of the differences, but some are unlikely to be overcome in the short term and will continue to lead to conflict and even war (the Hutus versus the Tutsis, the Kurds versus the Turks, the Palestinians versus the Israelis, French Canadians versus British Canadians, Serbs versus Kosovars, and so forth).

Huntington's conclusions also build on Kishore Mahbubani's phrase the "West versus the rest," describing the developing world's frustration and anger over Western paternalism and opportunism (the "West" being, primarily, the most advanced industrialized states). In neorealist terms (as discussed in Chapter 2), in the face of Western dominance, developing states' governments try to balance the great powers, uniting for more leverage (as OPEC did successfully in the 1970s), or they will bandwagon, using existing regimes and institutions to express their concerns or priorities. Developing states' populations might try to take advantage of globalization by holding demonstrations and rallies to garner worldwide public attention for their causes. The harsh reality, however, is that outside of the industrialized states lies little effective economic, political, or military power, creating the conditions under which frustrated states or disaffected individuals or groups can turn to asymmetric threats (like nuclear threats or terrorism). Although terrorism like the September 11, 2001, attack on U.S. targets is perhaps the most dramatic form of response, it is nonetheless the least common expression of the anger percolating in developing countries. Nonetheless, smaller scale terrorist attacks do take place worldwide relatively frequently. Ultimately, the disparity in power between "the West and the rest" causes a fundamental disconnect between Western and non-Western perceptions of rightful authority and the state of the world.

The most striking cultural divide in this view, one that several analysts have predicted will lead to continued conflict, is the gulf between Western culture and Islamic civilization.[3] Based on a strictly defined and strongly held set of religious and cultural principles, Islamic civilization often perceives the secularism and materialism of Western culture as a serious threat. In many Islamic states, Muslim clerics, who often play key political as well as religious roles, fear that Islamic social, cultural, and spiritual values are under constant attack from the West and conclude that democracy and capitalism must be resisted lest they undermine the Islamic foundations of society. Islamists are determined to prevent cultural change even at the cost of economic and political conflict with the secular West. This viewpoint, and consequently the potential for conflict with neighboring cultures, is strongest in states with avowedly Islamic governments, such as Iran, Saudi Arabia, and Sudan, and is widely held among Islamic insurgent or opposition groups in Algeria, Egypt, Afghanistan, the Philippines, and elsewhere in the Middle East, Africa, and Central Asia.

Civilizations have always been threatened by competition from other stronger, more dynamic, cultures. Once-great civilizations, such as the Egyptian, Classical Greek, and Arab societies, collapsed because they could not stand up to the economic, political, and ideological force of aggressive civilizations, such as the Roman or Ottoman empires, which in turn were destroyed or assimilated by other rising cultures. In today's globalized world, made small by technology, peoples can feel even more immediately and constantly threatened by other civilizations. Although liberals will argue that all civilizations—indeed, all people—share certain basic values on which mutually beneficial compromises can be built, and constructivists will argue that peoples can create less competitive identities over time through positive reinforcement of cooperative and trusting relations, realists tend to believe simply that conflict, whether military, economic, or cultural, is inevitable in an anarchic international system.

Globalization and fragmentation, as well as continued conflict and cooperation, dominate the post–Cold War landscape. The following sections will show how these competing trends have manifested themselves in relations between not only states but also nonstate actors. Chapter 3 highlighted the creation of the Westphalian state system and the dominance of sovereign states. Between 1991 and the present, some argue that the rise of numerous nonstate actors, such as **multinational corporations (MNCs)** and terrorist groups, has begun to erode state sovereignty and its relative influence in the international system.

A New World Order?

As mentioned earlier, in 1991 U.S. President George H. W. Bush spoke of a "new world order" that would replace the superpower rivalry of the Cold War with a system wherein states would cooperate against aggression and other common threats within the framework of international law. The post–Cold War world would therefore be less confrontational and more institutionalized. The end of the Cold War meant the end of the bipolar U.S.–Soviet military rivalry and its replacement by a system in which the United States was unchallenged in military capability. Although Russia retained a large stockpile of nuclear weapons; China, Britain, and France still possessed smaller nuclear arsenals; and many states maintained significant military forces in their respective regions, the United States became the only country with the ability to intervene in any conflict anywhere in the world. Although the size of its military establishment was reduced from the levels built up during the Cold War, the United States remained committed to maintaining the ground, naval, and air forces that would be needed should war again break out in Europe, the Middle East, or East Asia, together with the means to move and supply them, overseas bases to support them, and space-based reconnaissance systems to locate threats and guide weapons to their

▪ **Multinational corporation (MNC)** A large corporation with branches in many countries, headquarters in the developed world, and huge investments throughout the world. Examples include General Motors, PepsiCo, Sony, and Shell Oil.

targets. At the same time, the United States continued its military research and development efforts to keep its technological edge over potential challengers for as long as possible.

Some states, worried by well-armed regional rivals, welcomed this situation and sought new or continued alliances with the United States. Larger, ambitious regional powers such as Russia, China, and India, on the other hand, greeted the prospect of U.S. security leadership with trepidation or reserved judgment. Indeed, between 1995 and 2002, as Poland, Hungary, and the Czech Republic sought to join the NATO alliance (Bulgaria, Estonia, Latvia, Lithuania, Romania, Slovakia, and Slovenia joined in 2004), Russia viewed the expansion of NATO as a threat and an attempt to isolate Russia from Europe. Russian leadership, therefore, considered looking eastward, especially to China, for new security partners. Concurrent U.S. and international efforts to restrict the proliferation of nuclear weapons and ballistic missiles similarly produced negative reactions from India, Iran, and other regional powers. When the United States made it clear that it was willing to act unilaterally in Iraq in 2003, many states, particularly Russia, China, France, and Germany, balked at the prospect and sought to bring the United States back within the constraints imposed by the UN Security Council and other international organizations.

What follows in this chapter is a series of events in the post–Cold War world that highlight the concurrent processes of globalization and fragmentation, and cooperation and conflict. For example, the European Union, the genesis for which began much earlier than the post–Cold War period, is provided as an example of cooperation, while the discussion of the conflict between the Israelis and Palestinians is provided as evidence of fragmentation and conflict. As previously mentioned, these processes take place simultaneously—at one point bringing us together and another tearing us apart. It is important also to remember as you read through the description of these events that many of them can be traced back to the Cold War, the World Wars, and even centuries earlier. Peoples and states have long memories, and while enemies do often become friends and vice versa, history often looms large over relations between states.

War in the Gulf

The first global crisis after the Cold War ended came in the volatile and oil-rich Persian Gulf. The crisis had its roots in both the bipolarity of the Cold War and the long-standing regional rivalries of the Middle East. In 1980, Iraq, under the leadership of Saddam Hussein, invaded Iran. The attack was motivated in part to forestall the threat of the Islamic revolution that began in Iran in 1979 from spreading to its neighbors and in part to gain revenge for previous Iranian territorial gains. Iran put up a surprisingly stiff fight, not only halting the Iraqi attack but also going on the offensive. Fearing that Iraq might lose the war and that Iran might subsequently come to dominate the Persian Gulf, the wealthy oil-producing Arab states provided Baghdad with substantial economic aid. As the war bogged down into an eight-year struggle of attrition, the United States began to back Iraq, although it simultaneously secretly attempted to trade arms to Tehran in hopes of securing the release of American hostages (in what became known as Iran-Contra). By 1988 both sides were exhausted and agreed to a cease-fire, which was viewed as a victory for Iraq at the time.

Peace, however, proved very short-lived. After the Iran–Iraq War, the Gulf Arab states put pressure on Iraq to repay its debts. Faced with economic problems and possessing a huge military machine, Iraq invaded Kuwait in 1990, and in so doing threatened to gain a dominant position in the Persian Gulf (Saddam Hussein invaded Kuwait in part because he wanted control of the entire Ramallah oil fields and also because Iraq had always claimed Kuwait as part of its own country). This act of naked aggression, the first attempt by one Arab state to conquer another in the twentieth century, shocked the world. In an equally unprecedented move, the United States, diplomatically supported by the Soviet Union, spearheaded the formation of an international coalition (of thirty-four nations) under UN auspices to defend Saudi Arabia and oppose Iraq's invasion. The following year, after Iraq refused to implement UN Security Council resolutions demanding withdrawal, the coalition launched an offensive to evict Iraqi forces from Kuwait. The American-led coalition, equipped with the latest in military technology, including precision-guided weapons, won a stunning victory, ending the ground phase of its campaign after only four days of fighting. Coalition forces drove Iraqi forces from Kuwait and severely damaged Iraq's military capabilities and economic infrastructure. They halted their offensive short of Baghdad, however, and without deposing Saddam Hussein.

The terms of the cease-fire included requirements that Iraq disassemble its fairly advanced program to develop nuclear weapons and dispose of its large quantities of chemical and biological weapons. To verify its compliance, the UN established an inspections regime through the International Atomic Energy Agency (IAEA). At first, Iraq appeared to cooperate with the IAEA inspections and with the UN Special Commission (UNSCOM) that was in the country looking for chemical and biological weapons and ballistic missiles. Controversy dominated the landscape, however, throughout the 1990s as tension grew concerning the perception that Hussein was violating the terms of the agreement and moving forward with a WMD program. Once again, the seeds of future conflict were planted.

The European Union

Meanwhile, in Europe, which had been at the center of global conflict for more than 400 years, dramatic changes were taking place that highlight a spirit of cooperation. Freed from the political constraints and military competition of the Cold War, the nations of the European Community (Belgium, Denmark, France, Germany, Greece, Ireland, Italy, Luxembourg, the Netherlands, Portugal, Spain, and the United Kingdom) moved to form an economic and political union by removing trade barriers and building institutions to standardize policy (the European Community was formed during the Cold War and was the predecessor of the European Union). In 1993, the European Community became the European Union (EU), with a single market for capital, goods, services, and labor; a European Parliament with powers to pass legislation binding on all members; a European Commission to serve as an executive body; and a Court of Justice to adjudicate Union law. Austria, Finland, and Sweden joined the EU in 1995 and other countries, including the former Warsaw Pact states and Turkey, applied for admission. In 2002, a single currency, the euro, became legal tender in most member states, and in early 2003 the EU accepted ten more states (Cyprus, the Czech Republic, Estonia, Hungary, Latvia, Lithuania, Malta, Poland, Slovakia, and Slovenia) for membership. Union enthusiasts began drawing up plans for common foreign and defense policies, and many believed that the EU would soon rival the United States as a player in world politics.

The road to union was far from smooth, however. Critics charged that the EU suffered from a "democratic deficit" as laws and regulations affecting daily life were passed without giving enough consideration to the concerns of individual countries, provinces, or local communities. Popular votes in several countries delayed entry into the EU or rejected some parts of it, particularly the adoption of a common currency (Great Britain has refused to call a referendum on the euro). In 2005, France and the Netherlands rejected the EU's proposed constitution, which requires unanimous approval. Nevertheless, by the start of the

PHOTO 6.1   The European Parliament.

twenty-first century the EU provided the political and economic framework for an unprecedented era of peace and prosperity for its members, and a new chapter in European history.

U.S. Economic Hegemony Endures

During the same period, the U.S. role shifted from that of a traditional hegemon (assuming unilateral responsibility for the stability of the international financial system) to steward of an increasingly integrated international economic system. Its economic hegemony in the 1990s derived from its dominance in global trade and finance, from the size of its markets, and from the role of the dollar as a reserve currency and unit of international exchange.[4] The principal U.S. role in the IMF, the World Bank, the Group of 8 (G-8), and other international financial institutions also promoted its continued hegemony.

Contributing to U.S. dominance in the immediate aftermath of the Cold War, however, were other countries' misfortunes and obstacles to growth. Germany and Japan, rapidly rising economic powers in the 1980s, each experienced social, political, and economic setbacks that undermined their competitiveness. The other two rising economic powers, China and Russia, have serious structural weaknesses in their economies to overcome as they transition from communist systems to capitalist ones. China's economy is developing rapidly, but it is based on labor rather than technology and is handicapped by logistics, corruption, and the domestic economic system. Russia, too, has been hard hit by corruption, not to mention the long-term stultifying effects of Soviet policies. Although African nations finally experienced some impressive growth in the 1980s, they since have seen their economies destroyed by AIDS and loan interest payments. As will be discussed in Chapter 9, the Southeast Asian "Tigers" (Hong Kong, Singapore, South Korea, and Taiwan) have each experienced financial crises due to international currency speculation and steadily higher interest on accrued debts. The promising economies in Latin America, from Mexico to Chile to Venezuela, have also floundered, victims of the same dynamics that devastated Southeast Asian economies. Even the powerful U.S. economy is tenuous, based as it is on an enormous trade deficit. Nonetheless, bleak as this all may sound, the global economy has rebounded from the crises of the 1990s, new international regimes and institutions are in place to protect stability, and growth has touched every region.

The very globalization that has benefited the United States also threatens it, however. The country cannot hope to benefit long term from the turmoil surrounding it. Today it is tied deeply into the very international financial institutions and regional economic blocs that it helped to develop. It is dependent on other states' financial decisions for its own economic security. For example, Japan, China, and the United Kingdom now own billions of dollars in U.S. securities, a sign that the United States is dependent on foreign investors to maintain a certain standard of living.[5] Furthermore, it requires other states and regions to maintain solvency if its exports are to find lucrative markets. The situation is not unlike that in the late 1960s, when it seemed that the system the United States itself had promoted had begun to work against its interests. The benefits of interdependence are obvious, but the pitfalls cannot be overlooked. If markets collapse in one region, they affect producers in another; collapsing domestic economies have far-flung, global consequences that even a hegemon—even one deeply involved in the roots of the collapses—cannot long escape.

Enduring Regional and Internal Conflicts: The Middle East, South Asia, and the Korean Peninsula

The new era did not bring an end to long-standing, historical conflicts in regions around the globe, especially in the Middle East, South Asia, and East Asia. Although internal and regional conflicts took place during the Cold War, the superpowers understood them only in the context of their own competition. Thus local wars became proxies for the Cold War between the United States and the Soviet Union or were perceived as opportunities to expand one or the other superpower's sphere of influence. When the Cold War ended, however, such local conflicts persisted. Now, however, the United States and the international organizations to which it belonged had to deal with these crises as individual events, without the clarification and simplification that the Cold War had afforded. In the heady post–Cold War days, moreover, many of the more powerful states in the world shared an idealistic belief that the Cold War's end freed them to do what they had long hoped to do: promote peace and development (for more on collective security in the new era, see later in this chapter). Continuing tension, however, in the Middle East, South Asia, and the Korean Peninsula have proven to be tough to overcome.

The Middle East

Tension surrounding Iraq (see later in this chapter) and Iran (see Chapter 8) has, in turn, affected the Arab–Israeli peace process, which was already fluctuating dramatically from apparent near-success in the early 1990s to a point of uncertainty and confusion in 2010. The Arab–Israeli conflict emerged alongside—and was in part a product of—the Cold War (see At a Glance, "Arab–Israeli Confrontations," for the conflicts between the Arabs and Israelis). Despite a very few high-profile successes, notably the 1978 Camp David Accords (an Egyptian–Israeli negotiated peace agreement that led to a formal treaty in March 1979) and the 1994 Israel–Jordan peace agreement, Arab–Israeli relations have been characterized by intense distrust and animosity. The conflict between Zionism, or Jewish nationalism, and Arab and Palestinian nationalism form the core of the Arab–Israeli conflict.

The October 1991 Madrid Conference, however, seemed to represent serious progress. In its wake, Israel and its Arab neighbors began unprecedented direct bilateral negotiations supplemented by multilateral talks. After more

AT A GLANCE

Arab–Israeli Confrontations

War	Immediate Causes	Outcome
1948–1949 War	Israel (following its declaration of independence in 1948) is attacked by the Arab countries surrounding it.	Egypt captures Gaza; Jordan captures the West Bank and the Old City of Jerusalem; Israel also increases in size; many Palestinians become refugees and a Palestinian state does not emerge.
1956 War (Suez Crisis)	Israel, Great Britain, and France collude to invade Egypt because each country has serious distrust of the Nasser regime in Cairo. The United States bitterly opposes the invasion.	British and French influence declines in the Middle East, but Israeli access to the Gulf of Aqaba is guaranteed; a UN Emergency Force is stationed in Egypt's Sinai desert along Israel's border and Fedayeen attacks against Israel from Gaza cease.
The June 1967 War (The Six Day War)	Egypt evicts the UN peacekeeping force from the Sinai and closes Israeli access to the Gulf of Aqaba, and Arab armies mobilize and threaten to destroy Israel. In response, Israel launches a preemptive strike against Egypt. Jordan, Syria, and other Arab states join on the Egyptian side.	Israel captures the Sinai Peninsula and the Gaza Strip from Egypt, Jerusalem's Old City and the West Bank from Jordan, and the Golan Heights from Syria. UN Security Council Resolution 242 is issued following the war, calling for Israel to withdraw from occupied territories and for the Arab states to make peace with Israel in return.
October 1973 War (The Yom Kippur War; The Ramadan War)	Egypt and Syria launch a two-front surprise attack on Israel. The Jewish State is caught off guard and does not do well at first, but eventually its forces enter both additional territory in Syria and Egypt.	Through U.S. mediation, Egypt and Syria agree to disengagement accords with Israel that lead to Israeli withdrawal from small parts of Sinai and the Golan Heights. After Egypt's leader, Anwar Sadat, visits Jerusalem in November 1977, the first Arab leader to publicly step foot on Israeli territory, a process begins that ultimately leads to the signing of the Camp David Accords in 1978 and the Egyptian–Israeli peace treaty in 1979.

(continued)

AT A GLANCE   *Continued*

War	Immediate Causes	Outcome
1982 Lebanon War	Israel launches a major attack on the PLO in Lebanon during that country's civil war in an attempt to thwart a perceived Palestinian threat and to create a situation conducive to a Lebanese–Israeli peace.	After a ten-week siege of West Beirut, PLO guerrillas agree to evacuate, but Israel fails to create a new relationship with Lebanon. Hostilities continue; Israel retreats to southern Lebanon in 1985 and ultimately withdraws from that area in 2000.
1987 Intifada (war of Stones; "shaking off" in Arabic)	The climax of growing tension between the Israelis and Palestinians leads to a Palestinian revolt.	Violence gradually decreases, but the Oslo Accords (1993) in which Israel and the PLO mutually recognize each other mark the end of the Intifada.
2000 Al-Aqsa Intifada (Second Intifada)	After the failure of the July 2000 Camp David meetings, in which the Israelis and Palestinians did not succeed in reaching a final resolution of their conflict, the Palestinians initiate a second intifada. Palestinian suicide attacks against Israeli civilians are countered by Israeli retaliatory attacks against Palestinians in Gaza and the West Bank.	A trace of new hope appears in 2005 following the election of Mahmoud Abbas to replace the deceased Yasser Arafat and the Israeli unilateral disengagement from Gaza in August 2005, but it is shattered when Hamas wins the January 2006 elections and a serious rift develops between Fatah and Hamas, culminating in Fatah's expulsion from Gaza in June 2007.
2006 Second Lebanon War	Israel (in response to a raid in northern Israel by Hezbollah guerrillas from southern Lebanon that resulted in the death of three Israeli soldiers and the kidnapping of two others) launches air attacks and then a ground war against Hezbollah, which meanwhile bombards the northern section of Israel with rockets.	UN Resolution 1701 calls for the withdrawal of Israeli forces from Lebanon, the disarmament of Hezbollah, and the deployment of Lebanese troops and an expanded UN Mission (UNIFIL) in southern Lebanon.
War—Dec. 2008–Jan. 2009 (Operation Cast Lead)	In frustration at years of missile attacks from Gaza on nearby towns and villages, Israel launches a war against Hamas.	The controversial attack ends after about a month with much larger casualties (including civilians) suffered by Palestinians than Israelis, but missile attacks against Israelis from Gaza largely cease.

than four decades of violence, the possibility of a new order in this war-torn region appeared to have emerged. The primary process, parallel bilateral negotiations between Israel and Jordan, the Palestinians, Syria, and Lebanon, failed, but secret contacts in Oslo, Norway, resulted in a breakthrough in September 1993, when the Palestine Liberation Organization (PLO) and Israel recognized each other's legitimacy for the first time. Subsequent talks led to the withdrawal of Israeli forces from parts of the Palestinian territories and the turning over of these areas to the Palestinian Authority (PA) between 1994 and 1997. The Israel–PLO agreement broke a diplomatic logjam on the Israeli–Jordanian front, and a peace treaty between those two countries followed in 1994.

For a time, bilateral and multilateral contacts between Arabs and Israelis increased, and it appeared that an end to the conflict might be in sight. The conflict turned to a focus on the Israeli–Palestinian front, and extremists on both sides, bent on destroying the peace process, began to counterattack. Arab opponents intensified terrorist attacks against Israel, and in November 1995, an extremist Jewish student assassinated Israeli Prime Minister Yitzhak Rabin. A new wave of terrorism in 1996 resulted in the election of a conservative Israeli government. Conflicts over the implementation of Israeli withdrawals followed, and unresolved fundamental differences over such issues as Jerusalem and the possibility of a Palestinian state soon threatened to derail the process.[6] In 1998, at the Wye River Estate in Maryland, Israeli Prime Minister Binyamin Netanyahu and Palestinian Authority Chairman Yasser Arafat reached an agreement to move the peace process forward, but domestic differences on both sides made it impossible to implement.

When the electorate selected Ehud Barak as prime minister in 1999, the new Israeli government sought to reach a deal with Syria, but after unprecedented talks, the effort failed in March 2000. Barak then ordered a unilateral withdrawal from the "security zone" in southern Lebanon established by Israeli troops after their incursion into that country in 1982 to stop attacks against the northern sector of their country. Barak later attempted to achieve an end to the Israeli–Palestinian conflict in a dramatic meeting with Arafat and President Clinton at Camp David in July. At that historic occasion, the Israeli leader made several major concessions, which constituted the basis for a comprehensive and final deal between the Israelis and the Palestinians. Arafat rejected the proposal because he viewed the terms as unfavorable to the Palestinians. The negotiations then broke down. When conservative Israeli leader Ariel Sharon visited a Muslim-controlled area of Jerusalem sacred to both Muslims and Jews, militant Palestinian groups, with Arafat's acquiescence, incited a new popular uprising, the Al-Aqsa Intifada, which led to a new wave of violence and reprisals. The result was that Barak's government fell, and in 2001 Sharon was elected to head a new Israeli government. Conflict escalated in 2002 as Palestinian groups launched more suicide bomb attacks and Israel responded with major incursions into the West Bank and Gaza, blockading Arafat in his headquarters at Ramallah. The traditional site of the birth of Jesus became the scene of a tense drama when Israeli forces surrounded

Palestinian fighters occupying the Church of the Nativity in Bethlehem. With increasing clashes between Israelis and Palestinians and renewed tensions in the Persian Gulf, the conflicts that wracked the region in the twentieth century continued unabated into the twenty-first century.

In 2002, the United States, Russia, the UN, and the EU formed the "Quartet" and then developed a "road map" for peace between Israel and Palestine. Although the effort had obvious shortcomings from the outset, and for some time it appeared to have derailed, the death of Yasser Arafat on November 11, 2004, seemed to have created an opportunity for progress. In 2003, both the United States and Israel had refused to continue negotiations with Arafat, but the election of Mahmoud Abbas as president of the Palestinian National Authority in January 2005 allowed for the possibility of negotiations resuming. Abbas's moderate and pragmatic approach, coupled with his major role as an architect of the Oslo Accords, won him favor with the West and allowed Israel under Israeli Prime Minister Ariel Sharon to test the new waters. Sharon is a controversial figure whom some consider a hero (Israelis who believe he was tough on terrorism and doves who like his more moderate policies at the end of his career), others a murderer for his previous tough stances (particularly Arabs who wanted to see him tried for war crimes), and still others a traitor (Israeli settlers in the West Bank and Gaza who saw him giving up Israeli land in return for nothing).

In August 2005, a plan for Israeli unilateral disengagement from Gaza proposed by Sharon and accepted by the Israeli parliament came to fruition. In the face of protests and violence from Israeli settlers, the Israeli Defense Forces removed all Jewish settlers (and those who came to show their support) from the twenty-one Jewish settlements in Gaza (and four in the West Bank), turning the area over to the Palestinians (Israel maintains control of the borders and airspace). The action was applauded by many Western powers (including the United States and the European Union) as a step toward a final peace settlement. Right-wing Israelis and those suspicious of Sharon's motives objected to the action on security and religious grounds.

In January 2006 Ariel Sharon suffered a brain hemorrhage (through 2010 he remained in a coma and was not expected to recover) and was replaced by his deputy, Ehud Olmert. The most dramatic change of leadership, however, occurred on the Palestinian side. Later in January 2006, Hamas (the Islamist group branded as a terrorist organization by many in the international community) won a majority of the seats in a Palestinian parliamentary election. Israel and the United States (among others) immediately sought to isolate the Hamas government. Infighting began between the two Palestinian factions, Hamas and Fatah (originally the party of Yasser Arafat, Fatah has now become the moderate voice of the Palestinian government), culminating in the division of the Palestinian territories in June 2007. Hamas controls Gaza and Fatah controls the West Bank. What this development means for the future of a Palestinian state, or the Palestinian people, remains unclear. Although attempts by both the Bush administration in its last year and the Obama administration have

PHOTO 6.2 At the urging of U.S. President Barack Obama, in late 2009, Israeli and Palestinian leaders Benjamin Netanyahu and Mahmoud Abbas met face-to-face for the first time in New York City.

been made through 2010, reconciliation efforts between Fatah and Hamas have been fruitless. Coupled with the election of hard-liner Benjamin Netanyahu as prime minister of Israel in 2009 (taking office for the second time), the division between the Palestinians has left the Israeli–Palestinian peace process in a difficult and uncertain spot. Encouraged by U.S. President Obama, efforts are still being made to pursue peace between the Israelis and the Palestinians, including a concerted effort begun in late summer 2010 which succeeded in bringing Netanyahu and Abbas together to discuss the central issues separating the two sides. While President Obama announced he wants an agreement between the two sides within a year, tensions are often heightened in response to the construction of Israeli settlements in the West Bank and continued conflict between Israel and Hamas in Gaza. Hamas and other extremist Palestinian groups continue to fire rockets into southern Israel, to which Israeli forces respond, and an economic and military blockade of Gaza continues (some changes were made to the blockade following international condemnation of an incident in which Israel boarded and seized a series of ships attempting to violate the Gaza blockade and killed nine activists who Israel claims attacked boarding IDF soldiers in May 2010). What is certain is that resolution of the Israeli–Palestinian dispute is critical for progress in the region; without it, efforts to achieve regional stability will continue to be jeopardized.

PHOTO 6.3   In August 2005, Israel conducted its historic pullout from Gaza. Some settlers left willingly, but others had to be removed by force.

South Asia

Like the Middle East, South Asia has been a region marked by continual tensions with occasional outbreaks of violence, both within and between states. The international relations of South Asia have been dominated by the antagonism between India and Pakistan. The sources of instability stem from the colonial legacy (see Chapter 5), the efforts of the regional states to consolidate control, and ethnic and religious animosity. During the Cold War, both superpowers were actively involved in South Asia, but the direct involvement of China, through its border disputes with India and its ties with Pakistan, distinguishes South Asia from the Middle East.

To understand this enduring conflict, some historical background is necessary. As noted in Chapter 5, Britain had imperial control over virtually all of the Indian subcontinent prior to World War II. As pressure for independence became stronger between the two world wars, the Indians themselves increasingly became divided along religious lines, that is, between the Hindu majority and Muslim minority. The bases of these differences were in part theological, in part historical (Hindus resented the past Muslim domination of India), and in part political. Muslims eventually began demanding independence for the areas in which they constituted a majority. In 1947, these areas became the nation of Pakistan. In Britain's hasty withdrawal from India after World War II, however, borders were drawn that left many Muslims in India and Hindus in Pakistan.

Independence thus created a massive refugee problem, as more than 12 million Muslims and Hindus fled to their new "homelands." The migration of refugees was accompanied by widespread violence and deaths.

The most contentious area was and is Kashmir, where the population is primarily but not exclusively Muslim. In 1947, the Hindu prince of Kashmir was given the choice of joining Pakistan or India, but he procrastinated and even contemplated declaring independence as joining either would mean giving up power, and becoming part of India risked popular rebellion. When the prince's temporizing led to revolts among the Muslim population of Kashmir, Pakistani tribesmen infiltrated to give support. Facing a revolution, the prince joined India, which then sent troops to put down the rebellion and repulse the Pakistani tribesmen. In December 1947, India appealed to the United Nations, which called for a cease-fire and a vote to determine the wishes of the people. Instead, Pakistani troops intervened in early 1948 and occupied western Kashmir; a cease-fire was finally agreed to in 1949, but no vote was held.

India and Pakistan repeatedly clashed over the disputed region of Jammu and Kashmir and other issues during the Cold War, and full-scale wars between the two countries broke out in 1965 (in which India successfully countered early Pakistani attacks; later, with a military stalemate in effect and the implication clear that India would ultimately prevail, both sides agreed to a UN-mandated ceasefire) and 1971 (sprouting from the declaration of Bangladesh as an independent country in the eastern section of Pakistan and resulting in Pakistan acknowledging India's de facto control of Kashmir). As a result of the United States dispatching a nuclear-armed aircraft carrier to the Bay of Bengal as a sign of support for Pakistan during the 1971 conflict, India became concerned about its security from nuclear weapons. Both India and Pakistan had programs to develop nuclear weapons, with India placing a high priority on both civilian and military uses of nuclear energy. In 1974, India tested what it claimed was a "peaceful nuclear explosive," but the strategic implications of India's nuclear weapons potential were clear. Pakistan's Prime Minister Zulfikar Ali Bhutto declared that his country would "eat grass" if necessary to gain its own nuclear capability, and by 1992 Pakistan admitted that despite international efforts to prevent proliferation, it also had acquired the capability to produce nuclear weapons.[7]

Many hoped that the two regional rivals would stop there without moving toward a nuclear arms race, but this hope vanished in 1998. A government led by India's nationalist Bharatiya Janata party, which supported the open development of nuclear weapons, was elected in March, and two months later tested three nuclear weapons. Pakistan quickly responded by testing five weapons of its own. The first direct armed conflict between two nuclear-armed states followed in May 1999, when Pakistani troops infiltrated Indian-controlled Kashmir, and India responded with military operations against the Pakistani forces and Pakistani-armed Islamic fighters. Indian troops drove the Pakistani forces out after two months of fighting, and the crisis concluded without the serious threat of nuclear escalation. Another crisis erupted when Islamic militants attacked India's parliament in December 2001; this time, the crisis did not escalate into military conflict, but threats and tensions on both sides raised fears of another war. This is a clear example of the realist view of the security dilemma. Each state armed itself, resulting in a spiral of conflict.

After months of tension, progress toward improving relations began. In 2003, then-Indian Prime Minister Atal Behari Vajpayee offered the "hand of friendship" to Pakistan, bus service between Delhi and Lahore was resumed, and a cease-fire was ordered along the border between India and Kashmir. Peace talks began in 2004 with the aim of improving all aspects of the India–Pakistan relationship, including the conflict over Kashmir. Among the successes, both sides agreed to renew a ban on nuclear weapons tests, to set up a hotline to avoid escalation of crises (similar to the hotline between the United States and USSR after the Cuban Missile Crisis; see Chapter 4), and to give each other advance notice of ballistic missile tests (both sides continue missile tests that often result in heightened tension and international concern). Talks continued through 2010 on numerous topics, including combating terrorism (especially in light of the 2008 terrorist attacks in Mumbai, India, that killed over 100 people; see Chapter 8) and drug trafficking, the release of prisoners detained in both countries, water shortages, confidence-building measures, and the future of Kashmir.

Proponents of deterrence theory (see Chapter 7) say that the situation in South Asia proves their case: With both regional rivals armed with nuclear weapons, neither has an incentive to risk a major war that could unleash nuclear destruction. Others are not optimistic that the two regional powers, each with its own instabilities, will always be able to control their level of conflict, particularly when religious terrorism (covered in Chapter 8) is involved. Liberals, on the other hand, would argue that both sides recognized their mutual interests in avoiding a nuclear confrontation and thus proceeded to seek cooperative ways to reduce tension. Constructivists would argue that these cooperative efforts, if productive, can change the relationship between India and Pakistan and help promote peace. Regardless, the potential for nuclear crisis in South Asia remains one of the most serious challenges to international peace in the new era. Neither country possesses solid command-and-control structures, nor can they recall missiles fired in error. No one can. The internal situation in Pakistan is of the utmost concern as there is significant fear that radical elements will gain control of the government, and thus the nuclear arsenal. Thus, the ongoing talks between the two regional powers are crucial in avoiding a potential catastrophe.

The Korean Peninsula

On the Korean peninsula, the new era began hopefully with the first stages of a rapprochement between the two Koreas. Direct talks between North and South Korea and their entry into the UN in 1991 as member states muted tensions, at least for a while. Soon, however, North Korea's efforts to develop long-range missiles and nuclear weapons rekindled tensions. The death of North Korea's leader Kim Il-Sung in the summer of 1994 added further confusion. A crisis nearly erupted later that year when Pyongyang refused international inspectors access to its plutonium reprocessing plant and threatened to withdraw from the Nuclear Non-Proliferation Treaty. The situation was temporarily defused when North Korea agreed to cease some suspicious nuclear activities in return for assistance with its civilian nuclear power program from the United States, Japan, and South Korea in an arrangement known as the Agreed Framework. At that time, Pyongyang may have already accumulated enough plutonium to make two nuclear weapons, but it was hoped that the agreement would curb the North's nuclear ambitions and provide economic incentives for cooperation. Nevertheless, flooding and food shortages in North Korea from 1995 through 1997 further increased instability in the North and anxiety throughout the region, with many people in South Korea fearing that a desperate North Korea might attack across the demilitarized zone in a reckless attempt to reverse its fortunes.

Tensions increased further in 1998, when the North unexpectedly tested a "space launch vehicle" that could also be used as a long-range missile. In the late 1990s, South Korea's "sunshine policy" of engagement with the North and sporadic talks on a formal peace settlement offered glimmers of hope, but in 2002 it became apparent that neither the United States nor North Korea had fulfilled its obligations under the Agreed Framework. By that time, the Bush administration had referred to North Korea as part of the "axis of evil." The extent of North Korea's abrogation of the agreement became clear when it revealed that it had carried on a secret program to enrich uranium. Tensions shot up in the ensuing crisis, and North Korea defiantly restarted its production of nuclear material and withdrew from the NPT in January 2003. In April of that same year, the United States and North Korea finally sat down in China in an effort to defuse the crisis, but both sides left the negotiations with less resolved than they had hoped for; by the end of that year, Pyongyang announced it had processed enough nuclear material to make up to six nuclear bombs.[8]

Several rounds of six-party talks (between North Korea, the United States, Russia, Japan, South Korea, and China) produced an agreement in 2007 when North Korea agreed to close its main nuclear reactor (Yongbyon) in exchange for fuel (for more on proliferation and specifically North Korea, see Chapter 8). The IAEA reported that North Korea refused to allow inspectors into the Yongbyon facility in September 2008, apparently because of the U.S. failure to remove North Korea from the State Department's list of state sponsors of terrorism. The United States removed North Korea from this list in October 2008, but this failed to prompt North Korea to provide full disclosure of its nuclear weapons program. When North Korea launched a rocket attempting to place a communications satellite into space in April 2009, the United Nations admonished the state for this behavior. In response, North Korea officially abandoned the six-party talks and disallowed any inspections of its facilities. Numerous attempts have been made through 2010 to restart the six-party talks, but demands by one party or another have stalled the process. In the meantime, North Korea continues its nuclear program, tensions simmer with South Korea, and both threats and attempts at negotiations are made by all sides.

The People's Republic of China and Taiwan

No discussion of local crises would be complete without mentioning the Chinese-Taiwanese conflict. Although issues relating to North Korea have captured the headlines in recent years, the underlying tensions between Taipei and Beijing could erupt at any time. Almost six decades after the end of China's civil war, the People's Republic of China claims that the self-governing island of Taiwan is part of China and refers to it as a "renegade province." Some Taiwanese leaders support the eventual reunification with mainland China. However, others want to declare de jure independence and change the island's name to the Republic of Taiwan, a situation the PRC government has said it would never accept and will go to war to prevent. Taiwan, for it part, has evolved into a highly vibrant democracy with a very successful economy. As we saw in Chapter 4, the United States today recognizes the Peoples' Republic of China in Beijing but still maintains unofficial connections with Taiwan.

Collective Security

How the international community handles long-term as well as sudden crises is critical in the new era. While the United Nations cannot function as a global police force, it is the institution through which the international community comes together to discuss issues and often act in the face of threats to global security (see Chapter 13 for a broader discussion of the functions of the United Nations). During the Cold War the UN Security Council was often stymied because each superpower used its veto to protect its interests, allies, and satellites. The Gulf War, however, convinced many states that UN-mandated peace enforcement could really work, now that superpower rivalry was a thing of the past. At the same time, several events highlighted an urgent need for effective, unified international responses when diplomatic efforts at conflict resolution failed. Unfortunately the civil war that followed the breakup of Yugoslavia demonstrated the continued shortcomings of collective action in the new era. After World War II, Yugoslavia was organized as a federation of ethnically based republics. In the late 1980s, the country became increasingly divided politically, as conflicts appeared between the Belgrade government, dominated by Serbs, and Yugoslavia's other nationalities, including Croats, Slovenes, Albanians, and Bosnian Muslims. Following flare-ups of violence in the southern region of Kosovo in 1990, the republics of Slovenia and Croatia seceded from the federation in 1991. Intervention by the federal army did not prevent Slovenian and Croatian independence, but thousands of casualties resulted from the fighting, which ended in an uneasy truce in 1992. The republics of Bosnia and Macedonia seceded shortly afterward.

The most violent act in the tragedy opened in 1992 when a three-sided civil war broke out in Bosnia between Serbian nationalist forces backed by the federal army, Croatian militias receiving support from Croatia, and predominantly

Bosnian Muslim forces. The war was fought with a savagery that most modern Europeans would have liked to believe was a thing of the past on their continent. Bosnian Muslims in particular were terrorized by unspeakably brutal policies of "ethnic cleansing" (see Spotlight, "Definitional Discord: Genocide and Ethnic Cleansing," later in this chapter), wherein civilians were systematically driven from their homes, put into concentration camps, tortured, raped, or simply slaughtered.

The UN, the **Organization for Security and Cooperation in Europe (OSCE),** the EU, and NATO were slow to coordinate an effective response to the bloodshed. UN peacekeeping forces and relief convoys were deployed early in the conflict but were ineffective and, in some cases, counterproductive. It was not until 1994 that NATO deployed an Implementation Force (IFOR; including a sizable contingent of American troops) to guarantee the UN-ordered cease-fire. By that time, well over 70 percent of Bosnia had been carved up by Serbian and Croatian forces. In 1995, after intense pressure from the United States, the three parties signed the Dayton Accords, which provided for an independent multiethnic Bosnia with a collective presidency (in which a Muslim, a Serb, and a Croat serve together as chief executive). NATO deployed a Stabilization Force (SFOR) to police the implementation of the accords, but the halting response of the international community to the war in Bosnia augured poorly for the ability of international institutions to maintain peace.

Violent conflict flared up again in 1998 as Serbian troops fought with separatist forces in Kosovo, a region attached politically to the remnant Yugoslav state but populated mostly by Albanian Muslims. After diplomatic efforts to resolve the crisis failed, the United States led planning for a NATO military intervention, although Russia strongly opposed any military action against the Serbians, with whom Russia has strong cultural ties. Knowing Russia would veto any effort to get UN backing for military action (for more on voting in the UN, see Chapter 13), NATO launched air strikes against Serbian forces in 1999, effectively supporting the Kosovar Albanian rebels (although both Serbians and the Kosovo Liberation Army [KLA] committed atrocities). The Serbian forces relented and withdrew from Kosovo after eleven weeks of bombardment, and a NATO peacekeeping force, the Kosovo Force (KFOR), moved in. The human tragedy of the breakup of Yugoslavia proved that ethnic and nationalist conflicts in the post–Cold War world could be every bit as bloody as they were in the past.[9]

At the same time that Yugoslavia's disintegration was devastating Europe, the African country of Somalia was being torn apart by competing warlords who were using famine as a weapon against each other's populations. The United Nations attempted to intervene with a small humanitarian operation (UNOSOM I) that quickly failed, but U.S. President George H. W. Bush, who had just lost the 1992 election to Bill Clinton, noted the success of a U.S.-supported UN operation in Kurdistan following the 1991 Gulf War. International forces had been able to provide medical, logistical, and nation-building support to the Kurds who had fled to the region to avoid retribution from Saddam Hussein for their uprising during that war. President Bush therefore announced, in the face

▪ **Organization for Security and Cooperation in Europe (OSCE)**
Established in 1994 (formerly the Conference on Security and Cooperation in Europe [CSCE]) to encourage peace and wealth in Europe.

of the heart-wrenching humanitarian crisis in Somalia, that the United States would lead an international task force (UNITAF) to provide humanitarian assistance to the Somalis. In the face of considerable opposition from Congress, Bush promised that there would be no Somalia quagmire, as the purpose of the mission was only humanitarian in nature.

The challenges of coordinating forces from several countries, constantly changing objectives as the situation in the country proved to be more challenging and complex than initially understood, and disagreements about how best to implement the shifting goals all contributed to, ultimately, a fiasco. The UN took over the humanitarian efforts in Somalia from UNITAF in an operation called UNOSOM II. Anxious to expand from humanitarian assistance to peacemaking and nation-building, the UN pressured the United States to redirect its remaining forces in the country to capture or kill Mogadishu warlord Mohamed Farah Aideed but was unable to adequately coordinate support from other participating countries. On October 3, 1993, an attempt to capture close associates of Aideed by the elite U.S. Delta Rangers went horribly awry when two Black Hawk helicopters were shot down by rocket-propelled grenades. The end result was a firefight that killed hundreds (or by some estimates thousands) of Somalis and eighteen American soldiers. The video of a dead American soldier being dragged through the streets of Mogadishu caused the Clinton administration to order the March 31, 1994, withdrawal of U.S. troops. This episode marked a deterioration of relations between the United States and the UN, as well as a new U.S. policy that curtailed American involvement in humanitarian interventions.

Not long after the debacle in Somalia, the world was horrified as a chilling genocide in the African state of Rwanda culminated with nearly a million people viciously killed in a matter of a few short months. The ethnic conflict that led to genocide in Rwanda demonstrated a profound failure of collective action (see What Would You Do? later in this chapter). Rwanda had been a colony of Belgium, during which time the differences between the two ethnic groups of the area were stressed. The majority Hutu (85 percent of the population) were treated as an inferior group, whereas the minority Tutsi (15 percent of the population) were treated as the superior entity. When the Belgians withdrew in 1962, Rwanda was riddled with a series of Hutu uprisings and Tutsi reprisals. The trigger for the violence in 1994 was the assassination of Rwandan President Juvenal Habyarimana in April (along with the president of Burundi, Habyarimana was killed when his plane was shot down over Kigali, the capital of Rwanda). Habyarimana had ruled Rwanda under the banner of "Hutu Power" since 1973, and Hutu soldiers blamed Tutsis for his death. The Hutu government incited mobs to slaughter their fellow citizens with machetes, machine guns, spears, and clubs. Large groups were herded into buildings where they were shot or trapped as the building was set on fire. In the end, the Rwandan Patriotic Front (which had been formed in 1990 by Tutsis exiled to neighboring Zaire) fought its way into Kigali and assumed control of the government under the leadership of Paul Kagame.

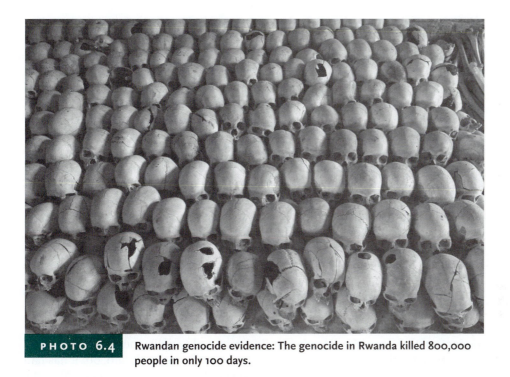

PHOTO 6.4 Rwandan genocide evidence: The genocide in Rwanda killed 800,000 people in only 100 days.

The international community stood by in 1994 and refused to act in the Rwandan genocide, in part because of the failure in Somalia. The UN actually reduced its Rwanda mission in the face of the violence. U.S. officials, burned by the experience in Somalia, did all they could to avoid using the word "genocide" to describe what was happening in Rwanda to prevent any obligation to intervene.[10] In the aftermath, Bill Clinton, Madeline Albright, and Kofi Annan have all expressed regret at the failure of the international community. In April 2000, the UN Security Council accepted responsibility for the failure to intervene. Clearly, although the UN was founded on the principle of collective response to aggression and breaches of the peace, and member states often supported that principle with speeches and rhetoric, it had been prevented from achieving its mission during the Cold War because of the superpowers' seats on the Security Council and had been unable to accomplish its mission in the Cold War's aftermath because of the almost insuperable challenges of coordinating member states to respond effectively and with unity in the face of international crises. The time had come, many argued, for UN members to put their money, and their soldiers, where their mouths had been for almost fifty years.

Since the international community's abject failure to respond in Rwanda, the genocide in the Darfur region of Sudan further called into question the international community's ability and willingness to respond to intrastate violence. Forces of the Sudanese government and ethnic militia (Janjaweed) that they employ began a systematic campaign of "ethnic cleansing" to crush rebel forces in Darfur (Sudanese Liberation Army/Movement [SLA/SLM], the Justice and Equality Movement [JEM], and other splinter groups) in 2003. Between 2003 and 2010, the UN estimates that the government forces and militias, combined with famine and disease, killed at least 300,000 people, raped and assaulted thousands of women and girls, and caused the displacement of approximately 2.7 million people living in camps in Darfur and another 200,000 living as refugees in neighboring Chad. [11]

In May 2006, the Sudanese government and a faction of the SLA agreed to the Darfur Peace Agreement (DPA), but the JEM and a second SLA faction refused to sign because the agreement failed to address key issues. Since the DPA was signed, fighting in Darfur "increased....The rebels who refused to sign the DPA continue to fight the government, which has launched an offensive against them, coordinated with militia and backed by aircraft."[12] On February 23, 2010, the Sudanese government signed a cease-fire with the JEM, but peace talks collapsed in May 2010. Despite this, there is hope for further discussion between the parties.

When it became apparent that the Sudanese government was targeting civilians (prompting the United States to declare the situation a genocide; see Spotlight, "Definitional Discord: Genocide and Ethnic Cleansing"), several components of the international community attempted to assist the people of Darfur. The African Union, for example, established the Mission in Sudan, but it has had limited success in protecting civilians and stabilizing the region. Since 2005, the United Nations has had a peacekeeping mandate for southern Sudan, but Sudan's president, Omar El Bashir, refused for more than two years to allow an international force to be deployed in Darfur (UN peacekeepers must be "invited" by the host country). In May 2007, the government of Sudan finally agreed to allow an international force of 20,000 UN peacekeepers in response to the United States imposing unilateral economic sanctions. On March 4, 2009, the International Criminal Court (ICC) issued a warrant for Bashir's arrest, citing that he committed crimes against humanity. Bashir has refused to submit to the jurisdiction of the ICC (Sudan has not ratified the Rome Statute and thus has no obligation to comply). and the ICC has no means to force his appearance to face the charges. (For more on the ICC, see Chapter 13.)

The UN Security Council, despite passing numerous resolutions to compel the Sudanese government to take certain actions (including ceasing attacks on civilians), has suffered the consequences of divergent interests. Both Russia and China (veto-wielding members of the Security Council) oppose intervention in Sudan. They have cited the rule of sovereignty (noninterference in the internal affairs of other states) to justify their actions, although economic reasons seem a more likely explanation. China imports 4 to 7 percent of its oil from Sudan, and China and Russia (as well as Ukraine, Belarus, and others) sell military supplies to Sudan. Although there is a limited UN ban on supplying arms to any of the warring parties in Sudan, it only applies to the territory of Darfur (thus states can continue to sell arms to Sudan as long as they are not used in Darfur).[13]

Definitional Discord: Genocide and Ethnic Cleansing

One of the reasons that the international community experiences difficulties in intervening in times of suspected genocide is that parties disagree on what constitutes the crime. The term "genocide" was coined in 1944 by Jewish-Polish lawyer Raphael Lemkin. He combined the Greek word for race or tribe (*genos*) with the Latin word for kill (*cide*). In 1946, the United Nations General Assembly described it as "a denial of the right of existence of entire human groups." In 1948, the definition was refined in the UN Convention on the Prevention and Punishment of Genocide. Article I of the convention binds the "Contracting Parties" to "undertake to prevent and to punish" the "crime" of genocide, "whether committed in time of peace or in time of war." Article II defines genocide as "any of the following acts committed with the intent to destroy, in whole or in part, a national, ethnical, racial or religious group, as such: killing members of the group; causing serious bodily or mental harm to members of the group; deliberately inflicting on the group conditions of life calculated to bring its physical destruction in whole or in part; imposing measures intended to prevent births within the group; forcible transferring children of the group to another group." Article III identifies punishable acts as genocide, conspiracy to commit genocide, direct and public incitement to commit genocide, attempt to commit genocide, and complicity in genocide.

The UN definition is often criticized for being too narrow. It fails to include targeted political and social groups (in other words, political killings and the annihilation of the culture itself). The definition also leaves one with the question, "How many deaths equal genocide?" As a result of this criticism, many scholars have attempted to refine the definition through expansion and typologies. One such attempt was made by Israel W. Charny.[i] His definition seeks to be inclusive and in the generic sense means "the mass killing of substantial numbers of human beings when not in the course of military action against the military forces of an avowed enemy, under conditions of the essential defenselessness and helplessness of the victims." He further identifies four categories within this broad definition: actual mass murder, attempted genocide, accomplices to genocide, and cultural genocide or ethnocide.

In certain instances, the term ethnic cleansing is used to bridge the gap between crimes against humanity and genocide. This term entered the English lexicon around 1992 to describe the wars of the former Yugoslavia and came from the Serbian/Croatian phrase *etnicko ciscenje,* meaning "ethnic cleaning." There are many different definitions of ethnic cleansing, ranging from very narrow to quite broad, but one author presents a relatively inclusive explanation: "a well-defined policy of a particular group of persons to systematically eliminate another group from a given territory on the basis of religious, ethnic or national origin. Such a policy involves violence and is very often connected with military operations. It is to be achieved by all possible means, from discrimination to extermination, and entails violations of human rights and international humanitarian law."[ii]

Unfortunately, there are numerous examples of genocide and ethnic cleansing throughout history, beginning in ancient times. Two of the major crimes of genocide in the twentieth century were the massacre of 400,000 to 1 million Armenians by the Ottoman Turks in 1915 and 1916 and the Nazi Holocaust from 1933 to 1945 that resulted in the murder of 6 million Jews and additional millions, including Soviet POWs, Germans deemed by the state to be mentally or physically handicapped or chronically ill, Roma and Sinti (Gypsies), German and Austrian male homosexuals, and Jehovah's Witnesses, among others. In the "new era," genocide and ethnic cleansing have occurred with alarming frequency. From the slaughter in the former Yugoslavia in the 1990s to the machete-wielding mobs in Rwanda in 1994 to the horror in the Darfur region of Sudan in the early twenty-first century, the practice of eliminating an "undesirable" population shows no sign of being eradicated.[iii]

---

i. Israel W. Charny, "Classification of Genocide in Multiple Categories," in *Encyclopedia of Genocide,* vol. 1, ed. Israel W. Charny (Oxford, UK: ABC Clio, 1999).

ii. Drazen Petrovic, "Ethnic Cleansing—An Attempt at Methodology," *European Journal of International Law* (1994): 352.

iii. For more on genocide, see Darren J. O'Byrne, *Human Rights* (New York: Longman, 2003).

Thus, although the new era at first appeared to have potential for a kind of collective security impossible during the Cold War, not to mention for global efforts to promote human rights and welfare, this did not materialize. The first difficulty that became apparent was the "free rider" problem: Many countries used the expectation of international action as an excuse to avoid acting themselves. States were understandably reluctant to commit resources and put their troops at risk in conflicts that did not immediately threaten their vital interests. Because all would reap the benefits of collective action whether they joined in or not, many preferred to wait for others to foot the bill. In a system with only one military superpower, it is not difficult to see why other states would wait to follow its lead.

What Would You Do?

Genocide in Rwanda

You are a permanent member (and thus a veto-wielding member) of the UN Security Council. In 1994, ethnic violence has erupted in Rwanda following the assassination of the Hutu president. As a consequence, Hutus are systematically slaughtering their rival ethnic group, the Tutsis, and any moderate Hutus who do not agree to participate in the violence. Thousands of people are being killed daily, and pictures of their dead and decomposing bodies are being shown on international television nightly. The UN Mission in Rwanda (originally placed there to monitor a cease-fire between the Hutu government and the Tutsi Rwandan Patriotic Front) is begging for reinforcements, without which they can do nothing to save the lives of innocent men, women, and children.

You must weigh the costs and benefits of voting to send more troops to Rwanda or to do nothing in response to the violence. If you choose to send reinforcements, you risk the loss of peacekeepers' lives (several have been lost in the violence already, and you are less than a year removed from the debacle in Somalia) and set a precedent for intervention in the internal conflicts of sovereign states. If you call the violence and killing genocide, you have obligated yourself to do something in response (due to the fact that you are a signatory of the 1948 Convention on the Prevention and Punishment of the Crime of Genocide). On the other hand, if you do nothing, you face a moral and ethical dilemma. The United Nations was founded, in part, on the principle of collective response to aggression and breaches of the peace. This is a clear case of aggression against civilians, and the members of the UN clearly have the capability to do something about it. You risk undermining the authority of the UN by failing to respond in the face of aggression as well as facing condemnation for your state and yourself personally for allowing the massacre to continue. Can you sit by and watch the death and destruction on the nightly news?

What Would You Do?

The second difficulty was the issue of national sovereignty. Deployment of UN peacekeeping forces requires the consent of the state in which they will operate. If the host country refuses to grant consent or withdraws its consent, international peace operations have no legal basis unless the UN Security Council takes the drastic step of authorizing military action to counter overt aggression. The UN has done so only twice in its fifty-year history (against North Korea in 1950 and Iraq in 1991), and the political circumstances in each case were extraordinary. Concerns for sovereignty also frustrated action in the former Yugoslavia from 1991 to 1995 and Rwanda in 1994. The clear message of these efforts to enforce peace is that if states are serious about collective security, they must be prepared to modify or violate the principles of national sovereignty that have been pillars of international law since the seventeenth century (see Chapter 3). States are understandably reluctant to set sovereignty aside, as doing so involves the surrender of some degree of national independence and might someday expose them to international intervention in circumstances they could not control.

Despite the obvious failures of collective security, however, the international community did successfully mobilize to provide humanitarian aid where the crises were the result not of war but of natural disasters. Missions to provide food, medicine, and other basic needs to the nations hit by the Indian Ocean tsunami of 2004, for example, have shown that the international community can carry out humanitarian assistance missions if its objectives are well defined and supported by participating states. Similarly, United Nations efforts to manage peaceful transitions to democracy in Namibia and Cambodia in the 1980s and 1990s also achieved some success against what many believed at the outset to be impossible odds. These missions had political, economic, and military components and involved long-term commitments.

The Terror of September 11

The landscape of world politics changed suddenly on September 11, 2001. Hijackers crashed two jet airliners into the World Trade Center in New York City and another into the Pentagon in Washington, DC. (Passengers overpowered the hijackers on a fourth jet, which crashed in rural Pennsylvania.) The Pentagon suffered serious damage, but the World Trade Center was completely destroyed; its twin towers disintegrated into smoldering rubble, killing roughly 3,000 people who could not be evacuated in time. The world saw the towers collapse live on television.

▪ **Al Qaeda**
A network of Islamic terrorist organizations, led by Osama bin Laden, that carried out the attacks on the U.S. embassies in Tanzania and Kenya in 1998, the *USS Cole* in Yemen in 2000, and the World Trade Center and Pentagon in 2001.

The 9/11 attacks were the work of **Al Qaeda,** a network of Islamic terrorist organizations led by Osama bin Laden (see Chapter 8).[14] Al Qaeda had struck at American targets before, killing U.S. military personnel in Saudi Arabia in 1996, bombing the U.S. embassies in Kenya and Tanzania in 1998, and nearly sinking the destroyer *USS Cole* at anchor in Yemen in a suicide bomb attack in 2000. This was not even the first time Al Qaeda had struck at the Twin Towers—a U.S.-based Al Qaeda affiliate set off a bomb at the World Trade Center in 1993. But the shock of a massive attack on America's largest city, the audacity of using airliners as missiles, and the spectacular destruction of a symbol of American economic strength signaled that global **terrorism,** too, had entered a new era. Many continue to fear that the next attack could use nuclear, chemical, or biological weapons, such as anthrax, which could cause casualties on an even more massive scale.

▪ **Terrorism**
The unlawful use—or threatened use—of force or violence against individuals or property to coerce or intimidate governments or societies, often to achieve political, religious, or ideological objectives.

The United States, under the leadership of President George W. Bush, responded quickly. By the end of 2001, a multinational military campaign spearheaded by U.S. airpower demolished the Taliban, the radical Islamic government of Afghanistan that had supported and provided a base of operations for Al Qaeda. This attack dealt the terrorist alliance a major blow (at least temporarily), but bin Laden escaped. In partnership with many states, both friends and former foes, the United States announced the start of a global "War on Terror" that would rely on international cooperation in diplomacy, law enforcement, intelligence, economic sanctions, and military operations to apprehend terrorists and thwart future attacks. Critics of the Bush administration urged more attention to what they believed were the root causes of terror, including poverty, lack of democracy and human rights, and resentment of the power and, some argued, arrogance of the United States, especially in the Islamic countries that supplied recruits for Al Qaeda and other radical Islamic groups.

War in Iraq

The United States soon determined to take action against another rogue state. In his 2002 State of the Union speech, Bush characterized Iraq, Iran, and North Korea as an "axis of evil" intent on developing nuclear weapons and likely to provide nuclear, chemical, or biological weapons to terrorists. Citing evidence that Saddam Hussein had not halted Iraq's efforts to acquire weapons of mass destruction and long-range ballistic missiles, as he had been required to do by the United Nations, the Bush administration attempted to put together a UN-backed coalition for military intervention in Iraq to force Hussein to disarm (as his father, George H. W. Bush, had done in 1990 and 1991).[15] The UN, however, proved reluctant to support military action, and the Security Council ordered a new round of inspections by the IAEA and the UN Monitoring, Verification and Inspection Commission before it would take further action. Despite adamant disapproval by many UN members, the U.S. administration said that the UN would prove itself "irrelevant" if it was not prepared to support military action to preempt the threat of weapons of mass destruction. Widespread protests in Europe, the Middle East, and elsewhere indicated that public opinion in many countries opposed any military action without UN approval, but despite protests in the United States, the majority of the U.S. public believed that the United States and its allies would be justified in acting independently of the UN.

Despite international opposition, President Bush ordered coalition military operations to begin on March 19, 2003, with a precision-guided air attack targeted directly at Hussein and other top Iraqi leaders. Unlike in 1991, when weeks of aerial bombardment preceded ground combat, U.S., British, Australian, Polish, and Danish units immediately began to advance toward Baghdad, and airborne troops dropped into northern Iraq to fight alongside Kurdish irregulars. Coalition forces (known as the "Coalition of the Willing") initially defied expectations that the war would soon become a "quagmire" similar to the Vietnam War by rapidly defeating disorganized Iraqi troops and seizing key cities, bridges, and oil fields. Predictions of massive civilian casualties and Saddam's inevitable use of chemical or biological weapons also went unrealized. On April 5, U.S. soldiers and Marines entered Baghdad, and on April 9 Hussein's ruling establishment lost its grip on power. Not all Iraqis welcomed coalition forces with open arms, but many celebrated the end of Saddam's brutal regime. Hussein was found hiding in a "spider hole" near his hometown of Tikrit at the end of 2003, and in 2006 he was found guilty of war crimes and crimes against humanity for the deaths of 148 Shiite Muslims in the town of Dujail in the late 1980s. He was executed by hanging on December 30, 2006.

The fact that the U.S.-led coalition achieved a stunning victory in a short time was undeniable, but what it will achieve in the long term is still, more than seven years later, uncertain.[16] No weapons of mass destruction were found in Iraq, lending credibility to the many who argued that the Bush administration's justification of needing eliminate Iraq's weapons program for overthrowing Hussein's regime was false. U.S. relations with allies and enemies suffered as a result of this action, and U.S. credibility took a significant hit. In addition, the challenge of building democracy in a country that has known only authoritarian rule has proven to be formidable. In October 2005, Iraqis went to the polls and ratified

PHOTO 6.5   **U.S., British, and allied forces quickly toppled Saddam Hussein's regime.**

the new Iraq constitution. Despite this progress, a complex set of insurgencies and terrorist movements has been wreaking havoc on coalition soldiers and Iraqi police and civilians.. In June 2010, Iraq Body Count, a group comprised of academics, human rights activists, and antiwar activists, reported that between 96,440 and 105,177 civilians had died as a result of the military intervention in Iraq. By June 2010, more than 4,700 coalition troops had been killed (with the vast majority being American soldiers) and more than 31,000 U.S. troops had been wounded. In 2006, Congress appointed a bipartisan panel, known as the Iraq Study Group, to assess the situation in Iraq. Despite this group's recommendations for a gradual withdrawal of U.S. troops and a dialogue with Iran and Syria, the Bush administration undertook a troop surge to protect Baghdad and the al Anbar province that consisted of more than 20,000 additional U.S. troops. Violence decreased in Iraq, and new U.S. President Barack Obama designed a strategy to withdrawal U.S. forces from Iraq, while at the same time increasing U.S. troop presence in Afghanistan, which was suffering from a resurgence of the Taliban. On August 31, 2010, President Obama officially announced the end of the U.S. combat presence in Iraq (although 50,000 U.S. troops remained for training and security). The impact both wars may have on the many conflicts in the Middle East, as well as the long-term impact on U.S. credibility abroad, is still far from clear.

Terrorism Redux

Despite these military campaigns and rhetoric touting successes of the war on terror, terrorists continue to shock the world with high death tolls. Great Britain has been a central target. On July 7, 2005, a coordinated series of bombings took place against London's transportation system. Bombs exploded within fifty seconds of each other on three tube trains and within one hour on a double-decker bus. The explosions were the work of four suicide bombers linked to Al Qaeda and resulted in fifty-six deaths (including the bombers) and hundreds injured. London was rocked a second time on July 21 when four bombs only partially exploded on four trains and a bus. No one was injured and the four would-be bombers were arrested days later by police. On June 29, 2007, there was a failed plot to explode car bombs (packed with gasoline and nails) in central London, followed the next day by a flaming car driven into the Glasgow International Airport. Terrorist incidents also took place in Bali, Indonesia, in October 2002 (in which 202 people were killed and more than 200 injured in the deadliest terrorist attack in Indonesian history); Madrid, Spain, on March 11, 2004 (in which 192 people were killed and nearly 1,500 wounded in ten coordinated explosions on commuter trains that constituted the worst terrorist assault in modern Spanish history); Sharm el-Sheikh, Egypt, on July 23, 2005 (which left 84 dead and more than 200 injured); and Mumbai, India, on November 26, 2008 (which

PHOTO 6.6   On November 26, 2008, terrorists attacked several locations in Mumbai, India, including the Taj Mahal Palace.

left at least 170 people dead and 250 injured in two five-star hotels, a train station, a Jewish center, a movie theater, and a hospital). While no major terrorist incidents have been successful in the United States since September 11, 2001, there have been failed attempts that highlight the failure of U.S. efforts to prevent terrorist attacks. On December 25, 2009, a Nigerian man boarded a Northwest flight in Amsterdam bound for Detroit and attempted to light an explosive device he had hidden in his pants (he burned himself, but the device did not explode and he was arrested in Detroit). In May 2010, a would-be bomber attempted to set off explosives in Times Square, and while this attempt also failed, the U.S. intelligence community has been under significant fire for mistakes critics charge they have made in handling alleged threats to U.S. security (in fact, National Intelligence Director Dennis Blair resigned in May 2010 in part due to criticism stemming from the Christmas Day bombing attempt). The internationalization and coordination of terrorism has thus become a major security concern of the early twenty-first century and has motivated a variety of international responses. The success of these responses, as well as alternative options, will remain a subject of debate, scrutiny, and discussion for years to come.

Conclusion

The terrorist attacks of 2001 and the continuing repercussions of the conflict in Iraq begun in 2003 have raised many questions for the future. Can the UN play a more active role in resolving future crises? Is the United States building a reputation as a force for global peace or as an international bully? Should Europe, Russia, and China ally with the United States or act as counterweights against it? The answers to these questions are likely to determine the character of world politics in the twenty-first century.

Comprehending the era that followed the Cold War has been difficult for world leaders and citizens alike. We can apply the paradigms discussed in Chapter 2 to help organize our thinking and evaluate policies (see At a Glance, "Levels of Analysis and Paradigms in Review: Examples from 1991 to the Present"). Thus, for some realists, the post–Cold War period is one of hitherto unimaginable U.S. dominance. To others, the world appears to have returned to a traditional realist balance-of-power system. Liberals, on the other hand, contend that world politics increasingly reflects the rise of nonstate actors, transnational interest groups, multinational corporations, international organizations, and global norms, all of which reflect and promote constructive interdependence. Constructivists would argue that the post–Cold War era has been hijacked by proponents of Huntington's clash of civilizations, people who interpret the events of the last decade and a half in terms of "us versus them" and new, insidious threats to their very survival (Islamic extremists versus Arab secularists, Al Qaeda versus the West, leftist Latin America versus capitalist North America, natives versus immigrants, and on and on). As the world never fits nicely into a single paradigm, the reality is likely to be somewhere in between. The following chapters will discuss major issues in world politics and delineate the complexity of the world today and the competing processes inherent in the distinctions between cooperation and conflict, and globalization and fragmentation.

AT A GLANCE

Levels of Analysis and Paradigms in Review: Examples from 1991 to the Present

	Realism	Liberalism	Constructivism
Individual	The warlords in Somalia, including Mohammed Farah Aideed, benefited from their cynical decisions to allow the situation in Somalia to devolve into a truly dog-eat-dog environment.	UN Secretary-General Boutros Boutros Ghali believed that through cooperation, the UN could assist troubled states in nation-building (creating institutions and stability).	By changing the terms of the discussion ("axis of evil," "War on Terror," "regime change," "preemptive war"), President George W. Bush was able to shift people's perceptions of the choice and challenges facing them.
Domestic	Ethnic conflict in Rwanda erupted in genocide in 1994 as the Hutus and the Tutsis competed for power. Their ethnic rivalry had intensified during the time of Belgian colonialism, and the Hutus and Tutsis had competed for power since the Belgian departure in the 1960s. In the end, the violence claimed more than 1 million lives.	Once relieved of the political and military constraints of the Cold War, the nations of the European Community moved to form an economic and political union by removing trade barriers and building institutions to standardize policy. The European Union created a single market and European executive, legislative, and judicial branches.	During the Cold War, the United States was perceived in the global economic system as the traditional hegemon. Internal economic difficulties in the United States altered its perception of its role, and, following the collapse of the Soviet Union, the U.S. role shifted to more of a steward of an increasingly integrated economic system.
Systemic	The United Nations proved unable to respond effectively to war-related crisis even after the collapse of the Soviet Union, not least because of the balance of power on the UN Security Council (the United States versus Russia and China), but also because states in general predictably sought their own relative interests rather than responding to the UN's calls for forces and support.	The continued coalescence of the European Union during this era supports an optimistic belief in the ability of countries to develop and adhere to a Lockean "social contract" that protects each member's interests.	By failing in its first post–Cold War attempts at collective security, the UN reinforced its identity as a toothless institution capable only of humanitarian assistance and development programs; this began a negative cycle in which states focused increasingly on the UN's corruption, weakness, and ineffectualness and became less willing to turn to it for guidance or to contribute to its operations.

Discussion and Review Questions

1. What are the arguments made by Francis Fukuyama and Samuel Huntington? Which argument do you find more persuasive? Why?
2. Do you believe peace is possible between the Israelis and Palestinians? Explain.
3. Explore the consequences of India and Pakistan openly joining the "nuclear club." Do you see this creating stability in their relationship, or is the possibility of nuclear war more a reality now than ever?
4. What are the impediments to successful collective action? Provide examples from the post–Cold War era of successful and failed collective action.
5. Discuss the What Would You Do? on page 227. How does being a permanent member of the Security Council affect your decision? What are the potential costs and benefits of intervening?
6. Discuss the international response to the terrorist attacks on September 11, 2001. Do you believe the response was satisfactory or not? If not, what more should have been done?

Key Terms

Al Qaeda 228
Clash of Civilizations 203
End of History 202
Multinational corporations
    (MNCs) 205
Organization for Security
    and Cooperation in
    Europe (OSCE) 221
Terrorism 228

PART II

The Major Issues in World Politics

CHAPTER 7

Security Theory and Practice

As part of the 1972 Strategic Arms Limitation Treaty (SALT I), the United States and Soviet Union agreed to limit ABM sites to two each (one around the capital and one to protect an ICBM complex). Although it required little strategic adjustment by either side, as both countries had become disenchanted with the utility of ABMs, this was a major breakthrough at the time and was one of the major examples of cooperation between the two superpowers during the Cold War. As an illustration of the importance of security, and of how Cold War–related issues have morphed in the new era, the ABM Treaty once again became an issue between the United States and Russia twelve years after the demise of the Soviet Union. Arguing that the treaty prevented the United States from addressing the threats of today's security environment, the United States announced the abrogation of the ABM Treaty in December 2001. This marked the first time in modern history that the United States renounced an international accord to which it was a party. Sounding very much like Cold War rhetoric, Russian President Vladimir Putin threatened retaliation ranging from increasing the number of warheads per missile to violating the provisions of numerous treaties that require missile limitations (START, for example). Thus a shining example of Cold War cooperation became a new symbol of fragmentation and conflict in the new era.

For better or for worse, nations have always been preoccupied with security. Although most of us have never personally experienced war in all its cruelty, violent conflict continues to be a fact of life, as exemplified by the bloody post–Cold War conflicts in the former Yugoslavia, throughout Africa, between Israel and Palestine, in Afghanistan, and twice between U.S.-led coalitions and Iraq. Economic interests, resource competition, humanitarian imperatives, ethnic and religious intolerance, and pure power grabs all continue to lead to violent internal and international conflicts. In the absence of an international authority, states must prepare themselves for such eventualities and focus not only on economic growth and quality of life but on security as well.

In many periods of history, national security was such an important value that people were expected to lay down their lives for it without question. The ancient Romans had an expression for this: *dulce et decorum est pro patria mori* ("how sweet and beautiful it is to die for the fatherland"). Today, even as economic interdependence and globalization link peoples together, states nonetheless continue to devote vast resources to protecting their sovereignty and independence. Despite optimism in the immediate post–Cold War period, the world's countries have continued to face the classic dilemma of "guns or butter"— the need to choose between security on the one hand and economic and social development on the other when allocating their scarce resources. This issue is clearly not new, but it continues to be an important component of state relations in the new era.

As introduced in Chapter 2, this chapter considers how nations try to manage the security dilemma by adopting strategies of self-protection and by trying to limit arms or prevent arms races from erupting into war. Each paradigm presented in Chapter 2 views this pursuit differently. Realists view this dog-eat-dog battle as one of self-interest dominated by the need to attain security from and over a nation's peers. As a consequence of anarchy, states are disposed to conflict rather than cooperation. Liberals, on the other hand, would contend that cooperation is not only possible in an anarchic world, but desirable. Rather than spending considerable time and money enhancing power against other states, security is more likely to be attained through interdependence, democracy, and international institutions. Constructivists would argue that the system is what states make it: The structure is created by the interaction of states over time. The behavior of states is driven by their own conception of the system and other states, and thus they are changeable over time. So, if states want to create a cooperative, variable-sum environment, rather than a zero-sum environment, they can. This chapter will also examine how the pursuit of security affects international politics, how states attempt to protect themselves from threats, and how their efforts at self-protection affect their relations with other states and organizations. Chapter 8 will present a series of contemporary security issues facing states, drawing on the strategies and efforts presented in this chapter.

The Many Faces of Security

Before looking at how states attempt to achieve security, however, it is necessary to understand what it is they are trying to achieve. In other words, what is national security? The term "security" is used much more frequently than it is precisely defined. In the absence of a generally agreed-on definition, virtually anybody can invoke the slogan of "national security" for any purpose. As one analyst wrote,

> National security is a modern incantation. As in any incantation the words have both power and mystery. In the name of national security, all things can be threatened. All risks can be taken. All sacrifices can be demanded....The ultimate catch-all term, it can mean anything the user chooses it to mean.[1]

Unfortunately, it is easier to point out why we need a precise definition of security than to actually offer one, partly because the concept of security has many different aspects and is constantly changing. Moreover, circumstances are likely to dictate how states think of security. Poor nations may count provision of adequate food and clean water among their primary security necessities, whereas more advanced, developing countries may simultaneously face ethnic separatism and foreign military threats, and industrialized countries may fear pollution and the loss of manufacturing jobs to other countries. Rich and poor states alike face the threat of terrorism, but some states may regard terrorism as a necessary evil, or even as a legitimate instrument of foreign policy, whereas others perceive it as a threat to their very existence. During the Cold War, the military aspects of security received the most attention, largely because of the ever-present risk of nuclear war. Now that the Cold War is history, decision makers are under more pressure to address the economic, environmental, and even cultural aspects of security. (Cultural security may seem a strange concept to Americans, but American rock music and fast food chains have "invaded" far more countries than have American troops.)

External and Internal Threats

When considering military security, most states must prepare for both internal and external security threats. Internal security threats, as one would expect, arise from within states and include domestic terrorism; insurgent groups, rebels, and militias; military coups; organized crime; and drug traffickers (see Chapter 8). Countries as diverse as the United States, India, Egypt, and Colombia deal with some combination of such internal threats on a daily basis, whereas other states, such as Canada, experience almost no internal political violence. External threats come from beyond a nation's borders and can involve anything from a full-on invasion to terrorist attacks to financial support for an insurgent group. Thus, a country such as Israel, which occupies a thin piece of hotly contested real estate along the Mediterranean Sea and is surrounded by adversaries, finds itself in a profoundly different security predicament than a country like Malta, an isolated island in the Mediterranean with few coveted resources.

External and internal threats to security are often interrelated. Countries' leaders go to great lengths to maintain their power and can face threats to this goal from outside forces. Throughout the world, neighbors compete with each other by supporting their opponents' internal insurgents as proxies. In the 1990s, South Africa, Tanzania, Zambia, and Namibia provided assistance to UNITA soldiers fighting for control over Angola. Armenia and Russia provided aid to Armenian separatists in Azerbaijan. In the conflict in the former Yugoslavia, Croatia provided assistance to Bosnian Croats, and Serbia provided assistance to Bosnian Serbs. Eritrea and Somalia both helped Ethiopia's rebel group (the Oromo Liberation Front), and Pakistan supported numerous separatist groups within India. Iran and the United States both offered help to the Iraqi Kurds, and Iran also supported the Shi'a Iraqis. The list of such external assistance for internal wars goes on and on, representing a blending of domestic and interstate conflicts that is repeated worldwide.

There are also security concerns that go beyond traditional domestic threats and bilateral competitions. The end of the Cold War and the pressures of globalization have drawn more attention to transnational security issues, including not just strictly military concerns but also the threats posed by international criminal organizations (which will be discussed in Chapter 8), the effects of HIV/AIDS and other diseases, and the spread of environmental pollution across borders (see Chapters 11 and 12, respectively). In addition, issues of **human security** are increasingly becoming topics of more central focus in the new era. From this perspective, security is not only a matter of state interests (sovereignty from external attack) as espoused by realists but is also a matter of freedom from poverty, hunger, dehydration, disease, lack of state capacity, and results of natural disasters. Human security calls for people to be free of both fear and want. Human security promotes the protection of individuals from war and other forms of violence (freedom from fear) as well as protection from life-threatening crises (freedom from want). Constructivists view an increased focus on human security as a reflection of values and norms in international society. As researchers build a case for the importance of considering the impact of human security, policymakers worldwide are acknowledging its importance and policy is following, albeit slowly.

Clearly, problems like environmental degradation, global warming, exhaustion of natural resources, rapid population growth, and migration can undermine a state's security by overtaxing its political, economic, and social systems, leading to instability or even the wholesale collapse of the state (see Chapter 11).[2] Many government and NGO officials, however, have been accused of calling all matter of issues and events security concerns to garner public support, national attention, and resources. Constructivists, as discussed in Chapter 2, term this phenomenon "securitization." If you will recall, this is the act of naming something a security concern so that it becomes an elevated priority. So, through the constructivist lens, something becomes an issue of

▪ **Human security**
Freedom from both fear and want.

security just because we say it is security-related.[3] This can certainly serve to draw attention to fundamental issues affecting states' citizens and lead to a distribution of resources to important global problems.

It is important to recognize, however, that there are dangers in expanding the concept of security to include every problem faced by a nation or the world. If we are not careful, we will broaden the concept of security so far that is encompasses nearly everything. Powerful bureaucratic players in many countries have a vested interest in broadening the definition of national security to include any activity that falls under their responsibility. Many ministers and cabinet secretaries responsible for health, education, the environment, or trade policy have been quick to claim that the issues they deal with are matters of national security to obtain more resources from the state. States do not possess an infinite amount of resources, and trade-offs have to be made. If the concept of security is broadened too far, there is a danger that nothing will receive the adequate resources. A more insidious potential danger in expanding the concept is that national security has traditionally been a favored excuse for governments to suspend or ignore civil liberties. Although states may be wise to give more attention to nonmilitary aspects of security, citizens should be alert to the potential for expanding definitions of national security to erode personal, political, and economic freedoms.

Subjective Versus Objective Aspects of Security

Another factor complicating the task of defining security is that security and insecurity frequently have a strong subjective dimension. In other words, security is in large part a perception or feeling. In the international system, some states (such as Stalin's Soviet Union) have at times behaved as if they were facing an imminent threat for reasons that outsiders could not understand. Conversely, some countries have felt unjustifiably safe in periods when they should have taken the threats that confronted them more seriously, and as a result suffered surprise attacks (such as the United States with respect to terrorism in 2001).

Subjective perceptions of security show up in nations' defense budgets. Defense spending may be thought of as an insurance policy against the vagaries of the international system. Just as people can take out different types of insurance policies for their cars, states also vary in their approach to risk: They can underestimate danger and not take out sufficient insurance, or they can be paranoid and overinsure. This relationship between objective threat and subjective perceptions of security may be represented as a matrix, as shown in Figure 7.1.

In this matrix, the right column represents cases of high objective threat, such as the presence of well-armed expansionist neighbors. Within this column, the top right corner of "underinsurance" (quadrant II) represents a dangerous situation in which a country is objectively in danger but believes itself to be secure. A country that fails to evaluate correctly the threats to its security is far less likely to invest sufficient resources into its defense, and it could therefore easily

		Objective Level of Threat	
		Low Threat	High Threat
Subjective Perception of Threat	Secure	I Pacificism (Malta, 2007)	II Underinsurance (France, 1940)
	Insecure	IV Overinsurance (North Korea, 2007)	III Prudence (Israel, 2007)

FIGURE 7.1   Objective and subjective aspects of security.

become a victim of aggression. For example, before World War II many European countries believed Hitler could be appeased and thus were not adequately prepared to resist when he attacked. France was especially unprepared; after Hitler invaded Belgium, he was able to bypass France's much heralded defensive fortification, the Maginot Line.

The lower right corner (quadrant III) depicts a state that is objectively in danger and, at the same time, is aware of its insecurity. Israel, for instance, has been surrounded by well-armed adversaries. However, because it remains acutely aware of its situation, committed to self-defense, and bolstered by the U.S. provision of significant amounts of security assistance and foreign aid, for more than six decades it has been able to survive.

The left column of the matrix represents countries that face few actual threats to their security. States that exist in low-threat conditions and perceive themselves to be secure have small defense budgets (quadrant I). In contrast, however, those states that are not objectively threatened but believe danger is imminent tend to plan on the basis of worst-case assumptions. This often results in "overinsurance" (quadrant IV). Such a country is likely to waste large amounts of resources against an illusory threat. The most salient example of security overinsurance is found in North Korea, a country that spends the bulk of its extremely limited resources on its enormous military. The energy-starved country produces less light at night than the Japanese fishing fleet, but it is nonetheless producing nuclear weapons and testing missiles. The problem with overinsurance is two-fold. It is extremely expensive domestically and can lead to the kinds of social stresses North Korea now faces as its population starves. More to the point, it can precipitate precisely the response internationally that it is intended to deter; in this case, other countries, seeing North Korea arm itself to the teeth, have become concerned about its intentions and have begun to respond accordingly, beefing up their own capabilities and shows of force in ways that only contribute to the spiral of insecurity.

The psychological mechanisms behind a country's perception of its security do not readily lend themselves to rational analysis. Intuitively, one might expect that as a country becomes more powerful, it would start to feel more secure. Historically, this proposition has been violated with astonishing regularity. Political scientist Karl Deutsch called this anomaly Parkinson's Law of National Security: "A nation's feeling of *insecurity* expands directly with its power" (italics added).[4] As most nations become more powerful, they acquire more interests that need defending, and more potential adversaries. The United States, for example, had few interests outside the Western Hemisphere when it was an isolationist power before World War I, and accordingly it spent little on defense. After World War II, however, the United States made commitments to defend its allies all over the globe. Its defense budgets rose to unprecedented levels, though few Americans felt any more secure than they had before World War II.

Working Definition of Security

Now that we understand how national security is a partly objective, partly subjective condition, the rest of this chapter examines the measures states take to survive as independent entities within the international system. Although the significance of internal threats is clear, and is the driving concern for many of the world's countries, this chapter focuses on transborder threats and international security (additional internal concerns will be addressed in Chapter 8). Thus, a country's security is defined herein as a condition in which the sovereignty and the territorial integrity of a country are guaranteed.

Given the anarchic nature of the international system, this condition has been difficult for states to achieve. It is an unfortunate but inescapable reality that the history of international relations has been punctuated by innumerable military conflicts, many of which resulted in massive bloodshed. Even in the new era, many states face threats against their sovereignty or territorial integrity, and as a result they have little choice but to try to protect themselves through various means.

Will the world ever reach a condition in which no country's independence or integrity is threatened? There are two distinct views on this. The first is that, as globalization persists and countries' development, democratic practices, and social and economic interdependence increase, military means of resolving conflict will eventually become obsolete. The other view is that people will always find something to fight about; conflict comes out of not just resource competition or the need for secure borders, but out of ideological differences, cultural and religious intolerance, and humans' natural drive for dominance. In this view, even as the world globalizes, it is rearranging itself into a different set of competitors.

Security Dilemma Revisited

States instinctively try to protect their sovereignty and territorial integrity. Every state uses a combination of protective strategies, including different degrees of militarization depending on the nature of the potential threat, the type of government making the decisions, and the available resources. The Roman author Vegetius summarized this idea in the fourth century b.c.e. with the famous adage *qui desiderat pacem, preparet bellum* ("let them that desire peace prepare for war"). As the North Korean case illustrates, sometimes such defensive efforts deter a potential aggressor, but other times they backfire and decrease the defender's security (as its neighbors arm themselves in response, and so on). Countries thus face the painful security dilemma discussed in Chapter 2: The measures a state takes to increase its own security are likely to decrease the security of other states. If all states take steps to increase their own security, the net effect may be that the security of all is actually diminished.

On the one hand, all nations understandably want to counteract the threat of an expanding neighbor, either by building up their own military strength internally or by allying with third powers who feel equally threatened by the rising state. By resorting to these actions, they may give the ascendant power an incentive (or excuse) to beef up its own military strength, which in turn decreases the other countries' security. As a result, states get trapped in this vicious spiral. Of course, some states will follow a deliberate policy of aggression or coercion, which makes matters even worse. As the old saying goes, even paranoids have real enemies. (For one theory on the conduct of war, see Spotlight, "Clausewitz on War and Politics.")

One might ask, why can't all these countries just act rationally? The problem is, from the realist perspective, they are acting rationally. In an anarchic environment where the possibility of conflict is ever present, it makes sense for each state to arm itself because the risk of preparing for armed conflict seems less than the risks incurred by remaining defenseless. It is therefore extremely difficult to escape from the security dilemma in an anarchic system, and as a result, all states have to adopt a security strategy of one kind or another. Liberals would focus on the fact that there are some partial solutions to the security dilemma, including confidence-building measures worked out diplomatically and, on a much larger scale, international organizations and regimes intended to create

Clausewitz on War and Politics

A number of strategists and military theorists have expounded their views on the conduct of war through the centuries. For example, the writings of the ancient Chinese General Sun Tzu on the art of war are still studied for their strategic insights. Most of these military thinkers have viewed the conduct of war as a specialized activity, outside the sphere of "normal" activities of a state or society. In the early nineteenth century, Prussian soldier Carl von Clausewitz (1780–1831) realized that holding this attitude was a good way to lose wars.

Born to a lower middle-class family, Clausewitz studied literature and philosophy and attended the War College in Berlin, but his experience of war was more than academic. He served in the field during the French Revolutionary and Napoleonic Wars, became a prisoner of war after the crushing Prussian

PHOTO 7.1 Carl von Clausewitz.

defeat by Napoleon at Jena in 1806, and joined the Russian army to fight against Napoleon's invasion of Russia in 1812. After Napoleon's final defeat inaugurated what became a century of relative peace in Europe, Clausewitz concentrated on the theoretical study of military affairs as a War College professor.

Unlike most other strategists, Clausewitz did not produce a system of guidelines for the conduct of battles or campaigns. Instead, his major work, *On War*, emphasized that mechanistic principles are of little value in carrying out military operations because war is inherently a risky and uncertain business. Chance, psychological factors, and the "fog of war" (the inability of commanders to have precise information about their own forces, let alone those of the enemy) make war a chaotic enterprise. To be successful, he argued, commanders must adapt to constantly changing conditions (on the battlefield and off) without losing sight of their strategic objectives.

Moreover, Clausewitz wrote, war is fought not just by armies, but by nations. To defend itself, a state must mobilize not only its military forces but also its resources and will to fight, and it must seek to reduce the enemy's army, industry, and national morale. His famous dictum, "War is nothing but the extension of politics by other means," reminds soldiers and statesmen alike that wars are fought for political objectives and that defeat is far more likely if the nation does not support the underlying goals of a military campaign.

Clausewitz's studies of war had a major impact on strategic thinking throughout the world, and many of his writings are still read at military academies and war colleges. Modern strategists, such as those on the American side in Vietnam, were foolish to ignore his conclusions that the political goals of war must be expressed and maintained. Although he wrote before the era of "total war," Clausewitz warned civilian and military leaders that national security is an activity to which the whole nation must contribute. Clausewitz thus anticipated, and may well have inspired, the well-known remark made by French Prime Minister Georges Clemenceau during World War I, "War is too important to be left to the generals."

a set of rules by which countries will interact. The problem, however, is that international law and organizations are nonbinding and adherence to them is voluntary (see Chapter 13). As was evident in 2003, when the United States went to war against Iraq in the absence of a UN Security Council resolution authorizing such action, global accords and regimes are only as strong as their members' commitment to them. Constructivists, on the other hand, would argue that the security dilemma is a product of realists' assumptions about anarchy. As states emerged as the primary actors, their relationships became competitive, resulting in a long-term negative tit-for-tat with the result that assumptions of self-help and the security dilemma became reified. If they had, in fact, engaged in positive, cooperative relationships, the system would have developed differently. Constructivists therefore challenge the security dilemma as a natural occurrence of international politics and posit that, through a process of complex learning (a positive tit-for-tat), states can deliberately overcome the security dilemma.

Military Power

The persistence of armed conflict reminds us that **military power** remains an essential component of security. Military power has been one of the traditional measurements of a state's capability to influence world politics directly or indirectly. Chinese leader Mao Zedong best expressed this view in his famous aphorism, "Political power grows out of the barrel of a gun." Likewise, when Stalin was once told that the Pope disapproved of one of his policies, he reportedly dismissed the criticism with the question, "How many divisions has the Pope?" Not all leaders share Mao and Stalin's realpolitik enthusiasm for military power, but its importance to world politics cannot be denied.

Military power derives from the size of a state's armed forces their quality and quantity of weaponry, and their training, morale, organization, and leadership. It thus consists of both "hardware" (weapons and equipment) and "software" (personnel and their direction). Because of the importance of the hardware, it is impossible to divorce military from economic power; throughout history the most developed states often have been the most militarily powerful ones (although there are striking exceptions, such as China and North Korea, each of which is militarily powerful but economically relatively underdeveloped).

As the largest armies are not necessarily the most effective, military expenditure is another means for gauging military power. These aspects of military power are relatively easy to quantify, but other components that are not so easy to express remain important to consider. These factors include training, leadership, morale, and power projection. Another crucial factor, technology, creates its own set of capabilities and challenges. It is rarely possible to know beforehand whether numbers, training, or technology will prove decisive in a conflict. Because of this uncertainty, states must pay attention to all elements of military power to maintain adequate forces for their security strategies.

Weapons of Mass Destruction

A country's ability to deploy weapons of mass destruction (WMDs)—nuclear, radiological, biological, and chemical weapons—continues to be a major determinant of military power, simply because of the threat such weapons pose and the expense and effort involved in countering them. Even countries with limited conventional capabilities must be considered serious opponents if they have WMDs and the means of delivering them. That said, a state is not considered a

▪ **Military power**
The factor of power relating to the size, organization, and training of a state's armed forces and to the quality and quantity of its weaponry.

global military power unless it has **strategic nuclear forces** (designed to attack long-range targets, including cities). The number of strategic nuclear warheads is a useful indicator of the size of a state's nuclear arsenal. The five states that tested nuclear weapons before 1967, not coincidentally, the permanent members of the UN Security Council, are considered nuclear weapon states under the **Nuclear Non-Proliferation Treaty** (NPT). In addition to strategic forces, most of the nuclear powers possess a number of **tactical nuclear weapons,** which are short- or medium-range weapons designed to be used primarily against military forces. Of these nations, the United States and Russia have the largest inventories. These large nuclear stockpiles are in many ways artifacts of the Cold War, when the superpower rivalry between the United States and the USSR was the driving force behind the buildup of their strategic arsenals. The end of the Cold War intensified efforts to reduce the arsenals of the two largest nuclear powers, and the numbers of weapons deployed by both states have decreased significantly in recent years (see the section on "Arms Control and Disarmament" later in this chapter). Table 7.1 shows the numbers of strategic nuclear warheads deployed by these states, along with the total number of warheads they are known or estimated to possess.

The states that deploy strategic nuclear weapons are not the only states that possess nuclear arms. Israel is generally believed to possess nuclear warheads as well, although it has never declared this openly. India first tested a nuclear device, which it claimed was a peaceful nuclear explosive, in 1974, and in May 1998 conducted five further explosions that were openly declared to be tests of nuclear weapons. Pakistan responded with its own series of tests a few weeks later. The numbers of nuclear weapons possessed by these states can be expressed only as a range of estimates, but Table 7.2 summarizes the forces that these other nuclear states are probably able to deploy. Although it may be assumed that India, Israel, and Pakistan have the means to use nuclear weapons against targets in their own and neighboring regions, they do not possess weapons that can strike intercontinental-range strategic targets. In addition, North Korea announced in 2005

▪ **Strategic nuclear forces**
Nuclear forces designed to attack long-range targets, including cities.

▪ **Nuclear Non-Proliferation Treaty**
Signed in 1968, the treaty provides that signatory nations without nuclear weapons will not seek to build them and will accept safeguards to prevent diversion of nuclear material and technology from peaceful uses to weapons programs. Nations in possession of nuclear weapons at the signing of the treaty agreed not to help nonnuclear states gain access to nuclear weapons but, rather, to offer access to peaceful nuclear technology.

▪ **Tactical nuclear weapons**
Weapons designed to attack short- or medium-range (95–310 miles) targets, primarily conventional military assets.

TABLE 7.1 Estimated Nuclear Arsenals of the Nuclear Weapons States, 2009		
State	**Total Active Weapons**	**Inactive Weapons**
United States	≈5,200	4,200
Russia	≈4,850	8,150[a]
France	300	0
United Kingdom	180	0
China	240	0

[a] The status of these weapons is unclear. A portion may be retired and awaiting disarmament.
Source: National Resources Defense Council, "Nuclear Notebook," Bulletin of the Atomic Scientists website, http://www.thebulletin.org/ (November/ December 2009).

that it possesses nuclear weapons (although it was suspected long before the announcement), but both the number of weapons and their delivery capability are unclear.

In addition to nuclear arms, many states have developed and maintain **chemical weapons** (nerve gas, poison gases like those used in World War I, or other deadly chemicals) for use against enemy troops or cities and **biological weapons** (weapons for germ warfare), even though such methods are now banned by international conventions. Saddam Hussein deployed chemical weapons both against Iran during the eight-year war between the two countries and against 5,000 Iraqi Kurds, whom he considered a threat to his regime. The United States invaded Iraq in 2003 claiming, in part, that it was doing so to ensure that Saddam Hussein could not deploy his WMDs against the United States or U.S. interests. Although the majority of Iraq's military capability had been destroyed during or after the 1991 war with the U.S.-led coalition that forced Iraqi troops out of Kuwait, the U.S. administration publicly declared that the possibility that Iraq might still have WMDs in 2003 was sufficient reason for invading the country, although no WMDs were found in Iraq after the invasion (see Chapter 6).

Because of their destructive potential, nuclear, chemical, and biological weapons are all indicators and signals of military strength. Map 7.1 shows the states known to possess, or suspected of possessing, these weapons. Although possession of these devices does not automatically make a state a major military power, it does show that the state perceives the need, or exhibits the desire, to develop military capabilities beyond those conferred by conventional forces.

Military Personnel

The overall number of military personnel is another important measure of military power. It indicates the total strength of a nation's ground, naval, and air forces, although it does not take into account the often vital factors of quality of equipment, technology, training, morale, command and control, and leadership.

TABLE 7.2	Estimates of Nuclear Weapons Possessed by Other States, 2009
Country	*Number of Weapons*
Israel	80–100
India	60–80
Pakistan	70–90
North Korea	?

Source: National Resources Defense Council, "Nuclear Notebook," Bulletin of the Atomic Scientists Website, http://www.thebulletin.org/ (November/December 2009).

■ **Chemical weapons** Weapons that use toxic chemical substances to cause death or severe harm to humans or animals. The active chemicals (chemical agents) in chemical weapons can be gases, liquids, or solid powders and include blister, nerve, choking, and blood agents.

■ **Biological weapons** Weapons that use living organisms, such as bacteria or viruses, or toxins produced by living organisms to cause death, disease, or injury to humans, animals, or plants.

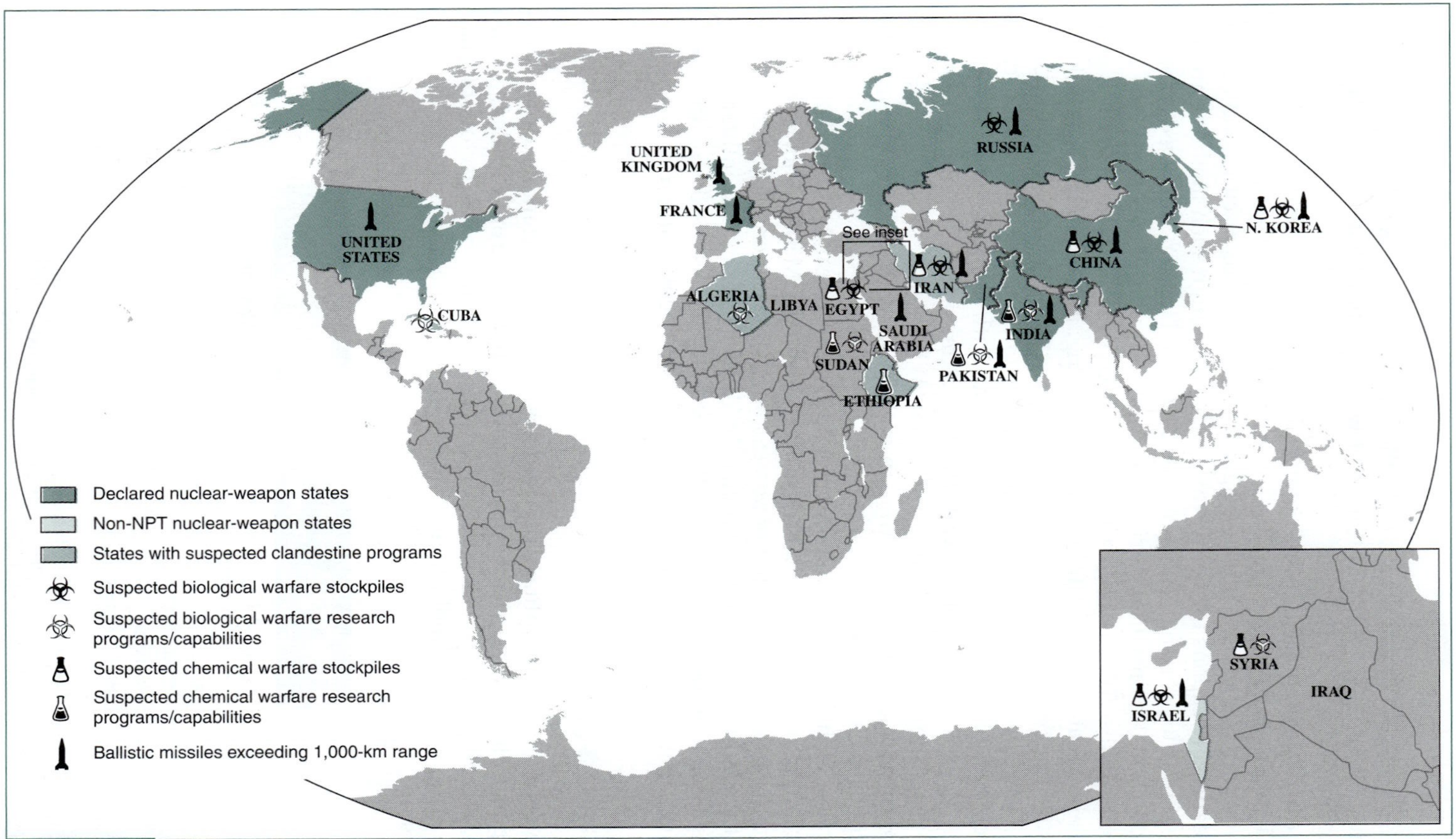
UNITED STATES
CUBA
UNITED KINGDOM
FRANCE
ALGERIA
LIBYA
EGYPT
See inset
SUDAN
ETHIOPIA
SAUDI ARABIA
IRAN
PAKISTAN
INDIA
RUSSIA
CHINA
N. KOREA
SYRIA
ISRAEL
IRAQ
Declared nuclear-weapon states
Non-NPT nuclear-weapon states
States with suspected clandestine programs
Suspected biological warfare stockpiles
Suspected biological warfare research programs/capabilities
Suspected chemical warfare stockpiles
Suspected chemical warfare research programs/capabilities
Ballistic missiles exceeding 1,000-km range

MAP 7.1 **Weapons of Mass Destruction**

Table 7.3 shows the number of military personnel fielded by selected countries in 1985 and 2010. Over this twenty-year period, China, the Soviet Union and its successor Russia, and the United States maintained large armed forces, consistent with their roles as leading military powers. Middle-rank military powers, such as India, Britain, France, and Germany, maintain sizable armed forces for both security and political reasons, but as a rising regional power India must "go it alone" on defense (thus necessitating a large active duty force), whereas Britain, France, and Germany can rely on the NATO alliance and so can get by with smaller, higher quality forces, particularly after the end of the Cold War. States like Japan that depend on alliances for their security and have no independent military ambitions can maintain relatively small forces. Significantly, all these states have reduced their force levels since the end of the Cold War, dramatically so in the case of the three major military powers, which are no longer locked in a global arms race. On the other hand, states in regions of tension, such as Israel, Pakistan, India, and the Koreas, have generally kept their force levels constant or increased their forces, as the Cold War's end did not greatly reduce the potential for conflict in these regions.

Note that the numbers in Table 7.3 indicate military personnel on active duty. Many smaller countries that cannot rely on military alliances, such as Israel,

TABLE 7.3	Military Personnel of Selected Countries, 1985 and 2010	
State	*Active Military Personnel, 1985*	*Active Military Personnel, 2010*
Major military powers		
United States	2,156,600	1,580,000
USSR (1985)/Russia (2010)	5,300,000	1,027,000
China	3,900,000	2,285,000
Middle-rank military powers		
India	1,260,000	1,325,000
France	464,300	255,000
Germany	478,000	353,000
United Kingdom	334,000	175,000
Japan	243,000	230,000
States in conflict regions		
Pakistan	482,800	617,000
Israel	142,000	177,000
Syria	402,000	325,000
North Korea	838,000	1,106,000
South Korea	598,000	687,000

Source: International Institute for Strategic Studies, *The Military Balance 2010*. http://www.informaworld.com. Reproduced with the permission of Taylor & Francis Ltd.

Switzerland, and Sweden, rely heavily on reserve forces that can be mobilized quickly in a crisis. Israel offers a noteworthy example of this strategy, fielding a standing army of 177,000 but maintaining about 565,000 well-trained reservists. Large reserve forces are important not only for smaller nations. The U.S. reserves, for example, have become increasingly important for the continuing wars in Iraq and Afghanistan. The United States maintains approximately 865,000 well-prepared reservists, many of whom have been called into active duty. Other countries carry huge reserve forces, some well trained, some not. Russia, for example, has a reserve obligation up to age fifty, and as a consequence boasts some 20 million reserves. North and South Korea also carry large reserve forces of 4.7 million and 4.5 million, respectively.[5]

Defense Expenditures

All these troops and weapons come at a price. By comparing defense expenditures, it is possible to see how much economic power a state is attempting to convert into military might. Table 7.4 gives the top fifteen military spenders in 2008. As we might expect, the largest military power (the United States) is at the top of the list, followed by France and the United Kingdom. China, a major military power, but otherwise a relatively poor developing country, is fourth, followed by Germany. Japan (which has a high GDP but strict constitutional limits on its defense expenditure) is sixth, and Russia, historically the second largest spender, has fallen to the seventh spot. The remaining positions in the top fifteen include

TABLE 7.4 Military Expenditures, 2008: Top Fifteen Countries		
State	**Military Expenditure, 2008 (in Billions)**	**% of GDP**
1. United States	$696.2	4.88
2. France	67.1	2.35
3. United Kingdom	60.7	2.28
4. China	60.1	1.36
5. Germany	46.9	1.28
6. Japan	46.0	0.93
7. Russia	40.4	2.41
8. Saudi Arabia	38.2	8.15
9. India	31.5	2.58
10. Italy	30.9	1.34
11. Brazil	26.2	1.66
12. South Korea	24.1	2.60
13. Australia	22.1	2.24
14. Canada	19.8	1.31
15. Spain	19.2	1.20

Source: International Institute for Strategic Studies, *The Military Balance 2010*. http://www. informaworld.com. Reproduced with the permission of Taylor & Francis Ltd.

contain several NATO members (Italy, Canada, and Spain) and an economically prosperous continent (Australia), but most are states in regions of high tension and potential for conflict. Table 7.4 also indicates military expenditure as a percentage of GDP for each of these states, indicating the fraction of national wealth each spends on security.

Table 7.5, which shows the ten countries with the highest defense burdens in terms of military expenditure as a percentage of GDP, tells quite a different story. Although the United States, Israel, and oil-rich Oman, Kuwait, and Saudi Arabia appear in the rankings, most of the other states in the top ten are poor countries that face serious internal or regional conflicts. Although the actual figures are not available, North Korea is believed to top the list and maintain high defense expenditures despite economic backwardness and even famine. Liberia, which ended a fourteen-year civil war in 2003 that continues to leave the country in a questionable security situation, and Burma (Myanmar), which is ruled by an antidemocracy military junta, are also believed to be high on the list, but again, data are unavailable. The list has changed considerably over the last several years, as countries like Iraq and Afghanistan that were formerly high on the list have had their governments toppled by U.S.-led coalitions and thus either no data on such expenditures are currently available (Iraq) or their defense expenditures are now relatively low (Afghanistan spends 1.51% of its GDP on defense).

The high defense burdens of strife-torn developing states underscore how poverty and violent conflict often create a vicious circle.[6] The military threats most of these countries face are significant, but considering that a stable economy is an important component of security, one cannot help but wonder if the overall security situation of many of these poor states might not be improved by spending less on guns and more on butter.

TABLE 7.5	Percentage of GDP Spent on Military, 2008: Top Ten Countries	
State	**Military Expenditure, 2008 (in Millions)**	**% of GDP[a]**
1. Jordan	$2,127	10.63
2. Oman	4,671	8.53
3. Saudi Arabia	38,223	8.15
4. Georgia	1,037	8.13
5. Burundi	83	7.48
6. Israel	14,772	7.41
7. United States	696,268	4.88
8. Kuwait	6,812	4.38
9. Singapore	7,662	4.20
10. Sri Lanka	1,793	4.15

[a] North Korea is believed to spend the largest percentage of GDP on defense, but the figures for its defense spending are not available.

Source: International Institute for Strategic Studies, *The Military Balance 2010.* http://www. informaworld.com. Reproduced with the permission of Taylor & Francis Ltd.

Logistics and Power Projection

Like police forces or fire brigades, military forces must arrive where they are needed, when they are needed, to accomplish their missions. The art and science of getting forces and supplies in the right place at the right time is known as logistics and is an extremely important component of military power. Wars are won, as one U.S. Civil War logistician put it, by the side that "gets there firstest with the mostest." States that can mobilize, supply, and transport sizable forces far from their own borders are in a position to use military power better than states that cannot. This capability for power projection, like other aspects of military power, requires both hardware (ships, transport aircraft, and land vehicles) and software (skill, experience, and the ability to analyze strategic data). Geography is also a major factor in power projection. States with port and free access to sea lanes, such as the United States or Britain, can more easily make their power felt all over the globe. Conversely, large nations with restricted access to the sea, such as Russia, often have difficulty getting their forces where they are needed to stop an invasion and must compensate by maintaining larger forces at home (which, in turn, makes their neighbors nervous).

One interesting and influential view of power-projection and geography is provided by John J. Mearsheimer. He contends that the "stopping power of water" restricts the attainment of global hegemony and that "large bodies of water profoundly limit the power-projection capabilities of land forces."[7] Further, he argues that "the presence of oceans on much of the earth's surface

PHOTO 7.2   Armored vehicles of the Irish guard in Basra, Iraq, in 2003.

makes it impossible for any state to achieve global hegemony" because "not even the world's most powerful state can conquer distant regions that can be reached only by ship." As a consequence, great powers can "dominate only the region in which they are located, and possibly an adjacent region that can be reached over land."[8] Thus, his conclusion is that land power is the principal component of military might.

Qualitative Factors: Equipment, Training, and Morale

The levels of nuclear forces, numbers of military personnel, and amount of money spent on defense are useful numerical indicators of military power. Nevertheless, there are qualitative components of these indicators that are equally important to consider. Aggregate numbers fail to reveal the accuracy, lethality, or reliability of weapons, for example, or the skills and morale of the troops who use them. Does one Israeli tank equal one Syrian tank? Does a twenty-five-year-old plane equal one that is only five years old? The same problem arises in attempts to compare nuclear weapons. During the Cold War it was hard to determine which side was ahead in nuclear capability because of the numerous ways of measuring the utility of nuclear warheads. Should comparisons be based on the numbers of launchers (missiles and aircraft), numbers of warheads, the yield (explosive power) of weapons, or their accuracy? Not surprisingly, by carefully choosing the indicators to examine, it was possible to argue throughout the later years of the Cold War that either the United States or the USSR had the superior nuclear arsenal.

Even if the preceding problems of measurement could be overcome, numbers could not adequately reflect some of the most important aspects of military power. The training and morale of armed forces have proven crucial to the outcome of many conflicts. For example, Allied Coalition forces in the Persian Gulf War of 1991 found that demoralized Iraqi troops surrendered almost faster than they could be captured. Small, professional forces that receive intensive training are usually far more capable than large numbers of draftees who are looking for the first opportunity to desert or surrender once combat has begun. Special forces, commando units such as the U.S. Green Berets and Navy SEALs and the British SAS, show what small groups of highly trained and expertly led soldiers can accomplish by slipping into hostile territory to destroy targets or rescue hostages.

Leadership at every level plays a critical role in both the effectiveness of training and the maintenance of morale under the debilitating stress of combat. Along with competent and experienced leaders, military power requires capabilities for command, control, communications, computers, and intelligence; essentially, this is the ability of leaders to get the information they need, determine how to use their forces, and transmit their orders to frontline units quickly and securely. The capacity to acquire, communicate, and utilize information is especially crucial. Reconnaissance satellites and unmanned aerial vehicles can give forces a decisive advantage by transmitting real-time intelligence to commanders, but forces in the field must be supplied with an increasing volume of data to maximize effectiveness and minimize casualties, creating challenges of information logistics. The bottom line is that no matter how plentiful or sophisticated its weaponry, any military force is useless without adequate training for those who use the weapons and competent leadership from the people who direct them in battle.

Soft Power

Another important qualitative measure of a nation's power is what Joseph S. Nye, Jr., has termed **soft power.** Whereas the traditional tests of power have been conducted in war (in other words, how well a nation fights and how often it wins), technology, education, and economic growth are more important today than they have been in the past. As a consequence, the true test of power "lies not in resources but in the ability to change the behavior of states." The questions facing a state that wishes to exert power are "to what extent it will be able to control the political environment and get other countries to do what it wants."[9] Thus, soft power is the "ability to attract others by the legitimacy of [national] policies and the values that underlie them."[10]

Nye contends that the response to the changing global environment should not be "to abandon the traditional concern for the military balance of power, but to accept its limitations and to supplement it with insights about interdependence." To gain and maintain power, states must cooperate and coordinate with a series of other actors, including transnational corporations, and consider new dimensions of security, including economic and ecological. Although traditionalists contend that if states wish to "preserve their independence" they must follow a "balancing strategy to limit the relative power of other states," today "economic and ecological issues involve large elements of mutual advantage that can be achieved only through cooperation."[11]

Although critics of soft power contend that it is merely a measure of popularity and such a consideration should not guide foreign policy, the effect of soft power can be seen in numerous cases. The U.S. role in Iraq is a case in point. International polls have shown that citizens around the globe disapprove of U.S. policies and believe that Washington has been detrimental in preserving peace, fighting global poverty, and protecting the environment.[12] As a consequence,

> when the United States becomes so unpopular that being pro-American is a kiss of death in other countries' domestic politics, foreign political leaders are unlikely to make helpful concessions.... And when U.S. policies lose their legitimacy in the eyes of others, distrust grows, reducing U.S. leverage in international affairs.[13]

Russia also provides an example of the effects of diminishing soft power. After the collapse of the Soviet Union, Chechnya declared its independence from Moscow, but then-President Boris Yeltsin refused to recognize the declaration. Russia's failure to defeat the rebels fighting for independence or its refusal

▪ **Soft power**
A term coined by Joseph Nye, Jr., that refers to a state's ability to attract allies through the legitimacy of its polices and their underlying values (cultural, political values, etc.).

to recognize Chechnya's independence (depending on your point of view) has diminished its standing in the international arena. Russia's inability to respond adequately to terrorist incidents, such as those in a Moscow theater in 2002 (during which more than 100 hostages were killed by the release of poisonous gas by government forces attempting to end the standoff) and a school in Beslan in 2004 (in which at least 335 hostages were killed by bomb blasts and gunfire by militants) make the state look weak and ineffective, and its underlying domestic and international polices are viewed the same way. As a consequence, fewer states see Russia as a major player with whom they would ally in a time of crisis.

Strategies for Security: Deterrence, Defense, and Compellence

States may use three basic strategies independently to protect their sovereignty and territorial integrity from external challengers: **deterrence, defense,** and **compellence.** These strategies are not mutually exclusive, but they are based on different assumptions and seek to protect the state through different means.

Deterrence

Deterrence attempts to prevent war by discouraging a potential aggressor from attacking. The primary goal for the defender is to convince the challenger that the probable cost of attacking will far exceed any anticipated gain. This is usually accomplished by threatening to retaliate militarily or punish the initiator if it commits the undesired action. More precisely, the defender must signal its commitment to punish or retaliate and its capability to do so to demonstrate the credibility of the deterrent threat. If the defender succeeds, the challenger will back down without a shot being fired; if it fails, the challenger will attack.

The concept of deterrence is commonly associated with nuclear weapons, but its application extends to any situation in which one side seeks to prevent another from taking some action that has not already been taken. When a five-year-old boy about to be accosted by bullies attempts to warn them off by threatening, "You better leave me alone or my big brother will beat you up," he is using a strategy of deterrence to deal with a security problem.

Deterrence can also be used by the strong to prevent the weak from trying to overthrow the established order. Its use dates back thousands of years. In 70 c.e., for example, a Jewish rebellion against Roman rule in Palestine was crushed, but a few Jews managed to escape to the mountain fortress of Masada. Although it could easily have chosen to ignore the remaining rebels, Rome painstakingly and expensively assaulted Masada to demonstrate that it "would pursue rebellion even to mountain tops in remote deserts to destroy its last vestiges,

■ **Deterrence**
The attempt to prevent war by discouraging a potential aggressor. The primary goal of the defender is to convince the challenger that the probable cost of attacking will far exceed any anticipated gain. For deterrence to function effectively, the defender must demonstrate the credibility of the deterrent threat through both capability and resolve.

■ **Defense**
A strategy that attempts to reduce an enemy's capability to damage or take something away from the defender. The purpose is to resist an attack and minimize losses after deterrence has failed.

■ **Compellence**
A strategy that attempts to force an adversary to reverse some action that has already been taken.

regardless of the cost."[14] Rome's purpose was to deter any other groups in the empire from rebelling.

Strategists identify four basic types of deterrence. Two kinds, general and immediate, have to do with the time frame of the strategy. **General deterrence** is a long-term strategy intended to "discourage serious consideration of any challenge to one's core interests by an adversary."[15] General deterrence operates all the time, aiming to prevent an adversary from attempting any kind of military challenge because of its expected consequences. **Immediate deterrence,** by contrast, is a response to a specific and explicit challenge to a state's interests. Once an aggressor has begun an attack, general deterrence has failed, but immediate deterrence may still convince the aggressor to stop what it is doing and go no further.

Two additional types of deterrence deal with the geographic scope of the intended strategy. **Primary deterrence** is intended to dissuade a challenger from attacking a state's own territory, whereas the objective of **extended deterrence** is to discourage a challenger from attacking an ally or partner. Through its commitments to NATO and Japan, the United States has used extended nuclear deterrence to protect its major allies. As one might guess, extended deterrence runs a greater risk of failure because challengers are more likely to doubt the willingness of one state to risk war (especially nuclear war) over its partner. For this reason, France developed its own nuclear arsenal during the 1960s, as French President Charles de Gaulle argued that France could never be sure that in a confrontation with the Soviet Union, the United States would be willing to "trade New York for Paris" and risk nuclear war to defend France.[16]

An example of extended nonnuclear deterrence was Israel's response to a Syrian threat in 1970. Israel believed that Syria would soon intervene in neighboring Jordan's civil war. Because Israel did not want Syrian troops so close to major Israeli cities, Israel dissuaded Syria from attacking Jordan by threatening direct retaliation against Syrian forces. Israel, in effect, made it clear that any attack on Jordan would be treated the same as an attack on Israel. Syrian forces, which had begun their intrusion, withdrew, and the Syrian air force did not attack.[17]

Defense

A defense strategy, in contrast to deterrence, attempts to reduce an enemy's capability to damage or take something away from the defender.[18] The purpose of defense is to resist an attack to minimize losses after deterrence has failed. It reduces the damage to the defender and denies the aggressor territory, raw materials, or other valued resources. Although a strategy of deterrence aims to provide security by raising the prospective costs of aggression to unacceptable levels, a strategy of defense attempts to thwart the aggressor's aims even if the aggressor decides to attack. Deterrence is primarily a psychological means of influencing the challenger's decision process, whereas defense is a tangible protective effort. These strategies can be combined, of course, but states have

▪ **General deterrence**
This long-term strategy operates at all times and attempts to prevent an adversary from attempting any kind of military challenge because of its expected consequences.

▪ **Immediate deterrence**
A strategy of response to specific and explicit challenges to a state's interests.

▪ **Primary deterrence**
A strategy intended to dissuade a challenger from attacking a state's own territory.

▪ **Extended deterrence**
A policy that seeks to discourage a challenger from attacking an ally or a partner.

finite resources to devote to security, and so must choose the mix of deterrence and defense that makes the best use of the resources available, keeping in mind that defensive measures typically also have some deterrent value and that they should not pursue one at the expense of the other.

With the exception of nuclear weapons, almost any type of military unit or matériel can be used for defense. They can also be used offensively, however, which is the very heart of the security dilemma. As long as a nation's soldiers, ships, tanks, artillery, and aircraft are capable of being used to attack as well as defend, its neighbors are likely to find it hard to believe that these forces are intended for purely defensive purposes. This caveat applies even to seemingly defensive concrete bunkers and trench lines. Rather than make one's neighbors less suspicious, they often increase suspicion by indicating to neighboring states that an attack on them is imminent.

Compellence

Whereas deterrence attempts to dissuade an adversary from a damaging action and defense attempts to reduce an enemy's capability to inflict damage, compellence attempts to force an adversary to reverse or undo some damaging action that has already been taken (some might refer to this as coercive diplomacy). If deterrence fails to prevent an invasion, for example, then the defender's next step is to convince or force the initial aggressor to withdraw from the territory it has occupied. Compellence is almost always more difficult than deterrence, as you are attempting to force an opponent to give back something that has successfully been gained.

The most cited case of successful compellence is the Cuban Missile Crisis (although some refer to it as a case of successful deterrence, it is actually a deterrence failure). In 1962, President Kennedy communicated a commitment to the Soviet Union that the United States would never allow offensive weapons to be stationed on Cuba. However, Premier Khrushchev decided to challenge Kennedy's commitment and proceeded to deploy ballistic missiles. This is a case of deterrence failure because despite U.S. warnings, the Soviets still placed missiles in Cuba; some part of the initial commitment was unclear or lacked credibility (this will be discussed later). After thirteen days of negotiations, threats, and military jousting by both sides, the United States was able to persuade the Soviets to withdraw the missiles, successfully executing a strategy of compellence.

More recently, a case of compellence failure can be seen in the U.S. (and UN) policy of attempting to compel Iraq and Saddam Hussein to relinquish the Iraqi WMD program after the Gulf War. At some point, the international community knew, without doubt, that Iraq possessed WMDs, as chemical weapons had been used against Iran in the Iran–Iraq War, as well as against the Kurds in Iraq. As explained in Chapter 6, after the Iraqi defeat in the Gulf War, Saddam Hussein was forced to agree to weapons inspections to ensure the destruction of the WMD program. After years of jousting between Hussein and IAEA inspectors

(UNSCOM), the Iraqi dictator finally expelled them in 1998. Six weeks later, President Bill Clinton ordered a bombing campaign against strategic targets in Iraq. In 1999, Clinton ordered a continual bombing campaign of targets within the no-fly zone of northern Iraq in an attempt to bring Iraq into compliance with its post–Gulf War agreements. In 2002, President Bush included Iraq in the "axis of evil" and the UN began revamping sanctions against Iraq in an effort to force compliance while limiting the harm to civilians. Ultimately, the attempt to compel Saddam Hussein failed and the United States resorted to war in 2003. (If you look at this a different way, one could argue it was a compellence success, but the international community simply did not realize it. After the invasion of Iraq and the overthrow of Saddam Hussein, no WMDs were found in Iraq, thus lending credence to the notion that the sanctions and bombing campaigns succeeded in compelling Hussein to cease his program.)

Requirements for Deterrence

As previously mentioned, three conditions must be met for deterrence to work. First, the defending state must define behavior that is unacceptable and communicate its commitment to punish the challenger. Second, the defender must possess the capability to punish an attacker. Finally, the defending state must demonstrate that it is willing to carry out its commitment to retaliate against the attacker; that is, the deterrent threat must have credibility.[19]

Commitment

As the first step in successful deterrence, the defending state must make a **commitment** to punish the challenger if the challenger takes a specified action. In other words, the defender must "draw a line in the sand" and warn the challenger that it will suffer if it crosses that line. This commitment must be stated clearly, unambiguously, and before the challenger commits the act of aggression. For example, Israel repeatedly stated that a blockade of the Strait of Tiran, the only waterway passage to its southern port of Eilat, would be regarded as an act of war, and Egyptian attempts to blockade the strait in 1955 and 1967 were contributing factors in both the 1956 and 1967 Arab–Israeli wars.

It is important that deterrence commitments be definite and specific, as ambiguity may elicit probes by challengers interested in testing a defender's resolve. For example, in 1950 the United States omitted South Korea from its announced defense perimeter in the Pacific, and this may have encouraged North Korea to believe that the United States would not respond if it attacked its southern neighbor.

Deterrence can easily fail when a defender does not properly signal a commitment to punish or fails to specify the precise retaliatory actions to be undertaken in case of aggression. There has been considerable debate over the mixed

▪ **Commitment**
The first step in deterrence, which must be stated clearly and unambiguously before a challenger carries out an act of aggression. The defending state must make clear its determination to punish a challenger if the challenger takes a specified action that the defender considers unacceptable.

signals that the United States sent Saddam Hussein prior to his 1991 invasion of Kuwait, specifically regarding the alleged comments that U.S. Ambassador April Glaspie made to Hussein shortly before the invasion. She reportedly stated that the United States had "no opinion" on Iraq's border dispute with Kuwait and did not warn Saddam Hussein of the consequences of using force against Kuwait.[20] In this case, deterrence appears to have failed because a defender did not state its commitment to punish or was ambiguous about its position.

Capability

The clearest commitment is useless if a state does not have the means to carry it out. Because deterrence revolves around convincing a challenger that the cost of a certain action is not worth the benefit, the challenger must be convinced (or at least strongly suspect) that the defender has the **capability** to retaliate. Even if a state's deterrent capability is weak, it may try to convince a challenger that its power to punish is greater than it actually is.

Deterrence with **conventional weapons** is difficult because aggressors can better estimate their capability to inflict punishment. America's naval strength in the Pacific in 1941 did not deter the Japanese attack on Pearl Harbor, and the combined armed forces of Egypt and Syria did not deter the Israeli attack in 1967 because both Israel and Japan gambled that they could each score a knockout blow with first strikes. Israel's gamble paid off; Japan's did not. Israel attacked because it was being encircled by Arab armies, and its leaders believed it might suffer a blow that would threaten its existence. That was a **preemptive strike,** designed to thwart an imminent attack. Japan believed it had a long-term problem with the United States because if it did not stop its aggression in Asia, war with the United States was inevitable. Because it was not prepared to change policies, the Japanese leadership figured it would be better off attacking "first," thus undertaking a **preventive strike.** This is also the approach the United States employed in its attack on Iraq in 2003 by invading and overthrowing Saddam Hussein in an effort to eliminate his suspected WMD program prior to him using it against the United States or its allies.

Credibility

A state must convince the aggressor of its resolve and willingness to carry out its commitment to punish. Even if a defender has clearly stated its commitment to punish and has the capability to do so, deterrence can still fail if the challenger doubts the willingness of the defender to risk war. As a result, this commitment to punish must be persuasive to keep it from sounding like a bluff. In part, the defender's success will depend on its reputation, past behavior, and image. With this in mind, Israel has consistently pursued a policy of harsh retaliation to foster its **credibility,** although its failure to respond to Iraqi Scud missile attacks during the Persian Gulf War (done so to prevent the unraveling

■ **Capability**
The aspect of deterrence that refers to the ability to do great harm to an aggressor; a state's ability to retaliate against a challenger should the defending nation deem the challenger's actions to be unacceptable.

■ **Conventional weapons**
Nonnuclear weapons such as tanks, artillery pieces, or tactical aircraft (troops that operate these weapons are referred to as conventional forces).

■ **Preemptive strike**
A defensive attack carried out when a fundamental threat to vital interests is identified or when an attack by an opponent is believed to be imminent. The underlying motivation holds that "the best defense is a good offense."

■ **Preventive strike**
A defensive attack carried out when an attack by the opponent is considered to be possible in the future but not an imminent threat.

■ **Credibility**
The resolve and willingness of the defending state to carry out its commitment to punish the aggressor state.

of the coalition spearheaded by President George H. W. Bush; see Chapter 6) was disturbing to many Israeli decision makers, who feared future deterrence would be eroded.

Ironically, the fearsome destructive power of nuclear weapons that makes their retaliatory capability unquestioned also leads to a credibility problem. Would the defender really be willing to sacrifice millions of people in a nuclear war? For example, in June 1948, one year before the Soviet Union exploded its first nuclear bomb, the American nuclear monopoly was still not able to prevent the Soviets from blockading Berlin. Similarly, in both the 1973 Arab–Israeli and the 1982 Falklands wars, nonnuclear challengers (Egypt and Syria, and Argentina, respectively) doubted the defenders' resolve to retaliate with their nuclear weapons. (As it turned out, neither Britain nor Israel had to resort to nuclear arms to turn back the aggressors.)

Deterrence can thus fail because a challenger doubts the defender's commitment, capability, or credibility to punish the aggressor. It can also fail, however, even if the three conditions are met if a challenger nonetheless calculates that the benefit or prize exceeds the punishment. In such a case, it is still rational for the challenger to choose to attack. In 1914, Austria-Hungary probably knew that an attack on Serbia would mean war with Russia, but it declared war on Serbia anyway because it believed it would win. If the government in Vienna had known that its empire would be destroyed as a result, it would not have attacked. Deterrence always involves risk and uncertainty.

Criticisms of Deterrence

The risks and uncertainties inherent in deterrence have prompted a number of scholars and policymakers to challenge the assumptions of deterrence theory and question its usefulness as a strategy for national security. The first criticism of deterrence questions the assumed **rationality** of leaders and their ability to make all the necessary cost–benefit analyses and calculations that deterrence requires. Deterrence theory assumes that decision makers are rational, that is, able to make comparisons among the possible options and rank them. Successful deterrence also requires that each party have sufficient, accurate, and up-to-date information about the situation at hand. Critics of deterrence, however, argue that policymakers are not the perfectly rational beings that deterrence theory makes them out to be. The problem is that humans have limited capacity to obtain, receive, process, and assimilate information about a situation and to evaluate all the policy options in the most thorough and accurate way. They must also have something of value that would be placed at risk by retaliation; that is, they must have something to lose. A desperate leader of a doomed regime might not hesitate to use WMDs, even if the destruction they would cause would accomplish nothing, to get revenge on his enemies. This critique of deterrence became especially relevant in the debate over U.S. nuclear and missile defense policy in the

▪ **Rationality**
Decision making based on informed cost–benefit analysis.

late 1990s and early 2000s. Supporters of building defenses against ballistic missiles (discussed later in the chapter) and of modernizing the U.S. nuclear arsenal contended that dictators such as Saddam Hussein and Kim Jong-Il, who could or did possess nuclear, chemical, and biological weapons, would not be deterred from using them by the prospect of thousands or even millions of citizens being killed in retaliation because these leaders, having already killed thousands of their own people to maintain their grip on power, were insensitive to civilian casualties.

A second bone of contention between proponents and opponents of deterrence is how to determine whether it has succeeded or failed. Proponents often point to the absence of war as proof of deterrence success, but the absence could be attributable to other factors. The fact that the Soviet Union never attacked western Europe or the United States during the Cold War does not conclusively demonstrate the effectiveness of deterrence. It may be that, despite all of NATO's military hardware, the Soviets never intended to attack western Europe or the United States in the first place. Instead, all they might have wanted was a secure buffer zone in eastern Europe. It is difficult to determine whether deterrence worked without knowing the objectives of potential aggressor states. Declassified Soviet records confirm that Stalin had designs on western Europe in the 1940s, but the means he was willing to use to expand the Soviet sphere of influence may have been limited to internal subversion.

A third criticism of deterrence is that even if the defender does everything right, the message the defender is trying to send may be misinterpreted by the challenger. To convince a challenger that you have the commitment, capability, and credibility to carry out a threat, you must at each stage send signals to the challenger, but these signals can be misinterpreted. First, it is particularly easy to misperceive the resolve of the defender if the challenger is strongly intent on taking a particular course of action. For example, prior to Iraq's invasion of Kuwait, the United Arab Emirates (UAE) and the United States held an air-refueling exercise to indicate American support for the security of the Gulf sheikdoms (of which Kuwait is one). However, because Saddam Hussein was bent on invading Kuwait, he may have interpreted the exercise as a signal of limited American interest in that it included only one tanker aircraft. Similarly, a challenger might underestimate the defender's intentions and believe the defender is bluffing when it actually intends to carry out its threat. During the Korean War, as UN troops pushed the North Korean army back and began to approach China, Chinese officials repeatedly issued warnings that Beijing would enter the conflict if the UN continued north. Discounting the likelihood of Chinese intervention, MacArthur ordered the advance to continue, whereupon China entered the conflict and sent UN troops into full retreat (see Chapter 4).

Additionally, aggressors can underestimate their adversaries' military capabilities and therefore expect an easier fight than actually occurs. When the USSR attacked Finland in 1939, Moscow expected that its 1 million soldiers would easily defeat the 200,000 Finnish troops but was stunned when Finnish forces dealt several heavy blows and held out for almost four months before being forced to meet Soviet demands.

Finally, states may get the impression that their opponents are actually preparing to attack rather than to resist a potential challenge. It can be difficult to convince other states that the tanks, aircraft, and missiles used for deterrence are really intended for that purpose, rather than for offense or intimidation. This problem bedeviled East–West relations throughout the Cold War, as both sides introduced new weapons that they claimed would be used only to deter attacks but that the other side perceived as an offensive threat. For example, the USSR built a large number of intermediate-range nuclear missiles (discussed later in the chapter) in the 1970s and early 1980s and deployed them in Europe, claiming that they were intended to dissuade NATO from launching a preemptive nuclear strike. NATO responded by developing and deploying "Euromissiles" of its own in the 1980s, which it likewise claimed were designed to deter Moscow from attacking with its own intermediate-range weapons. In an attempt to avoid this kind of misperception, states may take steps to reassure their rivals that their intentions really are defensive. Examples of such reassurance measures include taking aircraft and missiles and bombers off high alert and storing artillery or bridging equipment in depots far from border areas so they could not be used to mount a surprise attack.

Defensive Weapons Systems

As stressed earlier, a key aspect of deterrence is credibility, and anything that weakens credibility is destabilizing. For this reason, many strategists regard defensive weapons systems that shoot down incoming missiles as potentially destabilizing because they reduce the effectiveness of mutual deterrence. The controversies over ABMs, the Strategic Defense Initiative (SDI, or "Star Wars"), and missile defense illustrate this strategic paradox. These systems were designed to destroy incoming missiles. This, of course, defied the logic of mutual assured destruction (MAD), which held that possession of a secure **second-strike capability** by both sides was the bedrock of strategic stability. (This means that enough weapons would survive an initial attack to launch a retaliatory second strike that would inflict unacceptable damage on the enemy. For stable mutual deterrence, each side must have the ability to inflict massive damage on the other even if the other side strikes first.)

Nevertheless, in the 1960s the United States contemplated development of an ABM system that could protect U.S. cities from nuclear attack (thereby upsetting mutual deterrence), but eventually it scaled back its plans and settled on a limited system designed to protect missile silos rather than cities. The idea was to safeguard the U.S. second-strike capability without reducing the potential effectiveness of a Soviet second strike, which would have decreased strategic stability and increased Soviet threat perceptions. Both the United States and the USSR eventually agreed (in the ABM treaty signed as part of the SALT process; see the section on "Arms Control and Disarmament" later in this chapter) to deploy no

▪ **Second-strike capability**
Ability to retaliate, even after a nuclear attack, and thus punish the initiator of a nuclear war.

more than two ABM sites, one around the national capital and one near an ICBM base complex. The USSR went ahead with its system, but the U.S. system never became operational.

SDI, proposed in the 1980s, was intended from the start to create a space-based "peace shield" or "nuclear Astrodome" over the United States. Critics in both the United States and USSR immediately contended that such a system would be prohibitively expensive and dubiously reliable, would disrupt mutual deterrence, and would prompt a renewed arms race, as it would leave the USSR with no choice but to build more offensive missiles to overwhelm the system. Some critics of SDI, in fact, argued that deploying the system would encourage the Soviet Union to attack before it became completely operational, because once it was operational, the USSR would be unable to retaliate. SDI remained contentious until the end of the Cold War, when the plan was shelved but not entirely canceled, as the United States continued research into space-based missile defenses.[21]

In the 1990s and early 2000s, under the George H. W. Bush, Clinton, and George W. Bush administrations, the United States revived the idea of a defensive shield by developing several systems for ballistic missile defense. Various concepts for missile defense systems involved land-, sea-, air-, and space-based components, but all were made possible by the rapid improvement of information and sensor technologies in the last decade of the twentieth century. Although some systems utilized interceptor missiles with explosive warheads (similar to the Patriot missiles used to intercept Scuds in the 1991 Gulf War) and others proposed to use lasers to shoot down incoming missiles, most operated by directing an interceptor into a direct collision with the target, a concept known as "hit to kill." Plans to develop and deploy ground-, sea-, and space-based defenses that could intercept ICBMs precipitated a storm of protest both in the United States and internationally, particularly after the United States unilaterally withdrew from the ABM treaty in June 2002. Controversy erupted again when Russia responded unfavorably to a Bush administration plan to install defensive weapons in eastern Europe (the stated purpose of the plan was the protect U.S. allies in Europe from missiles launched from Iran). The tension did not subside even as President Obama was elected in the United States and the plan was modified. In 2009, President Obama canceled the Bush administration plan to station a radar facility in the Czech Republic and interceptors in Poland, but in November 2010, Obama announced that NATO would develop a missile defense system capable of covering both Europe and the United States. Any defensive weapons in eastern Europe are seen as a threat to Russia.

As discussed in the opening of this chapter, the global debate on missile defense and its effects on security, fueled by mixed test results and continued political controversy, continued well into the twenty-first century. Proponents of missile defense argue that the proliferation of ballistic missile technology to states such as North Korea and Iran, which have developed or are believed to be developing nuclear weapons and are overtly or potentially hostile to the United States, make missile defense essential to U.S. security. Opponents contend that

PHOTO 7.3   An Arrow anti-ballistic missile launched from Point Mugu Sea Range in California.

the systems will never work as intended, could be easily overcome with countermeasures, will cost too much, and will provoke new arms races.[22] Defenses designed to defend U.S. forces and allies from shorter range missiles were much less controversial, and the United States proceeded to develop such systems in cooperation with NATO allies, Japan, and Israel.

Technology and Security

The rapid pace of development of both nuclear and conventional weapons since World War II underscores the importance of technology to military power. During the Cold War, frequent innovations in Soviet and American strategic weaponry produced a rough technological parity between the two superpowers but at the same time broadened the gap between them and the smaller nuclear powers. The successful use of high-tech weapons and information technology in both the 1991 Persian Gulf War and the 2003 Iraq War suggest that advanced technology is increasingly important in conventional military operations as well. Although the pace of technological advance has been quite dramatic since World

War II, especially in aerospace and electronics, technical developments have revolutionized warfare many times over since the first time a primitive hominid picked up a rock. (See Spotlight, "Nukespeak," for definitions of different weapon technology)

Breakthroughs, Lead Times, and Cost

Historically, three aspects of technological advance have proven particularly important: breakthroughs, lead times, and cost. Technological breakthroughs refer to the introduction of new weapons with potential capabilities so great that they require a new calculation of military strength; in such cases, if other states do not keep up with the innovator, they are quickly left behind in the competition for military power. The introduction of the machine gun in the late nineteenth and early twentieth centuries was such a breakthrough, as was the development of nuclear weapons by the United States at the end of World War II. Technological revolutions can have unpredictable effects, however. In 1906 Britain introduced the dreadnought, a new type of battleship with high-caliber guns and steam turbine engines. Dreadnoughts were so fast and powerful that older battleships quickly became obsolete. This ultimately worked to Britain's disadvantage, however, because it led to intense German efforts to achieve parity with the Royal Navy. A new naval arms race ensued, and Germany proved better able to compete in the construction of the new warships. Ultimately, the expense of conducting a naval arms race damaged the British economy almost as much as the German submarines that were eventually produced.

Although new weapons may initially seem impressive, the effect of a technological breakthrough on warfare is often not realized until a dramatic event or military disaster occurs. Although tactical missiles had existed for decades, the 1982 Falklands War demonstrated for the first time their devastating effect in naval combat. Argentina was able to effectively use a French-made air-launched Exocet missile (costing $200,000) to disable a British destroyer (costing $50 million). Britain eventually won the war, but the use of advanced missile technology demonstrated the vulnerability of its naval surface forces to missile attack.

Lead time is the time required between the initial decision to produce a weapon and its operational deployment. The production of weapons systems with long lead times may allow an innovator to widen (or narrow) the gap with its nearest competition, but the whole process carries with it considerable risk. For instance, it may allow a state's closest competitor to neutralize that weapons system with an innovation of its own, or at least improve its existing weapons. During World War II, Germany devoted substantial technological and material resources to the development of jet fighter aircraft. When the aircraft were developed and deployed, they were clearly superior to anything the Allies could put in the air. While Germany was developing the new weapons, however, the Allies concentrated on the refinement and mass production of tried-and-true designs. By the time the German jet fighters became operational, Allied superiority in

▪ SPOTLIGHT ▪

Nukespeak

This is a quick reference guide to the weapons terminology used in this chapter.[i]

ABM Antiballistic missile; a missile designed to destroy incoming missiles or their warheads before they hit the designated targets.

ALCM Air-launched cruise missile; a cruise missile launched from an airplane. *See* Cruise missile.

Atomic weapon An expression used in the 1940s and 1950s to describe a nuclear weapon that derives its energy from nuclear fission.

Ballistic missile A vehicle that travels to its target unpowered after a short period of powered flight. Most ballistic missiles are powered by rocket engines. Part of the flight of longer range ballistic missiles may occur outside the atmosphere and involve the "reentry" of the missile. A ballistic missile may deliver a conventional warhead or a nuclear, chemical, or biological weapon.

Biological weapon A weapon that uses living organisms, such as bacteria or viruses, or toxins produced by living organisms to cause death, disease, or injury to humans, animals, or plants.

Chemical weapon A weapon that uses toxic chemical substances to cause death or severe harm to humans or animals. The active chemicals (chemical agents) in chemical weapons can be gases, liquids, or solid powders and include blister, nerve, choking, and blood agents.

Conventional weapon Nonnuclear weapon such as a tank, artillery piece, or tactical aircraft (troops that operate these weapons are referred to as conventional forces).

Cruise missile An unmanned, self-propelled guided vehicle that sustains flight through aerodynamic lift for most of its flight path. A cruise missile may deliver a conventional warhead or a nuclear, chemical, or biological weapon.

First strike Ability to destroy or decisively weaken an opponent's strategic weapons or to prevent retaliation with an initial attack.

GLCM Ground-launched cruise missile; a cruise missile launched from land.

Hydrogen bomb A thermonuclear weapon that uses a hydrogen or fusion reaction in which atoms are fused together to produce an energy release. These weapons require a fission reaction that uses uranium or plutonium to get the temperature high enough to have the hydrogen atoms react.

ICBM Intercontinental ballistic missile; a land-based missile able to deliver a nuclear payload to a target more than 3,400 miles away (in practical terms, capable of going directly from the United States to Russia, or vice versa).

IRBM Intermediate-range ballistic missile; a land-based missile with a range of 1,700 to 3,400 miles.

MAD Mutual assured destruction; a condition that exists when both sides are able to survive a first strike with sufficient forces to retaliate in a second strike and inflict unacceptable damage on their opponent. Thus both would be destroyed regardless of who struck first, and therefore neither has an incentive to initiate a nuclear war.

MIRV Multiple independently targeted reentry vehicle; a single ballistic missile with several warheads that can each hit a separate target.

Nuclear weapon An explosive device that derives its energy from the splitting of atomic nuclei (fission), the joining together of atomic nuclei (fusion), or both.

Second strike Ability to retaliate even after a nuclear attack, and thus punish the initiator of a nuclear war.

SLBM Submarine-launched ballistic missile; a long-range ballistic missile carried in and launched from a submarine. Examples include the U.S. Poseidon and Trident missiles.

SLCM Sea-launched cruise missile; a cruise missile launched from a ship or submarine.

Strategic weapon Weapon that strikes directly at a state's home territory and the industry, resources, population, or military forces located there.

Tactical weapon Weapon designed for use on the battlefield, often in support of ground troops.

Thermonuclear weapon Explosive device that derives its power from nuclear fusion, or the coming together of atoms (usually hydrogen or helium; this is the same process that gives the sun its energy).

Warhead The bomb that a missile delivers to its target.

---

i. For the technical definitions of this subject, see Norman Polmar, *Strategic Weapons: An Introduction* (New York: National Strategy Information Center, 1982); Lawrence Freedman, *The Evolution of Nuclear Strategy* (London: St. Martin's, 1983); Sheila Tobias et al., *The People's Guide to National Defense* (New York: Morrow, 1982); or Sheikh R. Ali, *The Peace and Nuclear War Dictionary* (Santa Barbara, CA: ABC-CLIO, 1989).

numbers made the air war no contest, and Germany's advanced weapons had little impact.

A third important aspect of technological development is cost. High technology usually requires big money, and political and military leaders often face difficult decisions as to whether the new weapons will justify their increased costs. Throughout the 1980s, the increasing costs of the U.S. SDI ballistic missile

"GOOD BOY, GEORGE... NOW GO BUILD ME A MISSILE DEFENSE SYSTEM IN EUROPE."

For numerous reasons, the United States has embarked on a comprehensive missile defense program.

defense system threatened that program's budgetary future in Congress, especially because it was not known whether the system would work. In the 1990s and 2000s, similar issues of cost-effectiveness added to the controversy over national missile defense and other advanced technologies (for example, the B-2 Stealth bomber costs $1–2 billion per aircraft). By the same token, countries may try to maximize their "bang for the buck" by buying technologies or developing capabilities that give them a decisive edge at a low cost. Unfortunately, biological and chemical weapons can achieve this, as can the ability to deliver even a single nuclear bomb. These are "asymmetrical strategies," intended to opt out of regular warfare to gain an advantage despite opponents' obvious superiority. Another form of asymmetrical threat is support for insurgents, rebels, or terrorists already within an opposing state. These are means by which low-tech states with a clear disadvantage in direct conflict can nonetheless increase their leverage and effect (as we have seen in Iraq since 2003).

The Offense/Defense Balance

Because wars are fought with the weapons of the time, the history of international security has been inextricably linked to the history of military technology. Changing military technology has made territorial acquisition and war more likely at certain points in time and less likely at others. In fact, the history of military technology can be interpreted as a struggle between offense and defense, referred to as the offense/defense balance. The argument is that certain periods in history can be characterized by a technological dominance of either the offense or the defense. Whenever the offense is dominant, wars are more likely to occur and can be expected to be shorter in duration and less costly. Conversely, when the defense is dominant, wars are less likely to occur, but if they do break out, they can be expected to last longer and to be more destructive. At the same time, territorial aggrandizement is unlikely to occur, although internal security challenges may arise.[23]

A technological shift, for instance, occurred in the late nineteenth century with the introduction of the breech-loading rifle and the machine gun. Prior to these developments, it was possible (albeit at an often staggering cost in human lives) to break through defensive lines with a well-organized large-scale offensive, as had been demonstrated many times during the wars of the eighteenth century and the Napoleonic Wars. However, with these new defensive weapons, frontal assaults became tantamount to mass suicide. This became painfully obvious during the American Civil War, but this lesson was ignored by the European powers until the massive carnage of World War I drove the point home. By World War II, the introduction of the tank and aircraft onto the battlefield again overturned defensive dominance. These new weapons allowed aggressors once more to break through defensive lines quickly and thus conduct rapid, short wars, most dramatically demonstrated by the German blitzkrieg attacks on Poland and France.

Although certain technological developments seem to make territorial conquest and empire building easier or harder, it is not always simple to classify a given historical period as offense or defense dominant, particularly during the period itself. Although the lessons to be drawn from the defensive wars of the end of the nineteenth century may seem fairly straightforward in hindsight, they were generally unappreciated at the time. In fact, most countries flatly ignored them and continued to believe in the possibility of offensive breakthroughs. It has been argued that this erroneous perception of the offense/defense balance (the "cult of the offensive") was one of the important factors leading to World War I, as Chapter 3 points out. Learning the right lessons from technological developments, particularly those that have not yet been extensively used on the battlefield, is a key challenge for strategists and military leaders.

The Cutting Edge

Four related trends illustrate how technology is likely to have an even greater impact on security as the new era progresses. The first trend is the emergence of space as a theater of military operations. Space has attained great economic and strategic importance through the increased use of satellites to collect and transmit data, the most precious cargo of the information age. Just as seventeenth-century navies struggled for control of the seas and twentieth-century air forces battled for control of the air, twenty-first-century space forces will contest the control of orbital space. This is no longer science fiction. The U.S. Space Command, which coordinates the operation and protection of U.S. military satellites, can deploy antisatellite missiles to destroy an opponent's space platforms. In 2007, China also demonstrated its capability to destroy spacecraft in antisatellite tests when it successfully destroyed an aging weather satellite. The growing reliance of military forces on satellites to locate targets, track friendly and hostile forces, transmit information, and coordinate movements will make "space power" as important to military success as sea power and airpower were in earlier periods.[24] The first potentially decisive actions of future wars may be silent battles fought high above the earth's atmosphere.

The second trend in security technology is the combination of advanced information systems with improved delivery systems, referred to by American analysts as the "revolution in military affairs." (The term itself shows an unfortunate lack of imagination, as the same expression was used more than forty years ago by Soviet theorists to describe the changes in military science brought about by nuclear weapons.) Satellite reconnaissance and navigation, "stealth" weapons capable of evading defenses, and "smart" weapons with uncanny accuracy make air, sea, and land battles deadlier than ever.[25] The lethality of these weapons systems was dramatically demonstrated during the Persian Gulf War of 1991, where missiles flew through doors and ventilation shafts to their targets while transmitting video images (keep in mind, however, that most of the missiles used by the United States in the Gulf War were traditional "dumb" bombs, many of which missed their targets). Weapons guided by computers and directed from space decimated the Iraqi army in the Gulf conflict, leaving the stunned survivors easy prey for coalition forces. NATO forces used unmanned, unarmed aerial vehicles (UAVs) to transmit real-time video and other data to headquarters thousands of miles away (using satellite communications links for reconnaissance) and to strike targets in Kosovo in 1999. In Afghanistan in 2002, U.S. troops used small, unmanned ground vehicles (UGVs) to search caves and bunkers for Al Qaeda fighters. Within a few years, UAVs, UGVs, and unmanned underwater vehicles (UUVs) will be able to travel the battle area, select targets, fire weapons, and return to their bases without receiving commands from human operators. In Kosovo, Iraq, and Afghanistan, the technological superiority of one side gave it clear advantages, but what will happen when two armies equipped with twenty-first-century technology clash is less clear, as are the potential effects of these new technologies on the balance between offense and defense (discussed earlier). Just as the machine gun stunned the European powers with its lethality at the start of World War I, the "revolution in military affairs" may hold some nasty surprises in future conflicts.

Even nastier surprises may come from a third high-tech trend, the emergence of **information warfare.** Heavy reliance on computers and instantaneous communications has a downside for both military and civilian users: What happens if hackers break into and disrupt the systems, or a computer virus causes everything to crash? Because so much of the security and productivity of modern states depends on information technology, strategists are busily devising ways to disable enemy information systems and to protect their own. Before the twentieth century, armies were often paralyzed by

▪ **Information warfare**
Military use of computer networks to attack an opponent's capabilities for receiving, processing, and communicating information.

epidemics, and disease killed more soldiers than the enemy did. In the coming century, computer viruses may lay armies low, and inadequate software safeguards may make aircraft and missiles fatally vulnerable to tampering. Terrorists might attempt information strikes also; consider what could happen if a nation's banking system were suddenly wiped out by a software "bomb." Military forces will often be able to rely on low-tech backup methods if their advanced equipment were suddenly put out of action, but civilian industry could be much more vulnerable. Future information attacks may be faster and stealthier than even the slickest stealth bomber, and computer defenses will have to react with equal speed and sophistication. Conceivably, states or terrorists might fight a future information war in minutes, winning a decisive victory by doing billions of dollars of damage to the enemy's economy without causing a single human casualty.[26]

A final, and unexpected, trend in high-tech weaponry in the twenty-first century is a growing emphasis on nonlethal weapons. When military forces are assigned to peacekeeping duties rather than traditional military operations, weapons that can neutralize immediate threats to peace while avoiding civilian casualties or, if possible, any casualties at all will become increasingly useful. The principles behind advanced nonlethal weaponry include beams of electromagnetic energy that heat the skin to cause pain without permanent injury, directional sound beams to irritate dug-in soldiers or criminals holed up with hostages, and chemical agents that disperse attacking troops or mobs with nauseating but harmless smells.

Arms Control and Disarmament

The creation and deployment of military forces is not the only means states have to achieve their security objectives. As the security dilemma reminds us, too much armament can be as dangerous as too little. The potential dangers of excessive arms became most obvious in the nuclear era, when many began to fear that the nuclear arms race between the Unites States and USSR would eventually lead to the destruction of civilization. For these reasons, just as nations have invested their resources in building up adequate defensive capabilities against real or perceived threats, some also have tried to cooperate to control the dangerous and wasteful arms race. The most common way to do so has been through negotiations on arms control and disarmament.

Definitions

Arms control can be defined as "measures, directly related to military forces, adopted by governments to contain the costs and harmful consequences of the continued existence of arms (their own and others), within the overall objective of sustaining or enhancing their security."[27] In other words, the main

▪ **Arms control**
Agreements between two or more states or unilateral actions to regulate the research, manufacture, or deployment of weapons or troops on the basis of number, type, and/or location.

ambition of arms control is to minimize the most dangerous consequences of the security dilemma by limiting, but not necessarily reducing or eliminating, weapons and armed forces. In this way, arms control differs from **disarmament**, in which states actually reduce their overall arms levels. Arms control may therefore be viewed as a managed compromise between armament and disarmament.

Even though disarmament might seem to be the more desirable path, certain types of injudicious disarmament could actually increase the danger of international conflict. Reducing arms below the level that states might need to deter aggression (see the earlier discussion of deterrence) could enable or encourage potential aggressors to attack. Highly asymmetrical disarmament initiatives imposed on a weakened opponent could also increase the opponent's feeling of subjective insecurity, leading to a renewed cycle of arms races. This is precisely what happened to Germany in the immediate aftermath of World War I.

To avoid such paradoxical effects of arms reductions, the primary aim of arms control is strategic stability, meaning a situation in which neither side has an incentive to launch an attack on an opponent or to increase its armaments because of the particular configuration of armed forces. As we will see, this concept was the basis for the Conventional Forces in Europe (CFE) talks, the U.S.–Soviet SALT and START negotiations, and the post–Cold War U.S.–Russian SORT treaty.

Early Efforts at Disarmament

At the turn of the twentieth century, there was already a widespread feeling in the international community that the existing level of armaments was excessive. Two international peace conferences were convened in The Hague in an attempt to restrict or prohibit the use of certain weapons systems in war, including chemical and germ weapons. The outbreak of war in 1914 ended this first effort at international disarmament, but the movement was revitalized through several disarmament initiatives following four years of World War I's unprecedented carnage and brutality. The most grandiose of these efforts was the Kellogg–Briand Pact (1928), in which almost all the states of the world agreed to renounce war as an instrument of national policy and instead settle all international disputes by peaceful means. In reality, however, various countries interpreted the obligations of the treaty differently (particularly the one that safeguarded a state's right to self-defense). Because there were no effective means to ensure compliance, the treaty was a dead letter.

A somewhat more successful set of arms control agreements were the naval treaties of the 1920s and 1930s, in which the world's leading naval powers (the United States, Britain, Japan, Italy, and France) agreed to quantitative and qualitative restrictions on certain types of warships. These agreements, too, were beset by problems. First, the signatories complied with the letter of the treaty but redirected their efforts into unregulated areas of warship construction (especially aircraft carriers, which were not covered in the treaties). Second, two major

▪ Disarmament
The reduction or elimination of a state's overall arms levels.

powers were not sufficiently involved: Germany was left out of the negotiations, and Japan withdrew from the treaties in 1934.

The end of World War II saw renewed attempts to achieve far-reaching arms control agreements. One of the most important efforts was the **Baruch Plan,** in which the United States proposed that all atomic energy activities fall under the control of an international atomic development authority. The Soviet Union rejected this plan primarily because it believed, with good reason, that the real goal of the plan was to codify and make permanent the existing U.S. monopoly over nuclear weapons.

The enthusiasm for far-reaching arms control agreements waned during the early years of the Cold War, although efforts to regulate the arms race were not abandoned altogether. Negotiations continued over two principal areas: control of WMDs (including strategic nuclear weapons, intermediate-range and tactical nuclear weapons, **nuclear proliferation,** and chemical and biological weapons) and conventional arms control.

Test Bans

The most important efforts to limit WMDs have been made in the area of nuclear weapons. The first significant achievement was the Limited (or Partial) Test Ban Treaty of 1963, which was inspired by the dangerous nuclear face-off during the Cuban Missile Crisis. The Limited Test Ban Treaty was supplemented in 1974 by the Threshold Test Ban Treaty, which limited the superpowers' underground explosions to an upper limit of 150 kilotons. After two decades of fits and starts, the Comprehensive Nuclear Test Ban Treaty (CTBT), which prohibits all tests of nuclear explosives, was signed in 1996 by more than 100 states, including the five strategic nuclear powers. Hopes for the treaty's rapid entry into force, however, were dashed when the U.S. Senate refused to ratify the treaty in 1999. (The United States cited concerns that testing would be needed to verify the safety and reliability of its nuclear weapons and the possible need to develop "mininukes" and "bunker busters" to use against underground sites for production of WMDs in countries such as North Korea and Libya.)

More hopefully, the United States and other states have declared their support for a Fissile Material Treaty, which would impose a global halt on the production of fissile material for use in nuclear weapons (including enriched uranium and plutonium). Nevertheless, significant resistance to test bans remains in the defense communities of the nuclear states, which contend that continued testing is necessary to maintain the safety and reliability of existing weapons.

SALT, START, SORT, and New START

In the late 1960s, the strategic nuclear arsenals of the two Cold War superpowers became symmetrical enough (that is, both states developed secure second-strike capabilities) to allow for talks on strategic nuclear arms control. The principal

■ **Baruch Plan**
A post–World War II U.S. proposal that would have placed all atomic energy activities under the control of an international atomic development authority. This proposal was rejected by the USSR primarily because it would have made permanent the existing U.S. monopoly over nuclear weapons.

■ **Nuclear proliferation**
States acquiring nuclear weapons that did not formerly possess them.

negotiations of the process, the Strategic Arms Limitation Talks (SALT), took place in two slow and protracted stages.

The first stage culminated in the signing of the Strategic Arms Limitation Treaty (SALT I) in Moscow in 1972 (see Chapter 4). SALT I consisted of the Interim Agreement and the Anti-Ballistic Missile (ABM) Treaty.[28] The Interim Agreement put a ceiling on the number of land- and sea-based strategic nuclear missiles the two sides were allowed to retain while they were negotiating a more substantive agreement, which was to be signed at a future date. This ceiling froze the number of offensive strategic missiles at their 1972 levels of 2,568 for the USSR and 1,764 for the United States. The disparity was justified by the exclusion of long-range bombers, of which the United States had many more.

Overall, the Interim Agreement did not require any sacrifices by either side; it simply froze the arsenals at their existing levels and left many loopholes for both superpowers to exploit. The most important of these was the failure to limit the number of warheads per launcher, which allowed for the creation of multiple-warhead missiles (MIRVs) throughout the 1970s. These loopholes aside, the Interim Agreement at least provided ways to verify arms limitations (that is, to make sure the other side did not cheat) through the use of orbital reconnaissance, or spy satellites. Because neither side wanted to admit officially that such satellites existed, they were referred to in the treaty as "national technical means" of verification.

The ABM Treaty of SALT I proved to be of greater long-term importance. Both parties were limited to not more than two ABM sites (one for the protection of the national capital, another to protect an ICBM complex), with not more than 100 interceptor missiles each. These restrictions did not result in any significant strategic adjustments by either side because both had become disappointed in the utility of ABMs. However, the ABM Treaty did prohibit the deployment of any space-based ABM system, which was an important element in the debate surrounding SDI (discussed earlier in this chapter).

The follow-up agreement to SALT I, creatively termed SALT II, was signed in 1979 but was never ratified by the U.S. Senate because of the Soviet invasion of Afghanistan (see Chapter 4). Even so, each side adhered to the guidelines of the treaty, while often accusing the other of noncompliance, sometimes justifiably and sometimes not. The provisions of the treaty were complex, but its central points were an aggregate ceiling of 2,250 launchers (including ICBMs, SLBMs, and heavy bombers) for both superpowers, as well as other limits on MIRVs. Unfortunately, the ceiling for MIRVed ICBMs still permitted both sides to increase their warheads by more than 40 percent from the initial signing of the treaty.

Indeed, a serious shortcoming of SALT II, as a whole, was that all of its aggregate limits were significantly higher than the levels existing at the time, thus allowing the superpowers to expand their arsenals to the treaty limits. Although it might have provided more predictability in the nuclear arms race, the SALT process was not particularly successful in curbing it; both qualitative improvements and quantitative increases in the superpower nuclear arsenals were permitted.

When Ronald Reagan assumed the presidency in 1981, the name of the negotiations was changed to the Strategic Arms Reduction Talks (START) to reflect his insistence on mutual and balanced reductions in strategic nuclear forces. The intellectual seeds of the START treaties were planted during the 1986 Reykjavik summit meeting between Reagan and Soviet Premier Mikhail Gorbachev, but it took negotiators more than four years to work out the final provisions of the January 1991 START I treaty. For the first time, an arms control treaty mandated genuine reductions in strategic arms, also addressing some of the weapons systems that are widely perceived to be destabilizing. The main parameters were set at 1,600 launchers and 6,000 warheads for each side.

On the negative side, the treaty suffered from several significant problems. It excluded certain weapons systems, had very permissive counting rules for some of the systems that were included, and placed far too few restrictions on modernization of existing systems. In a general sense, although strategic stability was one of the declared goals of the negotiations, the final result was somewhat disappointing because major steps like eliminating MIRVed ICBMs were not taken.

Significant as it was, START I was soon overshadowed by the collapse of the Soviet Union. Indeed, as the Cold War gave way to the new era, the arms race appeared to turn into an arms control race. Instead of trying to stay a step ahead of the adversary by developing new weapons systems, both the United States and Russia tried to outdo each other by advancing new proposals for nuclear arms reductions and even by unilaterally implementing cuts. This process led to the signing of START II in January 1993, whereby both sides pledged to reduce their strategic nuclear arsenals to no more than 3,500 warheads. In addition, START II fixed some of the problems with START I. For example, some of the permissive counting rules were tightened, and potentially destabilizing MIRVed ICBMs were to be eliminated.

The United States ratified START II in 1996, but Russia's ratification in 2000 attached conditions, including the Senate's acceptance of a 1997 agreement intended to demarcate the differences between theater and national missile defense systems (the latter falling under the limitations of the ABM Treaty). Russia regarded continued adherence to the ABM Treaty as an important aspect of strategic stability. Consequently, when the United States withdrew from the ABM Treaty in 2002, Russia stated that it would no longer consider itself bound by START II.

Proponents of arms control predicted a new U.S.–Russian arms race and other dire consequences, but Presidents George W. Bush and Vladimir Putin made continued discussions on arms control a priority for their administrations. In May 2002, barely one month after the United States had withdrawn from the ABM Treaty, these discussions culminated in the Treaty on Strategic Offensive Reductions, or SORT. SORT (also known as the Treaty of Moscow) obligates both parties to reduce their arsenals of operationally deployed offensive nuclear weapons to between 1,700 and 2,200 by 2012 but does not require them to dismantle or destroy the warheads taken out of service. Critics emphasized the omission of dismantlement and verification provisions as major weaknesses of the treaty, but the U.S. and Russian governments pledged to continue discussing measures to promote strategic stability.

Progress has continued into the administrations of Barack Obama and Dmitri Medvedev. Despite continued tension over missile defense, in April 2010 the two leaders signed an agreement (known as New START) that, if ratified, would reduce deployed strategic weapons to no more than 1,550 warheads or 800 launchers. These reductions, although not requiring the elimination of large numbers of warheads by either side, would need to be completed within seven years. The treaty reestablished an inspection regime (to monitor compliance) and could be the building block for a treaty including even further reductions. President Obama has made disarmament and the prevention of weapons proliferation a cornerstone of his administration.

The debates over the most recent arms control treaties show that just as during the Cold War, strategic arms control remains an inherently political process, and progress is difficult to achieve when it is linked to other political issues.

PHOTO 7.4   Barack Obama and Dmitri Medvedev sign the New START Treaty.

Nevertheless, through many disappointments and detours, bilateral negotiations between Washington and Moscow finally achieved significant agreements on the reduction of the two largest nuclear powers' strategic arsenals, and further reductions looked increasingly possible as the Cold War faded into distant memory.

Intermediate-Range and Tactical Nuclear Weapons

Strategic weapons were not the only nuclear forces considered for reductions in the waning days of the Cold War. In December 1987, after seven years of negotiations, the United States and the USSR signed the Intermediate-Range Nuclear Forces (INF) Treaty, which eliminated all nuclear missiles with a range of 310 to 3,400 miles. Although these weapons represented a relatively small portion of both superpowers' nuclear arsenals, the INF Treaty marked the first time that an entire class of nuclear weapons had been banned. By June 1991, all such weapons had been destroyed by both sides.

Another class of nuclear weapons lost much of their military significance after the disintegration of the Warsaw Pact and the reunification of Germany in 1990. Tactical nuclear weapons, with ranges between 95 and 310 miles, and battlefield nuclear weapons, with ranges of less than 125 miles, were no longer of any military importance in Europe. It was no great surprise, then, that both the Soviet Union (and subsequently Russia) and the United States announced unilateral steps to remove many of these weapons as the Cold War wound down to a close. After the August 1991 coup attempt in the Soviet Union, President George H. W. Bush declared that the United States would unilaterally reduce its short-range nuclear forces. In response, Gorbachev also announced similar steps. After the demise of the Soviet Union, the successor states agreed to transfer all of the tactical nuclear weapons on former Soviet territory to storage depots in Russia. By July 1992, the United States and former Soviet states had completed these steps, and by 1997 thousands of these weapons were dismantled without any type of formal arms control agreement. However, thousands more tactical nuclear weapons remain deployed, and concerns over the security of Russia's nuclear arsenal led many to conclude that reducing or eliminating these weapons should be an urgent priority.

Cooperative Threat Reduction

When the Soviet Union collapsed at the end of 1991, Russia and the other former Soviet states inherited the USSR's obligations to reduce its nuclear weapons. They also inherited widespread poverty and economic stagnation, compounded by the disintegration of the state-run economic system and the difficulties of building new economic, political, and social infrastructure. The newly independent states did not have enough funds to dismantle nuclear weapons safely and securely store their nuclear material, pay guards and other custodians of nuclear facilities, or take other steps to prevent theft or smuggling of plutonium or highly enriched uranium, which nuclear proliferators or terrorists could use to build nuclear weapons. Concerns rose that impoverished weapons specialists might sell their skills to the highest bidder, particularly countries intent on developing or expanding arsenals of ballistic missiles or nuclear, chemical, and biological weapons. A former Soviet general, Alexander Lebed, claimed that significant numbers of small "suitcase nukes" could not be accounted for and might have gone missing.

The United States and other countries responded to this unprecedented crisis by extending aid to Russia, Ukraine, Kazakhstan, and other former Soviet states through a partnership program known as Cooperative Threat Reduction (CTR). Starting in 1992, CTR and related programs provided funds, equipment, and technical assistance for dismantling missiles, submarines, nuclear warheads, and other strategic weapons. Plans for employing scientists and technicians formerly engaged in Soviet weapons programs in civilian occupations, and to convert military facilities for civilian research and production, were also put into operation. By 2002, the CTR program had removed all nuclear weapons from Kazakhstan, Ukraine, and Belarus and dismantled almost 6,000 nuclear warheads, more than 750 missiles, and twenty-four submarines. The Material Protection, Control, and Accounting (MPC&A) program had helped secure more than 200 tons of nuclear material.

The cooperative programs attracted criticism from both partners, however. The Russian side claimed that too much money was spent on American contractors and government workers and that programs for converting military industry were largely ineffective. American critics charged that Russia could not properly account for all the funds allocated to the programs and that the Russian side would not allow enough access to areas where weapons or nuclear material were stored to verify their security. Despite these criticisms, both partners remained committed to further cooperation to reduce the threat of "loose nukes."

Non-Proliferation Treaty

In addition to strategic nuclear weapons and intermediate-range and tactical nuclear weapons, a third major area of arms control after World War II concerned the proliferation of nuclear weapons. After the development of the atomic bomb and its use by the United States on Hiroshima and Nagasaki in 1945, the USSR, the United Kingdom, France, and China developed nuclear weapons. Many more countries embarked on research programs that gave them the potential to construct their own nuclear weapons.

To stem the danger of proliferation, the UN General Assembly adopted a resolution in 1961 calling on all states to sign a treaty prohibiting the transfer and acquisition of nuclear weapons. As mentioned in Chapter 4, the 1968 Treaty on the Non-Proliferation of Nuclear Weapons (NPT) prohibited states already in possession of nuclear weapons from helping other states to acquire them. Furthermore, nonnuclear weapon states were forbidden to manufacture or otherwise obtain nuclear arms and were to submit their nuclear programs to monitoring by the IAEA. Nuclear weapon states were allowed to facilitate the exchange of equipment, materials, and scientific and technical information on the peaceful uses of nuclear energy, and all states pledged to pursue further negotiations on arms control and disarmament.

Most of the countries signing the NPT had no intention of acquiring nuclear weapons in the first place. Several states with nuclear ambitions at the time (including India, Pakistan, South Africa, and Israel) refused to sign the treaty. Other countries, including Iran, Iraq, and North Korea, signed it but still continued their nuclear weapons programs. To prevent these countries from acquiring the weapons, the major nuclear suppliers began to meet in London in 1975 to develop a common approach to limit their nuclear exports. The Nuclear Suppliers Group eventually produced a set of guidelines for the transfer of peaceful nuclear technology. However, as the recent example of North Korea indicates, export controls remain insufficient to prevent nuclear proliferation. At the same time, many nonnuclear weapon states argued that the nuclear weapon states were not taking their obligation to pursue nuclear disarmament seriously, as none of them planned to dismantle their own nuclear arsenals. The nuclear weapon states responded by pointing out the progress made in strategic arms control (outlined earlier), which effectively ended the nuclear arms race (although it did not result in total elimination of nuclear weapons), and by contending that their commitment to nuclear disarmament was linked to progress on "general and complete" disarmament, which no parties to the treaty were seriously pursuing.

The fragmentation of the new era has led many states to rethink their policies toward nuclear proliferation. This has already happened with France and China, both of whom eventually signed the NPT after holding out for more than two decades. Setting other hopeful examples, Brazil and Argentina jointly agreed to halt their nuclear weapons programs in 1991, and South Africa revealed and destroyed its small nuclear capability in 1993. In 1995, the treaty was extended indefinitely, further strengthening the commitment of most states to preventing the spread of nuclear weapons. The NPT review conference of 2000 ended without making significant concrete progress, but it issued a declaration of thirteen practical steps, including ratification of the Comprehensive Nuclear Test-Ban Treaty, that states could take to strengthen nonproliferation and promote nuclear disarmament.

On the other hand, the dangers of new states gaining nuclear weapons in a more fragmented international arena have increased. As noted earlier, a number of states are known or believed to be continuing to develop nuclear weapons, even though some, such as Iran, are members of the NPT (to circumvent this problem, North Korea withdrew from the NPT in 2003 to pursue its nuclear weapons program). (Chapter 8 discusses current proliferation dangers.) Although the cause of nonproliferation has come a long way, the possibility that dictators or terrorists will build or buy nuclear weapons, or that nations that have not declared them will use them in regional conflicts, will continue to be serious security concerns in the new era.[29]

Chemical Weapons, Biological Weapons, and Missiles

As terrible as nuclear weapons are, they were neither the first nor the only WMDs. Chemical weapons, poisons designed to incapacitate or kill people after touching the skin or being inhaled, were first used as a weapon in World War I and have been employed in several wars since, such as in Yemen in the 1960s and in the Iran–Iraq War of the 1980s. The most common types of chemical weapons are vesicants, or blister agents, including the mustard gas that killed and blinded thousands of soldiers in World War I, and nerve agents, including sarin and VX, which are so toxic that a drop the size of a pinhead on the skin can cause death in a few minutes. In 1925, the Geneva Protocol prohibited the use but not the possession of chemical weapons, allowing many countries to build large stockpiles and continue their research and production programs. In 1980 the UN Conference on Disarmament began work on a treaty that would ban chemical weapons. Since January 1993, more than 150 nations have signed the **Chemical Weapons Convention (CWC),** which bans their possession, acquisition, production, stockpiling, transfer, and use. The treaty was finally ratified by a sufficient number of states (including the United States and Russia) in 1997, and signatory states were required to dispose of these weapons by 2007. In 2006, the United States requested an extension of this deadline to April 29, 2012, because as of March 31, 2006, the United States had succeeded in destroying only 36.4 percent of its stockpile.[30] In addition, Russia, which inherited 40,000 tons of chemical weapons material from the former Soviet Union, would be incapable of destroying this toxic legacy by the 2007 deadline. The CWC includes stringent provisions for verification, including challenge inspections of facilities suspected of producing chemical weapons, and the Organization for the Prohibition of Chemical Weapons was created to implement verification and facilitate compliance. However, Syria, North Korea, and other states refused to sign, and they maintain chemical weapons or programs to develop them despite the international convention.

As if chemical weapons were not bad enough, biological weapons use viruses, bacteria, or the toxins they produce to strike at an enemy's population through "germ warfare." Organisms that can be used as biological warfare agents include the deadly but noncontagious anthrax bacterium and weaponized strains of bubonic plague, smallpox, and other virulent diseases. Biological weapons can also be directed against crops or livestock, using diseases such as glanders, wheat rust, or rice blast. Many states, including the United States, Britain, the Soviet Union, Germany, and Japan developed biological weapons before 1945,

▪ **Chemical Weapons Convention (CWC)** Treaty signed in 1993 that prohibits the production, use, or stockpiling of chemical weapons.

PHOTO 7.5 The Chemical Weapons Convention (CWC) bans the possession, acquisition, production, stockpiling, transfer, and use of chemical weapons.

and Japan made limited use of crude biological weapons against China during World War II. Although many experts claim that biological weapons have never been successfully used as a military weapon, many countries continue to fund biological weapons programs, including Iran, Syria, and, until its breakup, the Soviet Union (see again Map 7.1). (Some experts maintain that a small, highly secret biological weapons program may still exist in Russia.) At the same time, the use of biological weapons by terrorists has become a major security concern in the new era, and many states began biodefense programs in the 1990s to counter this threat.[31]

The 1925 Geneva Protocol bans the use of biological weapons, and the 1972 Biological and Toxin Weapons Convention (BWC) prohibits the use, possession, and manufacturing of these weapons. Each signatory is formally committed not to develop, produce, stockpile, acquire, or transfer biological agents. In contrast to the CWC, the BWC has no provisions for verification, and therefore no way to catch cheaters, which would be difficult even with an intrusive inspection regime, because most biological research and production technology can be used for both peaceful and military purposes. In the 1990s, a group of verification experts drafted an inspection protocol for the BWC that would create a means to monitor compliance, but in 2001 the United States rejected the draft protocol and withdrew from negotiations on BWC verification. In rejecting the protocol, Washington expressed concerns that subjecting

U.S. biotechnology companies to inspections could allow competing firms to steal trade secrets and could facilitate false accusations of treaty violations. The United States proposed alternative means of strengthening the BWC, and discussions on how to improve and monitor compliance with the treaty continued into the 2000s.

As noted previously, chemical and biological weapons, like nuclear weapons, can be delivered by **ballistic missiles.** Throughout the 1980s, concerns rose about the proliferation of ballistic missiles in many regions of the world. In 1983 seven industrialized states began negotiations to limit the export of ballistic missile technology. Although they could not agree on a treaty, they did agree on the creation of the Missile Technology Control Regime (MTCR), a voluntary arrangement that restricts the export of ballistic missiles capable of carrying more than 500 kilograms (considered to be the minimum payload required for a nuclear warhead) over a distance of 300 kilometers or more. This agreement was subsequently strengthened by the inclusion of several key suppliers, including Russia, Israel, Argentina, and Brazil, and China, and other states have agreed to adhere to MTCR guidelines, but it is not clear whether Russia and China are fully committed to fulfilling its requirements. In 2001, MTCR members drafted a Code of Conduct designed to expand and reinforce the regime's guidelines.

The MTCR has not succeeded in eliminating missile deployment programs already existing in several countries. It does, however, offer the prospect of significantly restraining exports if its members adhere to their agreements and accept limitations that restrict potential sales. The involvement of a growing number of countries in efforts to control missiles and WMDs shows how the spread of military technology has become a global problem that can be addressed only through global cooperation.

Conventional Arms Control

The control of conventional arms has remained one of the most difficult areas for arms limitation. Throughout the Cold War, the Warsaw Pact maintained an overwhelming quantitative conventional superiority that led to corresponding NATO buildups. This resulted in a situation in which two enormous armies of more than 1 million troops each, equipped with the most sophisticated weapons, confronted each other for more than forty years along the East German–West German border. NATO's worst military nightmare was a Soviet surprise attack across this line with the vast Warsaw Pact army already in eastern Europe.[32] From 1973 until 1986 both alliances negotiated to little avail over reductions of conventional forces in the Mutual and Balanced Force Reductions (MBFR) talks.

As with the nuclear arms race, the end of the Cold War proved to be a major catalyst for change. In November 1990 NATO and the Warsaw Pact countries signed the CFE Treaty, one of the most intricate arms control agreements ever reached. The treaty called for the destruction or removal from Europe of more

▪ **Ballistic missile**
A vehicle that travels to its target unpowered after a short period of powered flight. Most ballistic missiles are powered by rocket engines. Part of the flight of longer range ballistic missiles may occur outside the atmosphere and involve the "reentry" of the missile. A ballistic missile may deliver a conventional warhead or a nuclear, chemical, or biological warhead.

than 125,000 tanks, artillery, armored vehicles, aircraft, and helicopters. In sharp contrast to the protracted MBFR negotiations, it took the twenty-two signatory states only twenty months to complete the treaty. The Soviet Union in particular made large concessions that removed the threat of a blitzkrieg-type Soviet invasion of western Europe even before the final collapse of the USSR. The demise of the communist superpower, ironically, created new difficulties in implementing the CFE Treaty, as the USSR's successor states argued among themselves over the allocation of the remaining weapons permitted under the agreement. Russia also argued that the treaty's "flank limits," which govern the equipment allowed in the northeastern and southeastern portions of the regions covered by the agreement, had to be revised to reflect its new security concerns, but this problem was resolved through the signing of an understanding with NATO in 1997. Difficulties erupted again in 2007 as Russian President Vladimir Putin announced the suspension of the CFE in July in response to

What Would You Do?

Nuclear Proliferation

You are the prime minister of Japan. The time is the present. Your intelligence services inform you that North Korea has completed a secret nuclear weapons assembly plant. The reports, confirmed by U.S. and South Korean intelligence, estimate that when the plant becomes operational, North Korea will be able to build ten to twenty nuclear weapons each year. They suspect, although they cannot be sure, that these weapons could be mounted on ballistic missiles with sufficient range to hit most cities in Japan, including Tokyo.

How should your country respond to this threat? You might ask the United States to destroy the plant with an air strike, but this could easily provoke a second Korean War, and Pyongyang would certainly retaliate, possibly by using terrorists to attack a Japanese city with chemical or biological weapons. You could secretly order the development of your own nuclear weapons to deter a North Korean nuclear attack, but your efforts would surely be detected and would distress the United States, anger China, and panic South Korea. You could cooperate with the United States and/or South Korea to develop and deploy theater missile defenses, but you could never be sure of their effectiveness, and Russia and China would probably try to block the program. Finally, you could reveal the existence of the plant in hopes of mustering international diplomatic pressure against Pyongyang, but the North Korean regime has never cared about world opinion, and the Japanese public may come to regard your moderate action as a sign of weakness or incompetence.

Each of these options has its own set of attendant risks, and all may seem unpalatable at best, but there are few easy choices where national security is concerned.

Perhaps you can come up with a better option, but the clock is ticking.

What Would You Do?

"extraordinary circumstances" affecting Russian security. Russian officials believe the CFE treaty is outdated, and negotiations continue as to the future of the accord.

Conventional arms control has far broader relevance beyond Europe and the United States, however. The developing world, in particular, where, over the course of the Cold War and since, the majority of combat casualties has taken place, has failed to undertake adequate arms control, so that even as defense spending has declined in most of the industrialized states, it has continued to increase in the developing world, particularly in the two poorest regions: sub-Saharan Africa and South Asia.[33] Part of the problem is that many developing countries rely on defense expenditures for growth, even though the linkage between military spending and economic benefits has yet to be conclusively proven. Some developing countries emphasize defense expenditures either because their leadership is largely military or as a means of appeasing the military and preventing coups d'état. The industrialized world is also culpable. Industrialized states tend to rely on the developing world as an arms market as their own demands decline, and they also use arms sales and military aid to developing countries as a means of diplomacy. When, in 2001, the United Nations held a conference about limiting the spread of illicit small arms worldwide, a problem that has exacerbated the numerous conflicts in Africa, in particular, but also nourishes conflicts elsewhere, none of the five permanent members of the Security Council was in favor. Although it is easy to focus on nuclear and conventional disarmament in the developed world, it would be irresponsible and dangerous to overlook the failure, thus far, of disarmament in the developing world, those volatile countries and regions most likely to experience violent conflict.

Conclusion

All nations face a security dilemma that they must manage, either through international negotiations, unilateral measures, or both. Regardless of their choices, the pursuit of the various goals that states include in their definition of "national security" consumes a significant portion of their available resources. This is understandable because one of the primary responsibilities of a state is the provision of security for its citizens. Beyond a certain point, however, the pursuit of security begins to have detrimental effects on a state's relations with its neighbors and the international community, and on the state itself. Determining the point where the proportion of a state's material and human resources devoted to security becomes self-defeating is a difficult task for its leaders, but an essential one.

Because many aspects of international security are fraught with uncertainty, there is no way to determine precisely how much security is enough.

The threats a state faces and the measures it should adopt in response depend heavily on perceptions. Ultimately, if national security is defined as the preservation of sovereignty and territorial integrity, the resources a state spends on national security are part of the price of independence. Just as an individual must decide how much health or accident insurance to purchase depending

Levels of Analysis and Paradigms in Review: Security Examples

	Realism	Liberalism	Constructivism
Individual	Chinese leader Mao Zedong believed that military power is essential for measuring a state's capability to influence world politics. As evidence, he once said, "Political power grows out of the barrel of a gun."	Individual world leaders have different views of the utility of arms control treaties. As a consequence, at certain times states pursue the reduction of weapons and at other times that notion has been rejected.	In the 1930s, Joseph Stalin perceived significant threats against himself and the Soviet Union that other actors could not understand. Stalin's perception of the international and domestic environment was conceived through his own paranoia and hostility.
Domestic	Carl von Clausewitz, in his famous dictum, "War is nothing but the extension of politics by other means," highlights the fact that wars are fought for political objectives and are far more likely to succeed if the nation supports the underlying goals of the military campaign.	In part as a consequence of widespread poverty and economic stagnation, the former republics of the Soviet Union that inherited nuclear weapons when the Soviet Union collapsed were willing to pursue cooperative solutions to dismantling these weapons and returning the components to Russia.	Beliefs about war were changing after World War I. Public opinion, especially in Europe and the United States, was heavily in favor of avoiding another massive conflict. As a consequence, states pursued arms control measures to curb the destruction and carnage of war.
Systemic	The potential for conflict is ever-present, and to protect itself a state must arm itself. The risk of preparing for armed conflict is less than remaining defenseless in a zero-sum game.	The security dilemma can be partially overcome through confidence-building measures, diplomacy, regimes, and international institutions. The world is a variable-sum game, and conflict can be avoided through cooperation.	The security dilemma is a product of realists' assumptions about anarchy. States can learn and change the negative environment by engaging in a positive tit-for-tat to create cooperative relationships.

on his or her specific needs, states must consider the threats confronting them and the strategies and resources available when they purchase their "security insurance." If they spend too little, they risk catastrophic losses from aggression not covered by their defense effort; if they spend too much, their other goals or values may suffer.

No matter how much attention a nation gives to these matters, absolute security is impossible to attain. Every security strategy involves risks of one sort or another, and the events of September 11, 2001, showed that even the most powerful state can never be totally secure. Consequently, each state must choose some combination of armament and disarmament, deterrence and defense, and multilateral cooperation and unilateral action to meet its security needs, and each option has its own inherent drawbacks. Considering the impact of advancing technology, military analysts describe how wars of the future will be different from wars of the past, but leaders mindful of the continuing threats posed by terrorism and WMDs realize that the peace of the future will be different from the peace of the past as well. As long as the possibility of conflict exists, and it always will, all states must assess the threats they face, decide how best to protect their land and people, and choose the sacrifices they will make and the risks they will accept in the name of national security.

Discussion and Review Questions

1. "War is nothing but the extension of politics by other means." What did Carl von Clausewitz mean by this statement? What are the perils of ignoring this dictum?
2. What is soft power, and how do states attain it? Which states possess soft power, and why? Which do not, and why?
3. How does the United States use the four types of deterrence (general, immediate, primary, and extended)? Provide examples of the application of each type.
4. Discuss the evolution of defensive weapons systems. What are the pros and cons of possessing such systems?
5. Discuss the What Would You Do? on page 287. What are the options, and what are the costs and benefits of each?

Key Terms

Arms control 275
Ballistic missile 286
Baruch Plan 277
Biological weapons 251
Capability 263

Chemical weapons 251
Chemical Weapons
    Convention (CWC) 284
Commitment 262
Compellence 259

Conventional weapons 263
Credibility 263
Defense 259
Deterrence 259
Disarmament 276

CHAPTER **8**

Contemporary Security Issues

Chapter 7 dealt with issues of traditional security, such as deterrence, defense, military power, and arms control. This chapter focuses on security issues that have dominated the post–Cold War landscape. In this new era, big power security issues, although still important, have taken a backseat to a series of more focused issues. Conflict and our concept of war have changed. The issues discussed in this chapter—terrorism, proliferation of WMDs (weapons of mass destruction, including nuclear, biological, chemical, and radiological weapons), and transnational crime—represent what political scientist John Mueller terms "the remnants of war." He claims that classic war, especially major war or war among developed countries, is in decline and has been replaced by wars that are "opportunistic predation waged by packs...of criminals, bandits and thugs.... [Thus] warfare has been reduced to its remnants—or dregs—and thugs are the residual combatants." The solution to dealing with these conflicts and the issues that arise from them, according to Mueller, is the development of "competent domestic governments," not necessarily international intervention.[1]

Yet that answer is too simple, given that these conflicts can have global effects so serious that the international community cannot simply wait for local governments to evolve to meet some standard of competence. Domestic conflicts can spill into neighboring states (as we have seen happen with Sudan, Somalia, Iraq, Afghanistan, and the Democratic Republic of Congo). (See Spotlight, "Human Costs of Modern Conflict," for more on domestic conflicts.) Transnational conflicts by definition transcend state boundaries (as do the conflicts between Shiites and Sunnis and between Arabs and Kurds). Even the smallest local conflicts can have worldwide repercussions, as is the case with the battle for control over the Niger Delta in Nigeria. Thus, though Mueller may well be right that in the absence of good governance conflicts will continue to arise and may not be resolved, the international community must nonetheless involve itself to some extent if only because its constituent states must protect their interests.

These challenges demonstrate perfectly the tangled relationship between the dual trends of globalization and fragmentation. Conflicts rooted in fragmentation can have global effects because of the interconnectedness of all states' economies and security. Globalization, in turn, can lead to pressures for fragmentation as groups feel threatened by encroachment of others' values, cultures, industries, or influence.

Although there are numerous security issues that could be included in this discussion, our selected topics—proliferation of WMD, **terrorism,** and organized crime—pose serious security threats in and of themselves, and combined they create a much more expansive problem. For example, issues surrounding the proliferation of nuclear weapons are compounded by the fear that they will be acquired and used by terrorist groups. Further, transnational criminal organizations (TCOs) engage in drug trafficking and arms sales. Terrorist organizations and TCOs are not always distinct from one another, especially as terrorist groups turn to crime to finance their operations. Thus, none of these security challenges exist in a vacuum. They each must be considered within the overall context of the post–Cold War environment and, more recently, the post–September 11 environment. These issues pose difficult and often related challenges for the international community, and combating them is a top priority of states, NGOs, and international organizations in the twenty-first century.

▪ **Intrastate conflict**
Discord occurring within the borders of a single state.

▪ **Terrorism**
The unlawful use—or threatened use—of force or violence against individuals or property to coerce or intimidate governments or societies, often to achieve political, religious, or ideological objectives.

Proliferation

Many internal, regional, and global conflicts are exacerbated by states developing and possessing nuclear weapons. Many of these states (such as North Korea and Pakistan) are ruled by tenuous regimes, and others (including Iran and Syria) are known or suspected to be major sponsors of terrorists. The status of the seven open nuclear weapons states (United States, Russia, France, Great Britain, India, Pakistan, and China) is widely accepted. (Israel's nuclear status is also widely known, although they fail to acknowledge it; many states, especially Arab states, continue to protest the existence of such weapons in Israel.) The international community is not comfortable with other states acquiring nuclear weapons

SPOTLIGHT

Human Costs of Modern Conflict

Many conflicts in the developing world are the consequence of **intrastate conflict** (occurring within the boundaries of a single state). These "failed states" cannot provide the minimally acceptable standards for domestic conditions, such as peace, order, and security. As Chapter 5 made clear, these states often "are a consequence of the end of empire. They are a price of unrestricted self-determination of former, usually colonial, dependencies."[i] Failed states are characterized by a complete breakdown of law and order, the rise of competing gangs (or warlords or strongmen), and the victimization of the general population.

If you watch the news on a regular basis, you will be familiar with the states that are in varying degrees of "failure." An annual index of failed states (compiled by the journal *Foreign Policy* and the Fund for Peace) ranks states according to twelve indicators, including movement of refugees or internally displaced persons creating complex humanitarian emergencies, sharp or severe economic decline, criminalization and/or delegitimation of the state, progressive deterioration of public services, and suspension or arbitrary application of the rule of law and widespread violation of human rights. The 2009 Failed States Index highlighted the fact that many of the most vulnerable (unstable) states are in Africa. The report includes 177 countries, with the most unstable being Somalia (as discussed in Chapter 6, instability has plagued this nation since the 1990s) and the most stable being Norway (the United States ranks 159th). The top ten failed states are Somalia, Zimbabwe, Sudan, Chad, Democratic Republic of the Congo, Iraq, Afghanistan, Central African Republic, Guinea, and Pakistan. It should not go without notice that the two countries whose governments have been overthrown by U.S.-led coalitions in the "War on Terror," Iraq and Afghanistan, both make the top ten. In addition, an important U.S. ally in the "war on terror", Pakistan, is also in the top ten.[ii]

Numerous conflicts in Africa highlight the problems of failed states. The majority of conflicts on the continent are intrastate, and often the dilemma for the international community is whether to intervene to stop the bloodshed or not. Somalia, for example, which was discussed in Chapter 6, has been wracked with internal clan warfare that has left that state in anarchy since 1991. A new Somali president, Abdullahi Yusuf Ahmed, came to power in 2004 and formed a new Transitional Federal Government (TFG), but in June 2006, the Union of Islamic Courts (UIC) took control of Mogadishu and appointed a hard-line Islamic leader to head the legislature. By the end of the year, with the help of Ethiopian forces, the TFG had recaptured Mogadishu. As a result, the Islamists, armed by Ethiopia's regional enemy Eritrea, adopted insurgent tactics, including the use of landmines, hit-and-run raids, and even suicide bombings. Somalia earned public attention again beginning in 2005 because of piracy in the Indian Ocean carried out by Somalis. Pirates have hijacked vessels from numerous countries, and many of these countries have responded with military measures. Thus violence continues to wrack the country and basic services continue to be denied. Similarly, the Republic of the Congo experienced a brief civil war in 1997, and although a peace accord was signed in 2003, the peace is tenuous and refugees continue to pose a humanitarian problem. In Chad, sporadic rebel activity has plagued the nation since a rebellion broke out in northern Chad in 1998. Although elections have been held several times, they are flawed and controversial, and rebel activity remains a significant threat to the population. The situation in Liberia is also tenuous. Fourteen years of civil war ended in August 2003 (after which Charles Taylor, the former president, was exiled to Nigeria; he was subsequently tried for crimes against humanity for the alleged support he gave to the rebel factions in Sierra Leone). The United Nations maintains a peacekeeping mission in the country, attempting to ensure security and disarm the former combatants, but the security situation is uncertain. Last, as highlighted in Chapter 6, Sudan continues to experience genocide despite numerous attempts at cease-fires and peace agreements. Many persons have been killed or remain displaced, both internally and in neighboring Chad.

Failed states highlight the concerns over human security, discussed in Chapter 7. If we believe that people should be free from fear and want, failed states truly represent a serious global problem in terms of the human condition. Conditions for the citizens who reside in states incapable of performing the basic functions of government are often horrendous. The case of Liberia in 1998 (eighteen months after the end of conflict) provides a classic example of conditions in a failed state:

> The country was without public utilities: no power, no running water, no functioning communications system, and no public transportation. Road systems were primitive at best, with most of the country served by seasonal roads that became completely impassable during the two rainy seasons. Government administration, whether at the local, county or national level, was almost nonexistent. There were no written or electronic records of residents, births, deaths, tax compliance, no drivers licenses, no government data bases, nothing left of the prewar criminal justice record system, and no functioning intelligence system.[iii]

As a consequence of these conditions, residents succumb to disease or are the victims of violent crime. Many flee their homes and take up residence in refugee camps inside the country or in neighboring countries. Human rights are routinely violated. In Sudan, for example, Amnesty International found that in 2007 the militias were attacking civilians and launching cross-border raids into Chad. Civilians were killed and displaced (some were forced to move several times), and they were frequently targeted by air force bombings. In addition, torture was widespread, government forces arbitrarily detained citizens, excessive force was used against demonstrators, and rape remained systematic.[iv]

The women and children who reside in failed states are subject to unspeakable horrors. Women are often the targets of domestic violence, rape, and genital mutilation. In at least twenty countries around the world, children (both boys and girls) are recruited to be active combatants in war. Human Rights Watch reported on these "soldiers":

> *Denied a childhood and often subjected to horrific violence, an estimated 200,000 to 300,000 children are serving as soldiers for both rebel groups and government forces in current armed conflicts. These young combatants participate in all aspects of contemporary warfare. They wield AK-47s and M-16s on the front lines of combat, serve as human mine detectors, participate in suicide missions, carry supplies, and act as spies, messengers or lookouts.[v]*

Many child soldiers are recruited by force, and because they are vulnerable and easily intimidated, they follow orders (although sometimes under threat of death). Others join willingly out of desperation when society breaks down, leaving them without access to schooling, often chased from their homes, and separated from their families.[vi]

In addition to the often unbearable existence of those who live in these states, failed states can be a haven for terrorists. The conditions in failed states, as already described, make them "very attractive venues for terrorists and terrorist groups seeking to avoid the reach of criminal justice systems and of military counterterrorist forces."[vii] This poses an obvious problem to those governments seeking to combat terrorism worldwide: If there is no control in failed states used as terrorist hubs, terrorists can train, equip themselves, and prepare for attacks uninterrupted. This concern increases dramatically when WMDs are added to the equation. Because WMDs are proliferating—nuclear weapons in particular—it becomes increasingly likely that these weapons could "find their way from state proliferators into the hands of terrorist groups."[viii] Thus, the conditions in failed states around the globe impact concerns about terrorism and proliferation, and thus lend credence to the arguments favoring a focus on human security.

---

i. Robert H. Jackson, "Surrogate Sovereignty? Great Power Responsibility and 'Failed States,'" Institute of International Relations, Working Paper No. 25 (November 1998), 2.

ii. The Fund for Peace, Failed State Index 2009, http://www.fundforpeace.org/web/index.php?option=com_content&task=view&id=99&Itemid=140, accessed June 1, 2010.

iii. Thomas Dempsey, "Counterterrorism in African Failed States: Challenges and Potential Solutions," Strategic Studies Institute (April 2006), 1.

iv. Amnesty International Report 2007: Sudan, http://thereport.amnesty.org/eng/Regions/Africa/Sudan, accessed July 25, 2007.

v. Human Rights Watch, "Child Soldiers," http://hrw.org/campaigns/crp/index.htm.

vi. Ibid.

vii. Dempsey, "Counterterrorism in African Failed States."

viii. Ibid.

(especially North Korea and Iran) or with the possibility that terrorist groups may access the knowledge or materials to develop nuclear weapons.

The possibility that nuclear material or the technical knowledge needed to make nuclear weapons might "leak" out of the former Soviet states, where security measures on nuclear facilities were revealed to be seriously inadequate, heightened proliferation concerns at the end of the Cold War, and major international efforts were launched to prevent this frightening possibility.[2] In the 1990s, as more states developed nuclear weapons programs (India, Pakistan, North Korea), the fear of nuclear knowledge and materials spreading intensified. The prevention of proliferation to both states and nonstate actors has become one of the highest security priorities of the new era.

The Debate over Proliferation

On its face, the idea of more states possessing nuclear weapons may seem like an obvious international hazard. However, as with most issues in international relations, there are two sides to this story. The proliferation debate breaks down into two sets of scholars, one group known as the optimists, the other known as the pessimists. Although there are many scholars on each side, the two most famous proliferation debaters are Kenneth Waltz (the optimist) and Scott Sagan (the pessimist). (In fact, their back-and-forth analysis appeared in their 1995 book, *The Spread of Nuclear Weapons: A Debate*, and again in 2003 with *The Debate Renewed*.) The optimists believe that proliferation is beneficial in the international arena and any negative aspects to proliferation can be contained. As discussed in Chapter 7, a credible deterrent can prevent crises, and the optimists believe that there is no better form of deterrence than nuclear weapons. Optimists point to the absence of war between the United States and Soviet Union during the Cold War to demonstrate the stabilizing aspect of nuclear deterrence. The superpowers existed in the highest stage of nuclear balance (MAD), thus ensuring mutual annihilation in a nuclear confrontation. It is undeniable that the costs of nuclear war are high (an understatement to say the least), and because the purpose of deterrence is to convince your adversary that the costs outweigh any potential gains, this argument seems to have some credibility.

Pessimists, on the other hand, argue that the likely hazards of proliferation far outweigh any potential deterrent capability. From this perspective, the main problem with the argument of the optimists is that it requires states to operate as unitary, rational actors. In a realist argument, Waltz (the optimist) asserts with confidence that states will always work to maximize their self-interest. Sagan (and other pessimists), however, challenges the belief that states can consistently recognize and act in accordance with what is in their best interests. In a domestic-level argument, Sagan contends that organizational and bureaucratic obstacles prevent states from always engaging in rational and coherent behavior. For example, Sagan argues that bureaucratic competition can undermine rational action, leading to the use of nuclear weapons, and poor countries will experience difficulties in the command and control of their arsenals.[3]

Although the debate is generally characterized by the arguments of Sagan and Waltz, there are additional concerns. First, if deterrence is to succeed, as discussed in Chapter 7, one's threat must be credible. Many view the threat of using nuclear weapons as empty, in that no state since the United States in 1945 has used them, and the repercussions in the international arena would be so detrimental as to make their use unfeasible. Second, newly emerging nuclear states find themselves in a very different situation than that of the superpowers during the Cold War. It is assumed that new nuclear weapons states (such as India and Pakistan) possess arsenals that are much smaller than what would be needed to create a situation of MAD between them. Thus the situation between these types of states may be highly unstable, as one might attempt to destroy the nuclear arsenal of another in a first strike or as nuclear weapons might be used against conventional forces.

Command and Control

Beyond the concern of states facing off with each other, ultimately, contemporary fears about the proliferation of nuclear weapons come down to issues of command and control. Once a state possesses nuclear weapons, there are three threats to the system: accidental use, unauthorized use, and inadvertent use.[4] Accidental use would be if "everyone is surprised" by its use, and such occurrences would fall into one of two categories: accidental detonation and accidental launch. An accidental detonation would be caused by "some mishap, such as a plane crash or fire," causing the warhead to explode, whereas "an accidental launch could result from a technical defect (such as faulty wiring) or unsafe procedures that caused the premature firing."[5] Pessimists believe that accidental use in proliferating states is a significant concern because the weapons will be relatively crude in design, the weapons will not have undergone the proper testing, and these states will most likely fail to implement proper safety procedures and technologies because of a lack of resources. Optimists, on the other hand, believe there is a relatively simple solution to this problem: Store the weapons disassembled. This solution is not likely to be accepted by any nuclear state, however, especially in unstable regions.[6]

Unauthorized use is of paramount concern in the new era. This "refers to the deliberate use by people who have access to the weapon, but who lack authority legitimately to order its use."[7] In states that lack adequate control over their nuclear weapons, it is possible that a rogue general or soldier could misuse a state's nuclear weapons. Of even more concern after September 11, this category covers the possibility of a terrorist group obtaining and using a nuclear weapon on its own (for more on terrorism and WMDs, see the section on "Terrorism" later in this chapter). There are several mechanisms for avoiding unauthorized use, such as a clear and reliable chain of command, rigorously screened and tested guards and military officers, and the implementation of the "two-person" rule in which every stage of use requires the approval of two persons.[8]

Finally, inadvertent use is "where the use is intentional and ordered by the people who have legitimate authority to order its use, but the order is based on misinformation."[9] This situation can result from "mistaken assessment of sensor data" or "a misinterpretation of the strategic situation or some combination of the two, especially in times of crisis generated either by domestic or international events."[10] Again, this problem is particularly acute in regions of conflict where tensions may be running high, leading to a false assessment of the situation.

Several factors undermine security procedures designed to prevent these three types of usage. First, organizational and bureaucratic constraints can lead to prioritizing that downgrades security interests and an unwillingness to implement changes in procedures. For example, some Russian bureaucrats have proven themselves unwilling to make security changes in relation to fissile materials to avoid admitting that the previous procedures were inadequate. Second, lack of availability or prohibitive cost prevents states from obtaining technologies necessary for sufficient command-and-control systems. Third, many proliferating states employ "denial and deception techniques" to hide their nuclear programs. Such techniques include hiding the facilities underground, claiming their WMD facilities are for dual-use technologies, and moving their facilities from location to location. Attempting to hide the program from others can lead to difficulties in controlling and accounting for nuclear materials and, in cases of domestic instability, can lead to a loss of control of these materials.[11]

Current Proliferation Concerns

In terms of states that are, or are suspected of, developing nuclear weapons, North Korea and Iran are of primary importance internationally. North Korea has been, and remains, one of the most secretive and oppressive regimes in the world. As seen in Chapter 6, North Korea's nuclear program sparked tension in 1994 and again from 2002 through 2010. In August 2003, the first round of six-nation talks began in Beijing among North Korea, the United States, Russia, Japan, South Korea, and China, but these talks, along with the subsequent three rounds, ended in failure. The fourth round began in July 2005; by August the parties became mired in a disagreement over North Korea's demand that it be allowed to use nuclear power for peaceful means. The United States was adamant that it could not allow such facilities because North Korea made bombs from a research reactor allowed under the 1994 Agreed Framework. However, the United States subsequently decided to renew the process with North Korea, and as a result, in February 2007 the six-party talks began again; as stated in Chapter 6, agreement was reached calling for North Korea to shut down its main reactor in exchange for fuel aid. The International Atomic Energy Agency (IAEA) confirmed the shutdown of the Yongbyon reactor in July 2007. The situation deteriorated, however, in 2008 when the IAEA announced North Korea's refusal to allow further inspections of the Yongbyon reactor, and ultimately the six-party talks collapsed. It remains to be seen in what direction negotiations with North

The international community has been attempting to rein in North Korea and its leader, Kim Jong-Il, who at times seems to be toying with his opponents.

Korea will go. There may be another pull back from the brink, or hostilities may continue to rise.

The situation has been complicated by the fact that North Korea announced in 2005 that it possessed plutonium-based nuclear weapons, although the number is unknown (see Chapter 7). In October 2006, a North Korean nuclear test was met with international condemnation, and strong diplomatic and economic pressure, including from China, may have contributed to the 2007 agreement. Pyongyang claims, however, that it requires this "defensive" component to its military power to counter the "hostile policy" of the United States. Although the international community does not want North Korea to take aggressive action against South Korea, the primary security challenge is preventing the communist regime from exporting nuclear technology. The international community must tread lightly in choosing military and economic actions. An overly aggressive military approach will invite crisis and confrontation, and economic sanctions may drive an already economically weak regime to seek the economic gain of exporting nuclear materials.[12]

Iran is another country of significant proliferation concern for nuclear as well as chemical and biological weapons. U.S. intelligence has long suspected Iran of engaging in a clandestine nuclear program. Iran ratified the NPT in 1970 (under the shah, who actually began the country's nuclear program) and, unlike North

Korea, remains a member of the nonproliferation regime. However, it is believed that Tehran responded to the Iraqi use of chemical weapons in the Iran–Iraq War of the 1980s with the establishment of a nuclear and chemical weapons program (Iran is believed to be manufacturing mustard gas and sarin, among other chemical agents). In 2003, the IAEA demanded a comprehensive declaration of all of Iran's nuclear activities, and in response the Islamic regime admitted "to having conducted various uranium enrichment efforts, and shortly thereafter the IAEA issued a report revealing the existence of a covert Iranian nuclear program dating back to 1986." In response, the IAEA declared that Iran was guilty of breaching the safeguard obligations in the NPT (although the IAEA has never provided any evidence that Iran has a nuclear weapons program).[13] After negotiations with France, Germany, and Great Britain, Iran signed the Paris Accord in November 2004, in which an agreement was reached to halt nuclear activity while a permanent deal was being negotiated. In August 2005, Iran violated this agreement when it broke the UN seal on its Isfahan nuclear plant and resumed activity. The situation was complicated by the fact that new leadership came to power in Tehran the same month—ultraconservative President Mahmoud Ahmadinejad.

In January 2006, Iran broke the IAEA seal on its Natanz nuclear research facility and claimed by April of that year that it had succeeded in enriching uranium at that facility. By the end of 2006, the UN Security Council had imposed sanctions on Iran, but Ahmadinejad vowed to speed up the enrichment of uranium. Mid-2007 brought some progress, as Iran agreed to allow inspectors into its Arak plant. In October 2009, Iran agreed to a plan that would call for Iran to export its uranium for processing (in other words, to be made into fuel) and then shipped back for energy use, thus preventing it from weaponizing the material. Citing distrust of the United States, Iran pulled out of the agreement weeks later. A similar plan has been discussed numerous times since, but Iran has declared that it requires fresh nuclear fuel to function a research reactor that provides isotopes for cancer treatment. Tensions remain high, and the United States continues to seek approval in the United Nations Security Council for tougher sanctions against Iran. Resolving this situation is critical, in part because the IAEA said in mid-2007 that Iran could produce a nuclear weapon in three to eight years and in February 2010 President Ahmadinejad proclaimed that Iran could build a nuclear weapon if it chose, but currently does not choose to do so.

Iran has denied (and continues to deny) the existence of a nuclear weapons program and claims that its uranium enrichment is for civilian nuclear reactors and research purposes (the right to pursue peaceful uses of nuclear power is a right granted by the NPT). Tehran claims that nuclear power is necessary in the face of rapid industrialization and population growth. The United States insists that Iran does not need nuclear power because of its large oil reserves, and thus assumes the nuclear plants must be for the purpose of developing weapons-grade materials.

Not all states are as concerned as the United States about Iran's intentions. Russia sells nuclear components to Iran, but adamantly insists that the nuclear program is for peaceful purposes (in the long run, Russia has no desire for Iran to possess WMDs, but in the short term, the former superpower benefits economically from the sale of materials intended for peaceful applications). China also opposes strict sanctions against Iran, and both China and Russia are permanent, thus veto-wielding members, of the UN Security Council. The situation in the Middle East is a sticky one. Iran does not recognize Israel's right to exist, and a prominent fear in the United States and Israel is that any nuclear weapons developed by Iran will be used against the Jewish state. Neighboring Arab states are also worried that an Iranian nuclear capability would upset the regional balance of power and threaten them. As a result, many of them have begun to talk about developing their own nuclear option. This development would likely lead to a nuclear arms race and would raise the threat of severe destabilization in the region. For these reasons, Iran's nuclear ambitions will be the subject of intense scrutiny for the foreseeable future.

Despite these problems, progress has been made in several proliferation areas. First, in the 1990s, Argentina, Brazil, South Africa, Kazakhstan, Ukraine, and Belarus (the last three are former Soviet republics that housed nuclear weapons during the Cold War) repudiated their nuclear ambitions. Second, as explained in Chapter 6, India and Pakistan have stepped back from the brink of war and made progress in improving relations between them. These improvements have also prompted increased acceptance in the international community (a fact that has raised ire in Tehran and accusations of a double standard). In fact, the United States no longer considers India and Pakistan nuclear pariah states. In 2005, Washington announced it would allow both India and Pakistan to buy military hardware from the United States. George W. Bush called India "a responsible state with advanced nuclear technology," and Pakistan earned praise for being a valuable ally in the War on Terror. Although the prospect of the two countries annihilating one another remains (in particular, over the territorial dispute of Kashmir; see Chapter 6), concern has shifted to controlling potential exports from the longtime rivals. The good news is that, unlike North Korea, both India and Pakistan have unilaterally developed significant policies to regulate their sensitive exports.[14] On the other hand, Dr. A. Q. Khan (Abdul Qadeer Khan), who is considered the "Father of the Pakistani Bomb," confessed to transferring nuclear technology to North Korea, Iran, and Libya, after heavy pressure on Pakistan resulted in an investigation of his activities. Further, internal strife in Pakistan is of the utmost concern to the outside world out of fear that nuclear weapons could fall into the hands of radical elements if the current government is overthrown.

Third, because no WMDs have been found in Iraq since the war's end, it is confirmed that Iraq has ended its nuclear program. Much of the 1990s was dominated by the concern about Iraq's potential WMD capabilities, with numerous UN resolutions and IAEA inspections. Thus, this development removes a significant proliferation concern from the international community. Finally, and perhaps most stunningly, in December 2003 it was announced that Libyan leader Mummar al-Qadhafi had renounced his country's WMD programs and pledged his cooperation with the international community in destroying them. Although significant concerns remain about the Libyan leader, the former pariah state has been rewarded for its new role as a partner in the War on Terror (discussed later in this chapter) and the battle against proliferation. (Libya ratified the Comprehensive Test Ban Treaty—ironically a move the United States is unwilling to take—and the Chemical Weapons Convention and allowed more rigorous IAEA inspections.) In response, Great Britain and the United States reestablished diplomatic relations with Libya and the EU lifted its near twenty-year arms embargo. (Prior to the announcement concerning WMDs, UN sanctions were lifted in September 2003, substantially because of Tripoli's acceptance of responsibility for terrorist attacks carried out by its intelligence units, in particular, the downing of Pan Am flight 103 over Lockerbie, Scotland.)

The Libya case demonstrates that if the international community uses all the tools at its disposal (for example, a combination of diplomacy and sanctions), broader adherence to nonproliferation norms is possible. It is important to remember, however, that numerous factors contributed to Libya's decision to comply with international norms (including economic hardship and a change in regional and economic dynamics).[15] Further, Qadhafi was a leader willing to take the dramatic step of announcing he would relinquish his program after decades of isolation, a step Saddam Hussein, for example, was not willing to take. Because no WMDs were found in Iraq, we can assume (for the sake of argument) that IAEA inspections and sanctions against Iraq were successful in halting Baghdad's weapons programs. From an individual-level perspective, if a different leader had ruled Iraq, it is possible that the 2003 war that toppled the Hussein regime would not have been necessary to counter an apparent proliferation threat. Thus, these two cases demonstrate that promoting nonproliferation does not have one formula for success and that this challenge will clearly continue throughout the new era.

Terrorism

As alluded to earlier, not all threats to states' security come from other states. Groups within countries, or international networks operating across national boundaries, can undermine a state's security and stability or achieve other political objectives. At its basic level, the use of violence to coerce a target group into meeting political demands is known as terrorism (more on the definition of terrorism later).[16] The attacks on the World Trade Center in New York and the Pentagon in Washington, DC, on September 11, 2001, were the first experience of devastating foreign terrorism on U.S. soil (an earlier attack on the World Trade Center occurred in 1993, killing six people), but terrorism in its modern form has plagued much of the rest of the world for decades.

Defining terrorism is not a simple task, but most people "know it when they see it." Individual states, international organizations, and nongovernmental groups have all tried their hand at defining the phenomenon, but there is no universally accepted definition. Terrorism is usually defined as some form of coercive intimidation; it is violence to make a point. The targets may be military or civilian (although some consider attacks on military personnel and equipment as acts of war, not terrorism), they may be inanimate objects of either real or symbolic importance (the oil pipeline in Colombia, for example, is a frequent target of terrorist attacks), or they may be people chosen for some affiliation or just randomly. The United Kingdom, for example, in Terrorism Act 2000, defines terrorism as "the use or threat of action" where there is serious damage to person or property (including death, serious risk to public health or safety, or disruption of the electronic system) and "the use or threat is designed to influence the government or to intimidate the public or a section of the public" and "is made for the purpose of advancing a political, religious, or ideological cause."[17] The U.S. Department of State defines terrorism as "premeditated, politically motivated violence perpetrated against noncombatant targets by subnational groups or clandestine agents, usually intended to influence an audience."[18] The European Union's definition is very specific, listing numerous acts such as kidnapping or hostage taking; causing damage to a public facility, transportation system, or infrastructure facility; seizing an aircraft or ship; manufacturing, possessing, or transporting weapons of mass destruction; releasing dangerous substances or causing fires or floods; and interfering with the water supply.[19] Some argue that the lack of a clear, widely accepted definition hinders states' ability to combat terrorism, whereas others argue that spending time on the fruitless attempts to create a universal definition takes away from the focus on combating the problem. This debate is sure to continue for the foreseeable future.

Historically, terrorism has been political, each attack an attempt to force a desired outcome, whether it be the release of political prisoners or a change of governmental policies. More recently, however, the nature of terrorism has been changing to be more punitive, more deadly, and more anonymous. The tools of terrorism remain largely the same—especially the use of suicide bombers or truck and car bombs—but whereas terrorists of the past were concerned about "political capital," or public opinion, and therefore tried to get the most attention for the least damage, terrorists of the early twenty-first century have demonstrated a willingness to commit more spectacular crimes as ends in themselves.[20] In fact, suicide attacks are efforts to "coerce the target government to change policy, to mobilize additional recruits and financial support, or both."[21]

Although terrorism is widespread, the ultimate effectiveness of terrorism is questionable. Although some claim that systematic campaigns of violence succeed in promoting the terrorists' message, others contend that negative reactions in the international community and the success of antiterrorism policies limit the ability of terrorists to achieve their aims.[22] The distinction between atrocious acts of terrorism and "legitimate" violence in support of a political cause or national goal is often blurred. One side's heroic revolutionaries are another's murderous thugs. The Contras, U.S.-backed insurgents against the socialist Sandinista regime in Nicaragua in the 1980s, exemplify this difference in perspective. Although the

Sandinistas perceived the Contras as criminal terrorists bent on the overthrow of a legitimate government, President Ronald Reagan viewed the Nicaraguan "freedom fighters" as "the moral equivalent of our Founding Fathers." Indeed, terrorists never refer to themselves as terrorists. They refer to themselves variously as holy warriors (for example, Mujahedeen), self-defense soldiers, militants for justice, commandos, rebels, guerrillas, and freedom fighters.

Terrorism has a long history. In Judea in the first century C.E., religious zealots revolted against Roman rule by creating an atmosphere where "no one was to be trusted and everyone was to be feared."[23] In the nineteenth and twentieth centuries, many nationalist groups sought to advance their aspirations through terrorism. Gavrilo Prinzip, the Serbian nationalist whose assassination of Archduke Franz Ferdinand was the spark that ignited World War I, was probably the world's most famous terrorist before Osama bin Laden. Many terrorist groups seek to create the same effect in the contemporary international system, but despite widespread condemnation of terrorism, effective international action to deal with the problem remains an elusive goal.

Contemporary Terrorism Around the World

Although most terrorist organizations have a regional base and political outlook, some have global reach, possessing capabilities to strike at targets far from their bases of operation. The September 11 attacks showed that no region is immune to international terrorism. Political and economic globalization, coupled with rapid improvements in technology, have given terrorists increased reach. International aviation, the opening of a railway tunnel from Britain to continental Europe, and other developments in transportation have created new vulnerabilities and given terrorists access to new targets. Improvements in communications, such as satellite broadcasting and the Internet, enable terrorists to publicize their motives and magnify the element of fear in regions far beyond their area of activity. Modern weapons technology, such as plastic explosives and small submachine guns, allows terrorists the use of less conspicuous and more destructive means of dealing in death. The possibility of terrorists obtaining nuclear, biological, or chemical weapons is one of the most frightening threats to international security.

According to counterterrorism specialists in the U.S. Department of State, there were forty-five foreign terrorist organizations as of January 2010. These groups include Hamas, Al Qaeda, Revolutionary Armed Forces of Colombia (FARC), Shining Path (Sendero Luminoso), Basque Fatherland and Liberty, and Real IRA.[24] (See Spotlight, "The Sheikh.") The State Department reported that there were 11,770 terrorist attacks in 2008, with the largest number of attacks (40 percent) occurring in the Near East. In these attacks, 15,765 persons were killed, and combined deaths, injuries, and kidnappings were over 54,000. The figures represent an 18 percent decrease in attacks and a 30 percent decrease in deaths over 2007. Violence against noncombatants in Africa, especially in Somalia and Democratic Republic of the Congo, rose by 140 percent in 2008.[25]

▪ SPOTLIGHT ▪

The Sheikh

The name Osama bin Laden has become synonymous with the globalization of terror. Born in 1957 in the Saudi Arabian city of Riyadh, bin Laden left his family's construction business to join the Afghan Mujahedeen fighting against the invading forces of the Soviet Union. He soon began to espouse a radical form of Islamic faith and to devote all his energy and most of his considerable personal fortune to a jihad (spiritual struggle or holy war) against not only the Soviets but also the West. By 1988, bin Laden established the nucleus of an organization known as Al Qaeda ("The Base"), which under his leadership grew into an international network with thousands of members, affiliated organizations across the globe, and sympathetic groups and "sleeper" cells in Europe and the United States.

PHOTO 8.1 Osama bin Laden, the founder of Al Qaeda and mastermind behind the September 11, 2001 attacks on the United States.

Bin Laden makes no secret of his goals: the overthrow of regimes he deems "non-Islamic" and the expulsion of non-Muslims, particularly Westerners, from Muslim countries (including, in his mind, the territory of the state of Israel). He particularly condemns the government of Saudi Arabia for allowing Western companies and military forces to operate within the kingdom. His rhetoric is unashamedly anti-American, anti-Western, and anti-Semitic. In February 1998, Al Qaeda issued a statement under the banner of "The World Islamic Front for Jihad Against the Jews and Crusaders," saying that all Muslims around the world had a duty to kill Americans and Israelis—civilian or military—and their allies. It is believed that bin Laden has financed and ordered some of the most destructive terrorist attacks in recent history, including the 1993 bombing of the World Trade Center in New York, the August 1998 bombings of the U.S. embassies in Kenya and Tanzania (which killed more than 300 people, although only a handful of Americans), and attacks on U.S. military forces in Saudi Arabia, Somalia, and Yemen. His terror network may have attempted to acquire chemical, nuclear, or biological weapons, although there is no evidence that it has any capability to use WMDs. Al Qaeda operated terrorist training camps in Afghanistan, where bin Laden became a major supporter of the radical Islamic regime, the Taliban, which attempted to stamp out all traces of Western influence and modernity in that war-torn country.

However, it was the attacks of September 11, 2001, that brought bin Laden and Al Qaeda into the center of international attention. On the morning of September 11, nineteen Al Qaeda suicide terrorists hijacked four U.S. commercial jets. Two of the jets crashed into the World Trade Center; one into the Pentagon in Washington, DC; and one in a field in Shanksville, Pennsylvania. Both towers of the World Trade Center collapsed; roughly 3,000 people were left dead or missing in the worst suicide terrorist attack in human history.

The attacks of 9/11 prompted global indignation and international action against Al Qaeda. When the Taliban refused to turn over or expel bin Laden, U.S. and allied military forces began air and ground operations against Taliban and Al Qaeda forces in Afghanistan, fighting alongside indigenous Afghan forces opposed to the ruling regime. The war was fought with a strange combination of ancient and modern military technology, as U.S. Special Forces troops rode to combat zones on horseback to identify targets for stealth aircraft and UAVs. The counterterrorist actions toppled the Taliban, which was replaced by an interim government led by Hamid Karzai (who became the first democratically elected president of Afghanistan in December 2004), and led to the capture or death of many Al Qaeda leaders. Bin Laden, however, was not located despite a massive manhunt for "the Sheikh," as he was known to his Afghan followers. A wave of arrests of Al Qaeda operatives and "sleepers" in Pakistan, the Middle East, Europe, and the United States quickly followed, but the world's most wanted terrorist was never found. As late as 2010, it was still unclear whether bin Laden was alive or dead. In the years following the September 11 attacks, numerous video and audiotapes purporting to be of bin Laden were released with messages directed at his followers, European nations, and the American people. Some believe he is alive and well in the mountains of Pakistan, others believe he is alive but not well (videotapes show a seemingly infirm bin Laden), and others believe he is dead. Regardless of the rumors regarding the possible whereabouts of bin Laden, the U.S. government is offering a $50 million reward for information leading to the capture of the world's most wanted man. Meanwhile, there is no question that Al Qaeda leaders have established new, secure hideouts in the mountainous border areas that Pakistan shares with Afghanistan.

Although terrorists can strike virtually anywhere, some areas of the world experience terrorist attacks more frequently than others. For example, in 2008, 35 percent of attacks occurred in South Asia, with attacks increasing in both Afghanistan and Pakistan (in fact, the attacks in Pakistan more than doubled over 2007). As mentioned earlier, 40 percent of attacks occurred in the Near East, but attacks in Iraq were on the decline.[26] Terrorism in Europe reached its peak in the 1970s, when terrorists such as the Red Brigades in Italy, the Red Army Faction in Germany, and Action Direct in France carried out terror attacks. In these cases, however, the terrorism was usually domestic, aimed at changing or overthrowing the existing governing structure.

The same pattern holds true in the rest of the world as well, where most terrorism consists of domestic attacks by ideological or separatist guerrillas. Examples include leftist revolutionary groups such as the Sendero Luminoso in Peru and ethnic insurgents such as the Liberation Tigers of Tamil Eelam (commonly referred to as the Tamil Tigers) in Sri Lanka. This terrorism can cross borders; the Tamil Tigers have conducted terrorist attacks against Indian targets, for example. Kashmiri militants likewise benefit from a safe haven in Pakistan, and the Kurdish PKK was dealt a serious blow when Syria withdrew support in the early 2000s. Serious issues exist between Turkey, Iraq, and the United States, however, as the PKK is attempting to use northern Iraq as a base.

Categories of Terrorist Groups

The extent and variety of terrorism across the globe shows that although terrorist organizations may use similar tactics, they have widely varying objectives and political orientations. Categorizing terrorist groups according to these characteristics is a useful first step in understanding terrorism, but it must be noted that many groups fall into more than one category. For example, Hamas, a separatist group dedicated to the eradication of Israel and the creation of an Islamic Palestinian state, has both ideological and nationalist motivations. At the same time, Hamas wages its struggle by peaceful means as well as violent methods, providing humanitarian relief for Palestinian refugees to further its cause and increase its political support (which in turn makes its terror campaign more effective). This approach helped Hamas sweep to victory in the 2006 Palestinian parliamentary elections. Most prominent terrorist organizations now have similar "legitimate" fronts through which they raise money, lobby governments, and curry public favor and converts to their causes with social outreach efforts.

State-Sponsored Terrorism

National governments sometimes engage in terror by subduing opposition within their own countries by cruel and violent means (a practice known as **enforcement terror**) or by sponsoring nonstate actors to carry out acts of violence abroad. States' use of fear and violence against their own citizens has a long and bloody history. In the sixteenth century, Russia's Tsar Ivan the Terrible employed terror not only to punish offenders but also simply to instill fear among his subjects. The French Revolution (see Chapter 3) was followed by the Great Terror, when an estimated 30,000 real and imagined opponents of the revolution were executed, many by guillotine.[27] In the twentieth century, the ruling regimes of Nazi Germany, Soviet Russia, and Communist China carried out state-sponsored domestic terror on a massive scale. Military governments in Argentina and Brazil, Shah Mohammed Reza Pahlavi's regime in Iran, and the apartheid regime in South Africa were other notorious users of enforcement terror.

In 2010, the U.S. Department of State listed Cuba, Iran, Sudan, and Syria as sponsors of terrorism. The list has undergone significant changes in recent years. North Korea's designation was rescinded in October 2008 after North Korea agreed to comply with verification requirements of its nuclear reactors. (It should be noted, however, that the U.S. Secretary of State Hillary Clinton publicly stated in 2009 that the United States was considering returning North Korea to the list. This is part of the ongoing tension and diplomatic maneuvering in response to North Korea's nuclear program, discussed earlier in this chapter). Iraq's designation was formally rescinded in October 2004, but the country continues to be a battleground in the war on terror as, although decreasing, an insurgency continues to conduct a violent terror campaign. Libya's designation was rescinded in June 2006 in response to its renunciation of terrorism and abandonment of its WMD programs. Libya's cooperation in the global War on Terror has earned it new legitimacy in the international community. Despite this progress, Cuba, Syria, Sudan, and Iran continue their support of terrorism.[28] Although Cuba has few resources for financial support of international terror, it provides refuge and training for terrorist groups ranging from Colombia's Revolutionary Armed Forces to Spain's Basque separatists. The Islamist government of Iran remains the most active sponsor of terror, supporting insurgent groups including the Kurdistan Workers' Party (PKK), Hezbollah, Hamas, and Islamic Jihad. Syria has decreased its sponsorship of international terrorism in

• **Enforcement terror**
Terrorism carried out by a government or a government-backed agency against its own citizens.

recent years but continues to provide funding, weapons, training, and other assistance to terrorist groups.

Despite the continued practice of state-sponsored terrorism, it has declined since the end of the Cold War. Terrorist groups are therefore turning to alternative sources of funding, including soliciting charitable donations, kidnapping for profit, working with criminal organizations, and becoming involved in drug trafficking.

Nationalist Separatists

Terrorist groups in this category have political objectives of national liberation or self-determination. Because nationalism gains momentum from the bond of a shared identity, terrorism instigated by separatist groups tends to have clear ethnic, cultural, or religious overtones. Conflicts between states over autonomy can continue for generations. By some definitions, the antagonism between Britain and Ireland goes back more than 800 years, and some scholars trace the Palestinian–Israeli dispute back to 1400 B.C.E.[29] Although separatists typically claim to be freedom fighters crusading for a separate homeland, their violent means and often indiscriminate targets can earn them reputations as terrorists of the most malicious nature. Notably, however, not everyone belonging to radical nationalist organizations espouses random violence, and many such groups are umbrella organizations for movements that include elements that support nationalist causes by peaceful means.

The conflict in Northern Ireland has given rise to some of the most feared nationalist terrorists. The Provisional wing of the Irish Republican Army (IRA) and Irish National Liberation Army carried out bombing campaigns, assassinations, and other attacks to achieve their goals of a British withdrawal from Northern Ireland. (Some radical groups of Unionists, who oppose this goal in the name of Northern Ireland's Protestant majority, also resorted to terrorist violence.) After decades of terrorist activity, the IRA declared a cease-fire in 1994, but this respite lasted only seventeen months. In 1997, a new IRA cease-fire, the renunciation of violence by Sinn Fein (the legal political party associated with the IRA), and the start of formal multilateral negotiations offered new hopes for peace. In April 1998, these negotiations culminated in an accord between the British and Irish governments and leading Catholic and Protestant groups that was overwhelmingly ratified by voters in both Northern Ireland and the Irish Republic. Widely regarded as an important step toward peace, the Good Friday agreement ended Ireland's constitutional claims on the northern counties, replaced direct British rule in Northern Ireland with an autonomous assembly, and established cooperative links between north and south. In September 2005, the Independent International Commission on Decommissioning confirmed that the IRA had decommissioned all of its weapons. Nevertheless, the Real IRA (RIRA) and the Continuity Irish Republican Army (CIRA) remain active as terrorist organizations seeking full British withdrawal from Northern Ireland. Despite continued terrorist activities, Gerry Adams of Sinn Fein and Ian Paisley of the Democratic Unionist Party agreed to a power-sharing arrangement between the Catholics and Protestants on March 26, 2007, thereby ushering in a new era of cooperation and reconciliation in Northern Ireland.

Terrorism also continues to play a role in the Palestinian–Israeli conflict. Before the creation of the state of Israel in 1948, both Jewish and Muslim terrorist groups operated in the mandated territory of Palestine. After 1967, when Israel occupied the West Bank and Gaza in the Six Day War, militant units of the Palestine Liberation Organization (PLO) stepped up their activities against Israeli targets and Palestinian "collaborators." Although the PLO officially renounced terrorism after signing the Oslo Accords in 1993, renegade groups including Palestinian Islamic Jihad (PIJ) (which concentrates on killing civilians and Israeli soldiers) and the al-Aqsa Martyrs Brigade (which targets Israeli officials and civilians) continue to conduct terrorist attacks.

In Europe, the separatist group Basque Fatherland and Liberty conducts terrorist operations, including attacks on tourists and a 1995 attempt to assassinate King Juan Carlos, to obtain independence for the Basque country of northern Spain. The Kurdistan Workers' Party in Turkey, Ansar al-Islam (a Kurdish group operating in northern Iraq), Sikh nationalists in India, and Tamil guerrillas in Sri Lanka also conduct separatist terrorism (the Tamil Tigers were recently defeated by the Sri Lankan military). Terror was also widely used by many sides in the conflicts in the former Yugoslavia in the 1990s (see Chapter 6).

Terrorism as a means to attain a national homeland remains as problematic as it was centuries ago. Feeding on ethnic tensions, this class of terrorism threatens the integrity and security of multinational states by perpetuating and rekindling old animosities. At the same time, nationalist groups are frequently used by rival states to further their own ends, thus combining separatist and state-sponsored terror. Especially in the Middle East, but in Africa and elsewhere as well, many states support rebel terrorists in neighboring countries in a deadly game of regional politics and nationalist ambitions.

Ideological Terrorism

Ideological terrorism refers to violence committed by groups influenced by extremist or revolutionary doctrines such as Marxism-Leninism or anarchism. These radical opposition groups work to overthrow a regime or political system. The rage that animates violent insurgencies often stems from the desire to overthrow oppressive governments or express anti-imperialist sentiments. The collapse of the Soviet Union decreased the support and motivation of many communist-inspired terrorists, but notable perpetrators of communist ideological terror included groups such as Action Direct in France, the Baader-Meinhof Gang in Germany, the Red Brigades in Italy, and the Japanese Red Army. Marxist terrorist groups do continue to exist in the twenty-first century, however, and some are gaining strength. One of the most persistent and violent opposition groups in Latin America, the Sendero Luminoso (Shining Path) guerrillas of Peru, espouses a Marxist ideology. The organization attempts to cultivate the support of farmers and impoverished rural residents for its antigovernment insurgency, but the strength of the group declined after the imprisonment of many top leaders in the 1990s. It regrouped in the new century and conducted terrorist activities that have caused the Peruvian government to refocus its counterterrorism campaign against the group. Other Marxist-inspired groups currently operating are Popular Front for the Liberation of Palestine (PFLP) (formerly receiving assistance from the Soviet Union but continuing to operate mostly in Israel with its goal to remove rightist Arab regimes and eliminate Israel), Communist Party of Philippines/New People's Army (a Maoist group that seeks to overthrow the country's regime), Revolutionary People's Liberation Party/Front (a Marxist-Leninist group that wants to create a socialist Turkey), and Revolutionary Organization 17 November (which seeks to isolate Greece from U.S. influence).

Although this loss of the Soviet Union as a backer was a serious blow to many of these organizations, two factors have helped many of these groups continue operating in the new era. On the one hand, some of them have represented traditionally disenfranchised elements of their states' populations and, Soviet Union or no, those elements continue to exist and seek attention and change. This appeared to have been the case with the Tupac Amaru revolutionary movement in Peru in the 1990s, which was believed to have weakened because of defections and the success of law enforcement. Tupac Amaru rose again to prominence in 1996 when the group took over the Japanese ambassador's residence in Lima, holding attendees of a diplomatic reception hostage for weeks, until the insurgents were wiped out by a commando raid. (Tupac Amaru has once again declined in strength and has not been included on the U.S. State Department's list of foreign terrorist organizations since 1999). On the other hand, once a terrorist organization has started, it can take on a life of its own and survive for the sake of survival, rather than for its original intent. Thus, it is unsurprising that some terrorist organizations have linked up with organized crime and drug traffickers to create much more powerful, wealthy, and deadly operations. In Colombia, the Marxist-inspired FARC maintains an estimated 9,000 to 12,000 combatants and has been deeply involved in every aspect of the narcotics trade since the mid-1980s, when they first began raising cash by offering protection to the drug cartels. In addition, the resurgence of Sendero Luminoso has been tied to the Peruvian cocaine trade. The group uses narcotrafficking to fund their operations.

Religious Terrorism

In the new era, religious radicalism has arisen as the prime ideological generator of international terrorism.[30] There are a host of grievances that lead people to commit acts of terror in the name of God. According to one scholar who interviewed numerous terrorists, these grievances include alienation (and the fostering of group identity, dehumanizing the enemy, and creating a person capable of killing innocent people), national humiliation (using the case of Palestinians living in desperation as an example), demographics (in particular, shifting demographics that spark violence between ethno-religious groups and immigrants), history (in particular, selective reading of history used to claim territory), and territory (using the dispute of Kashmir as an example of a territorial dispute that has given rise to much religious-based terrorism).[31] Religious terrorists tend to be obsessed with good and evil, yet they end up murdering innocent persons, and these groups tend to be more violent than organizations with other types of (secular) motives.[32]

As noted previously, Al Qaeda, a network of terrorist organizations headed by Osama bin Laden and motivated by a violently radical form of Islam, attained new levels of notoriety in 2001 by sponsoring the attacks of September 11, even though they had previously garnered attention for other bloody attacks on U.S. targets worldwide, including the 1998 bombings of U.S. embassies in Kenya and Tanzania. Their targets are not limited to U.S. holdings, however, as Al Qaeda cells are linked to the nightclub bombing in Bali (2002), train bombings in Madrid (2004), and transit bombings in London (2005). Other Islamic groups, such as Hamas in the West Bank and Gaza and Islamic Jihad, embody a deadly combination of ethnic nationalism and religious fanaticism directed primarily against Israel, demonstrated with tragic effects by suicide bombings since 1994. The Armed Islamic Group (GIA) in Algeria seeks to overthrow Algeria's secular regime and forcibly institute Islamic government and law and has murdered secularist teachers, journalists, women wearing Western dress, and other victims. (Although still included on the U.S. State Department's list of foreign terrorist organizations, GIA's activities have been limited in the twenty-first century.) In Egypt, Islamic extremists strike foreign tourists (killing sixty-two people at Luxor in November 1997 and at least eighty-four people in Sharm el-Sheik in July 2005) as well as Egyptian citizens to discredit and weaken the government. A radical Japanese religious sect, Aum Shinrikyo, used homemade nerve gas in an attack on the Tokyo subway in 1995. Other religiously motivated terrorists include Al-Shabaab (an Islamic faction seeking to oust the current regime in Somalia), Jemaah Islamiyah (a group seeking to create a pan-Islamic state in Southeast Asia), and Jaish-E-Mohammed (an Islamic group that wants to make Kashmir a part of Pakistan). In the United States, a similar combination of religious fanaticism and political separatism motivates Christian white supremacists such as the Posse Comitatus (and many other militias organized in defiance of the secular federal government), the Christian Patriots, and Aryan Nation. The 1995 bombing of the Oklahoma City federal building, a domestic terrorist attack, was carried out by an American white supremacist with militia ties who timed his attack to commemorate the FBI's assault on the Branch Davidian apocalyptic cult's compound two years previously.

Religious terrorism can attain especially frightening dimensions because religious terrorists typically regard violence as a morally justified, and even spiritually sanctified, means for the attainment of goals inspired by tenets of their faith. Islamic radicals do not consider the killing of nonbelievers to be murder, and they assert that fighters killed while committing terror strikes are assured of a place in heaven. Countering religious terror groups can be especially difficult because of their believers' fervent commitment and the support these groups often receive from disaffected religious or ethnic groups. At

PHOTO 8.2 After the September 11 attacks, the United States and other countries shifted their attention to the dangers posed by religious terrorism. The bombing of this Bali nightclub was an attack motivated by Islamic fundamentalism.

the same time, it is important to remember that people and countries sharing the same religious faith as terrorist groups do not automatically share the terrorists' goals or approve of their violent methods. Although a large number of terrorists justify their actions as a form of jihad, or spiritual struggle, most Muslim leaders and believers condemn the use of terror in the name of God, just as most Christians denounce the kinds of terrorist violence practiced by fanatical Christian movements.

Terrorism and Weapons of Mass Destruction

Terrorist attacks with firearms and conventional explosives are devastating enough, but the potential for terrorists to use nuclear, chemical, or biological weapons is even more frightening. WMDs are difficult to acquire and use; even large countries have trouble finding the financial and technical resources to build nuclear weapons, and biological weapons pose serious risks to anyone attempting to make and use them. (Chemical weapons, on the other hand, are not nearly as difficult to manufacture; for example, almost any factory that can produce organophosphate pesticides can also make nerve gas.) WMDs are also limited or banned outright by international treaties and are widely regarded as cruel and inhumane (see Chapter 7). Terrorists with political objectives who try to use nuclear, chemical, or biological weapons could easily destroy any public sympathy for their grievances or objectives, and they and the countries that harbor them could expect swift and powerful retaliation.

Perhaps for these reasons, the actual use of WMDs by terrorists has been very limited, the major exceptions being the 1995 attack on the Tokyo subway by religious fanatics using sarin nerve gas and the mailing of small quantities of anthrax to U.S. political leaders and media outlets in 2001.[33] Fortunately, the most frightening scenarios for terrorism are also the least likely. For example, terrorists manufacturing and detonating a nuclear weapon using stolen nuclear material is highly unlikely. Not even the most extensive terror network would have the resources and expertise to carry out such a plot without being detected and thwarted. Weapons that use conventional explosives to spread radioactive material, widely known as radiation dispersal devices or "dirty bombs," are much easier to make than nuclear weapons but would do far less damage.

Nevertheless, the possibility that terrorists might use these weapons remains a major concern among all states, and many countries have made major efforts to prevent mass destruction terror and to respond to nuclear, chemical, and biological incidents. International efforts to combat these forms of terrorism have also intensified. In 2001, the IAEA stepped up its efforts to work with member states to secure nuclear and radioactive material, and the nuclear power, chemical, and biotechnology industries pledged to work more closely with international organizations and national governments to protect their facilities from theft and sabotage. In another important effort, the 1992 U.S. Nunn-Lugar Act was established to destroy or safely store nuclear weapons and other WMDs (including chemical and biological weapons) in former Soviet republics (and now new states), including Russia, Kazakhstan, Ukraine, and Belarus, to prevent them from being obtained by terrorist organizations or rogue states. There have been impressive results (see Chapter 7), but more work is still left to be done.

Combating International Terrorism

Although almost all states publicly condemn terrorism, states differ greatly in their actual stance toward it. Although some governments actively combat terrorism, others just as actively support international terror or engage in it themselves, and still others do both as suits their political objectives. Nevertheless, the United States, the EU, and many governments and international organizations have attempted to cooperate to locate, thwart, and apprehend terrorists. In 2001, many countries increased their efforts to cooperate against terrorism in the wake of the September 11 attacks.

Efforts to combat terrorism fall into two categories: **antiterrorism** and **counterterrorism.** Antiterrorism refers to actions taken by diplomatic, law enforcement, and intelligence agencies to apprehend terrorists or thwart terror attacks before they can be carried out. Governments can cooperate on antiterrorism by sharing information on terrorist organizations, their known and suspected members, and especially on the transfer of money and weapons to terrorist groups.

With enough cooperation within and between governments, antiterrorism can be very effective, but much like undercover police work, most successful antiterrorist operations are not publicized to protect the sources and methods involved. In Britain, for example, the foreign intelligence service (MI6), the domestic intelligence agency (MI5), and the Police Special Branch work together to combat the RIRA, CIRA, and Islamic extremists attempting to attack British targets. When law enforcement and intelligence agencies fail to cooperate, however, antiterrorism has little chance of success. After the September 11 attacks, the U.S. Federal Bureau of Investigation (FBI), Central Intelligence Agency (CIA), State Department, and other organizations were criticized for not sharing bits of information that, if put together in a coordinated manner like pieces of a puzzle, might have given some warning of Al Qaeda's plans to strike.

In an effort to combat these intelligence-gathering problems, some states have reacted to terrorism by enacting new domestic legislation or rules. After the September 11 attacks, the U.S. Congress passed the Patriot Act, a set of regulations that enhance the government's surveillance powers. There are several controversial provisions in the act (parts of which were made permanent in 2005), including the ability to share information from criminal probes with intelligence agencies (critics fear this will lead to large-scale databases of innocent people) and roving wiretaps, record access, and "sneak-and-peek" warrants (which allow authorities to search a home or business without immediately notifying the target). Similarly, following the July 2005 Muslim terrorist bombings in London, Prime Minister Tony Blair announced a new antiterrorism package for Great Britain that included provisions to make deportations easier (a move that would require the amending of human rights laws), plans to ban certain Muslim organizations, and laws making the justification or glorification of terrorism a crime. Although many feel such moves make states safer, others feel that the abridgment of civil liberties is not worth the potential security gains.

Counterterrorism involves the use of military force against terrorist organizations. The use of force always involves inherent risks, but when military units cooperate with intelligence and law enforcement authorities, military operations can degrade or destroy terrorist organizations or retaliate against states that sponsor terrorism. Israeli forces achieved a famous counterterrorist success in 1976, when commandos rescued hostages taken in an airline hijacking and held at Entebbe Airport in Uganda. In 2001, U.S. forces led a multinational military

▪ **Antiterrorism**
Actions taken by diplomatic, law enforcement, and intelligence agencies to apprehend terrorists or thwart terrorist attacks before they can be carried out.

▪ **Counterterrorism**
Use of military force against terrorist organizations.

What Would You Do?

Response to Terrorism

You are the prime minister of Great Britain in 2005. Your capital city has been rocked by two series of coordinated bombings on your transit system. The first attacks resulted in the deaths of 56 persons on three tube trains and a double-decker bus. Two weeks later, you consider yourself lucky because the second set of attacks failed to cause any deaths as the bombs used only partially exploded on four trains and a bus. The four bombers in the initial attacks were killed in the blasts, and police have made numerous arrests, but your citizenry is still on edge. Two weeks after the second attack, Ayman al-Zawahri (Osama bin Laden's lieutenant), in a videotaped message appearing on al-Jazeera, blames your foreign policy for the attacks and vows that London will face further assaults in the future.

You face a two-front dilemma, one domestic (although with implications for foreign relations), the other international. On the home front, you outline a set of extended powers to deport those who pose a security threat and to lessen the rights of those suspected of terrorist activities. Many in Great Britain are critical of your plans on civil liberties grounds, and although you were recently reelected, you have faced severe scrutiny over the war in Iraq and for allegedly providing false information to muster support for the invasion. Others, however, believe that Great Britain has been too liberal with radical clerics and has become a center for militant Islam (nicknaming your capital "Londonistan"). You know you must strike a balance between freedom and security, but you also recognize that the rules of the game must change.

Your second dilemma revolves around your foreign policy. You have been a staunch supporter of U.S. President George W. Bush's War on Terror since its inception. You supported (rhetorically and militarily) the wars in Afghanistan and Iraq. Although there have been significant protests of your actions, you are heartened by the fact that both you and Bush won your respective bids for reelection. The situation in Iraq remains tenuous at best. The Iraqis have held an election and are moving forward with their constitution, thus providing some proof of the success of spreading democratic ideals, but the insurgency continues to kill Coalition troops and Iraqi civilians daily. On the one hand, pulling your troops out of Iraq would satisfy many of your critics and prevent any further loss of British life. On the other hand, any progress in Iraq might be lost if you cut bait and run, chaos may reign supreme in the region if Iraq is left unstable, and you may irreparably damage your close working and personal relationship with George W. Bush. Further, a change in foreign policy may make it appear that you are giving in to extremist demands in the face of terrorism, potentially promoting further violence in an effort to force additional changes in Britain's policies.

What Would You Do?

campaign in Afghanistan to defeat Al Qaeda fighters and forces of the country's radical Islamic regime, the Taliban. This military intervention achieved great initial success, overthrowing the Taliban and working with indigenous forces to build a new government, but Osama bin Laden, Taliban leader Mullah Omar, and other terrorist commanders escaped. The U.S. military continues to undergo a transformation of its military in response to the new challenges made evident by the September 11 terrorist attacks.[34] As then-Deputy Secretary of Defense Paul Wolfowitz described in 2003, "our operational emphasis now is on flexibility, speed and jointness."[35]

Counterterrorism is only one tool in the fight against terrorism, however, and must be augmented by both antiterrorism and follow-on efforts. For example, sustained international efforts will be crucial for rebuilding Afghanistan's shattered economy and political system, fractious in the best of times and damaged almost beyond repair after more than twenty years of civil war. In the absence of such follow-through, terrorism has a much better chance of resurfacing, as has been the case in the outlying areas of Kabul. With the election of President Barack Obama in the United States in 2008, Afghanistan became a more central focus of U.S. efforts, with the administration reducing troops in Iraq and increasing troop levels in Afghanistan to fight a resurgent Taliban. The 2003 War in Iraq also highlights this aspect of counterterrorism. Based partly on the fear that Saddam Hussein was aiding terrorists, the United States overthrew his regime. The aftermath of this effort, however, greatly increased terrorist activity in Iraq, resulted in a lengthy stay for U.S. soldiers, and highlighted the need for increased international cooperation.

Efforts to coordinate action against terrorism can be organized at the bilateral, regional, and international levels. Bilateral cooperation involves collaboration between two countries in areas ranging from exchange of intelligence information to joint police operations and border controls. For example, in the aftermath of the bombings in London in 2005, both Egypt and Italy cooperated with London officials and Scotland Yard in apprehending and questioning suspects in their countries. Although bilateral cooperation can be effective between states that share political objectives, problems often arise when two states differ in their ideological or strategic outlook. For example, Jordan and Israel agreed to cooperate against terrorism in their 1994 peace treaty, but cooperation was strained for several months after Israeli security services acknowledged responsibility for an attempt to assassinate Hamas leader Khaled Meshal in Amman in 1997. Bilateral cooperation can also encounter legal difficulties, such as tortuous procedures for extradition (turning over suspects to another country for trial). In an infamous incident in 1978, an agreement was under way to extradite four leading terrorists captured in Yugoslavia in exchange for the extradition of Yugoslav suspects held in Germany. The exchange was bungled, however, and Yugoslavia released the German terrorists instead of handing them over to German authorities.[36] The efforts of some law enforcement and intelligence agencies to nab terrorists can also raise serious questions of national sovereignty. Because so many states offer freedom from extradition or other forms of "safe haven" for terrorists, the techniques used to apprehend suspected terrorists have sometimes been likened to kidnapping. The United States has practiced the controversial policy of "extraordinary rendition," in which terrorism suspects are captured and sent to foreign countries or to U.S.-controlled sites outside of the United States, like Guantanamo Bay in Cuba or CIA "black sites." The purpose of this policy is that the protections of the American judicial system (including the restrictions on torture, critics argue) can be avoided outside of American soil.

Regional cooperation against terrorism is even more difficult to coordinate. Recognizing their common interests in countering terror, the Organization of American States and the South Asian Association for Regional Cooperation (SAARC) have attempted to organize regional responses to terrorism. Although these efforts have facilitated some police and intelligence cooperation and prompted dialogue on important issues, they have generally done little to suppress terrorist violence. Some SAARC countries were actually suspected of commissioning terrorist attacks on their regional neighbors even while they ostensibly cooperated in antiterrorist programs.[37] The North Atlantic Treaty Organization (NATO) conducts a number of operations related to fighting terrorism. In addition to its role in Afghanistan, for example, Operation Active Endeavor is a maritime surveillance operation. The operation undertakes antiterrorist patrols in the Mediterranean. The region that could benefit most from regional cooperation against terrorism, the Middle East, seems unlikely to achieve or even attempt it soon.

The success of international cooperation in combating terrorism depends on the efficacy of international law and organizations (see Chapter 13). Police and security agencies have attempted to coordinate their antiterrorist efforts at the international level, with modest success. Interpol, the International Criminal Police Organization, has fostered cooperation among national police forces for decades. Although the United Nations has passed many resolutions unanimously condemning terrorism, these declarations have had essentially no impact. In addition, according to the UN, numerous major conventions or protocols deal with terrorism (covering conduct aboard aircraft, taking hostages, control of nuclear material, and suppressing financing for terrorists), but their impact is also limited as many states are not party to the agreements. A proposed UN Convention Against Terrorism in All Its Forms languished in discussion, largely because member states could not agree on a common definition of terrorism (as discussed earlier) or on the kinds of groups to which it should apply. As mentioned earlier, one person's terrorist is often another's freedom fighter, and many UN member states denounce the activities of some groups while supplying others with money and weapons. The UN succeeded, however, in 2006 in adopting the Global Counterterrorism Strategy, marking the first time the General Assembly could agree on practical steps to prevent and combat terrorism.[38]

All states, whether they recognize it or not, have an interest in fighting terrorism. National, ethnic, ideological, and religious conflicts spill across state borders so easily that no state can consider itself immune from the pestilence of terrorism. Many of the mechanisms for cooperation against terrorism by police and security agencies are already in place; however, to take full advantage of these existing organizations, or to build new avenues for cooperation against terrorism, states will have to abandon the support of terrorism as a component of their foreign policies. States cannot completely prevent the victimization of innocent civilians by killers who want to publicize their causes, but governments, international organizations, and nonstate actors can come together to seek better ways of preventing terrorist attacks, apprehending suspected terrorists, and denying modern weapons to fanatics willing to kill and die for ancient hatreds and contemporary animosities. If they succeed, the threat posed by international terrorism may prove manageable; if they fail, the world may be faced with massive, punitive terror attacks more akin to those of September 11, 2001 (or worse), than to the more moderated terror of the past.

Organized Crime

When most Americans think of organized crime, they conjure up images of Tony Soprano protecting the "family business" in New Jersey. In reality, organized crime is a multibillion-dollar business of gambling, money laundering, loan sharking, theft, narcotics, and sex exploitation that has implications across the globe. Few regions of the world are outside the realm of organized crime; North America, South America, Europe, Africa, and Asia all experience the serious consequences of organized crime. Local, regional, and international efforts to combat organized crime are hindered by the conspiratorial nature of the crime, a lack of resources, and the constantly changing nature of organized crime activities.

What Is Organized Crime?

Much like the problem with terrorism discussed earlier, it is difficult to define organized crime and thus there is no universally accepted definition. In 2000, the United Nations Convention against Transnational Organized Crime defined the phenomenon as "structured groups of three or more people acting in concert to commit one or more serious crimes for material benefit." Michael Maltz points out that when we discuss organized crime, we are usually referring to a group of people, not an action. Thus, "organized crime is a crime in which there is more than one offender, and the offenders are and intend to remain associated with one another for the purpose of committing crimes." Although we may lack an accepted definition of organized crime, there is a widely accepted set of characteristics indicative of the phenomenon. These characteristics include nonideological, hierarchical structure, durability over time, self-perpetuating, limited or exclusive membership, diversified interests with specialization and division of labor, capital accumulation, reinvestment, access to political protection, use of illegal violence or bribery, monopolistic, and governed by explicit rules.[39] The most successful organized crime groups "have their own mystique, ensuring solidarity and loyalty through shared ethnicity, kinship, or allegiance to a code of behavior."[40]

Regardless of the definition, organized crime is a significant threat to international security. There are tens of thousands of organized crime groups worldwide. For example, there are roughly 4,000 such groups, boasting membership of approximately 40,000, in the EU alone. Further, estimates of profits are difficult to pin down, but some suggest between $750 billion and $1 trillion worldwide. In Russia alone, between 10 and 20 percent of GNP is siphoned off by organized crime. This money, of course, must be "counted, laundered, banked, and invested," and accountants, bankers, and investment houses across the globe take care of these aspects. "It is in the international finance system that underworlds and upperworlds unite and merge."[41]

Transnational Organized Crime Activities

The activities of organized crime were described by the Task Force on Organized Crime (1967) as "supplying of illegal goods and services—gambling, loan sharking, narcotics, and other forms of vice—to countless number of citizen customers." The main tenets of any good mob are **extortion** and **protection,** both of which make good fodder for movies and television plots. Extortion is defined as "demanding money from an individual or a business, which, if not paid, will result in the individual or business being physically or financially harmed," whereas protection is defined as "money paid on a regular basis to an organized crime group to 'protect' the individual or business from other criminals." An example of extortion is New York's Black Hand Gang forcing payment from immigrants arriving in the United States. An example of protection is a large company paying huge sums to the mob to ensure good labor relations. With modern technology, organized criminals can now conduct online protection rackets, for example, closing down a company's website and seeking substantial monetary compensation to prevent it from happening again.[42]

Beyond extortion and protection, organized crime manipulates people and money in other ways. Gambling has long been a mafia staple, including running "the numbers racket" (their own lottery) and exploiting online gambling (as a consequence, a bet that is illegal in one country can be made in another via the Internet). Many mobs also engage in loan sharking—charging very high interest rates for loans. This type of manipulation affects people who are desperately in need of money and cannot borrow from legitimate sources. Organized crime groups also engage in counterfeiting, both money (in fact, the Russian mob figured out how to counterfeit the "tamper-proof" $100 bill released in 1997)[43] and goods (including pharmaceuticals and vodka).[44] Further, organized crime groups will "finance frauds, swindles, or any conventional criminal activity that can bring in a profit substantial enough to make the effort worthwhile."[45]

Even more nefarious, organized crime is involved in the trafficking of persons for the sex industry and the trafficking of human organs. Females (both adult and children) as well as male children are known to have been enslaved

■ **Extortion**
Organized crime groups demanding money, behavior, or other goods and services from an individual or business that results in physical or financial harm if not paid.

■ **Protection**
Money paid to an organized crime group to protect the individual or business from other criminals.

PLANNER

MON	Prostitution racket
TUE	Money Laundering
WED	Hit Luigi's
THR	Gun running
FRI	Fix game
SAT	Rub out
SUN	Lie in.

"Now that's what I call organised crime."

"Organized crime planner." Transnational organized crime groups are involved in numerous activities, from sex exploitation to money laundering to gambling. (Goddard)

for sale by Italian, Albanian, Russian, Chinese, and Japanese groups. In addition, certain groups act as the middleman (and charge high prices) for those in need of organ transplants.[46] Organized crime groups also provide many illicit goods, from drugs (including heroin, cocaine, marijuana, and ecstasy; see Spotlight, "International Drug Trafficking," later in this chapter), tobacco (because it can be purchased more cheaply in one country and smuggled to another), arms (which has been a significant problem in the former Eastern bloc because of the opening of borders and currency devaluation), stolen automobiles, and even meat (including "bush meat," which refers to the flesh of endangered species).[47]

Once they have secured their profits, organized crime groups must find ways to legitimize their funds, and they do so through **money laundering.** This process involves "getting currency into the bank, around the reporting system, at home or abroad," in an action called placement. Then, "the launderer hides its criminal origins through a series of complex transactions" called layering. Finally, "the launderer then makes the proceeds available to the criminals in an apparently legitimate form" in a process called integration. The Cayman Islands, for example, are infamous for the establishment of "shell" companies to hide

■ **Money laundering**
The processing of criminal proceeds to hide the illegal origins of the money that includes three stages: placement, layering, and integration.

illegal activities. The island, located south of Cuba, has a population of 23,400 but houses 570 banks and 20,000 registered companies.[48]

The Globalization of Organized Crime

Globalization has had a dramatic impact on the reach of organized crime. "The globalization of organized crime has occurred in tandem with the globalization of the world economy. In the 1970s most organized crime groups were still anchored in their countries of origin," but during the 1980s, "traditional, cultural-bound organizations like the Japanese Yakuza, the Chinese Triads, and the Sicilian Mafia went global, becoming increasingly sophisticated and diversifying into new markets."[49] For example, the 40,000 organized crime groups in Europe include gangs from Europe itself, China, Vietnam, Colombia, Nigeria, North Africa, the Caribbean, Russia, Turkey, and Albania.[50] These groups are no longer bound to their homelands; instead they are operating across borders and wreaking havoc globally.

One of the strongest organized crime groups operating outside its country of origin is the Russian mob (or *Mafiya*). Although there was an extensive underworld in the Soviet Union (in fact, the roots of Russian organized crime are in the Soviet system, when the black market developed to provide goods that the state could not), the onset of a market economy, a new openness, and a weakening of the rule of law following the collapse of the communist regime have allowed the Russian mob to flourish. In fact, former Russian President Boris Yeltsin once referred to Russia as "the biggest mafia state in the world" and the "superpower of crime." Not satisfied with their power in their home countries, criminal elements have flocked over the borders of Russia and other post-Soviet republics such as Ukraine.[51] Russian gangsters have set up operations in more than fifty countries. According to Robert I. Friedman, "they smuggle heroin from Southeast Asia, traffic in weapons all over the globe, and seem to have a special knack for large-scale extortion." Further, the Russian mob has "plundered the fabulously rich gold and diamond mines in war-torn Sierra Leone, built dazzling casinos in Costa Rica with John Gotti Jr., and, through its control of more than eighty percent of Russia's banks, siphoned billions of dollars of Western government loans and aid." Of particular concern, U.S. intelligence believes that Russian mobsters could acquire WMDs and sell them to terrorist groups.[52]

The infiltration of the Russian mob has become a particular problem in the United States, as they have become "the FBI's most formidable criminal adversary," operating in at least seventeen U.S. cities (including New York, Miami, San Francisco, Los Angeles, and Denver). Their operations include "[invading] North America's financial markets, orchestrating complex stock scams, allegedly laundering billions of dollars through the Bank of New York, coolly infiltrating the business and real estate worlds," and penetrating the National Hockey League (see Spotlight, "The Red *Mafiya* Penalty Box and the NHL").[53]

▪ S P O T L I G H T ▪

The Red *Mafiya* Penalty Box and the NHL

Hockey has long been one of Russia's most popular sports, and the Russian *Mafiya* has played a significant role in the sport even back in the days of the Soviet Union. Either by force or cooperation, the *Mafiya* used hockey teams "for money laundering, as well as for many other illicit profits that could be sucked from stadium contracts, concessions, equipment procurement, ticket sales, player and management salaries, and tens of millions of dollars of untaxed vodka and cigarettes that the government gave to the teams."[i] With the collapse of communism in the late 1980s, the pool of wildly talented hockey players from the Soviet Union became available to the National Hockey League (NHL). NHL teams in Canada and the United States tripped over themselves to sign these players to lucrative contracts, but soon discovered "that they weren't importing only expert skaters and stickhandlers; they were also importing the brutal extortionists and gun-toters of the Russian *Mafiya* who followed in their wake."

The relationship of NHL players to the Russian mob has been twofold. First, the list of players "who have been secretly shaken down, beaten, and threatened by voracious Russian mobsters reads like a Who's Who of the NHL." Those suspected of being targets of extortion include Alexander Mogilny (New Jersey Devils), Alexei Zhitnik (Atlanta Thrashers), Vladimir Malakhov (who won the Stanley Cup with the New Jersey Devils in 2000), Sergei Fedorov (Columbus Blue Jackets), and Oleg Tverdovsky (Los Angeles Kings). In May 1996, a congressional investigation determined that the proportion of NHL players from the former Eastern bloc who have been forced to pay for protection could be as high as half. Alexei Zhitnik was allegedly beaten by mobsters under a Los Angeles pier, and Alexander Mogilny was abducted and shaken down for $150,000. Unlike Zhitnik, however, Mogilny went to the FBI, and as a result a Russian mobster was convicted and deported. Mogilny's action is an outlier, however, as NHL players universally deny that there is a problem. Despite the conviction, based largely on his testimony, even Mogilny refuses to acknowledge that there is an extortion problem in the NHL. This naturally prevents the FBI from prosecuting the mobsters.

On the other side of this coin, however, some NHL players have been personally linked to members of the Russian mob. This list also contains an impressive set of names: Slava Fetisov (who won the Stanley Cup with Detroit in 1997 and 1998), Valeri Kamensky (who won the Stanley Cup with Colorado in 1996), and, perhaps most famously, Pavel Bure (who is nicknamed the "Russian Rocket"). According to the FBI, Fetisov was listed as the president of a front company in

New York called Slavik Inc. that laundered money for the mob, Kamensky has close ties with the head of the Russian mob in Denver, and Bure has a wide array of mob friends, dating back to his childhood (in fact, Bure's ties are so extensive and public that in 1993 the Vancouver Canucks ordered Bure to stop associating with them, a demand he accepted but never honored).

In his book *Red Mafiya*, investigative reporter Robert I. Friedman questions why the NHL has not done more to protect its players and the reputation of the game. He writes, "Despite organized crime's frightening penetration into the sport, the NHL, according to several sources, stood by idly, even stonewalling the 1996 congressional investigation into the situation." He surmises that the reasons the NHL has failed to act include fear that the reputation of the game may be tarnished by acknowledgment of the problem (and thus a loss of revenue) and a lower set of moral standards in the NHL than in other sports leagues (for example, the NFL forced Joe Namath to sell a Manhattan restaurant because mobsters were known to frequent the establishment). As a consequence, "as long as everyone from the league's superstars to its own commissioner fails to speak out against it, the NHL will remain an irresistible opportunity for the world's most powerful and ruthless criminal cartel."

---

i. The information presented here was taken from Robert I. Friedman, *Red Mafiya: How the Russian Mob Has Invaded America* (Boston: Little, Brown & Company, 2000), Chapter 8, "Power Play," 173–201.

Asian gangs are also operating across borders. The Yakuza (in essence, the Japanese word for mafia) produce amphetamines in Japan, the Philippines, and Korea and act in the center of the international trade in sex slavery (they sell women and children throughout the developing world). The strongest group in Japan, the Yamaguchi-gumi, with roughly 17,500 members, dominates the major centers of the country. In China, the Triads (and their American offshoots, the Tongs) are believed to have originated in opposition to the Ch'ing dynasty in 1644 and have more than 100,000 members worldwide (any country with a sizable Chinese population has Triads). Groups of Triads in different countries may work together, but it is believed that there is no central control. Some Triads engage in the international drug trade, and others participate in people trafficking. In addition, there are several Vietnamese gangs located outside Vietnam, including Born to Kill (BTK) in New York City and numerous small groups operating in Germany.[54]

Also operating across borders, organized crime groups focusing on drug trafficking adversely affect efforts to combat the international drug problem (see Spotlight, "International Drug Trafficking"). Colombian organizations control the world's cocaine industry. Colombia grows its own coca; it also

PHOTO 8.3 The Japanese Yakuza have traditionally engaged in whole-body tattooing to demonstrate their endurance and loyalty.

receives it from Bolivia and Peru and then exports the processed drug to the United States. Colombian cartels, the most famous of which are the Medellin and Cali, do not hesitate to use violence, and this has allowed them to dominate rivals. Mexican criminal organizations are also involved in the drug trade and have actually succeeded in striking a deal with Colombian cartels that were moving their cocaine through Mexico. Numerous other cartels in Mexico oversee the growth and trafficking in drugs, including the Amezcuas Cartel (methamphetamines), the Herrera Family (heroin), the Sinaloa Cartel (cocaine), the Gulf Cartel (cocaine), La Familia (cocaine; formerly the paramilitary wing of the Gulf Cartel) the Juarez Cartel (cocaine), the Tijuana Cartel (cocaine, heroin), and the Sonora Cartel (marijuana, cocaine, amphetamine).[55]

Mexican President Felipe Calderon declared war on the country's drug cartels in 2006, and since then the drug cartels have been fighting each other and the Mexican authorities. The violence has been shocking, with thousands of drug-related murders each year. The cartels' behavior has been gruesome—individuals have been beheaded or dismembered, and there have been grenade attacks and gun battles—and targets have included Mexican authorities and their families, including children. The independence of the Zetas, formerly a part of the Gulf Cartel, has contributed to the increase in violence as this organization has become the most sophisticated and dangerous of the cartels in Mexico. Their activities are epitomized by the murder of the Veracruz police chief, his wife, and four children in July 2009, in which eight or nine gunmen with assault rifles and grenade launchers shot the chief, his wife, and their

▪ SPOTLIGHT ▪

International Drug Trafficking

Trafficking in illegal narcotics is a multibillion-dollar-a-year business connected to regional conflicts (the lack of government control in certain countries makes production and smuggling easier) and organized crime. The UN's Office on Drugs and Crime estimated that between 172 and 205 million people consumed illegal drugs in 2007 (18–34 million were "problem drug users," meaning they consume most of the drugs used each year).[i] World narcotics production is concentrated in four areas: Southeast Asia, the Middle East, Central America, and South America. Each region has its own specialty product, with Southeast Asia concentrating on opium and its derivatives (including heroin), the Middle East on hashish, Central America on marijuana/cannabis, and South America on cocaine. However, the lines of demarcation are not always clear. For example, heroin smuggled into the United States comes from several regions, including South America (Colombia), Southeast Asia (Burma/Myanmar), Mexico, and Southwest Asia and the Middle East (Afghanistan).[ii] In many cases, drug production in these regions is sustained or encouraged by insurgencies, civil war, and other violent internal conflicts.

The two main illegal drugs of concern to the international community are heroin or opium and cocaine, although according to the UN's Office on Drugs and Crime, cannabis is the largest illicit drug market, with between 143 and 190 million users in 2007.[iii] The vast majority of the world's opium is produced in two regions (Southeast and Southwest Asia): Burma/Myanmar, Laos, and Thailand, known collectively as the Golden Triangle; and Afghanistan, Iran, and Pakistan, together referred to as the Golden Crescent. Currently, the state of the heroin market is determined by conditions in southern Afghanistan, although in 2007 there was a decrease in the area under opium poppy cultivation.[iv] Cocaine is supplied mostly by three countries: Bolivia, Colombia, and Peru. Eradication efforts in Colombia have led to a decrease in the area under cultivation in that country (it fell by 52 percent between 2000 and 2006), but increases in Bolivia and Peru have been seen as a consequence of Colombia's decrease. Production appears to have leveled off as evidenced by the rising price and lower purity levels.[v] North America and western and central Europe are the two main cocaine consumption regions, and consumption has increased considerably in Europe over the past decade, doubling and even tripling in some countries.[vi] In terms of marijuana, which is the most extensively produced, trafficked, and used illegal drug globally, data are harder to come by given the geographic spread. However, the UN's

Office on Drugs and Crime *World Drug Report 2009* noted that "it is grown in most countries of the world and can be produced indoors or outdoors."[vii]

Because cocaine, heroin, marijuana, and other drugs are illegal in most countries, drug trafficking, the transportation of drugs from producers to consumers, has become a major international criminal enterprise, and official efforts to curb drug supply and abuse have attained moderate success. As the world's largest consumer of illicit drugs, by far, the United States has a large incentive to take the initiative in combating the international drug trade. Common American rhetoric, both within and outside of Washington, holds that the primary responsibility for the drug problem lies with pushers and criminal gangs who prey on vulnerable citizens. Accordingly, the United States has traditionally concentrated on restricting the supply of drugs rather than reducing demand for them. This may be done through interdiction (stopping drugs from coming into the country, primarily through customs inspection) or eradication (destruction of the crops that are processed into illegal drugs). The prime example of U.S. efforts is in Colombia, where the United States has provided Colombia with millions of dollars of aid for training, equipment, and intelligence to assist in the eradication of coca crops and the arrest of drug producers and traffickers. Proponents point to the decrease in coca crops in Colombia to highlight the success of this approach.

However, attempts by the United States to reduce drug production in cooperation with South American countries have frequently been stymied by four factors. First, the drug trade is a major source of employment and export revenues in many Latin American countries. Their governments have attempted to impress on the United States that one of the ultimate solutions to the drug trade is for the United States to import more of the legal goods of their countries.[viii] Second, efforts at drug eradication that do not provide for a transition to legal alternative employment for coca and marijuana growers or for balance-of-payments support for drug-producing countries encounter a great deal of resistance. The United States, with a dwindling pool of dollars to spend on international aid, has been reluctant to commit funds for agricultural and industrial development designed to supplant drug cultivation. Third, domestic resistance to what is perceived as Yankee imperialism has been exploited by drug traffickers to undermine joint U.S.–South American antidrug action. Finally, and perhaps most seriously, corruption, violence, and intimidation of political and judicial authorities within drug-producing countries continue to frustrate cooperative drug-control programs.

In the new era, an international consensus about how to deal with the drug problem has emerged. Efforts coordinated by the United Nations International Drug Control Program (UNDCP) to fight drug abuse and trafficking intensified in the early 1990s. At a special session of the General Assembly held in February 1990, the United Nations proclaimed a UN Decade Against Drug

Abuse (1991–2000) and unanimously adopted a thirty-point Political Declaration and Global Program of Action against illegal drugs. The declaration recognized that the drug problem in all its dimensions is linked to economic, social, and cultural conditions in affected countries and acknowledged links between drug abuse and the spread of AIDS, as well as the connection between drug trafficking and terrorism. Among its main recommendations, the Global Program suggested giving higher priority to drug-abuse prevention programs, especially those directed at children.[ix]

Drug-control experts argue that the contemporary global economy makes multilateral cooperation more important than ever because it relies heavily on the free exchange of goods, services, labor, and capital across sovereign borders. Importantly, disagreements between the United States and Latin American countries over drug-control strategy show how the drug trade exerts different effects on drug-producing and drug-consuming states. Rich drug-importing countries experience the health problems, crime, and economic harm attributable to addiction, whereas corruption and narco-terrorism become endemic in the poorer states that produce the narcotics. Because no country is immune to some of the ills created by drug abuse and trafficking, almost all states now regard the international war on drugs as an important and urgent cause. Efforts are complicated, however, by the fact that the drug trade is a hugely lucrative business, and traffickers have a strong motivation to match supply to demand. Unless individual states and the international community take further steps to reduce both the supply and demand sides of the drug equation, the global narcotics industry will continue to find ways to turn coca, marijuana, and poppies into gold.

i. United Nations Office on Drugs and Crime, *World Drug Report* (New York: United Nations, 2009), http://www.unodc.org/documents/wdr/WDR_2009/Executive_summary_LO-RES.pdf, accessed June 5, 2010.

ii. Drug Enforcement Administration, "Drug Trafficking in the United States," DEA Briefs & Background, http://www.usdoj.gov/dea/concern/drug_traffickingp.html.

iii. United Nations Office on Drugs and Crime, *World Drug Report.*

iv. Ibid.

v. Ibid.

vi. Ibid.

vii. Ibid.

viii. Bruce Michael Bagley, "Dateline Drug Wars: Columbia—the Wrong Strategy," *Foreign Policy* 77 (winter 1989–90): 159–60.

ix. "General Assembly Message to World: Reduce Drug Demand," *UN Chronicle* 27 (1990): 53–60.

son. They then set their house on fire, killing the three remaining children. The threat posed by this emerging cartel has caused other organizations in Mexico to ally together to combat them (including an alliance between the Gulf and Sinaloa cartels and La Familia). As a consequence, Mexico's tourism industry has taken a severe blow, and the violence has spilled over the border into the United States. Thus, the United States and Mexico have been collaborating on ways to combat this threat, but it is formidable to say the least.

Combating Organized Crime

Individual countries and the international community have taken several steps in an attempt to combat the problem of transnational organized crime. On the domestic front, countries have passed legislation to assist law enforcement agencies in investigating, arresting, and prosecuting members of organized crime groups. Japan, for example, has passed laws to strengthen its judicial system and aid law enforcement, including legislation to punish acts of child prostitution. Similarly, Canada has modernized its judicial system to expand police investigative powers and provide new offenses and sentences related to organized crime. In the United States, the Racketeer Influenced and Corrupt Organizations (RICO) statute of 1970 provided jurisdiction for the federal government in many issues relating to organized crime, including sports bribery, counterfeiting, loan sharking, contraband cigarettes, white slavery, and drug violations. This, in essence, made the FBI the lead agency in dealing with organized crime.[56]

Since the end of the Cold War, the international community has recognized that globalization has increased the destructive nature of organized crime. Cooperation is taking place both bilaterally and multilaterally. The United States and Canada, for example, hold an annual forum to set priorities in the fight against organized crime that helps enhance cooperation and information sharing. In addition, in 1996 the two nations established the Canada–U.S. Integrated Border Enforcement Teams (IBETs), which are designed to enhance border integrity and security. Germany has also concluded a series of bilateral agreements with countries in central and eastern Europe to combat organized crime.

Multilaterally, the United Nations adopted the Global Action Plan against Organized Transnational Crime in 1994 that was designed to enhance cooperation between member states. In 2000, the UN passed the Convention against Transnational Organized Crime, which provides a legal basis for cooperation between countries, and supplemented this with protocols against trafficking in persons and the smuggling of migrants. Regionally, the United States has partnered with Mexico, Central America, Haiti, and the Dominican Republic in the Merida Initiative. The purpose of this initiative is to strengthen institutions to combat criminal organizations through a variety of means, including equipping and training police, promoting and supporting judicial reform and education, and enhancing cross-agency cooperation. The United States has pledged hundreds of millions of dollars to this initiative. The EU has also taken action, with the Treaty of Amsterdam in 1997 expanding the possibility for cooperation between member states against organized crime. The EU employs the European Police Office (Europol) to act as the central agency for crime prevention. Europol collects and transmits information related to cross-border crimes and can make recommendations concerning investigations in member states.

The Group of 8 (G-8) has also made significant contributions to the fight against organized crime. In 1989, the then-G-7 set up the Financial Action Task Force (FATF). According to the FATF website, it is "an inter-governmental body whose purpose is the development and promotion of national and international policies to combat money laundering and terrorist financing. The FATF is therefore a 'policy-making body'...that works to generate the necessary political will to bring about legislative and regulatory reforms in these areas."[57] The Council of Europe also passed a convention to combat money laundering with the 1990 Convention on Laundering, Search, Seizure and Confiscation of the Proceeds from Crime. Finally, in 1995 the G-8 established the Lyon Group that drew up recommendations that have been widely implemented on how to utilize international agreements better in order to battle organized crime. Thus, the international community has taken significant action against organized crime. Despite these efforts, however, it remains a serious threat to international security that shows no sign of abatement.

Conclusion

Efforts to combat proliferation, terrorism, and organized crime are complicated by several factors. In many instances, there is a lack of resources to combat the problem at hand (organized crime), or the means to combat the problem are not universally accepted (as with the U.S. decision to overthrow the Iraqi regime to combat the spread of WMDs). There is general agreement that these issues pose a threat, but the solutions are not easily forthcoming.

In the globalized world, if progress is to be made, it must be international in scope. As Chapter 13 will discuss, international organizations have the potential to achieve lasting and substantial successes in many of these areas, but they are riddled with structural weaknesses. In 2003, Secretary-General Kofi Annan recognized the challenges for the UN in dealing with these problems.

> In many countries, terrorism has once again brought death and suffering to innocent people. In the Middle East, and certain parts of Africa, violence has continued to escalate. In the Korean peninsula, and elsewhere, the threat of nuclear

AT A GLANCE

Levels of Analysis and Paradigms in Review: Contemporary Security Examples

	Realism	Liberalism	Constructivism
Individual	India's test of a nuclear explosive prompted Pakistani Prime Minister Zulfikar Ali Bhutto to seek nuclear capability aggressively to counter that of his opponent. He was committed, at all cost, to keep pace with India, not allowing the enemy to gain a decisive advantage. This resulted in an arms race between India and Pakistan.	Libyan leader Mummar al-Qadhafi renounced his country's WMD program in favor of cooperation with the international community. Libya also ratified the CTBT and CWC and has become a partner in the War on Terror. Qadhafi realized that a successful future for Libya meant joining the international community and coming out of isolation.	Members of organized crime perceive themselves to be above the law, and as a consequence engage in activities that are inconceivable to others, for example, trafficking in people, human organs, and drugs.
Domestic	Pessimists in the proliferation debate argue that organizational and bureaucratic obstacles prevent states from always engaging in rational behavior. Bureaucratic competition, in which each organization is seeking its best outcome, may actually lead to an undesirable outcome (in this argument, the use of nuclear weapons).	According to political scientist John Mueller, competent domestic governance is required to overcome the conflicts of the new era. Because conflict, according to Mueller, is waged by criminals and thugs, domestic government is needed more than international intervention.	The recognition of the need to improve domestic laws and judicial systems to combat organized crime in many countries has evolved over time. As organized crime becomes more global, states have found cooperation essential to curbing the devastating effects of criminal activities.
Systemic	Optimists in the proliferation debate believe that a credible deterrent can prevent crises and that there is no better deterrent than nuclear weapons. Thus, proliferation is not a serious threat because states will always work to maximize their best interests.	States are cooperating on a myriad of security issues, such as combating terrorism and fighting organized crime, in an effort to seek mutually advantageous outcomes. These issues impact states across borders, and thus cooperation with others in the system is vital to ensuring success.	The international community has grown to accept the status of India and Pakistan as nuclear weapons states. States were initially reluctant and even hostile toward the idea of new nuclear states, but opinions evolved over time.

proliferation casts an ominous shadow across the landscape....All of us know there are new threats that must be faced—or perhaps, old threats in new and dangerous combinations: new forms of terrorism, and the proliferation of weapons of mass destruction....But, while some consider these threats as self-evidently the main challenges to world peace and security, others feel more immediately menaced by small arms employed in civil conflict, or by so-called "soft threats" such as the persistence of extreme poverty, the disparity of income between and within societies, and the spread of infectious diseases, or climate change and environmental degradation.[58]

The security challenges facing the international community have arguably changed as technology, interdependence, and shifting international norms have created mutual interests as well as new threats. Although nuclear war remains a terrible possibility, the circumstances that could bring about such a war have changed dramatically since the end of the Cold War. Although criminal activity is nothing new, worldwide networks arguably create unprecedented challenges of coordination and cooperation among the world's various policy and security forces. Truly we are in a new era, one in which the rules are shifting, the stakes are often incompatible, and the problems complex. At the same time, we have seen new forms of cooperation arise in the face of these difficulties, from the six-party talks involving North Korea to the peace agreement between Britain and Northern Ireland. We are watching both the threats and the responses to them evolve very rapidly as world politics flex and adapt in the first part of the twenty-first century.

Discussion and Review Questions

1. Should the international community do everything possible to prevent states from obtaining nuclear capabilities? Why or why not?
2. Why did Libyan leader Mummar al-Qadhafi agree to abolish his country's weapons of mass destruction program? Would you have done the same thing if in his shoes?
3. Discuss the definition of terrorism. What does terrorism mean to you?
4. Discuss the efforts to combat terrorism. What is being done, and is it enough? If not, what are some other options?
5. Define organized crime. What do you think of when you hear the term? What kinds of activities do you associate with organized crime?

Key Terms

CHAPTER 9

World Politics: Trade and Investment

Most studies of world politics seem to focus on military conflict for the same reason that public affairs broadcasts seem to devote most of their time to scandals, crime, earthquakes, and plane crashes: These developments are fascinating because they are out-of-the-ordinary, dramatic events. Just as earthquakes are rare and most planes do not crash, most states interact with each other peacefully most of the time, and much of that interaction is economic.

That is not to say that the economic arena is not competitive, or even conflictual. Economic power not only is tied closely to security but also can be wielded as effectively internationally as military power. A realist would therefore argue that states should seek relative economic gains rather than absolute profits because they will want to be stronger than their closest competitors. States should also, from this perspective, seek to gain some form of economic control over each other, whether through strategic investment or resource manipulation or some other form of economic leverage. Liberals, however, point out that there is a tremendous amount of economic cooperation, from trade agreements to regional blocs. They cite the benefits of unfettered trade and argue that everyone seeking their own self-interest leads to a healthier economic system for all.

For their part, constructivists remind us that there are efforts—like the United Nations Millennium Development Goals—that demonstrate people's deliberately evolving discussion of, and commitment to, **human security,** with all the implications that has for responsible trade and investment policies.

Trade and economic exchange have always accompanied the ongoing struggle for national power and security. Indeed, trade is the aspect of international relations that has the greatest impact on our individual lives. The range of options we have when we shop, the prices we pay, the jobs available to us, and even the health of our communities depend on trade. Investment also falls within the field of economics and has become increasingly significant as technological changes allow global investments that create deep interdependencies as well as vulnerabilities. With increased globalization, development becomes globally—rather than just locally or regionally—relevant. As will be discussed in the following chapter, an international system that perpetuates poverty and underdevelopment is not only problematic on ethical grounds, as many argue, but also limits global economic growth and creates security nightmares as criminals and terrorists take root where governments are too cash-strapped to assert control.

This chapter describes international trade and investment and relevant theories for each. It introduces key actors at all the levels of analysis. It is infused with the tensions between cooperation and conflict and globalization and fragmentation. It also begins to show how economic issues and concerns cut across all the fields of world politics.

Trade

Although some states have tried, none has ever achieved total economic self-sufficiency. Most states need goods and services that other states produce, and most produce goods and services that other states need. Thus, the only way for states to get all the goods and services they need (short of conquering other countries, which is usually very expensive as well as morally repugnant) is to trade for them.

This is especially true for certain natural resources that are unevenly distributed across states. For instance, just a few countries, such as Saudi Arabia, Iran, Venezuela, and Nigeria, produce large quantities of oil, but virtually all countries use oil in their economies for industrial processes, heating, generating electricity, and as fuel for automobiles. This is also true for many agricultural products. For instance, coffee grows best in highland tropical climates, so if Americans want to have a cup of coffee, it has to be imported from countries like Colombia, Brazil, or Kenya (although the United States does produce a small amount of coffee in Hawaii). Similarly, bananas do not grow well in the United States (although some farmers have tried) and must be imported from tropical countries like Ecuador or Honduras. This works both ways, of course. If Brazilians want apples or maple

▪ **Human security**
Freedom from both fear and want.

syrup, they must trade with temperate agricultural countries like the United States or Canada.

Even when countries can produce the same goods or services, trade may occur because states have different allocations of resources. Trade theory usually identifies three categories of resources: land, labor, and capital. A nation is land-abundant if it has a lot of land (agriculture and resources) relative to its population, and it is labor-abundant if wages are relatively low, usually caused by a large population. Similarly, a **capital-abundant** nation is relatively rich, both in terms of money and industrial plants and equipment.

Because nations have different allocations of resources, each enjoys a **comparative advantage** in producing those goods that use its abundant resource.[1] Some specialize in **labor-intensive** industries like textiles because they are abundant in labor. Others specialize in **capital-intensive** industries like airplane manufacturing because they are wealthy and can build factories and develop technology. Still others produce agriculture because their land is inexpensive. Comparative advantage is thus an explanation for how countries with different resources and skills engage in trade.

Ricardo's Model of Trade

It is logical to expect that a country will produce the goods it can make more efficiently than other countries. When a country is more efficient than others in producing a certain good, it is said to have an absolute advantage in production of that good. However, mutual gains from trade are still possible even if one party has an absolute advantage in all goods. David Ricardo (1772–1823), an English economist who contributed to the development of the fields of economics and political economy, demonstrated, using a simple model accounting for nations' varying labor productivity, how this could be so. His work provided a stepping-stone for the theoretical developments of a century later.[2]

Ricardo showed that even if one nation has an absolute advantage in the production of all goods, trade can still be mutually beneficial if the less efficient nation has a comparative advantage in one good over another. To see why this is so, let us consider the countries of Fredonia and Sylvania (two imaginary countries from the Marx Brothers' classic satire on international politics, *Duck Soup*). Both countries produce only two goods, wine and cloth. Table 9.1 shows the amount of labor (a cost of production) required to produce one bottle of wine and one bolt of cloth in each country.

The figures indicate that Sylvania has an absolute advantage in both wine and cloth; each is more costly to produce in Fredonia. Nevertheless, mutual gains from trade are still possible because of comparative advantage. The ratio of production costs for the two goods differs in the two countries. In Sylvania, one bottle of wine will exchange for one half-bolt of cloth (because the ratio of labor costs per unit of output of the two goods is 2:4), and in Fredonia, one bottle of wine will exchange for two bolts of cloth (because the ratio of labor costs for the two goods is 12:6). These ratios reflect the labor input to produce

■ **Capital-abundant**
Rich in terms of money, industrial plants, and equipment.

■ **Comparative advantage**
The ability of one business or entity to engage in production at a lower opportunity cost than another business or entity.

■ **Labor intensive**
Industry requiring labor as the main input.

■ **Capital intensive**
Industry requiring capital (money, plants, or equipment) as the main input.

TABLE 9.1	Comparative Advantage	
Worker Hours Needed to Produce One Unit of:		
Country	*Wine*	*Cloth*
Fredonia	12	6
Sylvania	2	4

each item. Cloth is relatively cheaper in Fredonia than in Sylvania; because one bottle of wine earns more cloth (12:6 versus 2:4), Fredonia has a comparative advantage in cloth making. Wine is relatively cheaper in Sylvania; because one bolt of cloth garners more wine (4:2 versus 6:12), it has a comparative advantage in wine making. Therefore, because of these relative prices, trade between these two countries will be mutually advantageous. Fredonia can sell one bolt of cloth for one half-bottle of wine domestically—or it can sell it for two bottles in Sylvania. Clearly, Fredonia will choose to trade with Sylvania. Sylvania can get one half-bolt of cloth per bottle of wine domestically, but it can trade with Fredonia for two bolts.

Each country gains by exporting the good in which it has a comparative advantage and by importing the good in which it has a comparative disadvantage. Mutual gains will lead to specialization within each country, making goods less expensive and production more efficient for both. However, the gains are not necessarily equal; because Fredonia has higher production costs for both goods, it gains more through trade and specialization. This is because trade and specialization allow nations to concentrate on the production of the goods they produce most efficiently. When goods are produced efficiently, they are produced at minimum cost. As Fredonia's costs decrease, so should the prices charged to consumers for those products. Of course, the same pattern occurs in Sylvania, but because it was more efficient to begin with, its gain from trade is less than that in Fredonia. Nevertheless, consumers in both countries benefit from trade.

Trade Barriers

Given the preceding discussion, it might seem counterintuitive for states to implement barriers to free trade. Yet governments often attempt to protect their domestic markets from international competition. Why? The trade theory just presented shows that national welfare improves when consumers purchase goods from the most efficient (least expensive) producer, whether it is foreign or domestic. However, competition may force domestic producers to go out of business if they become less efficient than foreign producers. Often, governments will not stand idly by while companies or entire industries go bankrupt. This is especially true if those industries employ many workers (whose jobs translate into domestic buying power and whose votes translate into domestic political power) or have tremendous political influence (like the U.S. steel industry). States may therefore impose **trade barriers** to protect domestic industries.[3] Governments also may use trade barriers as a form of leverage, exerting pressure against other governments to reduce their trade protections. This kind of tit-for-tat trade strategy can be very dangerous, resulting in escalating protectionism (as occurred between the World Wars, for example), and is therefore usually cautiously employed.

Barriers to free trade most often represent a conflict of domestic interests: consumers that want inexpensive products versus industries that want to stay in business (and workers in those industries, who want to retain their jobs). Because protection benefits a concentrated, politically powerful group of industrialists and workers and hurts an unorganized and disparate, albeit large, group of consumers, political support for protection can usually penetrate even the most ardent free-trade governments. One common form of protection is the **tariff,** a tax imposed on a good entering a country from abroad. This additional cost makes the foreign good more expensive than it was before. If domestic consumers are relatively price conscious, they will curb their consumption of foreign goods in exchange for locally produced goods. Thus, tariffs aid local producers who compete against foreign-produced goods. One negative consequence of a tariff is that consumers pay higher prices because they no longer have access to cheaper foreign products. Also, local firms have less incentive to become more efficient because they are subject to less international competition. Nevertheless, in the short term, the domestic economy might improve because the tariff encourages domestic production, albeit at the cost of higher consumer prices and less efficient production.

One famous example of a tax on imports is the Smoot-Hawley Tariff, mentioned briefly in Chapter 3. After the stock market crash of 1929, many in the United States feared that foreign competition would destroy even more U.S. jobs than had been lost as a result of the crash. In an attempt to protect remaining jobs, Congress in 1930 raised prices on all imports by 19 percent; by 1932, the average tariff reached 59 percent. Such a course of action is called a beggar-thy-neighbor policy. Foreign countries predictably responded to the Smoot-Hawley Tariff by raising their own tariffs, making U.S. exports more expensive abroad. As a result of these **countervailing tariffs,** export industries collapsed worldwide because they were increasingly shut out of the international market. Ultimately, this cycle of protection had a devastating impact on the world economy by accelerating and deepening the Great Depression.[4]

In addition to tariffs, there are other impediments to free trade, collectively known as **nontariff barriers.** The first is called an **import quota.** A state can put a limit on the number of imports it receives from the rest of the world. This is an explicitly protectionist barrier. However, sometimes a state will compel another nation to "voluntarily" limit its exports. These are called **voluntary export restrictions (VERs).** The importer might threaten to impose tariffs if the exporter does not comply. A government can demand VERs to protect its own industries from being pushed out of its own market. Between 1981 and 1994, for

■ **Trade barriers**
Means of preventing foreign goods from competing with domestic goods.

■ **Tariffs**
Taxes importers must pay before their goods can enter a country.

■ **Countervailing tariffs**
Tariffs levied by one country in response to tariffs imposed in another.

■ **Nontariff barriers to trade**
Eliminating foreign goods' competitiveness with domestic goods by imposing quotas or by putting a country in a position where it has no choice but to limit its exports.

■ **Import quota**
Restricting how much of a specific foreign product can enter the country.

■ **Voluntary export restrictions (VERs)**
Usually the result of political or economic leverage, VERs occur when states agree to limit how much of a specific product they will export to a given country.

PHOTO 9.1   Japanese auto worker.

example, the United States demanded that the Japanese restrict car exports to the American market to protect local automobile producers.

Japan complied, but Japanese automakers helped soften the blow of export restrictions by building factories in the United States and exporting higher value Japanese luxury cars to meet the VER quota. In another case, from 1996 to 2001, Canada agreed to limit its soft-lumber exports to the United States as part of a larger agreement aimed at ending a twenty-year trade dispute. When the agreement expired in September 2001 and Canada discontinued the VERs, the United States immediately responded with a tariff on Canadian soft lumber.

States also inhibit or prohibit foreign goods from competing with domestic products by imposing regulations ostensibly intended to protect domestic consumers. Agricultural products are hit frequently with these kinds of nontariff barriers, although other goods are also vulnerable. Sometimes the "consumer safety" concerns are particularly far-fetched, such as when, in the 1980s, Japanese trade officials restricted imports of skis, citing the purportedly unique character of Japanese snow. In 2000, in direct contravention of the NAFTA agreement, Mexico sought to protect its domestic salt industry by imposing scientifically questionable standards on salt imports (for example, becoming the only country in the world to prohibit the use of explosive-mined rock salt in food for humans and animals). In the 1990s, the EU banned genetically modified foods—despite an internal EU review finding such foods safe—in a move that served as a de facto trade barrier. The original ban was lifted but was replaced by eight national bans under an EU safeguard provision. Such policies can have trickle-down effects; in 2002, for example, despite its millions of starving citizens, Zimbabwe rejected U.S. food aid in fear that Europe would ban Zimbabwean exports if its farmers grew crops from the genetically modified U.S. seed.[5]

Just as specious claims of consumer protection can be used to block imports, so can labor and environmental regulations. Although the preponderance of such laws are well intended and, indeed, important, there are cases in which labor and environmental issues are used more cynically as a form of **protectionism.** Many developing countries, for example, claim that the United States benefits at their expense and undercuts their competitive advantage in the global market by imposing labor and environmental standards they cannot afford to meet.

Finally, governments can use **subsidies,** government funds, to support domestic industries. These government payments allow producers to price their goods below the cost of production without going out of business. Although the ostensible purpose of internal subsidies (called **price supports** in the United States) is to allow producers to compete against imports in the home market and that of external subsidies is to allow producers to compete in the international market, both in effect aid domestic producers. In the international system, it may be hard to distinguish between external subsidies and **dumping,** in which one country sells (or "dumps") its products in a foreign market so far below the costs of production that it causes other producers in that market to go out of business. In the last two decades, U.S. steel producers, for instance, have frequently brought antidumping suits against foreign steel producers before the U.S. Department of Commerce (to determine whether the products were "dumped" or unfairly subsidized) and the International Trade Commission (ITC) (to determine if dumping has occurred and whether it resulted in "material harm" to domestic producers). One of the problems with dumping is that after a domestic producer has been driven out of business, the foreign company may increase its prices, so both domestic producers and consumers ultimately lose.

Balance of Payments

Another important concept for understanding international economic relations is the **balance of payments.** Much like companies, states keep "balance sheets" that present their transactions with those of the rest of the world. These national

▪ **Protectionism**
Defending domestic industry from foreign competition.

▪ **Subsidies**
Government payments to domestic industries that allow them to produce at a lower cost, thus allowing them to sell more competitively in the international market.

▪ **Price supports**
Government action to uphold a domestic product's price, usually by buying it.

▪ **Dumping**
Exporting a product at below the cost of production and shipping.

▪ **Balance of payments**
The difference between the amount of money coming into a country and the amount of money going out.

accounts tell us a country's trade balance (exports of goods and services minus imports of goods and services), how much money locals earned overseas, the amount of foreign currency invested in the domestic economy, the level of official foreign aid given to other countries, and the amount of foreign currency held by the central bank (the Federal Reserve in the United States, for example, or the Bundesbank in Germany).[6]

The sum total of a nation's imports, exports, foreign aid and other government transactions, and investment income and payments is referred to as the **current-account balance.** This is the figure usually cited in news reports about a country's **balance of trade.** If the current-account balance is positive, the country enjoys a trade surplus, or a "net profit" from trade. If it is negative, the state has a "net loss," or trade deficit, even though consumers in the state may still be better off as a result of trade because they are able to buy less expensive and higher quality imported goods.

Accounting procedures guarantee that the balance of payments always equals zero. This is due to double-entry bookkeeping. For example, if an American purchases a foreign good, the import's value is recorded as a reduction from the balance of payments. However, once that foreign producer obtains U.S. dollars in exchange for that good, the producer usually deposits the money in a bank, the same way most people deposit paychecks. If the producer does a lot of business in the United States, it might deposit that money in an American bank. Once the producer deposits that money in the United States, the account's value is added to the plus side of the balance of payments. Even if the foreign producer deposits it in its own bank abroad, that foreign bank must eventually deposit it in a U.S. bank to redeem its value, that is, to get paid back. This has the effect of an addition to the balance of payments.

Money Makes the World Go Around

Our simplified discussion of international trade has focused on goods and services, but as we all know, almost all trade involves money in some form. Prior to the development of money, trade was conducted by barter, the mutual exchange of goods and services. This system was inefficient because, in the first place, it was difficult to establish rates of exchange between goods and services. Second, in a barter system there must be a coincidence of wants—every party must want exactly what the other has to offer. If you have a cow and want apples, then you need to find someone with apples who wants a cow; otherwise, you need another commodity to trade or a third person. Third, many commodities are perishable and might not last long enough to trade. Money solves all these inconveniences as a medium of exchange, unit of account for contracts, and store of value. Within countries, authorities have been established to ensure the legitimacy and stability of the currency and to deter counterfeiting and fraud; in the United States, for example, the Treasury Department has exclusive authority to issue paper and coin currency and to ensure that no one else does.

▪ **Current-account balance**
The difference between a state's total exports and total imports.

▪ **Balance of trade**
The value of exports minus the value of imports.

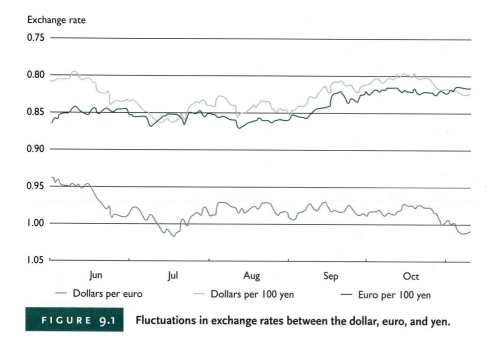

FIGURE 9.1   **Fluctuations in exchange rates between the dollar, euro, and yen.**

Exchange Rates

Of course, each state traditionally has its own currency, although the states of the EU have become an exception with the adoption of the euro as common currency. At any given moment, trade is being conducted somewhere using U.S. dollars, Japanese yen, Israeli shekels, Brazilian reals, South African rands, Norwegian krones, Malaysian ringgits, and so on (see Figure 9.1).

A way must always be found to exchange these currencies equitably. As those who have traveled abroad know only too well, rates change constantly; so, for example, the exchange rate between the U.S. dollar and euro may be altered daily. For the individual traveler, this is enormously inconvenient and potentially expensive. Such has not always been the case, however. During the periods from 1870 to 1914 and 1945 to 1973, countries agreed to fix their currencies' value so that they would not fluctuate daily. Although this might seem like a worthwhile system, there are benefits and costs to both **fixed** and **floating exchange rate systems**.

Fixed exchange rate systems arise when nations agree to establish a set of currency rules. Two examples of such a system are the gold standard (1870–1914) and the Bretton Woods system (1945–1973). During each period, all currencies were valued at fixed rates against one another. Aside from the benefits to travelers, it also encouraged international trade. Let us examine why this should be so. Suppose an American restaurant owner wants to buy fifty bottles of wine from a French vineyard next month. To do so, the restaurant owner must make the

▪ **Fixed exchange rate system**
When currency exchange rates are set and not responsive to supply and demand.

▪ **Floating exchange rate system**
When currency exchange rates are set by supply and demand.

purchase in euros. One bottle costs 5 euros, and today's exchange rate is $1 per 10 euros. If the American makes the purchase today; she pays $25. Under a fixed system, she will also pay $25 next month.

What if a floating exchange rate system is in effect? If the euro fluctuates during the month so that when the restaurant owner actually purchases the wine, $1 equals 5 euros, he or she would then owe $50, twice as much as before. Because prices can fluctuate, people might be less likely to trade because of its inherent risks. This problem, of course, is alleviated with fixed exchange rates because everyone can be confident about future currency values.

Given this problem, why would countries choose to have floating exchange rates, as the United States does today? There are surprising advantages to floating rates. Exchange rates are supposed to reflect the general health of an economy. If a nation goes into a prolonged recession, people expect its currency to weaken as well. In a fixed arrangement, however, exchange rate values cannot change. If a recession does occur, a government has two choices. First, it can pursue policies, like raising interest rates, that inflate the exchange rate to maintain its fixed value. Officials might choose to do this because they have made agreements with other states to defend their currency. The United States, for example, made this sort of agreement during the Bretton Woods period between 1945 and 1973.

However, artificially inflating a currency can worsen a country's domestic economy. For example, if a government attempts to shore up its exchange rate by raising interest rates, then foreign nationals will increase their demand for domestic investments, like savings accounts and certificates of deposit, because they will receive a good rate of return on their money. If interest rates are 10 percent in one country and 8 percent in another, money is likely to flow to the country giving a better deal. Citizens of the country with the 10 percent rate will also deposit their money at home. Thus, when domestic investments become more attractive (especially relative to foreign investments), people demand more local currency, increasing its value.

What are the drawbacks of this policy? Although high interest rates might help preserve a country's fixed currency rate, this policy decision also makes borrowing money more expensive. To the extent that borrowed funds help us buy goods like homes and cars, higher interest rates reduce the number of these purchases. When people choose to reduce their own spending on goods and services, it hurts the national economy. Therefore, to defend its currency's value internationally, a state often has to jeopardize its national economy.

A second option for policymakers is to stop defending their currency. This action reduces the exchange rate's value and does not have the same negative consequences on the economy that defending the currency might have. In fact, it might improve economic conditions by making exports less expensive. Under a fixed exchange rate system, however, if a country does not bolster its weakened currency, it will be reneging on its agreement with other countries, potentially affecting trade relations, security arrangements, and other related issues. Floating exchange rates thus have an advantage over fixed rates in that they accurately reflect a state's economic health and allow governments to pursue economic policies independent of exchange rate requirements.

The debate over fixed versus floating exchange rates pivots, much like the debate between free trade and protectionism, on the balance between domestic economic interests and the requirements of international trade. Although fixed exchange rates make the international economy more stable and predictable, they can also force governments to pursue harmful domestic policies when the currency's value goes in one direction and the economy's health in the other. Floating exchange rates accurately reflect an economy's well-being, but they create additional uncertainty in the world economy.

Capital Markets and Investment

Capital Markets

Exchange rates are influenced not only by national policies but also by international capital market forces beyond states' control. Underpinning the global economy are a variety of financial firms that invest internationally, including banks, securities firms, stock markets, and commodities exchanges. Of these, banks grant loans to foreign firms and foreign governments, sometimes opening branches around the world. Securities firms, which invest money for their clients, also open in foreign countries, even though they can also rely on the Internet to access financial information and make trades. Stock markets, in which companies' stocks are traded electronically and in **stock exchanges** (like the New York Stock Exchange, the London Stock Exchange, the Germans' Deutsche Börse, the Helsinki Stock Exchange, the Ghana Stock Exchange, the Ljubljana Stock Exchange in Slovenia, and the Kuala Lumpur Stock Exchange), are operating worldwide, facilitating international investments. However, of all the capital markets, **foreign exchange markets**—where currency is traded—stand out as the fastest growing (see Spotlight, "Day Traders Find New Outlet").

Under a floating system, exchange rates are affected in part by how popular national currencies are in foreign exchange markets. Factors influencing a currency's appeal are as diverse as weather, political stability, and even the money's own cachet (some people just love the British pound, for example). It is through these financial exchange markets that commercial banks, investment banks, other financial institutions, and individuals buy and sell currencies for profit. By 2004, the volume of trade in foreign exchange markets had reached $1.9 trillion per day and rates were changing every 4.8 seconds.[7]

Foreign exchange markets operate around the clock, with the major centers located in London, New York City, Hong Kong, Tokyo, and Singapore. Advances in technology have made transactions not only possible at all hours, but also cheaper and quicker than stock exchange trades. Partly because of this, foreign exchange trading is far greater than stocks trading and dwarfs trade in goods and

▪ **Stock exchange**
An organized marketplace where securities like stocks and bonds are bought and sold.

▪ **Foreign exchange market**
The global market for currency trading.

■ SPOTLIGHT ■

Day Traders Find New Outlet

At an hour past midnight, when he gets home after working as a disc jockey for a New York City classic-rock station, Marc Coppola checks the market and starts trading. . . .

Mr. Coppola, brother of actor Nicolas Cage and nephew of movie director Francis Ford Coppola, earlier this year pocketed about $1,400 on a $60,000 bet that the euro would rise against the dollar. In March, he reversed course, betting $40,000 that the euro would fall. Once it slipped to $1.30 from $1.31, he cashed in half of his investment, then soon after closed out the rest.

"I got scared out of the trade," Mr. Coppola says regretfully. "I should have said, 'The euro is going lower' and rode it down to the $1.20 area."

Welcome to the latest day-trading playground: the $1.9 trillion-a-day foreign-exchange market. Foreign-exchange traders can use any of a number of shops to set up online-trading accounts that—like the currency market itself—operate around the clock. Some of the most popular include Gain Capital Group and Forex Capital Markets, or FXCM, in the U.S., and Denmark's Saxo Bank.

China's announcement last week that it was revaluing the yuan and linking it to a basket of currencies further excited the house-bound currency traders. FXCM, for instance, saw daily trading volume spike to its highest ever at more than $12 billion Thursday as individual investors wagered correctly—that the yen would surge on the news. While the market awaits China's next move, more and more individuals may be tempted to place their bets.

Foreign-exchange veterans warn that the risks are huge. Traders can leverage their positions to place bets valued at as much as 200 times the money they put up. If a bet goes wrong, they can lose by a corresponding amount.

Foreign-exchange trading holds a certain unique appeal. The 24-hour market means that traders can participate whenever they want, not just between 9:30 a.m. and 4 p.m. Eastern time, as with the U.S. stock market where "after hours" trading is still just a small segment. Since transaction costs are lower, currencies also are cheaper to trade than stocks. And trading is simpler since six currency pairs—dollar versus euro, for instance, or yen versus dollar—account for nearly 90 percent of all trading volume, compared with thousands of stocks. Unlike stocks or bonds, there can never be a foreign-exchange bear market: Currencies are valued relative to one another, so some currencies have to be going up while some go down.

Perhaps most appealing of all, while stocks and bonds were gyrating up and down in recent years, most major currencies rallied steadily against the dollar between 2002 to 2004. The euro surged more than 50 percent during that period.

Still, the dollar's surprising rebound this year caught most professional currency managers off guard, causing them to lose a lot of money. But it doesn't require huge surprises for day traders to sustain losses.

"I had a bad streak," says Matthew Smith, a 23-year-old personal trainer in Colorado Springs, Colo., who lost more than half of the $10,000 he had in an online account while trading 17 currencies. Now that he focuses on the British pound versus the dollar, he thinks he can make it all back. "I'm hoping to do (currency trading) as my most significant source of income," Mr. Smith says.

Professionals don't think that is such a good idea. Kevin Morrison, head of the U.S. foreign-exchange desk for Citigroup Private Bank, says many of his clients trade currencies. But he advises that this trading come from the 10 percent of overall capital that investors put aside for riskier bets. "This is not a core asset," he says.

Even people running the trading shops warn clients against trying to time the market. "If 15 percent of day traders are profitable," says Drew Niv, chief executive of FXCM, "I'd be surprised."

And despite the Commodity Futures Modernization Act of 2000, regulating the foreign-exchange industry remains spotty and scams have been commonplace as "bucket-shop" hustlers seek to separate investors from their money. The government regulates individual trading firms but not the currency market itself. In pending cases, the Commodity Futures Trading Commission is charging 31 people and entities at six separate "boiler room" foreign-exchange operations that collected more than $25 million from customers but then allegedly misappropriated much of the money.

For decades, currency trading was reserved for only the biggest banks and companies. But Europeans and Asians—more used to crossing geographical borders and thus more attuned to currency fluctuations—began actively swapping currencies years ago. More recently, American investors such as Mr. Coppola have been piling in amid the dollar's well-publicized movements.

So far, currency trading has been good to Mr. Coppola, the father of two girls who also does some acting. He closed out last year with an 80 percent gain, he says.

His trading platform is Gain Capital. The Bedminster, N.J., firm initially catered to small money managers. But in a sign of how popular currency trading at home has become, Gain's individual-client business surpassed its institutional business late last year. Individuals now account for more than half of the firm's trading volume, which in the past nine months has soared 55 percent to more than $70 billion a month.

Mark Galant, Gain's chief executive and founder, says the firm's clients run the gamut from teachers, police officers, doctors and lawyers to former professional athletes and rock stars. "There are certainly a lot of George Soros wannabes," notes Mr. Galant, referring to the financier renowned for making $1 billion on the fall of the British pound in 1992. FXCM, based in Manhattan, also has seen its business surge in popularity. Of its 70,000 customers, the firm estimates nearly half of them signed up this year. Customers need a minimum of $2,000 to open an account and can borrow up to 100 times the value of the account, though Mr. Niv says 15 to 20 times leverage is more typical. FXCM's revenue in 2003 was $65 million, and jumped to $153 million last year. Mr. Niv projects around $300 million for 2005 revenue.

Excerpted from Craig Karmin and Michael R. Sesit, "Day Traders Find New Outlet in Foreign Exchange Wagers," *The Wall Street Journal*, July 26, 2005. Copyright © 2005, Dow Jones & Company.

services. Today, the volume of trade in foreign exchange markets has reached $1.9 trillion per day and the numbers of day traders—mostly stay-at-home investors who trade online through shops like Denmark's Saxo Bank and the American Forex Capital Markets (FXCM)—has increased exponentially.

This currency market is relatively unstable and unpredictable, however, precisely because so many factors go into influencing whether a state's money is appealing to investors and because so many different investors are looking for quick trades. The economists who convened at Bretton Woods in 1947 would not have been surprised (see Chapter 4). They saw how speculation in currency markets had been destabilizing in the 1920s and believed that floating exchange rates would be dangerous because of investors' irrational behavior. Their fears were played down by economists over the next two decades, who saw problems in fixed exchange rates and thought that speculators would actually stabilize the currency market as they sought profits. When fixed rates were abandoned in 1973 and speculation began anew, however, such hopes were dashed as it became obvious that speculators could not be completely rational, because—even with the benefits of the Internet—they could not base their decisions on complete information.[8]

This problem was one of many contributing to the devastating near-overnight collapse of the currencies of Thailand, Indonesia, and Russia in 1997 and 1998. A brief history is in order. Since the late 1980s, Thailand's baht, like many of the Southeast Asian countries' currencies, had been set at a fixed exchange rate tied to the dollar. This had worked well for a decade as the dollar lost value compared to Japan's yen; it meant that the Southeast Asian exports were more competitive and that their labor, land, and manufacturing plants were likewise more appealing to investors. Thailand, Indonesia, and the other Southeast Asian "Tigers" were therefore able to woo foreign trade and investment away from Japan, allowing their economies to grow rapidly. For a variety of reasons, including how their

PHOTO 9.2   The busy trading floor of the New York Stock Exchange.

societies and economies are structured, they showed very little foresight and put almost no protections in place. When Japan and the United States agreed in 1995 to devalue the yen vis-à-vis the dollar, a mere year after China had devalued its yuan, the Tigers' growth slowed precipitously and their currencies became viewed as overvalued. Thailand, which had depended on the Japanese market for its exports, found its goods no longer affordably priced. Because of the huge **structural weaknesses** underpinning its economy, Thailand was unable to adjust effectively. It was then that currency speculators began to attack the baht, seeing in its devaluation an opportunity for quick and colossal profits. "We are like wolves on the ridgeline looking down on a herd of elk," admitted a currency speculator interviewed by *Time* magazine.[9] Using financial tricks like forward contracts (in which they would enter into contracts with dealers to receive a certain number of dollars immediately in exchange for a specific amount of

▪ **Structural weakness**
Growth built on unsustainable economic practices (e.g., short-term borrowing for long-term needs) in the absence of effective governmental oversight and trade and monetary policies.

bahts they would pay back at an agreed-on point some months in the future), speculators put the Thai government on notice. The government, unprepared, was unable to protect its currency and soon, sensing the baht's collapse, investors sold off their Thai money, driving its value further down in a process likened to a run on a bank. Within months, the baht was worth only 60 percent of the dollar. Speculators began to rapidly sell off their other Southeast Asian currencies (Indonesia's rupiah, Malaysia's ringgit, and the Philippines' peso) and eventually created economic ripple effects from South Korea to Russia and Brazil.[10] Currency speculation was not the cause of the Asian crisis and its aftermath—that was a combination of huge private financial flows that were invested in short-term rather than long-term markets and imprudent banking activities—but it was an important contributing factor.[11]

The vulnerabilities of the foreign exchange market were duly noted and renewed discussion of the Tobin tax arose. The concept, first introduced in the 1970s by American economist James Tobin as a means of dampening currency market speculation, involves taxing global financial flows and using the money for development. Advantages would include stabilization of the currency market, income for development initiatives, and the potential political appeal of taxing the rich rather than the poor. The Tobin tax has therefore been seriously discussed in national legislatures, including a resolution in the U.S. Congress in 2000,[12] and the passage of a motion in Canada's parliament in 1999[13] and international organizations (including the G-7 and the United Nations). The tax has never been instituted, however, because of the challenges involved in assessing it, including getting a uniform tax implemented across all the relevant countries, coming to an agreement among them on how to collect and distribute the revenue, and—were all that to be accomplished—overcoming the market's natural tendency to open new financial exchange sites in countries not privy to (or not enforcing) the agreement.

In the absence of an international response to currency speculation, many countries instituted protections against **capital flight** on their own. These capital and exchange controls include policies dictating how foreign and local investment income can be exported, controlling domestic ownership of foreign assets and vice versa, limiting **currency convertibility**, and restricting financial flows related to local branches of foreign banks.[14] Here, domestic policies were intended to control international effects on domestic economies. Some analysts argue that such controls, many of which states had in place but eliminated at some point (either during the global push for economic liberalization in the 1980s or, ironically, following the financial crises of the late 1990s), are especially important for developing countries, which tend to suffer from inadequate regulatory administrations, shallow financial markets, and unreliable financial and monetary institutions.[15] Others, however, argue equally credibly that exchange and capital controls lend themselves to corruption and mismanagement without offering measurable positive effects.[16] In fact, the jury is still out on the best way—whether nationally or internationally—to deal with the volatility of the foreign exchange markets.

▪ **Capital flight**
A rapid outflow of financial assets when a country's economy appears to be in trouble.

▪ **Currency convertibility**
The ability to exchange a currency for gold or other currencies.

In addition to currency trading, capital markets include nongovernmental financial institutions like banks, stock and bond exchanges, commodities exchanges, and government securities markets. Each of these also influences world politics. Consider, for example, the bond market.

> A bond is a debt security, similar to an I.O.U. When you purchase a bond, you are lending money to a government, municipality, corporation, federal agency or other entity known as the issuer. In return for the loan, the issuer promises to pay you a specified rate of interest during the life of the bond and to repay the face value of the bond (the principal) when it "matures," or comes due.
>
> Among the types of bonds you can choose from are U.S. government securities, municipal bonds, corporate bonds, mortgage and asset-backed securities, federal agency securities, and foreign government bonds.[17]

U.S. Treasury bonds have long been considered one of the most secure investments in the world because the U.S. government is unlikely to default. The government sells the bonds to cover its debts; even if it did not have a budget deficit, it would likely have to sell the bonds to cover existing debts as they mature. However, the U.S. government has had a substantial budget deficit since 2001 and has relied primarily on Chinese and Japanese purchases of Treasury bonds to avoid raising interest rates. Indeed, in March 2010, the U.S. Treasury reported that China is the single-largest holder of U.S. Treasury securities, with holdings valued at $895.2 billion.[18] The Asian states and the United States both benefit—at least in the short term—from this symbiosis. It means that American consumers are likely to keep spending rather than salting away their wages to earn interest, something that works to the benefit of the Japanese and Chinese export sectors.

Look On The Bright Side

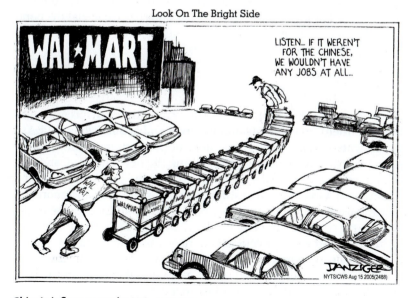

China's influence on the U.S. economy.

That, in turn, is a disincentive for either of the Asian countries to call in the U.S. debt. For Japan and China, it's as Jacques Rueff, a French economist, said in 1965: "If I had an agreement with my tailor that whatever money I pay him returns to me the very same day as a loan, I would have no objection at all to ordering more suits from him."[19]

That does not mean that China and Japan will not be tempted to diversify. In fact, in April 2007, China very tentatively began to diversify its portfolio, with the sale of $5.8 billion in U.S. Treasury securities, a small proportion of its then-$414 billion in holdings.[20] Since the 2008–2009 recession, however, and with the decline of the euro following the Greek credit crisis in early 2010, China has reinvested in U.S. Treasury securities, thus helping to revive confidence in the bonds. Nor has China been alone. One market follower observed that as of March 2010, "net foreign investment into the United States totaled $157.7 billion, a record figure. Of that total, $108 billion reflected net investment in Treasuries, including $80 billion from private-sector sources and $28 billion from such official sources as central banks."[21]

As mutually beneficial as this situation is, it is not stable. The United States cannot continue to accrue debt interminably and its bonds will be considered a risk if the Americans do not tackle their deficit. With pressures from Social Security and Medicare, the costs of the new healthcare legislation, and the potential for inflation, U.S. Treasury bonds may become "both credit- and interest-rate risks" with tremendous implications for the stability of the deeply interdependent international economy.[22] If American bonds became unacceptable risks, Japan and China would be tempted to liquidate their holdings. Such actions, however, would send the American economy into freefall and, as the recent worldwide recession has shown and as the 2010 events in Greece have demonstrated, the effects would be global and devastating. Thus it is clear that the bond market, rarely front-page news, has enormous implications for the health of the global economy and the stability of world politics.

Foreign Direct Investment

Foreign direct investment (FDI) is private corporate investment in foreign countries, including **greenfield investments** and **mergers and acquisitions (M&As)**. Greenfield investments involve the development of production facilities, often from the ground up, including construction, staffing the new business, and creating a customer base. In contrast, mergers and acquisitions simply involve buying existing businesses. Greenfield investments create more jobs and more tax revenues for local governments but are less popular with MNCs because of the startup costs.

Most FDI takes place between developed countries, although the percentage of FDI being spent in developing countries is on the rise (see Figure 9.2). Many developing countries have amended their rules and regulations to attract more FDI. Cash grants, tax concessions, and subsidies are popular incentives, although some countries go further, adjusting local infrastructure, training citizens in

▪ **Foreign direct investment (FDI)** Investment in business in one country by a firm from another country.

▪ **Greenfield investments** Developing an industry from scratch in a foreign country.

▪ **Mergers and acquisitions** Buying an existing business in a foreign company.

Chinese currency is called renminbi (the "people's currency"), the base unit of which is the yuan.

FIGURE 9.2   Foreign direct investment, inflows and outflows by region, 1970–2006.

useful skills, or even reworking existing bureaucracy to reduce red tape and improve timeliness. Some states create new staffs and governmental offices to smooth companies' efforts to invest in their country.

Indonesia, for example, created a special office with an Internet website dedicated to direct investors. On its website, Indonesia's Investment Coordinating Board lists the advantages of direct investment in the country. Among these are its fertile land, strategic location along sea lanes, large population (of workers and consumers), market-oriented economy, and democratic government. The site further offers a rundown of Indonesia's FDI-friendly laws, tax regulations, and specific incentives (tax concessions, import duty exemptions, allowances for importation of goods available locally, and special bonded zones with even further exemptions). It lists land and building rules, Indonesia's pro-FDI policies on investment guarantees and **intellectual property rights,** the country's immigration laws, and, finally, how environmental regulations are monitored.[23] Indonesia is far from unique in its approach to attracting FDI. Most countries in the world are now courting FDI, seeing in it a positive, long-term, stabilizing alternative to other forms of investment (like capital speculation). Furthermore, similar incentives programs are developed within countries, too, pitting regions and towns against each other in the competition for direct investment.

Despite all these efforts to attract FDI, there is no consensus that such efforts are merited. They tend to be costly, and there is evidence that MNCs look less at incentive packages and more at levels of local development and whether or not a state has good governance. Some analysts argue that states should focus more energy and resources on privatization, liberalization, and regulation if they wish to attract FDI. Such efforts are likely to create a more appealing environment for MNCs and also generally benefit the country. Moreover, some of the incentives governments offer actually can be harmful, such as when tax breaks cost the government more than the FDI brings in, when local businesses are displaced because foreign businesses are given systematic advantages, or when governments trade away labor rights and environmental protections. Mix a little corruption into this latter mix (with MNCs offering bribes to local leaders for deregulation and local leaders, in turn, trading away public goods like clean air and water), and the competition for FDI can prove extremely detrimental.[24]

Fortunately, although there are well-known instances of such corruption, studies seem to indicate that FDI does not promote nearly as much of this "race to the bottom" as originally believed. This is in part because the benefits and costs of FDI differ depending on the companies investing and on the local conditions. The worst-case scenario of corruption, regulation freezes and pollution havens seems to take place at the unfortunate nexus where special zones restricting collective bargaining attract corporations dependent on cheap labor and able to move easily to new locations.[25] Second, corruption seems more often to deter FDI, rather than stem from it. Corrupt governments raise the costs of business for MNCs by demanding payoffs for required government services. In this sense, corruption acts as an additional tax on business and is likely to dampen MNCs' interest in operating in a country. Thus, as countries struggle to bring in FDI, it

▪ **Intellectual property rights**
Legal entitlements attached to intellectual products with commercial value, including patents, copyrights, trademarks, industrial design rights, and trade secrets.

is likely that they will institute positive changes to reduce corruption, such as policies making decisions more transparent.

For the most part, economists find that FDI's benefits outweigh its costs. *The Economist* printed this glowing assessment of FDI in 2001:

> Economists and governments agree these days on the crucial importance of foreign direct investment. They see it both as the global market's "seal of approval" on a country's policies and prospects, and as a force, especially in developing countries, for far-reaching economic change. This consensus is surprising when you remember that FDI remains politically sensitive in many poor, and some not-so-poor, countries. But the benefits are so great that reservations on this account have been put aside. The point about FDI is that it is far more than mere "capital": it is a uniquely potent bundle of capital, contacts, and managerial and technological knowledge. It is the cutting edge of globalisation.[26]

FDI is not always welcome, however. Sometimes there are xenophobic responses to foreign efforts to invest. In the United States, for example, despite its own efforts to attract investment, some groups have thwarted Saudi efforts to develop American real estate or build factories.[27] In 2005, Americans rejected two high-profile Chinese investment attempts: The China National Offshore Oil Corporation (CNOOC) bid for American midlevel oil company UNOCAL (which instead accepted a lower offer from U.S. company Chevron) and Haier's bid for Maytag, which was countered and won by American company Whirlpool instead. Rejecting the Chinese bids in a nationalist fervor, the Americans dished out a bit of what they would receive in France in the same year, when the French became enraged at rumors that American company PepsiCo was planning a takeover bid of French national treasure Group Danone, of Dannon yogurt and Evian water.

Nationalist pressures to resist foreign investment can work against economic interests, however. In the case of the United States, at the same time that American companies were rejecting the Chinese bids, India displaced the United States as the second most popular FDI destination. China was the most attractive, followed by India, Hong Kong, and then the United States.[28] By 2010, the U.S. had regained its second-place ranking in terms of FDI confidence, but in 2005, given the country's already enormous budget deficit, losing FDI opportunities to other nations was a blow.[29] Yet, as mentioned in Chapter 2, these kinds of domestic pressures, often from interest groups lobbying policymakers, can influence foreign policy decisions and international relations more generally. Clearly, assuming that international investment and trade decisions are driven only by rational cost–benefit analyses would be problematic.

Economic Power

Cynics often argue that like domestic politics, international politics follows the Golden Rule: Whoever has the gold makes the rules. We do not have to be cynics to realize that regardless of our perspectives on international trade, control of resources, capital, and other productive assets usually translates into influence in the international system. This is why MNCs, for example, have been able to finagle such good terms in so many countries, bringing with them vast amounts of capital and financial incentives.

Even with their growing influence, however, MNCs cannot compete with states for real power in the international system because, in the case of states, economic power forms the material basis for military power as well as a means of leverage and political influence. Moreover, MNCs may gain access to raw materials, but they remain vulnerable to governments' reassertion of control over them, whether through nationalization or policies like taxation and regulation. States thus remain the most important actors in the international economy.

A state's raw materials, population, industrial capacity, technology, and geography all contribute to its strategic strengths and vulnerabilities. Some elements of economic strength, such as oil reserves and balance of trade, are relatively easy to calculate to allow comparison with other states. Other components of material power, such as the skills of a state's labor force and the creative potential of its research and development establishment, are equally important but more difficult to quantify.

For our survey of the sources of power, it is convenient to divide economic power into the three categories of territory, population, and trade and industry (again, rough equivalents for the economic factors of land, labor, and capital).

PHOTO 9.4   Rotterdam's harbor is one of the largest in the world in terms of capacity.

Although states can be competitive in world markets by maximizing their comparative advantage in specific economic "niches," a state must usually be strong in all three categories to remain a major player in the global economy over the long haul.

The territorial aspect of power does not need much elucidation. Based on geography and natural resources, it includes a country's size, location, proximity to major trade routes, and self-sufficiency in—or access to—key resources (food, water, energy). Likewise, the demographic requirements for power are clear: a population big enough to sustain power, neither too old nor too young, healthy, educated, and either homogeneous or effectively integrated. In fact, for the purposes of our discussion, economic power is most interesting in terms of trade and industry.

Trade and Industry

Economic power derives not only from geographic and demographic advantages (see Chapter 11) but also from a nation's ability to translate those into domestic production and foreign trade. Factors like technology, research and development capabilities, and capital mobility are all critical to trade and industry.

Gross national income (GNI) serves as a crude but convenient means of comparing the economic strength of various countries. GNI measures the market value of goods and services produced during a particular time period (usually a year) and provides an estimate of a nation's total agricultural, industrial, and commercial output. GNI differs from **gross domestic product (GDP)** in that the latter does not take into account income earned by a nation's citizens and corporations operating outside its borders, although it does give some sense of relative domestic productivity. GNI also is a useful way to compare the growth rates of states in both absolute and relative terms. For example, during the 1980s, although the U.S. economy was growing larger in terms of total output, its share of world production was declining relative to both Japan and Germany. Because power in international politics is relative, the relative size of national economies has more political significance than their absolute size.

Although it appeared that the relative economic power of the United States was declining precipitously during the 1980s, especially in light of the economic growth of West Germany and Japan, by the early 1990s, both Germany and Japan had suffered from recessions, exacerbated for Germany by the difficulties encountered in the absorption of the former communist East Germany. Over the next decade, the situation improved little for the two countries. Indeed, the Japanese government's 2002 debt stood at 130 percent of GDP and the Japanese banking system was burdened by more than $1 trillion in nonperforming loans. Meanwhile, Germany suffered from the lowest growth rate in the EU; China grew by about 9 percent a year after 1978, becoming one of the world's three largest economies (although rampant corruption and a centralized economy have prevented

■ **Gross national income (GNI)**
The total value of goods and services produced within a country, plus the income it receives from other countries, minus payments made to other countries.

■ **Gross domestic product (GDP)**
The total value of goods and services produced within a country.

it from reaching its full potential); and the U.S. economy improved tremendously, further widening the U.S. economic lead over its nearest competitors.

GDPs fell worldwide during the global recession that began in 2008. By late summer 2009, many countries had begun the process of recovery and some already were experiencing improvements in their GDPs. The U.S. GDP, however, was still in decline and only began a slow recovery in late 2009 and early 2010. Indeed, the recession set the U.S. back relative to the EU, India, and China, insofar as those countries were able to recover more quickly and experienced more rapid GDP growth than did the United States. The combined EU GDP surpassed that of the United States in 2009, though the total American GDP remains many times larger than individual EU members' and nearly twice the size of China's.[30]

GNI and GDP are not the only important indicators of a country's economic strength. Economists also look at **per-capita income (GNI/population),** for example, because a small country with the same GNI as a large country will have more wealth per person. Other key indicators include trade, industrial production, household savings rates, employment rates, and bankruptcies. Using these indicators to examine the present is helpful, but using them to accurately anticipate the future is notoriously difficult. This is true not only because the indicators can shift quickly but also, and even more so, because external, noneconomic factors can come into play. By all economic indicators, West Germany would have been an economic powerhouse by now; unification with the East, the product of political and social rather than economic strategy, slowed Germany's economic rise dramatically. Likewise, the United States, although still unequaled economically, changed its economic prospects by slipping from a budget surplus in 2001 to a huge deficit by 2005. What drove the change? Less economic planning than domestic politics (tax breaks) and foreign policies (the incredibly expensive war in Iraq).

Technology

Another factor that plays a major role in the creation and use of a nation's economic power is technology. Technology can create efficiencies (especially important as countries seek relatively higher profits) and spawn entire new industries (one need only consider the incredible exponential growth of the computer industry worldwide and of all the offshoot enterprises, from specialty mouse makers to software producers). Because of this, countries spend countless funds on research and development (R&D), trying to ensure that their technology is cutting edge.

The United States is unquestionably the world's R&D powerhouse. Between 1981 and 2004, the United States outspent the United Kingdom, France, Japan, and Germany combined. A 2008 study confirmed the U.S.'s continued lead in innovation.[31] This is partly a reflection of the enormity of the U.S. economy; U.S. R&D spending as a percentage of its total economy in that period was actually very similar to Japan's and Germany's, bearing out the adage "power begets

▪ **Per-capita income (GNI/population)** Income per person.

power."[32] Unlike advantages in natural resources and geography, however, technological advantages can dissipate quickly as new technologies are rapidly disseminated, reengineered, and reproduced worldwide. Indeed, the ability (and propensity) to steal and copy technologies has led to a surge in demand for protection of intellectual property rights. Meanwhile, concerns have arisen in the United States that it is losing its preeminence in research and development.[33]

Technology can be mechanical, industrial, or electronic. It can be related to medicine, weapons, entertainment, or any of a plethora of other fields. Arguably the most transformative technologies of the twenty-first century—those most likely to influence states' economic power—are those that involve moving and using information. Recognizing this, countries have made significant efforts to develop their technological and communications infrastructures, building "information superhighways" that allow information to flow faster and at higher volume than previously imaginable. Just as railroads and ports were the arteries of a nation's economic lifeblood in the nineteenth century, a nation's ability to use the Internet and other information networks will be vital to its economic health and growth in the twenty-first century. Although geography, natural resources, and population will continue to be major sources of economic power, knowledge, information, and communications will become increasingly important. The need for specialized data and skills is likely to result in increased specialization on the part of both firms and nations, which in turn may make economic alliances and unions more important as interdependence enables states to further maximize their comparative advantages.

In the meantime, however, the United States dominates in the realm of information technology. The largest U.S. corporations and smallest American mom-and-pop businesses have embraced the Internet's possibilities, making their goods easily available online. For example, more than 50 percent of U.S. companies sell their products online (in 1998, approximately 24 percent of companies did so; by 2000 this figure was 56 percent; today it is far higher). They are largely targeting American consumers because Americans have the education, language (an estimated 78 percent of Internet websites are in English), and access to make the Internet a useful daily tool. Estimates vary, but data show that at least two-thirds and perhaps as many as three-fourths of all U.S. households have Internet access, and the percentage is growing.[34] In a survey of 30,000 consumers in thirty states, the United States had the fastest growing number of Internet users as well as "the largest proportion of e-commerce consumers."[35] American children are educated at school in the use of computers and the Internet. In contrast, for much of the world, the lack of electricity to run a computer is the first and most basic obstacle to computer use, not to mention the lack of computers and the lack of education (in reading, much less in computing skills). And yet Internet access is increasing rapidly worldwide. In 2001, an estimated 5 percent of the world's population had Internet access and, of those, 60 percent were North Americans (and only 20 percent came from developing countries).[36] By 2009, 26.6 percent of the world's population had Internet access, representing an increase of almost 400 percent between 2000 and 2009. The greatest Internet penetration remained in North America, with Oceania/Australia trailing second and Europe a more distant third. The percent of Africa's population on-line was still very low (8.7), but it represented the most rapid increase (almost 1,810 percent over the nine year period).[37]

America's technological supremacy and its tremendous economic strength are closely related, but technology can also serve as an equalizer in the international economy. Technology has allowed for and underpinned the globalization of the job market (see Spotlight, "Technology Globalizes the Workforce"), spreading economic gains from the wealthiest countries to developing countries that adapted themselves to the changing world economy by educating and training a technologically savvy and computer-literate workforce. It has resulted in new industrial opportunities as countries shift from producing textiles to producing computer chips. It has helped overcome structural and logistical problems in developing countries via wireless communications and computer information technologies (for example, in 1978 there were no mobile telephones, but by 1998 there were more than 205 million worldwide, by 2005 there were an estimated 800 million,[38] and by 2010 there were more than 4.6 billion[39]). Even in its most basic forms technology has shortened distances and times among producers, manufacturers, and consumers. In all of these ways, technology enhances economic power not only in the industrialized countries but in developing ones as well.

There is an important caveat to the concept of economics as power: The processes of globalization and fragmentation both can act as intervening factors capable of stripping ostensible economic power from a country or enhancing it. Let us consider technology as an example. North Korea's ability to leverage its military technology—the only significant export produced within an otherwise decrepit and desperately dysfunctional economy—depends in large part on the global ramifications of its sales of nuclear and missile components. The United States and Europe are as deeply concerned about North Korea's proliferation as are its more immediate neighbors because, in a globalized world, the potential effects of such sales go far beyond the countries involved in the transaction. In this case, an economically weak country's economic power is enhanced by globalization. Ironically, North Korea's motivation for such sales reflects fragmentation at its extreme: Isolated deliberately from the international community, North Korea's leaders seek to ensure their country's continued seclusion from foreign influences and information. They can only do this, however, if they can earn enough income through weapons sales to appease their own military and to diminish the state's reliance on outside assistance and humanitarian aid. Fragmentation, too, can affect a country's economic power. A country with an otherwise potentially powerful economy in terms of population, resources and geography, technology, and trade can find its economic power diminished by fragmentation. Consider, for example, Turkey, which has tremendous economic potential but whose economic power is significantly reduced by two forms of fragmentation: the international response to the country's treatment of its Kurdish population and the EU's continued

▪ S P O T L I G H T ▪

Technology Globalizes the Workforce

In the early 2000s, big U.S., Japanese, and European corporations began outsourcing "knowledge work" to white-collar workers in developing countries. Enabled by digital technology, the Internet, and high-speed data networks, corporations are relying on workforces thousands of miles from their home offices to do everything from data processing and accounting to research and development. In fact, such foreign workers are taking on jobs in engineering, computer programming, internal finances, insurance claims processing, help-desk support, equity analysis, and even architectural work.

Cut to India. In dazzling new technology parks rising on the dusty outskirts of the major cities, no one's talking about job losses. Inside Infosys Technologies Ltd.'s (INFY) impeccably landscaped 22-hectare campus in Bangalore, 250 engineers develop IT applications for BofA [Bank of America]. Elsewhere, Infosys staffers process home loans for Greenpoint Mortgage of Novato, Calif. Near Bangalore's airport, at the offices of Wipro Ltd. (WIT), five radiologists interpret 30 CT scans a day for Massachusetts General Hospital.... About 1,500 km north, on an old flour mill site outside New Delhi, all four floors of Wipro Spectramind Ltd.'s sandstone-and-glass building are buzzing at midnight with 2,500 young college-educated men and women. They are processing claims for a major U.S. insurance company and providing help-desk support for a big U.S. Internet service provider—all at a cost up to 60% lower than in the U.S.... Behind glass-framed doors, Wipro voice coaches drill staff on how to speak American English. U.S. customers like a familiar accent on the other end of the line.

By exporting these office jobs to India, the Philippines, China, Costa Rica, South Africa, Bulgaria, and elsewhere, major corporations are spending one-third to half of what they would pay for equivalent labor in the United States. They are running more efficiently and keeping service prices down. Developing countries like India and China will be able to put some of their well-educated populations to work, bringing money into their local economies and creating new markets for other countries as well. The foreign workers may have lower salaries than they would have had for the same positions in the United States, Europe, or Japan, but in their own countries they can have comparable, if not better, lifestyles for far less money and they can be home with their families.

Of course, there is a potential downside to such outsourcing. The trend is in its early stages but, if it begins to appear that too many white-collar jobs are flowing out of the United States, Europe, and Japan, those countries might expect some political outcry. Though blue-collar jobs have been outsourced to foreign workers for decades, the blue-collar community has far less domestic political clout than do white-collar workers. In the face of increased competition from abroad, declining salaries, and limited opportunities at home, white-collar workers will have two options: insist on protections and adjust by shifting to other sectors or innovating. Probably, given the size of the white-collar workforce, both options will be exercised. The question for the industrial countries will be: Has there been a shift in comparative advantage and, if so, to what?

The issue may never become too pressing, however, because, though many jobs can be outsourced to foreigners, many cannot. At a time when corporate security is increasingly emphasized, many jobs will not be eligible for outsourcing. And there will always be those jobs that require meeting in person, whether it is providing medical care, negotiating deals, or conducting onsite audits.

Overall, this trend toward a "globally integrated knowledge economy" may change the face of business in both the industrialized and the developing countries. It is creating a new realm for real competition as services follow in the footsteps of manufacturing and should, ideally, have the same long-term benefits attributed to globalization more generally. And it was made entirely possible by technological developments in digitization, high-speed data networks, and the Internet.

———————

Excerpted from "The New Global Job Shift," *Business Week Online,* February 3, 2003, http://www.businessweek.com/print/magazine/content/ 03_05/b3818001.htm?mz.

PHOTO 9.5 Cell phones are ubiquitous, facilitating communication worldwide.

resistance to Turkish membership in part on the basis of the country's mostly Muslim population.[40]

Economics as Politics

The mention of international trade usually calls forth two sets of images. One is of leaders getting together in exotic places like Davos or Jakarta and signing trade agreements with much fanfare, conviviality, and talk of ever-expanding cooperation. The other is of businesses shutting down and factories closing because of overseas competition, as farmers block roads in protest against imported food and lobbyists and labor activists warn that jobs are being shipped overseas and that foreign goods are being "dumped" on the home market. Both of these images contain elements of truth. The global market is highly competitive, but rewards of cooperation between states and companies can be great for all concerned. There are, in short, incentives for both conflict and cooperation in world trade. Is it possible for states to overcome the incentives for conflict and realize the mutual benefits of cooperation? The three theoretical paradigms discussed in Chapter 2 each offer different prognoses.

Realism

Thomas Hobbes's *Leviathan* described the natural state of humankind as a "war of all against all," a no-holds-barred competition driven by vulnerability and

PHOTO 9.6   An oil well burns in the background during the 1991 War in Iraq.

fear. Anyone who has studied or worked in international trade will find this image all too familiar. Whereas states may fight wars with guns and rockets, they fight economic battles with tariffs and subsidies, weapons that can be as destructive to prosperity as their military counterparts. Realists thus believe that all states are in competition for bigger slices of the global economic pie. Because states seek to maximize their power to ensure their chances of survival, they are sensitive to any decline or loss in their relative capabilities. When also guided by the assumption that today's ally may well be tomorrow's enemy, states become reluctant to cooperate because they fear that they might be helping to strengthen a potential rival. The barrier, then, is that states are more concerned about any loss in their relative ranking in the international system of states. The question is not "Will both of us gain?" but "Who will gain more?" from cooperation. The implication is that in some instances, even when both states will obtain absolute gains, they will still fail to cooperate because one state fears that the other might disproportionately benefit from collaboration. Accordingly, states may give up increases in their absolute gains if doing so prevents others from achieving even greater gains. Additionally, in a world of dog-eat-dog competition, states have a natural distrust of one another. Because there is no world government or supranational body to guarantee that agreements are honored, states are reluctant to cooperate because they fear being duped by a partner who defects from an agreement.

From the realist perspective, therefore, economic policy should be a tool of power politics. Realists argue that economic decisions should enhance a state's relative overall standing in the international system, ensuring its security and influence. That is, the government should take measures to ensure a state's positive balance of trade with other states (as discussed earlier, that a state exports more than it imports). In its extreme, this approach to trade is known as **mercantilism,** and it dominated the first two centuries of the state-based international system. Although the concept of a zero-sum global volume of trade has been largely rejected since the end of the eighteenth century, elements of mercantilism have been revived, notably attention to the significance of balances of payments, an emphasis on production, and an embrace of selective government interventions in the market. Indeed, economist John Maynard Keynes (1883–1946) hoped to reinstate the discarded term mercantilism, but eventually became instead the father of **monetarism.**

Realists continue to advocate for positive balances of trade, production over consumption, and government intervention where necessary or even where advantageous. For example, the 2002 decision by the United States to protect its steel industry appeared to be not only the administration's response to domestic political demands (for which it was lambasted in both the American and foreign press) but also the creation of a bargaining chip with key competitors, namely the EU and Japan. Although each responded with the threat of retaliatory protectionism, the United States claimed that such rhetoric was hypocritical given each competitor's own tariffs and suggested a willingness to negotiate down the new steel taxes in exchange for a similar reduction of tariffs abroad. If indeed the

▪ **Mercantilism**
Economic approach involving governments attempting to ensure that they have a positive balance of trade.

▪ **Monetarism**
Supply and demand for money is the primary means of regulating economic activity.

administration protected steel as a means to enhance its global leverage, then its behavior was unabashedly realist.

Less controversially, realists suggest that states engaging in free trade under most circumstances nonetheless should be more protective of their strategic resources because the risks inherent in free trade become unacceptably high when survival requirements are at stake. In general, free trade states understand the possibility that uncompetitive domestic industries will fail and accept the less palatable fact that even competitive domestic industries might fold in the face of cheap foreign goods dumped on the market. They recognize, moreover, that each of these risks is accompanied by the likelihood that the affected industries will fall under foreign control. In the case of strategic resources, however, such as defense items or farm goods, these outcomes are not acceptable: Their ramifications go beyond pricing and consumer issues, beyond employment concerns, to affect national security directly. The country cannot be dependent on critical goods that are available only from foreign sources. In light of this, it is not surprising, from a realist's perspective, that the otherwise cooperation-oriented EU, United States, and Japan are hugely protectionist in terms of both their defense and agricultural industries.

Liberalism

Liberals' views toward trade are best characterized by their assumption that unhindered markets—those unfettered by governmental restrictions and protections—are the healthiest, most efficient, and most productive. Following Scottish economist Adam Smith's concept of the "unseen hand," described in his iconic 1776 book *The Wealth of Nations*, liberals argue that economic actors, operating in their own self-interests, not only dramatically increase wealth production but, in so doing, also unintentionally improve the general public good. Liberals thus strongly advocate free trade—the absence of tariffs, trade restrictions, trade protections, or any other governmental interference in the natural dynamics of the market.

The international norm has evolved over time from the mercantilism of the sixteenth to eighteenth centuries to a broadly accepted belief that global free trade will best serve the world economy while also most benefiting each of the states within it. Indeed, there is a clear correlation between the growth of free trade and the growth of the international market. Because of this, international organizations like the IMF, the WTO, and the World Bank have strongly encouraged—indeed, often pressured—developing countries to open their markets, reduce governmental interventions, privatize formerly nationalized industries, and otherwise decrease government involvement in trade.

Although this approach has many benefits, including efficiencies based on an emphasis on competitive advantages, we must consider several caveats. First, there is no pure free trade; even the most avid free-trade-promoting governments retain protections on strategic industries and often on industries with strong domestic constituencies as well. When great powers like the countries of western Europe, the United States, and Japan do this, the effects on developing countries are extraordinarily deleterious because these developing countries cannot afford to compete in the international market on the basis of the goods in which they have comparative advantages (more on this in Chapter 10). Second, even if there were pure free trade, this liberal approach to the market is not without cost. It depends on economies casting off their inefficient industries in favor of their more productive and competitive ones. The social, political, and immediate economic costs of the dislocations caused by eliminated protections—bankruptcies, industry collapse, joblessness, entire mini-economies gone under—can be tremendous. Disaffected workers can destabilize local or national governments, jobless rates can undermine local and national economies as unemployed workers have less to spend, and socially, people hurt by the policies can become ripe for radical ideologies, may turn to illegal activities (theft, robbery, drug-dealing) to make money, and can turn increasingly inward (more religious, more nationalistic, more focused on tribe or community or family), thus contributing to potentially volatile fragmentation. Third and finally, free markets may flourish with a lack of government intervention, but in the absence of some strong oversight mechanisms, protections for intellectual property rights, and defenses against predatory trade and investment practices, the economic system can suffer from a lack of confidence and from the costs of predation, as we saw with the economic crises of the 1990s discussed earlier.

In addition to advocacy for free markets, liberals believe in the possibility and benefits of cooperation. Although the liberal perspective on trade accepts many of the assumptions of realism, such as the supremacy of the nation-state and the anarchic character of the international system, liberals do not believe that trade is a zero-sum game in which one state's gain translates into another's loss. They see it, instead, as a variable-sum game; that is, through cooperation, all states can simultaneously and mutually benefit.[41] Cooperation allows states to benefit because the size of the pie is not fixed; it continues to grow. The greatest barrier to cooperation is not self-interest, but the difficulty of coordination and enforcement of cooperative agreements.

Indeed, some degree of economic cooperation among states has always occurred, and trade negotiators and businesspeople have worked out many innovative ways of managing competition and promoting mutually profitable exchange. Success in these efforts depends on the choice of an appropriate strategy for overcoming barriers to cooperation. Liberals, generally more optimistic about the prospects for cooperation, offer four basic options for surmounting the problems of cheating and relative gains: reciprocity, international regimes, international law, and interdependence. Reciprocity refers to states' iterated relations over time. If two parties expect to deal with each other only once, and they believe they can profit by cheating or deceiving each other, they will probably do so if they think they can get away with it. (Anyone who doubts this has not shopped for a used car lately.) However, if they expect to deal with each other on a regular basis (as supplier and manufacturer, for example, or family shopper and corner grocer), they can benefit from building a relationship of mutual trust if they both demonstrate that they are going to play fairly. In economists' terms, it is possible to achieve a mutually beneficial outcome by employing a tit-for-tat strategy if the transaction is the first of many and if both players value future gains from cooperation. This is accomplished by good-faith behavior during the initial transaction no matter what the other party does and then mimicking the other party's behavior on subsequent interactions—cooperating when it cooperates, cheating when it cheats. The purpose of this strategy is to convince the other side that you are willing to cooperate if it does but are also ready to cheat if it acts dishonestly. You show your willingness to take a chance on the first round by cooperating unconditionally, but you also demonstrate that you will not be taken for a sucker. This strategy shows that cooperation is possible, even in a decentralized and anarchic system, through a self-enforcing strategy of reciprocity.

Tit-for-tat can be an effective strategy for reducing trade barriers. As trade friction between the United States and Japan heated up in the early 1990s, with each side accusing the other of dumping, using import inspections and other bureaucratic delays as trade barriers, and other unfair trade practices, some of these tensions were eased through bilateral negotiations. Japan agreed to open its domestic market to U.S. exports of beef, citrus fruit, and other products, and the United States dropped plans to set import quotas and other restrictions on Japanese products. Although these measures did not resolve all issues outstanding between the two trading giants, they did use tit-for-tat reciprocity to prevent economic competition from escalating into a full-scale trade war.

Liberals' second solution to the problems of cooperation is to set up voluntary rules or institutions to detect and punish cheating. Many theorists advocate the creation of strong international institutions to help states work together in an otherwise anarchic world.[42] These institutions, more broadly called regimes, can range from informal customs to negotiated agreements to international organizations like the IMF and the WTO. Trade liberals contend that regimes influence and change the costs and benefits of individual state actions. More specifically, they alter states' interests or preferences by reducing the attractiveness of cheating, thereby allowing states to cooperate without fear of being taken advantage of. In exchange, states become willing to relinquish at least some independent decision making and instead agree to act according to established international norms.

International regimes establish the general rules and principles, or norms, of state behavior that facilitate cooperation. These norms are usually formalized in treaties, which in turn establish institutions and organizations to provide states with opportunities to meet and discuss their common problems. In the international system, institutions can emerge as a result of traditional international customs, such as freedom of the seas, or through a more specific process

East African Countries Form a Common Market

BUJUMBURA, Burundi—The world's newest common market was created Thursday when a regional bloc of five east African countries freed up the movement of people, products and capital across borders, furthering East Africa's dream of broad political unification.

The transformation and growth of the bloc, known as the East African Community, has been unfolding quickly after being reinvigorated just over 10 years ago. The bloc aims to become a monetary union by 2012 and have a common currency by 2015, with political federation to come soon after. Ultimately, leaders from the countries talk about becoming a single east African nation.

The East African Community was founded in 1967 by Kenya, Tanzania and Uganda but collapsed a decade later over political infighting between member states. Its resurrection, strengthened with the addition of Rwanda and Burundi and the creation of the common market, has been lauded by East African officials, though more work remains.

"What we have achieved so far is only the basic legal framework that outlines what needs to be done," Juma Mwapachu, the secretary general of the bloc, said in a press statement.

The agreement will allow citizens, products, capital and business services to move freely throughout the five countries, but Mr. Mwapachu said some national laws within member states would need to be harmonized with the regional agreement.

The agreement extends to 125 million people across a varied political, geographic and economic landscape, bordering some of Africa's worst war zones, from Somalia to the Democratic Republic of Congo.

Much of the region shares a common language, Swahili, and a history of previous agreements, which have promoted political will among the member states. Since its second founding in 1999, analysts say the community has developed swiftly. A customs union was formed in 2005.

The community has expressed interest in a common currency, as well as a single tourist visa. The member states are also collaborating on building a regional railway line that would run from the Indian Ocean to Burundi, bordering Lake Tanganyika.

"The idea of a United States of East Africa is less far-fetched than it was before," said Pratibha Thaker, regional director for the Economist Intelligence Unit.

Despite the significance politicians have attached to the common market, Ms. Thaker said economic growth was the most immediate interest for member states.

"It is critical for trade in service and trade in goods," she said. "Economics will make them come together faster than politics."

Article in its entirety from Josh Kron, "East African Countries Form a Common Market," *New York Times*, July 1, 2010, http://www.nytimes.com/2010/07/02/business/global/02africa.html?src=busln. Reprinted with permission.

of bargaining and negotiation over a set of issues. For example, at the end of World War II, a large group of countries negotiated GATT as a means to gradually lower trade barriers, and in 1994 they adopted an even more liberal trade regime that created the WTO. Members of another loose economic grouping, the Organization for Economic Cooperation and Development (OECD), often try to coordinate their monetary policies to stabilize the exchange rates between their national currencies, with some success. The Economic Community of West African States (ECOWAS) has sought, since 1975, to promote trade and cooperation in West Africa and, in 1993, its sixteen member states signed a revised treaty seeking, among other things, a common market and a single currency. Regimes, moreover, are not limited to formal institutions, but include informal cooperative programs. Before the 1967 Arab–Israeli War (see Chapter 4), for example, Israel and Jordan followed a tacit agreement to share the waters of the Jordan River even though they had no formal diplomatic relations and were technically at war.

Some analysts point out that, in contrast to national, state, or local governments, international regimes often lack any mechanism to enforce compliance. As a result, states may be unlikely to comply with regimes when they find it particularly inconvenient or costly.[43] Many theorists argue that this lack of enforcement power means that regimes reflect only a state's temporary interest and are thus unable to constrain national behavior. OPEC, lacking any enforcement mechanism, is frequently unable to force overproducers (i.e., cheaters) to comply with their quotas. Iraq's invasion of Kuwait in 1990 was in part caused by Kuwait's continued overproduction, which kept international oil prices down and thereby hurt Iraq, which needed prices to remain high to earn more income. In this case, the failure of an international regime to enforce its agreements prevented it from overcoming the barriers to cooperation. On the other hand, however, the WTO has become a very powerful actor in mediating disputes and demonstrates the extent to which an international organization can enforce international laws and norms through the use of sanctions (see Chapter 13 for more on the WTO). The WTO's power, in fact, is such that many states complain that it imposes on their sovereignty.[44]

International law is a third strategy for overcoming barriers to economic cooperation. Like domestic law, international law discourages states from selfishly acting against the common good or unfairly maximizing their individual gains at the expense of others. In particular, international law encourages all states to forgo short-term advantages gained by cheating and instead concentrate on the long-term benefits gained from cooperation.

Before 1945, international law focused on resolving disputes over navigation and shipping, abolishing the slave trade, and regulating the conduct of states in wars. In recent years, many attempts have been made to use international law to regulate the environmental consequences of international trade. The Montreal Protocol, signed in 1987, restricts the production and trade of chlorofluorocarbons (CFCs), chemicals that can damage the earth's ozone layer. Other international conventions prohibit trade in endangered species and regulate the shipment of nuclear and hazardous waste. These conventions include provisions for determining violations, resolving disputes, and penalizing states for noncompliance (usually through trade sanctions). Again, just like domestic laws, these international laws are not always obeyed, but they do set standards for proper behavior and create incentives for compliance.

Hegemonic Stability Theory: Bridging the Liberal–Realist Divide

Many analysts argue that the best means of guaranteeing stability in the international economic system is to have a hegemon in place: one major state that sets and enforces the rules for the global economy, providing certain public goods or "services" to ensure the international trading system's openness and stability. Such global services include making loans to countries in need, providing markets for various commodities, and defending the seas to make them safe for international trade. According to the theory, the hegemon's rationale for unilaterally providing these services is that, because it has the largest economy, it has the most to gain from free trade, even if the other states elect to free-ride. Likewise, it also has the most to lose if all other states impose tariffs and other trade barriers. Both realists and liberals would argue that because these global services are public goods, other states are tempted to free-ride, hoping that the hegemon alone will provide the service. However, if no state provides them, or if the hegemon cannot do it alone, then the international system will decline into disorder.

Thus, proponents of this theory contend that during the interwar period, when the previous hegemon, Britain, was exhausted and the United States, adhering to an **isolationist** strategy, had not yet accepted international economic leadership, the global trading system experienced increased protectionism, economic chaos, an accentuation of the Great Depression, and ultimately political and military upheaval.[45] In other words, periods of free trade tend to correspond with periods of hegemony, whereas economic protectionism and chaos often correspond with periods of hegemonic decline.

Some hegemonic stability theorists argue that decline is inevitable because hegemony is ultimately self-defeating. Although in the short run all trading partners gain because the hegemonic influence helps open markets and increases trade, the costs of hegemony tend to grow over time. As the hegemon's trading partners become more competitive relative to the hegemon, the hegemon becomes increasingly less capable of maintaining open markets for its partners' products, policing the open seas, and protecting access to crucial resources (e.g., oil) without its partners' help. As the hegemon begins to decline relative to its trading partners, it will be more willing to use its residual economic clout in coercive ways to get growing partners to pay for their share of the benefits they receive. For example, beginning in the 1970s, the United States began to demand that its European and Japanese allies help maintain a stable economic system and international security. By the time the Gulf War occurred in 1991, however, America's allies were paying much of the cost of sending U.S. troops into combat to protect oil supplies from the Middle East.[46]

Many hegemonic stability theorists worried that America's relative economic decline in the 1980s would lead to global instability in the absence of another hegemon or a unified coalition of states willing to provide similar services. Such concern was premature because the other states' faster growth was short-lived, leaving the U.S. status as economic hegemon unchallenged for the time being. In

▪ **Isolationist**
Withdrawn from
international affairs.

fact, the relatively strong growth of the United States led, between the mid-1990s and the early 2000s, to a trade imbalance of more than $339 billion. Ironically, in the face of this account deficit, the United States strongly encouraged its former competitors' economic growth.

Clearly, incentives currently exist for maintaining open markets, encouraging strong international economic development, and increasing cooperation. Trade liberals and realists are likely to agree that, as long as the United States remains in its position as hegemon, the international economy is likely to remain relatively stable. It appears inevitable, however, that the position of the United States will eventually be challenged, whether across the board or in certain key industries, leading to a redistribution of economic power internationally. How the international economy reacts—positively or negatively—will depend on several factors, including the success of regimes and laws put in place today, the level of interdependence that has developed between nations, and the ability or willingness of the most powerful state(s) to assume disproportionate costs for continued stability.

Constructivism

Constructivist scholar John Gerard Ruggie challenged hegemonic stability theory and liberal assumptions regarding the natural benefits of regimes in a 1982 article in which he introduced the concept of **embedded liberalism.**[47] Ruggie argued that a particular liberal view of the world, in which governments were responsible not only for prosperity but also for peace and well-being, emerged. The advanced industrial states embraced the idea that their political leaders needed to balance state, market, and democratic institutions in order to promote, simultaneously, economic growth, employment, and constituents' welfare.[48] This worked well for nearly three decades, from the end of World War II until the mid-1970s, but then, as the fixed exchange rate system established under Bretton Woods at World War II's end began to collapse, so did the architecture of logic and belief that had supported it. There was a jockeying for ascendancy among two competing ideas: socialism and free markets. In the end, the advocates of economic liberalization—free markets, reduced governmental oversight, increased corporate independence—won the day and their new philosophy, **neo-liberalism,** came to dominate domestic and international economies. Thus, ideas drove actions. When the philosophical consensus broke down and states' leaders begin to question the logic of embedded liberalism, new ideas emerged to replace it. This constructivist approach (as we would expect from our understanding of constructivism as discussed in Chapter 2) reverses the liberal and realist assumptions of cause and consequence so that the creation of the contemporary free trade system and the regimes that help sustain it are described as products of states' beliefs about the system rather than as products of the system itself. In very simplified terms, constructivists argue that structures are creations in response to ideas and, as ideas shift and change, people revise their institutions to reflect their new philosophies. This

(margin note, handwritten): rose w/ Britton's fall

▪ **Embedded liberalism**
The shared assumption among many states' leaders that governments should balance economic growth and social and economic welfare.

▪ **Neo-liberalism**
A theoretical perspective prioritizing open markets and international free trade.

means that as long as states maintain their contemporary assumption that the best international economic system is a free trade system, then even if the instruments for preserving the system break down (e.g., the hegemon declines), the system can nonetheless persist.

Conclusion

After considering the prevalence of barriers to economic cooperation and the difficulties inherent in overcoming them, readers may conclude that the prospects for economic cooperation are bleak and that it is a wonder that states trade with one another at all unless motivated by absolute necessity. Although the world economy can look shaky in theory, not even the global recession could not put the full brakes on it. International trade slowed, but it never stopped. Markets and investment opportunities contracted for only a short time before stubbornly expanding again. Although policy coordination remains difficult at the international level, trade flourishes at the level of the MNC, if only among units of the same company operating in different countries. Even small local firms and entrepreneurs can buy and sell products all over the world, placing orders over the Internet and receiving goods via international air express. Individual businesses may expand or fail, and government policies may lead to sustainable development and growth or to stagnation and near-total collapse. The globalized economy seems to press on regardless.

Adam Smith, for one, would not be surprised. More than two centuries ago, he argued that states were steered toward prosperity not by the firm hand of government but by the "unseen hand" of enlightened self-interest and individual enterprise. Governments, he was quick to point out, set the rules of economic interaction both within and between states, regulate currencies, enforce contracts and other agreements, and provide for public goods like law and order and defense. However, economic policy is executed locally, by individuals seeking to increase their welfare within their national economies and the global economic system.

The rules imposed by states and international organizations may change, resources may be scarce or plentiful, and markets may boom or crash, but individuals, at once interdependent and self-reliant, adapt and prosper as best they can.

Today, the pace of change is accelerating and the web of interdependence is growing ever tighter. Greater economic interdependence is likely to increase both the incentives and the risks of cooperation among states. The theories outlined in this chapter are basic tools for understanding how those incentives operate and how their attendant risks can be managed. Students may use them to understand how global economic forces affect their lives and for formulating informed opinions on national and international economic policy.

Levels of Analysis and Paradigms in Review: Trade and Investment

	Realism	Liberalism	Constructivism
Individual	Individual investors will behave as predatorily as possible; only government oversight, strict laws and regulations, and demonstrated ability to enforce them will prevent opportunistic investors from destabilizing trade and investment in general.	Rational political leaders will promote privatization over nationalization, will invite foreign direct investment in their countries' economies, and will encourage redirecting education and training from uncompetitive industries to those in which their countries have comparative advantages.	A single scholar, by offering new and compelling interpretations of trade relations, can change how states set their priorities, perceive themselves and other states, and behave internationally. For example, Adam Smith, John Maynard Keynes, and Karl Marx each not only observed but also contributed to countries' understandings of trade relations.
Domestic	The most powerful industrial interests domestically—as well as the most strategic—will be able to prevent total free trade by using their economic and political power to ensure continued government protections.	Social, political, and economic sacrifices are necessary at the domestic level if countries are to benefit from free trade internationally.	The structure and institutions of the international trading system will reflect states' interests and identities. If states' leaders agree that a liberal trading system is best, they will create means by which to bring it about.
Systemic	States will seek to protect their relative gains in the international market.	States will use regimes and institutions to enhance cooperation and promote free trade to ensure the greatest absolute gains.	The anarchy of the international system sets constraints and opportunities but does not determine institutions or states' identities.

What Would You Do?

The Sock Trade

You are the president of a country. The domestic sock industry, threatened by cheaper, better quality socks produced abroad, has sent lobbyists to you requesting protection. You are being pressured as well by the senators and congressional representative speaking for the town where most socks are made. They have already come to you with stories of individuals in the town who will be out of work and unable to support their families; they have regaled you with statistics about how local schools will deteriorate and local businesses will fail as workers lose their jobs. They are asking you to keep the domestic sock industry afloat, either by levying tariffs or by setting quotas on the foreign socks. Major retailers, on the other hand, are lobbying against any such trade barriers, arguing that if they can import higher quality socks at a lower price, it benefits both their bottom lines and domestic consumers. The international community, in the meantime, is pressuring you not to erect any barriers to trade, especially because your country has been at the forefront of the movement toward free trade and globalization.

What Would You Do?

Discussion and Review Questions

1. During the recent economic recession, many analysts wondered if, just as the failure of the fixed exchange rate in the 1970s led to shift from embedded realism to neo-realism, the current crisis would lead to a shift from neo-realism to a new paradigm, or way of thinking. Discuss.

2. Interdependence theorists believe trade raises the costs of conflict to prohibitive levels; realists argue that trade can lead to violent disputes. What current or recent events serve as examples of each of these dynamics?

3. In 2010, the euro was deeply stressed by Greece's economic crisis and yet, even before that problem was resolved, the EU and Estonia mutually agreed that the Baltic state could replace its national currency with the euro. What are the costs and benefits of a regional currency?

4. What international practices and ideas allowed the recession of the late 2000s to grow to such crisis-level proportions?

5. What in realist, liberal, or constructivist thought can account for the resilience of the international economy?

Key Terms

Balance of payments 343
Balance of trade 344
Capital-abundant 339
Capital flight 352
Capital intensive 339
Comparative advantage 339
Countervailing tariffs 341
Currency
  convertibility 352
Current-account
  balance 344
Dumping 343
Embedded liberalism 373
Fixed exchange rate
  system 345
Floating exchange rate
  system 345

Foreign direct investment
  (FDI) 354
Foreign exchange
  market 347
Greenfield
  investments 354
Gross domestic product
  (GDP) 359
Gross national income
  (GNI) 359
Human security 338
Import quota 341
Intellectual property
  rights 356
Isolationist 372
Labor intensive 339
Mercantilism 366

Mergers and
  acquisitions 354
Monetarism 366
Neo-liberalism 373
Nontariff barriers to
  trade 341
Per-capita income (GNI/
  population) 360
Price supports 343
Protectionism 343
Stock exchange 347
Structural weakness 351
Subsidies 343
Tariffs 341
Trade barriers 341
Voluntary export
  restrictions (VERs) 341

CHAPTER **10**

World Politics: Development

One of the debates sparked by globalization is whether it creates benefits for all the states in the international system or whether its rewards are unevenly distributed, going disproportionately to industrialized states at the expense of the **least and less developed countries (LDCs)**. As with other debates discussed in this book, your worldview is likely to color your perception of how globalization affects differently developed countries. Interestingly, in this debate, realists and world systems theorists are likely to make similar assumptions about the international economic system. They will argue, for slightly different reasons, that the developed states will take advantage of the LDCs to increase their own wealth and power. Realists will make this argument based on their assumptions about the anarchic international system's imperative to compete; world systems theorists will make the same argument based on their assumptions about the transcendence of the class system to the international level. Either of them will point, as evidence, to colonialism (one of the earliest forms of globalization) and, for more recent examples, to the **Washington Consensus** and other policies and behaviors they deem opportunistic and extractive. Liberals, in contrast, will make an entirely different argument, suggesting that free trade and liberalization are

■ **Least and less developed countries (LDCs)**
Countries with low average incomes relative to industrialized states, a reliance on primary product exports, limited technology, and few social services.

■ **Washington Consensus**
Initially, simply a list of ten recommendations economist John Williamson thought were most commonly offered by American and Bretton Woods institutions; came to be used as shorthand for a broader liberal economic philosophy.

| PHOTO 10.1 | Africa's share of global exports has declined since the 1980s. |

tides that "float all boats" higher, creating development opportunities for states that otherwise might have been left behind by the growth of the biggest economies. They will point to the benefits of labor and capital mobility, showing how people who, in the past, lived on the fringe of the world economy are now active participants in it, whether it is Indonesians working in Saudi Arabia and sending money home to their families or the opening of the London office of the China Telecom Corporation. Constructivists, finally, will argue that social relationships and normative structures determine development and that elites' beliefs about these, combined with their experiences with development, will drive development policies and processes. In other words, development may look like what realists, world systems theorists, or liberals predict, but that is because of political leaders' perceptions and the institutions they create. If their experiences and means of interpreting them lead them to believe that liberal regimes will promote development, then leaders will opt for liberal regimes. If, on the other hand, they believe it is a dog-eat-dog world and that they can only hope to improve it for themselves and those they care about, they will establish more predatory institutions as both realists and world systems theorists might expect.

Globalization has undoubtedly opened doors and facilitated development in places that otherwise would have had fewer opportunities; it has also, however, led to exploitation and, more neutrally, but perhaps most sadly, simply left some people behind. Africa's share of global exports, for example, at nearly 5 percent in the 1980s, had declined to less than 2 percent by 2004[1] and remained that low through 2009.[2]

One of the biggest debates about development is over where responsibility for promoting it lies. There are those who believe that development has been stymied by rapacious leaders who exploit their countries for personal gain and that no amount of international effort will help unless such individuals are removed. There are those who believe that development must take place naturally, from within countries and societies, because to work it must be a product of those countries. Others argue that some state structures and social systems preclude development and that external assistance is needed to overcome internal roadblocks. There are those who believe that no matter how hard states try to implement development efforts, no matter how well intentioned their leaders, if they have missed the development boat internationally, they have little chance of boarding without an international decision to throw them a life preserver.

As with all world politics issues, this one is more complex than these simplified arguments suggest. There are cases of exploitive leaders just as there are cases of exceptional leaders. Each of them works within a domestic structure that aids and constrains them at different junctures. Each of them is also dealing with the imperatives and limitations of an international economy that deemphasizes development in favor of the market—a market with rules and structures of its own, some of which may benefit them and others that may hurt them.

This chapter focuses on development: what it is, theories about how it might work, and where it stands today. The dichotomies previously discussed—globalization and fragmentation, conflict and cooperation—are as relevant to this discussion as are questions at each level of analysis: How much difference can an individual leader make? How important is governmental and political organization in determining how a state plays in the global economy? How important are natural endowments? How important is the structure of the global economy itself? How does economic development relate to human development more generally? Most of the current development theories discussed here focus on systemic- or domestic-level factors; indeed, individuals only work themselves back into the equation when we begin to discuss more contemporary thinking about development in terms of both practical steps that might be taken and the tolls of corruption.

What Development Means

Development clearly affects many sectors—education, industry, health, agriculture, politics, the environment, human rights—but it is a term and an occupation often laden with agendas and competing priorities. Advanced industrial states may want to help foster development worldwide as a means of opening markets, increasing stability, spreading capacities for democracy, promoting human rights and welfare, or stemming anticipated floods of refugees or immigrants. LDCs may seek development to promote their own economic competitiveness, to reduce the effects of pandemics, to strengthen themselves relative to their neighbors, to take care of and appeal to their electorates or sectors thereof, or to create bargaining chips for buying into the global economy.

One thing that is clear about development is that it is a constantly shifting goal. Economically, for example, the development process never stops. A country simply shifts its relative position along a continuum of growth, standard of living, and technological advancements. In the mid-nineteenth century, the "high-tech" industries were textiles and railroads, which were the foundation of Britain's industrial might. By the 1930s, one critical standard of development was the capacity to produce steel and heavy machinery. Today, of course, textiles and steel are increasingly produced in developing and **newly industrialized countries (NICs)** such as South Korea, whereas many factories in the English midlands, where the Industrial Revolution began, and the Ural Mountains, where Soviet Russia built the tanks to defeat the Nazi invasion, are obsolete by most international standards. Instead, most developed countries compete against each other in information-age technologies and services.

Development is a shifty subject, however, and trying to measure a country's development—even if the focus is primarily economic—can be challenging. China, for example, ranks among the LDCs in terms of standard of living, among the NICs in terms of its industrial growth, and among the most powerful countries in the world in terms of its economic influence. If the focus is broader, it becomes even more difficult to assess development. Russia, the hub of the former Soviet superpower, experienced strong economic growth after President Putin took office and implemented development-oriented reforms. The country also benefited in the 2000s from the upsurge in oil and gas prices (oil and gas are the country's largest exports). Nonetheless, Russia is far from an economic powerhouse. Its growth rate is heavily dependent on exports, making it vulnerable to fluctuations internationally; the economy relies on a few major energy and manufacturing industries (making it vulnerable to fluctuations in those industries); and the country is heavily indebted. More important, however, even as Russia's economy improved between 2000 and 2008, Russians' standard of living was in decline. Today, almost one-fifth of Russia's population lives below the poverty line, a number that increased dramatically with the 2008 recession;[3] the death rate is rising; and labor shortages limit productivity.[4] Furthermore, Russia's economy is threatened by growing capital flight, continued corruption, and decreasing transparency in government institutions.

It is evident from looking at these two powerful states in the international system that—even within a single state's borders—development can unfold differently in various sectors not only of the state's economy but also in its society and government more generally. Yet because the sectors are interwoven, the processes that lead to development in one are likely to affect the others, deliberately or not. A challenge for those promoting development is to understand and control the processes as much as possible, to maximize positive effects, and to avoid potential pitfalls.

▪ **Newly industrialized countries (NICs)** Social and economic classification recognizing states' industrialization but placing them on the development continuum somewhat below the most advanced industrialized states and above LDCs.

Human and Social Development

Development: A Holistic Approach

These dynamics of development are recognized in the UN's Millennium Development Goals for 2015. Those acknowledge that development crosses all the fields of world politics, touching on human issues (rights, equality, freedom), political issues (state structures, civil society), social issues (education, health, job opportunities), and economic issues (regulatory practices, tax systems, balance of agriculture, industry, and service), but focus primarily on human and social issues:

1. Eradicate extreme poverty and hunger.
2. Achieve universal primary education.
3. Promote gender equality and empowerment. [See Spotlight, "Gender Inequalities Harm Well-Being, Hinder Development".]
4. Reduce child mortality.
5. Improve maternal health.
6. Combat HIV/AIDS, malaria, and other diseases.
7. Ensure environmental stability.
8. Develop a global partnership for development.[5]

This is practical, as well as ethical and compassionate. Each objective represents a form of development in itself, but each also represents a requirement for broader development in the sense that the whole is larger than the sum of its parts.

For example, economic development should help lead to universal primary education, but universal primary education itself helps promote development. A more educated population is prepared for a broader diversity of economic roles, involves itself more intelligently and responsibly in politics, is less likely to be driven by destructive emotions (nationalism, xenophobia), and participates more effectively on the global stage. The assurance of environmental stability, likewise, ensures development over the longer term, promising that resources (to be put, perhaps, to new uses not yet conceived of) and a good quality of life will be available for future generations.

The UN chose these goals because of its leaders' belief in the connectivity of all the elements of human activity and society. Kofi Annan, former UN Secretary-General, wrote in 2005: "We will not enjoy development without security, we will not enjoy security without development, and we will not enjoy either without respect for human rights. Unless all these causes are advanced, none will succeed."[6]

This linkage is typified by the problems created by HIV/AIDS: The disease kills teachers, leaving fewer qualified people to provide education; it kills health-care workers, leaving fewer nurses and doctors to identify and care for those infected with HIV/AIDS; it kills parents, leaving orphans (often infected) to

▪ S P O T L I G H T ▪

Gender Inequalities Harm Well-Being, Hinder Development

Gender inequalities impose large costs on the health and well-being of men, women, and children and affect their ability to improve their lives. In addition to these personal costs, gender inequalities reduce productivity in farms and enterprises and thus lower prospects for reducing poverty and ensuring economic progress. Gender inequalities also weaken a country's governance—and thus the effectiveness of its development policies.

Well-Being

Foremost among the costs of gender inequality is its toll on human lives and the quality of those lives. Identifying and measuring the full extent of these costs are difficult—but a wealth of evidence from countries around the world demonstrates that societies with large, persistent gender inequalities pay the price of more poverty, malnutrition, illness, and other deprivations.

▪ *China, Korea, and South Asia have excessively high female mortality. Why? Social norms that favor sons, plus China's one-child policy, have led to child mortality rates that are higher for girls than for boys. Some estimates indicate that there are 60–100 million fewer women alive today than there would be in the absence of gender discrimination.*

▪ *Mothers' illiteracy and lack of schooling directly disadvantage their young children. Low schooling translates into poor quality of care for children and then higher infant and child mortality and malnutrition. Mothers with more education are more likely to adopt appropriate health-promoting behaviors, such as having young children immunized. Supporting these conclusions are careful analyses of household survey data that account for other factors that might improve care practices and related health outcomes.*

▪ *As with mothers' schooling, higher household income is associated with higher child survival rates and better nutrition. And putting additional incomes in the hands of women within the household tends to have a larger positive impact than putting that income in the hands of men, as studies of Bangladesh, Brazil, and Côte d'Ivoire show. Unfortunately, rigid social norms about the appropriate gender division of labor and limited paid employment for women restrict women's ability to earn income.*

- *Gender inequalities in schooling and urban jobs accelerate the spread of HIV. The AIDS epidemic will spread rapidly over the next decade—until up to one in four women and one in five men become HIV infected, already the case in several countries in sub-Saharan Africa.*

- *While women and girls, especially the poor, often bear the brunt of gender disparities, gender norms and stereotypes impose costs on males, too. In the transition economies of eastern Europe men have experienced absolute declines in life expectancies in recent years. Increases in male mortality rates—the largest registered in peacetime—are associated with growing stress and anxiety due to rapidly worsening unemployment among men.*

Productivity and Economic Growth

The toll on human lives is a toll on development—since improving the quality of people's lives is development's ultimate goal. But gender inequalities also impose costs on productivity, efficiency, and economic progress. By hindering the accumulation of human capital in the home and the labor market, and by systematically excluding women or men from access to resources, public services, or productive activities, gender discrimination diminishes an economy's capacity to grow and to raise living standards.

- *Losses in output result from inefficiencies in the allocation of productive resources between men and women within households. In households in Burkina Faso, Cameroon, and Kenya more equal control of inputs and farm income by women and men could raise farm yields by as much as a fifth of current output.*

- *Low investment in female education also reduces a country's overall output. One study estimates that if the countries in South Asia, sub-Saharan Africa, and the Middle East and North Africa had started with the gender gap in average years of schooling that East Asia had in 1960 and had closed that gender gap at the rate achieved by East Asia from 1960 to 1992, their income per capita could have grown by 0.5–0.9 percentage point higher per year—substantial increases over actual growth rates. Another study estimates that even for middle- and high-income countries with higher initial education levels, an increase of 1 percentage point in the share of women with secondary education is associated with an increase in per capita income of 0.3 percentage point. Both studies control for other variables commonly found in the growth literature.*

Governance

Greater women's rights and more equal participation in public life by women and men are associated with cleaner business and government and better governance. Where the influence of women in public life is greater, the level of corruption is lower. This holds even when comparing countries with the same income, civil liberties, education, and legal institutions. Although still only suggestive, these findings lend additional support for having more women in the labor force and in politics—since women can be an effective force for rule of law and good government.

Women in business are less likely to pay bribes to government officials, perhaps because women have higher standards of ethical behavior or greater risk aversion. A study of 350 firms in the Republic of Georgia concludes that firms owned or managed by men are 10 percent more likely to make unofficial payments to government officials than those owned or managed by women. This result holds regardless of the characteristics of the firm, such as the sector in which it operates and firm size, and the characteristics of the owner or manager, such as education. Without controlling for these factors, firms managed by men are twice as likely to pay bribes.

Excerpts from *Engendering Development: Through Gender Equality in Rights, Resources, and Voice*, a World Bank policy research report (21776) (Paris/New York: World Bank and Oxford University Press, 2001). Graphs and references to graphs have been removed. To see the complete original report, go to http://www.wds.worldbank.org/servlet/WDSContentServer/ WDSP/IB/2001/03/01/000094946_01020805393496/Rendered/PDF/multi_page.pdf.

---

make do in the streets or to crowd orphanages; it kills soldiers, leaving militaries understaffed and faced with increased training costs; it kills the workforce, leaving fewer people to run factories, offices, and services; it kills agricultural laborers, leaving fields and farms unable to produce to their potential; and it reduces family incomes, leaving children unable to go to school. By taking people in the primes of their lives, HIV/AIDS drains the most affected countries (all in sub-Saharan Africa, although the pandemic has spread to Asia and Russia) of every chance for development and, in some cases, has reversed development (in nine African countries, life expectancy has dropped to below forty years; none of the sub-Saharan African countries are currently expected to meet any of the UN's Millennium Development goals by 2015). Yet in a bitter catch-22, to end HIV/AIDS, some development must take place: People must be educated, clinics must be available, health-care workers must be trained and paid, drugs must be cheap enough, poverty must be reduced (one major element in the spread of HIV/AIDS in sub-Saharan Africa is that people exchange sex for food and basic necessities), and women must be accorded basic rights (HIV/AIDS is spread by prostitution, by cultural practices, by polygamy, by infected husbands who refuse to wear condoms, by husbands who will not allow their pregnant wives to be tested, etc.). To have a chance at development, states must fight HIV/AIDS; effectively fighting HIV/AIDS requires development. (For more on HIV/AIDS, see Chapter 11.)

To get out of this bind requires achievement of the final UN Millennium Development goal: a global partnership for development. Strapped states can turn to others for assistance. For example, Cuban nurses and doctors have spread out over Africa to help fight the HIV/AIDS crisis; the international NGO Population Services International has begun a campaign of educating people via cell phone in Mali; and the United Nations established UNAIDS, the UN AIDS Program, to organize efforts to combat the disease.

An international campaign has also pressured governments to reduce the poorest countries' **debt burdens**, thus theoretically giving them the financial flexibility to deal with crises like HIV/AIDS and famines. To this end, in the summer of 2005, a series of concerts took place in the **G-8 countries** and South Africa just as the G-8 itself was meeting in Gleneagles, Scotland. These Live 8 concerts, the goal of which was to rally world citizens to pressure their governments on the debt-burdens issue, represented concern about the lack of development in many parts of the world, the wish to help, and an incremental step toward a more sophisticated view of the requirements of development aid, not to mention development itself. Twenty years earlier, as thousands of people died of famine in Ethiopia, many of the same musicians and celebrities had put on Live Aid, an enormously popular concert intended to raise money to send to starving people in Africa. Between then and 2005, however, a growing number of people in the industrialized world realized that raising money was not enough, that famine usually was the product of politics as much as of nature, and that the only real way to make a significant positive difference was to force structural change. This meant addressing the underlying problems (the illness) rather than just responding to the crises as they arose (treating the symptoms). It required understanding the roadblocks to development—social, political, economic, and security-related—and systematically dealing with them. Although the musicians at Live 8 could do nothing to make the necessary systematic changes, and although many of the people in their audience were there for the music, the decision to hold worldwide concerts encouraging people to ask their governments to make structural changes in favor of the LDCs was a step forward in awareness if not effect. That said, the G-8 leaders—whether feeling pressure from music lovers or not—ultimately decided at the 2005 Gleneagles meeting to **forgive** eighteen of the world's poorest nations' debts to the World Bank, the IMF, and the African Development Bank (AfDB) and to double aid to Africa to $100 billion a year by 2010. The musicians declared themselves satisfied; others were more skeptical, claiming that waiting until 2010 to double aid would cost millions of lives and suggesting that the debt relief was little more than a financial sleight of hand.[7]

Ultimately, the outcome has been mixed: By 2008, the G-8 had met just one-third of the increase it pledged by 2010, that is, $7 billion of the $21 billion promised; in 2009, the outlook was only slightly better. Yet the story is more complex than the general numbers reflect. The United States and Canada, for example, are on track to surpass their pledges by significant amounts, with the United States providing 158 percent of the donations pledged and Canada providing 170 percent. The United Kingdom will keep close to the amount pledged, falling short by perhaps 7 percent. In contrast, Germany and France are each likely to pony

- **Debt burdens**
Multilateral debt, such as occurs when a government borrows from international institutions (IMF, World Bank), other governments, or foreign banks.

- **G-8 countries**
The Group of Eight (G-8) is comprised of the leaders of major industrial democracies and holds an annual summit to discuss mutual interests and concerns.

- **Forgive**
To excuse a heavily indebted country from paying its debts.

up only one-quarter of what they pledged, though to the Germans' credit, their initial pledge was very high. Italy, however, not only will not meet its pledge but has actually reduced the aid it is providing, thus bringing it to -6 percent of the pledge it made at Gleneagles.[8]

In fact, aid to Africa did increase, even if not by the amounts promised. And the G-8 summit in 2005 was remarkable for one more reason: It was the first at which members of civil society (NGOs) and representatives of developing countries and NICs were present. It represented a focus on human development issues and more involvement by a broader spectrum of stakeholders than ever in the past. The G-8, with its short meetings and limited membership (Britain, Canada, France, Germany, Italy, Japan, Russia, and the United States) is often disparaged as nothing more than an exclusive club for the world's great power leaders, but with its Gleneagles meeting it demonstrated the nexus of globalization and human development issues.

Civil Society and Development

Just as international human development efforts involve civil society, so does domestic development. Civil society (in the simplest possible terms) is a politically active, issue-organized public. A strong civil society is a flexible web of citizen groups that influences a government's decisions. At the international level, civil society includes NGOs, MNCs, and other nonstate actors. In democratic states, civil society includes special-interest groups, lobbies, and social movements. In a state with fewer freedoms, civil society includes prodemocracy groups, cultural heritage organizations, and other progressive assemblies, often flying under the official radar (they may disguise themselves as book clubs, music lovers' societies, or other less political groupings).

Among the development theories that focus on civil societies are structural-determinist approaches based on the assumption that civil societies will emerge along with middle classes. These theories, popular in the 1960s and 1970s, have largely been debunked as Eurocentric and underresearched, premised as they were on the belief that all states would go through the same pattern of development as did the western European countries. Other more constructivist theories focus on how the social mobilization embodied in civil society is self-reinforcing and identity-strengthening (i.e., once social mobilization starts, it gains momentum).

Often, however, proponents of the role of civil societies in development are just that: proponents. They make **normative** assumptions about the value of civil societies without taking into account potential counterarguments. Not all grassroots movements are equally laudable and some might seek power, profit, or the imposition of their own morality or special interest. Civil society, moreover, is unaccountable and, arguably, undemocratic in its efforts to impose special interests (whether it is "save the whales" or "save the farmers").

Despite these criticisms, civil society does appear to play a role in development, and understanding how and when it forms, the outer limits of its possible

▪ **Normative**
Prescribing a standard; involving an assumption of what should be.

influence, its relationship to government, and the extent to which it can grow are all important to understanding development more generally.

Modernization Theory

Another set of theories focused on human development—spanning economics, politics, standards of living, and civil liberties—emphasizes culture. These **modernization theories** contend that the most important factors contributing to development, and the primary causes of underdevelopment, are the economic, political, and cultural conditions within states.[9] In reaching this conclusion, the founders of modernization theory studied the experience of Europe and North America, long-established developing states such as Iran and Turkey, and the ex-colonies of Asia and Africa, including India, Pakistan, Côte d'Ivoire (Ivory Coast), Burma (Myanmar), Ghana, and many others.

Guided by the Western experience of development, modernization theorists contend that less developed states will develop only by shedding their traditional social, political, and economic institutions. Indeed, modernization theory draws a sharp distinction between traditional and modern societies. A traditional society is usually depicted as a culture in which customs, rituals, and knowledge are passed from generation to generation. Modern societies, in contrast, are more urban, dynamic, flexible, and innovative. To develop, modernization theorists contend, developing societies must undergo a process of transition from traditionalism to modernity.

From this perspective, the fundamental obstacle to development is traditional culture, which blocks the societal transformations necessary for rapid economic growth. Traditional societies are dominated by religious or aristocratic authority, are based on rural life, and are characterized by rigid social structures, such as the Indian caste system. Yet development requires the ability to achieve status through merit or success (rather than birth or caste) and tolerance of social and intellectual diversity. Politically, this translates into the emergence of democracy, the rule of law, political opposition, human rights, and basic freedoms. Economically, development means the creation of a market-based economy, a redistribution of wealth, and an openness to new technologies and industries. The process can take generations and, understandably, can produce enormous social tensions, as Europe experienced as a result of the Industrial Revolution.

From the modernization perspective, therefore, economic growth and democratization form a virtuous circle, each strengthening the other as well as social development, as they all progress. Industrialization, increased incomes, education, and **urbanization** all increase the likelihood of political democracy—which, in turn, protects and reinforces the market economy that is necessary for continued economic development.

For many modernization theorists, trade is the engine of economic growth. Accordingly, they call for free trade and open markets. In this relationship, MNCs and international investment play an important role in disseminating the capital,

■ **Modernization theories**
Socioeconomic theories of development involving assumptions about progress occurring in stages from traditional societies to modern ones.

■ **Urbanization**
Process by which a population shifts from the countryside and suburbs into cities.

managerial and technical skills, and technology necessary for the emergence of a modern industrial sector. Aid from the developed countries will help fill the resource gaps in underdeveloped states. At the same time, developing countries can "pull themselves up by their own bootstraps" by saving to accumulate financial capital, buying equipment and improving infrastructure to increase physical capital, and investing in education and training to improve human capital. One program for economic development in Puerto Rico, begun in 1948, was even called "Operation Bootstrap."

Social Impact of Modernization

At first glance, the path to development as prescribed by modernization theory may appear straightforward. In practice, however, modernization creates wrenching changes in a society. These changes lead to political, social, and economic problems that must be addressed for development to continue. The opportunities and challenges presented by development are illustrated by two trends characteristic of modernization: **demographic transition** and urbanization. (These trends occur in all developing societies, not just those in which development is guided by modernization theory. They are discussed here because modernization theory regards them as "growing pains" that societies must work through in the modernization process.)

Underdeveloped, traditional societies generally have very high birth and death rates, whereas in modern societies these rates are much lower. The change between high and low rates as countries develop from traditional to modern is termed "demographic transition." The change can be wrenching because death rates usually drop (with the introduction of the most current medicines) long before birth rates fall, leading to rapid population growth and all the social challenges that go along with a very young population (especially the increased demand for education, skills training, and jobs). As discussed in detail in Chapter 11, the world's poorest countries now have the youngest populations, whereas the world's wealthiest countries are "graying"; their populations are skewing toward the elderly, creating a whole new set of social problems (an aging, dependent population in societies with fewer workers and, concomitantly, fewer tax dollars).

A major consequence of the kind of demographic transition and industrialization that takes place with modernization is urbanization. One way that many families in traditional societies attempt to cope with the pressure of chronic overpopulation and the resulting unemployment is to send some children to urban areas to find cash employment. If work can be found, the proceeds can be sent back to the family to be used to educate younger siblings or support parents in their old age. There is no social security for the elderly in most LDCs, so parents often rely on their children for support. However, in many cases, work cannot be found, yet rural migrants nevertheless settle in urban areas, becoming part of the vast shantytowns that have grown up in cities such as São Paulo, Calcutta, Soweto, Cairo, and Jakarta.

The world's urban population grew from 30 percent of the population in the 1950s to almost 50 percent in 2000 and is projected to reach 60 percent by

▪ **Demographic transition**
Changes in the characteristics of human populations, including rate of growth, average age, literacy, and so forth.

the year 2025.[10] Although developed states have more people living in urban areas than do LDCs, urban population growth in LDCs is now outpacing that in industrialized countries. Eight-four percent of the Brazilian population lives in the cities, as does 87 percent of Chile's, 76 percent of French Guiana's, 77 percent of Mexico's, and 68 percent of Malaysia's.[11] In many cases, these newly burgeoning cities do not have the resources to provide the services such as fire protection, police protection, and sanitation that residents in industrialized countries take for granted. Whatever infrastructure Europeans built in the colonial era was quickly overwhelmed in postcolonial Asia and Africa. Therefore, shantytowns are often overcrowded, acutely poor, and persistently crime prone.

Despite these hardships, the modernization perspective generally views urbanization as an essential step in the development process away from subsistence agriculture and toward a modern economy. The newly urbanized migrant is undergoing a difficult but necessary introduction to new experiences, a modern economy, and an expanded worldview. This process of urbanization is never easy, but it has long been a stage in creating a modern society—the

PHOTO 10.2   These slums outside Jakarta suffer from inadequate housing and contaminated water.

Industrial Revolution produced vast slums in nineteenth-century Europe and the United States as well. Additionally, from the perspective of modernization theory, the city becomes the focus of the diffusion of new ideas, of science and technology, of social mobility based on productivity and the rise of a professional and middle class, of the development of a division of labor within society, and perhaps most important, the center of an industrial manufacturing and service-based economy.

Critiques of Modernization Theory

Modernization theory has been criticized on a number of fronts. First, its critics question whether earlier paths of development can be duplicated today.[12] Countries modernizing in the late twentieth century, they contend, are likely to face different kinds of problems (such as global environmental degradation and resource shortages) than those of the nineteenth century. In addition, although Britain, the United States, and Japan could borrow from one another and sell their goods amongst themselves or to their colonial empires, LDCs today are dependent on industrialized nations for markets and capital.[13] Also, industrializing countries in Europe faced little competition from already developed rivals, whereas today LDCs must compete with industrialized states with well-developed manufacturing sectors.

Second, critics of modernization theory stress that traditional social and political institutions are often difficult to change. As one author notes, "We have learned that in much of the Third World, so-called traditional institutions have, first of all, proved remarkably resilient, persistent, and long-lasting; rather than fading, crushed under the impact of change, they have instead proved flexible, accommodative, and adaptive, blending to the currents of modernization but not being replaced by them."[14] The survival of these traditional institutions can lead developing societies along very different development paths from those taken by industrialized states.

Third, many theorists and policymakers contend that modernization theory is Eurocentric. That is, this pattern of development is grounded essentially on the singular experience of western Europe. Similarly, some contend that modernization theory was a product of the Cold War mentality that sought to keep the developing world (then the Third World) out of the Soviet sphere by tying LDCs into a Western and liberal development pattern.

Finally, some political economists contend that the structure of the international trading system is biased and that, historically, wealth has not flowed from the rich states to the poor states through trade and aid; rather, just the opposite has occurred. This perspective on trade and development (closely related to world systems theory, discussed in Chapter 2, and to imperialism, discussed in Chapter 5) contends that, first through colonialism and later through MNCs and foreign lending, developed countries (or the core) have kept LDCs (or the periphery) in a perpetual state of underdevelopment. This criticism is the heart of the alternate school of thought on development known as **dependency theory** (more on this later in the chapter).

▪ **Dependency theory**
A socioeconomic theory based on the assumption that the process of the world economic systems development privileged a few countries while leaving the rest disadvantaged and vulnerable to exploitation.

Political Development

Not all assessments of development take a holistic view; in fact, many narrowly examine just one aspect of development. There are, for example, many theories focused expressly on political development. Political development is a touchy subject if only because there tends to be a level of self-congratulation in many analyses, the base assumption of which is that the analyst's country's own system is the most developed. Thus, democracies promote democracy as the solution to states' ills and as the "end of history." The Soviets, similarly, promoted communism as the inevitable endpoint of **economic determinism.** In the 1990s there was a short-term but vocal push for recognition of "Asian values," which were rooted in Confucianism and involved loyalty to family and nation, a focus on society over self, an emphasis on the work ethic, and a tendency to support authoritarianism. Lee Kuan Yew, former prime minister of Singapore, argued that freedom could only flourish in a well-ordered state and that Western insistence on individualism, the free market, **rationalism,** and **legalism** were anathema to Asians.[15] At the time this was hotly contested even within Asia itself, where Taiwan, Thailand, and South Korea were burgeoning democracies. The movement lost momentum with the Asian crisis of the late 1990s and the forced resignation in 1998 of Indonesian dictator Suharto, one of the concept's most powerful advocates. Some proponents of Islamic fundamentalism offer another alternative view of political development, arguing that Sharia, or Islamic law, which traditionally makes no distinction between religious and secular life, is incompatible with the rule of laws made by people in a democratic state. Many Muslims today consider such views extreme, however, and point out how comfortably Muslims can live in democracies like Indonesia, Senegal, Malaysia, Mali, Bangladesh, and India. In fact, of the 1.4 million Muslims in the world, half of them live in democratic states.[16]

Indeed, if by no other measure, democratization can be used as a measure of political development because of the spread of democracy worldwide. This is not a normative assessment that political development should be toward increased democracy but merely an observation of how world politics have evolved (although the number of states just claiming to be democracies would suggest a powerful belief in the appeal of such a system). Between 1986 and 2005, the number of electoral democracies in the world grew from 69 to 119 but then declined by 2010 to 116. Of course, some of these democracies are democracies in name only. **Freedom House** listed the number of free countries as having grown, however, from forty-two (27 percent of all countries) in 1974 to eighty-nine (46 percent of all countries) in 2004 (see Figure 10.1),[17] and the numbers remain the same in 2010.[18]

Requirements of Political Development

As events unfolded in Iraq early in the twenty-first century, it became clear that the term and concept of democratization were being used in many different

▪ **Economic determinism**
The theory, often attributed to Marx, that the economic structure, rather than politics, drives human development.

▪ **Rationalism**
Reliance on reason as a guide for action and beliefs.

▪ **Legalism**
Conforming strictly to the letter of the law, rather than the spirit of the law.

▪ **Freedom House**
A nonpartisan, nonprofit organization promoting worldwide freedom and democracy; perhaps best known for its country ratings.

TABLE 10.1	Free, Partly Free, and Not Free Countries of the World: 1979–2009					
	Free Countries		**Partly Free Countries**		**Not Free Countries**	
Year Under Review	*Number*	*%*	*Number*	*%*	*Number*	*%*
1979	51	32	54	33	56	35
1989	61	37	44	26	62	37
1999	85	44	60	31	47	25
2009	89	46	58	30	47	24

ways. The obvious question is this: When is democratization achieved? Is it when elections are held, when a constitution is written, or when a legislature is put in place? The very disparity between the numbers of electoral democracies and the number of free states listed by Freedom House's 2005 world report suggests that having the trappings of democracy—political parties, a constitution, separation of powers among different branches of government, elections, and so forth—simply is not enough. Democratization is achieved, by Freedom House's standards, when both political rights and civil liberties are present. Instructively, these measures reflect not governmental structure, but government's effect on and relationship with constituents. In other words, democratization requires certain institutional arrangements but extends beyond that to domestic political behaviors and relationships.

Democratization also suggests a process, rather than an endpoint, an evolution in which undemocratic practices give way to more democratic practices. There are innumerable theories about how this process works, however, and what its requirements are. These theories span the fields of world politics, the levels of analysis, and the various worldviews.

Domestic: Political Culture

Among the best known theories of political development are those that revolve around political culture. The fundamental assumption in these theories is that political values and beliefs represent a social framework that is independent of institutions, economics, or other factors and that explains political behavior at a group, rather than an individual, level. Gabriel Almond and Sidney Verba wrote the seminal book on political culture in 1963. *The Civic Culture: Political Attitudes and Democracy in Five Nations* was the result of five years of research and writing, 5,000 interviews, and comparative work in five countries. Almond and Verba saw political culture as a political group's belief structure. They assumed that individuals' behavior was **socialized** rather than rational and that their learned orientations moderated their perceptions of their political experiences. Ultimately, Almond and Verba argued, political culture fell

▪ **Socialized**
Taught how to behave through exposure to social customs, beliefs, and conduct.

into three types: parochial, subject, and participatory. Parochial political cultures were those in which people felt disassociated from politics, believed them to be a realm for the elite, and perceived the government as a mechanism for enforcement and collections. People were also disassociated in subject political cultures, but they were more politically aware and saw government as a source of infrastructure and services. Participatory political cultures, finally, were typified by people who believed their government was answerable to them and who even saw it as an extension of themselves. In such cultures, people participate actively and have high expectations of the government.

Almond and Verba's book was a groundbreaking work of political science. Closely related to the modernization school of thought, deeply liberal, and the first attempt to systematically apply the scientific method to political questions, their approach is laudable and their findings impressive. Yet, as with all political studies, the work raises as many questions as it answers. It is, for one thing, a product of its times, infused with assumptions about the desirability and superiority of democracy. It also overlooks issues of class, race, and gender in political culture. Another significant problem it has is with causality: It fails to explain why one society has one political culture and another has a different one; it suggests a relationship between political structure (democracy, authoritarianism, etc.) and political culture, but does not clarify which way the causality runs (does culture lead to structure or vice versa?); and it suffers from a disparity of focus (individuals within a system) and explanation (group), leaving it unable to adequately describe cases in which a state's political culture is fragmented. Yet despite all, *The Civic Culture* is an iconic book that begins an important discussion on the role of political culture in political development.

Indeed, in the four decades since that book was published, several different schools of political culture theory have emerged. The behavioralists, like Almond and Verba, see culture as the pattern of individuals' orientations. In their theories, political culture is an independent variable (that is, it is naturally occurring and influences other factors). The materialists (often Marxists) see people as being driven by material interests. In these theories, culture is the outcome of social class and, therefore, a dependent variable (i.e., social class creates culture). The rational choice theorists believe that culture is a consequence of many individuals' rational decisions coming together. In this case, culture is also a dependent variable. Finally, political culture can be conceived of as identity, collective vision, shared symbols, and memory. In this formulation, culture is a motivating force rather than an explanation (and, again, an independent variable). Preferences are learned and experience matters. This more constructivist approach offers an explanation for cultural diversity and evolution. In every one of these approaches, though, political culture is intrinsically related to political structure.

Empirical tests seem to validate this assumption. Ronald Inglehart wrote that political culture was a crucial link between economic development and democracy. He tested it against other explanatory variables and found that it remained important.[19] Robert Putnam, another political scientist, found after careful assessment that political culture was more compelling than institutional, structural, and class-based explanations for explaining when democracy works best. He found that when "civil community" is high—that is, there is a social pattern of trust, tolerance, and participation—democracy works well.[20]

That political culture and political structure are related does not, however, mean that political culture and political development are related. For that to be true, political culture would have to drive development somehow, or, alternatively, development would have to lead somehow to adjustments in political culture. One recent best seller in the United States made a case for the second notion. Amy Chua, in her 2003 book *World on Fire*, wrote that economic and political liberalization exacerbate cultural disparities between "market-dominant minorities"—the Chinese in Southeast Asia, Jews in Europe, "Whites" (Europeans or people of European descent) throughout Latin America, Indians in East Africa, Americans globally—and other groups less culturally equipped for trade. She points out, for example, the Chinese "spirit of capitalism" in comparison with the Burmese rejection of "greedy" profit-seeking and from there clearly narrates how globalization influences the relationship between these two ethnic groups.

In contrast to Chua, constructivists describe political culture not in terms of ethnicity, race, or nationality but as a unified understanding and interpretation of politics among states' elites. Constructivists argue that political culture drives the process of development by informing elites' decisions about which approaches

PHOTO 10.3   Chinese festival in Myanmar (Burma).

will work best for them and their constituents. One can see this in the emergence of **sustainable development**, the idea that today's development should not compromise future generations' needs. Sustainable development does not enhance countries' immediate relative power and thus does not fit neatly into the realist paradigm; its proponents warn against unfettered free trade and complete reliance on market institutions, thus rejecting some basic liberal tenets; and it requires international cooperation, not predation, thus falling outside the realm of world systems theorists' expectations (see Spotlight, "Tough Truths About Free Trade"). So what is motivating a disparate and growing group of countries like the United States, Britain, Colombia, Serbia, and India to undertake sustainable development programs? Constructivists argue that it is a shifting norm among international elites that emphasizes longer term planning and the placement of more value on future generations' likely needs.

Economic Development

Economic liberals tend to believe that encouraging economic development—improved standards of living, a shift from agriculture to industry, liberalization, and so forth—is the best way to stabilize the international system, promote democracy, and improve human welfare. That is a tall order for a single sphere of development, but it demonstrates their confidence that economic improvements inexorably lead to development in every field. Not all economists, however, see economic development as a universally positive process. In fact, one of the major, if waning, schools of economic development studies is dependency theory—a decidedly gloomy outlook for continued globalization and liberalization.

Systemic: Dependency Theory

Dependency theory is firmly rooted at the systemic level and is a denunciation of modernization theory (discussed earlier). Dependency theory rejects the premise that the source of development woes is domestic in nature.[21] Instead, it emphasizes the international context, contending that international institutions, MNCs, and industrialized states have deliberately kept the developing world in a dependent condition. In contrast to modernization theory, which has its roots in classical economics and the liberal perspective on world trade, dependency theory draws many of its insights on international economic relations from a branch of Marxist thought.

Dependency theorists argue that the existing international economic system is inherently biased against poor countries. This unequal relationship between the periphery and the core can be traced to the sixteenth century, when European countries began to colonize.[22] In this relationship, the periphery exported raw materials to the industrializing states of Europe (and later to

■ **Sustainable development** Fulfilling current needs while protecting the natural environment for future generations.

▪ SPOTLIGHT ▪

Tough Truths About Free Trade

It should be clear by now that the challenges of development are closely related to the dynamics of international trade and investment. The foregoing chapter introduced the main theories of international political economy. All too often, those theories and development theories are derived and examined independently of each other. As the following article from Newsweek International *makes clear, however, trade, investment, and development are intertwined and into their complex relationship factors everything from states' relative power to the roles of international organizations to the norms that elites both propagate and accept.*

"The word 'protection' is no longer taboo." This short sentence, uttered by French President Nicolas Sarkozy late last month, may have launched a new era in economic history. Why? For decades, Western leaders have believed that lowering trade barriers and tariffs was an inherent good. Doing so, they reasoned, would lead to greater economic efficiency and productivity, which in turn would improve human welfare. Championing free trade thus became a moral, not just an economic, cause.

These leaders, of course, weren't acting out of altruism. They knew their economies were the most competitive, so they'd profit most from liberalization. And developing countries feared that their economies would be swamped by superior Western productivity. Today, however, the tables have turned—though few acknowledge it. The West continues to preach free trade, but practices it less and less (especially in agriculture; this is why the Doha Round of trade talks is dying). Asia, meanwhile, continues to plead for special protection but practices more and more free trade. China and India have lowered tariffs significantly.

That's why Sarkozy's words were so important: He finally injected some honesty into the trade debate. The truth is that large parts of the West are losing faith in free trade, though few leaders admit it. For example, four U.S. senators—Max Baucus, Charles Grassley, Charles Schumer, and Lindsey Graham—introduced a new trade bill against China on June 13, portraying themselves as paragons of virtue. But the bill would require the Treasury Department to identify misaligned currencies based on International Monetary Fund criteria. This amounts to protectionism, since it would allow U.S. companies to appeal for antidumping duties on Chinese goods based on the distorted value of the yuan.

Raghuram Rajan, the IMF's former chief economist, has challenged the notion that the IMF can fairly judge exchange rates, arguing that it will be tempted "to follow the U.S. lead and accept that the only truly undervalued exchange rates are those where the government intervenes explicitly...not those where the exchange rate is 'market-determined.'" Such a standard would bias judgments against developing countries, since their governments naturally play a larger role. Rajan argues that powerful industrial countries should be equally liable to judgment by the IMF. Will the senators allow this?

Probably not. Indeed, few Western leaders are likely to acknowledge that they are becoming more protectionist, reflecting an intellectual dishonesty that plagues the trade debate today. Some economists are more honest. Paul Krugman is one of the few willing to acknowledge that protectionist arguments are returning. Krugman writes that "it's bad economics to pretend that free trade is good for everyone, all the time....The accelerated pace of globalization means more losers as well as more winners; workers' fears that they will lose their jobs to Chinese factories and Indian call centers aren't irrational. Addressing those fears...is essential [to] a realistic political strategy in support of world trade."

Krugman is right. In the short run, there will be winners and losers under free trade. This, of course, is what capitalism is all about. But more and more of these losers will be in the West. Economists in the developed world used to love quoting Joseph Schumpeter, who said that "creative destruction" was an essential part of capitalist growth. But they always assumed that destruction would happen over there. When Western workers began losing jobs, suddenly their leaders began to lose faith in their principles. Things have yet to reverse completely. But there's clearly a negative trend in Western theory and practice.

A little hypocrisy is not in itself a serious problem. The real problem is that Western governments continue to insist that they retain control of the key global economic and financial institutions while drifting away from global liberalization. Look at what's happening at the IMF. The Europeans have demanded that they keep the post of managing director. But all too often, Western officials put their own interests above everyone else's when they dominate these global institutions.

The time has therefore come for the Asians—who are clearly the new winners in today's global economy—to provide more intellectual leadership in supporting free trade. Sadly, they have yet to do so. Beijing, for example, does not want to frighten Washington by seeking leadership positions. Unless Asians speak out, however, there's a real danger that Adam Smith's principles, which have brought so much good to the world, could gradually die. And that would leave all of us worse off, in one way or another.

Kishore Mahbubani,"Tough Truths About Free Trade: The West Preaches Free Trade, but Practices It Less and Less," *Newsweek International,* July 30, 2007 issue, © 2007 Newsweek, Inc. Mahbubani is the dean of Singapore's Lee Kuan Yew School of Public Policy and the author of *Can Asians Think?* Reproduced with permission.

the United States and Japan), and in turn, those states exported manufactured goods to the periphery. More recently, MNCs have replaced the colonial powers in sustaining this relationship, as have international organizations like the IMF and the World Bank. According to *dependencistas* (adherents of dependency theory), this unequal relationship has ensured that LDCs remain the global "hewers of wood and drawers of water." This fundamental inequality, dependency theorists contend, fueled development in advantaged countries and stifled it in the disadvantaged ones.

Primary Product Exports

In dependency theory, LDCs' disadvantaged position stems from the fact that most of their economies depend heavily on the export of primary products—that is, raw materials such as timber, oil, and metals and agricultural goods such as coffee and bananas. Beginning in the sixteenth century, the periphery supplied the raw materials and foods for the economies of Europe, and then for the Industrial Revolution in Europe and later the United States. In turn, the periphery imported manufactured goods from the industrialized countries. Capitalist economists view this relationship as the operation of comparative advantage (as discussed in Chapter 9), but dependency theorists view it as an international division of labor wherein the LDCs do the "dirty work" of producing raw materials and the wealthy countries get the "good jobs" in manufacturing and services. They contend that this division of labor encourages developing countries to remain exporters of primary goods and discourages their development of modern manufacturing sectors.

Primary products make up a very high percentage of the exports of developing countries like Nigeria, which exports oil, and Côte d'Ivoire, which produces cocoa. Middle-income countries like Malaysia and Brazil have much more **diversified economies,** and therefore export a higher percentage of manufactured goods, whereas exports from more developed states like Singapore and Japan consist primarily of manufactured goods. To make matters worse, many LDCs' exports are dominated by a single commodity. These countries lack the diversity of goods and services that most industrialized countries have achieved in their exports and are thus vulnerable to fluctuations in the demand for or price of their main export. Perhaps the best examples of one-commodity countries are the oil-exporting states. Petroleum in its various forms accounts for virtually all of the exports of Saudi Arabia, Kuwait, Iraq, Iran, the Persian Gulf states, Libya, Nigeria, Gabon, Angola, and Brunei, and it is the most important export of Venezuela, Mexico, and Indonesia. When the world price for oil is high, these countries reap large rewards, but a drop in oil prices can lead to economic disaster. Many other developing countries depend on exports of a single commodity. Sugar dominates the exports of Cuba, Fiji, Mauritius, and, to a lesser degree, the Philippines. Coffee is the principal export of Colombia, El Salvador, Burundi, Rwanda, Uganda, Costa Rica, Kenya, and Ethiopia. Copper is the major export of Zaire, Zambia, and Chile. Jamaica, Guinea, and Surinam export bauxite, Honduras produces bananas,

▪ **Diversified economies** Economies based on several, if not many, products, industries, and services.

Niger mines uranium ore, Liberia exports iron ore, and Afghanistan's main export is an illegal drug—heroin.

Dependency theorists argue that this international division of labor—primary products in the developing countries, manufactured goods in the industrialized states—perpetuates LDCs' disadvantages. As long as they remain the exporters of primary products for the world, LDCs will not develop their own indigenous industries—and often their existing ones will be uncompetitive and fail—and so will remain dependent on industrialized states for manufactured goods and technology.

According to the dependency school, fluctuations in the prices of primary goods also perpetuate LDCs' dependency. They are very sensitive to sudden changes in external (and therefore uncontrollable) events, from natural phenomena to other states' decisions. Failed speculative ventures in response to these random external events can create disastrous ripples throughout LDCs' economies and cause depressions. The booms and busts that can result from external factors also make long-term planning difficult, especially for government expenditures in such areas as education, health, and infrastructure. Price fluctuations hit especially hard in countries that rely extensively on the export of a single commodity, such as oil, coffee, or rubber, and are at the mercy of the world market. In contrast, in industrialized states with large and diversified economies, fluctuations in the price of a few primary or finished products usually have little impact on the economy as a whole.

Unequal Terms of Trade

Dependency theory also argues that disadvantageous **terms of trade**—that is, the ratio of export prices to import prices—further impoverish the LDCs.[23] If the prices of a country's exports are rising faster than the prices of the goods it imports, its terms of trade are increasing; conversely, if import prices are increasing faster than export prices, its terms of trade are declining. For most developing countries, this means that if the prices of primary products decline and the prices of manufactured goods increase, the LDCs' terms of trade will worsen. Dependency theorists contend that prices of primary goods tend to decline over the long run relative to the price of manufactured goods.

At the same time, many dependencistas contend that in the global market, because there are often many sellers of raw materials and few buyers (a condition known as monopsony), it is easier for the buyers to impose artificially low prices. According to dependency theory, this monopsony power creates a buyers' market in which buyers can hold down the prices of primary goods. To give one example, sales of bananas in the United States, western Europe, and Japan are dominated by three corporations. When banana-producing countries formed the Union of Banana Exporting Countries and tried to impose an export tax in 1974, the buyers refused to purchase bananas from participating countries, stopped production at their plantations, and destroyed crates of bananas at the ports. Eventually, the banana-exporting countries backed down and the taxes were withdrawn.[24]

▪ **Terms of trade**
The ratio of export prices to import prices.

Multinational Corporations

By 2003, there were 63,000 MNCs worldwide with more than 821,000 subsidiaries, employing more than 90 million people and producing more than a quarter of the world's gross product (see Table 10.2); those numbers stayed fairly stable throughout the decade.[25] These companies wield a tremendous amount of power within developing countries, particularly because of their control over

TABLE 10.2	The World's Twenty Largest MNCs	
Rank	**MNC (Country)**	**Revenues (in $ millions)**
1	Wal-Mart Stores (USA)	378,799
2	Exxon Mobil (USA)	372,824
3	Royal Dutch Shell (Netherlands)	355,782
4	BP (Great Britain)	291,438
5	Toyota Motor (Japan)	230,201
6	Chevron (USA)	210,783
7	ING Group (Netherlands)	201,516
8	Total (France)	187,280
9	General Motors (USA)	182,347
10	ConocoPhillips (USA)	178,558
11	Daimler (Germany)	177,167
12	General Electric (USA)	176,656
13	Ford Motor (USA)	172,468
14	Fortis (Belgium)	164,877
15	AXA (France)	162,762
16	Sinopec (China)	159,260
17	Citigroup (USA)	159,229
18	Volkswagen (Germany)	149,054
19	Dexia Group (Belgium)	147,648
20	HSBC Holdings (Britain)	146,500

Karen Collins, *Exploring Business* (Boston: Addison Wesley Longman) 2006, available on-line at http://www.google.com/imgres?imgurl=http://static.flatworldknowledge.com/sites/all/files/imagecache/book/27984/fwk-collins-fig03_007.jpg&imgrefurl=http://www.flatworldknowledge.com/pub/1.0/exploring-business/40185&usg=__Mp_fvX7xKNeFXyQRSly9vT4F1NA=&h=504&w=412&sz=42&hl=en&start=1&itbs=1&tbnid=he1SnkqW7UlxrM:&tbnh=130&tbnw=106&prev=/images%3Fq%3D%252B%2522MNCs%2522%252B%2522largest%2522%26hl%3Den%26tbs%3DIsch:1

manufacturing. At one time, for example, MNCs controlled 70 percent of the manufacturing industry in Nigeria, 50 percent in Ghana, and 44 percent in Malaysia.[26] They also benefit from their mobility. Unhappy with taxes, labor policies, environmental regulations, or other costs of business in one country, they can move operations to another. Strikes hold little leverage because plenty of workers are available in other states. The result is that some MNCs, such as General Motors, IBM, Toyota, British Petroleum, and Siemens, are corporate giants, with total sales rivaling or surpassing the GDP of many countries.

Modernization theorists contend that MNCs promote development in LDCs, providing capital, technology, training, and managerial know-how. Dependency theorists, however, challenge this benevolent view of MNCs. They contend that MNCs exploit the poor countries, hinder their development, and contribute to the widening of the gap between rich and poor. According to dependency theory, MNCs have replaced the colonial system as the primary means of penetrating LDCs and extracting wealth from them. There are three primary complaints.

First, MNCs avoid paying their share of taxes by bookkeeping and accounting tricks devised to increase profits and minimize tax burdens. Because they have subsidiaries throughout the world, MNCs are able to use transfer-pricing mechanisms to transfer profits to countries where taxes are lower. Here is one author's description of a transfer-pricing scheme:

A U.S. manufacturer, for instance, might produce parts in a factory located in Texas but ship these parts to a plant in Mexico for assembly. In turn, the assembled product is transported back to the United States for final sale. The price that the home firm charges the Mexican subsidiary for the parts or that the subsidiary charges the home firm for the assembled product is essentially arbitrary because these transactions take place within the same company and are not exposed to market forces. If, let us say, Mexico imposes a higher tax on corporate profits than does the United States, then the MNC can lower its overall tax bill by overpricing the parts shipped to Mexico and underpricing the assembled products that are "sold" back to the home firm in the United States. By manipulating the prices on intrafirm trade in this way, the Mexican subsidiary will show little profit on its books, thus avoiding the high Mexican tax rate, as the profit of the home firm will be artificially boosted—allowing it to be taxed at the low U.S. rate.[27]

Of course, MNCs use transfer pricing to avoid taxes in industrialized countries as well. In addition, dependency theorists claim, MNCs remove scarce capital from LDCs by charging royalties and licensing fees for manufacturing products on which they hold copyrights and patents (as they do in industrialized countries). Finally, through bribery and lobbying, MNCs prevail on legislators to give them special tax breaks. For instance, when Honduras imposed a tax on the export of bananas, United Brands (formerly United Fruit) bribed a government official to reduce the tax.[28] In short, dependencistas claim that many business practices—legal and illegal—carried out by MNCs all over the globe cause more harm when they are applied in the resource-poor developing world.

Second, the technology that MNCs transfer to LDCs is often not appropriate for the region. In many instances, it is capital-intensive technology, which relies on expensive equipment and highly skilled workers and therefore does little to lower the often very high local unemployment rates. In addition, imported technology may stunt the development of local technology, discourage local research and development, and drive out local entrepreneurs. Developing areas, according to the dependency school, often do not need advanced technology; instead, they need appropriate technology that can be produced locally, run and maintained by local workers, and adapted to local conditions.

Third, MNCs do not bring capital into LDCs but instead often set up businesses that use up the limited supply of local capital. Bank loans to MNCs mean less money is available for local entrepreneurs to borrow. By using local capital, MNCs crowd out local entrepreneurs, and competition from MNCs often destroys existing domestic industries. In addition, top managers of MNC operations are often brought from the parent country, not recruited in the host country.

In general, dependency theorists allege that MNCs can control and manipulate the production of primary commodities in developing countries; in so doing, they act as industrialized states' instruments of control and subjugation over LDCs. This "neocolonial" exploitation of the developing world is actually more efficient and more profitable than the colonial system under which the United States and the European powers dominated most of Asia, Africa, and Latin America before World War II. Dependency theory concludes that although LDCs may have achieved political independence, they cannot achieve economic sovereignty because they are kept in a dependent state by the capitalist world economy.

Critiques of Dependency Theory

Critics assail dependency theory on several fronts.[29] The foremost criticism is that it has been proven false by the LDCs that have managed to industrialize and have done so with the help of investment and trade with developed states. These NICs have large, vibrant, and diversified industrial sectors and improving standards of living. By pursuing a strategy promoting the export of manufactured goods instead of isolating themselves from the global economic system, they have embraced international trade as a means of growth.

Second, the plight of primary product exporters may not be as bad as dependency theorists claim. Although world prices for primary commodities (except oil) have tended to decline since 1973, many developing countries that have improved productivity in their primary product industries have achieved substantial economic growth. Commodity producers that boosted agricultural productivity and lowered barriers to foreign trade and investment, such as Malaysia, Thailand, and Chile, have used primary product exports as a springboard to diversified economic development. By contrast, countries that raised barriers to imports of agricultural machinery and imposed export taxes on farm products (as have many in Africa) have remained dependent on primary products and lost market share to more efficient producers.[30]

PHOTO 10.4 India prepares mangoes for shipment to the U.S. India produces more mangoes than any other country.

Moreover, although dependency theory contends that the terms of trade are declining for LDCs, data do not clearly support this contention. Although some regions or categories of countries have gone through periods of sharp declines in terms of trade (such as sub-Saharan Africa in 1965–1973 and the oil exporters in 1980–1986), both developing and developed countries have experienced periods of declining terms of trade. The terms of trade for developing countries generally tend to fluctuate more than those of the industrialized countries. This may be attributed to greater reliance on primary products (with prices often subject to change without notice) in LDCs, whereas most industrialized countries have diversified economies less vulnerable to sudden changes in prices. Apparently, economic downturns and business cycles hurt both industrializing and developed states alike, although underdeveloped countries may be hurt more.

Third, dependency theory lays the blame for LDCs' poverty squarely on the more developed countries, with little if any discussion of factors within the developing world itself that contribute to economic stagnation and poverty. There can be little doubt that domestic factors such as rapid population growth, high rates of illiteracy, and corruption are partly responsible for persistent poverty and underdevelopment. Critics of dependency theory thus prefer to shift the discussion of economic development from the systemic level to the domestic level.

Domestic: Economic Development Theories

Economic development theories abound at the domestic level. Theories of geographical advantages (being an island, having deep-water ports, having enormous territories too large to absorb) and disadvantages (having no access to the sea, being fragmented by divisive mountain chains) are related to theories of natural advantages (having extensive oil deposits, having access to plenty of fresh water, having arable land and fertile soil) and disadvantages (suffering from desertification or floods; drought or storms; inaccessible fresh water; a lack of any energy supplies, gold or silver veins, or gemstone deposits). There are historical theories focused on the effects of colonialism, slavery, and tribal warfare. There are institutional theories focused on the rules, laws, norms, and structures of nations' economies. There are also theories focused on states' deliberate economic strategies: the decisions they make to advance economic development.

Import-Substitution Industrialization

Import-substitution industrialization (ISI) is a strategy of economic isolation intended to encourage domestic entrepreneurs to manufacture products otherwise imported from abroad. First, the exchange rate is overvalued, meaning that the rate at which currencies are exchanged makes imported goods relatively cheaper and exported goods relatively more expensive. Second, high tariff barriers are erected on consumer goods to block foreign competition. The intention is to make imports of capital goods (such as manufacturing equipment and spare parts) cheap and to make imported consumer goods (such as automobiles and appliances) expensive, so that consumers will buy from domestic producers.

Most countries pursuing an ISI strategy initially experience growth in domestic industries that produce consumer goods, just as planned. The next stage of the strategy, sometimes called deepening, is the development of manufacturing capabilities in intermediate industries such as steel. However, investments in these industries require more capital and more sophisticated technology from industrialized states, and an overvalued exchange rate hurts exports, which are necessary to earn foreign capital. Consequently, in practice ISI has often led to massive borrowing from foreign banks and growing external debt, resulting in even greater dependence on industrialized states for capital.

The trouble with ISI is that it typically requires a great deal of foreign capital to create and subsidize domestic industries. Because ISI undermines the profitable export sector, it tends to lead to a balance-of-payments deficit; that is, the nation's economy cannot earn enough through exports to pay for the imports it needs. This makes it difficult to purchase capital goods from industrialized countries, a problem that may defeat the whole purpose of the strategy.

Latin America offers the best examples of the successes and limitations of the ISI strategy.[31] The rapid decline in world trade that was a cause and effect of the Great Depression prompted Argentina (see At a Glance, "Argentina"), Brazil, and Chile to pursue de facto strategies of import substitution. In the years following World War II, ISI was formally adopted as a strategy of economic development and a way to reduce economic and political dependence. High tariffs were levied to protect new industries until they became established, and currencies were overvalued. The short-run impact was a shortage of foreign capital and a steep decline in the profitable export-oriented sector. Around 1960, through import and exchange controls, the initial, easy stage of industrialization characterized by the substitution of locally produced goods for imported consumer goods was successfully completed. In some cases, notably in Brazil, great strides were made in the domestic production of more durable consumer goods and some intermediate goods, including transportation and electronic equipment, metal fabrication, and chemicals.

The next stage of industrialization called for the development of capital goods, but, as noted previously, these goods require substantial foreign investment and technical capability. Because their export-oriented industries had declined as a result of the ISI strategy, Latin American countries lacked the foreign exchange necessary for the import of the appropriate technology from the North. This led to heavy foreign borrowing and severe indebtedness, which contributed to the "stalling out" of their industrial development.

In Africa, one country closely associated with import substitution was Tanzania, whose policies of *ujamaa* (unity) and *kujitegamea* (self-reliance) received great attention in the late 1960s. However, by the early 1980s Tanzania's economy was in severe crisis. Many of its state-owned industries were operating at roughly 10 percent capacity, and, because farmers were taxed so heavily to pay for critical imports, agricultural exports fell. Essentially, after a period of initial success, ISI had stalled and failed once again.

In short, ISI has not been very successful at either emancipating LDCs from economic dependence or providing a basis for long-term economic development. In most instances, it has resulted in greater dependence on capital and imports from the industrialized states without raising the general standard of living in underdeveloped countries.[32]

Export-Led Industrialization

The second principal strategy of growth promotes industrialization through trade. Export-led industrialization (ELI) seeks to promote development by working within, rather than against, the global economic system. Its advice to developing countries on their relationship to industrialized states is simple: "If you can't beat 'em, join 'em."

In the 1960s and 1970s, several developing countries, particularly Brazil and the NICs of East Asia, adopted an ELI strategy by giving substantial economic incentives to firms to export their products, particularly by undervaluing their foreign exchange rates, which made their exports cheap and their imports expensive.[33] For Japan, South Korea, Taiwan, Hong Kong, and Singapore, export promotion has proven to be a major impetus for exceptionally rapid economic development. In the course of less than two generations, these countries were transformed into industrialized nations poised to produce the high-tech products of the twenty-first century. Their tremendous growth rates have been

AT A GLANCE

Argentina

In the 1990s, Argentina was hailed by the IMF as a success story, a developing country that, because of its fiscal and trade policies, was on track to becoming a modern, industrialized state. Argentina had embraced the tenets of globalization. In a policy called convertibility, Argentina pegged its peso to the dollar, bringing inflation (which had reached as much as 200 percent a month) back under control while simultaneously encouraging confidence in the banking system. It generated enormous amounts of cash and cut spending by selling off state-owned enterprises—including social security, the post office, and utilities—to private, usually foreign, investors. Argentina's economy grew by almost 11 percent in 1991, $800 million in foreign investment poured into the country each month, and the IMF gave the government billions of dollars in support of its efforts. However, Argentina's rapid growth was built on a fragile foundation. Much of the investment money coming into the country could be pulled out just as quickly. The government's sales of assets funded government operations for a while (in lieu of the government's previous inflationary practice of simply printing money to cover costs), but once everything was sold off, there was no new means of generating income. Government spending, moreover, proved hard to curb. Because of an ongoing system of patronage, even after cutting back government-owned enterprises, the government still had the same number of employees. Because of the rules in place at the time, politicians with blank checks could and did still curry local favor by building large, expensive projects; at the same time, provincial governments refused to meet budgetary targets and spent recklessly, with the bills going to the federal government. Soon the government

was spending more than it was taking in, dollars were bleeding out of Argentina into foreign banks, and Argentina was forced to borrow money. This was toward the end of the 1990s, when interest rates were rising internationally. The IMF initially refused to give Argentina more loans to cover its debt but, after a news story appeared hailing the IMF's decision to loan the country another $8 billion, the organization capitulated and gave Argentina the money. It was too late, though. The government paid the money into the banks, the banks then used it to pay off their depositors, and the depositors then took the money back out of the country. The government tried to stem the run on the banks by imposing a limit on withdrawals, but this led to riots and looting and, soon thereafter, the resignations of the president and the economy minister. Argentina eventually defaulted on its debts to private creditors and allowed the peso to float freely again, ending convertibility just a decade after it was implemented. In 2002, Argentina's GDP dropped by an estimated 21 percent. In 2003, Argentina's unemployment stood at 22 percent and more than half of the population lived in poverty. As its economy foundered, so did Argentina's political institutions. The presidency, the congress, and the judiciary were discredited. Some police officers took to kidnapping. The country that had appeared on the brink of "First World" status had collapsed in on itself, apparently an example of the hazards of unreservedly applying liberal economic principles.

In this instance, the IMF, which had encouraged Argentina's actions, admitted some culpability, acknowledging in retrospect that it had made mistakes and had more to learn. Indeed, as late as 1999, the IMF officially had been predicting that Argentina would experience growth and be able to pull itself out of its economic tailspin, only to be proven terribly, and expensively, wrong. Of course, much of the blame for Argentina's failure rests with Argentina itself, a country in which corruption flourished and where there were no safeguards against rampant spending in the provinces. The sale of key assets was rash and dangerous and the planning all along was short term, with an eye to quick profits. Clearly the IMF should have recognized the problem far sooner than it did, but Argentina itself cannot be absolved of responsibility for its own economic implosion.

accomplished through intensive state intervention in the economy and society, borrowing of technology from industrialized states, and the promotion of research and development.

Some theorists have argued that the success of the NICs cannot be duplicated elsewhere, as those East Asian nations have saturated trading opportunities with industrialized states to such an extent that other LDCs have been squeezed out.[34] In essence, this perspective argues that trading opportunities with industrialized states are a fixed sum, and thus the gain in trade by one developing country forecloses openings for other developing countries. This view has some merit; as prices rise, international primary product markets can become glutted from increased production in other LDCs. However, global demand for most products is not static—as economies grow, they typically generate more demand for raw materials, consumer and capital goods, and services. LDCs might also find that markets are impenetrable because of protections put in place by industrialized states anxious to maintain some uncompetitive industries regardless of the domestic cost, whether for security, cultural, or domestic political reasons. Thus, African states find that their agricultural goods simply cannot compete against the subsidized farm products of the United States, the EU, and Japan. In fact, this concern was raised separately at the G-8 conference in 2005. Politically sensitive both domestically and internationally, farm protections undermine ELI in agriculture.

It must also be noted that industrial development in the Four Tigers (Taiwan, Singapore, Hong Kong, and South Korea) had significant social and environmental costs, just as it has everywhere else. Moreover, the striking success of the rapidly developing Asian economies was mitigated by their currency crises and recession in 1998, prices paid, in part, for earlier undervaluing of their exchange rates as part of ELI.

Washington Consensus

Clearly, there is little consensus on what economic steps to take to promote development. Countries and their foreign advisors have moved from one economic development fad to another.[35] The dependency theorists did not believe developing countries could benefit from free trade, and their thinking led to (unsuccessful) practices like **delinking, autonomous development, and the** UN's **New International Economic Order (NIEO)**. When such self-reliance proved unsupportable (in the absence of infusions of foreign investment), states turned to the Washington Consensus, itself a refutation of the power of external factors and a reaffirmation of states' abilities to control their economies. However, there never really was a consensus.

In 1989, economist John Williamson listed ten policy recommendations for developing countries on which he believed the majority of economists at the time agreed. These included:

- Fiscal discipline.
- A redirection of public expenditure priorities toward fields offering both high economic returns and the potential to improve income distribution, such as primary health care, primary education, and infrastructure.
- Tax reform (to lower marginal rates and broaden the tax base).
- Interest rate liberalization.
- A competitive exchange rate.
- Trade liberalization.
- Liberalization of inflows of foreign direct investment.
- Privatization.
- Deregulation (to abolish barriers to entry and exit).
- Secure property rights.[36]

▪ **Delinking**
Subjecting external relations to the imperatives of broad internal development.

▪ **Autonomous development**
Territorially based effort to meet a state's citizens' basic needs.

▪ **New International Economic Order (NIEO)**
An outgrowth of developing states' frustration and an evolutionary step from the nonaligned movement, the Group of 77, and the United Nations Conference on Trade and Development (UNCTAD), there was, in 1974, a Declaration of Principles for a New International Economic Order. Nothing came of it because of the LDCs' lack of influence, combined with their disunity of purpose and priorities.

Williamson never expected his list to become development's clarion cry of the decade, but it was quickly accepted as received wisdom. Many countries took these recommendations to heart, but how they interpreted and implemented them varied dramatically. Most of them soon found that these were but the threshold to the next steps that needed to be taken; they were not solutions in and of themselves. Nonetheless, talk continued about the Washington Consensus, and many different states' efforts were characterized as following its prescriptions.

During this period, the World Bank, the IMF, and the U.S. government encouraged states to undertake "shock therapy," rapidly implementing the Washington Consensus reforms. Many economists disagreed with this approach, even at the time, but states, sometimes under pressure from the international institutions and sometimes under their own steam, followed through. Their timing was auspicious, as it coincided with a flood of private investors in the global market (see Figure 10.1). Even as the countries liberalized and courted FDI, investors were searching for exactly such new ventures.

This led to rapid growth in many countries' economies, especially throughout Asia and Latin America. However, the economic advancements were not, in most cases, complemented by legal and regulatory, social, and political development. In fact, the opposite frequently occurred: The gap between rich and poor increased, countries' abilities to provide services decreased as they sold off government assets like water districts and postal services to private investors,

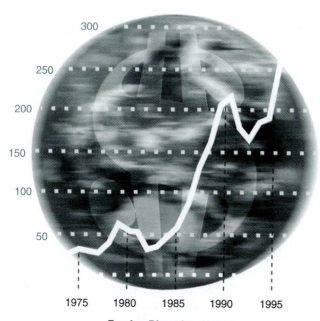

300

250

200

150

100

50

1975   1980   1985   1990   1995

**Foreign Direct Investment
1975-1995² ($ billions)**

FIGURE 10.1   **FDI burgeoned from the late 1980s to the mid-1990s.**

and liberalized—but unregulated—banks and financial institutions made themselves terribly vulnerable with short-sighted loans and policies. Ill-considered, rushed implementation of the Washington Consensus recommendations thus sent countries on a roller-coaster ride in which they rapidly improved their economies only to experience dramatic setbacks less than a decade later.

The late 1990s and early 2000s saw several economic crises that challenged the principles underlying the Washington Consensus rush to globalization via liberalization. Mexico's 1994 currency crisis resulted less from Mexico's behavior—although it left itself vulnerable by relying too heavily on short-term foreign loans running up to the crisis—than from external investors' actions. Foreign investors flooded into Mexico following NAFTA's signing, but, despite every indication that their investments would be profitable, they panicked after a routine depreciation of the peso. Creating a self-fulfilling prophecy, some of the famously capricious investment community immediately pulled out, creating panic among the rest, who rushed to follow them, thus quickly draining the country of capital and leaving it to deal with debts accumulated when growth appeared more certain.[37]

Asia's 1997–1998 economic crisis, as discussed in Chapter 9, also had its roots in Washington Consensus–based liberalization and globalization. The international troubles that crisis sparked were compounded in 1998 when Russia let the ruble float, defaulted on its external debts, and halted for three months its commercial banks' payments to foreign creditors. The Russian economy was in turmoil because of failed stabilization policies that had not taken the country's lack of central authority and other structural weaknesses into account. Furthermore, as in the situations already described, Russia had quickly accumulated an enormous amount of short-term debt over the course of the 1990s, its external terms of trade had deteriorated markedly as Russian exports' prices fell on the international market, and Russia also suffered from the fallout of the Asian crisis because investors burned in Asia were pulling their capital out of all emerging markets. Russia's default, in turn, was also contagious. The Brazilian economic crisis followed on its heels, arguably in large part because investors further fled emerging markets, leaving Brazil without capital and in much the same situation Russia had found itself in, and Southeast Asia and Mexico before it. The contagion did not stop with Russia and Brazil. The situation continued to deteriorate worldwide into the early years of the twenty-first century.

Clearly, in addition to the institutional failures of the affected governments, there were external factors at play. As discussed in Chapter 9, the foreign currency markets played a role. So, too, did the Bretton Woods institutions: the IMF and the World Bank (for more on these institutions, see Chapter 13). Critics of those two complain that they pressured states to make unhealthy domestic economic decisions. They make these claims in part because the Washington Consensus recommendations were lauded by the Bretton Woods institutions and in part because the recommendations were considered a continuation of the institutions' controversial **structural adjustment programs (SAPs)**.

Systemic-Domestic

Structural Adjustment Programs

In 1980, the World Bank shifted its emphasis somewhat from development projects to managing LDCs' debts, lending them funds and insisting on major economic reforms called structural adjustment programs (SAPs). SAPs were intended to lower LDCs' governments' debts by reducing their expenditures, to open LDCs' markets to investment and trade by eliminating barriers, and to promote exports as a means of bringing in foreign currency.

Although SAPs' objectives were consistent with liberal economic theory's assumptions about free trade and investment, their strict focus on the imperatives of global economics failed to account for domestic economic, social, and political concerns. Indeed, by opening their markets to external trade, LDCs often found their domestic industries unable to compete. By devaluing their currencies, LDCs' own products' values dropped and the costs of importing goods rose. By opening to investment, LDCs found their assets being bought and controlled by foreign corporations. Reducing government expenditures—including subsidies for faltering industries, civil service positions, and health, education, and housing programs—caused social unrest in LDCs as populations found

▪ **Structural adjustment programs (SAPs)** Application, often under some duress from the IMF, World Bank, or United States, of strict economic reforms rooted in liberal assumptions of the requirements of development.

themselves without any government safety net while prices rose, store shelves emptied, and jobs disappeared. This is perhaps best illustrated by the rise of populist leftist leaders in Argentina, Brazil, Ecuador, Uruguay, and Venezuela. SAPs also had political ramifications as populations rioted against government adherence to World Bank requirements at locals' expense. SAPs also failed to take the environment into account, often forcing ecological devastation in the pursuit of commerce because, for most LDCs, the most immediately promising exports are natural resources.

Development Today

Creating a New Paradigm

By 2000, following the collapse of the economies in South Korea, the Asian Tigers, Mexico, and Russia, leaders at the World Bank recognized that the Washington Consensus and SAPs more generally were not working and began to adjust the Bank's efforts accordingly.[38] Accused of lending incautiously, creating debts that further bind LDCs' governments' hands, the World Bank began to emphasize debt-relief programs and also made an effort to lend more judiciously, thus successfully reducing the number of "at-risk" projects in its portfolio. Already since the 1980s, the World Bank had attempted to have a "greener" policy in keeping with the global evolution toward sustainable development. It continued to fund projects such as open-pit coal mining, large-scale coal-fired power plants, and commercial logging in tropical forests, but it also began to undertake air quality improvement projects, carbon offset programs, and rainforest protection efforts, while generally increasing its funding for environmental projects. It also reduced its overall expenditures in the power sector from 21 percent of Bank lending in 1980 to approximately 7 percent of its total lending at the beginning of the twenty-first century. Criticized for focusing exclusively on economic growth as a means of promoting development and reducing poverty, the World Bank adjusted its own priorities to include greater spending on social programs including health, education, nutrition, and pension projects. In 1980, such efforts accounted for only 5 percent of the Bank's lending; in 2002, they accounted for 22 percent.

The Bank and its financial cousin, the IMF, have also attempted to implement the broader goals underpinning both SAPs and the Washington Consensus. In 2000, they replaced SAPs with what they called the Comprehensive Development Framework, of which the Millennium Development Goals are a part. In an enormous turnaround, the World Bank now claims that:

> [e]liminating poverty, reducing inequity, and improving opportunity for people in low- and middle-income countries are the World Bank Group's central objectives. The Comprehensive Development Framework is an approach by which countries can achieve these objectives. It emphasizes the interdependence of all elements of

development—social, structural, human, governance, environmental, economic, and financial.[39]

The World Bank regards this holistic approach as a second generation of reforms following, deepening, and allowing success for the first-generation SAPs.[40] Thus, although the Washington Consensus is still used as a buzzword for first steps at liberalization and reform, most economists, national leaders, and international organizations now acknowledge, after that stomach-lurching roller-coaster ride in the 1990s, that a much broader agenda and a much more sophisticated approach are required if LDCs are to develop and root themselves firmly in the international economy.

Searching for Practical Solutions: Technology

As analysts attempt to tease out how best to pursue development, some practical efforts are yielding intriguing results. Technology has created all kinds of opportunities for economic and political development that were unimaginable a couple of decades ago. The cell phone, for example, has completely changed power dynamics in countries where telephone landlines are limited, communication used to depend on transportation, and transportation was a luxury relegated to the rich or connected. This was the case in much of Africa up into the 1990s. There, governments, with their Land Rovers, had far more reach and access than did local NGOs or upstart political parties. Now, however, Africa has 135 million phone subscribers and is the fastest growing cell-phone market in the world.[41] The spread of mobile phones has facilitated the development and expansion of civil society and helped begin to shift countries' internal balances of power away from often corrupt and dictatorial governments. For those who believe that civil society is a necessary component of development, as discussed earlier, this technology-based sea change is an important step in the right direction.

The spread of the cell phone has been a function of the global market, but there have also been deliberate efforts to use technology to promote development. In one program, an NGO donates a solar-powered cell phone to a villager who then can open a business providing phone access to neighbors. In another, a development group provides crank-powered laptop computers to children. In India, corporate giant Intel has set up computer kiosks, a digital hospital, and support for 100 mobile computer labs in vans that will circulate through rural areas, providing scheduled computer access to villages.[42] These and many other programs like them, leveraging technological advancements, are changing the face of development by changing information and communication dynamics.

Innovations are showing up in other realms related to development, as well, especially agriculture. Consider the Green Revolution that began in the 1950s with the work of agronomist Norman Borlaug. The short, fertilizer-responsive grain varieties that Dr. Borlaug helped develop more than doubled harvests

TABLE 10.3	Green Revolution: Changes in Factors of Production in Developing Countries of Asia					
	Adoption of Modern Varieties					
	Wheat (Million ha*/% Area)	Rice	Irrigation (Million ha)	Fertilizer Nutrient Use (Million Tons)	Tractors (Millions)	Cereal Production (Million Tons)
1965	0/0%	0/0%	94	5	0.3	368
1970	14/20%	15/20%	106	10	0.5	463
1980	39/49%	55/43%	129	29	2.0	618
1990	60/70%	85/65%	158	54	3.4	858
2000	70/84%	100/74%	175	70	4.8	962
2005	72/87%	102/76%	178	77	6.4	1,017

* ha, hectares.

Source: FAOSTAT (Food and Agriculture Organization of the United Nations Statistics), March 2006, and author's estimates on modern variety adoption, based on CIMMYT (International Maize and Wheat Improvement Center) and IRRI (International Rice Research Institute) data.

wherever they were planted, staving off famines in India and Pakistan in the 1960s. Turkey and China were also early beneficiaries of the semidwarf Mexican wheat (see Table 10.3).

Dr. Borlaug, a Nobel laureate, was quick to point out that improvements in agricultural science are not themselves adequate to promote development. He credited individual leaders in 1960s India, Pakistan, and China for recognizing the potential of the new grain varieties and for putting in place policies that ensured that they would be disseminated and planted. He also noted that Africa has not benefited from the Green Revolution, not for lack of leaders but for lack of infrastructure: Without roads, farmers cannot get the required seeds and fertilizer nor move their crops to market; without irrigation, they cannot grow the crops; without subsidies they cannot afford to buy the seeds and fertilizer they need; and without education, people will not understand why it is imperative that they update their methods. Beyond those domestic requirements are international requirements, for the farmers' produce must also be competitive in the global market. This requires, in today's global market, that the small farmers in African states form large cooperatives. It also requires that the countries with which they are competing—largely the EU countries, the United States, and Japan—reduce their own protections enough to allow African farmers a foothold in international markets. Here, in microcosm, we can see that the Green Revolution requires individual, domestic, and systemic inputs, in addition to the pure science of improved genetics, to advance development. This same case can be interpreted from any of the worldviews. Realists will explain the global protections inhibiting African farmers' entrance into the international markets in terms of relative gains and security. Liberals will explain the Green Revolution's successes in terms of international cooperation among various governments and NGOs. Constructivists will explain the Green Revolution itself in terms of

▪ S P O T L I G H T ▪

Invention and Innovation

Rory Stear, founder and CEO of Freeplay Energy Corp., has focused on the problem that many developing regions lack an electricity infrastructure. In 1994, he saw on BBC-TV a demonstration of a wind-up radio by its inventor, Trevor Bayliss. Bayliss said that major corporations rejected the idea of marketing the product. That gave Stear the idea of starting a company based on the fundamental concept of "storing human energy and releasing it slowly to power consumer electronics and other products," he said. Stear bought the patent and marketing rights to the wind-up radio and launched Freeplay. His company is global, with its headquarters in South Africa, manufacturing operations in Asia, and major marketing channels in the United States and United Kingdom. He markets his products as high-priced specialty items in rich countries, which subsidizes the distribution of his products at no cost or low cost in poor nations. Only about half of Africa is electrified, and batteries are many times more expensive than electricity from the grid. "So there is a big barrier in access to energy," Stear said. With the AIDS pandemic spreading across Africa, countries in that region need a simple and inexpensive way to educate millions of people, many of whom don't know how to read. Freeplay's wind-up radio converts 30 seconds of hand cranking into energy that will last for 40 minutes of radio reception time. "We began selling these products at the Sharper Image, for camping and emergency preparedness," he says. In 1998, before the company was profitable, it began using that revenue to distribute its products in places like Zambia, Tanzania, Niger, Kenya, and Rwanda, where there are 65,000 child heads of household who need basic information on farming and about protecting their families from health threats. Freeplay has distributed about half a million of these wind-up radios for free to households, hospitals, and schools, with the help of the Red Cross and United Nations.

Over the next few years, there's clear demand for 50 million cell phones in Africa. "How do you power those phones?" reflected Stear. Freeplay is working with big corporations such as Vodaphone to develop and distribute products run on rechargeable batteries, solar power, as well as hand cranked chargers. Stear has also enlisted a wide range of investors in his company, including Ben Cohen of Ben & Jerry's and Anita Roddick of the Body Shop. General Electric invested $10 million for a 10 percent ownership stake in Freeplay and offered research help through its Schenectady, NY, laboratory. Stear is in the process of taking the company public in the United Kingdom.

Other current and future Freeplay products include foot powered starter motors for cars, low-energy medical instruments for hospitals, and $100 computers that run the free Linux operating system.

The case of Freeplay shows that there are economically viable ways to use invention and innovation to improve lives even in the world's poorest areas. Stear said that the innovation practices of leading companies must be deployed. Freeplay protects its intellectual property by filing for patents in the United States and Europe to fend off cheap knockoff products in developed markets. To spread its message to customers and investors, it doesn't spend money on ads but relies on public relations that has lead to free coverage on the BBC and in *Newsweek* and *The Wall Street Journal.* If sponsor companies want to put their brand logos on his products in order to pay for free distribution of those products in Africa, Stear is all for it. "We'll make red radios that say Coke on them," he said.

Excerpted from "Invention and Innovation for Sustainable Development" (report of a workshop sponsored by the Lemelson-MIT Program and LEAD International, London, November 2003), 13–14. Reproduced with permission.

elites' understanding that such a thing is both necessary and feasible. (For a discussion of innovation in another area, electricity, see Spotlight, "Invention and Innovation.")

Searching for Practical Solutions: Microfinance

In addition to all the work that is being done on technological and agricultural innovation, new financing practices that promote development from the bottom up have taken root. More than thirty years ago, a Bangladeshi economics professor named Mohammed Yunus began making small loans of a few dollars each to locals—mostly women—who wanted to start or sustain small businesses. His early efforts and successes eventually led him to establish the Grameen Bank, which over time has granted more than $5.1 billion worth of small loans to more than 5.3 million of the world's poorest people,[43] thus setting in motion the microcredit and broader microfinancing (including savings accounts, microinsurance, and other financial services) revolution that since has swept across the developing world. Since the start of the Grameen Bank, microfinance institutions (MFIs) have proliferated and taken on a variety of new forms, from government-run organizations to corporate entities to NGOs. It is difficult to determine the number of MFIs operating internationally. The IMF estimates the number as falling between 300 and 25,000, depending on how MFI is defined (the conventional wisdom is that the number is between 1,000 and 1,700). The number of borrowers is also debatable and could be anywhere between 30 million and 500 million.[44] The UN's Economic and Social Council proclaimed 2005 the "Year of Microcredit."[45] A year later, Dr. Yunus won the Nobel Peace Prize.

Dr. Yunus's initial concept turned development theory on its ear. He focused on the poorest of the poor rather than on elites, he emphasized local opportunities rather than international imperatives, and he recognized the intrinsic role of women in informal economies and in development and supported their active involvement.

The various innovations are far from mutually exclusive. Microfinancing, for example, benefits from the dispersal of mobile phones and the advancement of wireless computer technologies. In 2007, for example, Vodafone introduced a new program in Kenya making it possible to conduct financial transactions via cell phone. Likewise, Jamii Bora, the largest microfinance institution in Kenya, uses mobile technologies to reach the country's more remote areas. In a country without adequate roads and landline phones, these practices allow financial institutions to service isolated villages while remaining economically viable.[46]

Microfinance is hailed by many as the future of development, but the practice itself is continuing to evolve. Its success has led to an influx of microfinance institutions and even big loan organizations, and banks have begun to look at the world's poor as a market worth tapping into. In fact, with this evolution, problems have arisen, rooted in a lack of oversight of, and coordination among, MFIs. One of the challenges is preventing borrowers from taking out more than one loan at a time, thereby assuming an unrealistic debt burden. This practice is part of a deeper issue regarding borrowers' lack of knowledge about financial management and planning. Add to that the presence of illegitimate MFIs alongside trustworthy, established groups, and borrowers are positioned to be victims. Moreover, money-lending institutions have inherent limitations and do not provide services like money-saving and interest-accruing options. And social problems have also sometimes arisen. MFI loans are usually provided to women, but this can create tensions in households and communities that ultimately lead to dislocation if not violence.

Despite all, microfinance's successes have certainly exceeded many analysts' predictions. In 1998, the UN published a Secretary-General's report called "Role of Microcredit in the Eradication of Poverty," in which it warned:

> Furthermore, it is not clear if the extent to which microcredit has spread, or can potentially spread, can make a major dent in global poverty. The actual use of this kind of lending, so far at least, is rather modest: The overall portfolio of the World Bank, for example, is only $218 million. In recent international meetings, it has been stated that a target to reach 100 million families by the year 2005 would require an additional annual outlay of about $2.5 billion. This should be compared to the total gross domestic product (GDP) of all developing countries, which is now about $6 trillion. A certain sense of proportion regarding microcredit would seem to be in order.[47]

Yet, in 2005, microcredit was indeed reaching nearly 100 million families. That year, UN Secretary-General Kofi Annan remarked, "Microfinance has proved its value in many countries as a weapon against poverty and hunger," and Bangladesh's ambassador to the UN, Iftekhar Ahmed Chowdhury, called microcredit "a major instrument of poverty alleviation."[48]

There is some reason to be concerned that microfinance is perceived as a panacea—a cure-all—that will itself begin to wear away at poverty. Indeed, like the Green Revolution, microfinance can only be part of a larger effort to eradicate poverty and assist development. As the challenges listed here make clear, without combining microfinance with other poverty reduction activities (such as peer support, networking programs, and training), it cannot achieve its potential. As with the Green Revolution, microfinance has been far more effectively implemented in Asia than in Africa. In 2005, 90 percent of microloans were made within Asia; in Africa, less than 10 percent of the potential market was being served; in Latin American and the Caribbean a little less than 12 percent of the potential market was tapped.[49] That is not to suggest that microfinance does not have a constructive role to play in Africa or Latin America and the Caribbean, just that it can only be a part of a much more multifaceted approach that takes into account those regions' existing practices, structures, and requirements.

Corruption Versus Courage

Indeed, one of the factors that must be taken into consideration in those regions is corruption. No discussion of development—economic or more general—can be complete without mention of the dark, insidious effects of corruption. Gunnar Myrdal first wrote about the problem in 1968 in reference to Asia.[50] Since then, it has become common knowledge that corruption stifles development. Corruption can be institutionalized at the state level and can be a product of culture and social mores, so it is useful to examine it at the domestic level of analysis. However, corruption is also the accumulation of individuals' personal decisions, the most spectacular corruption enriching a very few at a cost to millions.

Corruption plagues developing countries. It permeates economic and political activities in states as diverse as Russia, Colombia, Nigeria, and Indonesia. It diverts resources from development, shifts local balances of power, and stymies growth. It taints international NGOs' efforts to provide humanitarian assistance as they buy access to victims of hunger, poverty, and conflict. It mocks bilateral and multilateral foreign investment efforts. It also contaminates diplomatic and security agreements as foreign governments make concessions to states' corrupt leaders to achieve their bigger objectives.

Efforts to fight corruption—to bring people to justice for abusing the system—require tremendous fortitude and courage. Those who corrupt the system do so by spreading complicity via money, opportunities, and fear. Those who would take them on often must deal with entrenched corruption, layers of people who have been bought into the system and who protect those at its foundation.

Corruption is institutionalized and socialized, although it comes down to individuals in every instance. Although each aspect is present whenever corruption occurs, in the following cases they are broken out for illustrative purposes.

- **Russia (institutional)** That corruption is at epidemic proportions in Russia is of no surprise to the Russians themselves. In a January 2005 poll, over 50 percent of the Russians polled listed corruption as the main impediment to development.[51] The numbers were even higher in a 2005 World Bank survey, which reported that 78 percent of Russian businesses stated that they have had to pay bribes. A research group in Moscow estimated in 2005 that Russians pay more than $3 billion in bribes each year and that businesses pay $316 billion. The total is more than twice as much as the Russian government brings in through taxes and represents billions of dollars that cannot be spent on development projects. President Putin recognized the problem and that it is structural. "The state as a whole and the law enforcement bodies, unfortunately, are still afflicted with corruption and inefficiency," he said in a 2004 interview. Accused of not doing enough to combat the problem, Putin instituted a number of minor fixes, including raising salaries for those in law enforcement and putting more teeth into the punishment of some corruption-related crimes, like issuing false passports.[52]

- **Colombia (social)** The 1961 *U.S. Army's Area Handbook for Colombia* offered a social explanation for the pervasiveness of corruption throughout the country based on the colonial concept of *fuero,* or local leaders' rules superseding rigorous applications of the law, part of the Free, Partly Free, and Not Free Countries of the World: 1979–2009 leaders' more general provision of privileges for their constituents.[53] More than forty years later, this concept of **patronage** continues to hold sway, although now the compromised congressional representatives, police, military leaders, and judges give privileges to whichever paramilitary, rebel group, or drug cartel holds sway in their district. In a 2005 court hearing, AUC (United Self-Defense Forces/Group) warlord Salvatore Mancuso asserted that his paramilitary controlled 35 percent of Colombia's national Congress, more than a third of the country's lawmakers.[54]

- **Individual** In a list of the ten most corrupt leaders of the modern era, Indonesia's Mohamed Suharto has the ignominious honor of standing head and shoulders above his competition, having embezzled between $15 billion and $35 billion from a country in which the per-capita GDP in 2001 was $695.[55] Although analysts argue that Suharto's efforts were less detrimental because they took place over decades, there is no question that the money stolen represented billions of dollars that could have

▪ **Patronage**
Corrupt use of public resources to advance the interests of a specific group in exchange for electoral support.

PHOTO 10.5 The late Sani Abacha, former military dictator of Nigeria (1993–1998), who embezzled more than $2 billion during his short tenure.

helped promote development in Indonesia. Sani Abacha, former president of Nigeria, moved more quickly, accumulating between $2 billion and $5 billion over the short five-year period he was in office. In Nigeria, the per-capita GDP was $319 in 2001. The damage these individuals did was enormous, not just because of the funds they redirected but also because of the culture of corruption they endorsed in their respective countries, the effects on their countries' reputations in the international community, and the resulting decisions made regarding aid and foreign direct investment.

Corruption, like development, spans economics, politics, security, and human welfare. It can be examined at each level of analysis. It involves civil society, institutions, governments, and culture. It is, in fact, a dark mirror image of development, as well as among the most significant factors stifling it. International institutions—especially the World Bank and the IMF, but others

What Would You Do?

Promoting Development

You are living in the West, but your family's roots lie in Burma (Myanmar). You are concerned about your relatives in the country: The regime is repressive, people are undernourished and living below subsistence (the average life span is less than fifty-seven years), and the country has been mostly closed to the outside world. Democracy movements in the country have been violently quashed, the economy is rife with corruption and is burdened by inefficient economic policies and government controls (not to mention U.S. sanctions), and HIV/AIDS is spreading, even as the population is already suffering from bacterial and protozoal diarrhea, hepatitis A, typhoid fever, dengue fever, and malaria. You would like to help promote development, but where do you start? What practical steps could you take? With whom might you work? What would be your priorities?

What Would You Do?

[handwritten margin note: World Bank IMF want to avoid corruption]

like the Pan-African Parliament, as well—focus on what they call **good governance,** or the absence of corruption. They seek to reward steps taken toward good governance and acknowledge its importance in the success of their development efforts. At the local level, spearheaded by individual leaders, there has been a renewed commitment in the twenty-first century to fighting corruption (e.g., Prime Minister Hun Sen in Cambodia, Argentine President Fernando de la Rua, Nigeria's President Olusegun Obasanjo, and Nepal's King Gyanendra). The results of these nascent efforts have been mixed. Although it is encouraging that these attempts are being made, there is still a long way to go, and many challenges endure.

Conclusion

▪ **Good governance**
Legislation and implementation free from corruption and with due regard for the rule of law.

Development is a difficult business and a difficult thing to measure. It is complicated by competing agendas and priorities. Efforts to promote it have evolved over time, but there is still no consensus on how best to advance it. Only recently has it become generally acknowledged that development must be a holistic process, that progress in one field can be undermined or mitigated by lack of

Levels of Analysis and Paradigms in Review: Development

	Realism	Liberalism	Constructivism
Individual	In an effort to increase the reach of Portugal, Prince Henry the Navigator formed a special center to focus the efforts of expert navigators, shipbuilders, and seamen on expanding Portuguese trade and dominion overseas.	Dr. Mohammed Yunus single-handedly changed the face of development by showing how microloans—to small businesswomen, in particular—could be profitable.	World leaders like Kofi Annan help change development processes by changing expectations. Annan did this by linking economic development to security and good governance and making a compelling argument for their interconnectedness.
Domestic	As Amy Chua argues in her book *World on Fire*, ethnic minorities culturally predisposed to successful business practices alienate ethnic majorities, who, feeling economically threatened, often turn to violence against the minorities to protect their interests.	Modernization theory holds that trade and open markets will lead inexorably to modernization, with which comes democratization.	Government funding for research into sustainable development in countries as varied as Serbia, Colombia, and the United Kingdom demonstrates a shift toward the longer term in how elites view development requirements.
Systemic	The projected failure of the UN to achieve its Millennium Development Goals is due in large part to the international institution's complete lack of authority and enforcement capability; states may sign up for the goals, but without oversight, they will subsume the UN's goals to their own agendas.	The UN's ambitious Millennium Development Goals reflect the hope that the international community can work together across a broad set of interrelated issues to promote development in a mutually beneficial way.	The presence of pro-development NGOs at the 2005 G-8 summit and the Live 8 concerts that aired worldwide the same summer may be evidence of a growing global civil society as people perceive their roles and options differently.

progress in another. This, combined with globalization, has had the salutary effect of raising human welfare higher on the world's agenda than it has ever been in the past. Nonetheless, complications and challenges—even potential reversals—persist as the international system and each of its members shift in spurts and starts along the development continuum.

Discussion and Review Questions

1. To what extent do the developed countries have a responsibility to help promote development in the LDCs? To what extent is it in their interest to do so? To what extent is it consistent or inconsistent with their mandates as state governments?
2. Although both SAPs and the Washington Consensus have gotten bad names, liberalization is generally accepted as a necessary step toward economic development (for example, in June 2010 Greece responded to its economic crisis in part by privatizing or partially privatizing some state-owned assets). Given the previous failures, why is this concept so strongly adhered to?
3. What are the benefits of a holistic development approach like the UN's Millennium Development Goals? What are the costs of such an approach?
4. What is the relationship between development, security, and governance? What are the implications of this relationship for international efforts to promote development in LDCs?
5. As discussed in Chapter 2, many LDCs consider the "right to pollute" a rite of passage for industrialization and development, regardless of the costs in terms of climate change. Discuss how this relates to colonialism and its aftermath, the resource curse, World Systems theory, "environmental reparations," international cooperation on climate change, the global commons, and the North–South divide.

Key Terms

Autonomous development 410
Debt burdens 387
Delinking 410
Demographic transition 390
Dependency theory 392
Diversified economies 400
Economic determinism 393
Forgive 387
Freedom House 393

G-8 countries 387
Good governance 422
Least and less developed countries (LDCs) 379
Legalism 393
Modernization theories 389
New International Economic Order (NIEO) 410
Newly industrialized countries (NICs) 382

Normative 388
Patronage 420
Rationalism 393
Socialized 394
Structural adjustment programs (SAPs) 412
Sustainable development 397
Terms of trade 401
Urbanization 389
Washington Consensus 379

CHAPTER **11**

Human Issues:
Demographic Trends

The preceding chapters have focused on security and economic issues, topics that have been the traditional mainstay of the study of international relations. In the following two chapters, we look at issues such as population, migration, and health and disease, as well as resource issues, the environment, energy consumption, food, and water. Importantly, the demographic issues addressed in this chapter, and the resources issues addressed in Chapter 12, are closely linked to security and economics as well as to each other. For example, we can think of the issue of population and migration, to be discussed in more detail later in the chapter. How do changes in population relate to the globalization and fragmentation and conflict and cooperation dichotomies? Many developing states, for example, face a youth bulge, "defined as large cohorts in the ages of 15–24 relative to the total adult population."[1] The issue for this cohort of young people is whether they can find jobs in their own countries. As the wealthier states in the world experience greater benefits of economic globalization relative to developing states, people living in the poorer states will seek those same benefits, thus the *pull* factor for people to migrate to wealthier states in search of a job and a better life. For example, a 2010 report by Gallup showed that "One-third of the educated, ambitious, creative and employed Arab youth, who form the bedrock of their countries' future prosperity, would like to leave their home countries permanently if they were given the opportunity."[2]

In the case of fragmentation, concerns arise as to whether this youth bulge leads to internal conflict, a security issue. A recent study found that "[y]outh bulges in the context of continued high fertility and high dependency make countries increasingly likely to experience armed conflict...while countries that are well underway in their demographic transitions are likely to experience a 'peace dividend.'"[3] Thus, fragmentation of societies is a possibility if younger people are not able to find employment and obtain an education and have no means to migrate.

In thinking of cooperation and conflict, we can look at refugees. Civil war can lead to the *push* factor in which people are compelled to flee from their homes as internally displaced people within their own country or as refugees fleeing to neighboring states to avoid the fighting. The ongoing conflict in Darfur, Sudan, illustrates this dynamic clearly. Fighting between the government and rebels that erupted in 2003 led hundreds of thousands of people to flee their homes to other parts of the country and neighboring Chad. The **United Nations High Commissioner for Refugees (UNHCR)** estimated that by the end of 2004, approximately 200,000 people fled to Chad and 1.6 million were displaced from their homes within Darfur (by 2010, the number of Sudanese refugees in Chad increased to 270,000).[4]

Conflict can lead to population movements, but cooperation at the international level can address these concerns. For example, the UNHCR, also known as the United Nations Refugee Agency, "is mandated by the United Nations to lead and coordinate international action for the worldwide protection of refugees and the resolution of refugee problems." As an impartial intergovernmental organization, the agency "works in partnership with governments, regional organizations, international and non-governmental organizations."[5] In the case of the Darfur crisis just noted, at the beginning of 2004, "UNHCR...mounted a major logistics operation to move the vast majority of the refugees to camps at a safer distance from the volatile border." The first camp opened in January 2004, and by September, ten were created. In these camps, UNHCR built small villages that include family shelters, clinics, wells, schools, and so forth. Within Darfur itself, the agency has mobile monitoring teams that visit settlements for internally displaced people to investigate the security situation they face.[6]

The increasingly interdependent world and the astounding pace of globalization are interrelated with the issues covered in this chapter: population growth and decline, migration, and health and disease. We explore the connections between these issues in the context of the globalization and fragmentation and conflict and cooperation dichotomies. We also see how the various theories introduced in Chapter 2 are evident here. For example, the fact that states can overcome their differences and cooperate to address AIDS/HIV provides support for liberalism. Alternatively, realism explains a state's reluctance to admit to an infectious disease pandemic for fears of the economic ramifications, such as

▪ **United Nations High Commissioner for Refugees (UNHCR)**
A UN agency that seeks to protect refugees as well as to respond to refugee problems.

a drop in tourism. Constructivism can tell us something about how states have redefined their security interests beyond military considerations to encompass "human security" such as health and disease.

A caveat is in order: It is impossible to examine any one of these issues in depth in a single chapter, and this book does not attempt to do so. Instead, it introduces some of the most salient issues in the community of states and how they are impacted by globalization and fragmentation as well as conflict. It also offers an overview of how the community cooperates in attempting to address and solve these issues. This chapter and the next do not examine every problem that each state faces, but they do show how pressing problems that cross state boundaries affect international politics and vice versa.

Population

Population Growth and Decline: Impact of Youth Bulges and Aging Populations

Between 1950 and 1955 approximately 98 million people were born per year. In the five-year period between 2005 and 2010, it is estimated that approximately 136 million people will have been born annually.[7] The rapid growth of the world's population is the root cause of many global problems. This section explores the issue of population growth historically, the trends for the future, and the implications of the growing number of people on the planet such as urbanization, development, and the international community's response to population.

According to the U.S. Bureau of the Census, "from the dawn of mankind to the turn of the nineteenth century world population grew to a total of one billion people." By 1900, the beginning of the twentieth century, the world population reached 1.7 billion. By the end of the twentieth century, the world population was nearly three times the size in 1900, at 6 billion people (world population doubled in size between 1960 and 1999).[8] The 2009 world population of 6.8 billion people is projected to increase to more than 9 billion by 2050, with 96 percent of the projected growth occurring in the developing states, namely in Africa, Asia, and Latin America. Although overall population growth has slowed since reaching its highest point in the mid-1990s (approximately 82 million people annually; see Figure 11.1), and while the expected population change for the developed countries is minor, it is estimated that the population of the 49 least developed states will grow 2.3 percent each year, doubling its population of 0.84 billion in 2009 to 1.7 billion by the year 2050.[9]

Why is the world's population increasing so fast? The phenomenon of demographic transition accompanies technological and economic development (see Chapter 10 for a discussion of demographic transition and modernization theory). Once a population gains access to rudimentary sanitation and medical services, the fertility (birth) rate quickly overtakes the mortality (death) rate,

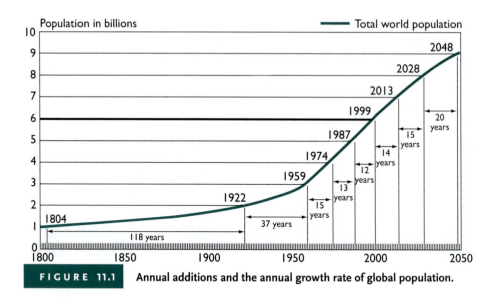

FIGURE 11.1 **Annual additions and the annual growth rate of global population.**

life expectancy increases, and the size of the population begins to increase steadily. Over time, as states industrialize, birth and death rates stabilize and population growth then levels off.[10] One need only look at the numbers in the industrialized states today. For example, the fertility rate in America is 2.09 children, which is needed to maintain population at a stable rate (**replacement level fertility** is where two parents replace two children, thereby stabilizing population growth). In the case of the states of the EU, the overall average fertility rate is 1.7. For particular countries, such as Italy and Spain, the fertility rate is approximately 1.3. If this rate continues for these two countries (without the added numbers from immigration), "the number of Spaniards and Italians [will] halve in 42 years." Importantly, as states become wealthier, life expectancy increases, and women become educated and enter the workforce, women "have fewer children and invest more in each one."[11] The result of a lower fertility rate is an aging population. In the case of the most developed states, there are now more people who are aged sixty years and older than there are people who are fifteen years and under.[12] Consequently, the demographic trend in developed countries is generally older and stable, slowly growing, or declining populations.

In the less developed countries of Asia, Africa, and Latin America, by contrast, medical advances such as vaccinations have reduced death rates, but families often remain large and birth rates remain high, mainly because children are needed to provide labor and income for the family. In fact, the dominant factor that determines the "future size, growth, and compositions of the populations of many developing nations" is a high fertility rate. As a result, the populations of many of these states remain younger and faster growing. According to the United Nations, "the numbers of children and young people in the less

▪ **Replacement level fertility**
Two parents are replaced by two children, which is an international goal to reduce overall population growth.

developed regions are at an all time high (1.7 billion children [under age 15] and 1.1 billion young people [aged 15–24])." In 1950, the less developed countries (LDCs) had double the population of the more developed countries (MDCs); at the present time, they have almost four times as many people, and by 2020 they are expected to have more than four-and-one-half times as many.[13] Concerns about development and potential for conflict arise for states with youth bulges, people in the age range of fifteen to twenty-four years old relative to the adult population as a whole. There is an association between a large youth group and the risk of domestic armed conflict, as well as riots, violent demonstrations, and terrorism.[14]

In addition, growing populations can impede economic development, furthering the gap between the developed and developing world. In the case of the Middle East, for example, with rapid population growth rates (second after sub-Saharan Africa), the youth bulge will make for difficult challenges for states in the region. This region is already beset with high youth unemployment, "a mismatch of jobs and skill levels, extensive government entitlements, and political instability." These factors will hinder the ability of the states in the Middle East to improve their economies. Moreover, in many Persian Gulf states, citizens face competition from foreign workers (in some of these countries "one-half or more of the labor force consists of foreign workers"). Governments' abilities to meet the needs of this growing demographic cohort depend on how well they are able to "invest in social, economic, and political institutions that meet their needs." According to a recent Population Reference Bureau article, "The fastest growth in youth population will be in places that are the least prepared economically: Iraq, the Palestinian Territory, and Yemen."[15]

A recent study examined China and India, two countries with large populations that are also succeeding in their economic development. The authors found that "the demographic experiences of China, India, and other developing societies show that relatively poor nations can achieve stable populations before major gains in income accrue. The possibility of a poverty trap can be contained and minimized by an effective political system." Thus, politics determines the fates of countries' development. When governments implement population control measures, namely reducing fertility rates, economic growth can occur, as demonstrated by the economic growth of China and India in recent years.[16]

As noted previously, developed countries have an aging population, but developing states are also beginning to confront this same dynamic (the UN named 1999 "The Year of the Older Person," in recognition of the global phenomenon of an aging population). According to the U.S. Bureau of the Census, "absolute numbers of elderly in developing nations often are large and everywhere are increasing. Well over half of the world's elderly (people aged 65 and over) now live in developing nations (59 percent, or 249 million people, in 2000). By 2030, this proportion is projected to increase to 71 percent (686 million)."[17] In fact, both developed and developing regions of the world will have an aging population: "During the next two generations, the number of the world's people older than 60 will quadruple, rising from 606 million now to 2 billion in 2050. For the first time in human history, the elderly will outnumber children."[18] This trend matters because states will need to take into account the economic costs of caring for their elderly citizens, and therefore the impact on economic development and growth for countries—both developed and developing. Given that many of these elderly people will want to lead independent lives, they "will need housing, streets and cityscapes that will accommodate their slower pace." For those who cannot afford to live independently, or are not able to do so, nursing homes will need to be constructed, all of which costs money. States will need to consider the implications for pensions as more people retire and will need that income to live.[19] In the case of Europe, for example, the EU states agreed in 2002 to attempt to increase the age of retirement from fifty-eight to sixty-three, thereby delaying paying pensions.[20] Increasing the age of retirement, according to a recent *Economist* article, "can make the difference between the solvency and insolvency of pensions."[21] Moreover, the EU hoped to have approximately 50 percent of its population aged fifty-five to sixty-five working by 2010 (a target that has been difficult to achieve). At present, only a third of those in this age group continue to work. The countries of the developing world confront the challenge of taking care of elderly people given the breakdown of "traditional family networks" as these states continue their path of urbanization.[22]

Urbanization and Megacities

As globalization continues, so does urbanization. The important point to recognize is that globalization benefits cities, which are the conduits to integration into the global economy. As people migrate to the cities for jobs, so too do investment opportunities and other economic activity.[23] Yet the world's fastest growing regions continue to be its poorest, and most of the growth is occurring in already overburdened urban regions. According to the UN Population Fund, in 2008, for the first time, more than half of the world's population lived in urban areas. It is estimated that by the year 2030, 5 billion people will call cities and towns home. In one generation, the urban population of Africa and Asia will double.[24] Given that this increase in the urban population will occur "in the poorest and least-urbanized continents, Asia and Africa," the challenges for these regions will be significant.[25] Whether these regions will be able to develop or instead face further poverty will be important considerations for individual governments and the international community alike.

With urbanization comes the emergence of "megacities"—cities with more than 10 million people (constituting 4 percent of the world's population), such as Mumbai, Tokyo, Mexico City, Sao Paolo, New York, and Shanghai. In 2007, the UN noted there were 19 such cities, with a projected increase in 2025 to 27 megacities. These megacities have exacerbated already acute difficulties in providing basic services in developing countries. Affordable housing is difficult to find, crime rates are on the rise, transportation and communication infrastructures are increasingly strained, and social tensions are more pronounced.[26]

Interestingly, it is projected that almost all the urban population growth will be in smaller cities and towns, and less so in the megacities. The problem is that smaller cities and towns are quite weak in their ability to plan for and implement polices to respond to this urban growth. Urban and national governments as well as international organizations and civil society at large will need to work together to take proactive steps to respond to the growing populations in the urban centers.[27] The point is that growth of urban areas in the developing states has global consequences. As the United Nations Population Fund noted in its 2007 *State of World Population* report, "What happens in the cities in the less developed world in coming years will shape prospects for global economic growth, poverty alleviation, population stabilization, environmental sustainability and, ultimately, the exercise of human rights."[28] This assessment remains as pressing as ever today.

International Responses to Population Dynamics: Importance of Family Planning

As demonstrated so far in this chapter, population trends affect the ability of countries to improve their economies and reduce poverty. Moreover, reducing overall population growth is linked to achieving the international goal of replacement level fertility, in which two parents are replaced by two children. Even though the results of their efforts will not be evident for a few generations, international organizations (such as the **United Nations Population Fund [UNFPA]** and International Planned Parenthood [IPP]) have concentrated on trying to create the social, economic, and political conditions necessary for reducing the birth rate.

Interestingly, under the auspices of the United Nations, several international conferences to address population have been held since 1954. The first, the World Population Conference, was held in Rome, Italy, "to exchange scientific information on population variables, their determinants and their consequences." The conference focused on ways to produce information about the demographic conditions in the developing states. The conference also sought to encourage the establishment of regional training centers that would concentrate on population issues as well as to train specialists in conducting analysis of demographics. Subsequent conferences held in 1965, 1974, and 1984 continued to focus on population and the analysis of fertility rates "as part of a policy of development planning" as well as the interdependence between population and development.[29]

However, it was the fifth UN conference (and largest conference on development and population at the time), the International Conference on Population and Development, held in Cairo, Egypt, in 1994 that explicitly made the link between population growth and development, particularly the importance of reducing or stabilizing population to attain economic growth. With more than

▪ **United Nations Population Fund (UNFPA)**
The largest organization that provides international assistance for programs promoting women's health around the world, in particular family planning. The organization also helps governments in support of policies to reduce poverty, recognizing that population size and structure are related to sustainable development.

180 countries participating, a new Program of Action was adopted, focusing on goals for the next two decades. Importantly, the program moved beyond looking at meeting particular demographic goals to a focus on the connection between population and development. The program also recognized the connection between individuals' needs and universally understood human rights principles. Further, according to the UNFPA, to fulfill these goals, it was important to empower women and provide them with better access to education, employment, health care, policymaking, and decision making. Moreover, the program called for universal access to family planning by 2015, education for girls, and so forth. In this, the program emphasized the role that governments and international organizations could play in ensuring the accomplishment of these goals.[30] A special session of the UN General Assembly in 1999 reiterated the Program of Action adopted in 1994.

From this brief overview of the various international conferences, one can thus see that the international community recognizes the importance of population for countries' well-being and that cooperation among states does occur. Yet the challenges remain daunting. Achieving replacement-level fertility where it is most urgently needed—the least developed countries—will require an increase in investments in human resource developments, particularly improvements in women's status and access to education on health and the means of family planning.

One means of reducing fertility, and hence population, is access to contraception, one of the goals of UNFPA as well as other international organizations addressing population. Currently, the UN estimates that approximately 215 million women in the developing countries want to prevent pregnancy. But the fear of side effects, lack of support from husbands and family, as well as lack of access to adequate and effective family planning services are obstacles women face in trying to use contraception. A 2004 UNFPA report anticipates a 40 percent increase in the number of contraceptive users between 2000 and 2015. According to most estimates, a 10 percent increase in contraceptive use results in roughly a 70 percent drop in the fertility rate. To attain the projected decline in birth rate for the next two decades, the proportion of couples using contraception worldwide must increase from the 62 percent in the early mid-2000s to at least 66 percent by 2025.[31] In the period from 1986 to 2004 data show that, regionally, North America had the highest rate of contraceptive use at 76.2 percent, with sub-Saharan Africa the lowest at 20.1 percent. These regional and national differences remain, with contraceptive use by married couples in the developing world continuing to lag behind that of the developed world.[32] Thus, the mission of international organizations such as the UN and IPP is clear: Design and implement effective family-planning programs throughout the world.

Yet family-planning programs have succeeded in fits and starts. Information provided by programs such as the UN-sponsored African Census Program in the 1970s illustrated to many governments the full dimensions of the population problem, and thus won their support for population programs. In fact, by 2001, according to the UN, government support for family planning programs was found in 92 percent of all states. However, government support does not automatically lead to successful program implementation. By the mid-2000s, only one in four Africans used contraceptives.[33] Moreover, two out of three Africans do not have "access to essential services, such as family planning, maternal health care, and HIV prevention and treatment."[34]

Contraceptive use clearly is not the only factor in fertility. Improving educational and economic opportunities for women also tends to lower birth rates and contributes to economic development. The United Nations has stated this most clearly in its Millennium Development Goals (MDGs), outlined at the 2000 Summit. For those goals to be met by their 2015 deadline (for example, universal access to reproductive health), "women's empowerment and gender equality" are front and center. As the executive director of UNFPA, Thoraya Ahmed Obaid, stated at the 2005 World Summit, "We will not be able to reduce poverty, slow the spread of HIV and AIDS, improve maternal health and reduce child mortality, unless greater investments are made in sexual and reproductive health."[35] Moreover, governments should enact policies that "address gender inequality," such as access to information about family planning, as well as "equal access to economic assets such as land and housing, increased primary school completion and expanded access to post-primary education for girls, equal labor market opportunities, freedom from violence, and increased representation at all levels of governance."[36]

Of course, the problem becomes one of money. Because many developing countries are chronically strapped for funds, they often have difficulty fully staffing and funding family-planning programs. Donations to UNFPA, for example, have not kept pace with the demand for reproductive health services. In 1995, 30 percent of the money contributed by donor states went toward reproductive health supplies, but a decade later, the amount decreased to 20 percent.[37] Estimates from UNFPA show that "each million shortfall in funding means" 800 women's deaths, 360,000 unwanted pregnancies, 11,000 infant deaths, and 14,000 more deaths of children under the age of five. This becomes an even more pressing problem given that more than 1 billion people are between fifteen and twenty-four years old, and this age group is "entering their reproductive lives as the largest-ever generation of young people."[38] Thus, funding to support family planning is vital. In 2006, for example, UNFPA received $360 million in contributions from 180 states, the "highest number of donor nations and the largest amount of contributions to UNFPA" since 1969 when the organization first launched its operations. Fortunately, the number of donor states has also increased in the last decade or so. In 1999, 69 countries contributed, and 172 did so in 2005, with 2006 the record year (180 donor countries). States continue to provide contributions to UNFPA for its work. In 2009 the top ten donors (the most recent data available, and provisional at this writing), in descending order, were the Netherlands, Sweden, Norway, the United States, Denmark, the United Kingdom, Japan, Finland, Germany, and Spain. Countries in Latin American, the Caribbean, and Africa also pledged contributions. Reflecting the global economic crisis that continued in 2010, many donors were unable to maintain the previous levels of contributions.[39] Yet the challenge remains: As the costs of these services and demand continue to rise, UNFPA and other organizations need to continue to obtain funding sources.

The Abortion Debate

According to UNFPA, over half a million women die needlessly every year as a result of complications due to pregnancy and childbirth. Most of these women live in developing countries. If they had access to health-care services as well as the necessary equipment and supplies, their lives could be saved.[40] In terms of maternal death rates, in North America a woman's risk is 1 in 2,566, compared to a woman in sub-Saharan Africa, where the risk is 1 in 16.[41] Moreover, an estimated 46 million abortions are performed each year, almost 19 million of which are done "in unsafe conditions and/or by unskilled providers," leading to the deaths of approximately 70,000 women and girls. These deaths "represent about 13 percent of all pregnancy-related deaths." Importantly, the vast majority of unsafe abortions are performed in developing countries, and it is in the developing countries "where 99 percent of abortion-related deaths occur."[42]

Thus, it seems clear that access to safe and effective family planning and health care is vital to women's health and a society's population as a whole. Although they have their detractors, government family-planning programs do reduce the rate of population growth.[43] In fact, most people support the goals of family planning—to reduce poverty, overcrowding, and other harmful effects of unrestrained population growth—but many object to some of the means employed. Religious objections to contraception restrict or prohibit the use of birth control in many countries, particularly those where a majority of the population is Roman Catholic or Muslim. The most controversial aspect of family-planning programs, however, is abortion. At one extreme are China's family-planning laws, by which government officials pressure or compel many women to have abortions to restrict couples to a single child. Most countries permit abortions to save the life of the mother, but there are some that do not, such as Chile and El Salvador, where abortions are prohibited—no exceptions are made for the life of the mother. Overall, developing states place more restrictions on access to abortion than do developed ones (67 percent of developed states permit abortion on request, whereas only 16 percent of developing states do). Of the world's population of women, 40 percent live in states in which their abortion laws are very restrictive. These states are found, for the most part, in the developing countries.[44]

To demonstrate the level of controversy surrounding abortion even in a developed state (and the controversy's impact on world politics), one need only look at the U.S. policies from the mid-1980s onward. During the Cold War, President Ronald Reagan, a staunch supporter of the American right-to-life movement, in 1984 ordered a cutoff of U.S. Agency for International Development (USAID) funding for NGOs working in other states, even if these organizations used their own funds to support abortion as a family-planning method.[45] International organizations such as the United Nations Population Fund also did not receive funds from the United States, which argued that the Fund supported abortion as a birth control means of last resort (UNFPA states that it "does not provide support for abortion services. It works to prevent abortion through family planning and to help countries provide services for women suffering from the complications of unsafe abortion"[46]). The controversy returned during the Clinton administration, but this time the administration favored full funding of family-planning programs that included abortion; many lawmakers in Congress objected. In 2002, President George W. Bush's administration withheld the $34 million U.S. contribution to the UNFPA, arguing, like Reagan, that the fund promoted abortion, particularly China's abortion policy.[47] Even though in 2002 the U.S. State Department sent a fact-finding team to China to investigate UNFPA-supported projects there and found "no evidence that UNFPA has knowingly supported or participated in the management of a program of coercive abortion or involuntary sterilization in the PRC [People's Republic of China]," the administration chose to withhold the funds anyway. As a result of the Bush administration's decision, two American women independently started a grass-roots movement, culminating in the "34 Million Friends" campaign in July 2002. This campaign sought to "find 34 million friends to help UNFPA continue its invaluable work as the largest multilateral provider of family planning and maternal health care."[48] Interestingly, although the United States was influential in UNFPA's creation, it is the only country that withholds funds from the organization for political reasons rather than financial ones. In other words, the United States has the ability to contribute, but sometimes does not do so. After the election of Barack Obama in 2008, the United States changed course again, calling for the restoration of U.S. funding for UNFPA.[49] Although the net impact of the U.S. debate over abortion in developing countries is difficult to assess, the controversy illustrates how cultural factors and domestic political disputes can affect international efforts to address global issues.

Migration

Migration—the movement of people from their homes, either within their countries or to other countries—occurs for several reasons: economic (jobs), family reunification, marriage, natural disasters (drought, earthquakes, tsunamis), environmental degradation, and man-made disasters such as famine, religious persecution, political repression, and war.[50] Migration has always played a major role in human history. This section focuses on patterns and problems of migration confronting the international community at the start of the twenty-first century as globalization continues at such a rapid pace.

Economic Migration

An imbalance between population and economic resources often leads to migration. In general, migration brings people from regions that suffer from a dearth of land or capital resources, such as Central America, Southeast Asia, or eastern Europe, to those that are richer, like North America and western Europe. Thus, with rare exceptions (such as the African slaves brought to Europe and the Americas before the nineteenth century), most people who have immigrated to the richer countries of the world have done so in search of a higher standard of living. Globalization (through improved transportation and communications; interdependence of the global economy) has both facilitated and motivated the movement of people from states with few economic prospects to those states in which labor supply is low and the gap needs to be filled.[51] This is hardly surprising, as higher birth rates in the developing world have produced an enormous population that has sought work in the industrialized world, with its comparative wealth, lower birth rates, and aging citizenry. Such migration, according to the UNFPA, "can play a key role in development and poverty reduction." It is estimated that as of mid-2010, approximately 214 million people lived in countries other than those in which they were born; this is more than double the number of migrants since the 1960s. If all international migrants lived in one place, they would constitute the world's fifth largest state by population (the top four in descending order are China, India, the United States, and Indonesia). Today women constitute almost 50 percent of international migrants, many of whom "migrate alone or as the primary income earners."[52]

Studies show that asylum migration to developed states, therefore, is largely the result of economic factors. This makes sense given that developed countries are wealthier than the developing states from which many migrants come.[53] The impact is that "[a]sylum migration creates conflict within developed countries between natives and asylum seekers, and it creates conflict between neighboring developed countries, with one trying to pass the burden of migration to another."[54] Importantly, as a result, as realism would demonstrate, states use asylum policies for their own national interests. For example, during the 1960s when people were fleeing eastern European communist regimes to get to the West, the western European countries did not turn them away. When those seeking asylum in the 1970s and 1980s were no longer mainly from eastern Europe, the western European countries became more restrictive and sought to decrease the number of asylum seekers they were willing to accept.[55]

In the decade between 1990 and 2000, approximately 67 percent of the growth in migrants occurred in North America, and this region remains the destination for a significant number of international migrants.[56] According to the UNFPA, "net migration accounts for a growing and major share of population growth in developed regions—three quarters in 2000–2005."[57] Despite attempts in many countries to restrict immigration, this influx of immigrants is surpassed in terms of the rate of migration only by the two surges of European immigration into the United States during the first two decades of the twentieth century, when the United States imposed very few immigration restrictions.[58]

The trend for people migrating for economic reasons will continue for the foreseeable future. Developed states need migrants from developing states to do many of the low-paying jobs that natives are unwilling or unable to do—and thus ensure that developed economies continue to grow. At the same time, developed states also need highly skilled professionals—engineers, scientists, and so forth. For developing countries, their migrants send back money—**remittance income**—which can increase consumption in the home state. Remittance income can be invested in businesses in the home country, thereby contributing to economic growth.[59] It has been estimated that in 2008, remittances amounted to $444 billion globally. Of that amount, $338 billion was sent to developing states. Foreign direct investment (FDI) is the largest source of external funds for developing states, but remittances follow close behind as the second largest source.[60]

The problem, as will be demonstrated clearly in the health section, is that many of those who migrate to the developed world bring their skills with them, which can have negative consequences for the economic growth and health of developing states, a "brain drain." For example, the Global Commission on International Migration reported that there are more doctors from Malawi practicing in one city in the United Kingdom (Manchester) than in all of Malawi.[61] As one can see, migration patterns have impacts on countries, both developed and developing ones, sometimes negative and sometimes not. Importantly, continued globalization of the world provides opportunities for those willing and able to migrate in search of economic opportunities.

Refugees

In addition to those seeking economic opportunity, migrants may also be fleeing from war and oppressive dictatorships. These individuals are collectively referred to as refugees because they are forced to flee their home countries for reasons not related to their economic standard of living. The UNHCR defines a refugee in its 1967 protocol as a person who, "owing to well-founded fear of persecution for reasons of race, religion, nationality, membership of a particular social group or political opinion, is outside of the country of his nationality and is unable or, owing to such fear, is unwilling to avail himself of the protection of that country."[62]

Refugees are either displaced within their own countries (**internally displaced people** [IDPs]) or flee to neighboring states or regions. Importantly, these refugees and IDPs in developing states flee primarily for security reasons—politicide or genocide—rather than long-term factors such as poverty, economic discrimination, civil war, and so forth.[63]

Although refugees and IDPs make up a small proportion of migrants compared to economic migrants, they are "some of the most vulnerable and

■ **Remittance income**
Money migrants send back to their home countries. This income can have a significant impact on the economies of the home state.

■ **Refugees**
People who are displaced from their own countries.

■ **Internally displaced people**
People who are displaced within their own countries.

PHOTO 11.1 In Dili, East Timor, a young girl too afraid to go home because of ongoing violence walks through a refugee camp crowded with people.

marginalized groups." Approximately 90 percent of refugees live in developing states.[64] As an indication of the dimension of the problem, there were 2.5 million refugees in 1970, 8 million in 1980, and 15.2 million at the end of 2008. Not surprisingly, refugees tend to be from poorer parts of the world, and developing states are also the host countries for 80 percent of all the world's refugees. Pakistan topped the list of countries that hosted refugees in 2008 (1.8 million), followed by Syria (1.1 million) and Iran (980,000). Nearly half of all refugees that are under the care of UNHCR came from Afghanistan (2.8 million) and Iraq (1.9 million).[65]

In the 1990s, African countries were particularly prominent as sources of internal refugees (South Africa, Sudan, Mozambique, Angola, and Liberia). The former Yugoslavia, Iraq, Myanmar (formerly Burma), the Philippines, and parts of the former Soviet Union were also identified as places where those who left or lost their homes remained, voluntarily or not, within their own country. Most of these people fled from conflicts within countries, especially Afghanistan, Rwanda, and Bosnia. Conflict in the last decade or so in Burundi, Somalia, and Eritrea, among others, added to refugee statistics. For example, conflict in Burundi and Congo drove hundreds of thousands of refugees to flee to Tanzania in the 1990s and early 2000s (Tanzania hosts approximately 276,000 refugees). The Tanzanian government urged those refugees to return home, especially given that a peace agreement, backed by the United Nations, ending the latest civil war in Burundi,

TABLE 11.1	Persons of Concern to UNHCR by Region
Region	**January 2009**
Africa	10,317,300
Asia	10,089,330
Europe	4,164,560
Latin America	3,400,190
Middle East	5,914,140
North America and the Caribbean	576,760
Total	34,462,280

Source: UN High Commissioner for Refugees, "UNHCR Global Appeal 2010–2011: Populations of Concern to UNHCR," December 1, 2009, http://www.unhcr.org/4b04002b9.html.

was signed in 2005 (the government recently gave more than 162,000 Burundi refugees Tanzanian citizenship in 2010—these were long-term refugees who had fled Burundi in 1976).[66]

In addition to fleeing because of conflict, in many other developing countries hundreds of thousands of people leave their home regions because of soil exhaustion, chemical contamination, lack of access to clean water, or inundation of towns and farms, becoming environmental refugees (see Chapter 12). The refugee problem is, therefore, growing at an alarming rate both within and between states. In fact, the numbers of IDPs are on the rise, and internally displaced persons are now considered the second largest group of people "of concern" to the UNHCR (see Table 11.1), after refugees fleeing to neighboring states or regions—14.4 million in 2008 who are protected or assisted by UNHCR (which estimates that there are a total of 26 million IDPs worldwide).[67] Clearly, the contemporary period is characterized by increased movement and, disturbingly, increased dislocation.

Consequences of Migration

The influx of immigrants, whatever their reasons for migrating, has periodically provoked backlashes by the host-country populations. Reactions are often racially motivated; nativist movements (political movements favoring the native-born and discriminating against immigrants) arise and gain strength during economic downturns, when immigrants are often blamed for unemployment and rising crime rates. Nativist pressure in the United States prompted the passage of the Immigration Act of 1924, which discriminated against potential immigrants from southern and eastern European countries and tightened already existing restrictions against Asians. The economic recession of the early 1990s in Europe and North America similarly prompted calls for limiting foreign immigration.

The current global economic recession has also led to pressure on governments to reduce immigration. Today, approximately 40 percent of the states in the world have policies intended to decrease levels of immigration.[68]

Examples in the developed world demonstrate the consequences of migration. Even though EU states face the challenges of aging populations and a dwindling domestic workforce, and thus need immigrants, they are concerned about the influx of migrants, both from new EU member states of central and eastern Europe and from beyond Europe's borders. Whereas citizens of EU member states are able to move freely from one country to another, existing EU member states have attempted to limit the influx of immigrants from the new EU member states, such as Romania and Bulgaria (which became the newest members of the EU in 2007). Treaties concluded between new members of the EU and existing members contain a "transitional" clause that permits existing EU member states to limit the movement of workers from new EU member states for up to seven years.[69]

Besides EU-wide efforts, individual European countries have also passed immigration laws. For example, until the 1990s, German asylum benefits were very generous. Although the German government took years processing an individual's request for asylum, it provided each asylum-seeker with housing, food, clothing, and medical expenses. In 1987, 57,400 people applied for asylum, and between 1988 and 1992 the number of applications totaled 1.1 million. By the mid-1990s, with unemployment persistently high, however, especially in the formerly communist East, the climate in Germany became increasingly conducive to racism and xenophobia, leading to hate crimes against "guest workers" and their families. The violence led to protests within Germany and abroad, but may also have contributed to Germany's tightened asylum laws in 1993. One can see the outcome of the laws in terms of the decreased number of asylum applications. In 2002 there were 71,127; this number declined further to 50,563 in 2003 (although this still ranked Germany number four in number of asylum applications submitted for the industrialized states). Concerns about high unemployment of foreigners and the state's capacity to assimilate and integrate foreigners remain. The issue of integration and assimilation of immigrants is not limited to Germany. Riots in predominantly Muslim suburbs in France in 2005, for instance, brought to the forefront the alienation that many Muslims experience (often a result of discrimination in education and employment). Moreover, Muslim extremists have found support from both the descendants of guest workers and new immigrants. Such extremist support has led, in recent years, to terrorist attacks by foreign and native-born extremist Muslims in states such as Spain (the bombing of the Madrid train station in 2004) and Britain (the bombings of the London underground in 2005). In the end, all the states of Europe are faced with the challenges of assimilation and integrating foreigners and descendants of immigrants.[70]

Even in the United States, where the Statue of Liberty beckons to immigrants, political pressure to restrict immigration is cyclical. It is not so much political

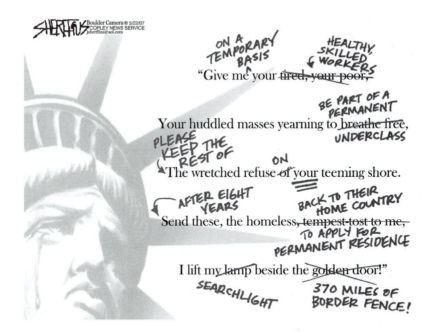

refugees that Americans mind, as the United States has historically granted asylum to people fleeing countries with which the United States has less than friendly relations. During the Cold War, for example, between 1975 and 1992, the United States admitted about 1.7 million political refugees, most from East Asia (particularly Vietnam) and the Soviet Union.[71] The United States had not always extended the same welcome, however, to people fleeing from noncommunist countries. Although almost 97 percent of Soviet and former Soviet asylum-seekers and 95 percent of Vietnamese refugees were admitted from 1975 to 1992, only 1.2 percent of people attempting to flee from impoverished, politically repressed Haiti were granted asylum. In 1992, hundreds of Haitian refugees, attempting to escape poverty and political violence by sailing to Florida in homemade rafts, were detained at sea and sent to the U.S. Naval station at Guantanamo Bay, Cuba.[72] President Clinton criticized this policy as inhumane during his 1992 campaign, but later he resumed the detention of Haitian refugees until 1994, when U.S. forces intervened to restore an elected government in Haiti. In contrast, virtually all those fleeing the communist island of Cuba interdicted at sea en route to Florida were granted asylum in the United States as political refugees. This policy changed, however, in 1994 when the United States refused to grant asylum to Cubans attempting to flee, instead sending them to havens in Guantanamo Bay and Panama. This exodus led to an agreement between Washington and Havana for controlled immigration from Cuba.

U.S. citizens' tolerance of economic migrants is cyclical: In weak economies, Americans begin to fear that immigrants are taking jobs away from U.S.

citizens (even though great numbers of immigrants accept low-paying jobs that few native citizens are willing to take). Nativists claim that new immigrants consume government services (such as Medicare and welfare) in excess of what they contribute in taxes, but these contentions are hotly disputed. Anti-immigrant sentiment contributed to the passage of a ban on welfare payments and Medicaid (low-income health insurance) coverage for immigrants in 1996, but these benefits were restored in 1997. Fear and resentment of immigrants and the inevitable friction caused by cultural diversity have taken other forms, ranging from "English-only" ballot initiatives in many areas to the 1992 presidential candidacy of David Duke, a reactionary former grand wizard of the Ku Klux Klan. Even with such anti-immigration policies, people continue to seek entry to the United States—in 2009 the United States was the top country for the resettlement of refugees and asylum applications.[73] The United States tightened its immigration rules for asylum-seekers and refugees as a result of the September 11, 2001, terrorist attacks. The passage of the USA Patriot Act (2001) and Real ID Act (2006) in the aftermath of the attacks meant that many people who had unknowingly, or as a result of coercion, provided support to armed groups that the United States considered terrorist organizations were denied entry into the United States. Most recently, immigration yet again became an issue in the forefront of U.S. politics, as the executive and legislative branches debated an immigration law that would allow amnesty to millions of illegal immigrants. The Obama administration has called immigration a top priority. The highly contested nature of the debate demonstrates that the issue of immigration and migration continues in an era of globalization—and provides impetus for conflict within and across societies.

International Solutions to Problems of Migration

Several international organizations have attempted to address the issues and problems surrounding economic migration. For instance, an international convention approved by the UN's General Assembly in 1990 seeks to protect the human rights of migrant workers. The convention recognizes that migration results in the scattering of the family; illegal, often secret movements; trafficking in human cargo (such as the smuggling of Mexican and Chinese people into the United States for exorbitant fees; see Spotlight, "Human Trafficking"); and the exploitative employment of undocumented workers. More important, it also codifies a series of rights to which migrant workers and their families are entitled. Countries such as Morocco and Mexico, both of which have many citizens who work abroad, have supported the convention, whereas many richer countries such as Oman, Japan, and Australia, worried about an influx of economic migrants, expressed reservations about adopting it.[74] With Guatemala's ratification of the United Nations Convention on the Protection of the Rights of All Migrant Workers and Members of Their Family in March 2003, the treaty entered into force in July 2003.[75]

Human Trafficking

In 2003 the United Nations Protocol against Trafficking in Persons entered into force. And yet, human trafficking remains a global problem. As the United Nations Population Fund's *State of World Population 2006* noted, "Trafficking is not only one of the most horrific manifestations of migration 'gone bad,' it also undermines national security and stability." Estimates from the International Labour Organization (ILO) are astounding to consider: "[A]t least 12.3 million adults and children are victims of forced labor, bonded labor and sex slavery each year." Of this 12.3 million, most are women and girls. Twenty percent of the total number of people trafficked are children.

What is very disturbing is that most women who are trafficked end up working as domestic help or in sweatshops. Many women also are forced to work in the sex trade. And many women are also traffickers of women. The economics of human trafficking are also staggering: With estimates of $7 billion to $12 billion a year, human trafficking is the third most profitable illicit industry after drugs and arms smuggling. The ILO asserts that these estimates are profits "from the *initial* sale of persons." Criminal organizations gain an additional $32 billion a year in profits once the person has entered the destination country.

How can trafficking and other forms of slavery be stopped? When women are desperate to put food on the table, provide shelter for their families, and so forth, they may be willing to cross international borders to find work. UNFPA, therefore, calls attention to the need for states to promote gender equality as well as to reduce poverty. Women must have better education and employment opportunities so that they do not become "easy prey for traffickers."

From UNFPA, "State of World Population 2006, A Passage of Hope: Women and International Migration," Press Summary, September 2006, http://www.unfpa.org/swp/2006/pdf/press-summary-en.pdf; Elise Labott, "Recession Boosts Global Human Trafficking, Report Says," June 16, 2009, http://www.cnn.com/2009/US/06/16/human.trafficking.report/index.html; United Nations Office on Drugs and Crime, "UNODC Report on Human Trafficking Exposes Modern Form of Slavery," February 12, 2009, http://www.unodc.org/unodc/en/frontpage/unodc-report-on-human-trafficking-exposes-modern-form-of-slavery-.html.

In terms of international cooperation to address refugees, the UNHCR "is mandated by the United Nations to lead and coordinate international action for the worldwide protection of refugees and the resolution of refugee problems." Moreover, the organization "strives to ensure that everyone can exercise the right to seek asylum and find safe refuge in another State, and to return home voluntarily. By assisting refugees to return to their own country or to settle permanently in another country, UNHCR also seeks lasting solutions to their plight."[76] UNHCR has carried out a number of programs designed to protect, resettle, and repatriate political refugees. The UN-sponsored 1989 International Conference on Central American Refugees, for example, obtained pledges of $156 million for aid and resettlement of more than 440,000 people displaced in that region.[77] The United Nations Relief and Works Agency (UNRWA) also operates a number of programs of education, relief, and humanitarian assistance for Palestinian refugees in Gaza, Jordan, Lebanon, Syria, and the West Bank. Ninety-eight percent of its funding comes from voluntary contributions from states, NGOs, and individuals. The United States is the largest bilateral donor to the organization (contributing a total of $268 million in 2009). However, meeting its budget goals has proved difficult for UNRWA; for example, in 2009 the agency's total budget was $1.2 billion, but it only received $948 million, thus facing a shortfall.[78]

States also have cooperated to promote efforts for voluntary repatriation of political refugees, and these attempts have achieved some notable successes. For example, after the Iraqi invasion of Kuwait in August 1990 displaced 5 million people from several countries of origin, an April 1991 Memorandum of Understanding between the UN and Iraq initiated a mass voluntary repatriation effort involving 1.5 million refugees. Most of these were Iraqi Kurds who had been displaced to squalid camps along the border with Turkey and Iran. While there, up to 800 people reportedly fell victim to disease and malnutrition every day.[79] Another international voluntary repatriation effort, the 1989 Comprehensive Plan of Action for Indochinese refugees, aided in repatriating thousands to their homelands in Cambodia, Laos, and Vietnam.[80]

Recent international efforts have made substantial progress in assisting refugees. In many other cases, however, displaced people find themselves with no place to go. Although many refugees return voluntarily to their homelands (such as the more than 5 million people from Afghanistan who have returned home since 2002 with the assistance of UNHCR), others are returned involuntarily.[81] For example, since the end of 2007, Kenya has forced refugees fleeing the violence in Somalia back to their home country. In that same year, Egypt sent 1,400 Eritreans back to Eritrea.[82]

Indeed, long-term migrants, whether economic migrants or political refugees, continue to pose major problems for their host countries and the international community. Although many economic migrants achieve the prosperity for which they came to their new homelands, thousands of others face discrimination and anti-immigrant violence. Until democracy, economic progress, and environmental protection catch up with population growth in the developing world, great numbers of people will continue to leave developing countries in search of political freedom and economic opportunity in the developed world. Industrialized nations can choose between turning away immigrants and welcoming them and can decide how and how much to promote economic development abroad, but they cannot ignore the crowds outside their gates forever. Developing nations also face the challenge of absorbing large numbers of refugees who have fled because of conflict and oppressive regimes. They also face the problem of highly skilled citizens leaving for better economic opportunities. As globalization progresses and the gap between the developing and developed world grows, how the international community as a whole and individual countries respond to the continuing cross-border movement of people matters for the future. As realism claims, states are fiercely protective of their sovereignty and, therefore, of who can enter their territorial boundaries. However, liberalism can also help us understand the role of international institutions in getting states to cooperate to address migration, as well as the institutions that deal with refugees and returnees. Constructivism can account for the emergence of international norms to protect refugees and IDPs.

Health and Disease

The Global Health Picture

At almost every stage of life, people in developing countries are more susceptible to health problems than those in richer ones because poverty, malnutrition, and poor sanitation contribute to the spread of disease. One broad measure of general health, life expectancy, is now about 67.6 years for the world as a whole, but on average, people in developed regions can expect to live longer than those in poorer states (for example, in 2008 the U.S. life expectancy at birth was 78 years, while life expectancy in the Democratic Republic of Congo was 53 years).[83] In 2009, the country with the highest life expectancy was Macau (84.36 years), while Angola had the lowest life expectancy (38.2 years).[84] Approximately 99 percent of child and infant deaths occur in the developing states (with 51 percent occurring in Africa and 42 percent in Asia, in 2008). Countries with the highest number of child deaths in 2007 included India, Nigeria, Pakistan, China, and Uganda.[85] Moreover, the lifetime risk of a woman dying in pregnancy or childbirth in sub-Saharan Africa is substantially higher than in the developed world (1 in 22 of women in sub-Saharan Africa versus 1 in 6,000 for women in the developed world).[86]

The prevalence of infectious diseases, which kill more than 17 million people per year worldwide (more than 10 million of them children under five years old), remains a serious global health problem and illustrates the distressing health conditions in much of the developing world. Nearly 90 percent of all deaths of children in developing countries are the result of six conditions: diarrhea, malaria, measles, neonatal causes, pneumonia, and HIV/AIDS.[87] There is also a connection to malnutrition. The **World Health Organization (WHO)** asserts that "the combination of communicable diseases (CDs) and malnutrition is the most prevalent public health problem in the world today; together they are responsible for millions of preventable deaths worldwide each year."[88] WHO estimates that 2.5 million children died in 2008 from vaccine-preventable diseases such as diphtheria, tetanus, hepatitis, yellow fever and polio.[89] While 106 million babies were vaccinated—a record—in 2008, nearly 20 percent of babies born annually do not receive "the complete routine vaccinations scheduled for their first year of life."[90] The lack of vaccination is concentrated in only a few countries: In 2008 approximately 23.5 million babies worldwide were not vaccinated with three doses of the vaccine for diphtheria–tetanus–pertussis (DTP3), 70 percent of whom were in ten developing states (Chad, China, Democratic Republic of Congo, Ethiopia, India, Indonesia, Iraq, Nigeria, Pakistan, and Uganda).[91]

Many developing countries face especially serious problems with tropical diseases such as malaria, "a public health problem today in more than 90 countries, inhabited by...40% of the world's population."[92] Worldwide, approximately 1 million people die each year of malaria, with 85 percent of all cases found in Africa ("malaria was present in 108 countries and territories" in 2008).[93]

Cholera, a deadly disease primarily transmitted by contaminated water and food, also claims a significant number of victims in developing areas (of the 236,896 cases worldwide, Africa accounted for 95 percent of all recorded cases in 2006). The disease, with a sharp increase since 2004 in reported cases, continues to claim lives (for example, between late 2008 and mid-2009, more than 4,200 people died from cholera in Zimbabwe).[94] Besides malaria and cholera, other **neglected tropical diseases (NTDs),** such as leprosy and schistosomiasis, affect 1 billion people in the world. They are called neglected because they affect people primarily "in the poorest and most marginalized populations of the world," areas in which housing, sanitation, and water supplies are inadequate.[95]

Acquired Immune Deficiency Syndrome (AIDS) is one of the world's most serious health problems—"the leading cause of death in sub-Saharan Africa" with women accounting for the majority of people "living with HIV/AIDS in the region."[96] Caused by the human immunodeficiency virus (HIV), it is actually a complex interaction between impairment of the immune system and opportunistic infections such as pneumonia, tuberculosis, syphilis, and other conditions. It is transmitted through blood (via intravenous drug use or, rarely, transfusion of infected blood) and sexual contact and from pregnant women to the fetuses they carry. Although intravenous drug use is said to carry the highest risk of HIV transmission, most recorded cases of AIDS are the result of unprotected sexual contact. The global AIDS epidemic began in the early 1980s; by the end of 2008, an estimated 33.4 million people were living with HIV/AIDS worldwide (of whom 2.1 million were children 15 years or younger), and 2.7 million people were newly infected. More than 25 million have died since the disease was first identified two decades ago. Approximately 2 million people died from HIV/AIDS in 2008.[97]

▪ **World Health Organization (WHO)** A humanitarian organization established in 1948 under the ECOSOC umbrella of the UN. WHO aids in the development of national health administrations and provides advisory services.

▪ **Neglected tropical diseases (NTD)** Diseases that affect people primarily in the poorest areas of the world in which housing, sanitation, and water supplies are deficient.

▪ **Acquired Immune Deficiency Syndrome (AIDS)** Complex interaction between impairment of the immune system and opportunistic infections such as pneumonia, tuberculosis, syphilis, or other conditions. It is transmitted through blood (via intravenous drug use or, rarely, transfusion of infected blood) and sexual contact and from pregnant women to the fetuses they carry.

As with other diseases, patterns of HIV infection differ around the globe. Africa has been hit especially hard by this insidious disease. As noted earlier, AIDS is the leading cause of death in sub-Saharan Africa, with UN estimates concluding that 67 percent of the global total of AIDS cases have occurred in this region (which has 12 percent of the world's population), where more than 22.4 million people were infected with HIV/AIDS in 2008. AIDS has led to more than 14 million children orphaned. The epidemic has also affected life expectancy in southern Africa: In the five-year period from 1990 to 1995, life expectancy was 61 years; in the period of 2005 to 2010, life expectancy decreased to 52 years. Recovery of life expectancy to levels of the early 1990s is not likely to occur before 2045.[98] Moreover, it is estimated that "by 2020, the AIDS epidemic will have claimed one-fifth or more of the agricultural labor force in most southern African countries."[99]

The epidemic continues to rise in eastern Europe and central Asia, as a result of both sexual transmission and intravenous drug use, with 1.5 million people living with HIV in 2008 (in 2001 that figure was 900,000, thus a 66 percent increase in the seven years).[100] The prevalence of AIDS in Asia has remained relatively stable over the last decade, but the region accounts for the second largest numbers of people with HIV/AIDS (after sub-Saharan Africa). The concern for many revolves around the economic impact of the disease, where it is estimated that "an additional 6 million households" will go into poverty by 2015 if governments do not respond more vigorously.[101] In 2008, the UN estimated that 4.6 million people in Asia were living with HIV, with more than 300,000 new HIV infections that same year.[102] In response to the disease, antiretroviral therapy drugs have been developed, but global coverage is not high. Fewer than half of those who needed treatment in 2008 were able get treatment.[103] Yet although therapies involving multidrug "cocktails" and recent experimental vaccines for HIV offer hope, the prospects for curing AIDS or curbing its spread still appear discouraging, especially in some developing regions. Not only are the pharmaceuticals less available in developing countries (in large part because of developed states' protection of their pharmaceutical companies), but social practices and customs in many developing states also make fighting HIV/AIDS particularly challenging.

Responses to Global Health Problems

Most responses to international problems depend on the individual reactions of single states, many of which are constrained by domestic financial considerations. Global health problems are no exceptions. AIDS is only the most recent of many deadly diseases to which the world community has tried to formulate a unified response. The ways in which the international community has dealt with these problems, ranging from immunization to attempts at eradication, illustrate the difficulties in securing international cooperation, even on the deadliest issues.

Immunization is one of the most cost-effective weapons for disease prevention. Since its founding in 1948, WHO has done much to control diseases through immunization. In 1980, for example, WHO announced that it had reached its 1965 goal of eradicating smallpox, a malady that killed millions worldwide for centuries. WHO is also making progress on eradicating polio, leprosy, and tropical diseases such as filariasis.[104] In 1998, WHO's stated goal was to eradicate polio within fifteen years; in fact, by the middle of 2010 there were only four countries in which polio was still endemic (Afghanistan, India, Nigeria, and Pakistan). Yet the concern remains that countries can be reinfected with the disease. For example, in Africa in 2003–2004, polio spread from northern Nigeria to fourteen previously polio-free states, such as Saudi Arabia and Sudan. The resurgence of this disease resulted from the suspension of vaccinations in the region in mid-2003 when Muslim clerics asserted that the polio vaccine was a plot by countries of the West to make Muslim girls infertile and that the vaccine contained HIV. By July 2004 the vaccinations were started again, with 80 million children receiving the vaccine. As a result of the actions in northern Nigeria, today 20–30 percent of Nigerian children under five years old have not been vaccinated against polio.[105]

Global efforts have worked to reduce the number of polio cases. As was just noted, today there are only four countries worldwide that continue to be polio-endemic (Afghanistan, India, Nigeria, and Pakistan), although a few other states have had reinfections (such as Tajikistan, which had not had a case of polio since 1997).[106] In 1974 WHO created the Expanded Programme on Immunization (EPI), which has achieved great success broadening its immunization coverage of the world's children. When it was first launched, fewer than 5 percent of the world's children less than one year of age were vaccinated against the six vaccine-preventable diseases (polio, diphtheria, tuberculosis, pertussis [whooping cough], measles, and tetanus). Today, because of the efforts of the EPI, 79 percent of children under the age of one have been vaccinated against these six diseases.[107]

Other diseases, such as malaria and AIDS, have been more resistant to eradication. The malaria virus, for instance, has proven resistant to a variety of treatments. One observer believes that the statement of the second Report of the Malarial Commission of the League of Nations in 1927 is still substantially valid today: "The history of special antimalarial campaigns is chiefly a record of exaggerated expectations followed sooner or later by disappointment and the abandonment of work."[108] In 1955 WHO launched a campaign to eradicate malaria, and while the disease was eliminated in some countries, it remained prevalent in others. As a result, WHO abandoned its goal of eradicating malaria, focusing instead on efforts of malaria control, although recently there has been an increased interest in pursuing eradication of the disease.[109]

Because multidrug treatments are still prohibitively expensive for developing countries and no vaccine is yet available, WHO has concentrated on promoting awareness of the high-risk behaviors associated with HIV infection (namely, unprotected sex with multiple partners and shared use of needles among intravenous drug users). In 1987, WHO established the Global Program on AIDS, with goals that include the prevention of HIV transmission, care for HIV-infected

PHOTO 11.2   Afghan child being vaccinated against polio.

people, and unification of national and international efforts against AIDS. Together with its scientific advisory body, the Global Commission on AIDS, the program supports national AIDS-control plans, which use education to try to curb the spread of the disease. With such an enormous undertaking resting on the shoulders of the WHO, the UN linked ten cosponsors to address the AIDS epidemic (including the United Nations Children's Fund [UNICEF], United Nations Development Program [UNDP], UNFPA, World Food Program [WFP], UNHCR, WHO, and the World Bank) under the heading of **UNAIDS,** the UN's AIDS agency. In 1997, UNAIDS implemented a country-by-country reporting system to track HIV/AIDS, which led, in June 1998, to the first ever country-by-country analysis of the disease. In 2000, the work of UNAIDS contributed to the decision by the UN Security Council to declare AIDS a security issue—the first time a health issue was so declared by that body.[110]

As with most global issues, the problem of AIDS has exacerbated international tensions as often as it has contributed to cooperation. Many governments have reacted to the spread of AIDS in their countries by denying it is "their" problem. In the United States, AIDS was initially perceived as a Haitian and gay disease. In Europe, it was first considered a disease of African and Caribbean people, whereas in many Asian countries AIDS was commonly regarded as a disease primarily afflicting "foreigners." As a result of these perceptions, governments have enacted more stringent travel restrictions and screening procedures. The United States, for example, extended its

▪ **UNAIDS**
With ten UN cosponsors, this is the umbrella agency that is entrusted with responding to the global HIV/AIDS crisis. UNAIDS coordinates and implements reporting systems to track HIV/AIDS around the world.

law prohibiting entry to people with a "deadly, infectious or contagious disease" to cover HIV in 1987. In 1999, an HIV-infected Canadian tourist was denied entry into the United States based on this law. The law was finally overturned by President Obama in January 2010.[111] It may be hoped that the stigma associated with AIDS will fade over time, but the initial difficulties in securing international cooperation to fight this devastating disease show how governments remain reluctant to combat diseases that they perceive to be somebody else's problem.

One of the most challenging aspects of dealing with such diseases is the ability to respond to outbreaks. WHO has attempted to do so through its Department of Communicable Disease Surveillance and Response. Importantly, WHO recognizes that at the beginning of the twenty-first century, the world confronts new and recurring diseases. Although countries can use traditional means to contain outbreaks, such as securing their borders and stockpiling vaccines, new methods are also needed—early warning systems, "epidemic preparedness plans," and a network of rapid communications and sharing of information—to contain epidemics. As a result, the Global Alert and Response (GAR) was created at an international meeting the department convened in 2000.[112] The system in place was tested and appeared to work well in 2002 and 2003 when Severe Acute Respiratory Syndrome (SARS), a new disease, spread rapidly from its outbreak in China to twenty-eight countries, including Canada, Germany, India, South Africa, Vietnam, and the United States. The situation looked dire: Between November 2002 and April 2003, more than 5,000 people were infected; by May the numbers reached more than 8,000 (with more than 700 deaths by the end of May 2003).[113] Those countries hardest hit included China, Taiwan, and Singapore. To deal with the outbreak, China and Taiwan quarantined approximately 27,000 and 12,000 people, respectively, in their homes and hospitals.[114] However, it was at the international level that cooperation kicked in to stop the disease in its tracks. The WHO coordinated an enormous international effort, establishing a new $200 million fund to help Asian countries (those hardest hit) to fight the virus, focusing on surveillance and analysis.[115] The effort was successful beyond people's expectations, and by 2005 SARS seemed to have stopped its spread, its effects contained.

As the example of SARS ably demonstrates, globalization's impact on infectious diseases cannot be underestimated. With increased economic integration, fluidity of state borders, and people on the move (estimates show that more than 2 million people cross international borders each day), diseases are more readily able to spread across the globe. As a result, some states see it in their interest not to report outbreaks for fear of the impact on their economies, especially if their economies are dependent on tourism.[116] It is imperative, though, that states cooperate, whether through WHO's Global Outbreak Alert and Response Network (GOARN) or through organizations such as the U.S. Centers for Disease Control (CDC) or Doctors Without Borders (Medecins Sans Frontieres), to deal with infectious diseases as well as overall health of the world's population.[117]

What Would You Do?

Avian Flu

An outbreak of avian influenza in the world began in Southeast Asia in mid-2003. According to WHO, this outbreak is considered to be the "largest and most severe on record. Never before in the history of this disease have so many countries been simultaneously affected, resulting in the loss of so many birds."[i] At present, humans have become infected by contact with birds in several countries, including Cambodia, Hong Kong, Indonesia, Thailand, and Vietnam. The problem is that once the human-to-human transmission of the virus becomes efficient and sustained, the threat of a pandemic is quite real. Also, although vaccines are manufactured annually for seasonal influenza, at present, there is no effective vaccine available for a pandemic.[ii]

As president of a country in the Southeast Asian region, you have been informed by your health ministry that an outbreak of the disease has been discovered in a small village. No humans have contracted the disease as of yet. You recognize the threat of this infectious disease to your domestic poultry as well as your citizens (although given the number of birds infected worldwide relative to the very small number of humans, the threat of a pandemic is quite small). You also are aware that the possibility of a larger pandemic exists. In addition, you must take into account the effect on your country's tourist industry, which is a major part of your economy, should the outbreak become public. Hong Kong experienced a severe drop in tourism as a result of its bird flu outbreak. Do you inform WHO?

i. World Health Organization, "Avian Influenza Frequently Asked Questions," December 5, 2005, http://www.who.int/csr/disease/avian_influenza/avian_faqs/en/index.html.

ii. Ibid.

What Would You Do?

Conclusion

This chapter demonstrates that population issues (growth and decline in developing and developed states, aging vs. youth bulges), migration (refugees, economic migrants), and health and disease affect all states in some way or another in the international community as the world becomes increasingly interdependent by means of globalization. These very issues, however, are also related to fragmentation, for example, when civil war leads to migration (people fleeing from the fighting) to other states, causing conflict with the local population. The problem is that with an anarchic international system in which there is no world government to address these issues effectively, states are protective of their sovereignty and often decide to solve (or not) problems on their own, very much as a realist would note. Yet as liberals would assert, cooperation at the international level is sorely needed to meet the challenges arising from these issues that transcend state borders. As constructivists claim, what may be needed is a redefinition of state interests and identity that includes human security.

AT A GLANCE

Levels of Analysis and Paradigms in Review: Demographic Issues

	Realism	Liberalism	Constructivism
Individual	Former president of Turkmenistan, President Niyazov, not only failed to inform the international community when there was an outbreak of the plague in his country but also made it illegal to acknowledge in any way that the plague was killing his citizens. This not only demonstrated his tremendous power at home but also had ramifications for Turkmenistan's neighbors, who were not given adequate information about the spread of the spread of the epidemic, and for the world in general, which had no opportunity to mobilize against the disease.	President Obama decided to restore U.S. funding to UNFPA in support of family-planning programs worldwide, demonstrating his support for international-level efforts to promote thoughtful population growth. This was clearly an individual-level decision because it reversed the decision by President Bush when he came to office.	Concepts such as human security only gain purchase with use and acceptance. When Nobel laureate and president of Costa Rica Oscar Arias makes speeches about globalization and human security, he is among the many influential individual leaders who are bringing this concept into common use, creating a shared understanding, and implying, in a normative way, a set of policy requirements.
Domestic	Worried about the influx of immigrants and high unemployment rates, groups within Germany pressured the government to tighten its asylum laws in the mid-1990s. This shows the impact domestic-level factors, such as unemployment, can have on particular government policies.	In response to the U.S. government's decision to withhold funds to UNFPA, the U.S. interest group Americans for UNFPA started a campaign to solicit funds to support the efforts of the organization as well as to pressure the U.S. government to resume funding.	Changes in state identities and interests that promote policies of gender equality enable women to have an education, access to family planning, and employment as a means to reduce overall poverty and for a state to develop economically.
Systemic	States use asylum policies for their own national interests, for example, western European countries increasing their restrictions on eligible asylum claims.	States look to international organizations, such as the World Health Organization, to respond to the challenges from global diseases.	International organizations redefine security threats, as evidenced by the UN Security Council's declaration in 2000 that HIV/AIDS is a threat to international peace and security.

Discussion and Review Questions

1. How would realism, liberalism, and constructivism explain the human issues covered in this chapter? Which theory of international relations is more likely to examine how states redefine security interests by encompassing the issue of human security?
2. Why is an aging global population of concern to states and the international community?
3. What is the connection between women's health and economic development?
4. What is the connection between globalization and migration?
5. How is the HIV/AIDS epidemic an example of cooperation, conflict, globalization, and/or fragmentation?

Key Terms

Acquired Immune Deficiency Syndrome (AIDS) 448
Demographic transition 429
Internally displaced people 439

Neglected tropical diseases (NTD) 448
Refugees 439
Remittance income 439
Replacement level fertility 430
UNAIDS 451

United Nations High Commissioner for Refugees (UNHCR) 428
United Nations Population Fund (UNFPA) 433
World Health Organization (WHO) 448

CHAPTER **12**

Resource Issues

Following India's independence in 1947, the new government constructed dams to ensure access to water for irrigation and navigation. These huge projects, particularly the Ganges River dam (Farakka), significantly affected India's relations with its neighbors, particularly Bangladesh. For example, following Bangladesh's independence in 1971, in constructing the Ganges River dam, India took unilateral action to secure water access through the diversion of the Ganges River dry-season flow (January–May). India did not confer with Bangladesh about its plans.[1] Given that the river crosses international boundaries, Bangladesh argued that the river should be controlled jointly by both countries. Interim agreements between the two countries were concluded in subsequent years, and in the early 1990s Bangladesh brought the issue to the UN as a means of garnering international backing for its claims to the water. The two countries were finally able to reach agreement in the mid-1990s with the signing of the 1996 Ganges River Treaty (of thirty-year duration), but a permanent treaty has not been concluded. The 1996 treaty is a water-sharing treaty, but India, as the upstream state, still holds more power.[2] More than a decade since the treaty was concluded, Bangladesh claims that it still does not receive sufficient water during the five dry months.[3]

This matters because around 35 million Bangladeshis rely on this particular water basin for their living. India's actions have negatively affected fishing and navigation, and they have introduced "salt deposits into rich farming soil." These actions, therefore, have had a negative impact on industrial and agricultural production.[4] Moreover, with predictions of a doubling of Bangladesh's population by the year 2025, population pressures on agricultural land will be significant given the considerable degradation of existing cropland.[5] The result of the negative impact on the lives of the Bangladeshis dependent on this basin has been the migration of Muslim Bangladeshis to India in search of better living conditions. This migration has led to conflict with the local population.[6] As the numbers of migrants from Bangladesh to neighboring states in India are quite large, the impact has been large as well. Land distribution has changed, as have economic conditions. Moreover, the political power between ethnic and religious groups (Hindus in India and the Muslims from Bangladesh) has changed, leading to intergroup conflict. A case in point is the Lalung tribe in Assam, India. The Lalung tribe claims that the Muslim migrants from Bangladesh have stolen the best farmland. An acrimonious election for federal offices in Assam in 1983 led to an outbreak of violence. In one village, members of the Lalung tribe killed almost 1,700 Bengalis in "one five-hour rampage."[7]

Another example is the current crisis in Darfur, Sudan. As noted in Chapter 6, millions of people have been displaced and several hundred thousand killed by the actions of the Arab Janjaweed (supported by the government) against the black Sudanese. Climate change, deforestation, and degradation of agricultural land have aggravated the conflict. Arable land has become a desert, and average rainfall has declined 40 percent in the last two-and-a-half decades. According to the World Resources Institute, "fewer pastures, smaller harvests, and increased tension between the various ethnic, religious, and political groups" are the outcome. An increasing population has also contributed to environmental stress.[8]

The India–Bangladesh and Sudan examples clearly demonstrate the concerns about fragmentation and conflict erupting as a result of resource issues. Importantly, the cases typify topics covered in this chapter. Of particular significance as you read this chapter, recognize the interrelated aspect of the issues, both within this chapter and the previous one. Environmental issues such as deforestation, climate change, and pollution are impacted by population growth and movements. These environmental issues also affect people's health and well-being, as well as their access to safe water and the ability to produce food. States competing in a global economy seek economic growth, often at the expense of the environment through the burning of fossil fuels such as coal that emit carbon dioxide into the atmosphere, leading to global warming. Given that these resource issues often cross state boundaries, states may no longer be able to claim sovereignty, but rather need to cooperate with other states and international organizations to solve many of these problems. This chapter, therefore, provides an introduction to resource issues that are increasingly important in light of the process of globalization and increased interdependence: environment, water, food, and energy.

The Environment

Environmental issues vividly demonstrate the impact of globalization and global interdependence. The spread of radioactive fallout from an accident at a nuclear reactor at Chernobyl (then in the Soviet Union, now in Ukraine) in 1986, the plumes of smoke from burning oil fields in Kuwait in 1991, the deadly smog created by catastrophic forest fires in Indonesia in 1997 and 1998, and the deaths of thousands of fish and other river life as a result of cyanide-tainted water that spilled into the Danube River in Europe from a gold mine in 2000 give striking examples of how environmental disasters can quickly cross national boundaries.[9]

Less dramatic but equally damaging environmental problems, such as **deforestation, desertification,** and acid rain, have pronounced effects on regional ecosystems but may also have a global impact. Although the international scope of environmental hazards is now well known, individual states have historically addressed environmental concerns mainly through domestic laws and regulations. Only recently have states begun to use international forums to address global environmental issues and promote collective solutions. We examine some of these solutions after a brief survey of two key global environmental issues: deforestation and pollution.

Deforestation

Deforestation occurs when people cut down trees without planting enough new ones to replace them. The demand for timber exports is one cause of deforestation. However, the primary cause of deforestation has been the clearing of forests for human settlement, cattle pasture, and farmland. According to the **Food and Agriculture Organization (FAO),** during the 1980s approximately 53,000 square miles of tropical forests were destroyed annually. Moreover, during the 1990s, deforestation translated into an annual loss of 0.4 percent of forests globally (tropical and primary forests), with deforestation highest in Africa and South America. From 1990 to 2005, there was a decrease of 3 percent of total forest area (approximately 0.2 percent each year).[10] Today although deforestation is occurring at an alarming rate, there has been a slowdown in net loss of forest because of the planting of new forests (reforestation) and natural growth of forests.[11]

The traditional slash-and-burn technique for clearing land for crop rotation and subsistence farming can also contribute to deforestation and desertification, as well as a host of additional environmental concerns, including topsoil erosion and increased emissions of nitrous oxide, methane, and carbon dioxide.[12] For example, by 2000, because of Madagascar's growing population and increased need for food, approximately 80 percent of its native coastal forests had been destroyed through slash-and-burn techniques to clear the vegetation for rice farming. The resulting deforestation threatens plants and animals exclusive to Madagascar, including the lemur.[13]

▪ **Deforestation**
Conversion of forested land to other uses, such as cropland, shifting cultivation, or urban and industrial use.

▪ **Desertification**
The process by which an area becomes a desert. The rapid depletion of plant life and topsoil at desert boundaries and in semiarid regions, usually caused by a combination of drought and overexploitation by humans of grasses and other vegetation.

▪ **Food and Agriculture Organization (FAO)**
UN humanitarian organization under the ECOSOC umbrella.

PHOTO 12.1   **Slash-and-burn techniques have led to the deforestation of an estimated 80 percent of indigenous forests, as shown in this photo of Madagascar from November 8, 2007.**

War and other unnatural disasters can also result in deforestation. It has been estimated that between 1955 and 1975, the Vietnam War leveled 2.5 million acres of forest and rendered at least 5 million acres unproductive because of the U.S. use of the defoliant Agent Orange and other chemical pollutants.[14] The ethnic civil war between Hutus and Tutsis in Rwanda in 1994 had an impact on the destruction of forests (see Chapter 6 for a discussion of the Rwandan genocide). The actual fighting is not what led to deforestation, but the actions of the refugees fleeing the fighting to neighboring Democratic Republic of Congo (DRC) did. The need for wood for fuel and subsistence hunting seriously damaged Virunga National Park in the DRC. The stress on the park's resources was immense given that more than 750,000 refugees were living in crowded and unsanitary conditions in a camp. In the end, more than 20,000 acres of protected park land were deforested.[15]

Deforestation does not just mean the loss of trees. It also contributes to a loss of wildlife. More than 34,000 plant species and at least 700,000 animal species live in only 3.5 percent of the earth's remaining primary forests. Loss of the forest cover in these wooded areas, occupying a mere 0.2 percent of the earth's surface, could mean the extinction of almost 7 percent of all plant and animal species on land. It is difficult to know exactly how fast species are disappearing, but some approximate the disappearance of up to 137 species every day worldwide.[16]

Additionally, the burning of forests produces carbon dioxide, which many ecologists fear contributes to global warming (see Spotlight, "Is the Earth Getting Warmer?"). In fact, tropical deforestation emits 1.5 billion tons of carbon into the atmosphere each year. The burning of fossil fuels (coal, gas, and oil) releases approximately 6 billion metric tons per year. Thus, deforestation plays a notable role in the increased amount of carbon dioxide in the atmosphere.[17] In fact, deforestation is the second biggest source of carbon dioxide emissions after power generation.[18] Specifically, scientists have estimated that the carbon in trees in the Amazon rainforest is greater than ten years of greenhouse gases produced as a result of human activity. Thus, with the clearing of these forests, carbon is released into the atmosphere, contributing to the greenhouse effect and climate change.[19] Some studies suggest that halting deforestation by 2050 could "save the emission of 50 billion tons of carbon into the atmosphere."[20]

Given the role that forests play in maintaining a healthy environment that transcends state borders, it is imperative that the international community meet the challenge of preventing or reducing deforestation. Governments and NGOs together will need to work with local communities to preserve tropical forests and also promote policies that minimize the negative impact of human activities on forests and yet enable societies to develop economically.[21]

Pollution

Although deforestation has become an increasing global concern in recent years, most people traditionally associate environmental damage with industrial pollution. After all, urbanization and industrialization create such familiar and readily noticeable environmental ills as smog, acid rain, and elevated levels of carbon dioxide and **chlorofluorocarbons (CFCs)**, which deplete the ozone layer. This air pollution is glaringly evident in smog-blanketed cities all over the world, from Mexico City to Los Angeles to Warsaw to Bangkok. The six countries emitting the most carbon dioxide are China, the United States, Russia, India, Japan, and Germany. Moreover, 2006 statistics show that six of the eight members of the G-8 economic group are among the top ten states in CO_2 emissions.[22] Such pollution not only worsens the problems of global warming and the depletion of the ozone layer (which shields the earth from harmful ultraviolet radiation) but also creates health problems. The World Health Organization (WHO) estimates that 1.5 billion people living in urban areas suffer from levels of outdoor air pollution greater than the maximum recommended levels. The World Bank estimates that air pollution leads to the premature death of approximately 2 million people worldwide each year. The United Nations Environment Program notes that every year, approximately 2 million children under the age of five die from acute respiratory infections, which are exacerbated by indoor and outdoor air pollution. The global health costs of air pollution are staggering. For developed states, the health cost from air pollution is estimated to be near 2 percent of GDP. For developing states, the costs range from 5 percent to 20 percent of GDP.[23]

▪ **Greenhouse effect**
An increase in the earth's average temperature caused by the emission of greenhouse gases (especially carbon dioxide and methane) that trap and retain the sun's heat in the atmosphere.

▪ **UN Intergovernmental Panel on Climate Change (IPCC)**
Established by the World Meteorological Organization and UN Environment Program in 1988, the IPCC assesses "the scientific, technical, and socioeconomic information" to understand the risks and impacts posed by human-induced climate change.

▪ **Chlorofluorocarbons (CFCs)**
A primary agent of ozone depletion found mostly in aerosols and refrigerants. The 1987 Montréal Protocol called for the phasing out of these chemicals.

Is the Earth Getting Warmer?

A well-publicized and controversial global environmental concern is the emission of gases such as carbon dioxide (CO_2) and methane, which can trap heat in the earth's atmosphere. In the 1990s, industry, transportation, and other human activities emitted more than 6 billion metric tons of CO_2 into the atmosphere each year, and total emissions of CO_2 continue to rise (see Map 12.1). In 2008, 31.8 billion tons of CO_2 were emitted into the atmosphere.[i] The source of carbon dioxide that has attracted the greatest environmental concern is the burning of fossil fuels for energy. It is estimated that the concentration of carbon dioxide in the atmosphere has risen from 277 parts per million by volume (ppmv) in 1744 to 387.35 ppmv in 2009.[ii]

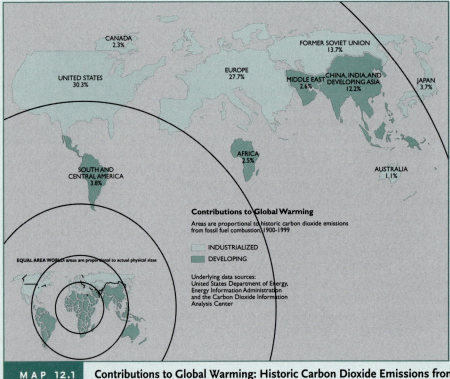

MAP 12.1   **Contributions to Global Warming: Historic Carbon Dioxide Emissions from Fossil Fuel Combustion, 1900–1999**

These statistics have many people worried. Scientists have argued that continued emission of greenhouse gases has increased the earth's average temperature, a phenomenon known as the **greenhouse effect.** Most climatologists agree that greenhouse gas emissions are probably responsible for at least part of a rise of about .74 degree Celsius, or 1.4 degree Fahrenheit, in the global average surface temperature since the late 1800s. The **Intergovernmental Panel on Climate Change (IPCC)** predicts that if production of greenhouse gases is not slowed, average world temperatures will rise by 1–3.5 degrees Celsius (about 1.8–6.3 degrees Fahrenheit) by 2100. (By way of comparison, the world has warmed by 5 to 9 degrees since the last Ice Age.) This may not sound like much, but it would be enough to cause persistent droughts in many areas, seriously affecting global food production, and could cause enough melting of the polar ice caps to raise the world's sea level by half a meter or more, causing serious flooding in low-lying areas. Moreover, there is increasing recognition that the affect of climate change will differ for men and women. Given that women do a large share of agricultural work, they are more vulnerable to natural disasters that are a result of weather changes. For example, if there's a drought or inconsistent rainfall, according to the United Nations Population Fund, women must "work harder to secure food, water and energy for their homes.... [T]his cycle of deprivation, poverty and inequality undermines the social capital needed to deal effectively with climate change."[iii]

There is evidence of recent global warming, evidence that is supported by climate scientists around the globe. The part of the Northern Hemisphere covered by snow has been shrinking, sea ice in the Arctic Ocean is receding toward the North Pole, expanses of the sea ice north of Greenland have thinned, and many glaciers in Alaska have also thinned. The Canadian and Alaskan permafrost has warmed by about 3.5 degrees since the 1960s. Land areas have warmed at a faster rate than the oceans. Global sea levels continue to rise at faster rates than in the past. Precipitation has increased in parts of North and South America, while precipitation declined in the Mediterranean, parts of southern Asia, and southern Africa.[iv] Thus, the effects of climate change are uneven; some areas have become warmer or drier, but others have become wetter or cooler. This trend is likely to continue in the future with continued CO_2 emissions in the atmosphere contributing to the warming of the earth's climate.

The decade from January 2000 to December 2009 was the warmest on record, further supporting the evidence that the earth's temperature continues to increase.[v] While there are a few experts who remain skeptical that a greenhouse effect even exists or, if it does, that it is as dangerous as most scientists and environmentalists contend, the vast majority of climate scientists agree that the earth is getting warmer and that much of the increase in the earth's temperature is a result of human activity. Because of climate change skeptics, persuading individuals to change their priorities and behavior and getting governments to agree on environmentally sustainable energy and industrial policies has been hard. But it's not impossible.

i. John Mulrow, "Climate Change Proceeds Down Worrisome Path," WorldWatch Institute, December 3, 2009, http://vitalsigns.worldwatch.org/vs-trend/climate-change-proceeds-down-worrisome-path; United States Department of Energy, Energy Information Administration, *International Energy Annual 1995* (Washington, DC: U.S. Department of Energy/EIA, 1996).

ii. World Resources Institute, EarthTrends Data Tables: Climate and Atmosphere, "Global Climate Trends 2005," 1, http://earthtrends.wri.org/text/climate-atmosphere/cli5_2005.pdf; CO2 Now, "What the World Needs to Watch: 392.39 ppm: Atmospheric CO2 for April 2010," April 2010, http://co2now.org.

iii. CO2 Now, "What the World Needs to Watch"; NASA, "2009: Second Warmest Year on Record; End of Warmest Decade," January 21, 2010, http://www.giss.nasa.gov/research/news/20100121; UNFPA, *State of World Population 2009: Overview*, 2009, 1, 4, http://www.unfpa.org/swp/2009/en/pdf/EN_SOWP09.overview.pdf.

iv. IPCC, "IPCC Fourth Assessment Report: Climate Change 2007: Synthesis Report," http://www.ipcc.ch/publications_and_data/ar4/syr/en/mains1.html; "Global Warming: Early Warning Signs—New Events" (2003), http://climatemap.org/newpoints.html.

v. Mulrow, "Climate Change Proceeds Down Worrisome Path."

Airborne pollutants can affect areas far from the cities and factories where they are emitted. For example, the burning of fossil fuels spews sulfur and nitrogen oxides into the air, which eventually fall back to earth in the form of acid rain. This combination of toxic chemicals and atmospheric moisture kills trees, erodes the surfaces of buildings, and acidifies bodies of water, making them inhospitable to the life therein and even creating a threat to safe drinking supplies. Tensions between the Canadian and U.S. governments over acid rain flare up periodically. The Canadian government insists that American industries, which produce most of the chemicals in acid rain that falls on both sides of the U.S.–Canadian border (the Canadian government estimates that around 50 percent of the sulphates come from the United States[24]), clean up their manufacturing processes. Attempts at doing so have run into political obstacles as companies ordered to reduce sulfur dioxide emissions contend that the increased costs would result in the elimination of many jobs. The two countries did manage to sign an agreement, the 1991 Canada–U.S. Air Quality Agreement. A similar problem from acid rain exists in northeast Asia, affecting China, Japan, South Korea, and Taiwan. Taiwan and Japan are feeling the affects of acid rain because of emissions from South Korean steel mills. South Korea, in turn, is experiencing acid rain from industrial emissions originating in China. As a result, these countries have created an international regime (see Chapter 2), an East Asian acid rain monitoring program to enhance regional cooperation on this issue.[25]

Efforts by the developed countries to get the issue of atmospheric pollution on the international agenda have not always been accepted by the developing countries, whose concern for preserving forests, wetlands, and the ozone layer pales in comparison to their desire to industrialize. Yet recent data show that the greenhouse gas emissions by the developing states are higher than emissions by the developed states as a result of the significant levels of emissions from China and India—the emerging economies. According to the U.S. Department of Energy's *International Energy Outlook 2010*, in 2007, emissions from developing (non-OECD) states was 17 percent greater than the developed (OECD) states. It is projected that by 2035 emissions from the non-OECD countries will double that of the OECD states.[26] Much of the rapid rise in pollution in developing countries is attributable to the fact that industries in poorer states tend to use dirtier fuels. China, for instance, relies on cheap, abundant, high-sulfur coal, which is among the most polluting energy sources known. The U.S. Energy Information Administration projects that China will be responsible for 26 percent of the world's total emissions by 2030.[27]

Development that produces more pollution will in the long run damage the global ecosystem, with potentially severe repercussions for international politics. For example, if significant changes in the climate were to occur, creating increased precipitation in some areas and desertification in others, the ability of many states to produce enough food for their people could be drastically reduced (see the discussion of food and hunger later in this chapter). In turn, this could cause huge population movements—in other words, environmental refugees (see Chapter 11 on refugees)—with potentially disruptive consequences, including internal and external conflicts.[28]

International Cooperation for Saving the Environment

International organizations began to focus their attention on environmental issues in the mid-twentieth century. The objectives of the Council of Europe (1949) included preservation of the environment and responsible uses of natural resources, goals the EU continues to advocate today. In 1949, the UN hosted the Scientific Conference on the Conservation and Utilization of Resources to discuss problems relating to natural resources. This was the first international forum convened to address the problem of resource conservation, although no major recommendations were issued.

During the late 1960s and early 1970s, the issue of the environment moved closer to the top of the UN's agenda. In 1968, the UN Economic and Social Council adopted an initiative calling for legislation to address the "human environment." The first result of this initiative was the Founex Report of 1971, which recognized the important relationship between development and the environment in the Third World and suggested that the poverty found in the developing world was directly related to environmental degradation. The 1972 Stockholm Conference helped to establish the UN Environmental Program, the main purpose of which was to promote international environmental cooperation. In 1974, the third UN

Convention on the Law of the Sea established a new law for protecting the marine environment. Overall, these international reports and conferences did much to raise awareness of environmental concerns, although very little progress was made in terms of finding practical solutions to the problems at hand.

International efforts in the 1980s and 1990s continued to link environmental concerns to issues of trade and economic development. Environmental programs sponsored by the United Nations, the World Bank, and other international organizations focused primarily on sustainable development—that is, strategies for increasing economic growth and raising standards of living in the developing world without exhausting natural resources or causing irreparable environmental damage.

By far, one of the most successful international environmental agreements is the 1987 **Montréal Protocol,** which required signatory states to phase out the use of CFCs (ozone-depleting chemicals) over a period of time and obligated them to prohibit importation of all products containing the offending chemicals. The protocol contained a loophole, however, that permitted developing countries to increase their per-capita use of CFCs, which could allow a 70 percent rise in CFC emissions by 2040.[29] The Protocol has been revised seven times (the last revision occurred in 1999), which helped address the problem, but CFC production remained a contentious issue between developed and developing states. Importantly, a 2006 study showed that the ozone layer was recovering and that the Protocol and its amendments contributed to that recovery, to the extent that by the middle of the twenty-first century the "global ozone layer could be restored to 1980 levels—the time that scientists first noticed the harmful effects human activities were having on atmospheric ozone."[30] In a further demonstration of the commitment by states to meet (or even beat) the scheduled deadlines for phasing out CFCs (and halon, another ozone-depleting chemical), by mid-2007 China, the largest producer of CFCs, closed down all but one of its plants, ahead of its 2010 deadline. As the UN Under-Secretary General and Executive Director of the UN Environment Program stated, "the Protocol is among the great success stories of recent years. This success underlines how, with political will, creative financing mechanisms, and the support of industry and NGOs, the international community can rise to the challenge of sustainable development."[31]

UN treaties such as the **UN Framework Convention on Climate Change (UNFCCC)** (signed in 1992 and reviewed in 1997 in Kyoto, Japan) and the Convention to Combat Desertification (signed in 1994) pointed the way toward increased international cooperation on environmental concerns. In 1997, a UN General Assembly special summit reviewed the progress made on the goals adopted at the first Earth Summit, held in Rio de Janeiro in 1992. Most delegates noted that although several conventions and treaties had been signed since the Rio Earth Summit, the overall progress on dealing with environmental problems was disappointing, in large part because of differences between the developed and developing states on concrete measures to address sustainable development. A decade after the first Earth Summit, the second Earth Summit was held in Johannesburg, South Africa, in 2002. The participating states reaffirmed their

▪ **Montréal Protocol**
Treaty signed in 1987 designed to phase out CFCs—chemicals that deplete the ozone layer.

▪ **UN Framework Convention on Climate Change (UNFCCC)**
An international treaty (entered into force in March 1994) that established a framework for international efforts to respond to the challenge from climate change.

▪ **Rio Earth Summit**
Meeting held in 1992 that led to treaties and conventions to deal with environmental problems and means to address sustainable development.

commitment to the idea of sustainable development but also recognized the challenges faced in terms of ending poverty, managing natural resources, and protecting the environment. At the 2002 Earth Summit, the states also acknowledged the impact of globalization on these challenges (namely, the uneven distribution of the benefits and costs of globalization).[32]

In response to the concerns about the global environment, the members of the G-8 have focused on the environment and climate change at their annual summits. At their 2007 summit, the leaders of the eight countries agreed that dealing with climate change is "one of the major challenges for mankind and it has the potential to seriously damage our natural environment and the global economy." The leaders of the EU, Canada, and Japan agreed to aim to reduce CO_2 emissions by half by 2050 (the United States and Russia did not). The leaders stressed the "shared responsibility" of all states that emit significant levels of CO_2, and thus the need to include large developing and emerging economies, namely, Brazil, China, India, Mexico, and South Africa, in achieving this goal.[33]

As a whole, these cooperative endeavors greatly increased awareness of these issues, but their attempts at practical problem solving have yielded mixed results. A typical example is the case of the 1997 **Kyoto Protocol,** which entered into force in February 2005. The Protocol called for more stringent limits on carbon emissions by industrialized countries (to reduce to 1990 levels by 2012); however, opposition by major emitters, most notably the United States (which is not party to the Protocol), will likely limit the eventual effectiveness of the Protocol, which is due to expire in 2012.[34] Parties to the Protocol, namely the EU states, have continued to pursue measures to reduce greenhouse gas emissions even without the participation of the United States, but the question remains about whether in the long term the momentum to continue to make significant reductions in greenhouse gas emissions can be sustained realistically after the Protocol's expiration.

Hopes for significant movement in addressing climate change, particularly in light of the impending expiration of the Kyoto Protocol, came with the UN Climate Change Conference in Copenhagen held in December 2009. At this summit of 193 states, leaders from both developing and developed countries met to discuss measures to reduce carbon emissions. (In the lead-up to the conference, the leaders of the major economies, both developed and developing, met in 2008 and 2009 to lay out national and international actions to reduce emissions.) The Copenhagen Accord, "for the first time, unite[d] the US, China and other major developing countries" to find a way to lower greenhouse gas emissions, including an annual fund of $100 billion by 2020 from developed countries for developing ones to help reduce emissions. The conference did not lead to any legally binding commitments by states to reduce their emissions, however, and "there is no global target for emissions reductions by 2050." While critics called the climate conference a failure, since no new treaty came out of the two-week-long conference, others noted the fact that countries came together and reiterated their commitments to reducing greenhouse gas emissions.[36]

▪ **Kyoto Protocol**
Treaty signed in 1997 that furthered the goals of the UN Framework Convention on Climate Change (1992) that places stringent limits on carbon emissions that cause the greenhouse affect; expires in 2012.

Some of the most effective efforts to preserve the environment have been carried out by NGOs through independent projects and through the pressure they apply on states and intergovernmental organizations. In the United States, one of the earliest environmental organizations, the American Forestry Association (founded in 1875), is still active in trying to preserve and manage natural resources. Another well-known environmental organization, the Sierra Club, was founded in 1892 to promote the conservation of public lands in the form of national parks. Following World War II and the recognition of the pollution resulting from industrialization and a perceived serious reduction in available natural resources, 1948 saw the creation of the International Union for the Protection of Nature, now the World Conservation Union. This organization consists of both governmental and nongovernmental actors and focuses on the use of science in working toward environmental goals, including the preservation of biodiversity, the creation of national parks, and the promotion of environmentally safe economic development. Other environmental NGOs emerged in the 1960s, including the World Wildlife Fund (now called the World Wide Fund for Nature, but still abbreviated WWF), which is concerned primarily with the conservation of biodiversity.[35]

Today, NGOs and other private groups are engaged in efforts to save all sorts of natural treasures. As a result of concerns about the future of the world's forests, environmentalists, foresters, loggers, and sociologists established the Forest Stewardship Council (FSC) in 1993. This NGO focuses on sustainable forestry. By setting forest management standards and a certification process, the FSC verifies whether logging companies have met the standards of sustainable forestry.[37] In addition to NGOs, many celebrities and corporations have campaigned for the environment. A recent example of celebrities bringing their fame to bear on environmental issues was the Live Earth concert on July 7, 2007. Partnered with the Alliance for Climate Protection (led by former U.S. Vice President Al Gore), the concert, held in eight venues around the world (Hamburg, Johannesburg, London, New Jersey, Rio de Janeiro, Shanghai, Sydney, and Tokyo), sought to raise awareness about climate change and its related impact on water scarcity, food shortages, and conflicts and promoted the idea that people should reduce their carbon emissions. Moreover, the concert organizers encouraged people to pressure governments and businesses to engage in practices that would reduce CO_2 emissions.[38] By using trade, rather than aid, to promote conservation of resources, these individuals and companies try to convince governments that the long-term economic benefits of environmental protection can exceed the short-run profits from environmentally destructive activities.

A Green and Pleasant Globe?

Many states and international organizations are convinced that economic incentives are the best way to address the problems of pollution and deforestation. Few incentives are great enough, however, to convince poorer countries to cease environmentally harmful development efforts (as realism would attest, many states see it in their national interest to develop at the expense of environmental damage), and a strategy of relying on the social consciousness of governments, private companies, and individuals is questionable at best. For these reasons, sustainable development is one of the most urgent items on the global economic and environmental agenda. At the same time, developed countries have a long way to go to put their own environmental houses in order, as shown by the problems with acid rain and carbon emissions. Despite the best of intentions, international environmental preservation efforts cannot succeed until both developed and developing countries adopt a long-term perspective in both global vision and local action. Efforts by the international community that include the major economies, such as the Copenhagen Summit, are steps in the right direction. This global vision and local action are also imperative for the next two issues that, besides a healthy environment, are vital for human life: water and food.

Water

Without water, life itself is impossible. A growing global population places strains on available fresh water supplies for industrial and agricultural use (which is 70 percent of all fresh water; in developing countries the rate is as high as 95 percent), as well as for basic household consumption. In the past seventy years, the world's population tripled but the demand for water grew sixfold.[39] An estimated 1.1 billion people lack clean and safe water, and approximately 2.5 billion live without adequate sanitation. By 2025, 3 billion people, or almost 40 percent of the world's population, will confront challenges in accessing fresh water, six times the number of people who had difficulty accessing fresh water in 2000. Nearly 80 percent of all cases of disease in developing countries have been linked to contaminated water. Approximately 2 million children, most under the age of five, die from water-related diseases, such as diarrhea, every year. For millions of women in the developing world, who spend many hours of their day getting water, access to safe water for food production is particularly vital.[40]

Water access is related to sanitation. For the world's poor people, getting access to water is one obstacle to overcome, but once that water is accessed, it also needs to be safe. According to the United Nations Development Program, nearly two in three people who do not have access to clean water live on less than $2 per day. One in three people live on less than $1 per day. In terms of sanitation, "more than 660 million people without sanitation live on less than $2 a day, and more than 385 million on less than $1 a day."[41] To get an even clearer picture of life for the world's poor one need only look at the data for Africa. Recent data (2007) show that 42 percent of those people living in rural areas had access to clean water. For the entire population, 63 percent did not have access to basic sanitation facilities.

What is disturbing about this number is that it is only a 5 percent decrease from the 68 percent that did not have access to such facilities in 1990.[42] The comparison of the developing world with the developed world makes this even more striking: 49 percent of people living in developing states have sanitation coverage. For the developed world sanitation coverage is double that number, at 98 percent.[43]

The price of water, which is increasing globally, is another factor in considering access and sanitation. Even in the developed world, the price of water has risen: Between 2002 and 2007, "municipal water rates have increased by an average of 27 percent in the United States, 32 percent in the United Kingdom, 45 percent in Australia, 50 percent in South Africa, and 58 percent in Canada." In the case of many developing countries, people do not have access to municipal water and therefore must buy water from private vendors. In some cities in Asia, "households forced to purchase water from a private vendor pay more than 10 times as much as middle-income families who are connected to the municipality's distribution system. The poorest households in Uganda spend 22 percent of their income on water, while those in El Salvador and Jamaica use more than 10 percent of their income to satisfy water needs."[44]

As discussed previously, climate change is a transboundary issue affecting all states. Climate change is also another area of concern as relates to water scarcity, particularly in the driest parts of the world. More than 2 billion people live in these regions, half of the world's poor people.[45] The impact of climate change in Africa, for example, is clear: "[B]etween 75 and 250 million people will be exposed to an increase in water stress. Without adequate preparation, the impact could be devastating on rural economies and the livelihood of the poor."[46] As noted in Chapter 11, with population growth occurring mostly in the developing world, states will have even more difficulty accessing water for their populations.

The connection between access to water and agricultural production of grain illustrates the dire situation for many countries in the world. If countries are no longer able to produce grain and then become grain importers, their relations with other states may be affected. At present, 26 percent of global grain imports are found in the water-stressed states in Africa, Asia, and the Middle East. With their populations growing, and thus the need for more grain to feed those populations, there will be an increased demand for grain from external sources. That could lead to states forming closer ties with states that are grain exporters to ensure an adequate supply of grain. Countries, such as those found in sub-Saharan Africa, without the financial resources to import grain will become more dependent on humanitarian aid to feed their people.[47]

All these factors—water access, sanitation, price of water, and climate change—are global issues, affecting different states differently. Not all states are water stressed, but many are. Those that are water stressed are likely to become more stressed as the temperature of the planet increases, making it difficult to grow food for their expanding populations. Moreover, without adequate access to water and sanitation, negative health effects are likely, affecting the ability of people to make a living and thereby hindering economic growth. As discussed next, water may provide the potential for intrastate and interstate conflict.

Water Scarcity and the Potential for Conflict

Given that water is a scarce resource, there is concern that conflicts resulting from competing claims for water are possible in the future. The past might or might not be an indication of the future. According to scholars, "the only recorded incident of outright war over water was 4,500 years ago between two Mesopotamian city-states, Lagash and Umma, in the region we now call southern Iraq." Interestingly, in the second half of the twentieth century there were nearly 2,000 interactions between states over water. Of these, only one-third led to conflict or violence. That means that two-thirds of these interactions were, therefore, cooperative. States have signed approximately 200 treaties, as well as joint scientific ventures. Thus, one could conclude that the possibility of a conflict over water would be small.[48]

Yet scholars caution that the past is not a good predictor of the future. Since the middle of the twentieth century, there has been a 58 percent decrease in the renewable supply of fresh water per person, but at the same time world population has grown tremendously (from 2.5 billion in 1950 to more than 6 billion today).[49]

Today there are 263 transboundary basins listed with the United Nations. This is in comparison to 214 in 1978. Of the 263 transboundary basins, about one-third are shared by two or more states, and nineteen basins are shared by five or more countries. Half of the world's population and half of the world's territory are found in these transboundary basins.[50] Given the number of transboundary basins, as well as the importance water plays in agriculture, industry, and overall health, access to water is likely to become an increasing source of conflict both within and between states. In fact, since 1950, 25 percent of "water-related interactions" were conflictual, primarily in the form of hostile words. However, in thirty-seven cases, conflict escalated to actions such as blowing up a dam or use of force.[51] Although water is not usually a direct cause of war, water has played a role in continued regional tensions (as well as impeded economic development). A recent example is the Tsang Po dam, which China wants to construct. The dam, however, affects water that China shares with India. In 2010, tensions between the two countries rose when China announced its intentions to build the dam. China claims that it needs the dam for electricity generation; India argues that the dam will reduce access to water, water it needs for its growing population.[52]

Within states, internal water stresses could potentially lead to violent protests as well as to migration to cities as farmers experience loss of access to irrigation water, thereby affecting their ability to earn a living. Migration to already crowded and stressed urban areas could fuel conflict. For example, in Pakistan farmers unable to produce food migrated to urban areas, leading to ethnic conflict.[53]

The mostly arid Middle East and northern Africa provide an example of a situation in which serious concerns over water supplies add to the potential for international conflict. This is the most water-scarce region on the planet (ten of the fifteen most water-scarce countries are in the Middle East), with 6.3 percent of the world's population but only approximately 1.4 percent of the world's renewable fresh water resources. Population growth puts significant pressure on gaining adequate access to water as countries need to grow crops for food to feed their populations, as well as sanitary and safe water for overall health of their populations. With a population growth of 2 percent per year (only sub-Saharan Africa has a higher population growth rate), inadequate rainfall, and boundaries of important water resources (rivers, lakes, aquifers, subterranean canals) shared by more than one state, some experts believe that the next war in the Middle East will be fought not for land, but for water.[54]

Consequently, states that control water have power over those that do not. For example, the upstream position of Turkey provides it with a lever of power in the Tigris-Euphrates basin. In 1987, Turkey imposed a water embargo on Syria over the latter's support for Kurdish terrorists in Turkey. In late 1989, Syria and Iraq were alarmed when the Turkish president announced that his country would temporarily block the flow of the Euphrates to fill Turkey's just-completed Ataturk dam, a mammoth project designed to turn the country into a food exporter.[55] Turkish "water pressure" is particularly feared by Syria, which has few water resources under its own control. In turn, Damascus has blocked World Bank funding for Turkey's $32 billion, thirteen-part Anatolia Project until Turkey signs a new agreement to share water, and in June 1996 Syria began massing armored units on its border with Turkey, declaring that the sharing of the water of the Euphrates was its "main quarrel" with Ankara.[56] Reluctant to relinquish its dominant status, in 1997 Turkey refused to sign a UN convention that "declared that international waterways should be divided reasonably and equitably, without causing unnecessary harm." In fact, Turkey remains committed to the Anatolia Project, despite objections expressed by its neighbors and social and environmental activists. Turkey's actions are consistent with realists' expectations about state behavior. Furthermore, the state increasingly appears to consider water a new and promising commodity. Indeed, in June 2002, Turkey and Israel closed an unprecedented deal in which Turkey agreed to provide Israel with 50 million cubic meters of fresh water annually for twenty years. Such agreements can only further antagonize those countries that live downstream from Turkey and depend on Ankara to let water through.[57]

International Responses to the Need for Water

In recent decades, the international community has responded to the concerns regarding this most valuable of resources. In 1977, the United Nations organized the first conference on water, requesting the formation of a worldwide inventory of availability of fresh water. The 1980s were declared the "International Drinking Water and Sanitation Decade," and in the early 1990s, the UN sponsored another conference, concluding "that water 'should be recognized as an economic good.'" In the 2000 UN Millennium Declaration, the organization stated as one of its goals "to halve, by the year 2015…the proportion of people who are unable to reach, or to afford, safe drinking water." Recognizing the decreased supply of safe water around the world, the United Nations declared 2003 the "International

Year of Fresh water" and, in a conference held in Japan, sought to determine the most effective ways to increase access to safe water, including privatization of water utilities and increased investment in technologies that would convert sea water into fresh water (a process known as desalination).[58] At the fifty-eighth session of the UN General Assembly, held in December 2003, the UN decided to proclaim 2005–2015 as the "International Decade for Action, 'Water for Life,' 2005–2015," starting with World Water Day, March 22, 2005 (World Water Day is every March 22). During this decade, the UN's various agencies (such as FAO, WHO, and the World Bank) will focus on providing a coordinated response to improving access to water for the world's population that desperately needs it. Access to a limited water supply is a challenge for the global community about how to allocate resources given that, by 2015, 100 million more people will need access to water each year (274,000 people per day).[59]

Several NGOs have supported and worked with international governmental organizations such as the UN and its various agencies in promoting water security for the world's population. For example, the WWF established a Freshwater Program with the goal of meeting several targets, including encouraging governments and industry alike to implement "policies and techniques that conserve life in rivers and reduce poverty for dependent communities."[60] Water Partners International, a not-for-profit organization, works with local communities in eight countries (including Bangladesh, India, and Kenya) to provide people in developing states safe drinking water and sanitation through the establishment of sustainable water projects.[61]

Water's Future

The past indicates that states have cooperated over water, for example, through the signing of treaties to share water. However, water stress seems to be becoming a zero-sum game, both within and between states, as realists would assert. As access to water becomes increasingly viewed as one's gain and the other's loss, conflict is increasingly likely. How individual states and the international community respond will determine whether water security is improved. Cooperating on developing new technology, planting of drought-resistant plants, and the use of drip irrigation (which significantly reduces the amount of water needed) are all possible means for improving access to water in an increasingly water-scarce and water-stressed world.[62]

Food

Feeding the World

As discussed previously, population increases impact access to safe water, and access to water is necessary for food. Thus there is the challenge of adequately feeding the more than 6 billion people that inhabit the planet. At the United

Nations 1996 World Food Summit, the goal was set to reduce the number of hungry people in the world by half by 2015 (to 425 million from the baseline of 850 million; at the 2000 UN Millennium Summit, the goal became to halve the proportion of hungry people in the world by 2015 rather than the number of people).[63] Yet more than a decade after the World Food Summit was held, there are more hungry people in the developing world than was the case in 1996. The Food and Agriculture Organization (FAO) estimates that, as of 2009, there are more than a billion hungry people in the world. By far the majority of hungry people live in the developing world, but hunger also affects people in the developed world, with approximately 15 million people who are considered undernourished in these countries.[64] Contrary to widespread belief, the problem is not a worldwide shortage of food but, rather, the difficulty in getting food to those who need it most, before hunger, malnutrition, and ultimately death result. Although world population has increased by 70 percent in the last three decades, "world agriculture produces 17 percent more calories per person.... This is enough food to provide every person worldwide with at least 2,720 kilocalories a day."[65] Distribution generally differs from developed to developing countries, and although developed countries are easily able to feed their populations, many developing states are not.

Daily per-capita caloric intake (i.e., how many calories each person, on average, consumes every day) serves as a rough indicator of the adequacy of a state's food supply. Although the global per-capita availability of food has increased despite population growth, great disparities exist between developed and developing regions in terms of daily caloric intake. In 2006, people living in high-income countries had a daily per-capita caloric intake of 3,348, while the numbers for middle-income countries and low-income countries were 3,000 and 2,608, respectively.[66]

These figures do not consider quality of diet; many people in developing countries have inadequate supplies of protein and other nutritional necessities. It will come as no surprise that residents of the richer countries consume diets vastly superior in quantity and quality from those of people in the developing ones. As developing countries become richer, their citizens typically want to eat more meat, leading some agricultural experts to question whether the world could produce enough meat if developing states' appetites demanded developed states' levels of consumption. For example, world meat consumption per capita in 2002 was 39.7 kilograms per person, but the difference between developed and developing regions shows the disparity: For the developed states the rate was 80.0 kilograms per person, and for developing states it was 28.9 kilograms per person. The World Resources Institute estimates that in the twenty-five-year period between 1995 and 2020, 85 percent of increased demand for "meat products and livestock feed grains" will be found in the developing world.[67]

Despite these differences in average consumption, food supplies in the developing world as a whole are adequate—few people will starve on an average of 2,000 calories per day. Nevertheless, the grave consequences of inadequate nutrition are readily apparent. As noted earlier, it is currently estimated that more than 1 billion people suffer from chronic malnutrition and that each year hundreds of thousands die from hunger-related diseases.[68] Chronic hunger leads to susceptibility to disease. People are weak and therefore have a reduced ability to work, leading to a cycle of hunger and poverty that affects countries' economies. Poor nutrition knows no bounds—undernourishment, overnourishment (eating too much), and an unbalanced diet lacking in nutrients are prevalent in developing states. Obesity and related diseases, such as heart disease and diabetes, are now problems for developing states, placing further social and economic burdens on these societies.[69]

Additionally, to understand a society's health, one need only look at the nutrition of women and children. Women comprise more than 60 percent of the chronically hungry people in the world.[70] Malnutrition increases a woman's risk of complications and death during pregnancy and childbirth. Malnutrition also affects children: The annual deaths of approximately 6 million children under the age of five are related to malnutrition. This malnutrition is linked to the poor nutrition of the mothers during their pregnancy. Further, children face deficiencies in essential nutrients such as vitamin A. Annually, approximately half a million children become partially or totally blind because they are vitamin A deficient. These deficiencies are preventable through supplements and fortified foods.[71]

Why are people suffering in the midst of such plenty? The answer is that although the quantity of food produced is generally adequate, its distribution is not. The major reason for chronic shortages of food is poverty—the lack of sufficient income to buy food or means to grow it. Soil exhaustion, depletion of water supplies, and other environmental problems can also lead to persistent shortfalls in food production. Flooding, drought, warfare, and misguided economic programs are the major causes of acute food shortages and famine. Areas prone to drought are especially vulnerable to drastic temporary shortages of food. If drought-stricken regions have poorly developed transportation systems and lack the cash to buy food from nearby sources, the result can be mass starvation. Given that droughts occur frequently and intensely in poor states, people are then unable to meet their basic needs, particularly access to food. In the ten-year period from 1988 to 1998 alone, the UN's **World Food Programme (WFP)** responded to 102 emergencies related to drought, more than 50 percent higher than food crises caused by floods (flooding ranks second behind drought as a serious natural disaster to which the WFP responds).[72]

The drought in Lesotho, Africa, in 2007, one of the worst in three decades, is a case in point. The drought led to a poor harvest, and, combined with extreme poverty, increasing cereal prices, and HIV/AIDS (with approximately 30 percent of the population infected), the population was in dire need of access to food. Here, an estimated 400,000 people (one-fifth of the population) faced food shortages. As a result, they need food assistance.[73]

In other cases, hunger results from man-made disasters, such as political chaos and intrastate warfare (the WFP estimates that food crises resulting from

▪ **World Food Programme (WFP)** UN agency whose mandate is to combat world hunger, provide emergency relief in response to both man-made and natural disasters, and promote development projects.

| PHOTO 12.2 | Despite food production adequate to meet the world population's needs, laissez-faire means of distributing food and political and military interruptions allow starvation to persist. This Ethiopian woman and child suffered from a famine in 1991; famine struck Ethiopia again in the 2000s. |

human causes rose from 15 percent to 35 percent since 1992—more than double).[74] For example, in 1991 and 1992, Somalia suffered a famine that threatened more than 4 million people with starvation. The cause was not only a severe drought but also the factional fighting and violent disputes over farmland that followed the collapse of the Somali government. Consequently, less food was grown, and much of the food that had been produced was hoarded by people afraid that they would not have enough to eat in the future and those eager to get a higher price for their foodstuffs in the short term. A tragic irony for Somalia was that there was food in the markets, but the prices were prohibitive for most people. Local strongmen and armed gangs took what they needed by force, but children, the elderly, and those who could not steal succumbed to hunger. At the start of 1993, Somalia relied on foreign aid for its food supply, and, despite the efforts of U.S. forces and the UN, more than one-sixth of the country's population still faced starvation. By the time the last of the U.S. troops departed in March 1994, leaving a weaker UN presence, these conditions had improved but the country still suffered from a serious economic and health crisis. More recently, the conflict in Darfur, Sudan, in which more than 1 million people have fled their homes, has led to a major food crisis, particularly given that agriculture is the foundation of the country's economy (approximately 87 percent of Sudan's population depends on agriculture for food security as well as their source of income). In 2010 alone, the WFP expected to feed nearly 11 million people in Sudan who were affected by conflict, drought, or both (a number twice what the WFP fed in 2009).[75]

International Food Aid and Famine Relief Efforts

Efforts to get food to countries that cannot feed themselves have been relatively successful, even though donating governments sometimes resort to using food as an inducement to try to get recipient countries to change their policies. Many states have acted independently to redress the balance between food production and consumption. The United States, rich in agricultural resources, has been active in fighting hunger and starvation on its own, as well as through contributions to UN relief agencies and other international relief efforts. However, the United States has also tried to use food as a political tool, most obviously in the grain embargo directed against the Soviet Union in 1980 as punishment for its invasion of Afghanistan the year before. This attempt to use food for political purposes failed, chiefly because the Soviet Union was able to purchase grain from other countries such as Canada and Argentina, and the embargo was lifted in 1981 after fifteen months (much to the relief of American farmers, who had profited from the sale of grain to the USSR throughout the Cold War). An embargo on trade with Iraq instituted during the 1991 Gulf War, intended to convince the regime to fully dismantle its capabilities to develop weapons of mass destruction, had discouraging results because the ruling elite found ways to treat itself to an extravagant lifestyle while the masses suffered. This was most clearly revealed following the U.S. invasion of Iraq in early 2003 and the numerous palaces that Saddam Hussein was able to build despite more than ten years of sanctions.

International organizations have taken a number of approaches to alleviate the problems of hunger and malnutrition. Several NGOs such as Oxfam (Britain's largest overseas charity) and the United Support of Artists for Africa (best known for its recording of the song "We Are the World" in 1985) concentrate on short-term relief of acute food shortages. Intergovernmental organizations, such as the UN's Food and Agriculture Organization (FAO), work toward long-term developmental solutions to problems of food production and distribution, providing technical and financial assistance for agricultural projects in developing countries. For example, as a result of the food crisis in Sudan, the FAO has donated seeds for families to grow vegetables for themselves and for the market. In addition, the agency has implemented projects that include crop and livestock production. The World Food Programme helps provide food in emergencies but also measures to prevent hunger in the long term. The WFP provides food for approximately 100 million people in 70 or more countries. In 2008, the UN Secretary-General established the Task Force on Global Food Security Crisis, as a result of the increased food prices that year, which threatened to derail the efforts to reduce hunger in the world. The Task Force includes the World Bank, IMF, WTO, and other UN agencies involved in the area of hunger and food (such as the FAO and WFP). The Task Force recognizes the link between climate change and food security, and its work is supported by governments, including the G-8 (which focused on the issue of global food security at its summit in 2009).[76]

Although all are well intentioned, some famine relief and agricultural development efforts generate a great deal of controversy. The UN's relief effort in Somalia, for example, was widely criticized for failing to create the necessary infrastructure for food distribution, primarily because of its difficulties in persuading Somalia's warlords to cooperate. Other famine relief efforts have been criticized for their shortsighted solutions. In Rwanda, for example, a high proportion of food aid intended for refugees went directly into the hands of corrupt officials and even suspected perpetrators of genocide. Often, because debt-ridden developing countries do not have adequate export earnings to pay for food imports, they are encouraged by international organizations to increase domestic food production. Bringing more land under cultivation, however, often entails clearing ecologically valuable forests for farming and ranching. The use of traditional farming and ranching methods on these lands leads to further deforestation or gradually turns arable lands into desert, thus paradoxically leaving countries more vulnerable to drought and famine. The ecological balance of the Brazilian Amazon, for example, has been upset by clear-cutting and the introduction of agricultural techniques to farm the land. Such land is unable to sustain itself for food growing over time, leaving the country more vulnerable than ever in the long term, with even less usable land.

World capabilities for food production continue to increase, and both governments and private donors are usually quick to support famine relief. However, because the world's population continues to expand, the longer that states and international organizations wait to adopt solutions, the more urgent the problem becomes. Both short- and long-term solutions to world hunger are relatively straightforward, but each has its costs. In the short term, the best solution to the food and hunger problem is to improve distribution networks and the type of aid given. Developed countries, which produce more than enough food to feed themselves and their less developed neighbors, usually prefer to donate surplus food (bulky, difficult to transport, and quick to spoil) instead of money (easy to transport and not perishable, but often subject to theft by corrupt officials or speculators). At the same time, free distribution of food aid to famine-ravaged areas undercuts the efforts of local farmers to increase production and improve long-term food security.[77] In the long term, economic development is the best solution to hunger and malnutrition, but economic development must proceed in such a way as to minimize environmental costs. Especially in developing countries, plans for sustainable agriculture must take soil exhaustion, renewable supplies of water, potential harm of clearing forest lands for cropland, and other environmental factors into account to ensure a bountiful, reliable, and affordable food supply for future generations. In the future, a global food crisis seems unlikely, but the world may still have to learn how to eat within its means.

Energy

As populations grow and economies industrialize, the world's available supplies of nonrenewable energy and natural resources become increasingly scarce. International forums such as the 1992 and 2002 Earth Summits have sought, with varying degrees of success, to promote widespread commitment to sustainable economic development. In the absence of an international agency to enforce accords that deal with energy use, states do not face many incentives to use resources in a manner that takes into account the needs of other countries and future generations. In this way, states are proving the realist argument that pursuing a state's national interest trumps international cooperation. The following section examines the various energy sources available that may cause more disputes, and therefore conflict and fragmentation, in the future.

The Need for Energy

Societies need energy to survive just as human beings do. In a sense, the course of technological progress is the story of the discovery, use, and conservation of new sources of energy. All societies consume energy in some form; before the Industrial Revolution, demand for wood fuel was a major reason for deforestation on every continent (as it still is today in many developing countries). As states attain higher levels of economic and technological development, they "graduate" to dependence on different sources of energy—from animal power to wood to coal to oil to nuclear power, and so on. Although a significant amount of the energy used by the developed world comes from nuclear fission and **hydroelectricity** (electricity generated by water power in dams), the main sources of energy for developed and developing countries alike are fossil fuels.

World energy consumption continues to increase each year. At the global level, there is a projected 57 percent increase in the period 2004 to 2030.[78] Energy consumption has increased in the industrialized countries in the last few decades, in large part because of "increased travel, larger homes with

▪ **Hydroelectricity**
Electricity generated by water power in dams, a frequently touted alternate energy source.

more appliances," and increased consumer spending.[79] The close relationship between economic growth and growth in consumption of energy resources means that much of the increased demand for energy resources in recent years comes from the developing countries. Importantly, the projected demand will be greatest in the states outside the Organization for Economic Cooperation and Development (OECD), particularly China.[80] Although the 1973 **Organization of the Petroleum Exporting Countries (OPEC)** oil crisis and the 1990 Persian Gulf War reinforced the importance of securing energy supplies in the developed world, economic growth in the developing world poses the possibility of a new struggle over supplies, especially among those countries that rely heavily on imports to meet their energy requirements. China, for example, recognizes the environmental dangers from continued fossil fuel consumption and recently focused on pursuing renewable energy sources to reduce its carbon dioxide emissions. In late 2009, in advance of the Copenhagen Summit, China gave actual targets in its intention to reduce its "carbon intensity" by 40–45 percent, in comparison to its 2005 levels, by 2020 (carbon intensity refers to "the amount of carbon dioxide emitted for each unit of GDP"). Yet at the same time, because its main source of energy is coal, which is highly polluting but which drives its economic growth, China has been reluctant to sign any international agreements that limit its ability to expand its consumption. China did, however, indicate its willingness to support the Copenhagen Accord (discussed earlier in the chapter).[81]

Oil's Critical Role

Since the invention of the automobile, oil has been the industrialized world's most important source of energy. However, the greater the reliance on oil to fuel the developed countries' economic (and automotive) engines, the greater the danger to their economies these countries face if the oil stops flowing. This danger was illustrated by the long lines at gas stations following the energy crises of 1973 and 1979. After the OPEC oil embargo of 1973, the OECD countries progressively reduced their dependence on oil. For example, in 1996, although total world demand for oil increased to record levels (more than 71 million barrels per day), it accounted for only 40 percent of total primary energy supplies, compared with 1973 when oil represented almost 55 percent of global energy demand. This decreased reliance on petroleum, combined with the glut on the world market, has lessened OPEC's power over the price of global oil supplies since the early 1980s. However, given that world oil demand is expected to increase from 86 million barrels per day in 2007 to 92.1 million barrels per day in 2020 to 103.7 million barrels per day in 2025 to 110.6 million barrels per day in 2035, OPEC's power may rise yet again. It is estimated that OPEC oil production will increase to 60.1 million barrels per day in 2025, more than twice the 30.8 million barrels per day produced in 2006.[82]

In general, demand for oil rises and falls with total economic activity. The recession of the early 1990s led to decreased demand for oil in North America

▪ **Organization of the Petroleum Exporting Countries (OPEC)** An intergovernmental cartel of oil-exporting countries that has the goal of raising collectively the price of crude oil on the world market.

and Europe (by 2 percent in 1990–1991 in North America). As soon as economic activity picked up, demand for oil did as well (by 1.5 percent in 1992 in North America). In eastern Europe and the former Soviet Union, by contrast, the convulsions caused by the collapse of the Soviet Union and the communist system led to a precipitous decline in oil use in the early and mid-1990s, but at the start of the new century demand for oil in these countries is increasing, and Russia is poised to play a role as a significant energy power. In fact, in 2008 Russia was the world's second largest oil producer (Saudi Arabia ranked first). In the developing countries, as noted earlier, demand for oil is rising with economic growth, especially in Asia; consequently, the demand for oil in the developing states is increasing much faster than in the industrialized countries.[83] OECD demand for oil increased from 49.80 million barrels per day (mb/d) in 2005 to 49.16 million barrels per day by 2007. Given the economic recession that followed, OECD demand dipped to 47.55 mb/d in 2008 and dropped even further to 45.36 mb/d in 2009. In 2010, with the global economy slowly coming out of the recession, OECD demand began to rise again. For non-OECD countries, the demand for oil increased from 34.24 mb/d in 2005 and continued to rise to 36.98 mb/d in 2007. Unlike the OECD countries, the demand from non-OECD countries continued to increase, despite the global economic recession. For these countries, their demand in 2008 stood at 38.20 mb/d and 38.66 mb/d in 2009. In 2009, world oil demand stood at 84.02 mb/d, with U.S. demand accounting for 18.6 mb/d of that world total and China at 8.22 mb/d (the world demand had decreased from 86.14 mb/d in 2007 and 85.75 mb/d in 2008).[84] World oil consumption is expected to grow by 1.6 mb/d in 2011. China's demand for oil is expected to increase 5.6 percent each year, reaching 10 mb/d by 2012. This will ensure China's spot as the second largest oil consumer (the United States is the largest; see Tables 12.1 and 12.2).[85]

TABLE 12.1	Top World Oil Producers, 2008	
Rank	*Country*	*Production (thousands of barrels/day)*
1	Saudi Arabia	10,782
2	Russia	9,790
3	United States	8,514
4	Iran	4,174
5	China	3,973
6	Canada	3,350
7	Mexico	3,186
8	United Arab Emirates	3,046
9	Kuwait	2,741
10	Venezuela	2,643
11	Norway	2,466
12	Brazil	2,402
13	Iraq	2,385
14	Algeria	2,180
15	Nigeria	2,169

Source: EIA: International Energy Data and Analysis, Country Energy Profiles (2008).
http://tonto.eia.doe.gov/country/index.cfm.

TABLE 12.2	Top World Oil Consumers, 2008	
Rank	*Country*	*Consumption (thousands of barrels/day)*
1	United States	19,498
2	China	7,831
3	Japan	4,785
4	India	2,962
5	Russia	2,916
6	Germany	2,569
7	Brazil	2,485
8	Saudi Arabia	2,376
9	Canada	2,261
10	South Korea	2,175
11	Mexico	2,128
12	France	1,986
13	Iran	1,741
14	United Kingdom	1,710
15	Italy	1,639

Source: EIA: International Energy Data and Analysis, Country Energy Profiles (2008).
http://tonto.eia.doe.gov/country/index.cfm.

Energy Crises and Global Responses

Since the early 1970s there have been three major oil crises—in 1973, 1979, and 1980—and a relatively minor crisis in 1990. The first involved a reduction of approximately 7 percent in world oil supplies following the decision of the Arab members of OPEC to impose embargoes on the United States and the Netherlands for their support of Israel during the 1973 Arab–Israeli war. The response of oil-consuming countries to the embargo was uncoordinated and competitive. Many countries sought to position themselves favorably by imposing restrictions on petroleum exports and by issuing pro-Arab statements in hopes of winning preferential treatment for their oil companies. This cacophony of national responses contributed to the quadrupling of official prices (from $3 to almost $12 per barrel) between the beginning of October 1973 and January 1974.[86]

Concerned with the effects of the embargo on its economy, the United States led an initiative to establish the **International Energy Agency (IEA) in 1974**—an example of international cooperation given the political conflicts over oil. The initial objectives of this agency were to develop an emergency system for sharing oil, establish an information system to monitor the oil market, facilitate long-term measures to reduce net demand for oil on world markets, and set up multinational energy research and development activities. The IEA program is designed to protect its member states from the economic difficulties that would result if their access to oil was significantly reduced. For example, if any member of the IEA suffers an oil supply shortfall exceeding 7 percent, it can ask the IEA secretariat to put into effect the emergency sharing system.[87]

The IEA was put to its first test in 1979, when the Iranian revolution resulted in a virtual cessation of Iranian oil exports. Oil-consuming states responded by scrambling to ensure supplies (usually by stockpiling) for themselves at whatever price had to be paid, and, as a result, prices doubled, even though production outmatched consumption for 1979 as a whole. When Sweden, suffering from an oil supply shortfall of more than 7 percent, requested that the emergency sharing system be activated in the winter of 1979, the IEA's governing board declined the request. In this case the IEA did not come through when it was needed.[88]

The third oil crisis resulted from the onset of the Iran–Iraq War in September 1980. This time, prices did not rise precipitously. In July 1981, they were only 5 percent higher than prewar levels. Oil prices remained stable, mostly because of weakness in demand and the Saudis' willingness to increase production, but also as a result of the IEA's efforts to persuade oil companies to sell oil inventories rather than stockpile them.[89]

Although no major oil shortage developed from the UN embargo on Iraq following its invasion of Kuwait in 1990, it did remove 4 million to 4.3 million barrels per day from the world's supply of crude oil. Initial uncertainties surrounding the invasion and fears of previous crises caused a temporary "spike" in oil prices. This complicated economic problems in eastern Europe and developing countries and damaged aviation and automobile industries in the industrialized

■ **International Energy Agency (IEA)** Created in 1974 to develop an emergency system for sharing oil, establish an information system to monitor the oil market, facilitate long-term measures to reduce net demand for oil on world markets, and set up multinational energy research and development activities.

nations. However, a more serious crisis was avoided by Saudi Arabia's willingness to increase production, reduced worldwide demand, and the IEA countries' decision to release oil from their strategic stocks.[90]

After the collapse of the Soviet Union, Western oil companies scrambled to develop the vast energy resources of Russia, Azerbaijan, and the Central Asian states, which many companies welcomed as a guarantee against future oil crises. For example, a British Petroleum-led consortium of oil companies constructed a pipeline in the territory of the former Soviet Union. In July 2006, the pipeline running from Azerbaijan, Georgia, and Turkey loaded its first tanker. By March 2009, the pipeline was carrying 1.2 million barrels per day (from the initial amount of 400,000 barrels per day).[91] Yet political disputes, instability in the region, an uncertain economic climate in many former Soviet countries, and the need to build long pipelines to transport petroleum for export have slowed the arrival of post-Soviet oil on the world market.

Coal and Natural Gas

Although petroleum is the energy resource that receives the most attention, other fossil fuels are also extremely important. The biggest share of electricity generation globally (60 percent of global supply) comes from coal and natural gas. Natural gas, for example, is used for cooking and heating of homes and offices. OECD states account for slightly more than 50 percent of total natural gas consumption, with non-OECD European and Eurasian states accounting for 25 percent. Importantly, nearly 75 percent of the world's natural gas reserves are located in Eurasia and the Middle East.[92] Yet because natural gas is difficult to transport by sea and can be expensive to transport over long distances by land, internationally traded gas still accounts for only 30 percent of total global gas consumption.[93] However, because of its many uses, relatively low emissions, and low cost when available nearby, natural gas will remain a significant source of energy. According to the U.S. Department of Energy, total world demand for natural gas is estimated to increase 1.9 percent annually between 2004 and 2030 as a result of demand for electricity (as "the world's fastest-growing energy source for electricity generation," it therefore is a significant issue in global energy needs).[94]

Another primary energy source is coal, especially for generating electricity (two-thirds of worldwide consumption of coal is used for electricity).[95] In 2006, coal contributed 42 percent of electricity generation worldwide (by far the largest energy source for electricity in comparison to other sources such as nuclear power, natural gas, and oil). Coal's contribution to electricity generation worldwide is expected to rise in 2030 to 43 percent.[96] Global coal consumption, which has grown steadily but slowly since the late 1980s, is expected to continue (with a projected annual increase of 1.9 percent between 2006 and 2015 and an annual increase of 1.6 percent between 2015 and 2030). Of particular importance is that in the developing world, coal will remain a dominant energy source. Projections from the Energy Information Administration estimate that, because of increased use of coal in non-OECD states, 94 percent of global coal consumption will occur in those states from 2006 to 2030. In particular, non-OECD Asian states, namely China and India, account for the significant percentage of increased global coal consumption in the future.[97]

As with other fossil fuels, coal has an environmental impact. Coal combustion leads to the emissions of carbon dioxide, sulfur dioxide, and nitrogen oxides, which, as discussed previously, can have harmful effects on the environment through climate change and acid rain, for example. In 2006 (the most recent data available as of this writing), China and the United States were the top two coal consumers worldwide as well as the leading emitters of carbon dioxide. In the same year, coal accounted for 42 percent of global carbon dioxide emissions (petroleum accounted for 39 percent, while natural gas accounted for 19 percent of CO_2 emissions). Importantly, coal surpassed petroleum as the largest source of carbon dioxide emissions and is projected to stay at the top spot in 2030 (coal will account for 45 percent of emissions; petroleum, for 35 percent).[98]

At the same time, the recognition of coal's environmental impact (as well as the possibility of other sources of electricity such as natural gas) has led some states, particularly in western Europe, to reduce consumption. Coal consumption in this region declined by 39 percent in the 1990s and is projected to decline an additional 23 percent by 2020.[99] Both Japan and OECD countries in Europe

PHOTO 12.3   Wind turbines in Copenhagen, Denmark.

are projected to continue to decrease their coal consumption as a result of factors such as declining or slowing population growth and use of natural gas and nuclear power for electricity.[100] However, given the energy demands for economic growth, particularly for countries such as China and India, it might be some time before the environmental effects of the energy source will lead other states to look to other sources of energy.

Renewable Energy

Not all sources of energy pollute the environment as much as fossil fuels do, but more environmentally friendly alternative energy sources remain a small part of global energy consumption. **Renewable energy** sources (such as hydro, solar, wind, geothermal, combustible renewables, and biomass for conversion into biofuels) contributes slightly more than 10 percent of the total energy supply in 2004, following fossil fuels and natural gas (around 6 percent of energy comes from nuclear energy). Renewable energy makes its greatest contribution in electricity generation (it is the third largest contributor, after coal and natural gas), predominantly in the form of hydroelectric power, which accounted for nearly 18 percent of the world total in 2007 and is projected to increase to 23 percent in 2035 as a result of increased consumption of coal and natural gas for electricity.[101]

Every alternative to fossil fuels has drawbacks, however. For example, nuclear power is relatively clean and safe but nuclear plants are expensive to build, and the possibility of spectacular accidents such as those that occurred at Three Mile Island in Pennsylvania in 1979 and Chernobyl in 1986 makes many people nervous about reliance on nuclear energy. Solar and wind power are unreliable in many areas. Some people find the wind turbines an eyesore and have campaigned against their installation, and, although their cost is steadily decreasing, they are still too expensive to compete on price with fossil fuels. Hydroelectric power is available only near major rivers and has significant environmental side effects, such as killing aquatic wildlife, reducing water quality, and inundating land under their reservoirs. Although environmentally friendly, the cost to produce electricity through the use of geothermal power plants is more expensive than traditional sources of energy. Concerns about biofuels—namely, the use of crops for energy rather than food, especially in light of the number of hungry people in the world today—also make this source of energy problematic.[102]

Almost all energy sources, apart from fossil fuels, are prohibitively expensive for developing countries, making coal and oil the most affordable energy options. The industrialized world will invest in fossil fuels in these countries, develop the infrastructure, and so on, in ways they will not do for other energy sources. Indeed, despite efforts to make the world more reliant on renewable energy, fossil-based fuels will continue as the dominant energy source and are projected to account for 83 percent of primary energy supplies in 2030 because of factors such as continuing growth in OECD transport demand, the lack

▪ **Renewable energy**
Environmentally friendly alternative energy sources such as hydro, solar, and wind power.

of substitution possibilities in other sectors, and rapid economic growth in the developing countries.[103]

In the long run, states will have to learn to do more with less energy to sustain economic growth without dangerously depleting world energy resources and causing further damage to the environment (one can think of the oil spill in the Gulf of Mexico in 2010 following an explosion on an oil rig—the worst oil spill in U.S. history—and the effects on the Louisiana coastline). In the short term, however, states have no choice but to use all means to conserve and safeguard their supplies of energy.[104]

Conclusion

Pressing global resource issues are the source of both cooperation and conflict among states. All states have common interests in each of the issue areas discussed in this chapter; all countries want access to energy sources to enable their economies to develop in a globalized world, as well as access to clean water, clean air, and enough food. At the same time, interests between and within states can conflict sharply.

What Would You Do?

Economic Growth Versus the Environment

You are the leader of a developing country that has economic growth occurring at a rapid pace. To be able to join the ranks of the industrialized and developed world, your economy relies on large quantities of coal for your industries. Your country does not have the resources to invest in environmentally cleaner energy sources if it is to continue on its current economic growth trajectory. At the same time, you recognize that coal consumption leads to carbon dioxide emissions, a significant source of global warming and pollution of the environment. The dilemma you face is whether to pursue environmentally sound policies (including signing international agreements agreeing to cap CO_2 emissions) or to prioritize economic development to catch up with the developed world.

What Would You Do?

Downstream countries are dependent on upstream states for access to water. If an upstream state unilaterally constructs a dam, the downstream state is then dependent for its water source. This can lead to tension and conflict between states, as shown by India and Bangladesh and their competition over the Ganges River. Within countries, pressures on infrastructure increase as more people migrate from rural to urban areas—adequate housing, sanitation, and so forth. Such migration can lead to conflicts (fragmentation) within states over scarce resources.

Countries attempting to address these resource issues have objectives that are simultaneously complementary and competing. Countries, however, have no global police force to call on when tensions emerge. Instead, they must work out agreements among themselves to enforce rules and strive for fairness in their transactions. The growing urgency of the problems discussed in this chapter makes it imperative for the international community to continue its coordinated efforts to tackle the related problems of environmental protection and resource conservation.

Many specific issues appear to place developed and developing countries in opposing camps. Rich countries tend to support restrictions on the use of coal and the preservation of tropical rainforests, for example, whereas many developing countries regard coal use for energy and clearing rainforests for farmland as economic necessities. In part, these differences suggest that although world politics in the second half of the twentieth century was dominated by the conflict between the democratic West and the communist East, global affairs now may see increasing contentiousness between the developed and developing states. Conflict may not be limited to this divide, however, because there are as many opposing interests and perspectives on global resource issues within both industrialized and developing states as between them.

Conflict can also arise as those states that control resources (Turkey and water, Russia and natural gas, Iran and oil, etc.) use that control as leverage in their political relationships (see Chapter 9). There will therefore be potential not only for contention over access to what can be perceived as zero-sum resources, but also for the deliberate wielding of resources as a form of economic power with both security and political ramifications. Both kinds of resource conflicts are completely consistent with predictions based on the realist paradigm.

Despite (or because of) this conflict potential, developed and developing countries alike are increasingly coming to the realization that collaborative efforts will be necessary and unavoidable to control problems that cross national and regional boundaries. This is, of course, completely consistent with what the liberal worldview would anticipate.

In the final analysis, there is only one world, and it appears to be shrinking with the rapid pace of globalization. More people, faster transportation, new technologies, and heightened awareness of transnational problems all promise to make interdependence a defining characteristic of world politics. However, interdependence does not guarantee cooperation. Leaders and citizens will be faced with difficult decisions as states are drawn closer together and interact more frequently (and on more levels) than previous generations would have thought possible, or even desirable.

It is far too early to tell whether such globalization will make world politics more or less conflictual and lead to increased fragmentation. Constructivists would argue that states' domestic perceptions of globalization—and, more specifically, of the availability of resources—will in large part determine their international behavior on this issue. If the nascent cooperative structures prove successful, they could lead to enhanced cooperation and a belief in the benefits of coordinated solutions; if the cooperative structures are undermined by predatory states or appear to give some states unfair advantages over others, then the pattern of behavior that emerges could be more conflictual.

What is abundantly clear, however, is that successful resolution of global resource issues requires states to recognize their responsibilities toward their neighbors. To deal successfully with the problems that confront them all, the

AT A GLANCE

Levels of Analysis and Paradigms in Review: Resource Issues

	Realism	*Liberalism*	*Constructivism*
Individual	Leaders faced with the tension between economic growth and environmental damage may choose not to sign international agreements that would constrain their state's economic growth. An example would be President George W. Bush's decision not to submit the Kyoto Protocol to the U.S. Senate for ratification.	At a G-8 Summit in July 2007, the leaders of the G-8 countries agreed to cooperate to address climate change while also promoting economic development. Specifically, the leaders of the EU, Canada, and Japan agreed to reduce carbon dioxide emissions by half by 2050.	Former U.S. Vice President Al Gore heads an organization, the Alliance for Climate Protection, that works with other organizations to promote awareness of the human impact on climate change. His goal is to redefine national and international interests such that protecting the environment is a global priority.
Domestic	Conflicts between ethnic groups may erupt within states as groups compete for land and resources. An example is the conflict between black Sudanese and Arab Janjaweed in Darfur, Sudan, which is further impacted by climate change, deforestation, and degradation of agricultural land.	Domestic actors initiate policies to protect the environment as a way of pressuring the government to act as well. For example, California's legislature passed the Global Warming Solutions Act in 2006, which requires a reduction of emissions to 1990 levels by 2020. In this way, the state of California hopes to pressure the federal government to take similar policy measures.	States' domestic perceptions of globalization, including the availability of resources, will in large part determine their international behavior on the issue of the environment. For example, at the UN Global Compact Leaders Summit in July 2007, executives of 153 businesses around the world called on states to work together and agree on legislation for climate market mechanisms (such as a stable price for carbon) after the Kyoto Protocol expires in 2012. These companies committed themselves to engaging in business practices that would reduce their carbon dioxide emissions and increase energy efficiency.

(continued)

AT A GLANCE	Continued	

	Realism	*Liberalism*	*Constructivism*
Systemic	Upstream states hold power over downstream states. Actions to prevent water access to the downstream states may lead to tensions and even conflict, as the tensions between India and Bangladesh over the Ganges River demonstrate.	States recognize that to control problems that cross national and regional boundaries, they will need to cooperate, as demonstrated by the Montréal Protocol phasing out CFCs.	The 1992 Rio Earth Summit advanced a new agenda linking protection of the environment to sustainable development. Prior to this, a UN conference in 1972 had focused on the challenge of environmental deterioration. This demonstrated the role that an international organization at the systemic level can play in changing existing norms.

countries of an increasingly interdependent world must develop and practice a code of global citizenship. In 1623 English poet John Donne described interdependence in the language of the seventeenth century: "No man is an island, entire of itself; every man is a piece of the continent, a part of the main." The international community would do well to recall his other words: "Any man's death diminishes me, for I am involved in mankind; and therefore never send to know for whom the bell tolls; it tolls for thee."

Discussion and Review Questions

1. Which theoretical paradigm suggests that states view economic development to be more important than environmental damage?
2. What are the major environmental issues facing the international system? How do environmental issues demonstrate the impact of globalization?
3. How can water scarcity lead to interstate and intrastate conflict?
4. What measures can the international community as a whole, and individual states, take to address global energy supply of both nonrenewable and renewable sources?
5. Discuss the application of realism, liberalism, and constructivism evident in resource issues. Which theory best explains state and international responses to these issues?

Key Terms

Chlorofluorocarbons 461
Deforestation 459
Desertification 459
Food and Agriculture
    Organization (FAO) 459
Greenhouse effect 461
Hydroelectricity 479
International Energy
    Agency (IEA) 483

Kyoto Protocol 467
Montréal Protocol 466
Organization of
    the Petroleum
    Exporting Countries
    (OPEC) 480
Renewable energy 486
Rio Earth Summit 466

UN Framework
    Convention on Climate
    Change (UNFCCC) 466
UN Intergovernmental
    Panel on Climate
    Change (IPCC) 461
World Food Programme
    (WFP) 475

CHAPTER **13**

Global Governance: International Law and Organizations

There is no central authority to determine how states should act toward one another and to enforce rules for such interactions unilaterally. Not surprisingly, as realism would assert, in this environment states often follow the principles of "kill or be killed" and "do unto others before they can do unto you," and the result has been frequent violent conflict and war.

Throughout history, many people have been profoundly disturbed by this state of affairs, and it is easy to understand why. The death, destruction, and suffering caused by war over the centuries are powerful arguments for making the international system less anarchic. From the seventeenth century onward, systematic efforts have been made to establish some form of authority in the international system in the hope that doing so might facilitate peace and cooperation among states (as liberal institutionalists would proffer). International law and organizations are manifestations of this hope, as mechanisms of global governance, for a more cooperative and peaceful world, particularly in an era of increasing globalization as well as fragmentation.

Global governance, thus, can be understood as "governance for a world without world government." To solve various global problems in a cooperative manner

■ **Global governance**
In a world without a world government, international law and institutions serve as mechanisms to address issues that transcend state borders, thereby fostering cooperation for mutually beneficial outcomes.

at a global level, rules (such as laws and norms) and organizations (both formal and informal) have been established.[1] The last few centuries have witnessed the development of an "idea of an international community bound together by shared values, benefits, and responsibilities and common rules and procedures."[2] Ideas about global governance, particularly "universal norms and international law," comprise the social identities of various actors in the international arena (such as state leaders and political activists) and subsequently "guide their behavior when they interact."[3] Constructivists would assert that the fact that states understand themselves to be members of an international community illustrates the changing nature of states' social identities and interests beyond that of narrow self-interests. Yet realists caution that as long as the international system remains anarchic and states are the dominant actors, global governance, which underlies international law and organizations, will be unsuccessful in constraining and determining state behavior.[4] States will thus, for example, follow international law only if it suits their national interests.

Consequently, this chapter explores these two manifestations of global governance and is divided into two main sections: international law and international organizations. In the section on international law, the chapter defines international law and provides an overview of how it is established and an assessment of how effective it is in the absence of a global authority to ensure compliance. Special attention is given to global conventions on human rights, which are among the most worthwhile and admirable components of international law; they are also, however, the most frequently violated and difficult to enforce. A second example of international law covered briefly in this chapter is war and aggression. Following this, the chapter turns to international organizations (IOs), of which there are two kinds: **intergovernmental (IGO)** and **nongovernmental (NGO) organizations.** IGOs are those comprised of states, and the chapter focuses on those that have attempted to replace international anarchy with systems of collective security and those that concentrate on global economic issues. The most recent of the organizations focusing on collective security is the United Nations (UN), whose structure, function, successes, and failures are all discussed in detail. Following a discussion of the UN, the Bretton Woods economic institutions are examined (see also Chapters 9 and 10 for a discussion of economic issues). Finally, the chapter looks at how NGOs attempt to exert varying degrees of influence on international politics.

▪ **Intergovernmental organizations (IGOs)** Groups of states or governments created through treaties and organized for a common purpose. Examples include OPEC, OECD, and NATO.

▪ **Nongovernmental organizations (NGOs)** Groups not directly related to governments but that are organized to take an active part in international affairs. Examples include religious orders, humanitarian organizations, and terrorist groups.

International Law

International law, also referred to as the law of nations, may be defined as "a body of rules which binds states and other agents in world politics in their relations with one another."[5] International law has evolved in tandem with the nation-state system, from the Peace of Westphalia to the present. It conforms to the decentralized nature of the international system and differs from domestic law in several ways. First, the law of nations reflects the lack of an international sovereign, or a single institution possessing a monopoly on coercive force. Because the international system lacks such a central authority, international law can be enforced only through reciprocity (doing unto other states as you would have them do unto you), individual or collective sanctions (such as freezing assets or imposing trade embargoes), or, when all else fails, reprisals (retaliation or response in kind).

Second, international law differs from domestic law in that there is no global legislature, or lawmaking body, to set down laws for all states. As will be discussed later, international law is an agglomeration of norms, treaties, conventions, accords, agreements, and resolutions rather than a comprehensive body of laws developed by a single organization. We are familiar with most of these, among the best known of which are the Geneva Conventions, the Universal Declaration of Human Rights, the Treaty on the Non-Proliferation of Nuclear Weapons, the Law of the Sea, and the UN Charter. These are not guided by a single constitution as are, for example, U.S. laws. Instead, they are specialized responses to perceived needs in the international system.

The third difference between domestic and international law is that in the international system there is no universal judiciary, nor is there an established, legitimate means of enforcement. Although there are international courts, such as the World Court and the International Criminal Court, not all states acknowledge their authority, and neither has credible means of compelling obedience. International law is, therefore, ultimately based on consent—states must accept its provisions, explicitly or implicitly, to be bound by them.[6] The array of issues addressed by international law is diverse and wide ranging. These areas include, but are not limited to, rules regarding human rights, warfare and aggression, the law of the sea, outer space, the environment, and international trade. Before looking at how international law attempts to promote cooperative solutions to these problems, it is necessary to examine the origins of international law and ask why states obey at all in a largely anarchic world.

Sources of International Law

Without a world legislature, who puts international law "on the books"? There are two primary sources of international law: **treaties** and **customary practices.** Essentially, signing a treaty constitutes explicit consent to be bound by international law, whereas customary practices establish international law through implied consent. In addition to treaties and customary practices, the writings of legal scholars, rulings of courts such as the International Court of Justice, and decisions of international organizations such as the UN help to refine, enrich, and expand on international law.

Customary Practices

International custom, or customary practices, refers to established and consistent practices of states in international relations. The notion of custom as a source

▪ **Treaties**
Documents similar to written contracts in that they impose obligations only on the parties that sign them. Also known as charters, pacts, conventions, or covenants, they are some of the main sources of international law.

▪ **Customary practices**
International customs represent the established and consistent practice of states in international relations; one of the sources of international law.

The First International Lawyer

Dutch jurist Hugo Grotius (1583–1645) is considered the "father" of international law. Grotius began life as a very gifted child—he wrote poetry in Latin at age eight and enrolled at Leiden University at eleven. Grotius gained firsthand experience in what would now be called human rights law when he was sentenced to life imprisonment for his political activities in 1618. He escaped to Paris in 1621, however, hidden in a box of books. In Paris, during the calamitous Thirty Years' War, he published *De Jure Belli ac Pacis (On the Law of War and Peace)*, an ambitious study of the rules of conduct applying to nations. This work publicized many of the emerging practices of customary law, especially attempts to humanize the conduct of war.

In his further writings, Grotius also formulated the legal basis for the principle of national sovereignty, which would later be codified in the Peace of Westphalia. When not devoting his energy to legal scholarship, he wrote works on history, linguistics, and theology as well as a prodigious amount of poetry. He served as the Swedish ambassador to France from 1634 until his death in a shipwreck in 1645, three years before the treaty ending the Thirty Years' War incorporated into its terms many of the concepts he developed. Although he achieved little fame during his lifetime, many of the ideas he espoused became the guiding principles of the Concert of Europe and the United Nations.

of law has its origins in the ancient Roman concept of *jus gentium*, the "law of the tribes," the common features Roman jurists identified among the subject peoples of their empire. Later, when states' adherence to unwritten rules of conduct or multilateral declarations became commonplace and widespread—that is to say, customary—they were regarded as binding on all states, even those that never expressly consented to them. The most prominent aspects of customary international law include **diplomatic immunity** and many provisions of human rights law, including the prohibition of slavery (later codified in the 1926 Slavery Convention), genocide (codified in the 1948 Genocide Convention), racial discrimination, and torture.

The concept of diplomatic immunity illustrates how international law develops from customary practice. For centuries in Europe, diplomats representing foreign states were accorded freedom of movement without fear of harassment from the governments with whom they were sent to negotiate. UN Resolution 43/167 and the 1961 Vienna Convention on Diplomatic Relations codified what

■ **Diplomatic immunity**
Freedom from arrest and prosecution for accredited diplomats.

had, by the nineteenth century, become the practice of diplomatic immunity, or extending freedom from arrest and prosecution to accredited diplomats. This practice has become crucial to the stability of interstate relations, as negotiators must be able to conduct diplomatic business without worrying about being harassed or arrested on trumped-up charges.

States violating this custom usually receive immediate international condemnation and political sanctions, as Iran did in 1979 when U.S. embassy personnel were kidnapped and held hostage. Controversy over this custom arises when embassy personnel fail to adhere to the provision of the 1961 Vienna Convention, which states that diplomats must abide by the laws of the host country. The inability of host countries to prosecute protected diplomats accused of serious crimes raises the question of how far the protection afforded by this custom should extend. If a foreign diplomat is suspected of committing an offense, all a state may do according to customary law is declare that individual *persona non grata* (an "unwelcome person") and expel him or her. To curb abuse of this practice, it is customary for the home country of the expelled diplomats to make a similar declaration regarding an equal number of the other country's envoys and order them out as well. (An interesting case occurred in the late 1990s when a diplomat serving in the Georgian Embassy in Washington, DC, was convicted in a U.S. court of involuntary murder as a result of a high-speed crash that killed an American teenager. In an unusual move, the Georgian government waived his diplomatic immunity and allowed the case to be prosecuted in the United States rather than having the diplomat recalled back to Georgia. Gueorgui Makharadze served several years in a U.S. federal prison before being sent back to Georgia to serve out the remainder of his sentence.[7]) In a recent case in June 2009, Britain and Iran expelled each other's diplomats. Iran expelled two British diplomats first, claiming that they were engaged in "activities incompatible with their status." The Iranian government did not clarify what these "activities" were, but most times, it usually refers to spying. Britain's response was to expel some Iranian diplomats in turn.[8]

Treaties

Also known as charters, pacts, conventions, or covenants, treaties represent the second main source of international law. Forming a large part of modern international law, treaties are similar to written contracts in that they impose obligations only on the parties that sign them. However, if the provisions of a particular treaty become customary practice, it can be argued that it has become a general law binding on all states. International law takes treaties very seriously; in practice it is assumed that agreements must be kept (*pacta sunt servanda*) and performed in good faith (*bona fide*). Also, a state's domestic laws cannot exempt it from compliance with international laws and often must be amended to comply with international agreements.

Some treaties become part of international law in a process quite similar to that of domestic legislation. UN conventions, for instance, become law in a three-stage process. Delegates from a member state must sign the treaty, the state's

As can be seen from this 1971 cartoon, the Indian–Pakistani conflict has become a perennial international problem.

national legislature must then ratify it, and domestic legislation must finally be enacted to bring the state into compliance. Article 18 of the 1969 Convention on the Law of Treaties stipulates that a state that has signed a treaty subject to ratification must refrain from acts that would defeat the object and purpose of the treaty.

Not all treaties are enacted through the United Nations, of course. Some are bilateral, or agreed on by two countries. Unless it later entered into that agreement between those two countries, a third country would not be bound by its provisions. For example, when the United States and the Soviet Union signed the bilateral START arms reduction agreement in 1991, it was binding only on these two countries. Problems arose when the Soviet Union broke up at the end of the same year, leaving four Soviet successor states with nuclear weapons deployed on their territory—Russia, Ukraine, Belarus, and Kazakhstan. Russia, the USSR's legal successor, was automatically bound by the treaty, but separate agreements, including offers of economic aid to defray the costs of transferring weapons to Russia, had to be concluded to bring the others into compliance.

As the volume of international transactions increases through the growth of global trade and communications, treaty making has tended to become multilateral, or conducted among more than two parties at the same time. Many multilateral treaties are now hammered out in common forums, such as special conferences (like the 1992 UN Conference on Environment and Development, or the Earth Summit), or in IGOs like the UN or the Organization of American States (OAS).

There is an accelerating trend toward multilateral treaty making, as global issues such as population growth, environmental degradation, resource depletion, and migration come to dominate the attention of governments (see Chapters 11 and 12). Treaty negotiations can strengthen customary practices by creating new organizational venues to disseminate information and foster international cooperation, thereby enhancing global governance. Overall, it appears that the trend toward globalization, interdependence, and greater cooperation among states will become more pronounced as global issues continue to dominate domestic agendas.

Violation and Compliance

Considering that there is no world legislature to make international law and no global authority to enforce it, it comes as no surprise that many states regularly flout international law when it runs counter to their national interests. In 1984, for instance, the government of Nicaragua (then ruled by the Soviet-backed Sandinista regime) won a unanimous decision from the International Court of Justice supporting its contention that the U.S. government's support of anti-Sandinista Contra rebels and mining of Nicaraguan harbors violated international law. However, the United States simply ignored the ruling. When Nicaragua took its claim to the UN Security Council, the United States vetoed its consideration.[9] Such flagrant disregard for international law reinforces the widespread notion that it rarely works.

As with domestic law, violations regularly make the headlines, whereas adherence to the law is much more common—and therefore does not make news. In fact, a wide variety of actors, including governments, private companies, and individuals, adhere to international law on a regular basis. For example, freedom of the seas is observed as a customary principle of international law. Thousands of ships with millions of dollars' worth of goods sail to hundreds of ports every day, unassaulted by pirates of other governments. Kidnapping or abuse of embassy personnel by host country governments is rare. Although international law may not always work as well as it is intended, it works much better than is often realized. This demonstrates the increasing trend toward global governance.

Today, most governments justify what they do in terms of international law, even when their actions are questionable. For instance, the United States argued that international law permitted the use of force to justify its invasion of Iraq in 2003. In speeches made in 2002, President George W. Bush argued that the doctrine of preemptive self-defense provided the legal justification for action. The United States asserted that Iraq's aggressive intentions toward the United States and its stockpile of weapons of mass destruction (in violation of previous UN Security Council resolutions in 1990, 1991, and 2002) were threats to the United States. The use of force is authorized by the UN Charter in only two conditions: when the UN Security Council authorizes such action and in cases of self-defense when an attack is imminent or has occurred. Given that neither of these conditions was present, other states and international lawyers argued that the United States did not have legal justification for the invasion.[10] (Interestingly, after the invasion, no such stockpiles of weapons of mass destruction were found.) The incident illustrates how the legality of an action under international law often depends on one's point of view—another effect of the lack of an internationally sovereign authority.

There are a number of reasons other than moral principle why states obey international law, particularly in a world of increased interdependence. First, international law provides a framework for the orderly conduct of international affairs. If norms of behavior such as the granting of diplomatic immunity were not followed, states would quickly find themselves unable to do business with one another. States adhere to international law because it is in their interest to preserve international order.

Second, states may adhere to the law of nations for fear of sanction or reprisal. For example, the use of chemical weapons in war was outlawed by the Geneva Protocol of 1925. Although both Germany and Britain possessed stockpiles of chemical weapons during World War II, both elected not to use poison gas against each other because both feared retaliation with potentially dire consequences to civilian populations and industry.

Third, international law may be enforced by reciprocity. In many cases, the long-term benefits of observing international law outweigh the short-term advantages of violating it. If states expect to interact with one another in the future and value their future relations highly enough, they will be more likely to follow laws and conventions as long as other states respond in good faith. This behavior is referred to as tit-for-tat, or doing as the other side does as long as the other side keeps doing it.[11] Many trade agreements are conducted on a tit-for-tat basis. The General Agreement on Tariffs and Trade (GATT), for example, specified that if one country raised discriminatory tariffs on goods coming in from another, the second country had the right to respond with "countervailing" tariffs.

Reciprocity in adhering to international law promotes an international environment in which, in the long run, cheaters never prosper. If a state routinely violates international norms, it may acquire a general reputation for lawbreaking, which could result in international humiliation and loss of opportunities for trade and cooperation with other countries. States that consistently prove they cannot be trusted may become **pariah** or **rogue states** and be ostracized. Although North Korea initially signed the Nuclear Non-Proliferation Treaty, it threatened to withdraw from the agreement in early 1993 and refused to allow international inspections of its nuclear facilities, despite mounting evidence of attempts to develop nuclear weapons, until the United States offered assistance with civilian energy programs in 1994. The North Korean government's reputation for untrustworthiness and unpredictability gave rise to serious doubts as to whether Pyongyang would live up to its end of the deal. In fact, in October 2002 the North Korean government admitted that it had a uranium-processing plant that could be used for building nuclear weapons, in violation of the 1994 Accord. In June 2003, North Korea officially withdrew from the Treaty.

■ **Pariah states**
States that consistently prove they cannot be trusted at their word and thereby become ostracized by the world community (also known as rogue states).

■ **Rogue states**
States that are considered untrustworthy and become ostracized by the international community (also known as pariah states).

PHOTO 13.1   One of the drawbacks of international law is poor compliance. For example, the Non-Proliferation Treaty includes a clause that allows member states to withdraw. Kim Jong-Il of North Korea took advantage of this clause and abandoned the treaty in 2003.

Areas of International Law

Human Rights Under International Law

The idea that sovereign governments should be subject to some form of international legal constraints to prevent them from abusing the rights of their citizens is a relatively new phenomenon, although the idea that human beings have certain inalienable rights is not new. In eleventh- and twelfth-century Europe, Christian canon lawyers debated the legal maxim that "an unjust law is not a law," which implies that even though a law has been enacted through due process, it might not be in accordance with accepted standards of justice. This developed from Roman and Greek philosophical principles that human beings have inherent rights regardless of the laws enacted by governments. These conceptions of human rights are grounded in the doctrine of **natural law,** which holds that certain human rights derive from a "higher law" rather than from the actions of rulers or governments. After the Reformation, philosophers like Thomas Hobbes, John Locke, and Jean Jacques Rousseau promoted the idea of a social contract that conferred rights as well as obligations on citizens and their rulers. The English Bill of Rights (1689), the American Declaration of Independence

▪ **Natural law**
Universal law that transcends man-made rules and regulations.

(1776) and Bill of Rights (1789), and the French Declaration of the Rights of Man (1789) offered lists of fundamental rights and freedoms regarded as inherent in all human individuals, by the sole virtue of their humanity, and as inalienable, or not capable of being taken away.

In the nineteenth century, international law began to develop a doctrine of humanitarian intervention when states committed shocking atrocities against their own subjects. For example, international collaboration pushed for the abolition of the slave trade (at the 1884 Berlin Conference on Africa) and then slavery (at the 1926 League of Nations Slavery Convention), set regulations for the conduct of war and treatment of prisoners (at The Hague and Geneva Conventions in the years before World War I), and offered protection from gross exploitation of workers (through the League of Nations International Labor Organization, founded in 1919).

Efforts to extend international law to cover human rights were hindered, however, by the doctrine of **positive law,** which held that rights could not derive from some unwritten "higher law," which the doctrine held to be a meaningless concept, but could originate only from human action, including the lawful acts of nation-states. Therefore, according to positivists, international law stems from the tacit or specific actions of states, and any law is meaningless without a sovereign authority to enforce it. Many positivists even denied the very existence of international law, contending that states could act however they wished in domestic affairs. The doctrine of positive law was taken to its cruel extreme in the National Socialist laws, enacted by the German Nazi government in 1936 at Nuremberg, which legalized first the persecution and then the wholesale murder of Germany's Jews.

During World War II, the Allies served notice on the Axis powers that trials for violations of international law would be held after the war. The St. James's Palace Declaration of 1942 stated, "There will be punishment, through the channels of organized justice, of those guilty or responsible for the crimes, whether they have ordered them, perpetrated them, or participated in them." After the Allied victory, Nuremberg was chosen in 1946 as the site of trials for Nazi officials accused of "crimes against humanity" in the Holocaust and other atrocities. The Charter of the International Military Tribunal of Nuremberg was endorsed by the fledgling UN in 1946. The charter defines crimes against humanity as "murder, extermination, enslavement, deportation, and other inhumane acts committed against any civilian population, before or during the war; or persecution on political, racial or religious grounds...whether or not in violation of domestic law of the country where perpetrated." The document thus asserts the superiority of international law over national law in questions of the grievous violation of human rights.[12]

Twenty-one of the top Nazi leaders were convicted and sentenced to death or to life imprisonment; ninety-eight lower ranking defendants were also convicted. Analogous trials were held in Tokyo for Japanese officials arraigned on similar charges. Two legal and moral principles became part of international law at Nuremberg: Orders given by one's superiors do not justify transgressions

▪ **Positive law**
A belief that international law exists only through those rules to which states have consented in writing, usually in treaties, or have otherwise clearly recognized.

against human rights, and individuals as well as governments may be held accountable for war crimes.

After the Holocaust and Nuremberg trials of 1946, the UN took the lead in codifying principles of human rights into international law. An early result was the 1948 Universal Declaration of Human Rights, a comprehensive statement of principles not binding on UN member states but generally recognized as customary law. In 1966 the UN General Assembly strengthened the declaration's provisions with three covenants: the International Covenant on Civil and Political Rights; the International Covenant on Economic, Social, and Cultural Rights; and the Optional Protocol, which allows citizens to sue governments for redress of human rights violations. The covenants received the required number of ratifications (thirty-five nations) and went into effect in 1976.

The UN has refined some of the basic principles through recent, more specific agreements. These include an agreement outlawing racial discrimination (1969), an accord forbidding torture (1984), and a convention on children's rights (1990). Not surprisingly, these and other agreements have not escaped controversy. Western, industrialized countries have tended to focus on individual civil rights and freedoms, whereas non-Western countries frequently stress collective economic rights.

In recent decades, the rights of women have acquired a special place in international human rights law, in large part a result of activism by women's groups. Gender equality in civil and political rights; equal access to education, economic opportunities, and health care; and prevention of violence against women have become international norms. For example, the 1948 Universal Declaration of Human Rights makes clear that all people are equal "without distinction of any kind such as race, color, sex, language...or any other status." Women's rights were reinforced with the 1979 Convention on the Elimination of All Forms of Discrimination Against Women (CEDAW) and the 1993 Declaration on the Elimination of Violence Against Women.[13] While these and other treaties and conventions promote women's rights, as with many other aspects of human rights, these principles are often violated in practice. The social construction of gender roles, which places women in the private sphere of the home rather than the public sphere, has led to the continued discrimination against women and girls around the world. Claims of "cultural values" and "cultural traditions," as well as strong political resistance in many countries, have made it difficult to abolish even the most egregious abuses of women's rights. For example, despite international condemnation, mass rape was used to terrorize women and children in the civil war in the former Yugoslavia in the early to mid-1990s, and practices such as female genital mutilation and the selling of women and girls into prostitution are still common in parts of Asia and Africa (see Chapter 11 and Spotlight, "Human Trafficking," in Chapter 11). Women continue to suffer from honor killings. Growing empowerment of women has made the rights, welfare, and status of women matters of global concern, as demonstrated by the World Conferences on Women (the most recent was held in 1995 in Beijing), but action on women's concerns within the framework of international law has been hampered by disputes over abortion, divorce, and other social controversies. Although there were still voices of opposition (representatives from the Vatican and many Islamic states opposed the sections on reproductive and sexual health that called for access to safe birth control and abortion), the Platform for Action adopted at the Beijing Conference sent a unified and powerful message that governments, NGOs, and the private sector must work together to remove all elements of discrimination, coercion, and violence from the lives of women and girls. (The UN General Assembly held a special session in 2000, "Beijing +5," reaffirming the Beijing Platform for Action.)[14] The push by women's groups and human rights groups for international law to respect and promote women's rights continues, particularly the violation of women's rights in times of conflict. In fact, in June 2008 the UN Security Council passed Resolution 1820, which focused on the link between women and sexual violence, noting that rape is a war crime (rape was first designated as such by the International Criminal Tribunal for the former Yugoslavia, established in 1993). As Amnesty International makes clear, "Women's rights and human rights are indivisible. All governments are obliged to uphold the basic human rights of each individual on an equal basis. States must recognize the unique context in which women experience human rights and take all necessary steps to protect women from discrimination and abuse in both the private and public spheres."[15]

At the end of the twentieth century the international community established two ad hoc tribunals to address gross human rights violations committed during the breakup of Yugoslavia (1991–1995) and the genocide in Rwanda (1994). The UN Security Council established these tribunals (the first such tribunals since the Nuremberg and Tokyo trials) as a means to prosecute individuals for particular crimes, including torture, willful killing, rape, and genocide. Most importantly, however, the international community recognized that such ad hoc tribunals raised the question of "selective justice"—for example, there have been no tribunals for the "killing fields" in Cambodia.[16] As a result, the international community went further in strengthening human rights law during the United Nations Conference on the Establishment of an **International Criminal Court** held in Rome, Italy, in 1998. Delegations from 160 states, fourteen specialized agencies of the UN, seventeen IGOs, and 124 NGOs participated in the conference. The International Criminal Court (ICC) statute was adopted with 120 in favor, 7 against (one of which was the United States), and 21 abstentions. The ICC has the power to try individuals accused of the most egregious crimes as a part of a systematic plan or policy, including war crimes, crimes against humanity, and genocide (crimes of aggression are also under the jurisdiction of the ICC, but there is yet to be a consensus on the definition of "aggression").[17] The statute entered into force on July 1, 2002 (as of May 10, 2010, 111 states are party to the ICC). Importantly, the ICC is seen as the "missing link in the international legal system." Whereas the International Court of Justice (World Court) deals with cases between states, the ICC deals with cases involving individuals, holding them accountable and responsible for their actions.[18] For example, in March 2009 the ICC issued an arrest warrant for Omar Al-Bashir, the president of Sudan, for

▪ **International Criminal Court**
Treaty signed in 1998 that created a permanent court that has the power to try individuals accused of the most egregious crimes as part of a systematic plan or policy, including war crimes, crimes against humanity, and genocide.

crimes against humanity and war crimes. These charges stem from the violence against civilians in Darfur that occurred during the conflict between the government and rebel forces.[19]

The establishment of the ICC, of course, has had its detractors. Of the five permanent members of the Security Council, two have signed and ratified it (France and the United Kingdom), one has signed but has not ratified (Russia), one has not signed (China), and one signed and then unsigned (United States). Although assured that the ICC will have jurisdiction only when governments are unwilling (when they lack the political will) or unable (when domestic judicial institutions may have collapsed) to prosecute individuals,[20] the United States fears that the ICC will be used by countries that oppose U.S. foreign and defense policy as a means to prosecute U.S. soldiers, the president, cabinet officers, and other high-level officials.[21] As noted previously, at the 1998 UN conference to establish the ICC, the United States voted against it. Yet interestingly, as President Bill Clinton prepared to leave office at the end of his second term, he signed the statute on December 31, 2000. On May 6, 2002, President George W. Bush "unsigned" the document, thus withdrawing from the statute, and then sought to weaken the ICC (for example, in an effort to punish states for joining the ICC, the United States withdrew military and economic assistance to various countries).[22] Those that support U.S. membership in the ICC were heartened by the election of President Barack Obama in November 2008, given his campaign focus on greater multilateral cooperation with other states. The Obama administration has taken slow steps to engage with the ICC, notably participating in the annual meeting of the ICC member states, held in November 2009, and participated in the work of the court when it sent a delegation to the ICC review conference in June 2010.[23] With the failure of three of the five permanent members of the UN Security Council to ratify the statute, the question arises as to whether the ICC can be an effective institution for implementing international law.

Finally, as another mechanism to promote human rights, the UN General Assembly adopted a resolution in June 2006 that led to the creation of the UN Human Rights Council (HRC). This 47-member state body, according to the resolution, "should address situations of violations of human rights, including gross and systematic violations, and make recommendations thereon. It should also promote the effective coordination and the mainstreaming of human rights within the United Nations system."[24] The HRC replaced the UN Human Rights Commission, a UN agency widely discredited over the years because of the poor human rights records of many of its members, such as Sudan and Zimbabwe. The General Assembly elects the member-states of the HRC. If any member is found to have committed human rights violations, their membership can be suspended. During the George W. Bush administration, the United States did not seek a seat on the body, but with the new Obama administration committed to a "new era of engagement" with the international community, the United States decided to participate and was elected in May 2009. Critics note, however, that because the elections are uncompetitive (before the election is held, states come to an agreement on who will run for election), states with poor human rights records can still win election and use their position on the Council to prevent others from investigating their human rights behavior.[25] While the council does have its critics, it has acted to promote human rights and call countries to task for their violations. In March 2010, the HRC adopted texts on areas such as torture, sexual violence against children, and the protection of journalists who are reporting in a conflict zone. More specifically, the council condemned the human rights violations of the people of Myanmar (formerly Burma), called for free and fair elections in the country, and extended the mandate of the UN Special Rapporteur for Myanmar, including a visit to the country.[26] Of course, whether the Myanmar government will respond favorably to the HRC's calls begs the question of the enforcement of international laws on human rights.

Can Human Rights Conventions Be Enforced?

Historically, when principles of human rights have clashed with the principle of state sovereignty, sovereignty has usually won out. Torture, imprisonment for political activity, and other abuses of human rights are practiced by governments in many parts of the world, despite protests from the UN and human rights organizations like Amnesty International.

During the Cold War, the issue of human rights became politicized along East–West lines, as UN member states disagreed fiercely over who was in violation of human rights law. When the United States accused communist and nonaligned regimes of human rights abuses, those regimes countered that such charges masked an "imperialistic" desire to interfere in their internal affairs and cited examples of human rights abuses in the West. In the late 1970s, for instance, the United States repeatedly accused the USSR of violating the human rights provisions of the 1975 Helsinki Accords, citing Soviet restraints on Jewish emigration and imprisonment of dissidents in psychiatric hospitals. In response, the Soviet Union maintained for years that Leonard Peltier, an activist for Native American rights convicted in the deaths of two FBI agents in a June 1975 shootout at Wounded Knee, South Dakota, was a political prisoner. Peltier's attorney even visited the Soviet Union in 1988 to seek aid on behalf of the jailed militant.[27] Recent controversies over the U.S. record on human rights include claims against the United States for holding alleged Taliban and Al Qaeda members at Guantanamo Bay, Cuba, as prisoners without recourse to legal representation since its invasion of Afghanistan in 2001. China and several African countries have pointed out the hypocrisy of the United States for accusing other countries of human rights violations given its own problems at home.

With the demise of the Cold War, countries have been more willing to consider enforcing human rights guarantees with multilateral intervention, at least in principle. In practice, however, the UN has been reluctant to commit troops to potential combat situations to safeguard human rights. The peacekeeping mission in the former Yugoslavia illustrates the difficulties inherent in preventing violations of human rights and bringing their perpetrators to justice. As discussed in Chapter 6, when fighting broke out over the secession of Croatia in 1991 and Bosnia in 1992, hundreds of thousands lost their lives and millions were driven from their homes.[28] Military, police, and militia forces carried out a policy of ethnic cleansing, entailing the forcible eviction, imprisonment, torture, rape, and murder of thousands of civilians. Although most of the reported incidents involved Serbian forces, Croatian and Muslim forces were accused of similar atrocities. The UN Security Council established an international tribunal to investigate and punish war crimes committed in the former Yugoslav republics, but little was done to stop the massive human rights abuses or apprehend those accused of ordering them until NATO forces intervened in 1995. However, arrests of suspected war criminals have often been fraught with political trouble, as one side's war criminal is often another's nationalist hero. The problems encountered in bringing war criminals to justice in the former Yugoslavia testify to the political and legal difficulties of enforcing international human rights law.

Warfare and Aggression

A second important area of international law concerns states' conduct during periods of warfare and aggression. Efforts to regulate the conduct of warfare have evolved from the task of articulating the legal obligations of belligerents to the relatively more difficult one of securing protection for individual noncombatants during wartime. An early agreement on the conduct of warfare was the 1856 Declaration of Paris, which clarified the rights of neutral vessels. However, it is the 1945 UN charter that contains the most universally accepted rules of warfare. The charter allows states to use force or other coercive methods (including economic sanctions) against other states in self-defense or as part of an organized peacekeeping effort. In an anarchic international system, however, aggression is still too often justified as self-defense when it is perceived as furthering a state's national interests.

Another set of conventions sets limits on the methods of warfare. The 1899 Hague Convention and the 1925 Geneva Protocol, in particular, prohibit the use of poisonous or asphyxiating gases. As of May 2010, more than 130 states have ratified the 1925 accord (the United States signed the accord in 1925 but the Senate did not ratify it until 1975). In January 1993, 125 states signed the Chemical Weapons Convention (CWC), which is much stronger—banning the possession, acquisition, production, stockpiling, transfer, and use of chemical weapons—and came into force in 1997 (as of June 2009, 188 states have signed and ratified the CWC). There is also an accord banning the use of biological weapons, the Biological Weapons Convention of 1972, which entered into force in 1975 (the CWC and BWC are discussed in Chapter 7).[29] Although party to the Geneva Protocol, Iraq violated the accord on poisonous gas use during the 1980s in its war with Iran and against its own Kurdish citizens, but the world community was slow to respond.

A third set of agreements seeks to protect human rights during warfare. Rules to protect sick and wounded combatants are laid out in the 1864 Geneva

Convention. The rights of prisoners of conventional war were refined most recently in 1977, extending protection to those involved in guerrilla warfare.

As can be surmised by the violations mentioned in the preceding paragraphs, efforts to regulate the conduct of warfare, protect combatants and noncombatants alike, and punish those who violate the rules have been only partially successful. The reasons for this limited success stem not only from the enforcement of international law in an anarchic environment but also from the inherent contradiction of trying to establish rules of conduct for violent, aggressive, and often desperate acts. Such rules work only when both sides fear retaliation should they violate them.

Effectiveness and Compliance: The Verdict on International Law

Given the foregoing discussion on international law, what can the various approaches, or paradigms, of world politics tell us about the effectiveness of and compliance with international law? As noted earlier, realism considers international law as merely a manifestation of the interests of the most powerful states in the international system. Structural realists go even further, asserting that international law is unimportant, given the anarchic international system and distribution of power. Liberalism, however, asserts that international law does influence the behavior of states (as well as leaders and groups). In responding to realism, liberal theory thus maintains that international law (and institutions) does matter. In addition, NGOs have been instrumental in promoting and encouraging international law as a mechanism for resolving various global issues, and thereby influencing governments to support legal measures.[30] Finally, constructivists claim that "international law both reflects and reinforces identities and interests," namely, the shared ideas, norms, and values of the international community, as demonstrated by the evolution of human rights law.[31]

In the end, the successes and failures of international law over the centuries suggest that the same attitudes toward law that prevail among individuals are shared by states. Some people obey the law because they believe it is their moral duty to do so, others disregard it whenever possible, and still others are swayed by circumstances. Similarly, some governments have taken great pains to abide by international law, others have repeatedly and flagrantly ignored it, and still others weigh the advantages of breaking the law against the risk and costs of enforcement sanctions in a given situation before deciding whether or not to obey. The vital role that effective enforcement plays in keeping honest people honest and making dishonest ones think twice before breaking the law thus has implications for international law. Generally speaking, elements of international law that have been readily enforced, such as diplomatic immunity and the prohibition of slavery, are less frequently violated than those provisions that states have been unwilling or unable to enforce, such as the Kellogg-Briand Pact (which outlawed war except in self-defense) or conventions against torture. Thus, as has been shown, the international system is not a totally anarchic environment. Good organization is the key to effective law enforcement and global governance in a society without a sovereign authority. This thought occurred to international jurists generations ago, prompting many to give first priority to the establishment and strengthening of international organizations. The next section examines how well their efforts have succeeded.

International Organizations

States may be the most important actors in the international system, but they are not the most numerous. The 2009–2010 edition of the *Yearbook of International Organizations* lists more than 30,000 entries of intergovernmental and nongovernmental organizations, as compared to the fewer than 200 nation-states.[32] Despite the proliferation of international organizations in the last few decades, a debate continues over whether they are in fact manipulated and controlled by governments. In either case, it is clear that international organizations try to make the world a less anarchic place by assuming tasks states cannot or will not undertake themselves, from humanitarian efforts to peacekeeping. They are both a cause and an effect of globalization in the contemporary era, and they are called on to deal with an increasingly wide array of political, social, and economic issues. In this way, IOs are manifestations of global governance, as they play an important role in promoting cooperation at the international level, creating norms, and providing information that enables states as well as other international actors to coordinate their behavior.[33]

IOs can be divided into two broad categories, intergovernmental organizations (IGOs) and nongovernmental organizations (NGOs). IGOs are associations of sovereign states that are established through formal agreements. IGOs include the United Nations, African Union, Arab League, and European Union (EU). There are also informal IGOs, such as the Group of 8 (or G-8). Scholars have attempted to determine the number of IGOs; the Yearbook of International Organizations lists 5,000, but other estimates count more than 300 formal IGOs and between 200 and 700 informal IGOs.[34]

NGOs are groups of institutions and individuals established through more informal means. Greenpeace, Amnesty International, and the International Olympic Committee are familiar examples. Even though NGOs do not include states in their membership, and so lie outside the structure of traditional international politics, many have exerted a significant impact on world affairs. Groups such as Amnesty International have influenced governments' policies through public pressure and lobbying, whereas organizations like Médecins Sans Frontières (Doctors Without Borders) have acted directly to provide humanitarian relief.

IOs can be further categorized by their membership base and intended purpose. Some, such as the International Committee of the Red Cross, seek members throughout the world, whereas others are oriented toward a particular region, like the Economic Community of West African States (ECOWAS). Multipurpose organizations such as the OAS handle a broad range of tasks, whereas specialized organizations like the International Criminal Police Organization (Interpol) perform more specific functions.

The primary reason IOs have taken on increasingly important roles in the nineteenth, twentieth, and now twenty-first centuries is because sovereign nation-states gradually came to the realization that they could not address all the problems that plague the international system by themselves. They came to acknowledge that institutions promoting and facilitating international cooperation are required to deal more effectively with problems that affect them all. Although various IOs frequently propose solutions for problems that confront states, states often ignore or fail to abide by the IOs' recommendations and decisions for fear of losing their sovereign powers. Because one of the most vital sovereign rights of a nation-state is that of self-defense, organizations formed to promote collective security as an improvement over the anarchic "every state for itself" security environment have found it difficult to achieve their objectives despite centuries of effort. The sections that follow reveal the constant tension that exists between sovereignty and cooperation, especially within IOs designed to provide collective security. In the end, international organizations need to be perceived as legitimate by states if they are to matter and be effective.[35]

International Governmental Organizations

Given that IGOs are comprised of states, scholars have debated whether they matter. Some argue, along the realist vein, that IGOs merely reflect and serve the interests of states (and reduce "the costs of making and enforcing agreements"), particularly the interests of the most powerful states in the system. If a state perceives that an IGO's mandate is not in alignment with that state's interest, the state can simply withdraw from the organization and join those states with which its interests will be served. As such, the influence and affect of IGOs on states are negligible, and state sovereignty is maintained. Others argue that IGOs do not just represent the interests of states but, in fact, "can and do exercise power autonomously." This is not to deny that states are still the dominant actors in the international system but, rather, to note that IGOs are independent actors that have influence, particularly in areas such as human rights. These IGOs are able to set "their own agendas, rules, and norms." Globalization further reinforces the autonomy and independence of IGOs.[36] Security and economic IGOs illustrate this dynamic, as will be discussed in the following sections.

Security IGOS: The United Nations

The United Nations is the most universal IGO today whose mandate is one of collective security as a means to ensure international peace and security. Its genealogy is a result of collective security institutions that emerged in the nineteenth and twentieth centuries. The Concert of Europe and League of Nations (see Chapter 3 for an overview of both) were the precursors to the UN. The experiences of these institutions informed the type of organization that the UN became and remains today.

The Concert of Europe was established in 1815 to restore the European balance of power after the Napoleonic Wars. However, the Concert was not an autonomous organization that could make rules for sovereign states in a disinterested manner. The Congress disposed of much European territory in a way that reflected the existing power relationships among the European great powers. The world's first collective security organization, therefore, did not start life in an unselfish spirit of international cooperation. The excessively elitist orientation of the Concert's concept of balance of power made it incapable of responding to the desire on the part of many subject peoples in Europe for national self-determination, and this elitism proved to be its Achilles' heel. The result was that the Concert deteriorated in the latter part of the nineteenth century, and the unstable peace it kept collapsed with the outbreak of World War I.

The successor to the Concert of Europe, as discussed in Chapter 3, was the League of Nations, created by the Treaty of Versailles at the end of World War I to prevent another catastrophic global war.[37] Unlike the Concert of Europe, which operated informally, the League was specifically chartered as a formal international organization dedicated to arbitration of international disputes, disarmament, and open diplomacy. Its founders were convinced that the nineteenth-century doctrine of the "balance of power," loosely maintained by the Concert, failed to prevent World War I because that doctrine was in disharmony with the ideals of national self-determination. As a result, a more active form of collective security, an "international police force," was deemed necessary for preventing future war. Collective security is an attempt to replace the "every state for itself" mindset of the anarchic international system with a "one for all, and all for one" mentality; in other words, "the organizing principle of collective security is the respect for the moral and legal obligation to consider an attack by any nation upon a member of the alliance as an attack upon all members of the alliance."[38] By ostensibly guaranteeing the security of all states in the international system regardless of their size or power, it was hoped that collective security would be a mechanism to pull states away from the brink of war in the nick of time.

In reality, collective security proved difficult to organize. States such as Britain and France continued to practice balance-of-power politics, as demonstrated by the way they handled the Italian invasion of Ethiopia in 1935. Additionally, the League did not include key global players in its membership. Original members Japan and Italy quit in 1933 and 1937, respectively. Germany also withdrew from the League in 1933 (Germany had been allowed to join in 1926). A few months after the Soviets signed the Nazi–Soviet Pact and Hitler invaded Poland in 1939, a League council resolution revoked the USSR's five-year-old membership. The United States never joined the League and thus missed many opportunities to exert its influence to avert the events that escalated into World War II.

The League of Nations' decision-making structure also hampered the organization's political power. There were four main components to the League: the Assembly, composed of representatives from all member states; the Council, consisting of permanent seats held by the most powerful states as well as rotating members chosen by the Assembly; the Secretariat, a primarily administrative organ; and the World Court, an international tribunal of judges to which states could appeal for rulings in international law. The Council, which during the history of the League ranged from eight to fourteen members, handled mainly political matters. These included major disputes likely to lead to war, as well as minor problems such as frontier adjustments. All decisions of substance required a unanimous vote of Council members, except for those directly involved in the dispute in question (whose votes did not count). However, any members of the League Assembly whose interests were concerned in the decision's outcome also had the right to veto League action.

Thus, the League was doubly constrained in taking action against belligerents. In the first place, the negative vote of any member (including one in the Assembly, not just the Council) sufficed to block any decision to authorize sanctions. Few of the Council's decisions were vetoed, if only because they tended to be watered down to be nearly meaningless. Second, even when the Council could manage to get a unanimous decision to use force, the League found it almost impossible to enforce the sanctions available to it, which ranged from trade embargoes to air and naval strikes against offending states. For example, the League's deficiencies rendered it powerless to stop Japan from invading Manchuria in 1931 and to stop Germany from its host of treaty violations and aggressive acts in the years before World War II.

In many respects, the structure of the League was an overreaction to the great-power politics that plagued the Concert of Europe. The feebleness of the League's collective security provisions reflected a forlorn hope that these measures could work through moral force alone, without the backing of the most powerful states. However, without the tangible support and concerted effort of the great powers, the organization's vacillations and meek declarations merely aggravated expansionist dictators, inviting further aggression. After such aggression led to a war even more horrible than World War I, world leaders attempted to construct an organization that could ensure the widest possible respect for and adherence to its decisions.

The United Nations Is Born

President Franklin D. Roosevelt and Secretary of State Cordell Hull coined the name of the League of Nations' successor organization in the 1942 Declaration of the United Nations. (British Prime Minister Churchill liked Roosevelt's proposed name United Nations better than his own suggestion of Associated Powers.) The new organization was officially established in June 1945 when fifty-one founding members signed the charter of the United Nations, which came into effect that October after the surrender of Germany and Japan ended World War II. The League of Nations quietly voted itself out of existence and transferred its assets to the UN in April 1946.

Thus, the UN supplanted the League of Nations as the preeminent collective security organization in the international system. Its primary purpose was, and still is, to maintain international peace and security. It is also dedicated to developing friendly relations among peoples; cooperating internationally in solving international economic, social, cultural, and humanitarian problems; and promoting respect for human rights. The UN charter established six primary organs of the United Nations, headquartered in New York City: the General Assembly, the Security Council, the Economic and Social Council, the Secretariat, the Trusteeship Council, and the International Court of Justice (ICJ). (The Trusteeship Council, organized to oversee the administration of non-self-governing areas assigned to member states for temporary administration before becoming fully independent, suspended operations in 1994 because all such territories had, in fact, become independent.) Although these organs and their auxiliary and subsidiary bodies are supposed to promote the widest possible cooperation among member states in the areas of collective security and peacekeeping, in practice, states have traditionally hewn to narrow definitions of their national interests in determining the desirability of international cooperation. This has often transformed the UN into an arena for political grandstanding and competition. The next section assesses the effectiveness of the UN's primary organs, looking at the effect of politics on decision making and at the nature of the political and economic difficulties that each body faces.

The United Nations: Structure, Functions, and Politics

General Assembly. From fifty-one original members, the UN General Assembly has expanded to include 192 nation-states (Montenegro became the most recent member in June 2006). Figure 13.1 shows the UN's organization and scope. All UN members have a seat in the General Assembly, and almost all independent states are members of the UN. Some states are not members, such as Taiwan, which is not a member because the PRC (People's Republic of China) government claims sovereignty over Taiwan (until 1991, Taiwan claimed that it was the rightful government of mainland China, which led to PRC vetoes of Taiwan's membership). In the past, a few other states had not been permitted to join: North and South Korea were denied membership until both joined simultaneously in 1991. Other entities that are not states are not members but have observer status, including the Holy See and Palestine.

The General Assembly is the UN's primary forum for the discussion of global issues. Operating according to the "one state, one vote" principle, it embodies the idea that the United Nations is based on the sovereign equality of all its members. Dominance of the General Assembly, defined as the ability to get one's resolutions passed by the required two-thirds vote, was first held by the United States, whose supremacy continued up until the 1960s, at which point the United States found itself at odds with the Assembly majority on a number of issues involving decolonization and development. (The USSR exploited this rupture to its advantage by taking the opposite stance.) The decline in U.S. influence began

The United Nations System

Principal Organs

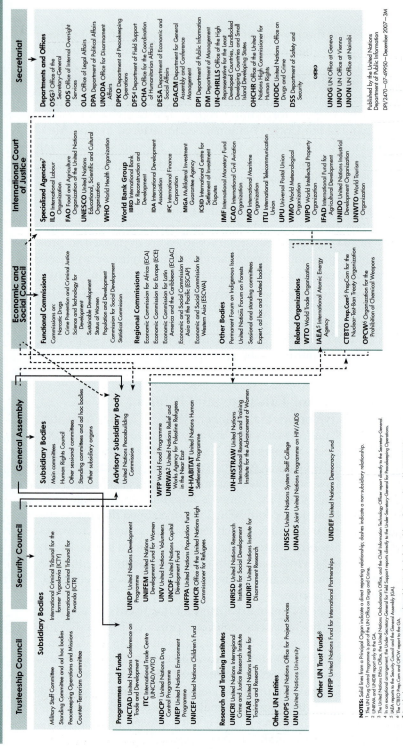

Trusteeship Council

Security Council

General Assembly

Economic and Social Council

International Court of Justice

Secretariat

Subsidiary Bodies (Security Council)

Military Staff Committee
Standing Committee and ad hoc bodies
Peacekeeping Operations and Missions
Counter-Terrorism Committee

International Criminal Tribunal for the former Yugoslavia (ICTY)
International Criminal Tribunal for Rwanda (ICTR)

Subsidiary Bodies (General Assembly)

Main committees
Human Rights Council
Other sessional committees
Standing committees and ad hoc bodies
Other subsidiary organs

Advisory Subsidiary Body

United Nations Peacebuilding Commission

Programmes and Funds

UNCTAD United Nations Conference on Trade and Development
ITC International Trade Centre (UNCTAD/WTO)
UNDCP[1] United Nations Drug Control Programme
UNEP United Nations Environment Programme
UNICEF United Nations Children's Fund

UNDP United Nations Development Programme
UNIFEM United Nations Development Fund for Women
UNV United Nations Volunteers
UNCDF United Nations Capital Development Fund
UNFPA United Nations Population Fund
UNHCR Office of the United Nations High Commissioner for Refugees

WFP World Food Programme
UNRWA[2] United Nations Relief and Works Agency for Palestine Refugees in the Near East
UN-HABITAT United Nations Human Settlements Programme

UN-INSTRAW United Nations International Research and Training Institute for the Advancement of Women

Research and Training Institutes

UNICRI United Nations Interregional Crime and Justice Research Institute
UNITAR United Nations Institute for Training and Research

UNRISD United Nations Research Institute for Social Development
UNIDIR[2] United Nations Institute for Disarmament Research

Other UN Entities

UNOPS United Nations Office for Project Services
UNU United Nations University

UNSSC United Nations System Staff College
UNAIDS Joint United Nations Programme on HIV/AIDS

Other UN Trust Funds[8]

UNFIP United Nations Fund for International Partnerships

UNDEF United Nations Democracy Fund

Functional Commissions

Commissions on:
Narcotic Drugs
Crime Prevention and Criminal Justice
Science and Technology for Development
Sustainable Development
Status of Women
Population and Development
Commission for Social Development
Statistical Commission

Regional Commissions

Economic Commission for Africa (ECA)
Economic Commission for Europe (ECE)
Economic Commission for Latin America and the Caribbean (ECLAC)
Economic and Social Commission for Asia and the Pacific (ESCAP)
Economic and Social Commission for Western Asia (ESCWA)

Other Bodies

Permanent Forum on Indigenous Issues
United Nations Forum on Forests
Sessional and standing committees
Expert, ad hoc and related bodies

Related Organizations

WTO World Trade Organization
IAEA[5] International Atomic Energy Agency
CTBTO Prep.Com[6] PrepCom for the Nuclear-Test-Ban Treaty Organization
OPCW[6] Organization for the Prohibition of Chemical Weapons

Specialized Agencies[7]

ILO International Labour Organization
FAO Food and Agriculture Organization of the United Nations
UNESCO United Nations Educational, Scientific and Cultural Organization
WHO World Health Organization

World Bank Group
IBRD International Bank for Reconstruction and Development
IDA International Development Association
IFC International Finance Corporation
MIGA Multilateral Investment Guarantee Agency
ICSID International Centre for Settlement of Investment Disputes

IMF International Monetary Fund
ICAO International Civil Aviation Organization
IMO International Maritime Organization
ITU International Telecommunication Union
UPU Universal Postal Union
WMO World Meteorological Organization
WIPO World Intellectual Property Organization
IFAD International Fund for Agricultural Development
UNIDO United Nations Industrial Development Organization
UNWTO World Tourism Organization

Departments and Offices

OSG[3] Office of the Secretary-General
OIOS Office of Internal Oversight Services
OLA Office of Legal Affairs
DPA Department of Political Affairs
UNODA Office for Disarmament Affairs
DPKO Department of Peacekeeping Operations
DFS[4] Department of Field Support
OCHA Office for the Coordination of Humanitarian Affairs
DESA Department of Economic and Social Affairs
DGACM Department for General Assembly and Conference Management
DPI Department of Public Information
DM Department of Management
UN-OHRLLS Office of the High Representative for the Least Developed Countries, Landlocked Developing Countries and Small Island Developing States
OHCHR Office of the United Nations High Commissioner for Human Rights
UNODC United Nations Office on Drugs and Crime
DSS Department of Safety and Security

UNOG UN Office at Geneva
UNOV UN Office at Vienna
UNON UN Office at Nairobi

Published by the United Nations
Department of Public Information
DPI/2470—07-49950—December 2007—3M

NOTES: Solid lines from a Principal Organ indicate a direct reporting relationship; dashes indicate a non-subsidiary relationship.

1 The UN Drug Control Programme is part of the UN Office on Drugs and Crime.
2 UNRWA and UNIDIR report only to the GA.
3 The United Nations Ethics Office, the United Nations Ombudsman's Office, and the Chief Information Technology Officer report directly to the Secretary-General.
4 In an exceptional arrangement, the Under-Secretary-General for Field Support reports directly to the Under-Secretary-General for Peacekeeping Operations.
5 IAEA reports to the Security Council and the General Assembly (GA).
6 The CTBTO Prep.Com and OPCW report to the GA.
7 Specialized agencies are autonomous organizations working with the UN and each other through the coordinating machinery of the ECOSOC at the intergovernmental level, and through the Chief Executives Board for coordination (CEB) at the inter-secretariat level.
8 UNFIP is an autonomous trust fund operating under the leadership of the United Nations Deputy Secretary-General. UNDEF's advisory board recommends funding proposals for approval by the Secretary-General.

FIGURE 13.1 The United Nations system.

in 1960, when seventeen new states, most of them African, joined the General Assembly. Many of these states identified the United States as the prime patron of their colonial oppression because of its alliance with all of the former colonial European powers.

By the 1980s, well over half of the 160 members of the General Assembly were either Asian or African, and these developing countries continued to use the UN as a forum to espouse their preferences and aims. For many smaller countries of the developing world, the General Assembly remains the most important channel to international diplomacy. However, since the breakup of the Soviet Union and the Persian Gulf War, there has been a marked increase in the American success rate, mirroring the end of the Cold War and America's status as "first among equals" in a new international environment.

Although disagreements between developed and developing states (and, during the Cold War, those between East and West) have inhibited the effectiveness of the General Assembly, budget disputes have been even more detrimental. Members are often delinquent in their payments; at other times, states have threatened to withhold money because of developments within the UN itself. In 1980, for example, the United States withheld more than $100 million in contributions, primarily because of its perceptions of anti-Western bias and repeated incidents of wasteful spending. By 1998, U.S. assessments to the UN were in arrears by more than $1.3 billion, or roughly half of the total owed to the UN by member states. Plans for the United States to pay its debt were hampered by the continuing argument between those who believe the country should fulfill its financial obligations immediately and others (especially in Congress) who hold that the UN should reform its organization and financial practices first. However, in 1999, Congress passed the Helms-Biden agreement for payment of U.S. arrears to the UN, totaling $926 million. The agreement stipulated three payments; the last occurred in September 2002.[39]

Still another concern affecting General Assembly effectiveness is the overloading of the assembly agenda when it convenes every September. Some argue that the General Assembly is losing its focus. For example, at the 61st General Assembly meeting held in 2006, the agenda contained more than 150 items, some of which were also on the agenda of the Security Council (which, by the UN charter, has precedence). The provisional agenda for the 62nd General Assembly meeting listed more than 160 agenda items. Proposals to reform the United Nations by limiting the bloating of the General Assembly agenda and thus enhancing its effectiveness include the consultation of the president of the General Assembly with member states to make recommendations to the UN Secretary General in advance of the agenda meeting, a time limit on speakers whose windy ramblings distort the proceedings, and more meetings between the support staffs of major powers before General Assembly sessions to become aware of their key positions sooner and thus save time. These recommendations reflect the perception by member states regarding the decline of the General Assembly's importance, as noted by a recent UN report.[40] Recognizing the continued need to make the UN more effective and efficient, in February 2010 informal consultations were carried out at a meeting at the UN on "System-wide Coherence." As explained by the Secretary-General, system-wide coherence refers to the way the UN functions as a whole "in order to improve the coordination, funding, accountability and the governance of operational activities for development." The activities in which the UN is engaged "remain fragmented, often duplicative with high transaction costs."[41] The continuing challenge for the UN is to implement reforms that will make it a better institution, improving its efficiency and effectiveness as it addresses many of the world's problems.

Security Council. The Security Council was designed to be the sword beside the UN's olive branch. It is charged with organizing collective security operations and dispatching observer missions and peacekeeping troops (defined later in this chapter) around the world at the request of one or more of the combatants involved. This body has the right to investigate any dispute or situation that might lead to international friction and to recommend methods of settlement. On all resolutions and proposals for action, the rule of **great-power unanimity** holds: A veto by any one of its five permanent members will kill any proposal. Every permanent Security Council member has used its veto power to protect what it has seen as its vital interests. Recent vetoes include two vetoes in 2006 by the United States that involved resolutions that condemned Israeli military operation in Gaza (as well as calling on the Palestinian Authority to take actions to end violence including firing of rockets into Israel). In 2007 China and Russia vetoed a proposal that called on the government of Burma to end its "military attacks against civilians in ethnic minority regions," allow international humanitarian organizations to operate unencumbered, and end forced labor. These same two countries exercised their veto in 2008 when a resolution that called for UN sanctions against Zimbabwe (a travel ban on the president, Robert Mugabe, and an international arms embargo) was brought to the Security Council.[42]

Over the past five decades, the Security Council has employed a wide variety of ways to maintain international peace. These have ranged from resolutions condemning violence to the establishment of peacekeeping forces and the implementation of sanctions. Through its debates, the Security Council has reflected the sentiment of the international community. Simply by allowing grievances to be aired, debates have often diffused tension. On the other hand, bitter debates in public view sometimes intensify disputes to the detriment of private negotiation. When such disputes result in resolutions that are perceived by member states as biased, the status of the Council is undermined, along with its ability to act (see Spotlight, "Conflict and Cooperation in the Security Council").

The Security Council also serves as a forum for negotiation. By arranging cease-fires or disengagements and by setting up fact-finding missions, the Security Council can "buy time" in crucial situations to allow participants in a given conflict to reconsider their positions. Even more so, resolutions passed by the Security Council can provide the framework for dispute settlement. For

■ **Great-power unanimity**
A concept that holds that on all resolutions and proposals before the UN Security Council, a veto by any one of the five permanent members (China, France, Russia, United Kingdom, and United States) will kill any proposal.

▪ S P O T L I G H T ▪

Conflict and Cooperation in the Security Council

In hindsight, it appears that the UN Security Council was not designed with a bipolar world in mind. Throughout the Cold War, the Security Council served as a forum in which the Soviet Union and the United States fought to influence world opinion in favor of their respective positions.

For nearly the first two decades of the UN's existence, the USSR had no allies in the Security Council and few in the General Assembly. As a result, the Soviet Union had to lean heavily on its veto power to prevent the passage of recommendations on peace and security matters with which it did not agree. In the first five years of the Security Council's existence, the USSR used the veto forty-seven times; the United States, zero. In fact, the United States did not veto a single Security Council resolution until 1970.

In the 1960s and 1970s, however, many newly independent African and Asian countries leaned toward the communist bloc or nonaligned movement because they resented the West for its colonial past. They began to pack the General Assembly and fill some of the two-year seats on the Security Council. As a result, fortunes began to reverse themselves in favor of the Soviet Union. By the mid-1980s, the votes of the General Assembly and the Soviet delegation were in agreement 79 percent of the time; during the same period, the U.S. figure had plummeted to 14 percent. In the early 1980s, the USSR used its veto power only twice, whereas the United States resorted to it twenty-eight times.[i] In the 1990s, however, the collapse of communism in the USSR broke the bipolar deadlock. The USSR did not veto the U.S.-led peace enforcement operation in the Persian Gulf War, and the United States and Russia accommodated each other's plans for peacekeeping in the Caucasus and Haiti in 1994. Finally, it seemed, the Security Council began to function more or less as its founders intended. However, great power interests still can conflict, as evidenced by the Russian, French, and Chinese opposition to the U.S.-led (and U.K.-supported) calls for military action against Iraq following the passage of UN Resolution 1441 on November 8, 2002.

Today, debate over whether the membership composition (numbers of both permanent and nonpermanent members) of the Security Council reflects the current global power structure has been renewed. In September 2006 then-UN Secretary-General Kofi Annan warned that if the status quo continued, "the whole process of transforming governance in other parts of the system is handicapped by the perception of an inequitable distribution of power."[ii] Serious consideration has been given recently to whether the Security Council should be expanded to include Japan and Germany, especially because other countries have become increasingly dependent on them to fund expanded UN programs. Reluctance to give Japan and Germany permanent seats both within and outside those countries is a reaction to their legacies of aggression, their postwar constitutional prohibitions against fielding large standing military organizations, and a general feeling that both states are not (or should not be) wholeheartedly committed to active participation in international politics.

The United States has anticipated that new admissions to the Security Council would reduce U.S. leverage, renew developing countries' demands for an end to the permanent members' veto power, and invite other large regional, developing states such as Brazil to seek permanent Security Council membership.[iii] Yet at the same time, the United States does support Japan's inclusion as a permanent member, arguing that by doing so, the council's effectiveness to address threats to peace and security will be enhanced. The argument the George W. Bush administration made was that as the second largest donor to the United Nations, Japan's status as a permanent member of the Security Council would reflect its commitment and support of the UN. Overall, the U.S. position is one in which it is open to expansion of the Security Council, but only if it is not at the expense of the effectiveness of the body.[iv] In 2009, Britain and France called for the need to increase the Security Council membership, arguing that the failure to do so weakens the legitimacy of the body. Russia has continued to oppose enlargement but has engaged in discussions about the issue. The Obama administration continued to express concerns about which countries would be considered for membership, although he recently stated his support for India's inclusion in the future.[v]

---

i. Robert E. Riggs and Jack C. Plano, *The United Nations: International Organization and World Politics* (Chicago: Dorsey, 1988).

ii. "General Assembly President Proposes Three Options on Security Council Reform," UN News Service (December 13, 2006), http://www.un.org/apps/news/story.asp?NewsID=20970&Cr=Security&CR1=Council#.

iii. For discussions of these issues, see James Weish, "The Partnership to Remember," *Time*, March 11, 1991, pp. 49–50; *New York Times*, September 27, 1992, and January 12, 1993.

iv. U.S. State Department, "U.S. Supports Japan as Permanent Member of U.N. Security Council," September 13, 2006, http://usinfo.state.gov/xarchives/display.html?p=washfile-english&y=2006&m=September&x=20060913180611esnamfuak3.509158e-02.

v. Colum Lynch, "Talks on Expanding U.N. Panel Called Off," *The Washington Post*, March 31, 2009, http://www.washingtonpost.com/wp-dyn-content/article/2009/03/30/AR2009093002919

---

example, the "land for peace" provisions in UN Resolutions 242 and 338 have served as a basis for negotiating the Arab–Israeli dispute.

If peaceful means fail, the Security Council can also impose harsh sanctions on a state or even launch military actions. Prior to the UN's authorization of the U.S.-led intervention to expel the Iraqi army from Kuwait in 1990, the only significant military action on which the Security Council was able to achieve a consensus was intervention in the Korean War in 1950 (see also Chapter 4). After three years the conflict ended in a stalemate, but because it was a successful collective effort to block aggression and limit its consequences, the Korean War was the first instance in which the UN acted as a "world policeman," just as its founders intended. U.S.–Soviet antagonism during the Cold War ensured that it would not do so again until the Persian Gulf War, forty years later.

Secretariat and Secretary-General

Headed by the secretary-general, who serves a renewable five-year term and reports to the General Assembly, the Secretariat is the UN's chief administrative body. The secretary-general is thus the "chief executive" of the UN, but has little power to act independently of the Security Council or General Assembly. However, the secretary-general can bring any matter that threatens world peace to the attention of the Security Council and can call special sessions of the General Assembly. In keeping with the tradition established by the League of Nations covenant, the UN Charter pledges the secretaries-general to strict impartiality in the discharge of their responsibilities.

The Secretariat includes nearly 40,000 staff members around the world in various positions such as at headquarters, regional commissions, peacekeeping missions, and tribunals. Although headquartered in New York City, the UN maintains offices all over the world.[43] Despite the large size of the staff, this administrative body has been hindered in the past by limited resources. The secretary-general is not authorized to engage in certain types of activities that might be perceived as violations of national sovereignty. One such example is that the secretary-general cannot order intelligence-gathering activities. If member states are not willing to provide sufficient information when a crisis erupts, the danger increases that the secretary-general's effectiveness as an impartial arbitrator will suffer. This problem became particularly acute when the UN Special Commission on Iraq (UNSCOM) was charged with verifying that Iraq had destroyed its weapons of mass destruction after the 1991 Gulf War. Iraq's attitude toward UNSCOM's efforts to gather information on its weapons and research facilities ranged from obstinacy to hostility, and safeguards had to be put in place to ensure that secret information sent to UNSCOM by other member states did not leak out. Some analysts suggest ways to get around these types of restrictions. For example, to accomplish intelligence gathering, the Secretariat could push for the development of UN satellite equipment capabilities, purchase commercially available satellite images, or perhaps just send special UN ambassadors to global capitals on a regular basis to gather information for the secretary-general.

These proposals would improve the resources available to the secretary-general but would not necessarily safeguard the desired impartiality of the office itself. Indeed, the process of selecting the secretary-general can be an especially political undertaking. Starting in 1956, the UN undertook consideration of geographic origins when selecting a secretary-general. This was to ensure that no one particular region of the world was more "represented" than others, although geographic distribution was still supposed to remain subordinate to questions of merit when selecting the most desirable candidate.

Of the eight individuals who have served as secretary-general, all have made significant contributions to the peaceful resolution of conflicts in many parts of the world. Some have been more activist than others in terms of leadership style, some more controversial than others, but all have been political figures dependent on the cooperation (and influence) of member nations (especially the five permanent Security Council members), and all have sought to wield influence over the membership as well as over the UN bureaucracy. For example, Kofi Annan (1997–2007) sought to build closer relationships between civil society and nonstate actors, including businesses, for pursuing the benefits of globalization. He also worked to strengthen the UN's traditional role in the "development and the maintenance of international peace and security" and to ensure human rights and the "values of equality, tolerance, and human dignity" espoused by the UN Charter.[44] Following the September 11, 2001, terrorist attacks on the United States, Annan played a principal role in the international struggle against terrorism through the General Assembly and the Security Council.[45] In December 2001, Annan and the United Nations were awarded the Nobel Peace Prize on the one hundredth anniversary of the award. The Nobel citation noted that Annan "had been preeminent in bringing new life to the Organization" and noted "that the only negotiable road to global peace and cooperation goes by way of the United Nations."[46]

International Court of Justice

Headquartered in The Hague, Netherlands, and permanently in session, the International Court of Justice (also known as the World Court, like its League of Nations predecessor) is the principal judicial organ of the UN. All questions brought before the court are decided by majority vote. Its fifteen judges are elected by the General Assembly and Security Council for nine-year terms. The election of the fifteen judges is one of individuals, not of states, chosen on the basis of their high moral character and their expert legal qualifications. Judges must come from different countries to ensure that most of the world's principal judicial and legal systems are represented on the court. The composition of the court, not free of political influences, changes periodically to ensure that the justices are drawn from leading states whose legal systems and institutions are well established, legitimate, and stable.

The court hears cases brought to it by the state involved. It also provides advisory opinions to the General Assembly and Security Council at their request. Although its decisions are formally binding between the parties concerned, there are no formal mechanisms to enforce its rulings. However, the UN charter provides that if a party fails to perform its obligations under a judgment, the other party may go to the Security Council, which may apply more pressure on the offending party to enforce the ruling.

The notion of state sovereignty also limits the effectiveness of court decisions. Because there is no formal obligation to accept the rulings, those that are perceived as violating state sovereignty are often brushed aside. Iran, for example, ignored the court's order to release the hostages held after the takeover of the U.S. embassy in Teheran in 1979, and the United States similarly dismissed an order to halt the mining of Nicaraguan harbors in the 1980s. In 2004, the ICJ ruled that Israel's security barrier in the West Bank (which surrounds more than seventy-eight Palestinian and Arab communities) was illegal and should be removed; the Israeli government ignored the ruling, arguing that the court does not have jurisdiction over issues pertaining to the occupation of the territories (interestingly, though, the Israeli Supreme Court did cite the ICJ's ruling in ordering the army to alter the barrier's route so as to lessen the harmful effects on Palestinians).[47]

Economic and Social Council

The **Economic and Social Council (ECOSOC)** is responsible for coordinating the work of the UN "family" of more specialized agencies and organizations, including the Universal Postal Union (UPU), International Children's Emergency Fund (UNICEF), the World Meteorological Organization (WMO), the World Health Organization (WHO), and the Food and Agriculture Organization (FAO). The ECOSOC "is responsible for promoting higher standards of living, full employment, and economic and social progress; identifying solutions to international economic, social and health problems; facilitating international cultural and educational cooperation; and encouraging universal respect for human rights and fundamental freedoms." In addition, the body issues reports related to these issues. "With its broad mandate the Council's purview extends to over 70 per cent of the human and financial resources of the entire UN system."[48]

The ECOSOC has been the most controversial organ of the UN as the specific tasks that several specialized agencies have sought to accomplish have drawn widespread criticism. Again, disputes between member states and ECOSOC specialized agencies seem to erupt most often when the question of state sovereignty becomes prominent. In 1992, for example, inspectors from the International Atomic Energy Agency (IAEA) endured verbal and physical harassment when trying to inspect alleged nuclear weapons production facilities inside Iraq. Inspectors were to determine whether Saddam Hussein was complying with UN prohibitions against such facilities there. Hussein opposed the inspections, claiming they violated Iraqi sovereignty. In response, President George H. W. Bush, in August 1992, threatened to bomb the Iraqi Ministry of Military Industrialization, largely responsible for Baghdad's nuclear programs, if inspections were not permitted. The confrontation fizzled as the IAEA team was allowed to complete its inspection without attempting to enter the national security ministry itself.

A second set of controversies over ECOSOC centers on the **UN Educational, Scientific, and Cultural Organization (UNESCO).** UNESCO promotes international collaboration among states in education, scholarship in the humanities and social sciences, and the arts. In 1984, the Reagan administration withdrew the

▪ **Economic and Social Council (ECOSOC)**
A UN organ responsible for coordinating the work of the UN "family" of more specialized agencies and organizations.

▪ **UN Educational, Scientific, and Cultural Organization (UNESCO)**
A specialized agency of the UN that attempts to improve literacy rates in the developing world, promote scientific and cultural exchange, and facilitate the distribution of information.

United States from UNESCO, charging it with anti-Western bias and economic mismanagement. Lack of American funding greatly reduced the effectiveness of the organization. The end of the Cold War led to renewed calls for the United States to rejoin UNESCO. In 1997, Britain, which dropped out at the same time as the United States, rejoined the organization. Meanwhile, the United States expressed its approval of a set of Japanese proposals to streamline and reform UNESCO's bureaucratic apparatus. In fact, in September 2002, President George W. Bush stated that the United States would rejoin the organization, which it did in October 2003.[49] Overall, much like their primary organs, UN cultural and educational agencies have not always lived up to the lofty goals proclaimed by their founders.

UN Peacekeeping Missions: Expectations and Experience

When UN collective security operations involve the use of force against a belligerent, UN peacekeeping and truce-supervision forces serve as armed sentries. Known as the Blue Berets and **Blue Helmets** because they retain their national uniforms but wear UN headgear, they are dispatched only at the invitation of parties to a local conflict (sometimes with great-power prodding), with their primary mission to separate armed combatants to make violation of a peace agreement more difficult. Peacekeeping forces are assigned to the UN by member states; the UN does not maintain a standing army, although this has been suggested. Since 1948, the Security Council has authorized sixty-three peacekeeping operations involving 600,000 troops, more than 2,000 of whom have died in the line of duty.[50] The Blue Helmets collectively received a Nobel Peace Prize in 1988 in recognition of their efforts.

The UN undertakes several kinds of missions, including observer, peacekeeping, and peace enforcement. **Observer missions** are international forces sent to observe a cease-fire that has been organized by the two opposing sides of a dispute. These forces are not usually large enough to make the cease-fire effective. **Peacekeeping missions** (see Table 13.1) not only observe the cease-fire but also act as a buffer between the two sides. **Peace enforcement missions** observe, act as a buffer, and, as a last resort, are allowed to use military force to keep the peace. Thus, peacekeeping operations differ from peace enforcement actions in that peacekeepers are dispatched to prevent combat, not take part in it. Also, significantly, peace enforcement missions do not require the invitation of the governments within whose territories the UN troops will be operating. Peace enforcement thus represents a decision to favor the greater good over state sovereignty. The UN-approved military operations in Korea, the Persian Gulf, and Somalia (discussed later) were undertaken without the respective countries' permission.

The end of the Cold War allowed ethnic conflicts to resurface in various regions of the world, just as the decline of Cold War politics within the UN encouraged the wider use of UN missions to mitigate these conflicts. However, expectations of what peacekeepers can now accomplish in a post–Cold War world frequently outpace what they can in fact achieve. The UN missions in the

▪ **Blue Helmets**
UN peacekeeping and truce-supervision forces dispatched at the invitation of parties to a local conflict. Their primary mission is to serve as armed sentries, separating combatants to make violation of a peace agreement more difficult. Also known as "Blue Berets," they wear UN headgear but retain their respective national uniforms.

▪ **Observer missions**
One of the types of UN missions; international forces that are present to observe a cease-fire organized by or for the opposing forces in a dispute.

▪ **Peacekeeping missions**
One of the types of UN missions; these troops not only observe a cease-fire but also act as a buffer between the two sides of a conflict.

▪ **Peace enforcement missions**
One of the types of UN missions; these troops observe, act as a buffer, and, as a last resort, are allowed to use military force to keep the peace in a particular locale.

TABLE 13.1	United Nations Peacekeeping Fact Sheet: Current Department of Peacekeeping Operations (DPKO)-led Peace Missions	
Year Launched	**Location**	**Name of Mission**
1948	Jerusalem	UNTSO (UN Truce Supervision Organization)
1949	India/Pakistan	UNMOGIP (UN Military Observer Group in India and Pakistan)
1964	Cyprus	UNFICYP (UN Peacekeeping Force in Cyprus)
1974	Syria	UNDOF (UN Disengagement Observer Force)
1978	Lebanon	UNIFIL (UN Interim Force in Lebanon)
1991	Western Sahara	MINURSO (UN Mission for the Referendum in Western Sahara)
1999	Kosovo	UNMIK (UN Interim Administration Mission in Kosovo)
1999	Democratic Republic of Congo	MONUC (UN Organization Mission in the Democratic Republic of Congo)
2002	Afghanistan	UNAMA (UN Assistance Mission in Afghanistan; a political mission administered by DPKO)
2003	Liberia	UNMIL (UN Mission in Liberia)
2004	Côte d'Ivoire	UNOCI (UN Operation in Côte d'Ivoire)
2004	Haiti	MINUSTAH (UN Stabilization Mission in Haiti)
2005	Sudan	UNMIS (UN Mission in the Sudan)
2006	Timor-Leste	UNMIT (UN Integrated Mission in Timor-Leste)
2007	Central African Republic and Chad	MINURCAT (UN Mission in the Central African Republic and Chad)
2007	Darfur, Sudan	UNAMID African Union (UN Hybrid Operation in Darfur)

Source: Based on data from http://www.un.org/en/peacekeeping/currentops.shtml and http://www.un.org/en/peacekeeping/list.shtml

former Yugoslavia and Somalia provide illuminating examples of mixed success (see Chapter 6 for a full account of the international community's involvement in both of these crises). Only NATO intervention in 1995, following an agreement among the warring parties, was able to provide effective intervention in the case of Yugoslavia, and the UN's inability to stabilize Somalia and ensure safe passage of humanitarian assistance contributed to the country's ongoing domestic anarchy.

Perhaps the biggest challenge facing UN peacekeeping missions in the future rests not on the battlefield but, rather, in the pocketbooks of member states. An independent advisory group concluded nearly two decades ago (although it still holds today) that the UN lacked the funding necessary for most effective peacekeeping and enforcement operations. To manage the ongoing problems of funding operations on such a scale, the report recommended the creation of a unified peacekeeping budget, annual assessments from member governments, and the establishment of a $400 million revolving fund for peacekeeping, to be financed by all member states.[51] The report reflected the increased international demands on the UN for peacekeeping in the 1990s. In 1991, about 15,000 UN peacekeepers were deployed around the world.[52] As of August 2010, nearly 100,000 military and civilian police from 116 states were serving in the current peacekeeping operations (this total does not include the more than 21,000 local and international civilian staff and UN volunteers). The peacekeeping budget for the period from July 2009 to June 2010 was estimated at $7.9 billion.[53]

Overall, despite the ongoing problem of inadequate funding, UN missions have played a vital role in bringing many conflicts to an end, especially in Africa, Central America, and the Middle East. Examples of successful peacekeeping include assistance in the transition to democratic rule in Namibia, El Salvador, and Cambodia. Because the end of the Cold War freed the community to focus on and respond to regional and ethnic conflicts all over the world, it is clear that UN forces will continue to be called on to play a major role in the resolution of these conflicts. In response to these concerns, the government leaders attending the 2005 World Summit called for the "Responsibility to Protect" (R2P) as part of their World Summit Outcome, in which the international community recognizes its responsibility to protect innocent people and prevent civilian deaths in times of conflict, when a state fails to protect its population from genocide, ethnic cleansing, crimes against humanity, and war crimes. The argument is that sovereignty implies responsibility—that states cannot argue that sovereignty trumps human rights violations. Thus, the international community, through the UN Security Council, has an obligation, a responsibility, to intervene to protect civilians. As a result of the World Summit outcome, both the General Assembly and Security Council adopted resolutions stipulating the responsibility to protect people from the four crimes noted. Of course, the "responsibility to protect" principle has its detractors, who argue that the concept would provide legitimacy to Western states to intervene in poorer ones and also that it reinforces the power of the five permanent members of the Security Council to determine when force might be used against another state. While the critics remain, the "responsibility to protect" has become increasingly viewed by the international community as an important norm.[54]

The question remains, however, whether UN forces should help settle conflicts, build new governments (peace building), protect personnel providing humanitarian relief, or just separate the combatants. These tasks have proven difficult to separate in practice, and the linkages between them have often

UN Peacekeeping

You are the secretary-general of the United Nations. Despite a broad international effort in the 1990s to end the civil war and establish democracy in Cambodia, the country is seized by a wave of violence as political factions begin fighting once again. Civilian casualties are mounting, and images of reported atrocities flash across television screens every night. Some UN observers, along with relief workers from many countries, are still in place, but they are increasingly threatened by the escalating conflict, and the head of the UN mission reports that their position may soon become untenable. The government in Phnom Penh is prepared to allow an expanded UN presence, but only if the government believes this will increase its chances of survival, which are uncertain. The United States is prepared to use its military forces to evacuate American civilians, and Japan has indicated that it would be willing to partially finance expanded humanitarian relief, but no other member states have made commitments. The Security Council has passed several resolutions calling for an end to the violence, but the warring factions have essentially ignored these resolutions.

You have no permanent forces under your command, so if you believe urgent action is necessary, you must rely on the Security Council and the member states. You cannot force member states to take action, but you can try to persuade them to act and can explain why expanded UN intervention would be in their own interest and in the interest of international security. However, most members of the Security Council regard Cambodia as an area of peripheral interest at best and will be very reluctant to spend money and risk lives in a conflict that does not directly affect them. The sole exception is China, but it lacks the logistical capability to transport large numbers of troops or quantities of supplies for humanitarian relief. Moreover, the other Security Council members would almost certainly veto a major operation in which China had the leading role, and even suggesting such a move would provoke strenuous opposition from Japan, South Korea, and other Asian states. Thus, a truly international effort is the only option for a renewed UN presence.

But should the UN try again where it has failed before? It will not be easy to justify another major UN effort at peacekeeping and nation-building even if all sides in the conflict agree to participate. The Security Council and other member states might find it difficult to justify spending more money and risking more troops in what they may now perceive as a lost cause. It might be better to evacuate the military and civilian observers now in place and use your influence to try to achieve a negotiated truce. This will take time, however, as long as one or more of the factions believes that they can gain something by fighting. If action is not taken soon, the death toll could rise, and a repeat of the horrors of the "killing fields" of the 1970s might not be out of the question.

Therefore, you are faced with some difficult choices. Should you ask for an expanded international commitment to stop the fighting, or should you withdraw UN personnel from this dangerous situation? If you ask for intervention, should you justify your request on the grounds of peacekeeping, humanitarian aid, or both? What precedents will your decision set for future UN peacekeeping? How could the actions you call for affect demands for political and financial reform of the UN—or should these even be considered at this time of urgent need?

The decisions you make and the actions you support could define the role of the United Nations at the beginning of the twenty-first century, but the potential victims of violence in Cambodia are your immediate concern.

What Would You Do?

resulted in "mission creep," as peacekeepers find that their initially modest objectives cannot be accomplished without undertaking more ambitious tasks, such as disarming warring factions. The commitment of the Blue Helmets to their missions has never been in question, but the negative response to former Secretary-General Boutros Boutros-Ghali's call for a predesignated reserve of peacekeeping forces, and the UN's bitter experiences in Yugoslavia, Somalia, and elsewhere, have cast further doubt on the extent to which UN member states will be willing to commit more troops and funds for their efforts.[55] Moreover, what happens once the fighting stops? The international community needs to consider what to do once the peacekeeping efforts have been successful in ending conflict, which means postconflict reconstruction and peacebuilding. As noted previously, the Security Council's mandate is one of responding to threats to peace and security, but "peacebuilding goes beyond the need to secure peace." What is needed is development, "which is the purview of the Economic and Social Council." To transition from peacekeeping to peacebuilding, for a more lasting peace, effective coordination must occur between the Security Council and ECOSOC.[56] In response, the UN established the Peacebuilding Commission in 2005, with a Peacebuilding Fund created in 2006, to assist countries in the postconflict stage in terms of both political reform (promoting democracy) and economic reform (promoting economic growth).[57] More recently, in February 2010 Secretary-General Ban Ki-moon acknowledged the lessons learned from the peacekeeping operations in the 1990s and the need to maintain "some type of follow-on presence to protect gains and continue the process of building durable peace," including the establishment of a UN Peacebuilding Office as part of the Peacebuilding Commission.[58] The challenge for continued and future peacekeeping operations continues—how to maintain and promote peace within and among the member states. With conflict and war a constant presence in the international system, the need for UN peacekeepers will continue for the foreseeable future.

United Nations' Effectiveness

Mindful of how the lofty expectations for the League of Nations had been dashed quickly, the founders of the UN sought to dampen expectations about what the new organization could accomplish. They believed that only the concerted will and strength of the great powers, reflected in agreement among the five permanent Security Council members, could rebuff aggression. Although it would seem that the veto power exercised by any permanent Security Council member could prevent the United Nations from taking any action and thus limit its effectiveness, the veto was intended to ensure that the UN would undertake only those actions that all the great powers would support. It was hoped that this "great-power government" would be adequate to meet any challenge presented to the postwar international system. In recognizing that the power of all states was not created equal, the UN's founders demonstrated a more realistic grasp of global power politics than the idealistic founders of the League of Nations.

Thus far, the UN appears to be the only existing organization with a chance of countering aggression in a legitimate and impartial manner. Its activities transcend those of the collective security organizations that preceded it, as its various agencies deal with a wide array of issues that transcend state borders. The power and effectiveness of the UN are still hamstrung, however, by its inability to claim sovereign authority over all states engaged in international affairs, given that action by the UN usually requires consent of the countries involved.

As was the case with the League of Nations, the UN cannot force any state to comply with its resolutions if the major powers are not committed to enforcing those resolutions with military might when necessary. Many argue that UN sanctions against Iraq for its invasion of Kuwait in 1990 would not have sufficed to compel Iraq to withdraw. Rather, a coalition of great powers (especially Britain, France, and the United States) was necessary to achieve that goal in the Persian Gulf, and would similarly have been required to put an end to the fighting in Bosnia in an expeditious manner. Might may not make right, but right is often impotent without might.

Lack of sovereign authority does not mean that UN sanctions are condemned to futility. In some cases, a UN sanctions resolution alone can inflict considerable costs on a state that is transgressing international law if the resolution's goals are shared by other states. Although many states find ways around sanctions, a state facing a UN-sanctioned embargo carries the stigma of being an international troublemaker, and few states wish to have their good standing tarnished by being associated with a stigmatized state. Arguably, for example, the governments of Rhodesia (now Zimbabwe) and South Africa were pressured to change their racist domestic policies by UN-sponsored sanctions.[59]

The UN's more than six decades of existence have proven that the objectives and expectations of the organization's founders were essentially correct. The UN was not designed to be all things to all states. It was created as a forum for the discussion of global issues, as a coordinating body for development aid and humanitarian relief, and as a means to facilitate collective security when the world's major powers agree on what should be done to meet specific threats. Overall, it has performed these functions remarkably well, even though it has been a target of justifiable criticism (as mentioned in this section). It has not brought about world peace; it cannot do so, and it was never intended to.

The UN is capable of doing more if its member states provide it with more resources, but its efforts will always be subject to the limitations imposed by national sovereignty as long as sovereignty remains a fundamental principle of international relations. Sovereignty constrains international organizations just as civil rights constrain national governments. In both cases, the governed cannot be blamed for thinking carefully before conceding more power to the government, even in the interest of law and order.

The UN's greatest challenge in the twenty-first century will be to adapt its structure and mission to the changing international system. It has risen to the challenge in some areas, placing new emphasis on sustainable development, famine relief, and programs to fight diseases such as AIDS (see Chapter 11).

In other areas, particularly peacekeeping, the need for further reform, division of responsibilities with other IOs and national governments, and finding a better balance between goals and resources is clear. Moreover, the institution needs to do a better job with promoting gender equality both in its own institution overall and in the countries in which it is involved in peacekeeping. For example, in 2000 the Security Council adopted resolution 1325, which called for women's involvement in peace negotiations and in the postconflict rebuilding of society. Yet women's roles in peace negotiations remain limited, if their presence is found at the negotiating table at all. With regard to UN peacekeeping operations, women experience sexual abuse and exploitation by peacekeepers, making women's lives even more insecure. Given that women are affected by conflict differently than men, their needs must be understood and addressed. The UN must be more proactive in including gender issues in all facets of its operations and activities.

Changing the UN Charter to reflect contemporary realities will be difficult, but the United States and other countries continue to call for organizational and financial reforms. The "Oil for Food" scandal reaffirms the arguments of UN critics that the organization is overly bureaucratic and "prone to fraud and abuse." Following the 1991 Gulf War, the Security Council imposed economic sanctions on Iraq. As a means to prevent starvation of the Iraqi people, the UN established the Oil for Food program, which allowed the Iraqi government to sell oil for food and medicine between 1995 and 2003. Rather than using the oil revenues to help his people, President Saddam Hussein collected nearly $2 billion in illegal oil revenue. It was discovered that UN officials received kickbacks from the Iraqi regime, thereby tarnishing the UN's reputation because of the significant mismanagement and level of corruption and fraud that took place.[60] An independent report that investigated the scandal found that over half of the 4,500 companies involved in the program "paid kickbacks or surcharges to the Iraqi government."[61] In many ways, it was the Oil for Food scandal that prompted then-Secretary-General Annan to push for serious reforms at the organization, as reflected by his report at the 2005 World Summit.[62]

The UN has furthest to go in reforming its political structure. Some reform proposals advocate expanding the Security Council; adding permanent seats for Germany, Japan, and major developing countries like Brazil and India; or changing the rules regarding vetoes. Such measures may help make the UN more effective, but, like its member states, the UN must find ways to adapt to economic globalization, regional integration, political fragmentation, and threats to security such as terrorism and ethnic conflict.[63] Otherwise, like its predecessors, the Concert of Europe and the League of Nations, it might soon discover that the world it was designed to serve has left it far behind.

As a response to the challenges faced by the UN in the twenty-first century, the General Assembly adopted Resolution 55/2, the United Nations Millennium Declaration. The Declaration adopted at the Millennium Summit held in New York in September 2000 by 147 heads of states and governments from the 191 member states established "the most comprehensive set of goals ever to receive global endorsement." These goals include peace and security, human rights, environmental protection, and targets for "reducing poverty, disease, hunger, illiteracy and gender discrimination" by 2015 (see also Chapter 10). The UN resolved to publish progress reports annually through 2015 indicating whether these goals have been met by the members of the international community. At the halfway mark, the UN noted that the results have been mixed.[64]

Economic IGOs

Whereas the UN is primarily focused on collective security and peace in the international system, other IGOs focus on economic issues, which are particularly important given the increased globalization and interdependence of the global economy, and are thereby further manifestations of global governance. As noted in Chapter 4, the Bretton Woods meeting in 1944 led to the creation of three important intergovernmental institutions to promote a stable international economic system. These organizations, the World Bank, International Monetary Fund, and GATT/WTO, discussed in detail next, are charged with encouraging development, reducing poverty, stabilizing exchange rates, and promoting and maintaining an open and free trade system (see Chapters 9 and 10 for more detailed examination of economic issues).

The World Bank
The World Bank's goal is to eliminate poverty. The World Bank is owned by 186 member countries, each of which is a shareholder with decision-making power. The Bank has become the primary financier of development projects in lesser developed countries, as well as the largest creditor. The World Bank burgeoned in the 1970s, funding enormous infrastructure development projects in developing countries worldwide, including dams, highway and road projects, education programs, commercial forestry efforts, cattle ranching, and export-oriented agricultural programs. By the 1980s it had become clear that a substantial proportion of these projects were deeply counterproductive, planned without taking into account local technologies, the environment, or sustainability. Moreover, few of these large-scale infrastructural development projects achieved their own economic objectives. The costs of such failures can be measured not just economically, but socially, ecologically, and politically as well.

Importantly, the World Bank has attempted to adjust to the changing requirements of the increasingly complicated international economy. It has learned from past mistakes, shifting its emphasis from development projects to social programs, paying more attention to the environment, and toning down its tendency to treat lesser developed countries as wayward children in need of strong discipline. Thus today, the World Bank provides billions of dollars in loans and grants per year and works with government agencies, NGOs, and the private sector in more than 100 developing countries, focusing on improving standards of living, reducing poverty, and developing more efficient, productive economic structures (in fiscal year 2009 the World Bank Group sponsored 767 projects, and in doing so committed $58.8 billion in credits, guarantees, grants, and loans). The Bank's programs are means to achieve the UN's Millennium Development Goals.[65] Still, despite such adjustments, the Bank's relevance and utility remain open to question. Concerned governments and NGOs have adopted various approaches to the World Bank's ongoing problems, perhaps the most important of which is the imbalance of influence among the Bank's members. Some seek to affect change from the inside, working within the established system under the assumption that such an institution, if reformed to be "faster, more flexible, and more accountable," holds promise for international economic cooperation (and, in fact, in 2010 the Bank shifted its voting power to give more to developing countries). Others see the Bank as moribund and unsalvageable, arguing that despite all efforts at reform, its structure benefits the richest countries at the expense of the poorest. Still others criticize the institution for a lack of focus, and yet in the last decade or so, given the effectiveness of the institution, the Bank has been pressured into providing funds for areas beyond its original intention, areas in which other IGOs are working, such as education (UNESCO) and HIV/AIDS (WHO).[66] For the time being, the Bank continues to grow and expand its efforts, all the while evolving to meet the needs of the world economic system.

The International Monetary Fund

The IMF is the World Bank's related institution: Whereas the World Bank was set up to provide funds for redevelopment, the IMF was created to regulate and liberalize the international monetary system to facilitate global trade and investment. As a secondary objective, the IMF, like the World Bank, also seeks to eradicate poverty. The IMF's goals include the promotion "of international monetary cooperation through a permanent institution that provides the machinery for consultation and collaboration on international monetary problems" as well as the promotion "of exchange stability, to maintain orderly exchange arrangements among members, and to avoid competitive exchange depreciation."[67]

The IMF's oversight and regulation of the international monetary system is important because each country's currency's relative value fluctuates in the global currency market, complicating transactions. Countries can also manipulate their currencies' relative values to gain advantages in paying off loans to other countries, in balance of trade, or in investment. IMF member states have therefore agreed to communicate and coordinate on domestic monetary policies that will affect exchange rates and payments between countries (rising interest rates, currency valuation, export taxes, import quotas, etc.) in the hopes that the IMF can help prevent monetary crises by promoting exchange rate stability and the orderly correction of balance-of-payments problems and by discouraging countries from competitively devaluing their currencies. The IMF and its members also ensure convertibility of currency on demand, allowing unrestricted international travel, commerce, and investment. Finally, much like

KÂR DEĞİL İNSAN!

DÜNYA BANKASI-IMF ☞ DEFOL!

PHOTO 13.2 Many believe that the IMF and the World Bank are not concerned with the well-being of the people they claim to help.

the World Bank, the IMF acts as a lender of last resort to members having difficulty making good on loans, as long as those countries are willing to undertake economic reforms along the lines of the structural adjustment programs (SAPs) described in Chapter 10. Whereas the World Bank lends for long-term development, the IMF provides shorter-term loans to help countries ride out economic crunches.

The IMF has prevented countries from economic free fall, stepping in as lender of last resort when it appears that governments have no alternative other than to default on their debts. This is most clearly seen in the example of the joint IMF–European three-year, $145 billion loan for Greece in May 2010 to prevent that country from defaulting on its debts.[68] Although bailing out governments is perhaps the IMF's most highly visible activity, the institution's most important role, arguably, has been its steady surveillance of member countries' economies, the better to discuss and assist in their steady economic development and stable inflation rates. Following the collapse of the Soviet Union, the IMF reorganized and hired staff to help the newly independent states make their transitions to market economies. Before long, Russia had accounted for nearly a quarter of all outstanding debts to the IMF. Since then, other states, including Brazil, Hungary, Romania, and Ukraine, have become large debtor states.[69] More than anything, however, beyond its role as lender and beyond its efforts to oversee and advise governments' financial decisions, the IMF "provides a key forum for exchange of ideas and best practices."[70]

Like the World Bank, perhaps even more so, the IMF has been criticized on a number of fronts. It has been charged with cutting developing countries out of key decisions; with making loans contingent on unreasonable and counterproductive "reforms"; with failing to control the effects of easy, fast convertibility (which leads to monetary speculation, arguably the cause of the Asian financial crisis of the late 1990s); and with "moral hazard," which creates the impression that private lenders can make incautious loans under the assumption that the IMF will step in and prevent defaults. Opponents of the IMF point to former IMF "golden children," from the Asian Tigers to Argentina, as examples of the IMF's failed approach, and to riots and other more serious forms of political and social unrest in countries that tried to subscribe to the institution's SAPs. Opponents also resent the IMF's decision-making process. IMF programs are run by a twenty-four-member executive board headquartered in Washington, DC. Because relative capital contributions to the Fund determine relative voting weight, the United States controls approximately 17 percent of all votes, almost three times as many as any other country.[71] This process leaves many countries feeling powerless and many observers concerned about the U.S. role in the organization.

IMF supporters make counterpoints for each of these complaints. They point out that the United States, because it makes the largest capital contribution (more than $50 billion), is entitled to have more influence over how, where, and under what conditions the money is disbursed than do other contributors. Supporters also make the point that most countries are able to pay back their debts to the IMF, demonstrating their continued solvency, a condition they could not have taken for granted absent the initial IMF assistance. They also argue that, without the IMF, many of those countries could well have defaulted on loans, leading to larger crises. IMF supporters further maintain that the IMF plays an irreplaceable role in promoting positive growth in global financial transactions while maintaining exchange rate stability.[72]

The GATT and the World Trade Organization (WTO)

The General Agreement on Tariffs and Trade (GATT) fell short of being a fullblown institution; rather, the agreement came into being by default. Initially, more than fifty countries agreed to a draft charter of the International Trade Organization (ITO), a third IGO that complemented the IMF and the World Bank. While work continued on the development of the ITO Charter, twentythree of the countries that agreed to the institution's draft charter got a jump start at removing some of the ongoing protectionist policies that led to World War II. They voluntarily opened a preratification round of tariff negotiations under the trade rules outlined in the charter. The substantial and significant tariff concessions made at that first round of negotiations and the provisional trade rules the participants accepted became the GATT and came into force in 1948. The agreement promoted free trade between member states not only by regulating and reducing barriers to trade but also by providing a shared mechanism for resolving trade-related disputes. In March 1948, a final version of the ITO Charter was finally approved at a UN Conference, but the organization—which went much further than the GATT in regulating employment, investment, and other aspects of trade—never came into being. The U.S. government announced that it would not submit the ITO Charter to Congress for ratification, and the ITO withered on the vine. Countries were thus left for forty-seven years with the highly provisional and voluntary GATT as the only mechanism moderating global trade.[73]

Yet the GATT was an ideal apparatus for the postwar years, helping to negotiate reductions in tariffs throughout the 1950s and 1960s that led to unprecedented rates of trade growth worldwide. The GATT's membership grew to more than 100 countries. Tariffs fell steadily as the GATT went through several different rounds. Then, in the 1970s and 1980s, the organization's shortcomings became increasingly obvious and problematic. As countries were hit by recession, they began to impose nontariff barriers to trade, policies over which the GATT had no authority. Loopholes in the GATT, particularly regarding agriculture and agricultural products, became more of an issue. At a higher level, the global economy had become more complex and larger, with rapid growth in international investment and trade-in-services (e.g., tourism), which were not covered under the GATT. In 1982, the GATT ministers came together to launch a new negotiating round but could not come to terms on agriculture. Although the 1982 meeting was considered a failure, it was there that the ministers set in motion the first steps for the Uruguay Round. Four years later the Uruguay Round began, and this time everything was on the table, from agriculture to trade-in-services. The negotiations took nearly eight years, but in April 1994 the Uruguay Round was successfully completed and the World Trade Organization (WTO) was born. Rather than abandon a multilateral mechanism that had fallen short, the GATT countries asserted their commitment to globalization by creating a new institution that improved on and expanded the GATT.[74]

The WTO is more than an expanded, updated GATT. It is a real institution with a structure and staff (as of 2010, 153 states are members). It covers a wider range of trade issues, including intellectual property rights and trade-in-services (GATT dealt with trade in goods). It precludes the kind of plurilateral and bilateral agreements among its members that undermined the GATT by letting its members break down into competing factions. It streamlined and improved the dispute settlement system.[75] In effect, it took up where the ITO planners had left off almost fifty years earlier.

The WTO, although not officially a Bretton Woods institution and the only one of the three that is not associated with the United Nations, has not been immune from the kinds of criticisms aimed at the World Bank and the IMF. In late 1999, riots broke out in the streets of Seattle as protesters came out in full force against the WTO. Labor organizations came to protest because the WTO refused to insist on labor safeguards, which can work against developing countries and can be perceived as a form of protectionism. Environmentalists came to protest because the WTO had not explicitly linked environmental protections to trade liberalization. Activists turned out in support of developing countries, arguing that the WTO was undemocratic (a charge that seemed to be supported at the WTO meeting as representatives from developing countries were repeatedly left out of negotiations) and motivated by corporate interests rather than concerns about development. The strange nexus of environmental and labor interests—usually diametrically opposed—highlighted the range of issues that WTO decisions and actions affect globally.[76]

WTO opponents claimed, in the aftermath of Seattle's drama, that the organization's days were numbered. Yet the Doha Round in Japan two years later proved to be uneventful and very successful. The WTO functions effectively as a trade authority and mediator. Several serious EU–U.S. trade disputes have been brought to the WTO, which then made rulings based on international trade rules. For example, the WTO deemed that the U.S. practice of giving rebates to American companies paying taxes on foreign sales constituted an illegal export subsidy and awarded the EU the right to impose $4 billion worth of countermeasures if the United States did not amend the relevant law. The United States, in response, agreed to amend the law and the EU deferred countermeasures while it waited to see how the United States implemented changes. Although the United States has been the most active in the WTO dispute system, with the EU coming in a close second, countries from all over the world, each with a very different economic system and culture, have availed themselves of the WTO dispute system. Korea, Chile, Argentina, Mexico, Australia, Brazil, India, Turkey, Japan, Guatemala, Indonesia, and Canada have all used the system to respond to perceived breaches in fair and free trade. This process—having a set of rules agreed to by consensus that can then be referred to in WTO adjudication—is largely understood to be the institution's biggest contribution to the stability of the international economy.

The WTO scored perhaps its biggest success to date when China gained entry in December 2001 following fifteen years of negotiations. China's entry was considered an enormous victory in the liberalization of the world economy, representing, as it did, an effort to transcend existing WTO members' domestic constituencies' concerns (particularly in the United States) and China's own transition from a strict command economy to a market economy with vast potential.

The Bretton Woods Institutions into the Future

To the dismay of some and the relief of others, the Bretton Woods institutions have not only survived since the end of World War II but have also expanded their missions and memberships, all the while adapting to the changing requirements of the international economic system and becoming increasingly important for global governance. Are the institutions tools of the great powers and corporations? They yield admittedly disproportionate influence on the institutions' policies. Have the industrialized states benefited disproportionately from globalization? They will continue to do so. Are there double standards, by which the industrialized nations can maintain price supports but require developing countries remove their own protections? Yes. Are the institutions democratic? Not entirely. Indeed, there is no question that each of the Bretton Woods institutions has at best contributed to, and at worst caused, economic, political, social, and even environmental crises. Yet it is also true that they have funded development, supported education and health, provided governments with profitable and constructive advice, bailed out countries on the verge of economic collapse, and, perhaps most important, created forums in which governments can come together to air complaints, seek commonalities, and develop confidence. In the meantime, they have each adjusted policies and programs in response to their failures, as have their members, demonstrating steep learning curves on many issues. Sticky moral dilemmas will continue: Should countries that depend on child labor be penalized or helped? What should the World Bank or IMF do when countries must undertake suboptimal, short-term economic policies to ensure that they can pay off their loans to the institutions? Are SAPs patronizing, counterproductive requirements that sidestep the real threats states face from outside, or are they the only way the Bretton Woods organizations can help countries reform self-defeating economic systems into productive, growing economies? These questions will persist. They are inevitable, given the complexities of international relations and the global economy. That they are being raised and discussed means that constructive, deliberate debate is taking place on all of these important topics. In the end, perhaps the one immutable, undeniable characteristic that these institutions share is their commitment to liberal economic policies and the belief that eventually, if not immediately, economic globalization will be the higher tide on which all boats rise.

Nongovernmental Organizations

Not all organizations taking an active part in international politics are directly affiliated with governments. These NGOs operate across national boundaries independent of governments. Like IGOs, they can be widely or narrowly focused with either more broadly based or narrowly restricted memberships. The Roman Catholic Church, the International Red Cross, Amnesty International, and Greenpeace are examples of NGOs with broad-based memberships (most scholars note that NGOs are nonprofit, so they often consider them separate entities from multinational corporations or MNCs). Because most NGOs cannot command resources as easily as states or IGOs, they tend to focus their efforts on specific projects to maximize their effectiveness. Through these projects or through global public support, they can exercise a profound influence on the conduct of states. This section discusses the power and influence that NGOs have and examines several types of NGOs as an illustration of their wide range of activities and interests.

NGOs, Power, and Global Governance

In light of the increased globalization of the international system, NGOs have come into their own as significant players on the world stage—and thus players in global governance. Scholars have examined how NGOs have been able to exert such influence and have focused on several points: NGOs have increased in both number and influence, are involved in more areas such that their functions are often those that were previously the domain of states, work not just with governments but also with IGOs and MNCs, and have profoundly affected state sovereignty.[77]

Given that the power, or influence, of NGOs has increased, from where does this power derive? As political scientist Maryann Cusimano Love notes, "NGOs trade in the currency of ideas, especially ideas of good and evil, right and wrong. The ideas compel, even when the organizations cannot. NGOs attract support more than they can enforce compliance."[78] In essence, NGOs have moral authority, whereas the authority governments possess is legal authority (of course, not all NGOs are agents of positive change—one can think of terrorist organizations; see Chapter 8). In addition to moral authority (versus the military power of governments or economic power of MNCs), NGOs also have information power. In this way, "NGOs may have access to grassroots information about how particular policies affect particular people, information that governments or IGOs overlook or do not have." NGOs thus promote transparency.[79] The UN, for example, relies heavily on NGOs to implement its projects, often as subcontractors, particularly in the field of humanitarian relief and aid, as these NGOs are better equipped and knowledgeable about local conditions on the ground. UN agencies provided more than $2 billion annually to NGO programs by the end of the 1990s.[80]

In addition, NGOs can use the media, which gives them power, especially if they have access to the global media to convey their message and goals. Moreover, the role of individuals, rather than states, matters; at their most basic level, NGOs look to individuals (as members and agents of change). Thus, rather than power held in the hands of states, power is held in the hands of individuals, the activists who are engaged in the work of NGOs. As a result of these aspects of the power NGOs wield, they are able to influence governments, MNCs, and IGOs, as well as individuals, and change their behavior and policies.[81] For example, women's rights NGOs were instrumental in the early 1990s when their efforts and activism led to the UN General Assembly's adoption of the Declaration on the Elimination of All Forms of Violence Against Women by unanimous consent. In doing so, as constructivists would assert, in these actions and others, women's rights NGOs were able to influence the idea of human rights to encompass women's rights. Women's rights NGOs also played a significant role in the adoption of UN Security Council Resolution 1325, which, as noted earlier, called for women's participation in the peace negotiations to end conflict and in the postconflict rebuilding of society.[82] In this way, NGOs have been instrumental in influencing international law.[83]

NGOs are able to garner political access and participation in international institutions, thereby facilitating the global governance system that includes many different actors. With international institutions more open to participation of NGOs, the ability of NGOs to influence policymaking increases. NGOs have increasingly become "official UN partners" when various UN conferences set forth plans of action, thereby further institutionalizing the role NGOs play in the global governance system.[84]

Moreover, globalization has contributed to the growing power and number of NGOs. For example, increased trade liberalization, in which money can transcend borders, provides NGOs with a means to solicit contributions more readily. Globalization of technology allows for the more rapid spread of ideas through the Internet and media.[85]

There are also limitations to the influence of NGOs. Given the array of NGOs, many of which are focused on the same issues, coordinating policies and action is difficult. Addressing problems and issues that transcend state borders means NGOs must be able to work with IGOs, MNCs, and states. However, the ability to work with these other international actors is often fraught with communication problems, as well as problems of coordination.[86]

In the end, however, states and IGOs are increasingly reliant on NGOs for information, implementation, and so forth in an increasingly globalized world. One can assert with certainty that the numbers and influence of NGOs will continue to increase for the foreseeable future. That said, we now turn to a brief discussion of examples of NGOs in action.

NGOs in Action

Many of the most famous NGOs engage in humanitarian activities. The International Committee of the Red Cross and Red Crescent (ICRC) acts as an international relief agency and maintains strict neutrality to alleviate suffering without becoming involved in politics. Its many activities include disaster and famine relief, immunization and public health programs, and efforts to ensure humane treatment of prisoners of war. Human Rights Watch investigates human rights abuses in more than seventy states around the world, publishing its findings in books and reports, and, through this publicity, aims to "embarrass abusive governments in the eyes of their citizens and the world." In meeting with government officials, Human Rights Watch members seek to encourage governments to change both "policy and practice."[87]

Other NGOs work to improve the environment, such as the World Wide Fund for Nature (WWF; formerly the World Wildlife Fund) and Greenpeace. With nearly 5 million supporters worldwide, WWF invests funding in various conservation projects aimed at conserving the globe's biodiversity, use of sustainable renewable natural resources, and promotion of pollution reduction. In all these efforts, WWF engages in scientific research, raises awareness of environmental issues, advises local and national governments on environmental policies, and works with corporations to promote conservation.[88] With 2.8 million supporters around the world and offices in forty-one states, Greenpeace's mission is to bring an awareness of various global environmental problems, whether sailing on the high seas to protect whales from Japan's "scientific" whaling experiment or pressuring companies such as Sony Ericsson, Samsung, and Nokia to phase out toxic chemicals in their electronic products.[89]

Economic and development issue-oriented NGOs include Oxfam and the International Chamber of Commerce. Oxfam, established in Britain during World War II as a famine relief organization, works to end poverty and injustice, evidenced more recently by its food distribution and water supply and sanitation efforts following the December 2004 Indian Ocean tsunami that killed more than 200,000 people and left 2 million homeless.[90] Founded in 1919, the International Chamber of Commerce, with membership of thousands of businesses in more than 130 states, promotes trade and investment, open markets, and the free flow of capital. The organization works with governments and IGOs "whose decisions affect corporate finances and operations worldwide."[91]

It is evident from this brief illustration of the variety of NGOs that these organizations play an important role in advancing many causes around the globe. Pressure on governments and IGOs as a result of raising awareness of these issues has made NGOs indispensable actors on the world stage and global governance.

Conclusion

In this chapter, we have seen how international law and organizations constitute a source of both conflict and cooperation in the international system. Although usually designed to promote cooperation or end conflict on some set of issues, international law and organizations sometimes generate new controversies. These unintended effects of attempts to reduce anarchy, coupled with the failures of international security organizations to prevent conflict and war, lead many people to question the whole enterprise of international law and organizations. It cannot be said that international law has worked perfectly or that the functioning of the UN and other global organizations has been above reproach. Still, these drawbacks are often apparent in domestic law and government as well, and few reasonable people would conclude that laws and governments in general should be abandoned. Sometimes both domestic and international institutions fail because they are poorly designed; at other times the laws and organizations are not themselves faulty, but failures result from weaknesses in the ethics or leadership of the individuals charged with running them. Many efforts to make the world less anarchic have failed for either reason, and sometimes both, but much good has come from the efforts nonetheless. If nothing else, international law sets ethical standards for the conduct of states and facilitates the coordination of action on various matters.

Like domestic law and government, international law and organizations tell us how we should act and why. Sovereign authority can give us powerful incentives to comply, but the decision to obey or disobey is ultimately ours, as is the responsibility for paying the penalty if we choose to break the law. Constrained as they are by national sovereignty, international law and organizations have weak enforcement mechanisms, but they can still give states and leaders incentives to behave in ways that benefit the global community without sacrificing vital national interests, as liberalism would attest.

Levels of Analysis and Paradigms in Review: Global Governance

	Realism	Liberalism	Constructivism
Individual	President George W. Bush "unsigns" the United States from the International Criminal Court, arguing that it would be detrimental to U.S. sovereignty.	President Bill Clinton signs the International Criminal Court treaty, thereby committing the United States to the international treaty.	Hugo Grotius (see Spotlight, "The First International Lawyer," earlier in the chapter) is considered the "father" of international law. His writings during the Thirty Years' War in Europe formulated the legal basis for the principle of national sovereignty, later codified in the Peace of Westphalia, and influenced the principles found in the Concert of Europe and the United Nations.
Domestic	Companies involved in the UN Oil for Food Program received kickbacks from the Iraqi regime in the mid- to late 1990s, reflecting the weakness of international law and organizations to constrain state behavior.	Domestic actors influence governments to participate in and support IOs. For example, the U.S. Congress passed the Helms-Biden Agreement in 1999 for payment of U.S. debts to the UN.	Domestic interest groups are able to change state interests and identities. For example, environmental groups have influenced their governments to include discussion of the environment when conducting trade talks at World Trade Organization meetings. In this way, trade issues (and therefore state interests and identities) expand to include the impact of trade on the environment and sustainable development.

(continued)

	AT A GLANCE *Continued*		
	Realism	**Liberalism**	**Constructivism**
Systemic	International governmental organizations and international law merely reflect the interests of the powerful states in the system.	International law and organizations provide states with the means to cooperate and reach mutually beneficial outcomes.	International women's rights NGOs have overcome opposition and have been able to promote the idea of women's rights as human rights and the need for specific treaties that end gender discrimination and other actions that violate women's rights. The 1993 UN General Assembly meeting led to the adoption of the Declaration on the Elimination of All Forms of Violence Against Women, demonstrating the role that NGOs play in the spreading of norms, ideas, and values, which are then incorporated by states and IGOs.

A word of caution: Not all international organizations seek to promote international cooperation. However, all of the organizations and agreements examined here have one thing in common. In one way or another, intentionally or not, they are all forces for globalization. International humanitarian relief agencies and collective security organizations alike attempt to mobilize opinion and gather resources for solving problems across state boundaries. Some treaties and organizations try to solve global problems at the global level, whereas other groups strive to globalize a local conflict in the hope that other states will intervene. It is clear, therefore, that although the successes attained by international law and organizations in making the world less anarchic are debatable, the increasing ability of various groups to voice their concerns on the world stage must be acknowledged. Although many have been slow to take hold, international institutions have become an integral part of global politics.

In his pivotal book *Leviathan*, seventeenth-century philosopher Thomas Hobbes argued that all-powerful sovereign authority is the only possible way to raise society above its "natural" state of "war of every one against every one."[92] As long as international relations are based on national sovereignty, the effectiveness of international law and organizations will be inherently limited. Nevertheless, through example and the threat of sanctions, international institutions have helped to advance the world a few steps beyond the near-anarchy that prevailed before the Peace of Westphalia set the foundations for the modern international system. In this new century, the world may face a new kind of anarchy, as interdependence promotes cooperation among regions, corporations, municipalities, individuals, and other nonstate actors outside the framework of nation-states and traditional international organizations. The model for future international organizations may be the Internet, which has no central controlling authority but nonetheless has rules and conventions enforced by reciprocity and common practice that enable it to function well despite exponential growth. This kind of "governance without government" may become an important part of the international system's adaptation to globalization and fragmentation. For Hobbes, "anarchy" connoted "chaos," and in the preindustrial and industrial eras the two generally went hand in hand. One of the paradoxes of the information age, however, may be that the world is becoming both more anarchic and more orderly.

Discussion and Review Questions

1. Why do states follow international law given that there is no enforcement mechanism?
2. How would a realist, liberal, and constructivist view the effectiveness of international law?
3. How does the structure of the UN Security Council and the General Assembly cultivate or help overcome conflict?
4. Which theoretical paradigm best explains the effectiveness (or ineffectiveness) of the United Nations?
5. What role do nongovernmental organizations (NGOs) play in the international community?

Key Terms

Blue Helmets 522
Customary
   practices 495
Diplomatic
   immunity 496
Economic and
   Social Council
   (ECOSOC) 521
Global governance 493
Great-power
   unanimity 516

Intergovernmental
   organizations
   (IGOs) 494
International Criminal
   Court 504
Natural law 501
Nongovernmental
   organizations
   (NGOs) 494
Observer missions 522
Pariah states 500

Peace enforcement
   missions 522
Peacekeeping
   missions 522
Positive law 502
Rogue states 500
Treaties 495
UN Educational,
   Scientific, and
   Cultural Organization
   (UNESCO) 521

CHAPTER **14**

World Politics in Context

What Have We Covered So Far?

This book is intended as a guide to world politics. We began with a discussion of conflict and cooperation, arguably the crux of international studies. Indeed, what are we attempting to explain, much less predict, when we analyze global relations if not the causes, expressions, and results of conflict and cooperation? We looked, too, at the intertwined yet conflicting processes of globalization and fragmentation, examining their relationship, their roots, and their effects. We followed that with a look at analytical tools, including the levels of analysis and the three leading theoretical paradigms: realism, liberalism, and constructivism. Throughout the book we showed how you can use those and other tools to parse the complexities of world politics, to break out and identify key actors and dynamics. The next several chapters described in detail how world politics have played out historically, from the Peace of Westphalia to the war in Iraq. Those chapters demonstrate how useful the analytical tools can be, how little is new, and how much we have to learn from the past. After the historical review, we focused in on the specific fields of world politics, including security and economics, and looked also at institutions, demographics, and resource issues. Throughout these chapters we introduced relevant theories, discussed trends, and highlighted the issues' interconnectedness. That interconnectedness—the linkages between the various fields of international affairs—is key. In the past couple of decades we have begun a steep learning curve regarding global relations, the most important component of which is recognition that advancements in one area of world politics—whether it is greater peace, economic development, or preventing pandemics—cannot be sustained without advancements across all fields.

What Have We Not Yet Covered?

Ethics

Thus far, we have not discussed in any detail how ethics relate to international relations, although ethics imbue every issue we have covered from globalization and fragmentation to demographics and resource use. The study of ethics is a field unto itself, and it breaks down into several categories: ethics of war, ethics of sovereignty and intervention, ethics of peace and reconciliation, ethics of trade and development, and ethics of competing interests. For each of these categories there is an entire literature, often rooted in philosophical writings, that provides a foundation for more contemporary debate.

Ethics are implied, to some extent, in the theoretical paradigms, each of which makes a normative argument: Realists favor pragmatism over idealism, which they portray as self-indulgent and irresponsible. Liberals favor natural law. Constructivists favor self-awareness and deliberate, considered behavior. Marxists favor the redistribution of wealth. In most instances, theoreticians of each stripe are not just identifying causal factors and the relationships between them but are also recommending an approach or tipping their hand to their preferred outcome. As will be evident later, adherents to each of the paradigms also have contributed to the vigorous debates that characterize studies of ethics across the aforementioned categories.

Ethics of War

▪ **Jus ad bellum**
Justice of war; the necessary conditions for undertaking a legitimate war.

▪ **Jus in bello**
Justice in war (the laws of war); acceptable and unacceptable behaviors during a war.

Considerations of morality permeate the theory and practice of war. They fall neatly into the two categories of *jus ad bellum* and *jus in bello*. *Jus ad bellum* translates from Latin into "justice of war," and *jus in bello* translates into "justice in war" or "the laws of war."

Jus ad bellum refers to the set of criteria that must pertain if war is to be just (legitimate and justifiable). The concepts underpinning *jus ad bellum* are as old as war itself, though the best-known early examination of these was Saint Thomas Aquinas's *Summa Theologicae*.[1]

The first two of the most often listed criteria are that the instigator must have just cause and rightful authority to undertake the war. Of course, what these terms mean is open to interpretation. Regarding just cause, is it acceptable to go to war over a transgression of sovereignty? Over an insult to one's country's honor? Over a competition for resources that has not been resolved diplomatically? Rightful authority is a more straightforward criterion and usually refers to the authority vested in the government of a sovereign state. There are nonetheless potential bones to pick here as well: Is the authority rightful if the legitimacy of the government itself—or the element within it opting for war—is questionable?

The third criterion is proportionality. This is the requirement that the state's use of war—and its military goals and means—must be proportional to the threat or attack. In other words, the state should not revert to war on the slightest provocation, nor undertake massive campaigns where smaller military operations will suffice.

The fourth criterion, interestingly, is that there must be a chance for success; an unwinnable war undertaken for retributive or other emotional rationales is not just. This latter requirement is realist in its emphasis on pragmatism but is nonetheless open to interpretation. For example, what is the measure of success? Must it be victory or nothing, or can it involve forcing a better position from which to negotiate at the end of the conflict or even fighting for one's honor rather than succumbing to an aggressor without any effort at defense?

The final *jus ad bellum* criterion is that war must be a last resort, the only option left after exhausting all other possibilities. Diplomacy, economic carrots or sticks, shows of force, and so on should be applied, and time for negotiations and crisis resolution allowed, before a country enters into war.

Jus in bello refers to the laws of war, those practices that are acceptable once a war begins. Among the most familiar of these are sparing noncombatants and other defenseless people, avoiding deliberately immoral tactics and strategies, ensuring that the military means are proportionate to the military goals, and attacking military capacity rather than civilian targets.

As with the *jus ad bellum* criteria, those associated with *jus in bello* are open to interpretation. Realists will argue, for example, that if targeting civilian populations will shorten a war, thus lowering the overall costs in lives, treasure, and suffering, then that should be done. That was the thinking behind the strategic bombing campaigns of World War II, in which the U.S. Army Air Force deliberately attacked noncombatants in the hopes of so diminishing their morale or so pressuring their political leaders that the war would end. The bombings of Hiroshima and Nagasaki, both large population centers, were the culmination of this. That decision went against all of the preceding admonitions but, at the time, was thought by many people to be the most prudent and, in fact, moral approach because it would shorten the war.

The laws of war are not universally applied, nor, given the anarchic international system, are transgressors likely to be punished for ignoring them (although they may suffer reprisals in kind). In many cases, the laws are flouted in conflicts

PHOTO 14.1   Prisoners being held at the U.S. detainment facility in Guantanamo Bay, Cuba.

between adversaries with no hopes of future productive interactions. In these instances, wars are more brutish, inhumane, and vicious. This is true of many ethnic wars, in which combatants on both sides have dehumanized their enemies, soldiers and civilians alike. The laws of war may also be rejected if they are considered too much of a constraint by either tacticians or strategists. This has been the case, recently, with the U.S. classification of fighters captured in Afghanistan and during the global War on Terror as enemy combatants. Classifying them in this way has released the United States, it argues, from a legal responsibility to apply to these captives the Geneva Conventions' rules regarding prisoners of war (POWs).

The Geneva Conventions are perhaps the most systematic delineation of the laws of war. They were adopted on August 12, 1949, by the Diplomatic Conference for the Establishment of International Conventions for the Protection of Victims of War. They entered into force on October 21, 1950. There are four Geneva Conventions, with 188 signatories. The first deals with wounded and sick field soldiers; the second with wounded, sick, and shipwrecked sailors; the third with POWs; and the fourth with civilians in times of war. Each is a list of proscriptions against torture, degradation, and other inhumane treatment and also includes specific positive behaviors to which each signatory must adhere. POWs, for example, must be provided with medical attention, access to people outside the camp, and appropriate religious activities.

The Geneva Conventions' forbears include the first international legal treaty, the Geneva Convention of 1864, as well as the 1899 Geneva Convention to War

Action at Sea, the 1907 Hague Convention's determination of categories of combatants, and the 1948 Universal Declaration of Human Rights. Since the 1949 Geneva
Conventions, moreover, two additional protocols were signed in 1977 (protecting
victims of international military conflicts and victims of local conflicts). In 1992,
the International Covenant on Civil and Political Rights was put into practice
and, in 1994, both the Convention Against Torture and Other Cruel, Inhuman or
Degrading Treatment or Punishment and the UN Standard Minimum Rules on
the Treatment of Prisoners were adopted.

Liberals point to these conventions and covenants as evidence that states recognize the benefits such agreements offer and can craft international law in such
a way that it builds trust and confidence. Realists disagree and point to the flout-
ing of such conventions as proof that states will only adhere to them when they
perceive it to be advantageous. When they are considered constraints, states will
simply ignore them, with no fear of international repercussions. Constructivists
will point out that there has been a process of social learning that influenced the
form and structure of these conventions and, indeed, of international law more
generally (see Chapter 13).

Ethics of Sovereignty and Positive Intervention

There is a huge and expanding literature on the ethics of interventions intended
to create peace (peace enforcement) or to protect human rights or human welfare
(humanitarian intervention).[2] There are two related debates fueling this outpour-
ing of articles and books. The first pivots on the relative importance of two often
competing interests: sovereignty and the moral imperative to protect life, reduce
suffering, prevent harm, and promote well-being. The second revolves around
the questionable efficacy of such interventions and, in light of that, whether they
do more harm or good.

The first debate touches on the crux of the entire international system: sovereignty. Since the Peace of Westphalia, the international system has functioned
because of the shared acknowledgment of the rules of sovereignty. It is, as constructivists would point out, the principal institution allowing for structured
global politics. Weaken sovereignty, and the system as a whole is threatened.
Yet there are situations in which the principle—the construction—of sovereignty
becomes obstructive, times that we might consider limiting it on behalf of deeper
moral obligations. The contemporary case of Darfur perhaps best illustrates this
ethical dilemma.

Sudan has been fraught with internal wars for more than forty years. A 1972
peace pact ended a war between the country's Arab-Muslim north (where the
mostly Arab government resides) and its larger African (non-Muslim) south.
Eleven years later, however, the conflict resumed as rebel groups in the south,
primarily the Sudan People's Liberation Army (SPLA), mobilized against the
imposition of Muslim law. A series of peace negotiations began in 2002, culminating in 2004 with a new north–south peace agreement. The success of those
negotiations, however, was tarnished by the crisis in Darfur, which first arose
in 2003 during the north–south negotiations when the people of Darfur realized

that the impending agreement divided the country's assets and opportunities between the warring parties, leaving out the African Muslims of Darfur. As mentioned in Chapter 12, the government's response to the rebellion in Darfur was reminiscent of its brutal tactics in its long war with the south, though escalated in pace: It undertook a massive bombing campaign while simultaneously arming and supporting the Janjaweed Arab militia's scorched earth operations, which involved not only the destruction of homes, businesses, farmland, and wells but also looting, mass killings, systematic rapes, and abductions.

As hundreds of thousands of residents of Darfur fled into neighboring Chad and even more became refugees within their own country, as the humanitarian situation declined and starvation and cholera spread throughout the displaced population, the international community was faced with precisely the ethical dilemma mentioned earlier: intervene and help the people of Darfur against the wishes of the Sudanese government or respect the country's sovereignty and spend precious time negotiating access to the people of Darfur as more suffered and died. In this case, sovereignty won out. Every step of the way the international community has accepted Sudan's restrictions on foreign involvement, its conditions for the insertion of peacekeeping troops, and foreign involvement and cooption of humanitarian assistance.

Yet we would be hard-pressed to make the argument that this was so because, when push came to shove, international leaders measured and considered and then deliberately chose sovereignty as a more important principle than human rights. Indeed, this case illustrates one of the abiding problems for ethics as a field: Given the various imperatives of international relations, ethics only seem to play a role when all other interests have already been met. That is, international behavior in Darfur was arguably determined by competing great power interests in the country (as mentioned earlier in the book, Russia, France, and especially China have close and lucrative economic dealings with the Sudanese government) and by the structure and rules of the United Nations more than it was by any conscious weighing of the costs and benefits of privileging sovereignty over human rights. Had three of the five UN Security Council members not been economically tied to Sudan, ethical debates arguably might have played a larger role in the international community's response, or so a realist would argue. A liberal might point out that the international community's response—driven by its sense of moral obligation—has been slowed, but not brought to a standstill, by the Sudanese government and that, moreover, it has succeeded in getting some humanitarian assistance through as well as what is hoped to be the first of many infusions of peacekeepers. And, a liberal might continue, doing so while respecting the government's sovereignty strengthens the legitimacy and, one might even argue, the efficacy and longevity of the humanitarian and peacekeeping operations. Meanwhile, a constructivist would likely bring us back to basics, reminding us to recognize both sovereignty and human rights as institutions and to consider the built-in assumptions and prescriptions of each.

Darfur can also be used to illustrate the second debate, over the morality of undertaking peace enforcement or humanitarian interventions that might not work, either because they slake immediate humanitarian needs but have longer term negative repercussions or because they simply fail, leading to a more complicated crisis with more actors involved. The question then becomes: Is it better to respond, to hope for the best, to deal with the short term and let the long term work itself out, or is it better to let an obdurate situation resolve itself without intervention? These questions were asked repeatedly throughout the 1990s as war-provoked humanitarian crises arose in Somalia, Haiti, Rwanda, Bosnia, and later Kosovo. Somalia quickly made clear that good intentions might not translate into positive outcomes and that, indeed, rushing in to provide solace and prevent suffering could contribute, over time and completely unintentionally, to deeper problems as those intervening worked unwittingly to exacerbate the conflict, strengthen the combatants, and weaken the local economy. More than a decade after intervening forces withdrew from Somalia, the country remains anarchic, desperate, and violent. And yet, as the 900,000 people killed over 100 days in Rwanda demonstrated, simply standing by might shorten the crisis but can have immeasurable and horrifying human costs.

So what to do in Darfur? It is unlikely that peace enforcement would work in a country of Sudan's geography and political complexity, and, moreover, any attempt to intervene forcibly on behalf of the people of Darfur would have incalculable political costs both within the country and internationally, given China's and other states' commitment to the Sudanese government. Yet as the world watches, genocide has taken place and the death toll continues to rise—some estimates are as high as half a million people dead, whereas others hover near 100,000.[3] Again, the decision of whether or not it is ethical to intervene, given the challenges and potential for negative consequences, has been more an academic one than a practical one. As the ethical debate has raged,[4] the international community's efforts appear to have been driven by a combination of pedestrian motivations, good intentions, immediate opportunities and pressures, and political maneuvering.

Ethics of Peace and Reconciliation

Ethical questions also permeate conflict resolution, both the process of negotiating peace and postwar behavior, including the establishment of **Truth and Reconciliation Commissions.** Among the most contentious of these questions is whether perpetrators of war—either states or individuals—should be punished for their actions or forgiven. Punishment can be a means of retribution, an effort at deterrence, or a way to bring closure to victims. Amnesty or a similar policy, alternatively, might speed reconciliation and prevent new or ongoing resentments from undermining peace. Although this is in many ways a practical question, the answer to which can probably be partially derived from past experiences and likely differs depending on the nature of the conflict and the form of its resolution, it is also an ethical question, in that it deals with justice.[5]

In fact, the question becomes more complicated when we ask what kind of justice people are seeking. Observers of conflict resolution break justice into two categories: retributive and restorative. Which is better—the former, requiring

■**Truth and Reconciliation Commission**
A group tasked with formally identifying the roots of a conflict, acknowledging the atrocities that took place during a conflict, and setting forth next steps for moving beyond the conflict; there have been fifteen such commissions internationally, including those in Sierra Leone, Liberia, South Africa (after apartheid), Peru, and El Salvador.

(to punish)
(retribution) or
to restore (restoration)

punishment of war criminals or belligerent states for their actions, or the latter, focused on winnowing out the truth of the conflict and healing the community—is a subjective question, completely open to interpretation.

The ethics of this issue are tremendously complicated in that they involve victims' rights, but perpetrators' options and intentions must also be taken into account. Even assuming that the perpetrators identified for prosecution committed atrocities above and beyond those of their fellow combatants, questions must be asked about whether they were forced to do so by threats to themselves or their families, whether they were (as is so often the case with child soldiers) conditioned to do so and under the influence of drugs and alcohol, and whether they themselves had suffered similarly at the hands of the people against whom they committed atrocities, thus acting on the principle of an eye for an eye. All of this is made yet more difficult by the "fog of war," or the near impossibility of determining who did what and for what reasons.

At the nexus of the practical and the ethical is the question with which we began: Even if a perpetrator is clearly identified as having committed terrible atrocities out of greed or self-interest—the worst possible scenario—we must still ask whether the greater good is served by punishing that person (or state) or by forgiveness. Will there be more healing if the instigators are punished, or will any remaining tensions between the parties to the conflict be better assuaged by amnesty?

The International Criminal Court described in Chapter 13 functions on the premise that war criminals should be caught, tried, and punished. Truth and Reconciliation Commissions, by comparison, often reduce or eliminate individuals' punishment in exchange for combatants' participation in telling the story of the war. States, too, have dealt with these issues. After the multinational coalition forced Iraq to leave Kuwait in 1991, the United Nations slapped punitive economic and military sanctions on the Baghdad regime, effectively isolating it and making clear that future such transgressions would not be allowed. Then again, one need only consider the effects of the Treaty of Versailles (see Chapter 3) to be reminded that if the penalties are too stiff and the reprisals too harsh, conflict may well reignite. So is it moral to punish or moral to forgive?

Ethics of Trade and Development

Questions of ethics are relevant not only to security issues but also to economics. Among these are debates over trade and development. We can see, looking even at the three main paradigms of international relations as introduced in Chapter 2 and then discussed in Chapters 9 and 10, where the dividing lines are on these debates. Realists, for example, see trade and development as opportunities to be seized so as to glean relative advantages and enhance a state's power. Using this perspective, trade and development are extractive, yielding unequal benefits to greater powers. Liberals, in contrast, see trade and development as natural processes that, even as each individual or state seeks gains, generate benefits across the board for everyone involved. Constructivists consider the institutions—such as free trade regimes—that have been created to foster trade and development and the assumptions underlying them. Marxists, for their part, see in trade and development structures and processes intended to enhance the power of the core at the expense of the periphery. Although these are each observations of international economic dynamics, they are also normative: Realists decry liberals' emphasis on cooperation in trade and development as idealistic and even dangerous, if security concerns are therefore overlooked; liberals decry realists' inability to recognize the positive potential of trade and development; Marxists decry a structure they perceive as unfair and that they anticipate (or used to anticipate) will be overthrown in favor of the periphery; and constructivists privilege complex learning and critical theory (self-reflection) and oppose predation, suggesting that they would argue, in terms of trade and development, for self-conscious efforts to create positive processes with mutual benefits.

That said, the ethical questions related to trade and development are more complex than this quick overview suggests. For example, which is more moral: creating a system in which more people can buy more goods at lower prices or preserving the world's variety of cultural traditions and local industries, from France's wines to Yoruba's textiles? As we discussed earlier in the book, achieving both is hugely challenging, if not impossible. The call is completely subjective; who is to say what the right answer is? We could ask an even more provocative question: Is the spread of capitalism and, with it, consumerism, doing more harm or good? The answer may seem obvious to you, but to many people in the developing world, especially in profoundly religious societies, the proliferation of consumerism runs directly counter to deeply held belief systems and cultural practices. Many Muslims have expressed dismay at the spread of capitalism, as has Pope Benedict the XVI, who said that it tends to "marginalize God."[6]

The ethical questions underpinning international economic dynamics are often given short shrift and laughed off. Liberals argue that capitalism is the natural economic order, letting them, in a sense, off the ethical hook, though they also believe that capitalism leads to economic gains for all participants. Realists and Marxists expect the system to be predatory; the former applaud such behavior, and the latter oppose it. However, constructivists remind us that capitalism is an institution, not an inevitability, and that we should recognize it as the product of an evolving process based on our interactions.

Ethics of Competing Interests

Although there are many ethical debates we have not covered, the one with which we close this brief overview is one of the most interesting, in that it involves all the fields of world politics as well as all the levels of analysis and the theoretical paradigms. Indeed, trying to identify the ethics of economics separately from the ethics of security as we have been doing is common but somewhat problematic because in the day-to-day complexity of global relations, these things are interrelated, making assessments of morality all the more challenging. Under such circumstances, it is not unusual that states' leaders must compromise, accepting a lesser evil to achieve a more dearly held objective. An oft-cited case in point is the deliberate, strategic decision by the United States to ally itself with dictators and

| **PHOTO 14.2** | **U.S. President Barack Obama and King Abdullah of Saudi Arabia in Riyadh, Saudi Arabia.** |

Sacrifice a small for a greater accomplishment.

other disreputable individuals in its quest to prevent the spread of communism. President Reagan's ambassador to the United Nations, Jeanne Kirkpatrick, even wrote a controversial article justifying such associations by making a distinction between authoritarianism and the more threatening (or so she argued) totalitarianism of the communists.[7] Let us consider another American example, one that involves security, economics, and resources: U.S. relations with Saudi Arabia.

The close U.S. relationship to the oppressive Saudi regime, including its sales of high-tech weaponry and its continuous military presence in the kingdom since World War II, should be surprising; the two countries' cultures are almost diametrically opposed.

The Saudi government, long resistant to democracy, is well known for its political repression and human rights violations. Israel, a close ally of the United States, perceives Saudi Arabia as a serious threat. More recently, the United States has been attacked by Osama bin Laden's Al Qaeda network; bin Laden is from a prominent Saudi family, and most of the 9/11 terrorists were Saudi dissidents. The Saudis have also been deeply critical of U.S. policies and actions in Iraq and Afghanistan. Yet the U.S.–Saudi relationship has flourished for nearly seven decades. It is a relationship based on the U.S. interest in oil and the Saudis' defense concerns, combined with their fierce determination to maintain control of their territory. During the Cold War, U.S. interests in the kingdom were enhanced by strategic considerations, but the relationship both predated and outlived the U.S.–Soviet rivalry.

Some might criticize the apparent U.S. double standard as hypocritical. Elsewhere in the world the country has pressured states to democratize, overthrown oppressive regimes, and applied strong sanctions against authoritarian governments. However, the United States, anxious for its continued access to Saudi Arabia, treats the country with diplomatic kid gloves. Is this unethical? We might argue that without affordable Saudi oil, the United States would not have become the economic powerhouse it is today and, had it not, would not have been able to serve as the engine of global economic growth, arguably boosting international standards of living and promoting political development. Without military bases on Saudi territory, the flexibility of the United States to defend its interests both during and after the Cold War would have been seriously circumscribed. Without the close relationship with the Saudis, the United States would have less access to valuable intelligence on Middle Eastern terrorism networks. If it had not been close to Saudi Arabia, the United States would be in the same position in which China finds itself today, working with a patchwork of terrible dictators and oppressive governments, mostly in Africa, to gain some limited and tenuous access to oil. So is the U.S.–Saudi relationship immoral and cynical, or does it represent an ethical decision to accept a lesser evil to promote a greater good? (For a discussion of another questionable ally of the United States, see Spotlight, "Bad Guys Make Even Worse Allies.")

PHOTO 14.3   China has made a concerted push to increase trade with Africa.

▪ S P O T L I G H T ▪

Bad Guys Make Even Worse Allies

The United States seems to be missing some guns in Iraq. Somehow, the U.S. military has lost track of 110,000 AK-47 assault rifles and 80,000 pistols that were supposedly delivered from our caches to Iraqi security forces.

It was classic bureaucratic bungling, the Government Accountability Office concluded last month in a report criticizing the Pentagon's failure to keep proper records and track weapons flows. But there may have been another factor—the government's dangerous and bumbling use of bad guys.

Consider the case of one particular bad guy, Viktor Bout—a stout, canny Russian air transporter who also happens to be the world's most notorious arms dealer.

When the U.S. government needed to fly four planeloads of seized weapons from an American base in Bosnia to Iraqi security forces in Baghdad in August 2004, they used a Moldovan air cargo firm tied to Bout's aviation empire. The problem is that the planes apparently never arrived. When Amnesty International investigators tried two years later to trace the shipment of more than 99 tons of AK-47s and other weapons, U.S. officials admitted they had no record of the flights landing in Baghdad.

The missing Bosnian weapons could simply be a paperwork problem (and it's not certain that they are among the missing weapons the GAO discovered; they may be an additional loss). But Bout's involvement as the transporter raises bleak possibilities far beyond bureaucratic error—including the possibility that the arms were diverted to another country or to Iraqi insurgents killing American troops.

That's because Bout is about as bad as bad guys get. For more than a decade before he landed on U.S. payrolls, Bout's air cargo operations delivered tons of contraband weapons—ranging from rifles to helicopter gunships—to some of the world's most dangerous misfits. He stoked wars across Africa, supplying Charles Taylor, the deposed Liberian president now on trial for war crimes. He ferried $50 million in guns and other cargo, and he even sold air freighters to the Taliban, whose mullahs shared their lethal inventories with Al Qaeda's terrorists in Afghanistan.

Bout also has a well-known record for working both sides of the fence. His planes armed both the Angolan government in Africa and rebel forces arrayed against it. He cut weapons deals with Afghanistan's Northern Alliance government before betraying it by arming the Taliban....

By the fall of 2004, . . . Bout had been targeted by a Treasury Department freeze in assets, prompted by a United Nations effort to use economic sanctions against Liberian dictator Taylor and his inner circle—which included Bout. But weeding out Bout's contracts was not a pressing problem to the Defense Department— even after he had become an official enemy of the U.S. government. ("We're talking about tens of thousands of contracts," said one Army official.) Worse, as late as 2005, after Bout's nefarious background and his role in Iraq were publicly exposed, military officials pressured Treasury Department officials to hold off on sanctions against his business empire until he had finished a final run of supply flights to Iraq. . . .

One thing about the Bout affair is certain. As of mid-2006, his firms were no longer flying for the U.S. in Iraq. But now he poses a new problem: "blowback," the blunt term espionage writers like to use for the deadly consequences of poor spycraft.

When the U.S. turned to the Bout network to mount its Iraq supply flights, it was already clear that Bout's network had aided the Taliban's extremist mullahs. How could the U.S. be absolutely certain he wouldn't fly for our enemies once he had left the payroll? We couldn't and, apparently, he is. Last summer, a jumbo Il-76 flying the Khazakh flag swooped down to a landing in Mogadishu to unload arms for radical Islamic leaders who briefly seized control of Somalia. It was one of Bout's planes, concluded U.S. military intelligence officials. Another bullet-point in a bad guy's resume.

———————

Excerpted from Stephen Braun, "Bad Guys Make Even Worse Allies: A Notorious Arms Dealer Was the Wrong Person to Enlist in the U.S. War Effort in Iraq," *Los Angeles Times*, August 13, 2007, http://www.latimes.com/news/opinion/la-oe-braun13aug13,0,1196900.story?coll=la-opinion-center.

China copes with similar ethical dilemmas by stressing its respect for sovereignty. It will deal with any country, withholding judgment of local politics. This has been the case as China expands its diplomatic and economic endeavors throughout Africa. It has found a niche in working with governments that other countries vilify, including, but not limited to, Sudan and Burma (Myanmar). Although China is often criticized for this blinkered approach to foreign policy, is it unethical? The Chinese need access to oil to fuel their rapid economic development. Economic development should help China lift much of its population out of poverty. How is this unethical? Oil simply is not available from democratic regimes in countries enjoying tolerant progressive cultures. The Soviets have oil and gas locked up in much of Europe; the United States and western European companies have control of the wells in most oil-producing states. China must work with the rogues or do without, and doing without means either increased reliance on coal, dangerous to produce and filthy to use, or foregoing development. Moreover, whoever casts a stone at China overlooks the relaxation of some social and political controls in the country as the economy grows (clearly something that liberals would both expect and espouse) and undervalues the potential benefits of an increasingly interdependent China as its economic ties flourish worldwide. Again, who is to say whether China is behaving immorally or morally in its economic dealings with oppressive regimes?

There are innumerable examples of ethical dilemmas caused by competing interests within and across the various fields of world politics. Global relations are so complex and interwoven that compromises are inevitable; countries will have to accept some unpalatable relationships or behaviors in exchange for achieving what they deem to be a more important objective. Realists count this as a cost of international relations; liberals hope that it will contribute to economic growth and exposure to democracy and democratic principles; constructivists remind us that our conceptions of morality shift over time.

Relationship of World Politics to Other Subdisciplines of Political Science

The second matter thus far omitted is an overview of how the study of world politics fits into the grander scheme of political science. You are probably aware that the discipline of political science is divided into subdisciplines: foreign policy, comparative politics, American politics (in the United States), and political theory. Academics tend to specialize in one subdiscipline or another, university and college departments often break down along these lines, and theories tend to fall within one area, rather than applying across them. Nonetheless, the subdisciplines are closely related and merit a brief overview.

Foreign Policy

The study of world politics involves examining the whole of global relations; the study of foreign policy, in contrast, emphasizes very specifically the factors contributing to selected U.S. policies. As with world politics, studies of foreign policy span the levels of analysis. The systemic level is considered mostly in terms of general opportunities and constraints. The domestic level receives the most attention, with emphasis on the policymaking structures, mechanisms, procedures, and institutions within the United States; the development of and readiness for policy options internationally, including diplomacy, economic carrots and sticks, and the full range of military actions, from humanitarian assistance and disaster relief to war; and potential foreign policy objectives across the various fields (economic, political, and security), in different regions, and with assorted global actors. The individual level comes into play in foreign policy as well, with examinations of decision-making processes, the role of character and charisma, the functions of belief and experience, and the influence of personal agendas and priorities. All three major worldviews are applied in foreign policy studies, too. Realism can be used to examine power relationships among various domestic political departments and offices or between the branches of government as well as to interpret foreign policy goals. Liberalism, too, can be used to analyze foreign policy objectives and can also be used to account for the rise and influence of domestic civil society, including NGOs. Constructivism is useful in the study of foreign policy in its attention to changing mores, assumptions, and even identity. Foreign policy and world politics are often confused because of their similarities; the key difference is that the subdiscipline of foreign policy is focused on American policy structures, goals, and methods, whereas the study of world politics looks more broadly at global relations.

Comparative Politics

The objective of comparative politics is to identify and explain patterns of governance, development, civic involvement, modernization, and so forth, across states. Most academics in this field have an area specialty and speak one or more foreign languages. Although at first blush comparative politics seems to have little in common with world politics, focused as it is on states' domestic structures and functions, there is quite a bit of overlap between comparative theories and domestic-level world politics theories as discussed in Chapter 2 with reference to the concept of political culture. And comparativists' sociohistorical institutionalism is very similar to bureaucratic theories in world politics. Both focus on the structures, processes, norms, and dynamics of government. Likewise, comparative politics theories focused on civil society identify many of the same dynamics observable in domestic-level world politics theories dealing with lobbies, NGOs, and other advocacy groups. In all of these instances, the main difference is that comparativists are looking primarily for generalizable explanations for domestic structures and dynamics, whereas the world politics analysts are seeking to explain how these things influence international relations.

American Politics

The study of American politics has more in common with foreign policy than with world politics, although there are some shared concepts. Perhaps most importantly, the political dynamics observed at the domestic level are often mirrored at the international level, and vice versa. Balance-of-power politics function among and within the branches of U.S. government much as they do among states in the international system. Also, the social contract on which the United States is based is similar to efforts to create social contracts internationally. The unbridgeable gap between American politics and world politics, however, is that the former are hierarchically organized whereas the latter are anarchic. Thus, although the social contracts and the concepts underpinning them might be alike in many ways, in American politics they are enforceable by a structure that includes not only a legislature but an executive and a judiciary as well, whereas in world politics adherence to social contracts is strictly voluntary and depends entirely on states' continued belief that such contracts (whether it be the UN Charter, the Geneva Convention, the Laws of the Sea, the Kyoto Protocol, or the Nuclear Non-Proliferation Treaty) work in their interests.

Political Theory

Last, but not least, is the subdiscipline of political theory. Political theory examines, in depth, the texts and ideas that underpin the rest of political science, including world politics. The roots of realism and liberalism can be found here in the works of Thucydides, Hobbes, Grotius, Locke, and Rousseau. The terrible challenges of ethics are contemplated; conflict and cooperation are dissected, scrutinized, and appraised; and the dueling trends of globalization and fragmentation are anticipated. World politics does not overlap with political theory as much as it springs from it, the contemporary musings of students of world politics elaborating, updating, and building on the foundations provided by political theory. Indeed, many of the best-known political theorists have been introduced in this book, their relevance undiluted by time and history.

The Future

Our last omission thus far in the book is an assessment of what the future of world politics most likely holds. There is tremendous speculation on this topic, not surprisingly, and it includes everything from anticipation of the decline of the state as the predominant international actor as MNCs, NGOs, and IOs rise in prominence to predictions of Chinese **hegemony,** first in Asia, but eventually in the world at large. Rather than listing the plethora of hypotheses about what the coming decades will bring, we structure our brief final discussion around the worldviews.

Realist Projection

Realists will not anticipate a future much different than the present. Human nature has not changed. The system remains anarchic. The security dilemma still holds. Indeed, looking at the present suggests that we should expect more of the same. The liberals' beloved institutions, especially the United Nations, are foundering under corruption scandals and criticisms of being undemocratic, leaving us no closer to global governance than we ever were. Nuclear weapons are spreading, not being reduced, and the treaties that have held proliferation and development in check have been abandoned. States remain the key actors in international relations, their associations with IOs and their adherence to international law strictly voluntary and far from universal (even terrorists depend on states for protection and support). The world continues to suffer wars, both international (the United States and its coalition members in Afghanistan) and internal (a short list includes the Philippines, Sudan, Pakistan, and Somalia).

The great powers, especially the United States, still put their own interests first—China in Sudan, the United States in Iraq, Russia in Kosovo—and can do so without suffering any consequences. Realism is a paradigm that anticipates stasis rather than change, and a realist's projection for the future would

▪ **Hegemony**
Dominance or leadership, usually with regard to a preponderant world power in a unipolar system.

PHOTO 14.4   **Some consider the ongoing Muslim insurgency in the Philippines another front in the War on Terror; others see it as a function of the Philippine government's resistance to locals' demands.**

be consistent with that: Based on what we have seen in the past and what we see today, world politics will remain a dog-eat-dog arena in which power is the greatest asset and security the motivating ambition.

Liberal Projection

Not surprisingly, liberals' predictions for the future differ drastically from those of realists. For decades liberals have pointed to the rise of global civil society (and the concomitant diminishing of states' power), increasing interdependence, and the burgeoning world economy as evidence that the world is changing, that anarchy is being overcome, and that states are learning the benefits of living in peace. With exponential improvements in technology, combined with pressures to cope intelligently with global challenges (like the effects of global warming, pandemics, resource shortages, migration, pollution, terrorism, etc.), liberals anticipate even more cooperation.

Like realists, liberals extrapolate from current events; unlike realists, liberals see trends. The international community has mobilized to promote sustainability, reduce greenhouse gases, preserve species and protect the environment, address pollution, combat HIV/AIDS, ally against terrorism, stabilize international markets, and fight poverty. People are more aware now than ever before,

PHOTO 14.5   **What is the future of world politics?**

courtesy of an internationalized media; they can become more easily involved than ever before, courtesy of the Internet. Moreover, there is a positive synergy between awareness and the international market, evident in the emergence of hybrid and electric cars, pressures to reduce waste in packaging, and the greater interest in and availability of **green** building and production. Liberals believe that these trends will continue and that the future will be one of greater, smarter cooperation intended to ensure a healthy, functioning world for all international actors.

Constructivist Projection

As we have discussed before, the constructivists differ dramatically from the realists and the liberals in that they do not credit either the anarchic nature of the international system or the liberal international economic order with independent effects on world politics. Instead, they argue that global political institutions are the result of decision-making elites' identities, assumptions, and interpretations of the world around them and the consequent processes created by their interactions. For constructivists, therefore, the future can be more radically different than either realists or liberals would predict. It is not rooted in the system; it is free to morph as people's and their representative groups' identities and interpretations of the world change, thus leading to potentially very different sets of interests and political interactions, especially if new ideas are introduced and take root. Constructivists therefore offer a potentially more revolutionary, but simultaneously far less clear, prediction of the future of world politics.

▪ **Green**
Designed to be
environmentally friendly.

Conclusion

We began this book by describing the complexity of world politics, from the number and diversity of international actors to the range of competing, conflicting, and overlapping agendas to the plethora of variables (resources, geography, demographics, etc.) that create obstacles, opportunities, and imperatives. We considered these in terms of the predominant processes of world politics: conflict, cooperation, globalization, and fragmentation. We went on to promote the value of simplifying—deliberately selecting one or a few variables to examine, within a single level of analysis, from a specific worldview—but also warned that observers of world politics often see only what they are looking for. Indeed, this is obvious when one considers the artificial chasm between realism and liberalism or between security studies and international political economy. Adherents to each approach look at precisely the same circumstances but interpret them differently based on their assumptions and preferences. So, as you continue your examination of global relations, teasing out what is important, identifying dynamics and trends, and learning more about the various actors and their roles and interactions, have a realist's pragmatism and a liberal's optimism, and keep the open mind and self-awareness that constructivists espouse.

What Would You Do?

The Future of the UN

You are the new secretary-general of the United Nations. Your organization is being challenged as undemocratic because of the five veto-holding permanent Security Council members. Your predecessor left a legacy of corruption. UN peacekeeping troops are being accused of raping women under their protection. Sudan first rejected UN peacekeepers for Darfur and then placed unrealistic conditions on such a force. The United States, your most powerful member, in the name of defending UN legitimacy, flouted UN power by invading Iraq against the organization's wishes. Now, as the United States seeks a way out of the quagmire it created, it is requesting a greater UN presence. The UN Millennium Development Goals laid out with such optimism are far behind schedule. Your organization's bureaucracy is bloated and obstructive. As you grapple with these challenges, you are expected to begin your tenure with a speech that will reinvigorate people's hopes in and respect for the United Nations. You must present to the world your vision of the organization's future: its structure, its capacity, and its mission. There are people who anticipate your organization's demise and others who pin their hopes for the future on it. What will you say?

What Would You Do?

Discussion and Review Questions

1. The various subfields of political science are, like the paradigms and levels of analysis within them, simply academic constructs meant to help facilitate and simplify analysis through categorization. What are the costs and benefits of breaking down the study of politics along these lines? Where do the lines blur?
2. To what extent should deliberate considerations of ethics drive international practices?
3. Globalization appears to be a trend; is fragmentation an equal and opposite trend? If so, what will happen in the long run?
4. Where in your own life do you see the effects of globalization and fragmentation? How are those a function of your own government's policies? How are they a function of the international system more generally?
5. Last but not least, which of the theoretical paradigms introduced in this book would provide the most useful guidance in the event of alien contact? What assumptions along these lines do many books, films, and comics make? How does this question relate back to more immediate global political issues like climate change and nationalism?

Key Terms

Green 560
Hegemony 558

Jus ad bellum 544
Jus in bello 544

Truth and Reconciliation
   Commission 549

Notes

Chapter 1

1. If you see a reference to a global event with which you are unfamiliar, it is always a good idea to follow up. Search the Internet for more information on the topic, look in the library for a book or articles on the subject, or ask a professor or instructor.
2. Zhang Ye, "Hope for China's Migrant Women Workers," *The China Business Review*, April 26, 2002, http://www.chinabusinessreview.com/public/0205/ye.html.
3. Eurasianet.org, "Uzbek Authorities Crack Down on Another Foreign NGO in Tashkent," Eurasianet.org, http://www.eurasianet.org/departments/civilsociety/articles/eav091704. shtml.
4. Lionel Wijesiri, "NGOs or New Gods Overseas?," *Sunday Observer*, May 8, 2005, http://www. sundayobserver.lk/2005/05/08/fea29.html.
5. Michal Roberge and Youkyung Lee, "China-Taiwan Relations," *Backgrounder*, Council on Foreign Relations, August 11, 2009, http://www.cfr.org/publication/9223/chinataiwan_ relations.html.
6. Jan Scholte, *Globalization: A Critical Introduction* (New York: St. Martin's, 2000), 64–65.
7. J. A. Foreman-Peck, *A History of the World Economy: International Economic Relations Since 1850*, 2nd ed. (Upper Saddle River, NJ: Prentice-Hall, 1995), 116.
8. Taylor B. Seybolt, "Major Armed Conflicts," in *SIPRI Yearbook 2001: Armaments, Disarmament, and International Security* (Oxford, UK: Oxford University Press, 2001), http:// editors.sipri.se/pubs/yb01/ch1.html.
9. Eric Bellman, "McDonald's to Expand in India," *Wall Street Journal,* June 30, 2009, http:// online.wsj.com/article/SB124628377100868055.html; McDonald's, "Novel Menu Promotions Throughout the Years…(Since 1993)," McDonald's, http://www.mcdonalds.com/countries/ singapore/food/foodpromo/food promo.html; http://www.mcdonalds.com/countries/ india/index.html.
10. Uzbek Radio Youth Channel, "Senior Uzbek Official Urges New Approach to Youth to Counter Foreign Influence," Uzbek Radio Youth Channel, http://www.uzland.uz/2001/ february/02_02.htm#youth.
11. Allison Jackson, "Match of the Day May Go to Court," *The Age*, January 20, 2001, National News.

Chapter 2

1. J. David Singer, "The Level-of-Analysis Problem in International Relations," *World Politics* 14 (1961): 77–92; Kenneth N. Waltz, *Man, the State, and War* (New York: Columbia University Press, 2001).
2. Thomas C. Schelling, "The Retarded Science of International Strategy," *Midwest Journal of Political Science* 4 (May 1960): 2108.

3. Graham T. Allison, *Essence of Decision: Explaining the Cuban Missile Crisis* (Boston: Little, Brown, 1971); Ole R. Holsti, "Review: *Essence of Decision: Explaining the Cuban Missile Crisis,*" *The Western Political Quarterly* 25 (1972): 136–140.

4. "The Clash of Civilizations?" Samuel P. Huntington, *Foreign Affairs* (Summer 1993), http://www.foreignaffairs.com/articles/48950/samuel-p-huntington/the-clash-of-civilizations.

5. Amy Chua, *World on Fire: How Exporting Free Market Democracy Breeds Ethnic Hatred and Global Instability* (New York: Doubleday), *2002.*

6. Ferdinand Mueller-Rommel, ed., *New Politics in Western Europe: The Rise and Success of Green Parties and Alternative Lists* (Boulder, CO: Westview Press, 1989).

7. "Global Warming Seen as a Major Problem Around the World: Less Concern in the U.S., China, and Russia," Pew Global Attitudes Project, Pew Research Center Publications, December 2, 2009, http://pewresearch.org/pubs/1427/global-warming-major-problem-around-world-americans-less-concerned.

8. "Australia Ratifies Kyoto Protocol," *The Sydney Morning Herald,* 3 December 2007, http://www.smh.com.au/news/environment/rudd-signs-kyoto-deal/2007/12/03/1196530553203.html.

9. Kenneth N. Waltz, *Theory of International Politics* (Cambridge, MA: McGraw-Hill, 1979).

10. Hans J. Morgenthau, *Politics Among Nations: The Struggle for Power and Peace,* 5th ed., rev. (New York: Alfred A. Knopf, 1978).

11. Modern classics of the realist paradigm include Edward Hallett Carr, *The Twenty Years' Crisis: 1919–1939* (New York: Harper & Row, 1964); Morgenthau, *Politics Among Nations.*

12. See Waltz, *Theory;* Joseph Grieco, *Cooperation Among Nations: Europe, America, and Non-Tariff Barriers to Trade* (Ithaca, NY: Cornell University Press, 1990); David A. Baldwin, ed., *Neorealism and Neoliberalism: The Contemporary Debate* (New York: Columbia University Press, 1993).

13. John Mearsheimer, "Back to the Future: Instability in Europe After the Cold War," *International Security* 15 (1990): 12.

14. John H. Herz, "Idealist Internationalism and the Security Dilemma," *World Politics* 2 (1950): 157–180; Robert Jervis, "Cooperation Under the Security Dilemma," *World Politics* 30 (1978): 167–214; Charles Louis Glaser, "The Security Dilemma Revisited," *World Politics* 50 (1997): 171–201.

15. Gideon Rose, "Neoclassical Realism and Theories of Foreign Policy," *World Politics* 51 (1998): 144–172.

16. Fareed Zakaria, *From Wealth to Power: The Unusual Origins of America's World Role* (Princeton, NJ: Princeton University Press, 1998); Randall L. Schweller, *Deadly Imbalances: Tripolarity and Hitler's Strategy of World Conquest* (New York: Columbia University Press, 1998).

17. Daniel S. Geller and Joel David Singer, *Nations at War: A Scientific Study of International Conflict* (Cambridge, UK: Cambridge University Press, 1998).

18. Randall L. Schweller, "Bandwagoning for Profit: Bringing the Revisionist State Back In," *International Security* 19 (1994): 72–107.

19. Morgenthau, *Politics Among Nations: The Struggle for Power and Peace,* Brief Edition, revised by Kenneth W. Thompson (Boston: McGraw Hill, 1993), 11.

20. John Locke, *The Second Treatise of Civil Government* (1690), http://www.constitution.org/jl/2ndtreat.htm.

21. Immanuel Kant, *Perpetual Peace: A Philosophical Sketch, trans.* Ted Humphrey (Indianapolis: Hackett, 2004).

22. Robert O. Keohane, "The Demand for International Regimes," *International Organization* 36 (1982): 325–355; Oran R. Young, "Regime Dynamics: The Rise and Fall of International Regimes," *International Organization* 36 (1982): 277–297; Oran R. Young, "Review: International Regimes: Toward a New Theory of Institutions," *World Politics* 39 (1986): 104–122; Andreas Hasenclever, Peter Mayer, and Volker Rittberger, "Interests, Power, Knowledge: The Study of International Regimes," *Mershon International Studies Review* 40 (1996): 177–228.

23. Oran R. Young, *International Cooperation: Building Regimes for Natural Resources and the Environment* (Ithaca, NY: Cornell University Press, 1989), 32.

24. Robert Keohane, ed., *After Hegemony: Cooperation and Discord in the World Political Economy* (Princeton, NJ: Princeton University Press, 1984).

25. Robert O. Keohane and Lisa L. Martin, "The Promise of Institutionalist Theory," *International Security* 20 (1995): 42.

26. Thomas Hobbes, *The Leviathan* (1660).

27. John Locke, *The Second Treatise of Civil Government* (1690).

28. These are but a few of the books and articles published on this subject: Richard N. Rosecrance, *The Rise of the Trading State: Commerce and Conquest in the Modern World* (New York: Basic Books, 1986); Solomon W. Polachek, John Robst, and Yuan-Ching Chang, "Liberalism and Interdependence: Extending the Trade-Conflict Model," *Journal of Peace Research* 36 (1999): 405–422; Susan M. McMillan, "Interdependence and Conflict," *Mershon International Studies Review* 41 (1997): 33–58; Mark J. Gasiorowski, "Economic Interdependence and International Conflict: Some Cross-National Evidence," *International Studies Quarterly* 30 (1986): 23–38; Mark J. C. Crescenzi, "Economic Exit, Interdependence, and Conflict," *The Journal of Politics* 65 (2003): 809–832.

29. Dean V. Babst, "Elective Governments—A Force for Peace," *The Wisconsin Sociologist* 3 (1964): 9–14; Dean V. Babst, "A Force for Peace," *Industrial Research* (1972): 55–58; Melvin Small and David J. Singer, "The War Proneness of Democratic Regimes, 1816–1965," *Jerusalem Journal of International Relations* 1 (1976): 50–69; Michael W. Doyle, "Kant, Liberal Legacies, and Foreign Affairs," *Philosophy and Public Affairs* 12 (1983): 205–235; Michael W. Doyle, "Kant, Liberal Legacies, and Foreign Affairs, Part 2," *Philosophy and Public Affairs* 12 (1983): 323–353.

30. John Gerard Ruggie, "What Makes the World Hang Together? Neo-Utilitarianism and the Social Constructivist Challenge," *International Organization* 52 (1998): 855–885; Alexander Wendt, "Constructing International Politics," *International Security* 20 (1995): 71–81.

31. "Geo-Engineering: A Bad Idea Whose Time Has Come," NPR, May 29, 2010, http://www.npr.org/templates/story/story.php?storyId=127245606; "The Global Warming Fix Stinks," Elizabeth Svoboda, *Wired*, 21 August 2006, http://www.wired.com/science/discoveries/news/2006/08/71613.

32. A Google search of "securitization" and "climate change" yields over 79,000 hits, including Michael Brzoska, "Securitization of Climate Change and the Power of Conceptions of Security," paper presented at the ISA's 49th annual convention, Bridging Multiple Divides, San Francisco, CA, March 26, 2008, http://www.allacademic.com/meta/p253887_index.html; Ole Waever, "All Dressed Up and Nowhere to Go? Securitization of Climate Change," paper presented at the ISA's 50th annual convention, Exploring the Past, Anticipating the Future, New York, February 15, 2009, http://www.allacademic.com/meta/p311899_index.html; Avilash Roul, "Beyond Tradition: Securitization of Climate Change," Society for the Study of Peace and Conflict, Article No. 112, May 1, 2007, http://sspconline.org/article_details.asp?artid=art124.

33. Robert Axelrod, *The Complexity of Cooperation: Agent-Based Models of Competition and Collaboration* (Princeton, NJ: Princeton University Press, 1997).

34. Eric Brahm, "International Regimes," BeyondIntractability.org, September 2005, http://www.beyondintractability.org/essay/international_regimes/.

35. See Rebecca Grant and Kathleen Newland, *Gender and International Relations* (Bloomington: Indiana University Press, 1991); Judith Ann Tickner, *Gender in International Relations: Feminist Perspectives on Achieving Global Security* (New York: Columbia University Press, 1993); and V. Spike Peterson and Anne Sisson Runyan, *Global Gender Issues* (Boulder, CO: Westview Press, 1993).

36. Kyla Bender-Baird, "Feminism and Climate Change," The National Council for Research on Women, http://www.ncrw.org/public-forum/real-deal-blog/feminism-and-climate-change.

37. Immanuel Wallerstein, "The Rise and Future Demise of World Systems Analysis," paper presented at the 91st annual meeting of the American Sociological Association, New York, August 16, 1996.

38. "Greenhouse Gas Inventory," Chapter 3, *U.S. Climate Action Report* 2010, http://www.state.gov/documents/organization/140009.pdf (this document shows the increase in U.S.

greenhouse gas emissions between 1990 and 2007); *IPCC Fourth Assessment Report: Climate Change 2007*, 1.3.1.2 Intensities, http://www.ipcc.ch/publications_and_data/ar4/wg3/en/ch1s1–3-1–2.html (this document shows that CO2 emissions reductions in most of Western Europe and some transitional states have been offset by increases in China and India).

39. Patrick Bond, "Climate Debt Owed to Africa: What to Demand and How to Collect?" *Links: International Journal of Socialist Renewal*, 5 May 2010, http://links.org.au/node/1675.

40. Rachel Godfrey Wood, "Banking on Coal in the Global South?" International Institute for Environment and Development, 28 April 2010, http://www.iied.org/sustainable-markets/blog/banking-coal-global-south; Ben Webster, "Greenhouse Gas Emissions Study Highlights Need for Tighter National Targets," *TimesOnline*, 18 November 2009, http://www.timesonline.co.uk/tol/news/environment/article6920778.ece.

Chapter 3

1. For analyses of political and economic trends during this period, see W. H. McNeill, *The Rise of the West* (Chicago: University of Chicago Press, 1967), and *The Pursuit of Power: Technology, Armed Forces and Society Since 1000 AD* (Chicago: University of Chicago Press, 1983); Albert Hirschmann, *The Passions and the Interests* (Princeton, NJ: Princeton University Press, 1977); and E. L. Jones, *The European Miracle* (Cambridge, UK: Cambridge University Press, 1981).

2. On the causes and nature of wars in the eighteenth century, see Kalevi J. Holsti, *Peace and War: Armed Conflicts and International Order 1648–1989* (Cambridge, UK: Cambridge University Press, 1991); Geoffrey Parker, *The Military Revolution* (Cambridge, UK: Cambridge University Press, 1988); and Jeremy Black, *European Warfare, 1660–1815* (New Haven, CT: Yale University Press, 1994). For an overview of the major wars in eighteenth-century Europe, see Michael Howard, *War in European History* (New York: Oxford University Press, 1976).

3. For more on the development of the idea of nationalism and its role in the French Revolution, see Eric Hobsbawm, *Nations and Nationalism Since 1780* (Cambridge, UK: Cambridge University Press, 1990) and Liah Greenfeld, *Nationalism* (Cambridge, MA: Harvard University Press, 1992). For more on the spread of revolutionary ideas, see George Rude, *Revolutionary Europe 1783–1815* (London: Collins, 1964).

4. There are more books on Napoleon than any other real person, with the possible exception of Jesus of Nazareth. Some of the most useful works on the man and his time are Louis Bergeron, *France Under Napoleon*, trans. R. R. Palmer (Princeton, NJ: Princeton University Press, 1981); J. C. Herold, *The Age of Napoleon* (London: Weidenfeld & Nicholson, 1963); J. M. Thompson, *Napoleon Bonaparte: His Rise and Fall* (Cambridge, MA: Blackwell, 1990); David Chandler, *The Campaigns of Napoleon* (New York: Macmillan, 1966); and Alistair Horne, *How Far from Austerlitz? Napoleon 1805–1815* (New York: St. Martin's, 1996).

5. Carl von Clausewitz, *On War*, rev. ed., ed. and trans. Michael Howard and Peter Paret (Princeton, NJ: Princeton University Press, 1984), 69.

6. Quoted in Henry W. Littlefield, *History of Europe Since 1815* (New York: Barnes & Noble, 1963), 48. The life and career of the Iron Chancellor are presented in Edward Crankshaw, *Bismarck* (New York: Viking, 1981); and Otto Pflanze, *Bismarck and Development of Germany: The Period of Unification, 1815–1871* (Princeton, NJ: Princeton University Press, 1973).

7. For more on the changes wrought by the Industrial Revolution, see W. O. Henderson, *The Industrial Revolution in Europe, 1815–1914* (Chicago: Quadrangle, 1961); David S. Landes, *The Unbound Prometheus* (Cambridge, UK: Cambridge University Press, 1969); and Sidney Pollard, *Peaceful Conquest: The Industrialization of Europe, 1760–1970* (New York: Oxford University Press, 1981).

8. For more details, see Rondo Cameron and Larry Neal, *A Concise Economic History Fourth Edition* (New York: Oxford University Press, 2002), 163–190; and Landes, *The Unbound Prometheus*, 41–123.

9. Robert Gilpin, *The Political Economy of International Relations* (Princeton, NJ: Princeton University Press, 1987), 31.

10. P. J. Cain and A. G. Hopkins, "The Political Economy of British Expansion Overseas," *The Economic History Review* 33 (1980): 475.

11. Cameron, *A Concise Economic History,* 279.

12. For more background, see Sidney Pollard, *The Industrialization of Europe, 1760–1970* (Oxford, UK: Oxford University Press, 1982), 172–183.

13. L. L. Farrar assesses the effectiveness of Bismarck's policies and the system of European alliances in general in *Arrogance and Anxiety: The Ambivalence of German Power, 1848–1914* (Iowa City: University of Iowa Press, 1981).

14. A. G. Kenwood and A. L. Lougheed, *The Growth of the International Economy 1820–2000* (London, UK: Routledge, 1999), 70–73.

15. Aaron Friedberg, *The Weary Titan: Britain and the Experience of Relative Decline* (Princeton, NJ: Princeton University Press, 1988).

16. For more on the balance of power leading to World War I, see John Mearsheimer, *The Tragedy of Great Power Politics* (New York: W.W. Norton Press, 2003).

17. For contending perspectives on the expansion of German power before World War I, see Fritz Fischer, *War of Illusions: German Policies from 1911 to 1914,* trans. Marian Jackson (New York: Norton, 1975); and John A. Moses, *The Politics of Illusion: The Fischer Controversy in German Historiography* (New York: Barnes & Noble, 1975). For more on the Anglo–German naval arms race, see Robert K. Massie, *Dreadnought: Britain, Germany, and the Coming of the Great War* (New York: Random House, 1991).

18. R. Albrecht-Carrié, *A Diplomatic History of Europe, Since the Congress of Vienna* (New York: Harper E Brothers, 1958), 212–214.

19. A. J. P. Taylor, *The Struggle for Mastery in Europe* (Oxford, UK: Clarion, 1957), 427; and Paul Kennedy, *The Rise and Fall of the Great Powers* (New York: Vintage, 1987), 215–219.

20. James L. Stokesbury, *A Short History of World War I* (New York: Morrow, 1981), 11.

21. Taylor, *The Struggle for Mastery in Europe,* xxix–xxxi.

22. These trends are discussed in Kennedy, *The Rise and Fall of the Great Powers,* 194–249.

23. For more on this subject, the reader is referred to J. Gallagher and Ronald Robinson, *Africa and the Victorians: The Climax of Imperialism in the Dark Continent* (New York: St. Martin's, 1961); and Wilfred Baumgart, *Imperialism: The Idea and Reality of British and French Colonial Expansion* (New York: Oxford University Press, 1982).

24. Quoted in Gordon A. Craig, *Germany, 1866–1945* (Oxford, UK: Clarendon, 1978), 246.

25. For more on this belief and its origins, see Stephen Van Evera, "The Cult of the Offensive and the Origins of the First World War," *International Security* 9 (1984): 58–107.

26. For a discussion of Germany's goals in fighting a preventive war, see Dale Copeland, *The Origins of a Major War* (Ithaca, NY: Cornell University Press, 2001).

27. An outstanding comprehensive account of World War I is B. H. Liddel Hart's *History of the First World War, 1914–1918* (London: Faber & Faber, 1938). John Keegan presents a gripping ground-level description of trench warfare in *The Face of Battle* (New York: Penguin, 1976).

28. Estimates taken from D. H. Aldcroft, *From Versailles to Wall Street: The International Economy in the 1920s* (Berkeley: University of California Press, 1977), 13–14.

29. For a firsthand account of the squabbling, see Harold Nicolson, *Peacemaking 1919* (London: Constable, 1933).

30. For more on the Versailles settlement's impact on the Middle East and Eastern Mediterranean, see David Fromkin, *A Peace to End All Peace: The Fall of the Ottoman Empire and the Creation of the Modern Middle East* (New York: Avon, 1989).

31. Mussolini, his party, and his fascist philosophy are described by James Gregor in *Italian Fascism and Developmental Dictatorship* (Princeton, NJ: Princeton University Press, 1979) and *Young Mussolini and the Intellectual Origins of Fascism* (Berkeley: University of California Press, 1979).

32. Thomas D. Lairson and David Skidmore, *International Political Economy: The Struggle for Power and Wealth* (Fort Worth, TX: Harcourt Brace, 1993), 52.

33. Barry J. Eichengreen, *Golden Fetters: The Gold Standard and the Great Depression, 1919–1939* (New York: Oxford University Press, 1992).

34. For more on the causes and effects of the Great Depression, see C. P. Kindelberger, *The World in Depression, 1929–1939,* rev. ed. (Berkeley: University of California Press, 1986).

35. For more on this misunderstanding, see Dale Copeland, *The Origins of Major War* (Ithaca, NY: Cornell University Press, 2001).

36. John Mearsheimer makes this argument in *The Tragedy of Great Power Politics* (New York: W.W. Norton Press, 2003).

37. For more on the German concern over Russia's growing power, see Dale Copeland, *The Origins of Major War* (Ithaca, NY: Cornell University Press, 2001).

38. These approximate figures, estimated by Soviet and Western sources, are cited in Kennedy, *The Rise and Fall of the Great Powers,* 362.

39. The strained relations between the Soviet Union and the Western Allies are discussed from different perspectives in John Lewis Gaddis, *Strategies of Containment* (New York: Oxford University Press, 1982), 3–24; and Walter LaFeber, *America, Russia and the Cold War 1975–1990* (New York: McGraw-Hill, 1991), 8–28.

40. Hannah Arendt, *Eichman, in Jerusalem: A Report on the Banality of Evil* (New York: Penguin Books, 1977).

41. For a superb account of the development of the first atomic weapons, see Richard Rhodes, *The Making of the Atomic Bomb* (New York: Simon & Schuster, 1988).

42. For alternative views on the decision to use the atomic bombs, see Barton M. Bernstein, "Roosevelt, Truman, and the Atomic Bomb, 1941–1945: A Reinterpretation," *Political Science Quarterly* 3 (1975): 23–69; Martin J. Sherwin, *A World Destroyed: The Atomic Bomb and the Grand Alliance* (New York: Random House, 1987); Paul Fussell, *Thank God for the Atom Bomb, and Other Essays* (New York: Ballantine, 1988); and Gar Alperovitz, "Hiroshima: Historians Reassess," *Foreign Policy* 99 (1995): 15–34.

Chapter 4

1. Quoted in David Holloway, The *Soviet Union and the Arms Race* (New Haven, CT: Yale, 1983), 20.

2. A sample of the range of views on the origins of the Cold War can be found in John Lewis Gaddis, *We Now Know: Rethinking Cold War History* (New York: Oxford University Press, 1998) and *The United States and the Origins of the Cold War,* rev. ed. (New York: Columbia University Press, 2000); Martin Walker, *The Cold War: A History* (New York: Holt, 1995); Walter LaFeber, *America, Russia, and the Cold War, 1945–1996,* 9th ed. (New York: McGraw-Hill, 2001); Daniel Yergin, *Shattered Peace: The Origins of the Cold War,* 2nd ed. (New York: Penguin, 1990); Thomas G. Paterson and Robert J. McMahon, eds., *The Origins of the Cold War,* 3rd ed. (Lexington, MA: D. C. Heath, 1991); Melvyn P. Leffler and David S. Painter, eds., *Origins of the Cold War: An International History* (London: Routledge, 1994); and R. C. Raack, *Stalin's Drive to the West, 1938–1945: The Origins of the Cold War* (Stanford, CA: Stanford University Press, 1995).

3. Winston Churchill, "The Sinews of Peace," *Vital Speeches of the Day* 12 (1946): 332.

4. William Fox exemplifies this perspective in *The Super-Powers: The United States, Britain, and the Soviet Union—And Their Responsibility for Peace* (New York: Harcourt Brace, 1944).

5. Adapted from Dean Acheson, *Present at the Creation* (New York: Norton, 1969), 196.

6. William A. Williams, *The Tragedy of American Diplomacy,* rev. ed. (New York: Delta, 1962), 269–270.

7. Harold F. Gosnell, *Truman's Crises: A Political Biography of Harry S. Truman* (London: Greenwood, 1980), 351.

8. Department of State Bulletin, June 15, 1947, 1159–1160.

9. See in telegram from U.S. Embassy, Moscow to Secretary of State Marshall, May 26, 1947, papers of Joseph Jones, Truman Library.

10. Joan Spero, *The Politics of International Economic Relations* (New York: St. Martin's, 1985).

11. See Alan Milward, *War, Economy and Society, 1939–1945* (Berkeley: University of California Press, 1977), 67.

12. A. G. Kenwood and A. L. Lougheed, *The Growth of the International Economy 1820–2000* (London, UK: Routledge, 1999), 245.

13. For more on the establishment of the Bretton Woods institutions, see Thomas D. Lairson and David Skidmore, *International Political Economy: The Struggle for Power and Wealth* (Fort Worth: Harcourt Brace, 1997), 65–66; and Joan Edelman Spero, *The Politics of International Economic Relations*, 4th ed. (New York: St. Martin's, 1990), 21–27.

14. For details, see Spero, *The Politics of International Economic Relations*, 68–73.

15. Chen Jian, *Mao's China and the Cold War* (Chapel Hill: University of North Carolina Press, 2001), 41.

16. Ibid., 47–48.

17. Ibid., 44.

18. Ibid., 54–55. For a further discussion of the role of the Soviet Union and China in the beginning of the Korean War, see Chen Jian, *China's Road to the Korean War: The Making of Sino-American Confrontation* (New York: Columbia University Press, 1994); and Sergei N. Goncharov, John W. Lewis, and Xue Litai, *Uncertain Partners: Stalin, Mao, and the Korean War* (Stanford, CA: Stanford University Press, 1993).

19. Dwight David Eisenhower, *Mandate for Change* (New York: Doubleday, 1963), 181.

20. Tom Gervasi, *The Myth of Soviet Military Supremacy* (New York: Harper & Row, 1986), 411–412.

21. Walter LaFeber, *America, Russia, and the Cold War: 1945–2002* (New York: McGraw-Hill, 2002), 212.

22. Ibid., 238.

23. For more on the Cuban Missile Crisis, see Graham T. Allison, *Essence of Decision: Explaining the Cuban Missile Crisis* (Boston: Little, Brown, 1971); and James G. Blight and David A. Welch, *On the Brink* (New York: Hill & Wang, 1989).

24. R. Ernest Dupuy and Trevor N. Dupuy, *The Encyclopedia of Military History, from 3500 B.C. to the Present*, rev. ed. (New York: Harper & Row, 1977), 1221.

25. John Odell, *U.S. International Monetary Policy* (Princeton, NJ: Princeton University Press, 1982), 203–205.

26. John Lewis Gaddis, *The United States and the End of the Cold War* (New York: Oxford University Press, 1993), 231.

27. Ronald Reagan, remarks to the National Association of Evangelicals, March 8, 1983, in Strobe Talbott, *The Russians and Reagan* (New York: Vintage, 1984), 116.

28. For a range of analytical perspectives on the end of the Cold War, see Michael R. Beschloss and Strobe Talbott, *At the Highest Levels* (Boston: Little, Brown, 1993); Raymond L. Garthoff, *The Great Transition* (Washington, DC: Brookings, 1994); Richard Ned Lebow and Janice Gross Stein, *We All Lost the Cold War* (Princeton, NJ: Princeton University Press, 1994); Ralph Summy and Michael E. Salla, eds., *Why the Cold War Ended: A Range of Interpretations* (Westport, CT: Greenwood, 1995); and Jay Winik, *On the Brink: The Dramatic, Behind-the-Scenes Saga of the Reagan Era and the Men and Women Who Won the Cold War* (New York: Simon & Schuster, 1996).

Chapter 5

1. Columbus's "discovery" of America is debated by many. In fact, a Chinese map claiming to be a 1763 copy of a 1418 map suggests that the Chinese mapped the Americas decades before Columbus's journey.

2. For an overview of imperial motives and strategies, see Carlo Cipolla, *Guns and Sails in the Early Phase of European Expansion* (London: Pantheon, 1965); D. K. Fieldhouse, *Economics and Empire, 1830–1914* (Ithaca, NY: Cornell University Press, 1973); D. K. Fieldhouse, *Colonialism, 1870–1945: An Introduction* (New York: St. Martin's, 1981); Bernard Semmel, *The Rise of Free Trade Imperialism* (Cambridge, UK: Cambridge University Press, 1970); Immanuel Wallerstein, *The Modern World-System, Part I: Capitalist Agriculture and the Origins of the European World-Economy in the Sixteenth Century* (Orlando, FL: Academic, 1974).

3. The Spanish Empire is described in C. Gibson, *Spain in America* (New York: Harper & Row, 1966); and J. H. Parry, *The Spanish Seaborne Empire* (London: Hutchinson, 1966).

4. For a discussion of different classes in the colonies, see J. Lockhart, *Early Latin America* (New York: Cambridge University Press, 1983).

5. For more on the establishment of the Portuguese Empire, see B. W. Diffie and C. D. Winius, *Foundations of the Portuguese Empire 1415–1580* (Minneapolis, MN: Minneapolis Press 1977).

6. For the story of the Anglo–French imperial rivalry, see J. H. Parry, *Trade and Dominion: The European Overseas Empire in the Eighteenth Century* (London: Weidenfeld & Nicolson, 1971); and C. G. Reynolds, *Command of the Sea: The History and Strategy of Maritime Powers* (New York: Morrow, 1974).

7. France's colonial policies are discussed in Winfried Baumgart, *Imperialism: The Idea and Reality of French Colonial Expansion* (New York: St. Martin's, 1961).

8. For an analysis of the political problems that decolonization posed for France, see R. von Albertini, *Decolonization* (New York: Doubleday, 1971); and Jean-Pierre Rioux, *The Fourth Republic, 1944–1958*, trans. Godfrey Rogers (Cambridge, UK: Cambridge University Press, 1989). For more on the case of Algeria, see Alastair Horne, *A Savage War of Peace* (New York: Viking, 1978). For Indochina, see Bernard Fall, *Street Without Joy* (Harrisburg, PA: Stackpole, 1964).

9. British Colonialism in North America up to the time of the American Revolution is described in Ian K. Steele, *The English Atlantic, 1675–1740* (New York: Oxford University Press, 1986); and Lawrence H. Gibson, *The Coming of the Revolution, 1763–1789* (New York: Harper, 1954).

10. The establishment of British rule in India is outlined in Henry H. Dodwell, ed., *British India, 1497–1858* (Cambridge, UK: Cambridge University Press, 1929).

11. J. Gallagher and Ronald Robinson examine this phase of British imperialism in *Africa and the Victorians: The Climax of Imperialism in the Dark Continent* (New York: St. Martin's, 1961), as does Bernard Porter in *The Lion's Share: A Short History of British Imperialism 1850–1970* (London: Longman, 1976).

12. C. Barnett, *The Collapse of British Power* (London: Eyre Methven, 1972), is a noteworthy study of Britain's retreat from its empire.

13. For more on the history of the prerevolutionary Russian Empire, see Nicholas V. Riasanovsky, *A History of Russia*, 4th ed. (New York: Oxford University Press, 1984).

14. The achievements and repressions of Soviet communism are discussed in Basil Dmytryshin, *USSR: A Concise History*, 4th ed. (New York: Charles Scribner's, 1984). Both Lenin and Stalin became famous under their revolutionary *noms de guerre*: Lenin was born Vladimir Ulyanov, and Stalin was originally called Iosif Dzhugashvili.

15. Outstanding among the many works on American imperialism in the late nineteenth and early twentieth centuries are Walter LaFeber, *The New Empire: An Interpretation of American Expansion 1860–1898* (Ithaca, NY: Cornell University Press, 1963); Ernest R. May, *American Imperialism: A Speculative Essay* (New York: Atheneum, 1968); W. A. Williams, *The Roots of the Modern American Empire* (New York: Random House, 1969); and Robert Dallek, *The American Style of Foreign Policy* (New York: Mento, 1983).

16. The rise and decline of the Ottoman Empire is covered in M. A. Cook, ed., *A History of the Ottoman Empire to 1730* (Cambridge, UK: Cambridge University Press, 1976).

17. For the impact of the collapse of Ottoman power on Middle Eastern politics, see David Fromkin, *A Peace to End All Peace: The Fall of the Ottoman Empire and the Creation of the Modern Middle-East* (New York: Avon, 1989).

18. Ronald Robinson, "The Non-European Foundations of European Imperialism: Sketch for a Theory of Collaboration," in *Studies in the Theory of Imperialism,* ed. E. R. J. Owen and R. Sutcliffe (London: Longman, 1972).

19. Samuel Popkin, *The Rational Peasant: The Political Economy of Rural Society in Vietnam* (Berkeley: University of California Press, 1979).

20. The wrenching events that led up to these reforms are recounted in W. G. Beasley, *The Meiji Restoration* (Stanford, CA: Stanford University Press, 1972).

21. See Ronald Robinson and John Gallagher, "The Imperialism of Free Trade," *The Economic History Review* (new series) 6 (1953): 1–15.

22. For differing views on the economic impact of imperialism on the developing world, see William Woodruff, *Impact of Western Man: A Study of Europe's Role in the World Economy, 1750–1960* (New York: St. Martin's, 1967); W. Mommsen and J. Osterhammel, eds., *Imperialism and After: Continuities and Discontinuities* (London: Allen & Unwin, 1986); and Daniel Headrick, *The Tentacles of Progress: Technology Transfer in the Age of Imperialism, 1850–1940* (New York: Oxford University Press, 1988).

23. See Crawford Young, *The Politics of Cultural Pluralism* (Madison: University of Wisconsin Press, 1976), for an excellent survey of the cultural diversity in the developing world.

Chapter 6

1. Francis Fukuyama, *The End of History and the Last Man* (New York: Free Press, 1992).

2. In his 2002 book *Our Posthuman Future,* Fukuyama argues that our growing ability to manipulate human DNA could have a profound effect on our political order and undermine the principles of liberal democracy.

3. This viewpoint is articulated in Mark Juergensmeyer, *The New Cold War? Religious Nationalism Confronts the Secular State* (Berkeley: University of California Press, 1993); and Graham E. Fuller and Ian O. Lesser, *A Sense of Siege: The Geopolitics of Islam and the West* (Boulder, CO: Westview, 1995).

4. Gary A. Dymski, "Post-Hegemonic U.S. Economy Hegemony: Minskian and Kaleckian Dynamics in the Neoliberal Era," http://www.economics.ucr.edu/papers/2002papers.html.

5. Major Foreign Holders of Treasury Securities, 2007, http://www.treas.gov/tic/mfh.txt.

6. For more on the Middle East peace process since the end of the Cold War, see William B. Quandt, *Peace Process: American Diplomacy and the Arab-Israeli Conflict Since 1967,* rev. ed. (Washington, DC: Brookings, 2001); and David Makovsky, *Making Peace with the PLO* (Boulder, CO: Westview, 1996).

7. For the origins of the Indo–Pakastani conflict over Kashmir, see Mushtaqur Rahman, *Divided Kashmir* (London: Lynne Rienner, 1996). On Indo–Pakistani relations after the Cold War, see Hafeez Malik, ed., *Dilemmas of National Security and Cooperation in India and Pakistan* (New York: St. Martin's, 1993). George Perkovich offers a fascinating account of India's effort to develop nuclear weapons in *India's Nuclear Bomb,* updated ed. (Berkeley: University of California Press, 2001).

8. The story of relations between the two Koreas and North Korea's nuclear program are told in Michael J. Mazarr, *North Korea and the Bomb* (New York: St. Martin's, 1995) and Don Oberdorfer, The *Two Koreas: A Contemporary History,* rev. ed. (New York: Basic Books, 2002).

9. For more on the many conflicts in the former Yugoslavia, see Misha Glenny, *The Fall of Yugoslavia* (New York: Penguin, 1992); James Gow, *Triumph of the Lack of Will: International Diplomacy and the Yugoslav War* (New York: Columbia University Press, 1997); Robert Kaplan, *Balkan Ghosts* (New York: St. Martin's, 1993); Sabrina Petra Ramet, *Balkan Babel* (Boulder, CO: Westview, 1996); and Susan Woodward, *Balkan Tragedy* (Washington, DC: Brookings, 1995).

10. For more on the international response to the genocide in Rwanda, see Samantha Power, "Bystanders to Genocide," *Atlantic Monthly,* September 2001.

11. BBC News, "Q & A: Sudan's Darfur Crisis," BBC News, http://news.bbc.co.uk/2/hi/africa/3496731.stm, accessed May 31, 2010.
12. Ibid.
13. Ibid.
14. On the Al Qaeda network and its leadership, see Rohan Gunaratna, *Inside Al Qaeda* (New York: Columbia University Press, 2002); Peter L. Bergen, *Holy War, Inc.: Inside the Secret World of Osama bin Laden* (New York: Free Press, 2001); Peter Bergen, *The Osama bin Laden I Know: An Oral History of Al Qaeda's Leader* (New York: Free Press, 2006); and Michael Scheuer, *Through Our Enemies' Eyes: Osama bin Laden, Radical Islam, and the Future of America,* rev. ed. (Dulles, VA: Potomac Books, 2006).
15. Iraq's program to develop weapons of mass destruction is detailed in Khidir Hamza and Jeff Stein, *Saddam's Bombmaker: The Terrifying Inside Story of the Iraqi Nuclear and Biological Weapons Agenda* (New York: Scribner, 2000); Shyam Bhatya and Daniel McGrory, *Brighter Than the Baghdad Sun* (New York: Regnery, 2000); and Richard Butler and James Charles Roy, *The Greatest Threat: Iraq, Weapons of Mass Destruction, and the Crisis of Global Security* (New York: Public Affairs Press, 2001). For a skeptical view, see William Rivers Pitt and Scott Ritter, *War on Iraq: What Team Bush Doesn't Want You to Know* (New York: Context, 2002). Kenneth M. Pollack discusses the strategy of regime change in "Next Stop Baghdad?," *Foreign Affairs* 81 (March–April 2002): 32–47.
16. For an assessment of the U.S. war in Iraq, see Thomas E. Ricks, *Fiasco: The American Military Adventure in Iraq* (New York: Penguin, 2007); and Rick Fawn and Raymond A. Hinnebusch, eds., *The Iraq War: Causes and Consequences* (Boulder, CO: Lynne Rienner, 2006).

Chapter 7

1. Richard J. Barnet, "Challenging the Myths of National Security," *New York Times Magazine,* April 1, 1979, 25.
2. A broad definition of security is articulated in Norman Myers, *Ultimate Security: The Environmental Basis of Political Stability* (New York: Norton, 1993). For good discussions of the military, environmental, economic, and human aspects of national security, see Sean M. Lynn-Jones and Steven E. Miller, eds., *Global Dangers: Changing Dimensions of International Security* (Cambridge, MA: MIT Press, 1995); and Michael E. Brown et al., eds., *Theories of War and Peace* (Cambridge, MA: MIT Press, 1998).
3. For more on the concepts of human security and securitization, see Michael C. Williams, "Words, Images, Enemies: Securitization and International Politics," *International Studies Quarterly* 47.4 (December 2003): 511–531; Stefan Elbe, "Should HIV/AIDS Be Securitized? The Ethical Dilemmas of Linking HIV/AIDS and Security," *International Studies Quarterly* 50.1 (March 2006): 119–144; and James Busuntwi-Sam, "Development and Human Security: Whose Security, and from What?," *International Journal* 57.2 (Spring 2002): 253–272.
4. Karl W. Deutsch, *The Analysis of International Relations* (Englewood Cliffs, NJ: Prentice-Hall, 1968), 88. "Parkinson's Law" was formulated by British historian Cyril Parkinson, who observed that work expands to fill the time available for its completion.
5. International Institute for Strategic Studies, *The Military Balance 2010* (London, UK: Routledge), 462–468.
6. The concentration of armed conflict in poor regions is noted in Dan Smith, *The State of War and Peace Atlas,* 2nd ed. (New York: Penguin, 1997).
7. John J. Mearsheimer, *The Tragedy of Great Power Politics* (New York: Norton, 2001), 83–84.
8. Ibid., 84.
9. Joseph S. Nye, Jr., "Soft Power," *Foreign Policy* 80 (Autumn 1990), 155.
10. Joseph S. Nye, Jr., "The Decline of America's Soft Power," *Foreign Affairs* 83 (2004): 16–20.
11. Nye, "Soft Power," 156–158.

12. Nye, "The Decline of America's Soft Power."

13. Ibid.

14. Edward Luttwak, *The Grand Strategy of the Roman Empire* (Baltimore: Johns Hopkins University Press, 1976), 4.

15. Patrick Morgan, *Deterrence: A Conceptual Analysis* (Beverly Hills, CA: Sage, 1977), 24–47. For comprehensive analyses of deterrence in the new era, see Keith B. Payne and Colin S. Grey, *Deterrence in the Second Nuclear Age* (New York: University Press of Kentucky, 1996); Keith B. Payne, *The Fallacies of Cold War Deterrence and a New Direction* (New York: University Press of Kentucky, 2001); and Stephen J. Cimbala, *Russia and Postmodern Deterrence: Military Power and Its Challenges for Security* (Washington, DC: Potomac Books, 2007).

16. An outstanding work on primary and extended deterrence and the policies designed to achieve both is Alexander L. George and Richard Smoke, *Deterrence in American Foreign Policy: Theory and Practice* (New York: Columbia University Press, 1974).

17. Paul Huth, *Extended Deterrence and the Prevention of War* (New Haven, CT: Yale University Press, 1988), 86–97. Although technically a limited number of Syrian tanks and troops had already intervened, the Israelis clearly deterred a full-scale invasion.

18. Glenn H. Snyder, *Deterrence and Defense: Toward a Theory of National Security* (Princeton, NJ: Princeton University Press, 1961), 3.

19. For more on these requirements, see Richard Ned Lebow and Janice Gross Stein, *When Does Deterrence Succeed and How Do We Know?* (Toronto: Canadian Institute for International Peace and Security, 1990).

20. See "Missed Signals in the Middle East," *Washington Post Magazine*, March 17, 1991, 19–41. Glaspie challenges the accuracy of the Iraqi transcript and contends that it excluded her warnings that the "United States would protect its vital interests in the area."

21. The heated debate over SDI produced a large number of works for and against the system. For reasonably balanced summaries of these arguments, see The Ethics and Public Policy Center, *Promise or Peril: The Strategic Defense Initiative* (Washington, DC: Rowman and Littlefield, 1986), or Steven W. Guerrier and Wayne C. Thomson, eds., *Perspectives on Strategic Defense* (Boulder, CO: Westview, 1987).

22. The debate over ballistic missile defense became even more heated than the controversy over SDI. For overviews of the various positions, see Michael O'Hanlon et al., *Defending America: The Case for Limited National Missile Defense* (Washington, DC: Brookings, 2001); Melvin A. Goodman et al., *The Phantom Defense: America's Pursuit of the Star Wars Illusion* (New York: Praeger, 2001); and Bradley Graham, *Hit to Kill: The New Battle over Shielding America from Missile Attack* (New York: Public Affairs Press, 2001).

23. For an overview of this concept, see Jack S. Levy, "The Offensive/Defensive Balance of Military Technology: A Theoretical and Historical Analysis," *International Studies Quarterly* 28 (1984): 219–238. For a broader survey of how technology has impacted warfare and vice versa, see Martin Van Creveld, *Technology and War from 2000 bc to the Present*, rev. ed. (New York: Free Press, 1991).

24. Concepts of war in space, and how it will influence traditional theaters of war, are presented in Thomas Karas, *The New High Ground* (New York: Simon & Schuster, 1984); United States Air Force, "New World Vistas," *Air and Space Power for the 21st Century, Summary Findings Volume*, December 15, 1995, http://www.fas.org/spp/military/docops/usaf/vistas/vistas.html; and Norman Friedman, *Seapower and Space* (Annapolis, MD: Naval Institute Press, 2001).

25. Charles C. Moskos et al., eds., *The Postmodern Military: Armed Forces After the Cold War* (New York: Oxford University Press, 2000), and Martin Van Creveld, *The Transformation of War* (New York: Free Press, 1991), offer visions of how these technologies will affect warfare.

26. For more on information warfare, see Winn Schwartau, *Information Warfare: Chaos on the Electronic Superhighway*, 3rd ed. (New York: Thunders' Mouth Press, 1996); Stuart J. D. Schwartzstein, ed., *The Information Revolution and National Security, Significant Issues Series*, Vol. 18 (Washington, DC: Center for Strategic and International Studies, 1997); and Anthony Cordesman (with Justin G. Cordesman), *Cyber-threats, Information Warfare, and Critical Infrastructure Protection: Defending the U.S. Homeland* (Westport, CT: Praeger, 2002).

27. Patrick Morgan, "Elements of a General Theory of Arms Control," in *Conflict and Arms Control: An Uncertain Agenda*, ed. Paul Viotti (Boulder, CO: Westview Press, 1986), 285.

28. For details on the SALT I agreement and the negotiations that led up to it, see John Newhouse, *Cold Dawn: The Story of SALT* (New York: Holt, Rinehart, & Winston, 1973).

29. For good discussions of the challenges of proliferation and some possible responses to them, see Joseph Cirincione et al., *Deadly Arsenals* (New York: Carnegie Endowment for International Peace, 2002); T. V. Paul, Richard J. Harknett, and James J. Wirtz, eds., *The Absolute Weapon Revisited: Nuclear Arms and the Emerging International Order* (Ann Arbor: University of Michigan Press, 2000); and United States Department of Defense, Office of the Secretary of Defense, *Proliferation: Threat and Response* (Washington, DC: DOD, 2001).

30. Bureau of International Security and Nonproliferation (ISN),"Fact Sheet: U.S. Request to Extend Chemical Weapons Convention (CWC) Deadline for Complete Destruction of Chemical Weapons Stocks," http://www.state.gov/t/isn/rls/fs/64874.htm.

31. For more information on chemical and biological weapons, see Eric Croddy et al., *Chemical and Biological Warfare: A Comprehensive Survey for the Concerned Citizen* (New York: Copernicus Books, 2001); Judith Miller et al., *Germs: Biological Weapons and America's Secret War* (New York: Simon & Schuster, 2001); and Roland Langford, *Introduction to Weapons of Mass Destruction: Radiological, Chemical, and Biological* (Hoboken, NJ: Wiley-Interscience, 2004). For the shocking story of the Soviet biological weapons program, see Ken Alibek and Steven Handleman, *Biohazard* (New York: Delta, 2001).

32. Not all analysts agree that Warsaw Pact forces held the upper hand throughout this period. For a contrary argument, see Tom Gervasi, *The Myth of Soviet Military Supremacy* (New York: Harper & Row, 1986).

33. Mahbub ul-Haq, "The New Deal," *The Internationalist*, December 1994.

Chapter 8

1. John Mueller, "Policing the Remnants of War," *Journal of Peace Research* 40 (2003): 507.

2. The threat of "leakage" of nuclear material from the former USSR and means to address it are discussed in Oleg Bukharin, Matthew Bunn, and Kenneth N. Luongo, *Renewing the Partnership: Recommendations for Accelerated Action to Secure Nuclear Material in the Former Soviet Union* (Princeton, NJ: Russian American Nuclear Security Advisory Council, 2000); U.S. Department of Energy, Secretary of Energy Advisory Board, Russia Task Force (Howard Baker, Lloyd Cutler, Co-Chairs), *A Report Card on the Department of Energy's Nonproliferation Programs with Russia* (Washington, DC: U.S. Department of Energy, 2001); and Jon Brook Wolfstahl, Cristina-Astrid Chuen, and Emily Ewell Daughtry, eds., *Nuclear Status Report: Nuclear Weapons, Fissile Material, and Export Controls in the Former Soviet Union* (Washington, DC: Carnegie Endowment for International Peace and Center for Nonproliferation Studies, 2001).

3. Scott D. Sagan and Kenneth N. Waltz, *The Spread of Nuclear Weapons: A Debate Renewed* (New York: Norton, 2003).

4. Nathan E. Busch, *No End in Sight: The Continuing Menace of Nuclear Proliferation* (Lexington: The University Press of Kentucky, 2004), 6–19.

5. Ibid., 15.

6. Ibid., 7.

7. Peter D. Feaver, "Command and Control in Emerging Nuclear Nations," *International Security* 17 (1992–1993): 164. Quoted in Busch, *No End in Sight*, 6.

8. Busch, *No End in Sight*, 17.

9. Ibid., 6.

10. Rumsfeld Commission to Assess the Ballistic Missile Threat, Report to Congress, Section IIc2, July 15, 1998. Quoted in Busch, *No End in Sight*, 6.

11. Busch, *No End in Sight*, 27–31, 295–298.

12. Dinshaw Mistry, "Nuclear Asia's Challenges," *Current History* 104 (2005): 177. For more on North Korea's nuclear program, see James T. Laney and Jason T. Shaplen, "How to Deal with North Korea," *Foreign Affairs* 82 (March–April 2003): 16; and Anonymous, "The Nuclear Crisis on the Korean Peninsula: Avoiding the Road to Perdition," *Current History* 102 (2003): 152–169.

13. Busch, *No End in Sight*, 264–265.

14. Anupam Srivastava and Seema Gahlaut, "Curbing Proliferation from Emerging Suppliers: Export Controls in India and Pakistan," *Arms Control Today* 33 (September 2003): 12–16.

15. Gawdat Bahgat, "Oil, Terrorism, and Weapons of Mass Destruction: The Libyan Diplomatic Coup," *The Journal of Social, Political, and Economic Studies* 29 (2004): 373–394; and Paul Kerr, "Libya's Disarmament: A Model for U.S. Policy?" *Arms Control Today* 34 (June 2004): 36–38.

16. This definition of terrorism comes from Sean Anderson and Stephen Sloan, *Historical Dictionary of Terrorism* (London: Scarecrow Press, 1995), 8.

17. United Kingdom Government, "Terrorism Act 2000," http://www.opsi.gov.uk/Acts/acts2000/20000011.htm.

18. U.S. Department of State, "Patterns of Global Terrorism, 2003" (April 2004), xii. http://www.state.gov/s/ct/rls/crt/2003/c12153.htm.

19. The Council of the European Union, "Council Common Position of 27 December 2001 on the Application of Specific Measures to Combat Terrorism" (2001/931/CFSP), http://eur-lex.europa.eu/smartapi/cgi/sga_doc?smartapi!celexapi!prod!CELEXnumdoc&lg=EN&numdoc=32001E0931&model=guichett.

20. Bruce Hoffman, *Inside Terrorism* (London: Victor Gollancz, 1998).

21. Robert A. Pape, "The Strategic Logic of Suicide Terrorism," *American Political Science Review* (August 2003): 344.

22. Kent Layne Oots, *A Political Organization Approach to International Terrorism* (Westport, CT: Greenwood Press, 1986), 22.

23. Anderson and Sloan, *Historical Dictionary of Terrorism*, 8.

24. For a complete list of terrorist organizations designated by the United States, see U.S. Department of State, Foreign Terrorist Organizations, Office of the Coordinator of Counterterrorism, January 19, 2010, http://www.state.gov/s/ct/rls/other/des/123085.htm, accessed June 5, 2010.

25. U.S. Department of State, Office of the Coordinator of Counterterrorism, Country Reports on Terrorism 2008, Annex of Statistical Information, March 20, 2009, http://www.state.gov/s/ct/rls/crt/2008/122452.htm, accessed June 5, 2010.

26. Ibid.

27. Anderson and Sloan, *Historical Dictionary of Terrorism*, 9.

28. U.S. Department of State, Office of the Coordinator of Counterterrorism, State Sponsors of Terrorism, http://www.state.gov/s/ct/c14151.htm, accessed June 5, 2010.

29. John Dinse and Sterling Johnson, "Ideologies of Revolutionary Terrorism," in *Terrorism and Political Violence*, ed. Henry Han (New York: Oceana Publications, 1993), 61–76.

30. For more on religion as a motivational element of terrorism, see Mark Juergensmeyer, *Terror in the Mind of God: The Global Rise of Religious Violence* (Berkeley: University of California Press, 2001).

31. Jessica Stern, *Terror in the Name of God: Why Religious Militants Kill* (New York: Harper Collins Publishers, 2003).

32. Ibid., xxii.

33. For analyses of the possibilities for terrorists to acquire and use weapons of mass destruction, see Jessica Stern, *The Ultimate Terrorists* (Cambridge, MA: Harvard University Press, 1999); Gavin Cameron, *Nuclear Terrorism* (London: Palgrave Macmillan, 1999); and Jonathan B. Tucker, ed., *Toxic Terror: Assessing Terrorist Use of Chemical and Biological Weapons* (Cambridge, MA: MIT Press, 2000).

34. For more on the U.S. military's transformation, see http://www.defenselink.mil/transformation/.

35. Paul D. Wolfowitz, speech to Naval War College graduates, June 20, 2003.

36. D. P. Sharma, *Countering Terrorism* (New Delhi: Lancers, 1992), 154. For more on possible responses to terrorism, see Russell Howard and Reid Sawyer, *Terrorism and Counterterrorism: Understanding the New Security Environment* (New York: McGraw-Hill, 2002).

37. Sharma, *Countering Terrorism*, 157–158.

38. To read the entire UN Global Counterterrorism Strategy, access http://www.un.org/terrorism/strategy-counter-terrorism.html.

39. Definitions and characteristics were compiled from Howard Abadinsky, *Organized Crime*, 7th ed. (Belmont, CA: Wadsworth, 2003), 1–2, and Paul Lunde, *Organized Crime: An Inside Guide to the World's Most Successful Industry* (London: DK, 2004), 8–11.

40. Lunde, *Organized Crime*, 11.

41. Ibid.

42. Ibid., 38, 50.

43. Robert I. Friedman, *Red Mafiya: How the Russian Mob Has Invaded America* (Boston: Little, Brown, 2000), xviii.

44. Lunde, *Organized Crime*, 44–50.

45. Abadinsky, *Organized Crime*, 240.

46. Abadinsky, *Organized Crime*, 243; and Lunde, *Organized Crime*, 27.

47. Lunde, *Organized Crime*, 28–37.

48. Abadinsky, *Organized Crime*, 271, 275.

49. Lunde, *Organized Crime*, 11–12.

50. Ibid., 12.

51. For more on Russian organized crime, see Abadinsky, *Organized Crime*, 191–205; Lunde, *Organized Crime*, 85–91. For more on organized crime in Ukraine, see James O. Finckenauer and Jennifer L. Schrock, eds., *The Prediction and Control of Organized Crime: The Experience of Post-Soviet Ukraine* (New Brunswick, NJ: Transaction, 2004).

52. Friedman, *Red Mafiya*, xvii–xix.

53. Ibid.

54. Abadinsky, *Organized Crime*, 211–219.

55. Ibid., 167–186.

56. Ibid., 318.

57. Website of the Financial Action Task Force, http://www.fatfgafi.org/pages/0,2987,en_322503 79_32235720_1_1_1_1_1,00.html.

58. Address to the UN General Assembly by Kofi Annan (New York, September 23, 2003).

Chapter 9

1. This is the standard definition of comparative advantage using the Heckscher–Ohlin model. For an in-depth analysis of comparative advantage and other variants of the concept, see Paul Krugman and Maurice Obstfeld, *International Economics: Theory and Policy* (New York: HarperCollins, 1991), 9–118; and James R. Markusen et al., *International Trade: Theory and Evidence* (New York: McGraw-Hill, 1995).

2. David Ricardo, *The Works and Correspondence of David Ricardo, ed. Piero Sraffa* (Cambridge, UK: University Press for the Royal Economic Society, 1951).

3. Hundreds of books and thousands of articles have been written from both sides of the free trade versus protectionism debate. Good surveys of the arguments from both sides are collected in Jeffry A. Frieden and David A. Lake, eds., *International Political Economy: Perspectives on Global Power and Wealth*, 3rd ed. (New York: St. Martin's, 1995). For a strong presentation of the case for free trade, see Jagdish Bhagwati, *The World Trading System at Risk* (Princeton, NJ: Princeton University Press, 1991); for arguments critical of free trade, see Paul Krugman, *Rethinking International Trade* (Cambridge, MA: MIT Press, 1990); William

Greider, *One World, Ready or Not: The Manic Logic of Global Capitalism* (New York: Simon & Schuster, 1997); and Dani Rodrik, *Has Globalization Gone Too Far?* (New York: Institute for International Economics, 1997).

4. For more on the Great Depression's effect on the world economy, see Charles Kindelberger, *The World in Depression, 1929–1939* (Berkeley: University of California Press, 1973).

5. That is not to say that there are not legitimate questions to be raised about genetically modified foods, both scientific and social. There is a great deal of debate on the long-term effects of some of the genetic modifications. More immediately, however, there are concerns about the corporate control of genetically modified organisms and the effects such controls have on farmers who buy those products. In India, in 2010 there was an uproar at the planned commercial release of a genetically modified eggplant, Bt brinjal. The government halted the product's release until further studies could be undertaken. The concerns raised in India mirrored broader worries: that the crop had not been adequately scientifically tested and that its introduction would enrich and empower the Monsanto corporation while hurting poor farmers. About 45 percent of India's population relies on agriculture for a living and most live on small family farms. "A Hungry India Balks at Genetically Modified Crops," Erika Kinetz, AP, February 16, 2010, http://www.etaiwannews.com/etn/news_content.php?id=1181902&lang=eng_news.

6. There is also a statistical discrepancy because of some inaccuracy in measuring this data. For more on the balance of payments, see Thomas D. Lairson and David Skidmore, *International Political Economy* (Belmont, CA: Thomson Wadsworth, 2002), 15–20.

7. *Economic Report of the President,* Council of Economic Advisors Publications, February 2007, Chapter 7, "Currency Markets and Exchange Rates," http://www.whitehouse.gov/cea/ch7-erp07.pdf; "The Foreign Exchange Market Overview," Worldwide Times, http://www.worldwidetimes.com/overview.htm; "History of the Foreign Exchange Market," AFEX: Associated Foreign Exchange, http://afex.com/forex-history.html.

8. Paul Krugman, "Exchange Rates," in *The Concise Encyclopedia of Economics,* http://www.econlib.org/library/Enc/ExchangeRates.html.

9. Eugene Linden, "How To Kill a Tiger: Speculators Tell the Story of Their Attack Against the Baht, the Opening Act of an Ongoing Drama," *TIME Magazine Asia,* November 3, 1997, http://www.time.com/time/magazine/1997/int/971103/asia.how_to_kill_a.html.

10. "Lessons from Thailand," Federal Reserve Bank of San Francisco Economic Letters, 97–33, November 7, 1997, http://www.frbsf.org/econrsrch/wklyltr/el97-33.html; Jeffrey Sachs, "Proposals for Reform of the Global Financial Architecture" (paper prepared for the United Nations Development Programme Meeting on Reform of the Global Financial Architecture, New York, December 8, 1998), http://www.undp.org/rblac/documents/poverty/archit/harvard.pdf.

11. Christian Weller, "Currency Speculation: How Great a Danger?" *Dollars & Sense,* 217 (May–June 1998), http://www.dollarsandsense.org/archives/1998/0598weller.html.

12. "U.S. Congress Concurrent Resolution on Taxing Cross-Border Currency Transactions to Deter Excessive Speculation," H. Con. Res.301, introduced April 11, 2000, http://www.ceedweb.org/iirp/ushouseres.htm.

13. "Tobin Tax Motion Passes Canada's Parliament," http://www.ceedweb.org/iirp/canadames.htm.

14. Patrick Bond, "A Case for Capital Controls" (paper commissioned by the Nedlac Labour Caucus, September 1999, published by the International South Group Network), http://www.isgnweb.org/pub/01–007.htm.

15. Barry Eichengreen, "Capital Controls: Capital Idea or Capital Folly?," http://business.baylor.edu/Tom_Kelly/Capital%20Controls.htm.

16. Sebastian Edwards, "The Mirage of Capital Controls," http://www.anderson.ucla.edu/faculty/sebastian.edwards/for_aff.pdf.

17. "Bond Basics: What Are Bonds?" The Bond Market Association, http://www.investinginbonds.com/learnmore.asp?catid=46&id=2.

18. "World's Largest Holders of U.S. Treasury Bonds," May 24, 2010, http://business.rediff.com/slide-show/2010/may/24/slide-show-1-worlds-largest-holders-of-us-treasury-bonds.htm.

19. "A Fair Exchange," *The Economist*, October 2, 2004, http://www.bjreview.com.cn/200443/ViewPoint-200343.htm.

20. David Cohen, "Is Beijing Bailing on Treasuries?" *Business Week*, June 20, 2007, http://www.businessweek.com/investor/content/jun2007/pi20070620_210310.htm?chan=search.

21. "U.S. Treasury Bonds: The 'Not-So-Safe' Safe Haven," Money Morning, Daily Markets, May 26, 2010, http://www.dailymarkets.com/economy/2010/05/26/us-treasury-bonds-the-not-so-safe-safe-haven/.

22. Ibid.

23. Indonesia's Investment Coordinating Board, The Site for Direct Investors, BKPM (an investment service agency of the Indonesian government), http://www.bkpm.go.id/en/info.php?mode=baca&cat=7&info_id=16.

24. José Manuel Martins Caetano and António Caleiro, "Corruption and Foreign Direct Investment, What Kind of Relationship Is There?" (Economics Working Papers 18_2005, University of Evora, Department of Economics, 2005), http://ideas.repec.org/p/evo/wpecon/18_2005.html.

25. *International Trade and Core Labour Standards*, OECD Publishing, October 12, 2000, http://www.oecdbookshop.org/oecd/display.asp?lang=EN&sf1=identifiers&st1=222000041p1; Dr. Valpy Fitzgerald, "Regulatory Investment Incentives," OECD Publishing, November 20, 2001, http://www.oecd.org/dataoecd/32/17/2510459.pdf.

26. "The Cutting Edge," *The Economist*, February 22, 2001, http://www.economist.com/displaystory.cfm?story_id=S%26%28H%28%2EPA%2F%27%0A.

27. Tanya C. Hsu, "The United States Must Not Neglect Saudi Arabian Investment," Saudi-American Forum, September 23, 2003, http://www.saudi-american-forum.org/Newsletters/SAF_Essay_22.htm.

28. Freny Patel, "Manufacturers Prefer India to US in FDI Stakes," Rediff.com, http://inhome.rediff.com/money/2005/aug/16fdi.htm.

29. A. T. Kearney, "2010 Foreign Direct Investment (FDI) Confidence Index," http://www.atkearney.com/index.php/Publications/foreign-direct-investment-confidence-index.html.

30. *The World Fact Book*, U.S. Central Intelligence Agency, https://www.cia.gov/library/publications/the-world-factbook/rankorder/2001rank.html, with updated 2009 estimates.

31. "Is U.S. Innovation Headed Offshore?" Pete Engardio, *Bloomberg Businessweek*, May 7, 2008, http://www.businessweek.com/innovate/content/may2008/id2008057_518979.htm?campaign_id=rss_topStories_msnbc.

32. Table 14, "International Research and Development Expenditures and Research and Development as Percentage of Gross Domestic Product, by Selected Country and for All Organisation for Economic Co-operation and Development Countries: 1981–2004," in National Patterns of R&D Resources, 2002 Data Update, NSF 06–327 (Arlington, VA: National Science Foundation, Division of Science Resources Statistics, 2006), http://www.nsf.gov/statistics/nsf06327/pdf/tab14.pdf.

33. "The Failed Promise of Innovation in the United States," Michael Mandel, *Bloomberg Businessweek*, June 3, 2009, http://www.businessweek.com/magazine/content/09_24/b4135000953288.htm.

34. The 2007 U.S. Census Bureau report showed just over 60 percent of all U.S. households having access to the Internet, http://www.census.gov/population/www/socdemo/computer/2007.html.

35. Wenhong Chen, Jeffrey Boase, and Barry Wellman, "The Global Villagers: Comparing Internet Users and Uses Around the World" (paper, Department of Sociology, University of Toronto, 2002), http://www.chass.utoronto.ca/~wellman/publications/villagers/gdd13-final.PDF, 8.

36. Ibid., 4.

37. "Internet Usage Statistics," Internet World Stats, http://www.internetworldstats.com/stats.htm.

38. Jan Aart Scholte, *Globalization: A Critical Introduction* (Basingstoke/New York: Palgrave Macmillan, 2005), 86; Sonja Sharp, "Cell Phones Could Send Real-Time Safety Data," *The Daily Californian*, September 21, 2005, http://www.dailycal.org/sharticle.php?id=19586.

39. "Number of Cell Phones Worldwide Hits 4.6B," CBS News, February 15, 2010, http://www.cbsnews.com/stories/2010/02/15/business/main6209772.shtml.

40. Ambrose Evans-Pritchard, "Turkey's Muslim Millions Threaten EU Values, Says Commissioner," Telegraph.co.uk, August 9, 2004, http://www.telegraph.co.uk/news/main.jhtml?xml=/news/2004/09/08/wturk08.xml.

41. Joseph Grieco, *Cooperation Among Nations: Europe, America, and Non-Tariff Barriers to Trade* (Ithaca, NY: Cornell University Press, 1990), 22.

42. This position is taken in Susan Strange, "Cave! Hic Dragones: A Critique of Regime Analysis" in S. Krasner, ed., *International Regimes* (Ithaca, NY: Cornell University Press, 1983), 337–354.

43. Charles Kindelberger, *The World in Depression, 1929–39* (Berkeley: University of California Press, 1973).

44. John H. Jackson, *Sovereignty, the WTO and Changing Fundamentals of International Law* (Cambridge, UK: Cambridge University Press, 2006).

45. See Robert Keohane, *After Hegemony: Cooperation and Discord in the World Political Economy* (Princeton, NJ: Princeton University Press, 1984); and Krasner, ed., *International Regimes.*

46. Stephen Krasner, "State Power and the Structure of Foreign Trade," *World Politics* (1976): 371–347.

47. John Gerard Ruggie, "International Regimes, Transactions, and Change: Embedded Liberalism and the Postwar Economic Order," *International Organization* 36 (1982): 379–415.

48. David Harvey, *A Brief History of Neoliberalism* (Oxford: Oxford University Press, 2005), 10.

Chapter 10

1. K. Y. Amoako, "Comment: World Trade Liberalisation Still Excludes Africa," *Financial Times*, November 23, 2004.

2. "United States Seeks Expanded Economic Growth in Africa," Merle David Kellerhals, Jr., America.gov, June 25, 2009, http://www.america.gov/st/business-english/2009/June/20090625114929dmslahrellek0.8004114.html.

3. "Millions More Russians Shunted into Poverty," Luke Harding, Guardian.co.UK, August 31, 2009, http://www.guardian.co.uk/world/2009/aug/31/russia-economy-poverty-increase-putin; "Poverty Rate Rises by a Third in Russia," *The Times of India*, August 28, 2009, http://timesofindia.indiatimes.com/NEWS/World/Europe/Poverty-rate-rises-by-a-third-in-Russia/articleshow/4945939.cms.

4. Judy Dempsey, "And What Now, Mr. Putin?" *International Herald Tribune*, August 6, 2005, http://www.iht.com/articles/2005/08/05/business/wbrussia.php.

5. The UN Millennium Development Goals, available at http://www.un.org/millenniumgoals/.

6. United Nations Population Fund, "Quotes on Human Rights," http://www.unfpa.org/rights/quotes.htm.

7. "To Give or Forgive," *The Economist*, June 16, 2005.

8. "Africa: G7 Country Overall Assessments," AllAfrica.com, May 25, 2010, http://allafrica.com/stories/201005250348.html; "The Data Report 2010: Monitoring the G8 Promise to Africa," ONE International, May 25, 2010, http://www.one.org/c/international/hottopic/3331/; "The Data Report 2009," ONE International, http://one.org/international/datareport2009/downloads.html.

9. Classic works of modernization theory include Gabriel Almond and James Coleman, eds., *The Politics of Developing Areas* (Princeton, NJ: Princeton University Press, 1960);

W. W. Rostow, *Stages of Economic Growth: A Non-Communist Manifesto* (Cambridge, UK: Cambridge University Press, 1960); David Apter, *The Politics of Modernization* (Chicago: University of Chicago Press, 1965); Samuel Huntington, *Political Order in Changing Societies* (New Haven, CT: Yale University Press, 1968); Lucian Pye, *Communications and Political Development* (Princeton, NJ: Princeton University Press, 1963); and Dankwort Rostow, *A World of Nations: Problems of Political Modernization* (Washington, DC: Brookings, 1967).

10. "Urbanization and Global Change," University of Michigan, April 3, 2005, http://www. globalchange umich.edu/globalchange2/current/lectures/urban_gc/.

11. "Urban Population (Percent of Total Population Living in Urban Areas) 2009," U.S. Global Health Policy, http://www.globalhealthfacts.org/topic.jsp?i=85&srt=1#table.

12. Leading critiques of modernization theory are offered in Gunnar Myrdal, *Economic Theory and Underdeveloped Regions* (New York: Harper & Row, 1971); Ragnar Nurske, *Problems of Capital Formation in Underdeveloped Countries* (New York: Blackwell, 1953); and Raul Prebisch, "Commercial Policy in the Underdeveloped Countries," *American Economic Review* 49 (1959): 251–273.

13. This criticism is advanced in Arrighi Emmanuel, *Unequal Exchange: A Study of the Imperialism of Trade* (New York: Monthly Review Press, 1972), rebutted in Paul Samuelson, "Illogic of Neo-Marxist Doctrine of Unequal Exchange," in *Inflation, Trade, and Taxes*, ed. David Belsey et al. (Columbus: Ohio State University Press, 1976), 96–107; and discussed in Sven Grassman and Erik Lundberg, eds., *The World Economic Order—Past and Prospects* (London: Macmillan, 1981).

14. Howard Wiarda, "Toward a Nonethnocentric Theory of Development: Alternative Conceptions from the Third World," *Journal of Developing Areas* 17 (1983): 437.

15. Lee Hong-jong, "Development, Crisis, and Asian Values," *East Asian Review* 15 (Summer 2003): 27–42.

16. "Freedom in the World, 2004," Freedom House, http://www.freedomhouse.org/research/freeworld/2004/countries.htm.

17. "Freedom in the World, 2005," selected data from Freedom House's annual global survey of political rights and civil liberties, Freedom House, http://www.freedomhouse.org/research/freeworld/2005/charts2005.pdf.

18. "Freedom in the World 2010: Erosion of Freedom Intensifies," Freedom House, http://www.freedomhouse.org/uploads/fiw10/FIW_2010_Tables_and_Graphs.pdf.

19. Ronald Inglehart, "The Renaissance of Political Culture," *The American Political Science Review* 82 (1988): 1203–1230.

20. Robert Putnam, with Robert Leonardi and Raffaella Y. Nanetti, *Making Democracy Work: Civic Traditions in Modern Italy* (Princeton, NJ: Princeton University Press, 1994).

21. Outstanding works on dependency theory include Henrique Cardoso and Enzo Faletto, *Dependency and Development in Latin America* (Berkeley: University of California Press, 1979); David Collier, *The New Authoritarianism in Latin America* (Princeton, NJ: Princeton University Press, 1979); Theotonio Dos Santos, "The Structure of Dependence," *American Economic Review* 60 (1970): 235–246; Peter Evans, *Dependent Development: The Alliance of Multinational, State, and Local Capital in Brazil* (Princeton, NJ: Princeton University Press, 1979); Andre Gunder Frank, *Latin America: Underdevelopment or Revolution* (New York: Monthly Review Press, 1969); and Osvaldo Sunkel and Pedro Paz, *El Subdesarrollo Latinoamericano y la Teoria del Desarollo* (Mexico City: Siglo Veintiuno, 1970).

22. See Immanuel Wallerstein, *The Modern World-System: Capitalist Agriculture and the Origins of the European World-Economy in the Sixteenth Century* (New York: Academic, 1976).

23. This argument is set forth in Joseph L. Love, "Raul Prebisch and the Origins of the Doctrine of Unequal Exchange," *Latin American Research Review* 15 (1980); and Joan Robinson, "Trade in Primary Commodities," in *International Political Economy: Perspectives on Global Power and Wealth*, 2nd ed., ed. Jeffry A. Frieden and David Lake (New York: St. Martin's, 1991), 376–385.

24. Robinson, "Trade in Primary Commodities," 378–379.

25. Medard Gabel and Henry Bruner, *Globalinc.: An Atlas of the Multinational Corporation* (New York: The New Press, 2003); "Multinational Companies and Collective Bargaining:

Employment Profile of MNCs," *European Industrial Relations Observatory On-line*, July 2, 2009, http://www.eurofound.europa.eu/eiro/studies/tn0904049s/tn0904049s_2.htm.

26. Rhys Jenkins, *Transnational Corporations and Uneven Development* (New York: Methuen, 1987), 10.

27. Thomas Lairson and David Skidmore, *International Political Economy: The Struggle for Power and Wealth* (Fort Worth, TX: Harcourt Brace, 1993), 260.

28. Joan Spero, *The Politics of International Economic Relations*, 4th ed. (New York: St. Martin's, 1990), 287.

29. For critical reviews of dependency theory, see David Ray, "The Dependency Model of Latin American Underdevelopment: Three Basic Fallacies," *Journal of Interamerican Studies and World Affairs* 15 (1972): 4–20; Sanjaya Lall, "Is Dependence a Useful Concept in Analyzing Underdevelopment?" *World Development* 3 (1975): 799–810; and Tony Smith, "The Underdevelopment of the Development Literature: The Case of Dependency Theory," *World Politics* 32 (1979): 247–288.

30. See World Bank, *Global Economic Prospects and the Developing Countries 1994* (Washington, DC: World Bank, 1994); and "Poor Relations: Are Third-World Commodity Producers Condemned to Eternal Poverty?" *The Economist*, April 16, 1994, 76.

31. See Guillermo O'Donnell, *Modernization and Bureaucratic-Authoritarianism* (Berkeley: University of California Press, 1979).

32. Robert Alexander offers an evaluation of import-substitution industrialization in "Import Substitution in Latin America in Retrospect," in *Progress Toward Development in Latin America: From Prebisch to Technological Autonomy*, ed. James L. Dietz and Dilmus D. James (Boulder, CO: Lynne Rienner, 1991), 15–28.

33. John Macomber discusses this strategy in "East Asia's Lessons for Latin American Resurgence," in *International Political Economy*, ed. Jeffry A. Frieden and David Lake (New York: St. Martin's, 1991), 386–395.

34. Robin Broad and James Cavanagh, "No More NICs," *Foreign Policy* 72 (1988): 81–103.

35. Moises Naim, "Washington Consensus or Washington Confusion?" *Foreign Policy* 118 (2000): 86–103; Moises Naim, "Fad and Fashion in Economic Reforms: Washington Consensus or Washington Confusion?" working draft of a paper prepared for the IMF Conference on Second Generation Reforms, Washington, DC, October 1999.

36. John Williamson, "What Washington Means by Policy Reform," in *Latin American Adjustment: How Much Has Happened?*, ed. John Williamson (Washington, DC: Institute for International Economics, 1990), 7–38.

37. Jeffrey Sachs, Aaron Tornell, and Andres Velasco, "The Collapse of the Mexican Peso: What Have We Learned?" (paper presented at National Bureau of Economic Research, Project on Exchange Rate Crises in Emerging Market Countries, *Currency Crises: Lessons from Mexico* conference, Cambridge, MA, May 6, 1999).

38. World Bank, *World Development Report 1991: The Challenge of Development* (Washington, DC: The World Bank, 1991), 114.

39. The World Bank Group, 2005, http://web.worldbank.org/WBSITE/EXTERNAL/PROJECTS/STRATEGIES/CDF/0,,pagePK:60447~theSitePK:140576,00.html.

40. For links to an excellent and diverse set of papers from one such conference, see IMF Conference on Second Generation Reforms, November 1999, http://www.imf.org/external/pubs/ft/seminar/1999/reforms/.

41. Binyavanga Wainaina, "Generation Kenya," *Vanity Fair*, July 2007, http://www.vanityfair.com/culture/features/2007/07/wainaina200707?currentPage=1.

42. "Digital Transformation for Rural India," XTVWorld.com, http://press.xtvworld.com/article15164.html.

43. "Nobel Winner Yunus: Microcredit Missionary," *Business Week*, December 26, 2005, http://www.businessweek.com/magazine/content/05_52/b3965024.htm.

44. Ina Kota, "Microfinance: Banking for the Poor," *Finance and Development: The Quarterly Magazine of the IMF* 44.2 (June 7, 2007), http://www.imf.org/external/pubs/ft/

fandd/2007/06/basics.htm; "Microfinance Benchmarks of MFIs," Mix Market, 2008, http://www.mixmarket.org/mfi/benchmarks.

45. John Paul, "Microfinance: Fighting World's Poverty Through Investment," Nextbillion.net, June 9, 2006, http://www.nextbillion.net/newsroom/2006/06/09/microfinance-fighting-worlds-poverty-through-investment.

46. Chris Nicholson, "In Poorer Nations, Cellphones Help Open Up Microfinancing," *New York Times*, July 9, 2007, http://www.nytimes.com/2007/07/09/business/worldbusiness/09micro.html?ex=1186372800
&en=4f46414d8fd414d0&ei=5070.

47. "Role of Microcredit in the Eradication of Poverty," Secretary-General's Report, A/53/223, August 10, 1998, http://www.un.org/documents/ga/docs/53/plenary/a53-223.htm.

48. Ayesha Gooneratne, "Development: Microcredit Poised to Reach 100 Million Families" IPSNews.net, December 2005, http://ipsnews.net/news.asp?idnews=31341.

49. "International Cooperation at a Crossroads: Aid, Trade, and Security in an Unequal World," *Human Development Report 2005*, United Nations Development Programme, http://hdr.undp.org/reports/global/2005/.

50. Gunnar Myrdal, *Asian Drama: An Inquiry into the Poverty of Nations*, vol. II (New York: Pantheon, 1968), 951–958.

51. Russian News and Information Agency NOVOSTI, January 7, 2005, http://en.rian.ru/society/20050701/40827814.html.

52. Steven Lee Myers, "Pervasive Corruption in Russia Is 'Just Called Business,'" *New York Times*, August 13, 2005.

53. *U.S. Army's Area Handbook for Colombia* (Washington, DC: American University, 1961), cited in Anthony P. Maingot, "Studying Corruption in Colombia," National Defense University, September 30, 2002.

54. "Colombia This Week News Summary," August 8, 2005, ABColombia Group, London, http://colhrnet.igc.org/newitems/August05/CTW%20080805.htm.

55. Transparency International, "Plundering Politicians and Bribing Multinationals Undermine Economic Development, Says TI," press release, Transparency International, March 25, 2004.

Chapter 11

1. Henrik Urdal, "A Clash of Generations? Youth Bulges and Political Violence," *International Studies Quarterly* 50 (2006): 608.

2. Cited in Jumana Al Tamimi, "Educated Arab Youths Keen on Emigration," Gulfnews.com (March 21, 2010), http://gulfnews.com/news/region/educated-arab-youths-keen-on-emigration-1.600650.

3. Urdal, "A Clash of Generations?," 619.

4. United Nations High Commissioner for Refugees (UNHCR), "Chad-Darfur Emergency," http://www.unhcr.org/cgi-bin/texis/vtx-chad?page=intro; United Nations High Commissioner for Refugees, "2010 UNHCR Country Operations Profile—Chad" (2010), http://www.unhcr.org/cgi-bin/texis/vtx/page?page=49e45c226.

5. UNHCR, "Global Appeal 2007: Mission Statement," http://www.unhcr.org/publ/PUBL/4565a5742.pdf.

6. UNHCR, "Chad-Darfur Emergency."

7. United Nations, "World Population Prospects: The 2008 Revision Population Database (births per year both sexes combined)" (March 11, 2009), http://esa.un.org/unpp/p2k0data.asp.

8. U.S. Department of Commerce, Bureau of the Census, "World Population Profile: 1998—Highlights," http://www.census.gov/ipc/www/wp98001.html; Bureau of the

Census, "Global Population at a Glance: 2002 and Beyond," March 2004, 1, http://www.census.gov/ipc/prod/wp02/wp02–1.pdf.

9. Bureau of the Census, "Total Midyear Population for the World: 1950–2050," http://www.census.gov/ipc/www/worldpop.html; United Nations Population Fund (UNFPA), "State of World Population 2004: The Cairo Consensus at Ten: Population, Reproductive Health and the Global Effort to End Poverty," 2004, 8, http://www.unfpa.org/swp/2004/pdf/en_swp04.pdf; UNFPA, "New Population Projections Underline Urgency of Family Planning Needs in Developing Nations," March 13, 2007, http://www.unfpa.org/; UNFPA, "World Population to Exceed 9 Billion by 2050: Developing Countries to Add 2.3 Billion Inhabitants with 1.1 Billion Aged Over 60 and 1.2 Billion of Working Age" (March 11, 2009).

10. Tadeusz Kugler and Siddharth Swaminathan, "The Politics of Population," *International Studies Review* 8 (2006): 583.

11. "Now We Are 300,000,000," *The Economist*, October 12, 2006, http://www.economist.com/world/na/Printerfriendly.cfm?story_id=8031359.

12. "Aging Summit Hears Global Warming," CNN.com, April 8, 2002, http://archives.cnn.com/2002/HEALTH/04/08/madrid.ageing/index.html.

13. Bureau of the Census, "World Population Profile 1996," 1–2; Bureau of the Census, "Global Population at a Glance: 2002 and Beyond," March 2004, 3, http://www.census.gov/ipc/prod/wp02/wp02–1.pdf; UNFPA, "State of World Population 2004," 76; UNFPA, "World Population to Exceed 9 Billion by 2050: Developing Countries to Add 2.3 Billion Inhabitants with 1.1 Billion Aged over 60 and 1.2 Billion of Working Age" (March 11, 2009).

14. Urdal, "A Clash of Generations?," 623.

15. Farzaneh Roudi-Fahimi and Mary Mederios Kent, "Challenges and Opportunities— The Population of the Middle East and North Africa," Population Reference Bureau (2007), http://www.prb.org/Publications/PopulationBulletins/2007/ChallengesOpportunitiesinMENA.aspx.

16. Kugler and Swaminathan, "The Politics of Population," 583–584.

17. Bureau of the Census, "An Aging World: 2001," 1, http://www.census.gov/prod/2001pubs/p95–01-1.pdf.

18. Ginanne Brownell and Carla Power, "The Golden Age," *Newsweek International*, November 28, 2004, http://www.msnbc.msn.com/id/6597549/site/newsweek/.

19. Ibid.

20. "Aging Summit Hears Global Warning."

21. "Suddenly, the Old World Looks Younger," *The Economist*, June 14, 2007, http://www.economist.com/world/europe/displaystory.cfm?story_id=9334869.

22. "Aging Summit Hears Global Warning."

23. UNFPA, "State of World Population 2007: Unleashing the Potential of Urban Growth," June 27, 2007, http://www.unfpa.org/swp/2007/english/chapter_1.html.

24. UNFPA, "State of World Population 2007"; UNFPA, "UNFPA-2008 Annual Report" (2008), http://www.unfpa.org/about/report/2008/en/ch4.html.

25. "The World Goes to Town," *The Economist*, May 3, 2007, http://www.economist.com/surveys/PrinterFriendly.cfm?story_id=9070726.

26. UN Population Division, "World Urbanization Prospects: The 2001 Revision," 2002, http://www.un.org/esa/population/publications/wup2001/WUP2001report.htm; UN Population Division, "Future World Population Growth to Be Concentrated in Urban Areas of the World According to New Report Issued by United Nations Population Division," 2002, http://www.un.org/esa/population/publications/wup2001/WUP2001-pressrelease.pdf; UNFPA, "State of World Population 2004," 24; United Nations, *World Urbanization Prospects: The 2007 Revision (Executive Summary)*, February 26, 2008, http://www.un.org/esa/population/publications/wup2007/2007WUP_ExecSum_web.pdf.

27. UNFPA, "State of World Population 2007."

28. Ibid.

29. United Nations, "Key Conference Outcomes on Population," http://www.un.org/esa/devagenda/population.html.

30. UNFPA, "International Conference on Population and Development," September 1994, http://www.unfpa.org/icpd/icpd.htm.

31. Nafis Sadik, "The 1990s: The Decade of Decision," *Populi* 17 (1990): 10–19; UN Population Division, "Levels and Trends of Contraceptive Use as Assessed in 1998: Key Findings," May 2002, www.un.org/esa/population/pubsarchive/contraceptives1998/contraceptives1998.htm; United Nations, "Majority of World's Couples Are Using Contraception," May 2002, http://www.un.org/esa/population/publications/contraceptive2001/WallChart_CP2001_pressreleaseUN.htm; UNFPA, "State of World Population 2004," 7; UNFPA, "State of World Population 2004," press summary (2004), 4, http://www.unfpa.org/swp/2004/pdf/summary.pdf; UNFPA, "Contraceptives Save Lives" (2009), http://www.unfpa.org/webdav/site/global/shared/safemotherhood/docs/contraceptives_factsheet_en.pdf.

32. World Resources Institute, "Population, Health and Human Well-Being—Public Health: Contraceptive Prevalence Rate," http://earthtrends.wri.org; United Nations, Department of Economic and Social Affairs, Population Division, "2010 Update for the MDG Database: Contraceptive Prevalence (POP/DB/CP/A/MDG2010)" (2010).

33. UN Population Division, "Levels and Trends of Contraceptive Use as Assessed in 1998: Key Findings"; UNFPA, "State of World Population 2004," 13, 39.

34. UNFPA, "New Push to Promote Women's Health in Africa: Health Ministers Adopt Measures to Curb Maternal Death," September 22, 2006, http://www.unfpa.org/news/news.cfm?ID=8702language=1.

35. As quoted in UNFPA, "Make Women and Young People Your Top Priority, UNFPA Chief Urges World Leaders," September 14, 2005, http://www.unfpa.org/news/news.cfm?ID=677.

36. UNFPA, "UNFPA's Contribution to Meeting the MDGs: Findings from the United Nations Millennium Project," September 2005, http://www.unfpa.org/icpd/gender.htm.

37. UNFPA, "Reproductive Health Commodity Security—Challenges," October 19, 2006, http://www.unfpa.org/news/news.cfm?ID=887.

38. UNFPA, "The Need for Steady Funding," http://www.unfpa.org/supplies/funding.htm.

39. UNFPA, "Record Number of Countries Contribute Record Amount to UNFPA in 2006," January 15, 2007, http://www.unfpa.org/news/news.cfm?ID=925; United Nations, "United Nations Population Fund: Report on Contributions by Member States and Others to UNFPA and Revenue Projections for 2010 and Future Years," April 30, 2010.

40. UNFPA, "Family Planning Essentials," http://www.unfpa.org/supplies/family.htm; United Nations Children's Fund, *The State of the World's Children 2009* (December 2008), 2.

41. Population Reference Bureau, *Unsafe Abortions: Facts and Figures* (Washington, DC: Population Reference Bureau, 2006), 9.

42. Ibid., 3.

43. One widely quoted study found that at any level of social development, the stronger the family planning effort, the greater the decline in the birth rate. In developed countries, for example, birth rate decline between 1965 and 1980 in countries with strong family planning programs was three times faster than in those with weak or nonexistent programs. See McGeorge Bundy, "Population: An Inescapable Problem," *Populi* 17 (1990): 20–24.

44. Population Reference Bureau, *Unsafe Abortions: Facts and Figures*, 26; Rebecca Wind, "Abortion and Unintended Pregnancy Decline Worldwide as Contraceptive Use Increases," Guttmacher Institute (2009), http://www.guttmacher.org/media/nr/2009/10/13/index.html.

45. Julia L. Ernst, Laura Katzive, and Erica Smock, "The Global Pattern of U.S. Initiatives Curtailing Women's Reproductive Rights: A Perspective on the Increasingly Anti-Choice Mosaic," Center for Reproductive Rights, http://www.reproductiverights.org/pub_art_mosaic4.html.

46. UNFPA, "The Power of Two Women, One Idea and 34 Million Friends," http://www.unfpa.org/support/friends/34million.htm.

47. Americans for UNFPA, "International Women's Health & Dignity Act Introduced House Bill Would Restore U.S. Commitment to Women Everywhere," June 7, 2007, http://www.americansforunfpa.org/NetCommunity/Page.aspx?&pid=2268&srcid=356; "US Cuts UN

Funds in Abortion Row," BBC News, http://newsvote.bbc.co.uk/mpapps/pagetols/print/newsbbc.co.uk/1/hi/world/americas/3902311.stm.

48. UNFPA, "The Power of Two Women."

49. Americans for UNFPA, "International Women's Health & Dignity Act"; UNFPA, "UNFPA Welcomes Restoration of U.S. Funding," January 23, 2009, http://www.unfpa.org/public/site/global/lang/en/pid/1562.

50. Maryann Cusimano Love and Dorle Hellmuth, "People on the Move: Refugees, IDPs, and Migrants," in *Beyond Sovereignty: Issues for a Global Agenda*, 3rd ed., ed. Maryann Cusimano Love (Belmont, CA: Thomson Wadsworth, 2007), 187; UNFPA, "State of World Population 2006: A Passage to Hope: Women and International Migration, Chapter 1," 2006, http://www.unfpa.org/swp/2006/english/chapter_1/index.html.

51. United Nations Development Fund for Women (UNIFEM), "Women Migrant Workers," 2006, http://www.unifem.org/gender_issues/women_poverty_economics/women_migrant workers.php; UNFPA, "State of World Population 2006, Chapter 1," http://www.unfpa.org/swp/2006/English/chapter_1/index. html.

52. United Nations Development Fund for Women (UNIFEM), "Women Migrant Workers," 2006, http://www.unifem.org/gender_issues/women_poverty_economics/women_migrant workers.php; UNFPA, "State of World Population 2006, Chapter 1," http://www.unfpa.org/swp/2006/English/chapter_1/index.html; United Nations, "International Day of Families 2010: 'The Impact of Migration on Families Around the World,'" May 15, 2010, http://www.un.org/esa/socdev/family/idf/2010/backgroundnote.pdf.

53. Eric Neumayer, "Bogus Refugees? The Determinants of Asylum Migration to Western Europe," *International Studies Quarterly* 49 (2005): 395–396.

54. Ibid., 389.

55. Ibid., 390.

56. International Migration Organization, "Facts and Figures: Global Estimates" (2010), http://www.iom.int/jahia/Jahia/about-migration/facts-and-figures/lang/en; UNFPA, "State of World Population 2004," 25.

57. UNFPA, "State of World Population 2006, Chapter 1."

58. For data on migrant populations in 2010, see International Migration Organization, "Regional and Country Figures" (2010), http://www.iom.int/jahia/Jahia/about-migration/facts-and-figures/regional-and-country-figures. For discussion on European immigration to the U.S. in the early twentieth century, see Organization on Economic Cooperation and Development, *Trends in International Migration* 1996.

59. UNFPA, "State of World Population 2006, Chapter 1."

60. International Migration Organization, "Facts and Figures: Global Estimates"; UNFPA, "State of World Population 2006," press summary, 2006, http://www.unfpa.org/swp/2006/pdf/press-summary-en.pdf.

61. UNFPA, "State of World Population 2006."

62. Anne-Christine D'Alesky, "UNHCR: Facing the Refugee Challenge," *UN Chronicle* 28 (1991): 43.

63. Neumayer, "Bogus Refugees?," 405.

64. UNFPA, "State of World Population 2006, Chapter 1."

65. UNHCR, *2008 Global Trends: Refugees, Asylum-seekers, Returnees, Internally Displaced and Stateless Persons* (June 16, 2009); "Iraq Drives up Refugee Count, U.N. Says," CNN.com, June 19, 2007, http://www.cnn.com/2007/WORLD/meast/06/19/un.refugees/index.html; UNHCR,"Refugees by Numbers (2006 Edition)," September 1, 2006, http://www.unhcr.org/cgi-bin/texis/ttx/print?tbl=BASICS&id=3b028097c.

66. "Tanzania Urges Burundian Refugees to Go Home," CNN.com, June 19, 2007, http://www.cnn.com/2007/WORLD/africa/06/19/tanzania.refugees.reut/index.html; "Tanzania Gives Citizenship to 162,000 Burundi Refugees," BBC News, April 16, 2010, http://news/bbc.co.uk/2/hi/8625429.stm.

67. UNHCR, *2008 Global Trends: Refugees, Asylum-seekers, Returnees, Internally Displaced and Stateless Persons*; UNHCR, "Refugees by Numbers (2004 Edition)," 2004, http://www.unhcr.ch/cgibin/texis/vtx/basics.

68. UN Population Division, "Number of World's Migrants Reaches 175 Million Mark," UN press release POP/844, 2002, http://www.un.org/esa/population/publications/ittmig2002/press-release-eng.htm.

69. Catherine Drew and Dhananjayan Sriskandarajah, "EU Enlargement in 2007: No Warm Welcome for Labor Migrants," Migration Information Source, January 1, 2007, http://www.migrationinformation.org/Feature/display.cfm?ID=568.

70. Veysel Oezcan, "Germany: Immigration in Transition," Migration Information Source, July 2004, http://www.migrationinformation.org/Profiles/display.cfm?ID=235; Rainer Munz, "New German Law Skirts Comprehensive Immigration Reform," Migration Information Source, August 1, 2004, http://www.migrationinformation.org/Feature/display.cfm?ID=241; UNHCR, "Refugees by Numbers (2004 Edition)"; Robert S. Leiken, "Europe's Angry Muslims," *Foreign Affairs* 84.4 (July/August 2005): 120–35; "Europe's Muslims: A Year After the French Riots, Their Alienation Is Growing," *Washingtonpost.com*, October 25, 2006, http://www.washingtonpost.com/wpdyn/content/article/2006/10/24/Ar2006102401148.html.

71. U.S. Committee for Refugees and Immigrants, *Refugee Reports*, December 31, 1992, 9–13.

72. Ibid.

73. Fatoumata Lejeune-Kaba, "Number of Asylum-seekers Remains Stable over 2009, UNHCR Figures Show," UNHCR, March 23, 2010, http://www.unhcr.org/4ba8d8239.html; UNHCR, "A New Beginning in a Third Country," UNHCR, http://www.unhcr.org/pages/4a16b1676.html.

74. "Convention on Migrant Worker Rights Adopted," *UN Chronicle* 28 (1991): 80–81.

75. UNHCR, "Convention on Protection of Rights of Migrant Workers to Enter into Force Next July," March 19, 2003, http://www.unhchr.ch/huricane/huricane.nsf/view01/B87E9E85C7147498C1256CEF00385E50?opendocument.

76. UNHCR, "UNHCR Global Appeal 2007: Mission Statement," http://www.unhcr.org/pub/PUBL/4565a5742.pdf.

77. D'Alesky, "UNHCR: Facing the Refugee Challenge," 46.

78. UNRWA, "About UNFWA: Frequently Asked Questions," 2010, http://www.unrwa.org/etemplate.php?id=87.

79. "Iraqi Refugee Tragedy Steers UN on New Path to Humanitarian Aid," *UN Observer & International Report* 13, August 1991, 4.

80. D'Alesky, "UNHCR: Facing the Refugee Challenge," 53–54.

81. UNHCR, "Returnees: Going Back Home," 2010, http://www.unhcr.org/pages/49c3646c1ca.html.

82. U.S. Committee for Refugees and Immigrants, "World Refugee Survey 2009: Best and Worst Places for Refugees," http://www.refugees.org/FTP/WRS09PDFS/BestandWorst.pdf; "World Refugee Survey 2004: Returns and Expulsions," http://www.refugees.org/data/wrs/04/pdf/involuntary.pdf.

83. Population Reference Bureau, "2008 World Population Data Sheet" (August 19, 2008), http://www.prb.org/Publications/Datasheets/2008/2008wpds.aspx?p=1; United Nations, Population Division of Economic and Social Affairs, "World Population Prospects: The 2008 Revision Population Database," March 11, 2009, http://esa.un.org/unpp/p2k0data.asp; see also World Resources Institute, "Demographics: Life Expectancy 2005–2010," http://www.earthtrends.wri.org.

84. Central Intelligence Agency, "The World Factbook—Country Comparison: Life Expectancy at Birth," https://www.cia.gov/library/publications/the-world-factbook/rankorder/2102rank.html.

85. Global Health Council, "Where Do Child Deaths Occur?" (2010), http://www.globalhealth.org/child_health/child_mortality/where_occur.

86. Population Reference Bureau, "2008 World Population Data Sheet."

87. WHO, "MDG 4: Reduce Child Mortality," 2007, http://www.who.int/topics/millennium_development_goals/child_mortality/en/index.html.

88. WHO, "Communicable Diseases and Severe Food Shortage Situations," August 25, 2005, http://www.who.int/hac/crises/ner/sitreps/CDs_severe%20food%20shortages_FINAL_25082005.pdf.

89. WHO, "Global Immunization Data" (October 2009), http://www.who.int/immunization/newsroom/GID_english.pdf.

90. Center for Disease Control and Prevention, "State of the World's Vaccines and Immunizations," (October 21, 2009), http://www.cdc.gov/features/GlobalImmunizations/.

91. WHO, "Global Immunization Data."

92. WHO, "State of the Art of New Vaccines Research & Development: Initiative for Vaccine Research," 2003, 24, http://www.who.int/vaccine_research/documents/new_vaccines/en/index1.html.

93. WHO, "Malaria," April 2010, http://www.who.int/mediacentre/factsheets/fs094/en/print.html.

94. WHO, "Initiative for Vaccine Research (IVR): Cholera," February 2009, http://www.who.int/vaccine_research/diseases/diarrhoeal/en/index3.html; Voice of America, "World Health Organization Reports New Death from Cholera in Midlands, Zimbabwe," January 11, 2010, http://www1.voanews.com/zimbabwe/news/health/Zimbabwe-Another-Cholera-Death-Reported-in-Midlands-11Jan10–81153597.html

95. WHO, "WHO Marks Turning Point for 1 Billion People: Partners Commit to Global Action Against Forgotten Diseases," April 19, 2007, http://www.who.int/mediacentre/news/releases/2007/pr19/en/index.html; WHO, "10 Facts on Neglected Tropical Diseases," April 17, 2007, http://www.who.int/features/factfiles/neglected_tropical_diseases/en/index.html.

96. The Kaiser Family Foundation, "The HIV/AIDS Epidemic in Sub-Saharan Africa," November 2009, http://www.kff.org/hivaids/upload/7391–08.pdf.

97. UNAIDS, "Global Facts and Figures: The Global AIDS Epidemic," 2009, http://data.unaids.org/pub/Factsheet/2009/20091124_FS_global_en.pdf; The Kaiser Family Foundation, "The HIV/AIDS Epidemic in Sub-Saharan Africa."

98. UNAIDS, "Global Facts and Figures: The Global AIDS Epidemic"; UNFPA, "World Population to Exceed 9 Billion by 2050."

99. World Food Programme, "Facts & Figures: Hunger Facts," 2007, http://www.wfp.org/aboutwfp/facts/hunger_facts.asp?section=1&sub_section=5.

100. UNAIDS, "Eastern Europe and Central Asia," 2009, http://www.unaids.org/en/CountryResponses/Regions/EasternEuropeAndCentralAsia.asp.

101. UNAIDS, "Asia," 2009, http://www.unaids.org/en/CountryResponses/Regions/Asia.asp.

102. UNAIDS, "Global Facts and Figures: The Global AIDS Epidemic."

103. Ibid.

104. WHO, "Statue Commemorates Smallpox Eradication," May 17, 2010, http://www.who.int/mediacentre/news/notes/2010/smallpox_20100517/en/index.html; WHO, "Control of Neglected Tropical Diseases," June 2010, http://www.who.int/neglected_diseases/en/.

105. Global Polio Eradication Initiative, "Wild Poliovirus Weekly Update," May 26, 2010, http://www.polioeradication.org/casecount.asp; Celia W. Dugger, "$630 Million Donated Toward Polio Eradication Efforts," *New York Times*, January 22, 2009, http://www.nytimes.com/2009/01/22/world/africa/22polio.html; Jeffrey Kluger, "Polio's Back. Why Now?" *Time*, May 16, 2005, 46.

106. Global Polio Eradication Initiative, "Wild Poliovirus Weekly Update," May 26, 2010.

107. UNICEF, "Expanding Immunization Coverage," 2010, http://www.unicef.org/immunization/index_coverage.html.

108. Jose Antonia Najera-Morrondo, "Malaria Control: History Shows It's Possible," *World Health* (September–October 1991): 32.

109. WHO, "Malaria: Key Facts," 2010, http://www.who.int/mediacentre/factsheets/fs094/en/index.html.

110. UNAIDS, "Tracking, Monitoring and Evaluation," http://www.unaids.org/en/Coordination/FocusAreas/track-monitor-evaluate.asp; UNAIDS, "Cosponsors," http://www.unaids.org/en/AboutUNAIDS/Cosponsors_about/default.asp; UN AIDS, "UNAIDS 10-Year Anniversary," 2006, http://data.unaids.org/pub/FactSheet/2006/20060428_FS_UNAIDS10Years_en.pdf.

111. Sharon Lerner, "Banned from Pride: The INS Blocks a Visitor with HIV (Ken: Singled Out at the Canadian Border)," *Village Voice*, June 30–July 6, 1999, http://www.aegis.com/news/vv/1999/VV990601.html; BBC News, "US Lifts HIV/AIDS Immigration Ban," January 4, 2010, http://news.bbc.co.uk/go/pr/fr/-/2/hi/americas/8438865.stm.

112. WHO, "Global Outbreak Alert and Response: Report of a WHO Meeting," 2000, http://who.int/csr/resources/publications/surveillance/WHO_CDS_CSR_2000_3/en/.

113. WHO, "Update 62—More Than 8000 Cases Reported Globally, Situation in Taiwan, Data on In-Flight Transmission, Report on Henan Province, China," May 22, 2003, http://www.who.int.csr/ don/2003_05_22/en/print.html.

114. "CDC Expert Sickened with SARS," MSNBC, May 22, 2003, http://www.msnbc.com.

115. "Developments Concerning the SARS Virus," *Miami Herald*, May 22, 2003, http://www.miami.com/mld/miamiherald/news/world/5919463.htm.

116. Dennis Pirages and Paul Runci, "Ecological Interdependence and the Spread of Infectious Disease," in *Beyond Sovereignty: Issues for a Global Agenda*, 3rd ed., ed. Maryann Cusimano Love (Belmont, CA: Thomson Wadsworth, 2007), 234, 240–243, 247–248.

117. Ibid., 246.

Chapter 12

1. Ashok Swain, "Displacing the Conflict: Environmental Destruction in Bangladesh and Ethnic Conflict in India," *Journal of Peace Research* 33 (1996): 191.

2. "River Ganges," The Water Page, 2000–2001, http://www.africanwater.org/ganges.htm.

3. Interestingly, Bangladesh and India share fifty rivers but have only been able to come to agreement on the Ganges River. Waliur Rahman, "Bangladesh-India Water Talks Fear," BBC News, September 19, 2005, http://news.bbc.co.uk/go/pr/fr/_/1/hi/world/south_asia/4261320.stm.

4. Swain, "Displacing the Conflict," 192–193.

5. Thomas F. Homer-Dixon, "Environmental Scarcities and Violent Conflict: Evidence from Cases," *International Security* 19 (1994): 21.

6. Swain, "Displacing the Conflict," 194, 198.

7. Homer-Dixon, "Environmental Scarcities and Violent Conflict," 22.

8. Chris Ward, "Environmental Degradation and Political Instability: Lessons from Sudan," World Resources Institute, http://www.earthtrends.wri.org/updates/node/217.

9. "Romanian Mine Re-opens After Environmental Disaster," BBC, June 14, 2000, http://news.bbc.co.uk/1/hi/world/europe/790547.stm; Michael Kidron and Ronald Segal, *The New State of the World Atlas*, 4th ed. (New York: Simon & Schuster, 1991), 106–107.

10. Gerald Urquhart, Walter Chomentowski, David Skole, and Chris Barber, "Tropical Deforestation," 3, http://www.earthobservatory.nasa.gov/Library/Deforestation; Food and Agriculture Organization (FAO), "Deforestation Continues at a High Rate in Tropical Areas; FAO Calls Upon Countries to Fight Forest Crime and Corruption," press release, October 3, 2001, http://www.fao.org/WAICENT/OIS/PRESS_NE/PRESSENG/2001/pren0161.htm; FAO, "Global Report Cites Progress in Slowing Forest Losses," March 13, 2007, http://www.fao.org/newsroom/en/news/2007/1000506/index.html.

11. FAO, "World Deforestation Decreases, but Remains Alarming in Many Countries," March 25, 2010, http://www.fao.org/news/story/en/item/40893/icode/; "Scientific Facts on Forests," *Green Facts: Facts on Health and the Environment*, March 7, 2007, http://www.greenfacts.org/en/forests/index.htm#2.

12. Paul Harrison, "Beyond the Blame-Game: Population-Environment Links," *Populi* 17 (1990): 14–21.

13. NASA, "New Images: Northern Madagascar," NASA, May 2000, http://earthobservatory.nasa.gov/Newsroom/NewImages/images.php3?img_id=4731.

14. Paul Shaw, "Population Growth: Is It Ruining the Environment?" *Populi* 16 (1989): 22.

15. "War," Mongabay.com, http://rainforests.mongabay.com/0810.htm.

16. Urquhart et al., "Tropical Deforestation," 6; estimates cited in U.S. Council on Environmental Quality and Department of State, *The Global 2000 Report to the President*, vol. 2 (Washington, DC: U.S. Council on Environmental Quality and the Department of State, 2000), 331.

17. Earth Observatory, NASA, "Deforestation Plays Critical Climate Change Role," May 11, 2007, http://earthobservatory.nasa.gov/Newsroom/view.php?id=32686; Urquhart et al., "Tropical Deforestation," 5.

18. "Indonesia Pledges Two-Year Deforestation Moratorium," BBC News, May 27, 2010, http://news.bbc.co.uk/2/hi/world/asia_pacific/10167038; "Where to Start," *Economist*, September 7, 2006, http://www.economist.com/surveys/PrinterFriendly.cfm?story_id=7852974.

19. Rebecca Lindsey, "Reference: Tropical Deforestation," NASA Earth Observatory, March 30, 2007, http://earthobservatory.nasa.gov/Library/Deforestation/printall.php.

20. Earth Observatory, NASA, "Deforestation Plays Critical Climate Change Role."

21. Lindsey, "Reference: Tropical Deforestation."

22. "China Tops US in Carbon Emissions," *The Boston Globe*, June 21, 2007, A16; World Resources Institute, *World Resources 1996–1997* (New York: Oxford University Press, 1996); Union of Concerned Scientists, "Each Country's Share of CO2 Emissions," May 13, 2009, http://www.ucsusa.org/global_warming/science_and_impacts/science/each-countrys-share-of-co2.html; U.S. Department of Energy, Energy Information Administration, "World Carbon Dioxide Emissions from the Consumption and Flaring of Fossil Fuels, 1992–2001," *International Energy Annual 2001*, http://www.eia.doe.gov/emeu/iea/tablehI.html; United Nations, http://millenniumindicators.un.org/unsd/mifre/mi_series_results.asp?rowID=749&FID=r15&cgID=.

23. WHO, "Air Quality and Health," August 2008, http://www.who.int/mediacentre/factsheets/fs313/en/index.html; Worldwatch Institute, "Global Fossil Fuel Consumption Surges," Worldwatch Institute, http://www.worldwatch.org/node/1811; United Nations Environment Program, *Key Facts About Cities: Issues for the Urban Millennium*, (Nairobi, Kenya: United Nations Environment Program, 2005), http://www.unep.org/wed/2005/english/Information_Material/facts.asp.

24. Environment Canada, "Acid Rain FAQ," http://www.ec.gc.ca/air/default.asp?lang=En&n=7E5E9F00–1#wsEFF855FF.

25. U.S. Department of Energy, Energy Information Administration, "South Korea: Environmental Issues," http://www.eia.gov/emeu/cabs/skoren.html.

26. U.S. Department of Energy, Energy Information Administration, "International Energy Outlook 2010: Highlights," http://www.eia.doe.gov/oiaf/ieo/highlights.html; "Fossil Fuel Carbon Dioxide Emissions Up by 29 Percent Since 2000," *ScienceDaily*, November 17, 2009, http://www.sciencedaily.com/releases/2009/11/091117133504.htm.

27. Energy Information Administration, "International Energy Outlook 2007," 74, http://www.eia.doe.gov/oiaf/ieo/pdf/em missions.pdf; Seth Dunn, "Climate Change: Can the North and South Get in Step?" in *The Global Agenda: Issues and Perspectives*, 6th ed., ed. Charles W. Kegley, Jr., and Eugene R. Wittkopf (New York: McGraw-Hill, 2001), 440.

28. For excellent work on the connection between conflict and the environment, see Homer-Dixon, "Environmental Scarcities and Violent Conflict"; and Swain, "Displacing the Conflict."

29. See Harrison, "Beyond the Blame-Game," 17; Bruce Babbit, "Earth Summit," *World Monitor*, January 1990, 30.

30. National Aeronautical and Space Administration, "News: NASA, NOAA Data Indicate Ozone Layer Is Recovering," press release, August 30, 2006, http://www.jpl.nasa.gov/news/news-print.cfm?release=2006–102.

31. United Nations Environment Programme (UNEP), "China Closes Ozone Depleting Chemical Plants: A Contribution to Avert a Global Health Catastrophe," July 1, 2007,

http://www.unep.org/Documents.Multilingual/Default.Print.asp?DocumentID=5
14&ArticleID=5624&l=en.

32. United Nations Environment Programme (UNEP), "Workmanlike Plan Agreed to Fight Against Poverty and Fight for Sustainable Development Says Klaus Toepfer," September 4, 2002, http://www.unep.org/Documents.Multilingual/Default.asp?DocumentID=264&Artic leID=3120; World Summit on Sustainable Development, http://www.rrcap.unep.org/wssd/ Political%20declaration_4%20Sep%2002.pdf.

33. G-8 Summit 2007, "Growth and Responsibility in the World Economy," June 7, 2007, 13, http://www.whitehouse.gov/g8/2007/g8agenda.pdf; "Breakthrough on Climate Protection," June 7, 2007, http://www.g-8.de/nn_94646/Content/EN/Artikel/__g8-summit/2007–06-07- g8-klimaschutz__en.html; Environment News Service, "G8 Summit Extends Environmental Work Beyond Climate," June 8, 2007, http://www.ens-newswire.com/ens/jun2007/ 2007–06-08–05.asp.

34. Neelesh Misra, "Climate Session Ends Without New Deadline," *The Boston Globe*, November 2, 2002.

35. "Q&A: The Copenhagen Climate Summit," *BBC News*, December 21, 2009, http://news. bbc.co.uk/go/pr/fr/-/2/hi/science/nature/8278973.stm; "UN says Copenhagen deal 'a start,'" *BBC News*, December 19, 2009, http://news.bbc.co.uk/go/pr/fr/-/2/hi/science/ nature/8422133.stm.

36. Sierra Club, http://www.sierraclub.org; World Conservation Union, http://www.iucn.org; World Wildlife Fund, http://www.worldwildlife.org.

37. Forest Stewardship Council, "What Is FSC-US?" http://www.fscus.org/faqs/ what_is_fsc.php; Forest Stewardship Council, "The History of FSC-US," http:// www.fscus.org/about_us/.

38. World Resources Institute, "Live Earth: The Concerts for a Climate in Crisis," 2007, http:// earthtrends.wri.org/updates/node/219; Alliance for Climate Protection, http://www. climateprotect.org/about.

39. UNESCO, "Facts and Figures Extracted from the 2nd United Nations World Water Development Report," 2006, http://www.unesco.org/water/wwap/wwdr2/facts_figures/ index.shtml; Douglas Jehl, "In Race to Tap the Euphrates, the Upper Hand Is Upstream," *New York Times*, August 25, 2002, http://www.nytimes.com/pages/world/worldspecial/ index.html; Food and Agriculture Organization, "Coping with Water Scarcity: Q&A with FAO Director-General Dr. Jacques Diouf," March 22, 2007, http://www.fao.org/newsroom/ en/focus/2007/1000521/index.html.

40. "Water Facts," Water.org, http://water.org/learn-about-the-water-crisis/facts/; UNICEF, "Billions Still Lack Clean Water and Sanitation," in *The Progress of Nations 2000*, http:// www.unicef.org/pon00/billions.htm; Mary H. Cooper, "Water Shortages," *Global Issues: Selections from the CQ Researcher* (Washington, DC: CQ Press, 2005), 321, 330; United Nations Development Programme (UNDP), *Human Development Report 2006—Beyond Scarcity: Power, Poverty and the Global Water Crisis* (New York: United Nations Development Programme, 2006), v.

41. United Nations Development Programme, *Human Development Report 2006*, 7.

42. United Nations, *Africa and the Millennium Development Goals: 2007 Update* (New York: United Nations, 2007), http://ww.un.org/millenniumgoals/docs/MDGafrica07.pdf.

43. UNESCO, "Facts and Figures Extracted from the 2nd United Nations World Water Development Report."

44. Edwin H. Clark, II, "Water Prices Rising Worldwide," *Earth Policy Institute*, March 7, 2007, http://www.earth-policy.org/Updates/2007/Update64_printable.htm.

45. FAO, "Coping with Water Scarcity."

46. UN, "Africa and the Millennium Development Goals: 2007 Update."

47. Sandra L. Postel and Aaron T. Wolf, "Dehydrating Conflict," *Foreign Policy* 126 (September– October 2001): 62. See also Clifton Coles, "Water Pressure Builds Worldwide: Skyrocketing Water Consumption Is Leaving Many Countries High and Dry," *The Futurist* (January– February, 2003): 9.

48. Postel and Wolf, "Dehydrating Conflict," 60; UNESCO, "Sharing Water Resources," http://www.unesco.org/water/wwap/facts_figures/sharing_waters.shtml.

49. Postel and Wolf, "Dehydrating Conflict," 60.

50. UNESCO, "Sharing Water Resources," http://www.unesco.org/water/wwap/facts_figures/sharing_waters.shtml; United Nations, Department of Economic and Social Affairs, "International Rivers and Lakes," June 2003, 2, http://www.un.org/esa/sustdev/sdissues/water/rivers_lakes_news39.pdf.

51. Postel and Wolf, "Dehydrating Conflict," 60.

52. Postel and Wolf, "Dehydrating Conflict," 61; David Axe, "War Is Boring: China Dam Project Stokes Regional Tensions," *Global Policy,* April 28, 2010, http://www.globalpolicy.org/security-council/dark-side-of-natural-resources/water-in-conflict/49047.html.

53. Postel and Wolf, "Dehydrating Conflict," 62.

54. For the population statistics, see Farzaneh Roudi-Fahimi, Liz Creel, and Roger-Mark De Souza, *Finding the Balance: Population and Water Scarcity in the Middle East and North Africa* (Washington, DC: Population Reference Bureau, 2002), 1–2, http://www.prb.org/pdf/FindingTheBalance_Eng.pdf; Population Resource Center, "Executive Summary: The Middle East," 2004, http://www.prcdc.org/summaries/middleeast/middleeast.html. For the discussion on water conflicts, see Peter H. Gleick, "Water and Conflict: Fresh Water Resources and International Security," *International Security* 18 (1993): 79–112; Joyce R. Starr, "Water Wars," *Foreign Policy* 82 (Spring 1991): 17–36; Jon B. Altermam, "Clear Gold: Water and Conflict in the Middle East," *Global Policy,* April 19, 2010, http://www.globalpolicy.org/security-council/dark-side-of-natural-resources/water-in-conflict/48960.html. For a contrary view, see Peter Beaumont, "The Myth of Water Wars and the Future of Irrigated Agriculture in the Middle East," *Water International* 10 (1994): 9–21.

55. Serdar Guner, "The Turkish–Syrian War of Attrition: The Water Dispute," *Studies in Conflict & Terrorism* 20 (1997): 105–106; Starr, "Water Wars," 28–31.

56. Servet Multu, "The Southeastern Anatolia Project (GAP) of Turkey: Its Context, Objectives, and Prospects," *Orient* 37 (1996): 59–86; Robert Olson, "Turkey–Syria Relations Since the Gulf War: Kurds and Water," *Middle East Policy* 5 (1997): 168–193.

57. Jehl, "In Race to Tap the Euphrates."

58. Cooper, "Water Shortages," 322, 332.

59. United Nations, "Water: It's Attitude That Counts," statement from the World Water Assessment Programme on the occasion of World Water Day, March 22, 2005, http://www.unesco.org/water/wwap/news/wwap_wwd_05.shtml; United Nations, "World Water Day 2005," press release, http://www.worldwaterday.org/page/130.

60. World Wildlife Fund, "Preserving Fresh Water—WWF's Work and What You Can Do to Help," 2006, http://worldwildlife.org/earthday/freshwater-work.cfm.

61. Water Partners International, "Thirsty Planet: Coping with Water Scarcity," press release, March 21, 2007, http://water.org/news/releases/PDF/NR_2007_03_21_WWD.pdf.

62. Postel and Wolf, "Dehydrating Conflict," 65–66; Alex Kirby, "Water Scarcity: A Looming Crisis?" *BBC News*, October 19, 2004, http://news.bbc.co.uk/go/pr/fr/hi/science/nature/3747724.stm.

63. FAO, "The Spectrum of Malnutrition," 2002, http://www.fao.org/worldfoodsummit/english/fsheets/malnutrition.pdf; FAO, "Hunger: Frequently Asked Questions (FAQs)," 2010, http://www.fao.org/hunger/faqs-on-hunger/en/.

64. FAO, "Hunger at a Glance," 2010, http://www.fao.org/hunger/hunger_home/hunger_at_a_glance/en/; FAO, "Hunger: Frequently Asked Questions (FAQs)," 2010, http://www.fao.org/hunger/faqs-on-hunger/en/.

65. Frederic Mousseau and Anuradha Mittal, "Food Sovereignty: Ending World Hunger in Our Time," *The Humanist,* March–April 2006, 24, http://www.americanhumanist.org.

66. World Resources Institute, "Earth Trends: The Environmental Information Portal: Agriculture and Food (Nutrition: Calorie Supply per Capita)," http://earthtrends.wri.org/. Elizabeth Frazao, Birgit Meade, and Anita Regmi, "Conversing Patterns in Global Food Consumption and Food Delivery Systems," *United States Department of Agriculture,*

February 2008, http://www.ers.usda.gov/amberwaves/february08/features/covergingpatterns.htm.

67. World Resources Institute, "Earth Trends: Agriculture and Food," http://earthtrends.wri.org/features/view_feature.php?theme=8&fid=24.

68. FAO, "The Numbers: SOFI 2004 Hunger Statistics," http://www.fao.org/newsroom/en/focus/2004/51786/printable_51791en.html.

69. FAO, "The Spectrum of Malnutrition."

70. WFP, "Facts and Figures: Hunger Facts" (2007), http://www.wfp.org/aboutwfp/facts/hunger_facts.asp?section=1&sub_section=5.

71. FAO, "The Spectrum of Malnutrition;" FAO, "Hunger Slows Progress Towards Millennium Development Goals," November 22, 2005, http://www.fao.org/newsroom/en/news/2005/1000151/index.html.

72. FAO, World Food Programme, "Food Aid to Save and Improve Lives," 2000, http://www.fao.org/worldfoodsummit/english/fsheets/wfp.pdf.

73. FAO, "Lesotho Faces Deep Food Crisis After One of Its Worst Droughts in 30 Years; One Fifth of Population Will Need Assistance," June 13, 2007, http://www.fao.org/newsroom/en/news/2007/10000597/index.html.

74. WFP, "Why Does Hunger Exist?" 2007, http://www.wfp.org/aboutwfp/introduction/hunger_causes.asp?section=1&sub_section=1.

75. FAO, "FAO Component of the 2007 Work Plan for Sudan," 2007, http://www.fao.org/tc/tce/app_sudan_07_intro_en.asp; WFP, "Fighting Hunger Worldwide" February 4, 2010, http://documents.wfp.org/stellent/groups/public/documents/communications/wfp215812.pdf.

76. Global Food Security Crisis, "Background," 2009, http://www.un-foodsecurity.org/background; WFP, "Overview," 2010, http://www.wfp.org/our-work; FAO, "FAO Component of the 2007 Work Plan for Sudan"; FAO, "UN Reports Fresh Fighting in Sudan's Darfur Region," December 2, 2004, http://www.fao.org/world/regional/rne/news/news294_en.htm.

77. For a detailed explanation of why this occurs, see *Somalia, Operation Restore Hope: A Preliminary Assessment* (London: African Rights, 1993); and Peter Madden, *Brussels Beef Carve-up: EC Beef Dumping in West Africa* (London: Christian Aid, 1993).

78. U.S. Department of Energy, Energy Information Administration, "Table E1, World Primary Energy Consumption (Btu), 1992–2001," 2003, http://www.eia.doe.gov/emeu/iea/tablee1.html; U.S. Department of Energy, Energy Information Administration, *International Energy Outlook 2007* (Washington, DC: U.S. Department of Energy, Energy Information Administration, 2007), 1, http://www.ei.doe.gov/oiaf/ieo/index.html.

79. Vaclav Smil, "The Energy Question, Again," *Current History* 99 (2000): 409.

80. U.S. Department of Energy, Energy Information Administration, *International Energy Outlook 2007*, 1.

81. Smil, "The Energy Question, Again," 411; "China Unveils Emissions Targets Ahead of Copenhagen," *BBC News*, November 26, 2009, http://news.bbc.co.uk/2/hi/asia-pacific/8380106.stm.

82. U.S. Department of Energy, Energy Information Administration, *Annual Energy Outlook 2003 with Projections to 2025*, Report #DOE/EIA-0383 (2003), 2, http://www.eia.doe.gov/oiaf/aeo/index.html; International Energy Agency, "IEA Director Releases Latest World Energy Outlook, Says Current Energy Trends 'Call for Urgent and Decisive Policy Responses,'" October 26, 2004, http://www.iea.org/Textbase/press/pressdetail.asp?PRESS_REL_ID=137; Energy Information Administration, *International Energy Outlook 2006*, "Table A4. World Oil Consumption by Region, Reference Case, 1990–2030," 87, http://www.eia.doe.gov/oaif/ieo/pdf/ieoreftab_4.pdf; Energy Information Administration, "International Petroleum Monthly: Table 4.2 OPEC Crude Oil Production (Excluding Lease Condensate), 1980–2006," June 2007, http:www.eia.doe.gov/emeu/ipsr/supply.htm; Energy Information Administration, *International Energy Outlook 2010—Highlights*, May 25, 2010, http://eia.doe.gov/oiaf/ieo/highlights.html.

83. Figures for the 1990s taken from UN World Economic and Social Survey, 1996; Energy Information Administration, *International Energy Annual* (2000–2004), *International Petroleum Monthly* (2005–2006), http://www.eia.doe.gov/emeu/cabs/topworldtables3_4.html.

84. Energy Information Administration, "Table 2.4, World Oil Demand, 1998–2002," *International Petroleum Monthly* (December 2002), http://www.eia.doe.gov/emeu/ipsr/t24.xls; Energy Information Administration, "Table 3. International Petroleum Supply and Demand: Base Case," July 2007, http://www.eia.doe.gov/emeu/steo/pub/3tab.html; Energy Information Administration, *April 2010: International Petroleum Monthly*, "Table 2.1 World Oil Balance, 2005–2009," May 11, 2010, http://www.eia.doe.gov/emeu/ipsr/t21.xls.

85. "China Oil Demand Seen Rising to 9.96 Mln BPD by 2012 from 7.59 Mln This Yr—IEA," Forbes, July 9, 2007, http://www.forbes.com/afxnewslimited/feeds/afx/2007/07/09/afx3893219.html; Energy Information Administration, "Short-Term Energy Outlook," May 11, 2010, http://www.eia.doe.gov/emeu/steo/pub/.

86. Robert O. Keohane, *After Hegemony: Cooperation and Discord in the World Political Economy* (Princeton, NJ: Princeton University Press, 1984), 223.

87. *Ibid.*, 224–229.

88. Ibid., 229–230.

89. *Ibid.*, 231–237.

90. See Robert J. Lieber, "Oil and Power After the Gulf War," *International Security* 17 (1992): 155–176.

91. British Petroleum, "BTC Celebrates Full Commissioning," July 13, 2006, http://www.bp.com/genericarticle.do?categoryId=2012968&contentId=7019835; British Petroleum, "Baku-Tblisi-Ceyhan Timeline," March 2009, http://www.bp.com/sectiongenericarticle.do?categoryId=9029481&contentId=7053999.

92. CEDIGAZ, The International Association for Natural Gas, "Natural Gas in the World—2009 Edition," 2009, http://www.cedigaz.org/Fichiers/NGW.pdf; U.S. Department of Energy, Energy Information Administration, *International Energy Outlook 2007: Natural Gas* (Washington, DC: Energy Information Administration 2007), 39–40, http://www.eia.doe.gov/oiaf/ieo/pdf/nat_gas.pdf; U.S. Department of Energy, Energy Information Administration, *International Energy Outlook 2009: Chapter 1—World Energy Demand and Economic Outlook* (Washington, DC: Energy Information Administration 2009), http://www.eia.doe.gov/oiaf/archive/ieo09/world.html.

93. CEDIGAZ, The International Association for Natural Gas, "2006 Natural Gas Year in Review: CEDIGAZ' First Estimates," press release, April 26, 2007, http://www.cedigaz.org/Fichiers/PREstimates2006.pdf.

94. U.S. Department of Energy, Energy Information Administration, *International Energy Outlook 2007*, 7.

95. Ibid., 3.

96. U.S. Department of Energy, Energy Information Administration, *International Energy Outlook 2009—Electricity* (Washington, DC: U.S. Department of Energy, Energy Information Administration, May 27, 2009), http://www.eia.doe.gov/oiaf/archive/ieo09/electricity.html.

97. U.S. Department of Energy, Energy Information Administration, *International Energy Outlook 2009: Coal* (Washington, DC: U.S. Department of Energy, Energy Information Administration, 2007), http://www.eia.doe.gov/oiaf/archive/ieo09/coal.html.

98. U.S. Department of Energy, Energy Information Administration, *International Energy Outlook 2006*, "Table A6. World Coal Consumption by Region, Reference Case, 1990–2030," 2006, 89, http://www.eia.doe.gov/emeu/international/coalconsumption.html; U.S. Department of Energy, Energy Information Administration, *International Energy Outlook 2009: Chapter 8—Energy-Related Carbon Dioxide Emissions* (Washington, DC: U.S. Department of Energy, Energy Information Administration, May 27, 2009), http://www.eia.doe.gov/oiaf/archive/ieo09/emissions.html.

99. U.S. Department of Energy, Energy Information Administration, *International Energy Outlook 2002: Coal,* Report #DOE/EIA-0484 (Washington, DC: U.S. Department of Energy, Energy Information Administration, 2002), 7, http://www.eia.doe.gov/oiaf/archive/ieo02/index.html.

100. U.S. Department of Energy, Energy Information Administration, *International Energy Outlook 2009: Chapter 1—World Energy Demand and Economic Outlook.*

101. International Energy Agency, "Renewables in Global Energy Supply: An IEA Fact Sheet," January 2007, 3, 5, http://www.iea.org/textbase/papers/2006/ renewable_factsheet.pdf; U.S. Department of Energy, Energy Information Administration, *International Energy Outlook 2010—Highlights,* May 25, 2010, http://www.eia.doe.gov/oiaf/ieo/highlights.html.

102. U.S. Department of Energy, Energy Information Administration, "Electricity—A Secondary Energy Source," November 2006, http://www.eia.doe.gov/kids/energyfacts/sources/electricity.html.

103. International Energy Agency, "World Energy Outlook 2006: Fact Sheet—Global Energy Trends," 2006, http://www.worldenergyoutlook.org/fact-sheets/fs_GlobalEnergyTrends.pdf.

104. Daniel Yergin explores the role of oil and energy in international politics in *The Prize: The Epic Quest for Oil, Money & Power* (New York: Simon & Schuster, 1991).

Chapter 13

1. Ramesh Thakur and Luk Van Langenhove, "Enhancing Global Governance Through Regional Integration," *Global Governance* 12 (2006): 233.

2. Ibid.

3. Yakub Halabi, "The Expansion of Global Governance into the Third World: Altruism, Realism, or Constructivism?" *International Studies Review* 6 (2004): 36.

4. Ibid., 25.

5. This definition comes from Hedley Bull, *The Anarchical Society* (New York: Columbia University Press, 1977), 127.

6. For a more detailed introduction to these principles of international law, see Paul Sieghart, *The International Law of Human Rights* (Oxford, UK: Clarendon, 1983), 10ff.

7. "Georgian Diplomat Convicted in Fatal Crash Goes Home," CNN.com, June 30, 2000, http://archives.cnn.com/2000/US/06/30/georgia.diplomat/.

8. Paul Reynolds, "Britain and Iran's Fraught History," BBC News, June 29, 2009, http://news.bbc.co.uk/go/pr/fr/-/2/hi/uk_news/8116245.stm.

9. Robert F. Drinan, *Cry of the Oppressed: The History and Hope of the Human Rights Revolution* (San Francisco: Harper & Row, 1987).

10. Hilary Charlesworth, "Is International Law Relevant to the War in Iraq and Its Aftermath?" National Press Club, Canberra, October 29, 2003, 2–3, http://www.globalpolicy.org/empire/un/2003/1029charlesworth.pdf.

11. For more on the use of the tit-for-tat (TFT) strategy in international relations, see Robert Axelrod, *The Evolution of Cooperation* (New York: Basic Books, 1984).

12. Web Genocide Documentation Centre, "Resolution on German War Crimes by Representatives of Nine Occupied Countries, January 12, 1942," http://www.ess.uwe.ac.uk/genocide/trials.htm; "Charter of the International Military Tribunal," http://www.ess.uwe.ac.uk/documents/chtrimt.htm.

13. Amnesty International, "Women's Rights," http://www.amnestyusa.org/violence-against-women/stop-violence-against-women-svaw/womens-rights/page.do?id=1108231.

14. For good discussions of the special human rights concerns of women, see World Health Organization, *Women's Health: Across Age and Frontier* (New York: United Nations Press, 1992); "Violence Against Women," *UN Chronicle,* June 1995, 48; Oloka Onyango, "Women, War, and Rape," *Human Rights Quarterly* 17 (1995): 650–690; and Julie A. Mertus, *War's*

Offensive on Women: the Humanitarian Challenge in Bosnia, Kosovo, and Afghanistan (Bloomfield, CT: Kumarian Press, 2000).

15. Amnesty International, "Women's Rights," http://www.amnestyusa.org/violence-against-women/stop-violence-against-women-svaw/womens-rights/page.do?id=1108231.

16. "Judging Genocide," in *World Politics 02/03*, 23rd ed., ed. Helen E. Furkitt (Guilford, CT: McGraw-Hill/Dushkin, 2002), 217–218; "Rome Statute of the International Criminal Court: Overview," *United Nations, 1998–1999*, 3, http://www.un.org/law/icc/general/overview.htm.

17. "UN Diplomatic Conference Concludes in Rome with Decision to Establish Permanent International Criminal Court," UN press release L/ROM/22, July 1998, http://www.un.org/icc/pressrel/lrom22.htm.

18. "Rome Statute of the International Criminal Court: Overview," 2.

19. ICC-Darfur, Sudan, "Situations and Cases," http://www.icc-cpi.int/Menus/ICC/Situations+and+Cases/Situations/Situation+ICC+0205/.

20. "Rome Statute of the International Criminal Court: Overview," 3.

21. "Statement of John R. Bolton," in *Taking Sides: Clashing Views on Controversial Issues in World Politics*, 11th ed., ed. John T. Rourke (Guilford, CT: McGraw-Hill/Dushkin, 2004), 299.

22. Amnesty International, "US Threats to the International Criminal Court," http://web.amnesty.org/pages/icc-US_threats-eng.

23. Blake Evans-Pritchard and Simon Jennings, "US Takes Cautious Steps Towards ICC," May 6, 2010, http://www.globalpolicy.org/component/content/article/164-icc/49067-us-takes-cautious-steps-towards-ICC.html. The International Criminal Court Takes Steps to End Aggression" (June 2010), http://www.globalsolutions.org/issues/2010_icc_review_conference.

24. United Nations General Assembly, "Resolution Adopted by the General Assembly," 60/251. Human Rights Council, April 6, 2006.

25. "Rights Body 'Clean Break' for UN," BBC News, June 19, 2006, http://news.bbc.co.uk/go/pr/fr/-/2/hi/europe/5093590.stm; "UN Elects New Human Rights Body," BBC News, May 9, 2009, http://news.bbc.co.uk/go/pr/fr/-/2/hi/americas/4754169.stm; "US Elected to UN Rights Council," BBC News, May 12, 2009, http://news.bbc.co.uk/go/pr/fr/-/2/hi/americas/8046676.stm.

26. Office of the High Commissioner of Human Rights, "Human Rights Council Extends Mandate of Special Rapporteur on Myanmar, Adopts Resolutions on Guinea and Democratic Republic of the Congo," United Nations, March 26, 2010, http://www.ohchr.org/EN/NewsEvents/Pages/DisplayNews.aspx?NewsID=9944&LangID=E.

27. For more on the Peltier case, see *New York Times*, April 3, 1988, 6A.

28. For estimates of the casualties caused by the fighting in the former Yugoslavia, see Milan Andreevich, "Bosnia & Herzegovina: In Search of Peace," Radio Free Europe/Radio Liberty Research Report, June 5, 1992, 5–9; and Patrick Moore, "Ethnic Cleansing in Bosnia: Outrage but Little Action," Radio Free Europe/Radio Liberty Research Report, August 28, 1992, 11–15.

29. Organization for the Prohibition of Chemical Weapons, http://www.opcw.org/factsandfigures/index.html#participation; Center for Nonproliferation Studies, "Inventory of International Nonproliferation Organizations and Regimes," June 18, 2009, http://www.nti.org/e_research/official_docs/inventory/pdf.

30. Richard H. Steinberg and Jonathan M. Zasloff, "Power and International Law," *The American Journal of International Law* 100 (2006): 64, 74, 79, 81.

31. Ibid., 65, 82.

32. Union of International Associations, *Yearbook of International Organizations 2009/2010*, 46th ed. (Munich: K. G. Saur Verlag, 2007), http://www.uia.be/ybvol1.

33. Allen Buchanan and Robert O. Keohane, "The Legitimacy of Global Governance Institutions," *Ethics & International Affairs* 20 (2006): 405–438.

34. Maria Green Cowles, "Intergovernmental Organizations: Global Governance and Transsovereign Problems," in *Beyond Sovereignty: Issues for a Global Agenda*, 3rd ed., ed.

Maryann Cusimano Love (Belmont, CA: Thomson Wadsworth, 2007), 42–43; Thomas J. Volgy, Elizabeth Fausett, Keith Grant, and Stuart Rodgers, "Ergo FIGO: Identifying Formal Intergovernmental Organizations," Working Paper Series in International Politics, Department of Political Science, University of Arizona (December 2006).

35. Buchanan and Keohane, "The Legitimacy of Global Governance Institutions."

36. Cowles, "Intergovernmental Organizations," 43–44.

37. For more on the objectives and formation of the League, see E. H. Carr, *The Twenty Years' Crisis* (New York: Harper & Row, 1964).

38. Hans Morgenthau, *Politics Among Nations*, 5th ed. (New York: Knopf, 1978), 200.

39. UNA-USA, "Status of US Financial Obligations to the United Nations," June 2002, 2, http://www.globalpolicy.org/finance/unitedstates/2002/06status.htm.

40. United Nations, "Report to the President of the General Assembly on the Consultations Regarding Revitalizing the Role and Authority of the General Assembly," August 2, 2007, 5–10, http://www.un.org/ga/president/61/follow-up/revitalization/Facilitators-Report-GARev.pdf. See also "On the Lines: The UN Role in Preventing and Containing Conflict," United Nations Association of United States of America News, 1985; "Report of the 18 UN Issues Conference," 1987, Stanley Foundation.

41. UN General Assembly, "In the Informal Consultations of the Plenary on System-wide Coherence," February 4, 2010, http://www.un.org/ga/president/64/statements/SWC4210.stml.

42. Global Policy Forum, "Subjects of UN Security Council Vetoes," http:///www.globalpolicy.org/security/membship/veto/vetosubj.htm; UN Security Council, "United Kingdom of Great Britain and Northern Ireland and United States of America: Draft Resolution," January 12, 2007, http://www.globalpolicy.org/security/veto/2007/14.pdf; UN Security Council, "Qatar: Draft Resolution," November 10, 2006, http://www.globalpolicy.org/security/veto/2006878.pdf.

43. United Nations, "Secretariat," 2004, http://www.un.org/documents/st.htm; United Nations General Assembly, "Composition of the Secretariat: Report of the Secretary-General," September 15, 2009.

44. United Nations, "Biography of Kofi A. Annan," 2000–2002, http://www.un.org/News/ossg/sg/pages/sg_biography.html.

45. The Nobel Foundation, "Kofi Annan—Biography," 2001, http://www.nobel.se/peace/laureates/2001/annan-bio.html.

46. United Nations, "Biography of Kofi A. Annan."

47. Andrew Rubin, "We Are No Longer Able to See the Sun Set," *Al-Ahram*, July 7, 2005, in Global Policy Forum, http://www.globalpolicy.org/intljustice/icj/2005/0707israel.htm; "World Court Marks 6th Anniversary, as Its Case-Load Gets Heavier and Tougher," Associated Press, April 11, 2006, http://www.globalpolicy.org/intljustice/icj/2006/0411anniversary.htm.

48. ECOSOC, "Background Information," http://www.un.org/ecosoc/about/.

49. U.S. State Department, "United States Rejoins UNESCO: President Bush Announced This September 12," September 12, 2002, http://usinfo.state.gov; U.S. State Department, "America's Principles and Multilateral Commitment," August 2003, http://usinfo.state.gov/products/pubs/unesco/.

50. United Nations Department of Peacekeeping Situation Centre, "Fatalities by Year: Up to June 2007," July 5, 2007, http://www.un.org/Depts/dpko/fatalities/StatsByYear%201.pdf.

51. *UN Chronicle*, June 1993, 73.

52. See *The Blue Helmets: A Review of United Nations Peacekeeping*, 2nd ed. (New York: United Nations, 1997).

53. UNA-USA, "Status of US Financial Obligations to the United Nations," 4; United Nations, "Monthly Summary of Military and Police Contribution to United Nations Operations," April 2010, http://www.un.org/Depts/dpko/dpki/contributors/index.htm; United Nations Department of Peacekeeping Operations, "United Nations Peacekeeping Fact Sheet" (March 2010).

54. "An Idea Whose Time Has Come—and Gone?" *The Economist*, July 23, 2009, http://www.economist.com/world/international/displaystory.cfm?story_id=E1_TQDRSSRR; United

Nations General Assembly, "Implementing the Responsibility to Protect: Report of the Secretary-General," A/63/677, January 12, 2009; "Secretary-General Addresses International Peace Academy Seminar on 'The Responsibility to Protect,'" February 2, 2002, http://www.un.org/News/Press/docs/2002/sgsm8125.doc.htm; *The Responsibility to Protect* (Ottawa, Canada: International Commission on Intervention and State Sovereignty, 2001).

55. The possibilities and problems with UN peacekeeping are debated in William Durch and Barry Blechman, *Keeping the Peace: The United Nations in the Emerging World Order* (Washington, DC: Henry L. Stimson Center, 1992); John Q. Blodgett, "The Future of UN Peacekeeping," *Washington Quarterly* 14 (1991): 207–20; and a special issue of *Survival* 32 (May–June 1990), which includes contributions from Brian Urqhardt, Aleksandr Belonogov, Augustus Norton, and Thomas Weiss, among others.

56. Crispin Grey-Johnson, "Beyond Peacekeeping: The Challenge of Post-Conflict Reconstruction and Peacebuilding in Africa," *UN Chronicle*, Online ed. (2006), http://www.un.org/Pubs/Chronicle/2006/issue1/0106p08.htm#.

57. "New Peacebuilding Fund Reflects Commitment to Sustained Engagement in Countries Emerging from Conflict, Says Secretary-General at Fund's Launch," General Assembly PBC/4, October 11, 2006, http://www.un.org/News/Press/docs/2006/pbc4.doc.htm.

58. United Nations, "Secretary-General Ban Ki-moon's Remarks to Security Council Open Debate on Transition and Exit Strategies for Peacekeeping Operations," February 12, 2010, http://www.un.org/en/peacekeeping/articles/sg_article12022010.htm.

59. See David Baldwin, *Economic Statecraft* (Princeton, NJ: Princeton University Press, 1985).

60. Cowles, "Intergovernmental Organizations," 51.

61. "Iraq Scandal Taints 2,000 Firms," BBC News, October 27, 2005, http://news.bbc.co.uk/go/pr/fr/-/1/hi/world/americas/4382820.stm.

62. United Nations, "Reform at the United Nations: UN Reform Highlights Since 1997," 2006, http://www.un.org/reform/highlights/shtml.

63. Cowles, "Intergovernmental Organizations," 50–53.

64. United Nations, "UN Reform Dossier: 1997–2000," 6, http://www.un.org/reform/dossier.htm; United Nations, "Progress Towards Development Targets Is Mixed, UN Finds," The Millennium Development Goals Report 2007, July 2007, http://www.un.org/millenniumgoals/pdf/mdg2007-globalpr.pdf.

65. World Bank, http://www.worldbank.org; World Bank, "World Bank Group Fiscal Year Highlights, 2009; Sebastian Mallaby, "Saving the World Bank," *Foreign Affairs* 84 (2005): 75.

66. Mallaby, "Saving the World Bank," 84; World Bank, "2010 Spring Meetings Endorse $86 Billion Capital Increase, Voting Reform," April 25, 2010, http://web.worldbank.org/WBSITE/EXTERNAL/NEWS/0,,contentMDK:22556192~menuPK:34457~pagePK:34370~piPK:34424~theSitePK:4607,00.html.

67. Article I, Articles of Agreement of the International Monetary Fund.

68. International Monetary Fund, "IMF Approves €30 Bln Loan for Greece on Fast Track," IMF Survey Magazine: In the News, May 9, 2010, http://www.imf.org/external/pubs/ft/survey/so/2010/NEW050910A.htm; Bob Davis, "Who's on the Hook for the IMF's Greek Bailout?" *Wall Street Journal*, May 5, 2010, http://online.wsj.com/article/SB10001424052748704866204575224421086866944.html/.

69. James M. Boughton, "Michael Camdessus at the IMF: A Retrospective," *Finance & Development: A Quarterly Magazine of the IMF* 37(2000): 2–6.

70. Kenneth Rogoff, "The IMF Strikes Back," *Foreign Policy* (2003): 46.

71. Cowles, "Intergovernmental Organizations," 53–55; Rogoff, "The IMF Strikes Back," 41; Lawrence J. McQuillan, "The Case Against the International Monetary Fund," in *Essays in Public Policy* (Stanford, CA: Hoover Institution Press, 1999).

72. Rogoff, "The IMF Strikes Back," 41–42.

73. World Trade Organization (WTO), "What Is the WTO?" http://www.wto.org/english/thewto_e/whatis_e/tif_e/fact4_e.htm.

74. Ibid.

75. Ibid.

76. See Cowles, "Intergovernmental Organizations," 56–58.

77. Maryann Cusimano Love, "Nongovernmental Organizations: Politics Beyond Sovereignty," in *Beyond Sovereignty: Issues for a Global Agenda*, 3rd ed., ed. Maryann Cusimano Love (Belmont, CA: Thomson Wadsworth, 2007), 70–71.
78. Ibid., 72.
79. Ibid., 73.
80. Kim D. Reimann, "A View from the Top: International Politics, Norms and the Worldwide Growth of NGOs," *International Studies Quarterly* 50 (2006): 49.
81. Love, "Nongovernmental Organizations," 73–77.
82. Jutta Joachim, "Framing Issues and Seizing Opportunities: The UN, NGOs, and Women's Rights," *International Studies Quarterly* 47 (2003): 247.
83. Steve Charnovitz, "Nongovernmental Organizations and International Law," *The American Journal of International Law* 100 (2006): 348–372.
84. Reimann, "A View from the Top," 55, 60.
85. Love, "Nongovernmental Organizations," 80–81.
86. Ibid., 77.
87. "Human Rights Watch: Who We Are," Human Rights Watch, http://www.hrw.org/about/whoweare.html.
88. "WWF—The Global Conservation Organization," http://www.panda.org/about_wwf/who_we_are/index.cfm; "How Is WWF Organized," WWF, http://www.panda.org/about_wwf/who_we_are/offices/organization.cfm.
89. Greenpeace, "Questions About Greenpeace in General," http://www.greenpeace.org/international/about/faq/questions-about-greenpeace-in; Greenpeace, "Toxic Tech Victory: Sony Ericsson Announces Phase Out of Toxic Chemicals," April 29, 2005, http://www.greenpeace.org/international/news/toxic-tech-victory; Greenpeace, "Arctic Sunrise," http://www.greenpeace.org/international/about/ships/the-arctic-sunrise.
90. Oxfam, "History of Oxfam," http://www.oxfam.org.uk/about_us/history/index.htm; "One Programme: One Goal," http://www.oxfam.org.uk/about_us/history/history8.htm; "Tsunami Crisis," http://www.oxfam.org.uk/oxfam_in_action/emergencies/tsunami.html.
91. International Chamber of Commerce, "ICC Membership," http://www.iccwbo.org/home/intro_icc/membership.asp; International Chamber of Commerce, "What Is ICC," http://www.iccwbo.org/home/menu_what_is_icc.asp.
92. Thomas Hobbes, *Leviathan*, ed. Michael Oakeshott (New York: Collier, 1962), 100.

Chapter 14

1. Contemporary writings on just war include the following: Michael Walzer, *Just and Unjust Wars: A Moral Argument with Historical Illustrations* (News York: Basic Books, 1977); Barrie Paskins and Michael Dockrill, *The Ethics of War* (Minneapolis: University of Minnesota Press, 1979); Richard Norman, *Ethics, Killing, and War* (New York: Cambridge University Press, 1995); and Mark Evans, *Just War Theory: A Reappraisal* (New York: Palgrave Macmillan, 2005).
2. André Pasquier, "Humanitarian Action: Is Its Legitimacy in Question?" in *Making the Voice of Humanity Heard: Essays on Humanitarian Assistance and International Humanitarian Law*, Liesbeth Lijnzaad, Johanna van Sambeek, Bahia Tahzib-Lie, Corinne A A Packer, and Margriet, Princess daughter of Juliana Queen of the Netherlands (Herndon, VA: Nijhoff, 2004), 465–472; Ian Forbes, ed., *Political Theory, International Relations and the Ethics of Intervention* (London: St. Martin's Press, 1993); Stanley Hoffmann, *The Ethics and Politics of Humanitarian Intervention* (Notre Dame, IN: Notre Dame University Press, 1996); Oliver Ramsbotham and Tom Woodhouse, *Humanitarian Intervention in Contemporary Conflict* (Cambridge, UK: Polity, 1996); Antonia Tanca, *Foreign Armed Intervention in Internal*

Conflict (Dordrecht, Netherlands: Martinus Nijhoff, 1993); William J. Buckley, ed., *Kosovo: Contending Voices on Balkan Interventions* (Grand Rapids, MI: Eerdmans Publishing, 2000); David Chandler, *From Kosovo to Kabul: Human Rights and International Intervention* (London: Pluto Press, 2002); Walter Clarke and Jeffrey Herbst, *Learning from Somalia: The Lessons of Armed Humanitarian Intervention* (Boulder, CO: Westview Press, 1997); Gareth Evans and Mohamed Sahnoun, *The Responsibility to Protect: Report of the International Commission on Intervention and State Sovereignty* (Ottawa, Canada: The International Development Research Centre, 2001); Martha Finnemore, *The Purpose of Intervention: Changing Beliefs About the Use of Force* (Ithaca, NY: Cornell University Press, 2003); Katharina P. Coleman, *International Organisations and Peace Enforcement: The Politics of International Legitimacy* (Cambridge, UK: Cambridge University Press, 2007); Richard N. Haass, *Intervention: The Use of American Force in the Post-Cold War World* (Washington, DC: Carnegie Endowment for International Peace, 1994); J. L. Holzgrefe and Robert O. Keohane, eds., *Humanitarian Intervention: Ethical, Legal and Political Dilemmas* (Cambridge, UK: Cambridge University Press, 2003); Gene M. Lyons and Michael Mastanduno, eds., *Beyond Westphalia: State Sovereignty and International Intervention* (Baltimore: Johns Hopkins University Press, 1995); Nicolaus Mills and Kira Brunner, eds., *The New Killing Fields: Massacre and the Politics of Intervention* (New York: Basic Books, 2002); Jonathan Moore, ed., *Hard Choices: Moral Dilemmas in Humanitarian Intervention* (Lanham, MD: Rowman & Littlefield, 2000).

3. J. R. Minkel, "Darfur Dead Much Higher Than Commonly Reported," *Scientific American*, September 15, 2006, http://www.sciam.com/article.cfm?articleID=00037EE7-D970–150A-997083414B7F0000; "No More Delay on Darfur," editorial, *New York Times*, April 19, 2007, http://www.nytimes.com/2007/04/19/opinion/19thu2.html?ex=1334635200&en=3f412665d4cc9b5f&ei=5088&partner=rssnyt&emc=rss; Julian Borger, "Darfur Conflict Heralds Era of Wars Triggered by Climate Change, UN Report Warns," *Guardian Unlimited*, June 23, 2007, http://www.guardian.co.uk/environment/2007/jun/23/sudan.climatechange.

4. Regan Morris, "Sudan: A Growing Grassroots Movement Strives Toward an Ethical Response," Changemakers.net, June 2005, http://www.genocideintervention.net/about/press/coverage/index.php/archives/6; Nicholas Kristof, "OpEd: Kristof Responds," *New York Times*, June 1, 2005, http://www.genocideintervention.net/about/press/coverage/index.php/archives/10; Alex J. Bellamy and Paul D. Williams, "The UN Security Council and the Question of Humanitarian Intervention in Darfur," *Journal of Military Ethics* 5 (2006): 144–160; Thomas G. Weiss, "Halting Genocide: Rhetoric vs. Reality," *Genocide Studies and Prevention* 2 (2007): 7–30; Nsongurua J. Udombana, "When Neutrality Is a Sin: The Darfur Crisis and the Crisis of Humanitarian Intervention in Sudan," *Human Rights Quarterly* 27 (2005): 1149–1199; Nick Grono, "Briefing—Darfur: The International Community's Failure to Protect," *African Affairs* 105 (2006): 621–631; Alec Barker, "Between Conscience and Self-Interest: The United States, Sudan, and Darfur," *BC Journal of International Affairs* 9 (2006), http://bcjournal.org/2006/between-conscience-and-self-interest/.

5. Andrew Rigby, *Justice and Reconciliation: After the Violence* (London: Lynne Rienner, 2001); Jonathan Allen, "Balancing Justice and Social Unity: Political Theory and the Idea of a Truth and Reconciliation Commission," *The University of Toronto Law Journal* 49 (1999): 315–353; Robert L. Rothstein, *After the Peace: Resistance and Reconciliation* (Boulder, CO: Lynne Rienner, 1999); Donald W. Shriver, Jr., "The Long Road to Reconciliation: Some Moral Stepping-Stones," in *After the Peace: Resistance and Reconciliation*, ed. Robert L. Rothstein (Boulder, CO: Lynne Rienner, 1999).

6. Ian Fisher and Larry Rohter, "The Pope Denounces Capitalism and Marxism," *New York Times*, May 13, 2007, http://www.nytimes.com/2007/05/14/world/americas/14pope.html?ex=1336881600&en=7618945a33b6ff6c&ei=5124&partner=newsvine&exprod=newsvine; Mark McCallum, "Muslim Call to Thwart Capitalism," BBC News, July 12, 2003, http://news.bbc.co.uk/2/hi/europe/3061833.stm.

7. Jeanne Kirkpatrick, "Dictatorship and Double Standards," *Commentary* (1979): 34–45.

Glossary

Absolute gains: Absolute increases in wealth or strength, regardless of others' increases.

Absolute power: Total amount of power.

Acquired Immune Deficiency Syndrome (AIDS): Complex interaction between impairment of the immune system and opportunistic infections such as pneumonia, tuberculosis, syphilis, or other conditions. It is transmitted through blood (via intravenous drug use or, rarely, transfusion of infected blood) and sexual contact and from pregnant women to the fetuses they carry.

Al Qaeda: A network of Islamic terrorist organizations, led by Osama bin Laden, that carried out the attacks on the U.S. embassies in Tanzania and Kenya in 1998, the *USS Cole* in Yemen in 2000, and the World Trade Center and Pentagon in 2001.

Anarchic: Lacking a legitimate, hierarchical structure.

Antiballistic missile (ABM): A missile designed to destroy incoming missiles or their warheads before they hit the designated targets.

Antiterrorism: Actions taken by diplomatic, law enforcement, and intelligence agencies to apprehend terrorists or thwart terrorist attacks before they can be carried out.

Appeasement: One-sided concessions to a potential opponent.

Arms control: Agreements between two or more states or unilateral actions to regulate the research, manufacture, or deployment of weapons or troops on the basis of number, type, and/or location.

Autonomous development: Territorially based effort to meet a state's citizens' basic needs.

Balance of payments: The difference between the amount of money coming into a country and the amount of money going out.

Balance of trade: The value of exports minus the value of imports.

Balancing: When states seek to prevent another state's or other states' domination of the international system either by ensuring through domestic development that they are equally powerful or by creating alliances that are equal to a state's or another alliance's power.

Ballistic missile: A vehicle that travels to its target unpowered after a short period of powered flight. Most ballistic missiles are powered by rocket engines. Part of the flight of longer range ballistic missiles may occur outside the atmosphere and involve the "reentry" of the missile. A ballistic missile may deliver a conventional warhead or a nuclear, chemical, or biological warhead.

Bandwagoning: When (usually weak) states seek to ally themselves with rising powers to take advantage of their strength.

Baruch Plan: A post–World War II U.S. proposal that would have placed all atomic energy activities under the control of an international atomic development authority. This proposal was rejected by the USSR primarily because it would have made permanent the existing U.S. monopoly over nuclear weapons.

Bilateral: Between two countries; two-sided.

Biological weapons: Weapons that use living organisms, such as bacteria or viruses, or toxins produced by living organisms to cause death, disease, or injury to humans, animals, or plants.

Bipolar: An international structure dominated by two superpowers.

Bismarckian system: A succession of alliances sought by Otto von Bismarck in the twenty years after the unification of Germany in 1871; these were pursued to moderate the demands of Germany's allies, prevent the formation of opposing coalitions, and prevent local conflicts from escalating into general war.

Blue Helmets: UN peacekeeping and truce-supervision forces dispatched at the invitation of parties to a local conflict. Their primary mission is to serve as armed sentries, separating combatants to make violation of a peace agreement more difficult. Also known as "Blue Berets," they wear UN headgear but retain their respective national uniforms.

Capability: The aspect of deterrence that refers to the ability to do great harm to an aggressor; a state's ability to retaliate against a challenger should the defending nation deem the challenger's actions to be unacceptable.

Capital-abundant: Rich in terms of money, industrial plants, and equipment.

Capital flight: A rapid outflow of financial assets when a country's economy appears to be in trouble.

Capital intensive: Industry requiring capital (money, plants, or equipment) as the main input.

Carbon sink: Forests, oceans, and other reservoirs that absorb and store carbon.

Casualties: Members of the armed forces who have been killed, wounded, or captured or are interned, sick, or missing and, therefore, are no longer a part of active duty.

Causality: The relationship of cause and effect.

Chemical weapons: Weapons that use toxic chemical substances to cause death or severe harm to humans or animals. The active chemicals (chemical agents) in chemical weapons can be gases, liquids, or solid powders and include blister, nerve, choking, and blood agents.

Chemical Weapons Convention (CWC): Treaty signed in 1993 that prohibits the production, use, or stockpiling of chemical weapons.

Chlorofluorocarbons (CFCs): A primary agent of ozone depletion found mostly in aerosols and refrigerants. The 1987 Montréal Protocol called for the phasing out of these chemicals.

Clash of Civilizations: A theory that suggests that the future of international politics will be characterized not by the state-against-state or ideological conflicts of the past but, rather, by clashes of civilizations as they seek to defend their traditions, beliefs, territory, and general interests against competing cultures.

Codex Alimentarius: International food standards and guidelines.

Collective action: Efforts undertaken by a group in its members' mutual interests.

Colonialism: A policy by which a nation maintains or extends its control over foreign dependencies. The two main types of colonialism are movement of people from the mother country to form a new political institution in the designated distant land and external powers' rule over indigenous peoples.

Commitment: The first step in deterrence, which must be stated clearly and unambiguously before a challenger carries out an act of aggression. The defending state must make clear its determination to punish a challenger if the challenger takes a specified action that the defender considers unacceptable.

Comparative advantage: The ability of one business or entity to engage in production at a lower opportunity cost than another business or entity.

Comparativists: Those who work within the field of comparative politics, a subfield of political science.

Compellence: A strategy that attempts to force an adversary to reverse some action that has already been taken.

Complex learning: Learning from experience; learning by imitation.

Concert of Europe: A special system of consultation used by the great powers of Europe after the Napoleonic Wars. A great power could initiate international conferences when it believed that the security and peace of Europe were compromised.

Confidence-building measures: Stipulations built into treaties or agreements to reduce the likelihood of defection and to enhance communication.

Conflict: A state of disharmony or opposition.

Containment: U.S. foreign policy during the Cold War aimed at halting Soviet expansion through American military and economic power.

Conventional weapons: Nonnuclear weapons such as tanks, artillery pieces, or tactical aircraft (troops that operate these weapons are referred to as conventional forces).

Cooperation: Joint operation or action.

Core: Central, or innermost, part.

Corn Laws: A set of tariffs and other restrictions on agricultural imports that protected British landowners in the late 1700s and early 1800s. Repeal of these laws in 1846 helped facilitate a boom in international trade.

Correlation: A relationship between two variables.

Counterterrorism: Use of military force against terrorist organizations.

Countervailing tariffs: Tariffs levied by one country in response to tariffs imposed in another.

Credibility: The resolve and willingness of the defending state to carry out its commitment to punish the aggressor state.

Crusade: A holy war sanctioned by the Pope; a Christian military expedition to recover the Holy Land from the Muslims.

Currency convertibility: The ability to exchange a currency for gold or other currencies.

Current-account balance: The difference between a state's total exports and total imports.

Customary practices: International customs represent the established and consistent practice of states in international relations; one of the sources of international law.

Dawes Plan: A plan to alleviate the economic pressure on Germany caused by reparations imposed after World War I. Under this agreement, American banks would lend money to Germany for its reparations payments to the Allies. These payments could then be transferred to the U.S. government from the Allies to service war loans.

Debt burdens: Multilateral debt, such as occurs when a government borrows from international institutions (IMF, World Bank), other governments, or foreign banks.

Defense: A strategy that attempts to reduce an enemy's capability to damage or take something away from the defender. The purpose is to resist an attack and minimize losses after deterrence has failed.

Deforestation: Conversion of forested land to other uses, such as cropland, shifting cultivation, or urban and industrial use.

Delinking: Subjecting external relations to the imperatives of broad internal development.

Demographic transition: Changes in the characteristics of human populations, including rate of growth, average age, literacy, and so forth.

Dependency Theory: A socio-economic theory based on the assumption that the process of the world economic systems development privileged a few countries while leaving the rest disadvantaged and vulnerable to exploitation.

Deregulate: Reduce or remove government involvement in the private sector; reduce or remove governmental oversight and control of the private sector.

Desertification: The process by which an area becomes a desert. The rapid depletion of plant life and topsoil at desert boundaries and in semiarid regions, usually caused by a combination of drought and overexploitation by humans of grasses and other vegetation.

Détente: French for "relaxation of tensions." During the Cold War, détente between the United States and Soviet Union referred to cooperation on areas such as arms control, trade, and technology.

Deterrence: The attempt to prevent war by discouraging a potential aggressor. The primary goal of the defender is to convince the challenger that the probable cost of attacking will far exceed any anticipated gain. For deterrence to function effectively, the defender must demonstrate the credibility of the deterrent threat through both capability and resolve.

Diaspora: The dispersion of people throughout the world from their original homeland.

Diplomatic immunity: Freedom from arrest and prosecution for accredited diplomats.

Disarmament: The reduction or elimination of a state's overall arms levels.

Diversified economies: Economies based on several, if not many, products, industries, and services.

Dumping: Exporting a product at below the cost of production and shipping.

Economic and Social Council (ECOSOC): A UN organ responsible for coordinating the work of the UN "family" of more specialized agencies and organizations.

Economic determinism: The theory, often attributed to Marx, that the economic structure, rather than politics, drives human development.

Elite colonialism: Indigenous rulers are replaced by a European political and economic elite but the native population remains essentially in place; much of the culture thus remains intact.

Embedded liberalism: The shared assumption among many states' leaders that governments should balance economic growth and social and economic welfare.

End of History: A theory that posits that the apex of human political and social development is reached by successfully democratizing, guaranteeing human rights, achieving stability, and implementing economic liberalization.

Enforcement terror: Terrorism carried out by a government or a government-backed agency against its own citizens.

The Enlightenment: The period in European history (most associated with the eighteenth century) when philosophers sought to "enlighten" their counterparts by explaining how human reason could overcome tyranny, ignorance, and superstition; often perceived as a threat to religion and religious thought.

Exogenously given: Determined externally; imposed, rather than derived from within.

Extended deterrence: A policy that seeks to discourage a challenger from attacking an ally or a partner.

Extortion: Organized crime groups demanding money, behavior, or other goods and services from an individual or business that results in physical or financial harm if not paid.

Factor: Variable; something with some measure of influence over an outcome.

Fascism: A doctrine promoted by the far right seeking an authoritarian society built around the rule of an elite led by a dictator or supreme leader.

Feminist: One who believes in equality of the sexes.

Feudal: Rulers of smaller political units, such as city-states, counties, or duchies, often owed allegiance to the rulers of larger principalities or kingdoms and were granted title over their lands in exchange for promises of money or military service.

Fixed exchange rate system: When currency exchange rates are set and not responsive to supply and demand.

Flexible response: The Kennedy administration's military doctrine that replaced massive retaliation and focused on countering the Soviet threat across the entire spectrum, from operations other than war to conventional warfare to nuclear exchange.

Floating exchange rate system: When currency exchange rates are set by supply and demand.

Food and Agriculture Organization (FAO): UN humanitarian organization under the ECOSOC umbrella.

Foreign direct investment (FDI): Investment in business in one country by a firm from another country.

Foreign exchange market: The global market for currency trading.

Forgive: To excuse a heavily indebted country from paying its debts.

Fragmentation: Used here to mean adherence to or embracing of regional and even local political authority, economic development, social and cultural associations, ethnic or national divisions, and so on; more generally, the act, process, or result of breaking something into smaller pieces.

Free trade zone: A group of states that have agreed to significantly reduce or eliminate trade barriers for all group members; an area in which goods can flow freely across borders without being subjected to taxes, tariffs, or other trade restrictions or efforts to protect domestic producers of those goods.

Freedom House: A nonpartisan, nonprofit organization promoting worldwide freedom and democracy; perhaps best known for its country ratings.

G-8 countries: The Group of Eight (G-8) is comprised of the leaders of major industrial democracies and holds an annual summit to discuss mutual interests and concerns.

General Agreement on Tariffs and Trade (GATT): An agreement established in 1947 to encourage freer trade. Several rounds of GATT rules negotiations since its founding progressively lowered tariffs and nontariff barriers to trade among member states.

General deterrence: This long-term strategy operates at all times and attempts to prevent an adversary from attempting any kind of military challenge because of its expected consequences.

Generalizable: Applicable to other situations, issues, and cases.

Genocide: The systematic and deliberate extermination of a specific group of people, usually an ethnic, racial, religious, national, or political group.

Glasnost: Russian for "openness," referring to the political policies that followed Mikhail Gorbachev's 1985 rise to power in the USSR.

Global commons: Ungoverned areas shared by all countries, such as the seas, space, and the atmosphere.

Global governance: In a world without a world government, international law and institutions serve as mechanisms to address issues that transcend state borders, thereby fostering cooperation for mutually beneficial outcomes.

Globalization: Used here to mean increasing general connectivity and interdependence globally (culturally, technologically, politically, militarily, economically, etc.); often used in purely economic terms in reference to the increased mobility of goods, services, labor, technology, and capital throughout the world.

Gold standard: A fixed exchange-rate system in which each nation's currency value is set to gold.

Good governance: Legislation and implementation free from corruption and with due regard for the rule of law.

Great power: A state that possesses, exercises, and defends interests throughout the world. Great-power status may be quantitative, such as a certain level of gross national product or the size of its armed forces. It may also be qualitative, demonstrated by a high level of industrialization or the capability to make and use nuclear weapons. Great powers may also be distinguished by institutional recognition, such as that accorded by the League of Nations or the UN.

Great-power unanimity: A concept that holds that on all resolutions and proposals before the UN Security Council, a veto by any one of the five permanent members (China, France, Russia, United Kingdom, and United States) will kill any proposal.

Great powers: The few states in the international system whose economic and military power set them qualitatively apart from the next tier of states.

Green: Designed to be environmentally friendly.

Greenfield investments: Developing an industry from scratch in a foreign country.

Greenhouse effect: An increase in the earth's average temperature caused by the emission of greenhouse gases (especially carbon dioxide and methane) that trap and retain the sun's heat in the atmosphere.

Gross domestic product (GDP): The total value of goods and services produced within a country.

Gross national income (GNI): The total value of goods and services produced within a country, plus the income it receives from other countries, minus payments made to other countries.

Gross national product (GNP): The total sum of all goods and services produced by a nation.

Hegemon: Predominant world power.

Hegemony: Dominance or leadership, usually with regard to a preponderant world power in a unipolar system.

Human security: Freedom from both fear and want.

Hydroelectricity: Electricity generated by water power in dams, a frequently touted alternate energy source.

Hyperinflation: An extreme, rapid, and uncontrolled rise in prices and concomitant decline in a currency's value.

Idealism: Belief that people can make the world a better place.

Immediate deterrence: A strategy of response to specific and explicit challenges to a state's interests.

Imperialism: A superior-inferior relationship in which one state controls the people and territory of another area.

Import quota: Restricting how much of a specific foreign product can enter the country.

Independent variable: A causal factor; that which acts on something else, rather than being acted on. The dependent variable is that which is acted upon.

Information warfare: Military use of computer networks to attack an opponent's capabilities for receiving, processing, and communicating information.

Institution: An international norm, law, agreement, treaty, group, or organization formed around a common interest or region; synonymous with regime.

Intellectual property rights: Legal entitlements attached to intellectual products with commercial value, including patents, copyrights, trademarks, industrial design rights, and trade secrets.

Intercontinental ballistic missile (ICBM): A land-based missile able to deliver a nuclear payload to a target more than 3,400 miles away (in practical terms, capable of going directly from the United States to Russia or vice versa).

Interdependence: Symbiosis; a relationship of mutual dependence between two or more entities in which changes in one entity affect the other entities.

Intergovernmental organizations (IGOs): Groups of states or governments created through treaties and organized for a common purpose. Examples include OPEC, OECD, and NATO.

Internally displaced people: People who are displaced within their own countries.

International Bank for Reconstruction and Development (IBRD, or World Bank): Established as part of the Bretton Woods system, the World Bank was initially created to help finance reconstruction after World War II. Since the 1950s and 1960s, it has lent money to developing countries to finance development projects and humanitarian needs.

International Criminal Court: Treaty signed in 1998 that created a permanent court that has the power to try individuals accused of the most egregious crimes, as part of a systematic plan or policy, including war crimes, crimes against humanity, and genocide.

International Energy Agency (IEA): Created in 1974 to develop an emergency system for sharing oil, establish an information system to monitor the oil market, facilitate long-term measures to reduce net demand for oil on world markets, and set up multinational energy research and development activities.

International Labor Organization (ILO): Specialized UN agency that seeks the promotion of social justice and internationally recognized human and labor rights.

International Monetary Fund (IMF): Established as part of the Bretton Woods system, the IMF is a global lending agency that originally was to aid industrialized nations in stabilizing their economies after the shocks of the Great Depression and World War II. Its goals today are promotion of market economies, free trade, and high growth rates.

International organization (IO): An international institution involving many different countries (e.g., the United Nations).

International regimes: International laws or norms that set the rules for cooperation.

Intervening variables: Factors that influence but don't determine an outcome; factors that filter the effects of an independent variable.

Intrastate conflict: Discord occurring within the borders of a single state.

Inverse correlation: A relationship in which an increase in one factor corresponds to a decrease in another.

Isolationist: Withdrawn from international affairs.

Jus ad bellum: Justice of war; the necessary conditions for undertaking a legitimate war.

Jus in bello: Justice in war (the laws of war); acceptable and unacceptable behaviors during a war.

Just War: A specific set of criteria about when resorting to the use of force is acceptable (*jus ad bellum*) and a set of criteria about how combatants should behave (*jus in bello*).

Kyoto Protocol: Treaty signed in 1997 that furthered the goals of the UN Framework Convention on Climate Change (1992) that places stringent limits on carbon emissions that cause the greenhouse effect; expires in 2012.

Labor intensive: Industry requiring labor as the main input.

Least and less developed countries (LDCs): Countries with low average incomes relative to industrialized states, a reliance on primary product exports, limited technology, and few social services.

Legalism: Conforming strictly to the letter of the law, rather than the spirit of the law.

Leviathan: Per Hobbes, an absolute sovereign; a benevolent dictator.

Liberal democracy: A representative democracy moderated by a constitution, protecting the freedom and rights of individuals and the minority, guided by the will of the majority, and with an accountable government.

Liberalization: In general, the reduction of government involvement, interference, or oversight; in economic terms, the reduction of government rules and regulations with regard to the private sector.

Liberalize markets: Reduce government intervention in the private sector; reduce laws and other restrictions.

Limited war: A conflict in which states with nuclear weapons choose to limit combat to conventional means.

Linkage: Negotiating more than one issue concurrently, so that concessions on one might be made up by gains on another.

Maginot Line: An extensive system of defensive fortifications built by France in 1930 along its border with Germany.

Massive retaliation: The Eisenhower administration's strategic doctrine that Soviet-sponsored aggression would be countered with large-scale nuclear retaliation.

Mercantilism: Economic approach involving governments attempting to ensure that they have a positive balance of trade.

Mergers and acquisitions: Buying an existing business in a foreign company.

Metropole: A home country in relation to its colonies.

Military power: The factor of power relating to the size, organization, and training of a state's armed forces and to the quality and quantity of its weaponry.

Modernization theories: Socioeconomic theories of development involving assumptions about progress occurring in stages from traditional societies to modern ones.

Monetarism: Supply and demand for money is the primary means of regulating economic activity.

Money laundering: The processing of criminal proceeds to hide the illegal origins of the money that includes three stages: placement, layering, and integration.

Montréal Protocol: Treaty signed in 1987 designed to phase out CFCs—chemicals that deplete the ozone layer.

Multilateral: Among three or more countries; many-sided; more than two-sided.

Multinational corporation (MNC): A large corporation with branches in many countries, headquarters in the developed world, and huge investments throughout the world. Examples include General Motors, PepsiCo, Sony, and Shell Oil.

Multipolar: An international structure dominated by several great powers.

Mutual assured destruction (MAD): A condition that exists when nuclear states can survive a first strike with sufficient nuclear forces to retaliate in a second strike and inflict unacceptable damage on their opponent. Because any nuclear strike would result in both opponents' destruction, there is no incentive to initiate a nuclear war.

Nation: A group of people who share a common culture, history, and (often) language.

Nationalism: A love of, and pride in, one's nation; the belief in one's nation's superiority and, often, in its related rights and privileges (and sometimes responsibilities) internationally.

Natural law: Universal law that transcends man-made rules and regulations.

Necessary and sufficient variables: Factors that are adequate for determining—and that must be present to achieve—a specific outcome.

Neglected tropical diseases (NTD): Diseases that affect people primarily in the poorest areas of the world in which housing, sanitation, and water supplies are deficient.

Neo-liberalism: A theoretical perspective prioritizing open markets and international free trade.

New International Economic Order (NIEO): An outgrowth of developing states' frustration and an evolutionary step from the nonaligned movement, the Group of 77, and the United Nations Conference on Trade and Development (UNCTAD), there was, in 1974, a Declaration of Principles for a New International Economic Order. Nothing came of it because of the LDCs' lack of influence, combined with their disunity of purpose and priorities.

Newly industrialized countries (NICs): Social and economic classification recognizing states' industrialization but placing them on the development continuum somewhat below the most advanced industrialized states and above LDCs.

Nonaligned Movement: Refers to those state leaders who, during the Cold War, chose not to align their countries with either superpower, instead playing one off against the other in the pursuit of their own interests.

Nongovernmental organization (NGO): An association of individuals or groups independent of government, but active in international affairs. Examples include religious institutions and humanitarian organizations.. NGOs are an element of civil society.

Nontariff barriers to trade: Eliminating foreign goods' competitiveness with domestic goods by imposing quotas or by putting a country in a position where it has no choice but to limit its exports.

Norm: A generally accepted rule or standard.

Normative: Prescribing a standard; involving an assumption of what should be.

NSC-68: A document prepared by the U.S. National Security Council in early 1950 to counter the spread of international communism. NSC-68 called for expansion of America's armed forces, adding an important military dimension to the economic and political means of containment.

Nuclear Non-Proliferation Treaty: Signed in 1968, the treaty provides that signatory nations without nuclear weapons will not seek to build them and will accept safeguards to prevent diversion of nuclear material and technology from peaceful uses to weapons programs. Nations in possession of nuclear weapons at the signing of the treaty agreed not to help nonnuclear states gain access to nuclear weapons but, rather, to offer access to peaceful nuclear technology.

Nuclear proliferation: States acquiring nuclear weapons that did not formerly possess them.

Objective: Unbiased, neutral, independent, dispassionate.

Observer missions: One of the types of UN missions; international forces that are present to observe a cease-fire organized by or for the opposing forces in a dispute.

Operation Barbarossa: The invasion of the Soviet Union ordered by Hitler on June 22, 1941.

Operational code: Cognitive roadmap; complex tracking of belief system.

Organization for Security and Cooperation in Europe (OSCE): Established in 1994 (formerly the Conference on Security and Cooperation in Europe [CSCE]) to encourage peace and wealth in Europe.

Organization of the Petroleum Exporting Countries (OPEC): An intergovernmental cartel of oil-exporting countries that has the goal of raising collectively the price of crude oil on the world market.

Pariah states: States that consistently prove they cannot be trusted at their word and thereby become ostracized by the world community (also known as rogue states).

Parsimony: Simplicity, thrift.

Patronage: Corrupt use of public resources to advance the interests of a specific group in exchange for electoral support.

Peace enforcement missions: One of the types of UN missions; these troops observe, act as a buffer, and, as a last resort, are allowed to use military force to keep the peace in a particular locale.

Peace of Westphalia: The 1648 treaty that ended the Thirty Years' War and marked the beginning of the modern international system by legitimizing the state as the ultimate sovereign authority over people and geographic territory.

Peacekeeping missions: One of the types of UN missions; these troops not only observe a cease-fire but also act as a buffer between the two sides of a conflict.

Per-capita income (GNI/population): Income per person.

Perestroika: Mikhail Gorbachev's policy for restructuring the economy of the Soviet Union, it promoted democratization, privatization of the economy, and free markets.

Periphery: Outer area.

Positive law: A belief that international law exists only through those rules to which states have consented in writing, usually in treaties, or have otherwise clearly recognized.

Power projection: Influence, often by force, beyond one's borders.

Preemptive strike: A defensive attack carried out when a fundamental threat to vital interests is identified or when an attack by an opponent is believed to be imminent. The underlying motivation holds that "the best defense is a good offense."

Preventive strike: A defensive attack carried out when an attack by the opponent is considered to be possible in the future but not an imminent threat.

Price supports: Government action to uphold a domestic product's price, usually by buying it.

Primary deterrence: A strategy intended to dissuade a challenger from attacking a state's own territory.

Private sector: The realm of nongovernmental economic activity; business.

Process: Series of interactions over time.

Protection: Money paid to an organized crime group to protect the individual or business from other criminals.

Protectionism: Defending domestic industry from foreign competition.

Ratification: A country's legislative approval of a treaty signed by the executive.

Rational actor: An IR simplifying assumption in which states are presumed to make the best possible decision based on their set priorities.

Rationalism: Reliance on reason as a guide for action and beliefs.

Rationality: Decision making based on informed cost–benefit analysis.

Reagan Doctrine: The Reagan administration's abandonment of détente and return to an assertive form of containment. This was characterized by direct U.S. intervention and indirect support of anticommunist insurgencies.

Realpolitik: Interest-based (rather than ethics-based or ideals-based) foreign policy.

Reductivism: Using domestic- or individual-level variables in an analysis of world politics; looking beyond systemic level factors for explanations.

Referendum: Direct popular vote on a proposed public measure or law.

Reforestation: The opposite of deforestation; the planting of trees to act as carbon sinks.

Refugees: People who are displaced from their own countries.

Regime: An international norm, law, agreement, treaty, group, or organization formed around a common interest or region; synonymous with institution.

Reification: Fallacy of treating something man-made (an object or idea) as if it were naturally occurring.

Relative gains: Increases in wealth or strength relative to others.

Relative power: Amount of power compared to other entities.

Remittance income: Money migrants send back to their home countries. This income can have a significant impact on the economies of the home state.

Renewable energy: Environmentally friendly alternative energy sources such as hydro, solar, and wind power.

Replacement level fertility: Two parents are replaced by two children, which is an international goal to reduce overall population growth.

Republican: Based on popular consent and representation.

Revisionist state: A state that is dissatisfied with its position in the international system and therefore intent on changing the system itself.

Rio Earth Summit: Meeting held in 1992 that led to treaties and conventions to deal with environmental problems and means to address sustainable development.

Rogue states: States that are considered untrustworthy and become ostracized by the international community (also known as pariah states).

Romantic nationalism: Increases, during the Romantic period, in the embrace throughout Europe of national pride, including nationalistic ritual, propaganda, and symbolism based on language, ethnicity, and history.

Romanticism: The period in European history that followed the Enlightenment, in which politics and the arts reverted "romantically" to the ideals of the Middle Ages.

Schlieffen Plan: Developed by German Chief of Staff Alfred von Schlieffen and put into operation at the beginning of World War I, this strategic plan directed German forces to knock out France with a fast-moving offensive, then shift by rail to the eastern front to fight Russia.

Scientific: Systematic and logical; replicable.

Secession: A group's, territory's, or other subnational entity's withdrawal from political association with a country; breaking away.

Second-strike capability: Ability to retaliate, even after a nuclear attack, and thus punish the initiator of a nuclear war.

Secular: Nonreligious.

Securitization: Most simply, securitization is the act of naming something a security concern so that it becomes an elevated priority justifying greater national attention and resources.

Security dilemma: When distrust runs so high between states that when each seeks to increase its defensive capabilities, the other perceives that as a threat and increases its own, creating an arms race.

Self-help: When there is no higher authority to which to appeal.

Self-reinforcing: Initial perceptions or assumptions lead to preferences that will satisfy those perceptions or assumptions.

Settler colonialism: Immigrants seize land from the indigenous population and become the dominant population.

Signatories: States that have signed a treaty or international agreement.

Social contracts: Agreements between people, groups, or states, in which the parties defer some autonomy to an authority they form to act on behalf of the group as a whole.

Socialized: Taught how to behave through exposure to social customs, beliefs, and conduct.

Soft power: A term coined by Joseph Nye, Jr., that refers to a state's ability to attract allies through the legitimacy of its policies and their underlying values (cultural, political values, etc.).

Solidarity: A popular labor union begun in the 1970s in Poland led by Lech Walesa. Solidarity made political and economic demands on the communist government for many years before winning elections and assuming power under a new constitution in 1989.

Sovereignty: Exclusive political authority over a defined territory and the people within it.

Sphere of influence: A region influenced by one great power. In a sphere of influence, the dominant power does not have sovereignty but imposes its will over several neighboring states, restricting the maneuverability of local territorial leaders.

Stagflation: A combination of low or stagnant economic growth coupled with high rates of inflation.

State of Nature: A metaphor for a world in which there is no higher authority to which to turn and in which each individual can depend only on himself or herself.

Stock exchange: An organized marketplace where securities like stocks and bonds are bought and sold.

Strategic Defense Initiative (SDI): A 1980s U.S. program that proposed the creation of a highly ambitious ballistic missile defense system that would provide a total defense against strategic nuclear weapons and missile systems. Also known as "Star Wars," SDI threatened to upset the nuclear balance of power by giving the United States an ability to launch a first strike without fear of a Soviet counterattack. Its potential effectiveness was controversial.

Strategic nuclear forces: Nuclear forces designed to attack long-range targets, including cities.

Structural adjustment programs (SAPs): Application, often under some duress from the IMF, World Bank, or United States, of strict economic reforms rooted in liberal assumptions of the requirements of development.

Structural weakness: Growth built on unsustainable economic practices (e.g., short-term borrowing for long-term needs) in the absence of effective governmental oversight and trade and monetary policies.

Structure: The ordering of units (usually states) within the system.

Subjective: Prejudiced, skewed, biased.

Submarine-launched ballistic missile (SLBM): A long-range ballistic missile carried in and launched from a submarine.

Subnational groups: Usually interest groups, often nongovernmental organizations, sometimes based on identity (ethnicity, religion, nationality, etc.), and always within a state.

Subsidies: Government payments to domestic industries that allow them to produce at a lower cost, thus allowing them to sell more competitively in the international market.

Superpowers: One or two states whose powers are so great that they cannot be effectively challenged for domination of the international system.

Supranational: Transcending sovereign states' established borders.

Sustainable development: Fulfilling current needs while protecting the natural environment for future generations.

Tactical nuclear weapons: Weapons designed to attack short- or medium-range (95–310 miles) targets, primarily conventional military assets.

Tariffs: Taxes importers must pay before their goods can enter a country.

Terms of trade: The ratio of export prices to import prices.

Terrorism: The unlawful use—or threatened use—of force or violence against individuals or property to coerce or intimidate governments or societies, often to achieve political, religious, or ideological objectives.

Theocracy: A government ruled by or subject to religious authority.

Theoretical paradigm: Worldview; *Weltanschauung;* set of theories based on shared assumptions.

Third World: During the Cold War, terminology evolved in which the world was divided between the First World (the United States and its friends and allies), the Second World (the Soviet Union and its sphere of influence), and the Third World, unaligned states that sought to use their neutrality to insulate themselves from the U.S.–Soviet competition or to manipulate the two superpowers.

Trade barriers: Means of preventing foreign goods from competing with domestic goods.

Trading blocs: Groups of states that set trade rules cooperatively, usually involving the reduction or elimination of trade restrictions within the bloc (perhaps the most famous example is the European Union; NAFTA is another).

Transaction costs: The costs of doing business.

Treaties: Documents similar to written contracts in that they impose obligations only on the parties that sign them. Also known as charters, pacts, conventions, or covenants, they are some of the main sources of international law.

Treaty of Tordesillas: A 1494 treaty between Spain and Portugal that purported to divide up the world. It drew an imaginary line that ran north to south approximately 300 miles west of the Azores Islands. Spain was granted possession of all lands to the west of this line, Portugal the lands to the east.

Truman Doctrine: Pledged U.S. military and economic aid to countries (initially Greece and Turkey) to resist communism.

Truth and Reconciliation Commission: A group tasked with formally identifying the roots of a conflict, acknowledging the atrocities that took place during a conflict, and setting forth next steps for moving beyond the conflict; there have been fifteen such commissions internationally, including those in Sierra Leone, Liberia, South Africa (after apartheid), Peru, and El Salvador.

Typology: Method of classification.

UN Educational, Scientific, and Cultural Organization (UNESCO): A specialized agency of the UN that attempts to improve literacy rates in the developing world, promote scientific and cultural exchange, and facilitate the distribution of information.

UN Framework Convention on Climate Change (UNFCCC): An international treaty (entered into force in March 1994) that established a framework for international efforts to respond to the challenge from climate change.

UN Intergovernmental Panel on Climate Change (IPCC): Established by the World Meteorological Organization and UN Environment Program in 1988, the IPCC assesses "the scientific, technical, and socioeconomic information" to understand the risks and impacts posed by human-induced climate change.

UNAIDS: With ten UN cosponsors, this is the umbrella agency that is entrusted with responding to the global HIV/AIDS crisis. UNAIDS coordinates and implements reporting systems to track HIV/AIDS around the world.

Unipolar: An international structure dominated by a single power.

Unitary actor: An International relations (IR) simplifying assumption in which states are treated as if they are unified entities rather than composites of many domestic actors.

United Nations High Commissioner for Refugees (UNHCR): A UN agency that seeks to protect refugees as well as respond to refugee problems.

United Nations Population Fund (UNFPA): The largest organization that provides international assistance for programs promoting women's health around the world, in particular family planning. The organization also helps governments in support of policies to reduce poverty, recognizing that population size and structure are related to sustainable development.

United Nations Security Council (UNSC): The fifteen-member council that makes binding decisions for the United Nations as a whole; it is composed of five permanent veto-holding members (the United States, China, Russia, France, the United Kingdom) and ten nonpermanent members who have staggered two-year terms; for a resolution to pass, it must receive nine affirmative votes and not be vetoed by any of the five permanent members.

Urbanization: Process by which a population shifts from the countryside and suburbs into cities.

Variable: Factor.

Variable-sum: Potential for expanding, and mutual, benefits; opposite of zero-sum.

Voluntary export restrictions (VERs): Usually the result of political or economic leverage, VERs occur when states agree to limit how much of a specific product they will export to a given country.

Warsaw Pact: An alliance between the Soviet Union and its client states in eastern Europe signed in 1955 in response to the 1949 creation of NATO.

Washington Consensus: Initially, simply a list of ten recommendations economist John Williamson thought were most commonly offered by American and Bretton Woods institutions; came to be used as shorthand for a broader liberal economic philosophy.

Weapons of mass destruction (WMD): Chemical, biological, radiological, or nuclear weapons.

World Food Programme (WFP): UN agency whose mandate is to combat world hunger, provide emergency relief in response to both man-made and natural disasters, and promote development projects.

World Health Organization (WHO): A humanitarian organization established in 1948 under the ECOSOC umbrella of the UN. WHO aids in the development of national health administrations and provides advisory services.

World Trade Organization (WTO): International body dealing with the rules of trade between nations.

Worldview: *Weltanschauung;* perspective on human nature.

Zero-sum: One entity's loss is another's gain and vice versa.

Bibliography

Abadinsky, Howard. *Organized Crime,* 7th ed. Belmont, CA: Wadsworth, 2003.

Acheson, Dean. *Present at the Creation.* New York: Norton, 1969.

"Africa: G7 Country Overall Assessments." AllAfrica.com, May 25, 2010. http://allafrica.com/stories/201005250348.html.

"AIDS and Violent Conflict in Africa." Special report by the United States Institute of Peace. In *World Politics 02/03 Annual Editions,* edited by Helen E. Purkitt, 188–195. Guilford, CT: McGraw-Hill/Dushkin, 2002.

Al Tamimi, Jumana. "Educated Arab Youths Keen on Emigration." Gulfnews.com. March 21, 2010. http://gulfnews.com/news/region/educated-arab-youths-keen-on-emigration-1.600650.

Albertini, R. von. *Decolonization.* New York: Doubleday, 1971.

Albrecht-Carrié, R. *A Diplomatic History of Europe Since the Congress of Vienna.* New York: Harper & Brothers, 1958.

Aldcroft, D. H. *From Versailles to Wall Street: The International Economy in the 1920s.* Berkeley: University of California Press, 1977.

Alexander, Robert. "Import Substitution in Latin America in Retrospect." In *Progress Toward Development in Latin America: From Prebisch to Technological Autonomy,* edited by James L. Dietz and Dilmus D. James, 15–28. Boulder, CO: Lynne Rienner, 1991.

Alibek, Ken, and Steven Handleman. *Biohazard.* New York: Delta, 2001.

Allen, Jonathan. "Balancing Justice and Social Unity: Political Theory and the Idea of a Truth and Reconciliation Commission." *The University of Toronto Law Journal* 49 (1999): 315–353.

Allison, Graham T. *Essence of Decision: Explaining the Cuban Missile Crisis.* Boston: Little, Brown 1971.

Almond, Gabriel, and James Coleman, eds., *The Politics of Developing Areas.* Princeton, NJ: Princeton University Press, 1960.

Alperovitz, Gar. "Hiroshima: Historians Reassess." *Foreign Policy* 99 (1995): 15–34.

Altermam, Jon B. "Clear Gold: Water and Conflict in the Middle East." Global Policy. April 19, 2010. http://www.globalpolicy.org/security-council/dark-side-of-natural-resources/water-in-conflict/48960.html.

Americans for UNFPA. "International Women's Health & Dignity Act Introduced House Bill Would Restore U.S. Commitment to Women Everywhere." June 7, 2007. http://www.americansforunfpa.org/NetCommunity/Page.aspx?&pid=2268&srcid=356.

Amnesty International. "Report 2007: Sudan." http://thereport.amnesty.org/eng/Regions/Africa/Sudan.

Amnesty International. "US Threats to the International Criminal Court." http://web.amnesty.org/pages/icc-US_threats-eng.

Amoako, K. Y. "Comment: World Trade Liberalisation Still Excludes Africa." *Financial Times,* November 23, 2004.

"An Idea Whose Time Has Come—and Gone?" *The Economist.* July 23, 2009. http://www.economist.com/world/international/displaystory.cfm?story_id=E1_TQDRSSRR.

Anderson, Sean, and Stephen Sloan. *Historical Dictionary of Terrorism.* London: Scarecrow Press, 1995.

Andreevich, Milan. "Bosnia & Herzegovina: In Search of Peace." Radio Free Europe/Radio Liberty Research Report. June 5, 1992.

Anonymous. "The Nuclear Crisis on the Korean Peninsula: Avoiding the Road to Perdition." *Current History* 102 (2003): 152–169.

Apter, David. *The Politics of Modernization.* Chicago: University of Chicago Press, 1965.

Arendt, Hannah. *Eichman in Jerusalem: A Report on the Banality of Evil.* New York: Penguin Books, 1977.

Associated Foreign Exchange. "History of the Foreign Exchange Market." AFEX: Associated Foreign Exchange. http://afex.com/forex-history.html.

"Australia Ratifies Kyoto Protocol." *The Sydney Morning Herald.* December 3, 2007. http://www.smh.com.au/news/environment/rudd-signs-kyoto-deal/2007/12/ 03/1196530553203.html.

Axe, David. "War Is Boring: China Dam Project Stokes Regional Tensions." Global Policy. April 28, 2010. http://www.globalpolicy.org/security-council/dark-side-of-natural-resources/water-in-conflict/49047.html.

Axelrod, Robert. *The Complexity of Cooperation: Agent-Based Models of Competition and Collaboration.* Princeton, NJ: Princeton University Press, 1997.

———. *The Evolution of Cooperation.* New York: Basic Books, 1984.

Babbit, Bruce. "Earth Summit." *World Monitor,* January 1990.

Babst, Dean V. "Elective Governments—A Force for Peace." *The Wisconsin Sociologist* 3 (1964): 9–14.

———. "A Force for Peace." *Industrial Research* (1972): 55–58.

Bahgat, Gawdat. "Oil, Terrorism, and Weapons of Mass Destruction: The Libyan Diplomatic Coup." *The Journal of Social, Political, and Economic Studies* 29 (2004): 373–394.

Baldwin, David A. *Economic Statecraft.* Princeton, NJ: Princeton University Press, 1985.

———., ed. *Neorealism and Neoliberalism: The Contemporary Debate.* New York: Columbia University Press, 1993.

Barker, Alec. "Between Conscience and Self-Interest: The United States, Sudan, and Darfur." *BC Journal of International Affairs* 9 (Spring 2006). http://bcjournal. org/2006/between-conscience-and-self-interest/.

Barnet, Richard J. "Challenging the Myths of National Security." *New York Times Magazine,* April 1, 1979, 25.

Barnett, C. *The Collapse of British Power.* London: Eyre Methven, 1972.

Baumgart, Winfried. *Imperialism: The Idea and Reality of French Colonial Expansion.* New York: St. Martin's, 1961.

Baumgart, Wilfred. *Imperialism: The Idea and Reality of British and French Colonial Expansion.* New York: Oxford University Press, 1982.

BBC News. "China Unveils Emissions Targets Ahead of Copenhagen." November 26, 2009. http://news.bbc.co.uk/2/hi/asia-pacific/8380106.stm.

———. "Indonesia Pledges Two-Year Deforestation Moratorium." May 27, 2010. http://news.bbc.co.uk/2/hi/world/asia_pacific/10167038.

———. "Iraq Scandal Taints 2,000 Firms." BBC News. October 27, 2005. http://news.bbc.co.uk/go/pr/fr/-/1/hi/world/americas/4382820.stm.

———. "Q & A: Sudan's Darfur Crisis." http://news.bbc.co.uk/2/hi/africa/3496731.stm.

———, "Tanzania Gives Citizenship to 162,000 Burundi Refugees." April 16, 2010. http://news/bbc.co.uk/2/hi/8625429.stm.

———. "US Cuts UN Funds in Abortion Row." BBC News, http://newsvote.bbc.co.uk/mpapps/pagetols/print/newsbbc.co.uk/1/hi/world/americas/3902311.stm.

———. "US Lifts HIV/AIDS Immigration Ban." January 4, 2010. http://news.bbc.co.uk/go/pr/fr/-/2/hi/americas/8438865.stm.

Beasley, W. G. *The Meiji Restoration.* Stanford, CA: Stanford University Press, 1972.

Beaumont, Peter. "The Myth of Water Wars and the Future of Irrigated Agriculture in the Middle East." *Water International* 10 (1994): 9–21.

Bellamy, Alex J., and Paul D. Williams. "The UN Security Council and the Question of Humanitarian Intervention in Darfur." *Journal of Military Ethics* 5 (2006): 144–160.

Bellman, Eric. "McDonald's to Expand in India." *Wall Street Journal,* June 30, 2009. http://online.wsj.com/article/SB124628377100868055.html.

Bender-Baird, Kyla. "Feminism and Climate Change." The National Council for Research on Women. http://www.ncrw.org/public-forum/real-deal-blog/feminism-and-climate-change.

Bergen, Peter L. *Holy War, Inc.: Inside the Secret World of Osama bin Laden.* New York: Free Press, 2001.

Bergen, Peter L. *The Osama bin Laden I Know: An Oral History of al Qaeda's Leader*. New York: Free Press, 2006.

Bergeron, Louis. *France Under Napoleon*. Translated by R. R. Palmer. Princeton, NJ: Princeton University Press, 1981.

Bernstein, Barton M. "Roosevelt, Truman, and the Atomic Bomb, 1941–1945: A Reinterpretation." *Political Science Quarterly* 3 (1975): 23–69.

Beschloss, Michael R., and Strobe Talbott. *At the Highest Levels*. Boston: Little, Brown, 1993.

Bhagwati, Jagdish. *The World Trading System at Risk*. Princeton, NJ: Princeton University Press, 1991.

Bhatya, Shyam, and Daniel McGrory. *Brighter Than the Baghdad Sun*. New York: Regnery, 2000.

Black, Jeremy. *European Warfare, 1660–1815*. New Haven, CT: Yale University Press, 1994.

Blight, James G., and David A. Welch. *On the Brink*. New York: Hill & Wang, 1989.

Blodgett, John Q. "The Future of UN Peacekeeping." *The Washington Quarterly* 14 (1991): 207–20.

"Bond Basics: What Are Bonds?" The Bond Market Association. http://www.investinginbonds. com/learnmore.asp?catid=46&id=2.

The Bond Market Association. "Bond Basics: What Are Bonds?" http://www.investinginbonds. com/learnmore.asp?catid=46&id=2.

Bond, Patrick. "A Case for Capital Controls." Paper commissioned by the Nedlac Labour Caucus, September 1999. Published by the International South Group Network. http://www.isgn-web.org/pub/01–007.htm.

Borger, Julian. "Darfur Conflict Heralds Era of Wars Triggered by Climate Change, UN Report Warns." *Guardian Unlimited*, June 23, 2007, http://www.guardian.co.uk/environment/2007/jun/23/sudan.climatechange.

Boughton, James M. "Michael Camdessus at the IMF: A Retrospective." *Finance & Development: A Quarterly Magazine of the IMF* 37 (2000): 2–6.

Brahm, Eric. "International Regimes." BeyondIntractability.org. September 2005. http://www.beyondintractability.org/essay/international_regimes/.

British Petroleum. "BTC Celebrates Full Commissioning." July 13, 2006. http://www.bp.com/genericarticle.do?categoryId=2012968&contentId=7019835.

———. "Baku-Tblisi-Ceyhan Timeline." March 2009. http://www.bp.com/sectiongenericarticle.do?categoryId=9029481&contentId=705399.

Broad, Robin, and James Cavanagh. "No More NICs." *Foreign Policy* 72 (1988): 81–103.

Brown Michael E., Owen R. Cote, Jr., Sean M. Lynn-Jones, and Steven E. Miller., eds. *Theories of War and Peace*. Cambridge, MA: MIT Press, 1998.

Brownell, Ginanne, and Carla Power. "The Golden Age." *Newsweek International*, November 28, 2004. http://www.msnbc.msn.com/id/6597549/site/newsweek/.

Brzezinski, Zbigniew. *The Ethics and Public Policy Center, Promise or Peril: The Strategic Defense Initiative*. Washington, DC: Rowman and Littlefield, 1986.

Brzoska, Michael. "Securitization of Climate Change and the Power of Conceptions of Security." Paper presented at the annual meeting of the International Studies Association's 49th annual convention, "Bridging Multiple Divides," San Francisco, CA. March 26, 2008. http://www.allacademic.com/meta/p253887_index.html.

Buchanan, Allen, and Robert O. Keohane. "The Legitimacy of Global Governance Institutions." *Ethics & International Affairs* 20 (2006): 405–438.

Buckley, William J., ed. *Kosovo: Contending Voices on Balkan Interventions*. Grand Rapids, MI: Eerdmans Publishing, 2000.

Bukharin, Oleg, Matthew Bunn, and Kenneth N. Luongo. *Renewing the Partnership: Recommendations for Accelerated Action to Secure Nuclear Material in the Former Soviet Union*. Princeton, NJ: Russian American Nuclear Security Advisory Council, 2000.

Bull, Hedley. *The Anarchical Society*. New York: Columbia University Press, 1977.

Bundy, McGeorge. "Population: An Inescapable Problem." *Populi* 17 (1990): 20–24.

Busch, Nathan E. *No End in Sight: The Continuing Menace of Nuclear Proliferation*. Lexington: The University Press of Kentucky, 2004.

Busuntwi-Sam, James. "Development and Human Security: Whose Security, and from What?" International Journal 57. 2 (Spring, 2002): 253–272.

Butler, Richard, and James Charles Roy. *The Greatest Threat: Iraq, Weapons of Mass Destruction, and the Crisis of Global Security.* New York: Public Affairs Press, 2001.

Caetano, José Manuel Martins, and António Caleiro. "Corruption and Foreign Direct Investment, What Kind of Relationship Is There?" Economics Working Papers 18_2005, University of Evora, 2005. http://ideas.repec.org/p/evo/wpecon/18_2005.html.

Cain, P. J., and A. G. Hopkins. "The Political Economy of British Expansion Overseas." *The Economic History Review* 33 (1980): 463–490.

Cameron, Gavin. *Nuclear Terrorism.* London: Palgrave Macmillan, 1999.

Cameron, Rondo. *A Concise Economic History of The World.* New York: Oxford University Press, 1993.

Cardoso, Henrique, and Enzo Faletto. *Dependency and Development in Latin America.* Berkeley: University of California Press, 1979.

Carr, Edward Hallett. *The Twenty Years' Crisis: 1919–1939.* New York: Harper & Row, 1964.

"CDC Expert Sickened with SARS." MSNBC. May 22, 2003. http://www.msnbc.com.

CEDIGAZ, The International Association for Natural Gas. "2006 Natural Gas Year in Review: CEDIGAZ' First Estimates." Press release. April 26, 2007. http://www.cedigaz.org/Fichiers/PREstimates2006.pdf.

———. "Natural Gas in the World—2009 Edition." 2009. http://www.cedigaz.org/Fichiers/NGW.pdf.

Center for Disease Control and Prevention. "State of the World's Vaccines and Immunizations." October 21, 2009. http://www.cdc.gov/features/GlobalImmunizations/.

Center for Environmental Economic Development. "Tobin Tax Motion Passes Canada's Parliament." http://www.ceedweb.org/iirp/canadames.htm.

———. "U.S. Congress Concurrent Resolution on Taxing Cross-Border Currency Transactions to Deter Excessive Speculation." http://www.ceedweb.org/iirp/ushouseres.htm.

Center for Nonproliferation Studies. "Inventory of International Nonproliferation Organizations and Regimes." June 18, 2009. http://www.nti.org/e_research/official_docs/inventory/pdf.

Central Intelligence Agency. "The World Factbook—Country Comparison: Life Expectancy at Birth."https://www.cia.gov/library/publications/the-worldfactbook/rankorder/2102rank.html.

Chandler, David. *The Campaigns of Napoleon.* New York: Macmillan, 1966.

———. *From Kosovo to Kabul: Human Rights and International Intervention.* London: Pluto Press, 2002.

Charlesworth, Hilary. "Is International Law Relevant to the War in Iraq and Its Aftermath?" October 29, 2003. http://www.globalpolicy.org/empire/un/2003/1029charlesworth.pdf.

Charnovitz, Steve. "Nongovernmental Organizations and International Law." *The American Journal of International Law* 100 (2006): 348–372.

Charny, Israel W. "Classification of Genocide in Multiple Categories." In *Encyclopedia of Genocide,* vol. 1, ed. Israel W. Charny. Oxford, UK: ABC Clio, 1999.

Chen, Wenhong, Jeffrey Boase, and Barry Wellman. "The Global Villagers: Comparing Internet Users and Uses Around the World." Paper, Department of Sociology, University of Toronto, 2002. http://www.chass.utoronto.ca/~wellman/publications/villagers/gdd13-final.PDF.

"China Oil Demand Seen Rising to 9.96 Mln BPD by 2012 From 7.59 Mln This Yr-IEA." Forbes.com. July 9, 2007. http://www.forbes.com/afxnewslimited/feeds/afx/2007/07/09/afx3893219.html.

"China Tops US in Carbon Emissions." *The Boston Globe,* June 21, 2007, A16.

Chua, Amy. *World on Fire: How Exporting Free Market Democracy Breeds Ethnic Hatred and Global Instability.* New York,: Doubleday, 2002.

Churchill, Winston. "The Sinews of Peace." *Vital Speeches of the Day* 12 (1946): 332.

Cimbala, Stephen J. *Russia and Postmodern Deterrence: Military Power and Its Challenges for Security.* Washington, DC: Potomac Books, 2007.

Cipolla, Carlo. *Guns and Sails in the Early Phase of European Expansion.* London: Pantheon, 1965.

Cirincione, Joseph, Jon Wolfsthal, and Miriam Rajkumar. *Deadly Arsenals.* New York: Carnegie Endowment for International Peace, 2002.

Clark, Edwin H., II. "Water Prices Rising Worldwide." Earth Policy Institute. March 7, 2007. http://www.earth-policy.org/Updates/2007/Update64_print able.htm.

Clarke, Walter, and Jeffrey Herbst. *Learning from Somalia: The Lessons of Armed Humanitarian Intervention.* Boulder, CO: Westview Press, 1997.

CNN. "Aging Summit Hears Global Warming." April 8, 2002. http://archives.cnn.com/2002/HEALTH/04/08/madrid.ageing/index/html.

———. "Iraq Drives up Refugee Count, U.N. Says." June 19, 2007. http://www.cnn.com/2007/WORLD/meast/06/19/un.refugees/index.html.

———. "Tanzania Urges Burundian Refugees to Go Home." June 19, 2007. http://www.cnn.com/2007/WORLD/africa/06/19/tanzania.refugees.reut/index.html.

Cohen, David. "Is Beijing Bailing on Treasuries?" *Business Week,* June 20, 2007. http://www.businessweek.com/investor/content/jun2007/pi20070620_210310.htm?chan=search.

Cohen, Mike. "Worldwide Hopes, Rallies Commemorate AIDS Day." *Boston Globe,* December 2, 2002.

Coleman, Katharina P. *International Organisations and Peace Enforcement: The Politics of International Legitimacy.* Cambridge, UK: Cambridge University Press, 2007.

Coles, Clifton. "Water Pressure Builds Worldwide: Skyrocketing Water Consumption Is Leaving Many Countries High and Dry." *The Futurist,* January–February 2003, 9.

Collier, David. *The New Authoritarianism in Latin America.* Princeton, NJ: Princeton University Press, 1979.

Collins, Karen. *Exploring Business.* Boston: Addison Wesley Longman, 2006.

"Colombia This Week News Summary." ABColombia Group, London. August 8, 2005. http://colhrnet.igc.org/newitems/August05/CTW%20080805.htm.

Cook, M. A., ed. *A History of the Ottoman Empire to 1730.* Cambridge, UK: Cambridge University Press, 1976.

Cooper, Mary H. "Water Shortages." In *Global Issues: Selections from the CQ Researcher,* 319–339. Washington, DC: CQ Press, 2005.

Copeland, Dale. *The Origins of a Major War.* Ithaca, NY: Cornell University Press, 2001.

Cordesman, Anthony (with Justin G. Cordesman). *Cyber-Threats, Information Warfare, and Critical Infrastructure Protection: Defending the U.S. Homeland.* Westport, CT: Praeger, 2002.

Council of Economic Advisors. "Currency Markets and Exchange Rates." In *Economic Report of the President.* Washington, DC: Council of Economic Advisors Publications, 2007. http://www.whitehouse.gov/cea/ch7-erp07.pdf.

The Council of the European Union. "Council Common Position of 27 December 2001 on the Application of Specific Measures to Combat Terrorism" (2001/931/CFSP). http://eur-lex.europa.eu/smartapi/cgi/sgadoc?smartapi!celexapi!prod!CELEXnumdoc&lq=EN&numdoc=32001E0931&model=guic:hett.

Cowles, Maria Green. "Intergovernmental Organizations: Global Governance and Transsovereign Problems." In *Beyond Sovereignty: Issues for a Global Agenda,* 3rd ed. edited by Maryann Cusimano Love, 41–67. Belmont, CA: Thomson Wadsworth, 2007.

Craig, Gordon A. *Germany, 1866–1945.* Oxford UK: Clarendon, 1978.

Craig, Gordon A. and Alexander L. George. *Force and Statecraft.* New York: Oxford University Press, 1983.

Crankshaw, Edward. *Bismarck.* New York: Viking, 1981.

Crescenzi, Mark J. C. "Economic Exit, Interdependence, and Conflict." *The Journal of Politics* 65 (2003): 809–832.

Croddy, Eric, Clarisa Perez-Armendariz, and John Hart. *Chemical and Biological Warfare: A Comprehensive Survey for the Concerned Citizen.* New York: Copernicus Books, 2001.

"The Cutting Edge." *The Economist,* February 22, 2001. http://www.economist.com/displaystory.cfm?story_id=S%26%28H%28%2EPA%2F%27%0A.

D'Alesky, Anne-Christine. "UNHCR: Facing the Refugee Challenge." *UN Chronicle* 28 (September 1991): 40–47.

Dallek, Robert. *The American Style of Foreign Policy.* New York: Mento, 1983.

"The Data Report 2009." ONE International. http://one.org/international/datareport2009/downloads.html.

"The Data Report 2010: Monitoring the G8 Promise to Africa." ONE International, May 25, 2010. http://www.one.org/c/international/hottopic/3331/.

Dempsey, Judy. "And What Now, Mr. Putin?" *International Herald Tribune*, August 6, 2005. http://www.iht.com/articles/2005/08/05/business/wbrussia.php.

Dempsey, Thomas. "Counterterrorism in African Failed States: Challenges and Potential Solutions." *Strategic Studies Institute* (April 2006).

Department of State Bulletin, June 15, 1947, 1159–1160. Quoted in telegram from U.S. Embassy, Moscow to Secretary of State Marshall. Papers of Joseph Jones. Truman Library.

Deutsch, Karl W. *The Analysis of International Relations.* Englewood Cliffs, NJ: Prentice-Hall, 1968.

"Developments Concerning the SARS Virus." *Miami Herald.* May 22, 2003. http://www.miami.com/mld/miamiherald/news/world/5919463.htm.

Diffie, B. W., and C. D. Winius. *Foundations of the Portuguese Empire 1415–1580.* Minneapolis, MN: Minneapolis Press, 1977.

"Digital Transformation for Rural India," XTVWorld.com, http://press.xtvworld.com/article15164.html.

Dinse, John, and Sterling Johnson. "Ideologies of Revolutionary Terrorism." In *Terrorism and Political Violence*, edited by Henry Han, 61–76. New York: Oceana Publications, 1993.

Dmytryshin, Basil. *USSR: A Concise History.* 4th ed. New York: Charles Scribner's, 1984.

Dodwell, Henry H., ed. *British India, 1497–1858.* Cambridge, UK: Cambridge University Press, 1929.

Dos Santos, Theotonio. "The Structure of Dependence." *American Economic Review* 60 (1970): 235–246.

Doyle, Michael W. "Kant, Liberal Legacies, and Foreign Affairs." *Philosophy and Public Affairs* 12 (1983): 205–235.

———. "Kant, Liberal Legacies, and Foreign Affairs, Part 2." *Philosophy and Public Affairs* 12 (1983): 323–353.

Drew, Catherine, and Dhananjayan Sriskandarajah. "EU Enlargement in 2007: No Warm Welcome for Labor Migrants." Migration Information Source. January 1, 2007. http://www.migrationinformation.org/Feature/display.cfm?ID=568.

Drinan, Robert F. *Cry of the Oppressed: The History and Hope of the Human Rights Revolution.* San Francisco: Harper & Row, 1987.

Dugger, Celia W. "$630 Million Donated Toward Polio Eradication Efforts." *New York Times.* January 22, 2009. http://www.nytimes.com/2009/01/22/world/africa/22polio.html.

Dunn, Seth. "Climate Change: Can the North and South Get in Step?" In *The Global Agenda: Issues and Perspectives*, 6th ed., edited by Charles W. Kegley, Jr. and Eugene R. Wittkopf, 434–445. New York: McGraw-Hill, 2001.

Dupuy, R. Ernest, and Trevor N. Dupuy. *The Encyclopedia of Military History, from 3500 B.C. to the Present*, rev. ed. New York: Harper & Row, 1977.

Durch, William, and Barry Blechman. *Keeping the Peace: The United Nations in the Emerging World Order.* Washington, DC: Henry L. Stimson Center, 1992.

Dymski, Gary A., "Post-Hegemonic U.S. Economy Hegemony: Minskian and Kaleckian Dynamics in the Neoliberal Era." http://www.economics.ucr.edu/papers/2002papers.html.

Dyson, Stephen Benedict. "Drawing Policy Implications from the 'Operational Code' of a 'New' Political Actor: Russian President Vladimir Putin." *Policy Sciences* 34 (2001): 329–346.

Edwards, Sebastian. "The Mirage of Capital Controls." May 1999. http://www.anderson.ucla.edu/faculty/sebastian.edwards/for_aff.pdf.

Eichengreen, Barry. "Capital Controls: Capital Idea or Capital Folly?" November 1998. http://business.baylor.edu/Tom_Kelly/Capital%20Controls.htm.

———. *Golden Fetters: The Gold Standard and the Great Depression, 1919–1939.* New York: Oxford University Press, 1992.

Eisenhower, Dwight David. *Mandate for Change.* New York: Doubleday, 1963.

Elbe, Stefan. "Should HIV/AIDS Be Securitized? The Ethical Dilemmas of Linking HIV/AIDS and Security." International Studies Quarterly 50.1 (March 2006): 119–144.

Engardio, Pete. "Is U.S. Innovation Headed Offshore?" *Bloomberg Businessweek*, May 7, 2008. http://www.businessweek.com/innovate/content/may2008/id2008057_518979.htm?campaign_id=rss_topStories_msnbc.

Emmanuel, Arrighi. *Unequal Exchange: A Study of the Imperialism of Trade.* New York: Monthly Review Press, 1972.

Environment Canada. "Acid Rain FAQ." September 12, 2003. http://www.ns.ec.gc.ca/msc/as/acidfaq.html.

Environment News Service. "G8 Summit Extends Environmental Work Beyond Climate." June 8, 2007. http://www.ens-newswire.com/ens/jun2007/2007–06-08–05.asp.

Ernst, Julia L. Laura Katzive, and Erica Smock. "The Global Pattern of U.S. Initiatives Curtailing Women's Reproductive Rights: A Perspective on the Increasingly Anti-Choice Mosaic." Center for Reproductive Rights. http://www.reproductiverights.org/pub_art_mosaic4.html.

Eurasianet.org. "Uzbek Authorities Crack Down on Another Foreign NGO in Tashkent." (2004). http://www.eurasianet.org/departments/civilsociety/articles/eav091704.shtml.

"Europe's Muslims: A year after the French Riots, their alienation is growing." *Washingtonpost.com.* October 25, 2006. http://www.washingtonpost.com/wp-dyn/content/article/2006/10/24/AR2006102401148.html.

Evans, Peter. *Dependent Development: The Alliance of Multinational, State, and Local Capital in Brazil.* Princeton, NJ: Princeton University Press, 1979.

Evans-Pritchard, Ambrose. "Turkey's Muslim Millions Threaten EU Values, Says Commissioner." Telegraph.co.uk, August 9, 2004, http://www.telegraph.co.uk/news/main.jhtml?xml=/news/2004/09/08/wturk08.xml.

Evans, Gareth, and Mohamed Sahnoun. *The Responsibility to Protect: Report of the International Commission on Intervention and State Sovereignty.* Ottawa, Canada:The International Development Research Centre, 2001.

Evans, Mark. *Just War Theory: A Reappraisal.* New York: Palgrave Macmillan, 2005.

"A Fair Exchange." *The Economist*, October 2, 2004. http://www.bjreview.com.cn/200443/ViewPoint-200343.htm.

Fall, Bernard. *Street without Joy.* Harrisburg, PA: Stackpole, 1964.

Farrar, L. L. *Arrogance and Anxiety: The Ambivalence of German Power, 1848–1914.* Iowa City: University of Iowa Press, 1981.

Fawn, Rick, and Raymond A. Hinnebusch, eds. *The Iraq War: Causes and Consequences* Boulder, CO: Lynne Rienner, 2006.

Feaver, Peter D. "Command and Control in Emerging Nuclear Nations." *International Security* 17 (1992–1993): 160–187.

Federal Reserve Bank of San Francisco. "Lessons from Thailand." Federal Reserve Bank of San Francisco, Economic Letters, 97-33, November 7, 1997. http://www.frbsf.org/econrsrch/wklyltr/el97-33.html.

Feng, Huiyun. "The Operational Code of Mao Zedong: Defensive or Offensive Realist?" *Security Studies* 14 (2005): 637–662.

Fieldhouse, D. K. *Economics and Empire, 1830–1914.* Ithaca, NY: Cornell University Press, 1973.

———. *Colonialism, 1870–1945: An Introduction.* New York: St. Martin's, 1981.

Finckenauer, James O., and Jennifer L. Schrock, eds. *The Prediction and Control of Organized Crime: The Experience of Post-Soviet Ukraine.* New Brunswick, NJ: Transaction Publishers, 2004.

Finnemore, Martha. *The Purpose of Intervention: Changing Beliefs About the Use of Force.* Ithaca, NY: Cornell University Press, 2003.

Fischer, Fritz. *War of Illusions: German Policies from 1911 to 1914.* Translated by Marian Jackson. New York: Norton, 1975.

Fisher, Ian, and Larry Rohter. "The Pope Denounces Capitalism and Marxism." *The New York Times*, May 13, 2007. http://www.nytimes.com/2007/05/14/world/americas/14pope.html?ex=1336881600&en=7618945a33b6ff6c&ei=5124&partner=newsvine&exprod=newsvine.

Fitzgerald, Valpy. "Regulatory Investment Incentives." Paris: OECD Publishing, 2001. http://www.oecd.org/dataoecd/32/17/2510459.pdf.

Foege, William H. "International Health Developments after the Elimination of Smallpox." *World Medical Journal* 38 (1991): 7–8.

Food and Agriculture Organization (FAO). "Coping with Water Scarcity: Q&A with FAO Director-General Dr. Jacques Diouf." March 22, 2007. http://www.fao.org/newsroom/en/focus/2007/1000521/index.html.

———. "Deforestation Continues at a High Rate in Tropical Areas; FAO Calls Upon Countries to Fight Forest Crime and Corruption." Press release. October 3, 2001. http://www.fao.org/WAICENT/OIS/PRESS_NE/PRESSENG/2001/pren0161.htm.

———. "FAO Component of the 2007 Work Plan for Sudan." 2007. http://www.fao.org/tc/tce/app_sudan_07_intro_en.asp.

———. "Food Aid to Save and Improve Lives." 2000. http://www.fao.org/world foodsummit/english/fsheets/wfp.pdf.

———. "Global Report Cites Progress in Slowing Forest Losses." March 13, 2007. http://www.fao.org/newsroom/en/news/2007/1000506/index.html.

———. "Hunger at a Glance." 2010. http://www.fao.org/hunger/hunger_home/hunger_at_a_glance/en/.

———. "Hunger: Frequently Asked Questions (FAQs)." 2010. http://www.fao.org/hunger/faqs-on-hunger/en/.

———. "Hunger Slows Progress Towards Millennium Development Goals." November 22, 2005. http://www.fao.org/newsroom/en/news/2005/1000151/index.html.

———. "Lesotho Faces Deep Food Crisis After One of Its Worst Droughts in 30 Years; One Fifth of Population Will Need Assistance." June 13, 2007. http://www.fao.org/newsroom/en/news/2007/10000597/index.html.

———. "The Numbers: SOFI 2004 Hunger Statistics." http://www.fao.org/newsroom/en/focus/2004/51786/printable_51791en.html.

———. "The Spectrum of Malnutrition." 2002. http://www.fao.org/worldfoodsummit/english/fsheets/malnutrition.pdf.

———. "UN Reports Fresh Fighting in Sudan's Darfur Region." December 2, 2004. http://www.fao.org/world/regional/rne/news/news294_en.htm.

———. "World Deforestation Decreases, but Remains Alarming in Many Countries." March 25, 2010. http://www.fao.org/news/story/en/item/40893/icode/.

Forbes, Ian, ed. *Political Theory, International Relations and the Ethics of Intervention.* London: St. Martin's, 1993.

"The Foreign Exchange Market Overview." *Worldwide Times.* http://www.worldwidetimes.com/overview.htm

Foreman-Peck, J. A. *A History of the World Economy: International Economic Relations Since 1850,* 2d ed. Upper Saddle River, NJ: Prentice Hall, 1995.

Forest Stewardship Council. "The History of FSC-US." http://www.fscus.org/about_us/.

———. "What Is FSC-US?" http://www.fscus.org/faqs/what_is_fsc.php.

Fox, William. *The Super-Powers: The United States, Britain and the Soviet Union—And Their Responsibility for Peace.* New York: Harcourt Brace, 1944.

Frank, Andre Gunder. *Latin America: Underdevelopment or Revolution.* New York: Monthly Review Press, 1969.

Frazao, Elizabeth Birgit Meade, Anita Regmi. "Converging Patterns in Global Food Consumption and Food Delivery Systems." *United States Department of Agriculture.* February 2008. http://www.ers.usda.gov/amberwaves/february08/features/covergingpatterns.htm.

Freedman, Lawrence. *The Evolution of Nuclear Strategy.* New York: St. Martin's, 1983.

Freedom House. *Freedom in the World, 2004.* http://www.freedomhouse.org/research/freeworld/2004/countries.htm.

———. *Freedom in the World, 2005.* http://www.freedomhouse.org/research/freeworld/2005/charts2005.pdf.

———. *Freedom in the World 2010: Erosion of Freedom Intensifies.* http://www.freedomhouse.org/uploads/fiw10/FIW_2010_Tables_and_Graphs.pdf.

Friedberg, Aaron. *The Weary Titan: Britain and the Experience of Relative Decline.* Princeton, NJ: Princeton University Press, 1988.

Frieden, Jeffry A., and David A. Lake, eds. *International Political Economy: Perspectives on Global Power and Wealth,* 3rd ed. New York: St. Martin's, 1995.

Friedman, Norman. *Seapower and Space.* Annapolis, MD: Naval Institute Press, 2001.

Friedman, Robert I. *Red Mafiya: How the Russian Mob Has Invaded America.* Boston: Little, Brown, 2000.

Fromkin, David. *A Peace to End All Peace: The Fall of the Ottoman Empire and the Creation of the Modern Middle-East.* New York: Avon, 1989.

Fukuyama, Francis. *The End of History and the Last Man.* New York: Free Press, 1992.

———. *Our Posthuman Future.* New York: Farrar, Strauss, and Giroux, 2002.

Fuller, Graham E., and Ian O. Lesser. *A Sense of Siege: The Geopolitics of Islam and the West.* Boulder, CO: Westview, 1995.

The Fund for Peace. *Failed State Index 2009.* http://www.fundforpeace.org/web/index.php?option=com_content&task=view&id=99&Itemid=140.

Fussell, Paul. *Thank God for the Atom Bomb, and Other Essays.* New York: Ballantine, 1988.

G-8. "Breakthrough on Climate Protection." June 7, 2007. http://www.g-8.de/nn_94646/Content/EN/Artikel/__g8-summit/2007-06-07-g8-klimaschutz__en.html.

Gabel, Medard, and Henry Bruner. *Globalinc.: An Atlas of the Multinational Corporation.* New York: The New Press, 2003.

Gaddis, John Lewis. *Strategies of Containment.* New York: Oxford University Press, 1982.

———. *The United States and the End of the Cold War.* New York: Oxford University Press, 1993.

———. *The United States and the Origins of the Cold War,* rev. ed. New York: Columbia University Press, 2000.

———. *We Now Know: Rethinking Cold War History.* New York: Oxford University Press, 1998.

Gallagher, J., and Ronald Robinson. *Africa and the Victorians: The Climax of Imperialism in the Dark Continent.* New York: St. Martin's, 1961.

Garthoff, Raymond L. *The Great Transition.* Washington, DC: Brookings, 1994.

Gasiorowski, Mark J. "Economic Interdependence and International Conflict: Some Cross-National Evidence." *International Studies Quarterly* 30 (1986): 23–38.

Geller, Daniel S., and Joel David Singer. *Nations at War: A Scientific Study of International Conflict.* Cambridge UK: Cambridge University Press, 1998.

"Geo-Engineering: A Bad Idea Whose Time Has Come." National Public Radio. May 29, 2010. http://www.npr.org/templates/story/story.php?storyId=127245606.

George, Alexander. "The 'Operational Code': A Neglected Approach to the Study of Political Leaders and Decision-Making." *International Studies Quarterly* 23 (1969): 190–222.

George, Alexander L., and Richard Smoke. *Deterrence in American Foreign Policy: Theory and Practice.* New York: Columbia University Press, 1974.

"Georgian Diplomat Convicted in Fatal Crash Goes Home." CNN.com. June 30, 2000. http://archives.cnn.com/2000/US/06/30/georgia/diplomat.

Gervasi, Tom. *The Myth of Soviet Military Supremacy.* New York: Harper & Row, 1986.

Gibson, C. *Spain in America.* New York: Harper & Row, 1966.

Gibson, Lawrence H. *The Coming of the Revolution, 1763–1789.* New York: Harper, 1954.

Gilpin, Robert. *The Political Economy of International Relations.* Princeton, NJ: Princeton University Press, 1987.

Glaser, Charles Louis. "The Security Dilemma Revisited." *World Politics* 50 (1997): 171–201.

Gleick, Peter H. "Water and Conflict: Fresh Water Resources and International Security." *International Security* 18 (1993): 79–112.

Glenny, Misha. *The Fall of Yugoslavia.* New York: Penguin, 1992.

Global Economic Prospects and the Developing Countries 1994. Washington, DC: World Bank, 1994.

The Global Fund to Fight AIDS, Tuberculosis and Malaria. "A Force for Change: The Global Fund to Fight AIDS, Tuberculosis and Malaria." 2006. http://www.theglobalfund.org/en/files/malaria_information_sheet_en.pdf.

Global Health Council. "Where Do Child Deaths Occur?" (2010). http://www.globalhealth.org/child_health/child_mortality/where_occur.

Global Policy Forum. "Qatar: Draft Resolution." November 10, 2006. http://www.globalpolicy.org/security/veto/2006878.pdf.

———. "Subjects of UN Security Council Vetoes." http:///www.globalpolicy.org/security/membship/veto/vetosubj.htm.

———. "United Kingdom of Great Britain and Northern Ireland and United States of America: Draft Resolution." January 12, 2007. http://www.globalpolicy.org/security/veto/2007/14.pdf.

———. "World Court Marks 6th Anniversary, as Its Case-Load Gets Heavier and Tougher." Associated Press. April 11, 2006. http://www.globalpolicy.org/intljustice/icj/2006/0411anniversary.htm.

Global Polio Eradication Initiative. "Wild Poliovirus Weekly Update." May 26, 2010. http://www.polioeradication.org/casecount.asp.

Goncharov, Sergei N., John W. Lewis, and Xue Litai. *Uncertain Partners: Stalin, Mao, and the Korean War.* Stanford California: Stanford University Press, 1993.

Goodman, Melvin A., Craig Eisendrath, and Gerald E. Marsh. *The Phantom Defense: America's Pursuit of the Star Wars Illusion.* New York: Praeger, 2001.

Gooneratne, Ayesha. "Development: Microcredit Poised to Reach 100 Million Families." IPSNews.net, December 2005. http://ipsnews.net/news.asp?idnews=31341.

Gosnell, Harold F. *Truman's Crises: A Political Biography of Harry S. Truman.* London: Greenwood, 1980.

Gow, James. *Triumph of the Lack of Will: International Diplomacy and the Yugoslav War.* New York: Columbia University Press, 1997.

Graham, Bradley. *Hit to Kill: The New Battle over Shielding America from Missile Attack.* New York: Public Affairs Press, 2001.

Grant, Rebecca, and Kathleen Newland. *Gender and International Relations.* Bloomington Indiana University Press, 1991.

Grassman, Sven, and Erik Lundberg, eds. *The World Economic Order—Past and Prospects.* London: Macmillan, 1981.

Greenfeld, Liah. *Nationalism.* Cambridge, MA: Harvard University Press, 1992.

"Greenhouse Gas Inventory." *U.S. Climate Action Report 2010.* http://www.state.gov/documents/organization/140009.pdf

Greenpeace. "Arctic Sunrise." http://www.greenpeace.org/international/about/ships/the-arctic-sunrise.

———. "Questions About Greenpeace in General." http://www.greenpeace.org/international/about/faq/questions-about-greenpeace-in.

———. "Toxic Tech Victory: Sony Ericsson Announces Phase Out of Toxic Chemicals." April 29, 2005. http://www.greenpeace.org/international/news/toxic-tech-victory;

Gregor, James. *Italian Fascism and Developmental Dictatorship.* Princeton, NJ: Princeton University Press, 1979.

———. *Young Mussolini and the Intellectual Origins of Fascism.* Berkeley: University of California Press, 1979.

Greider, William. *One World, Ready or Not: The Manic Logic of Global Capitalism.* New York: Simon & Schuster, 1997.

Grey, Colin S. *Modern Strategy.* New York: Oxford University Press, 1999.

Grey-Johnson, Crispin. "Beyond Peacekeeping: The Challenge of Post-Conflict Reconstruction and Peacebuilding in Africa." *UN Chronicle,* Online ed. (2006). http://www.un.org/Pubs/Chronicle/2006/issue1/0106p08.htm#.

Grieco, Joseph. *Cooperation Among Nations: Europe, America, and Non-Tariff Barriers to Trade.* Ithaca, NY: Cornell University Press, 1990.

Grono, Nick. "Briefing—Darfur: The International Community's Failure to Protect." *African Affairs* 105 (2006): 621–631.

Guerrier, Steven W., and Wayne C. Thomson, eds. *Perspectives on Strategic Defense.* Boulder, CO: Westview, 1987.

Gunaratna, Rohan. *Inside Al Qaeda*. New York: Columbia University Press, 2002.

Guner, Serdar. "The Turkish–Syrian War of Attrition: The Water Dispute." *Studies in Conflict & Terrorism* 20 (1997): 105–16.

Haass, Richard N. *Intervention: The Use of American Force in the Post-Cold War World*. Washington, DC: Carnegie Endowment for International Peace, 1994.

Hackett, James, ed. *The Military Balance, 2007*. London: International Institute for Strategic Studies, 2007.

Halabi, Yakub. "The Expansion of Global Governance into the Third World: Altruism, Realism, or Constructivism?" *International Studies Review* 6 (2004): 21–48.

Hamza, Khidir, and Jeff Stein. *Saddam's Bombmaker: The Terrifying Inside Story of the Iraqi Nuclear and Biological Weapons Agenda*. New York: Scribner, 2000.

Harding, Luke. "Millions More Russians Shunted into Poverty." Guardian.co.UK. August 31, 2009. http://www.guardian.co.uk/world/2009/aug/31/russia-economy-poverty-increase-putin.

Harrison, Paul. "Beyond the Blame-Game: Population–Environment Links." *Populi* 17 (1990): 14–21.

Harvey, David. *A Brief History of Neoliberalism*. Oxford: Oxford University Press, 2005.

Hasenclever, Andreas, Peter Mayer, and Volker Rittberger. "Interests, Power, Knowledge: The Study of International Regimes" *Mershon International Studies Review* 40 (1996): 177–228.

———. *Theories of International Regimes*. New York: Cambridge University Press, 1997.

Hass, Mark L. *The Ideological Origins of Great Power Politics, 1789–1989*. Ithaca, NY: Cornell University Press, 2005.

Headrick, Daniel. *The Tentacles of Progress: Technology Transfer in the Age of Imperialism, 1850–1940*. New York: Oxford University Press, 1988.

Henderson, W. O. *The Industrial Revolution in Europe, 1815–1914*. Chicago: Quadrangle, 1961.

Herold, J. C. *The Age of Napoleon*. London: Weidenfeld & Nicholson, 1963.

Herz, John H. "Idealist Internationalism and the Security Dilemma." *World Politics* 2 (1950): 157–180

Hirschmann, Albert. *The Passions and the Interests*. Princeton, NJ: Princeton University Press, 1977.

"History of the Foreign Exchange Market." AFEX: Associated Foreign Exchange. http://afex.com/forex-history.html.

Hobbes, Thomas. *The Leviathan*. The text edited by A. R. Waller, Cambridge: at the University Press, 1904.

Hobsbawm, Eric. *Nations and Nationalism Since 1780*. Cambridge, UK: Cambridge University Press, 1990.

Hoffman, Bruce. *Inside Terrorism*. London: Victor Gollancz, 1998.

Hoffman, Stanley. *The Ethics and Politics of Humanitarian Intervention*. Notre Dame, IN: Notre Dame University Press, 1996.

Holloway, David. *The Soviet Union and the Arms Race*. New Haven, CT: Yale University Press, 1983.

Holsti, Kalevi J. *Peace and War: Armed Conflicts and International Order 1648–1989*. Cambridge, UK: Cambridge University Press, 1991.

Holsti, Ole R. "Review: *Essence of Decision: Explaining the Cuban Missile Crisis*." *The Western Political Quarterly* 25 (1972): 136–140.

Holzgrefe, J. L., and Robert O. Keohane, eds. *Humanitarian Intervention: Ethical, Legal and Political Dilemmas*. Cambridge, UK: Cambridge University Press, 2003.

Homer-Dixon, Thomas F. "Environmental Scarcities and Violent Conflict: Evidence from Cases." *International Security* 19 (1994): 21.

Horne, Alastair. *A Savage War of Peace*. New York: Viking Press, 1978.

Howard, Michael. *War in European History*. New York: Oxford University Press, 1976.

Howard, Russell, and Reid Sawyer. *Terrorism and Counterterrorism: Understanding the New Security Environment*. New York: McGraw-Hill, 2002.

Hsu, Tanya C. "The United States Must Not Neglect Saudi Arabian Investment." Saudi-American Forum, September 23, 2003. http://www.saudi-american-forum.org/Newsletters/SAF_Essay_22.htm.

Human Rights Watch. "Human Rights Watch: Who We Are." http://www.hrw.org/about/whoweare.html.

———. "Child Soldiers." http://hrw.org/campaigns/crp/index.htm.

Huntington, Samuel P. "The Clash of Civilizations?" *Foreign Affairs* 72 (1993): 22–49.

———. *Political Order in Changing Societies.* New Haven, CT: Yale University Press, 1968.

Huth, Paul. *Extended Deterrence and the Prevention of War.* New Haven, CT: Yale University Press, 1988.

IMF Conference on Second Generation Reforms. November 1999. http://www.imf.org/external/pubs/ft/seminar/1999/reforms/.

Indonesia's Investment Coordinating Board. The Site for Direct Investors, BKPM (an investment service agency of the Indonesian government). http://www.bkpm.go.id/en/info.php?mode=baca&cat=7&info_id=16.

Inglehart, Ronald. "The Renaissance of Political Culture." *The American Political Science Review* 82 (1988): 1203–1230.

International Chamber of Commerce. "ICC membership." http://www.iccwbo.org/home/intro_icc/membership.asp.

———. "What Is ICC." http://www.iccwbo.org/home/menu_what_is_icc.asp.

"International Cooperation at a Crossroads: Aid, Trade, and Security in an Unequal World." *Human Development Report 2005,* United Nations Development Program. http://hdr.undp.org/reports/global/2005/.

International Energy Agency. "IEA Director Releases Latest World Energy Outlook, Says Current Energy Trends 'Call for Urgent and Decisive Policy Responses.'" October 26, 2004. http://www.iea.org/Textbase/press/pressdetail.asp?PRESS_REL_ID=137.

———. "Renewables in Global Energy Supply: An IEA Fact Sheet." January 2007. http://www.iea.org/textbase/papers/2006/renewable_factsheet.pdf.

———. "World Energy Outlook 2006: Fact Sheet—Global Energy Trends." 2006. http://www.worldenergyoutlook.org/fact-sheets/fs_GlobalEnergyTrends.pdf.

International Institute for Strategic Studies, *The Military Balance 2010.*

International Migration Organization. "Facts and Figures: Global Estimates." 2010. http://www.iom.int/jahia/Jahia/about-migration/facts-and-figures/lang/en.

"International Research and Development Expenditures and Research and Development as Percentage of Gross Domestic Product, by Selected Country and for All Organisation for Economic Co-operation and Development Countries: 1981–2004," Table 14 in National Patterns of R&D Resources, 2002 Data Update, NSF 06-327. Arlington, VA: National Science Foundation, Division of Science Resources Statistics, 2006. http://www.nsf.gov/statistics/nsf06327/pdf/tab14.pdf.

International Trade and Core Labour Standards, OECD Publishing, 2000. http://www.oecdbookshop.org/oecd/display.asp?lang=EN&sf1=identifiers&st1=222000041p1.

"Internet Usage Statistics." Internet World Stats. http://www.internetworldstats.com/stats.htm.

"Inuit Leader Wins UN Award for Activism Against Climate Change." UN News Centre. June 20, 2007. http://www.un.org/apps/news/story.asp?NewsID=22973&Cr=climate&Cr1=change.

IPCC Fourth Assessment Report: Climate Change 2007. http://www.ipcc.ch/publications_and_data/ar4/wg3/en/ch1s1-3-1-2.html.

"Iraqi Refugee Tragedy Steers UN on New Path to Humanitarian Aid." *UN Observer & International Report* 13 (1991).

Jackson, Allison. "Match of the Day May Go to Court." *The Age* (2001).

Jackson, John H. *Sovereignty, the WTO and Changing Fundamentals of International Law.* Cambridge, UK: Cambridge University Press, 2006.

Jackson, Robert H. "Surrogate Sovereignty? Great Power Responsibility and 'Failed States.'" Institute of International Relations, Working Paper No. 25 (November 1998).

Jehl, Douglas. "In Race to Tap the Euphrates, the Upper Hand Is Upstream." *The New York Times,* August 25, 2002. http://www.nytimes.com/pages/world/worldspecial/index.html.

Jenkins, Rhys. *Transnational Corporations and Uneven Development.* New York: Methuen, 1987.

Jensen, Kenneth M., ed. *Origins of the Cold War: The Novikov, Kennan, and Roberts "Long Telegrams" of 1946.* Washington, DC: United States Institute of Peace, 1993.

Jervis, Robert, "Cooperation Under the Security Dilemma." *World Politics* 30 (1978): 167–214.

Jian, Chen. *China's Road to the Korean War: The Making of Sino-American Confrontation.* New York: Columbia University Press, 1994.

———. *Mao's China and the Cold War.* Chapel Hill: University of North Carolina Press, 2001.

Joachim, Jutta. "Framing Issues and Seizing Opportunities: The UN, NGOs, and Women's Rights." *International Studies Quarterly* 47 (2003): 247–274.

Jones, E. L. *The European Miracle.* Cambridge, UK: Cambridge University Press, 1981.

"Judging Genocide." In *World Politics 02/03,* 23rd ed., edited by Helen E. Purkitt, 216–18. Guilford, CT: McGraw-Hill/Dushkin, 2002.

Juergensmeyer, Mark. *The New Cold War? Religious Nationalism Confronts the Secular State.* Berkeley: University of California Press, 1993.

———. *Terror in the Mind of God: The Global Rise of Religious Violence.* Berkeley: University of California Press, 2001.

The Kaiser Family Foundation. "The HIV/AIDS Epidemic in Sub-Saharan Africa." November 2009. http://www.kff.org/hivaids/upload/7391-08.pdf.

Kant, Immanuel. *Perpetual Peace: A Philosophical Sketch.* Translated by Ted Humphrey. Indianapolis, IN: Hackett, 2004.

Karas, Thomas. *The New High Ground.* New York: Simon & Schuster, 1984.

Kaplan, Robert. *Balkan Ghosts.* New York: St. Martin's, 1993.

Kaysen, Karl. "Is War Obsolete?" In *The Cold War and After,* edited by Sean Lynn-Jones and Steven E. Miller, 81–103. Cambridge, MA.: MIT Press. 1993.

Kearney, A. T. "2010 Foreign Direct Investment (FDI) Confidence Index." http://www.atkearney.com/index.php/Publications/foreign-direct-investment-confidence-index.html.

Keegan, John. *The Face of Battle.* New York: Penguin, 1976.

Kellerhals, Merle David, Jr. "United States Seeks Expanded Economic Growth in Africa." America.gov. June 25, 2009. http://www.america.gov/st/business-english/2009/June/20090625114929dmslahrellek0.8004114.html.

Kennan, George F. "The Sources of Soviet Conduct." *Foreign Affairs* 20 (1947): 556–582.

Kennedy, Paul. *The Rise and Fall of the Great Powers.* New York: Vintage, 1987.

Kenwood A. G., and A. L. Lougheed. *The Growth of the International Economy 1820–2000.* London, UK: Routledge, 1999.

Keohane, Robert O. *After Hegemony: Cooperation and Discord in the World Political Economy.* Princeton NJ: Princeton University Press, 1984.

———. "The Demand for International Regimes." *International Organization* 36 (1982): 325–355.

Keohane, Robert O, and Lisa L. Martin. "The Promise of Institutionalist Theory." *International Security* 20 (1995): 39–51.

Keohane, Robert O, and Joseph S. Nye, Jr. "The Club Model of Multilateral Cooperation and the World Trade Organization: Problems of Democratic Legitimacy." Working Paper No. 4, Visions, The John F. Kennedy School of Government. http://www.ksg.harvard.edu/visions/publication/keohane_nye.pdf.

Kerr, Paul. "Libya's Disarmament: A Model for U.S. Policy?" *Arms Control Today* 34 (June 2004): 36–38.

Kidron, Michael, and Ronald Segal. *The New State of the World Atlas.* 4th ed. New York: Simon & Schuster, 1991.

Kindelberger, Charles. *The World in Depression, 1929–1939.* Berkeley: University of California Press, 1973.

———. *The World in Depression, 1929–1939,* rev. ed. Berkeley: University of California Press, 1986.

Kinetz, Erika. "A Hungry India Balks at Genetically Modified Crops." AP, February 16, 2010. http://www.etaiwannews.com/etn/news_content.php?id=1181902&lang=eng_news.

Kirby, Alex. "Water Scarcity: A Looming Crisis?" BBC News. October 19, 2004. http://news.bbc.co.uk/go/pr/fr/-/hi/science/nature/3747724.stm.

Kirkpatrick, Jeanne. "Dictatorship and Double Standards." *Commentary* (1979): 34–45.

Kluger, Jeffrey. "Polio's Back. Why Now?" *Time*, May 16, 2005, 46.

Kota, Ina. "Microfinance: Banking for the Poor." *Finance and Development: The Quarterly Magazine of the IMF* 44 (2007). http://www.imf.org/external/pubs/ft/fandd/2007/06/basics.htm.

Krasner, Stephen. *International Regimes*. Ithaca, NY: Cornell University Press, 1983.

———. "State Power and the Structure of International Trade." *World Politics*, 28 (April 1976): 317–347.

Kristof, Nicholas. "OpEd: Kristof Responds." *New York Times*, June 1, 2005. http://www.genocideintervention.net/about/press/coverage/index.php/archives/10.

Krugman, Paul. "Exchange Rates." In *The Concise Encyclopedia of Economics*. http://www.econlib.org/library/Enc/ExchangeRates.html.

———. *Rethinking International Trade*. Cambridge, MA: MIT Press, 1990.

Krugman, Paul, and Maurice Obstfeld. *International Economics: Theory and Policy*. New York: HarperCollins, 1991.

Kugler, Tadeusz, and Siddharth Swaminathan. "The Politics of Population." *International Studies Review* 8(2006): 581–596.

LaFeber, Walter. *America, Russia, and the Cold War, 1945–1996*, 9th ed. New York: McGraw-Hill, 2001.

———. *America, Russia, and the Cold War: 1945–2002*. New York: McGraw-Hill, 2002.

———. *America, Russia and the Cold War 1975–1990*. New York: McGraw-Hill, 1991.

———. *The New Empire: An Interpretation of American Expansion 1860–1898*. Ithaca, NY: Cornell University Press, 1963.

Lairson, Thomas D., and David Skidmore. *International Political Economy: The Struggle for Power and Wealth*. Fort Worth, TX: Harcourt Brace, 1993.

———. *International Political Economy: The Struggle for Power and Wealth*. Fort Worth, Harcourt Brace, 1997.

———. *International Political Economy*. Belmont, CA: Thomson Wadsworth, 2002.

Lall, Sanjaya. "Is Dependence a Useful Concept in Analyzing Underdevelopment?" *World Development* 3 (1975): 799–810.

Landes, Davids. *The Unbound Prometheus: Technological Change and Industrial Development in Western Europe from 1750 to the Present*. Cambridge, UK: Cambridge University Press, 1969.

Laney, James T., and Jason T. Shaplen. "How to Deal with North Korea." *Foreign Affairs* 82 (March–April 2003): 16–31.

Langford, Roland. *Introduction to Weapons of Mass Destruction: Radiological, Chemical, and Biological*. Hoboken, NJ: Wiley-Interscience, 2004.

Lebow, Richard Ned, and Janice Gross Stein. *We All Lost the Cold War*. Princeton, NJ: Princeton University Press, 1994.

———. *When Does Deterrence Succeed and How Do We Know?* Toronto: Canadian Institute for International Peace and Security, 1990.

Lee, Hong-jong. "Development, Crisis, and Asian Values." *East Asian Review* 15 (2003): 27–42.

Leffler, Melvyn P., and David S. Painter, eds. *Origins of the Cold War: An International History*. London: Routledge, 1994.

Leiken, Robert S. "Europe's Angry Muslims." *Foreign Affairs* 84, 4 (2005): 120–35.

Leites, Nathan. *The Operational Code of the Politburo*. New York: McGraw-Hill, 1951.

Lejeune-Kaba, Fatoumata. "Number of Asylum-seekers Remains Stable over 2009, UNHCR Figures Show." March 23, 2010. http://www.unhcr.org/4ba8d8239.html.

Lerner, Sharon. "Banned from Pride: The INS Blocks a Visitor with HIV (Ken: Singled Out at the Canadian Border)." *Village Voice*, June 30–July 6, 1999. http://www.aegis.com/news/vv/1999/VV990601.html.

"Lessons from Thailand." Federal Reserve Bank of San Francisco, November 7, 1997. http://www.frbsf.org/econrsrch/wklyltr/el97-33.html.

Levy, Jack S. "The Offensive/Defensive Balance of Military Technology: A Theoretical and Historical Analysis." *International Studies Quarterly* 28 (1984), 219–238.

Liddel Hart, B. H. *History of the First World War, 1914–1918*. London: Faber & Faber, 1938.

Lieber, Robert J. "Oil and Power After the Gulf War." *International Security* 17 (1992): 155–176.

Linden, Eugene. "How to Kill a Tiger: Speculators Tell the Story of Their Attack Against the Baht, the Opening Act of an Ongoing Drama." *Time Magazine Asia,* November 3, 1997. http://www.time.com/time/magazine/1997/int/971103/asia.how_to_kill_a.html.

Lindsey, Rebecca. "Reference: Tropical Deforestation." NASA Earth Observatory. March 30, 2007. http://earthobservatory.nasa.gov/Library/Deforestation/printall.php.

Littlefield, Henry W. *History of Europe Since 1815.* New York: Barnes & Noble, 1963.

Locke, John. *The Second Treatise of Civil Government*, edited by C. B. MacPherson. Indianapolis: Hocket Publishing Company, Inc., 1980.

Lockhart, J. *Early Latin America.* New York: Cambridge University Press, 1983.

Love, Joseph L. "Raul Prebisch and the Origins of the Doctrine of Unequal Exchange." *Latin American Research Review* 15 (1980).

Love, Maryann Cusimano. "Nongovernmental Organizations: Politics Beyond Sovereignty." In *Beyond Sovereignty: Issues for a Global Agenda*, 3rd ed., edited by Maryann Cusimano Love, 68–90. Belmont, CA: Thomson Wadsworth, 2007.

Love, Maryann Cusimano, and Dorle Hellmuth. "People on the Move: Refugees, IDPs, and Migrants." In *Beyond Sovereignty: Issues for a Global Agenda*, 3rd ed., edited by Maryann Cusimano Love, 186–210. Belmont, CA: Thomson Wadsworth, 2007.

Lunde, Paul. *Organized Crime: An Inside Guide to the World's Most Successful Industry.* London: DK, 2004.

Luttwak, Edward. *The Grand Strategy of the Roman Empire.* Baltimore: Johns Hopkins University Press, 1976.

Lynn-Jones, Sean M., and Steven E. Miller, eds. *Global Dangers: Changing Dimensions of International Security.* Cambridge, MA: MIT Press, 1995.

Lyons, Gene M., and Michael Mastanduno, eds. *Beyond Westphalia: State Sovereignty and International Intervention.* Baltimore: Johns Hopkins University Press, 1995.

Macomber, John D. "East Asia's Lessons for Latin American Resurgence." In *International Political Economy*, edited by Jeffry A. Frieden and David Lake, 386–395. New York: St. Martin's, 1991.

Madden, Peter. *Brussels Beef Carve-up: EC Beef Dumping in West Africa.* London: Christian Aid, 1993.

Mallaby, Sebastian. "Saving the World Bank." *Foreign Affairs* 84 (2005): 75–85.

Mandel, Michael. "The Failed Promise of Innovation in the United States." *Bloomberg Businessweek,* June 3, 2009. http://www.businessweek.com/magazine/content/09_24/b4135000953288.htm.

Markusen, James R., James R. Melvin, William M. Kacmpfer, and Keith Maskus. *International Trade: Theory and Evidence.* New York: McGraw-Hill, 1995.

Massie, Robert K. *Dreadnought: Britain, Germany, and the Coming of the Great War.* New York: Random House, 1991.

May, Ernest R. *American Imperialism: A Speculative Essay.* New York: Atheneum, 1968.

McCallum, Mark. "Muslim Call to Thwart Capitalism." BBC News, July 12, 2003. http://news.bbc.co.uk/2/hi/europe/3061833.stm.

McLellan, David S. "The 'Operational Code' Approach to the Study of Political Leaders: Dean Acheson's Philosophical and Instrumental Beliefs." *Canadian Journal of Political Science* 4 (1971): 52–75.

McMillan, Susan M. "Interdependence and Conflict." *Mershon International Studies Review* 41 (1997): 33–58.

McNeill, W. H. *The Pursuit of Power: Technology, Armed Forces and Society Since 1000 AD.* Chicago: University of Chicago Press, 1983.

———. *The Rise of the West.* Chicago: University of Chicago Press, 1967.

McQuillan, Lawrence J. *"The Case Against the International Monetary Fund," Essays in Public Policy.* Stanford, CA: Hoover Institution Press, 1999.

Mearsheimer, John J. "Back to the Future: Instability in Europe After the Cold War." *International Security* 15 (1990): 5–56.

———. "Back to the Future: Instability in Europe After the Cold War." In *The Cold War and After: Prospects for Peace*, edited by Sean M. Lynn-Jones, 141–192. Cambridge, MA: MIT Press, 1991.

————. *The Tragedy of Great Power Politics*. New York: Norton, 2003.

————. *The Tragedy of Great Power Politics*. New York: Norton, 2001.

Merriam-Webster. *Webster's Ninth New Collegiate Dictionary*. Springfield, MA: Merriam-Webster, 1989.

Mertus, Julie A. *War's Offensive on Women: The Humanitarian Challenge in Bosnia, Kosovo, and Afghanistan*. Bloomfield, CT: Kumarian Press, 2000.

"Microfinance Benchmarks of MFIs." Mix Market, 2008. http://www.mixmarket.org/mfi/benchmarks.

Miller, Judith, Stephen Engelberg, and William Broad. *Germs: Biological Weapons and America's Secret War*. New York: Simon & Schuster, 2001.

Mills, Nicolaus, and Kira Brunner, eds. *The New Killing Fields: Massacre and the Politics of Intervention*. New York: Basic Books, 2002.

Milward, Alan. *War, Economy and Society, 1939–1945*. Berkeley: University of California Press, 1977.

Minkel, J. R. "Darfur Dead Much Higher Than Commonly Reported." *Scientific American*, September 15, 2006, http://www.sciam.com/article.cfm?articleID=00037EE7-D970-150A-97083414B7F0000.

Misra, Neelesh. "Climate Session Ends Without New Deadline." *The Boston Globe*, November 2, 2002.

Mistry, Dinshaw. "Nuclear Asia's Challenges." *Current History* 104 (2005): 176–182.

Mommsen, W., and J. Osterhammel, eds. *Imperialism and After: Continuities and Discontinuities*. London: Allen & Unwin, 1986.

Moore, Jonathan, ed. *Hard Choices: Moral Dilemmas in Humanitarian Intervention*. Lanham, MD: Rowman & Littlefield, 2000.

Moore, Patrick. "Ethnic Cleansing in Bosnia: Outrage but Little Action." Radio Free Europe/Radio Liberty Research Report. August 28, 1992.

Morgan, Patrick. *Deterrence: A Conceptual Analysis*. Beverly Hills, CA: Sage, 1977.

————. "Elements of a General Theory of Arms Control." In *Conflict and Arms Control: An Uncertain Agenda*, edited by Paul Viotti, 283–310. Boulder, CO: Westview Press, 1986.

Morgenthau, Hans J. *Politics Among Nations: The Struggle for Power and Peace*, 5th ed. revised. New York: Knopf, 1978.

Morris, Regan. "Sudan: A Growing Grassroots Movement Strives Toward an Ethical Response." Changemakers.net, June 2005. http://www.genocideintervention.net/about/press/coverage/index.php/archives/6.

Moses, John A. *The Politics of Illusion: The Fischer Controversy in German Historiography*. New York: Barnes & Noble, 1975.

Moskos, Charles C., John Allen Williams, and David R. Segal., eds. *The Postmodern Military: Armed Forces after the Cold War*. New York: Oxford University Press, 2000.

Mousseau, Frederic, and Anuradha Mittal. "Food Sovereignty: Ending World Hunger in Our Time." *The Humanist* (March–April 2006). http://www.americanhumanist.org.

Mueller, John. "Policing the Remnants of War." *Journal of Peace Research* 40 (2003): 507–518.

Mueller-Rommel, Ferdinand. *New Politics in Western Europe: The Rise and Success of Green Parties and Alternative Lists*. Boulder, CO: Westview Press, 1989.

Multu, Servet. "The Southeastern Anatolia Project (GAP) of Turkey: Its Context, Objectives, and Prospects." *Orient* 37 (1996): 59–86.

Munz, Rainer. "New German Law Skirts Comprehensive Immigration Reform." Migration Information Source. August 1, 2004. http://www.migrationinformation.org/Feater/display/cfm?ID=241.

Myers, Norman. *Ultimate Security: The Environmental Basis of Political Stability*. New York: Norton, 1993.

Myers, Steven Lee. "Pervasive Corruption in Russia Is 'Just Called Business,'" *The New York Times*, August 13, 2005.

Myrdal, Gunnar. *Asian Drama: An Inquiry Into the Poverty of Nations*, vol. II. New York: Pantheon, 1968.

————. *Economic Theory and Underdeveloped Regions*. New York: Harper & Row, 1971.

Naim, Moises. "Fad and Fashion in Economic Reforms: Washington Consensus or Washington Confusion?" Working draft of a paper prepared for the IMF Conference on Second Generation Reforms, Washington DC, October 1999.

———. "Washington Consensus or Washington Confusion?" *Foreign Policy* 118 (2000): 86–103.

Najera-Morrondo, Jose Antonia. "Malaria Control: History Shows It's Possible." *World Health,* September–October 1991.

Nakajima, Hiroshima. "Epidemiology and the Future of World Health." *Epidemiological Bulletin* 12 (1990): 589–94.

NASA. "New Images: Northern Madagascar." May 2000. http://earthobservatory.nasa.gov/Newsroom/NewImages/images.php3?img_id=4731.

———. "Deforestation Plays Critical Climate Change Role." May 11, 2007. http://earthobservatory.nasa.gov/Newsroom/view.php?id=32686.

———. "News: NASA, NOAA Data Indicate Ozone Layer Is Recovering." August 30, 2006. http://www.jpl.nasa.gov/news/news-print.cfm?release=2006-102.

National Resource Defense Council, "Nuclear Notebook," Bulletin of the Atomic Scientists Web site (November/December 2009). http://www.thebulletin.org/.

Neumayer, Eric. "Bogus Refugees? The Determinants of Asylum Migration to Western Europe." *International Studies Quarterly* 49 (2005): 389–409.

Neustadt, Richard E., and Ernest R. May. *Thinking in Time: The Use of History for Decision-Makers.* New York: The Free Press, 1986.

Newhouse, John. *Cold Dawn: The Story of SALT.* New York: Holt, Rinehart, & Winston, 1973.

Nicholson, Chris. "In Poorer Nations, Cellphones Help Open Up Microfinancing." *The New York Times,* July 9, 2007. http://www.nytimes.com/2007/07/09/business/worldbusiness/09micro.html?ex=1186372800&en=4f46414d8fd414d0&ei=5070.

Nicolson, Harold. *Peacemaking 1919.* London: Constable, 1933.

"No More Delay on Darfur," editorial. *New York Times,* April 19, 2007. http://www.nytimes.com/2007/04/19/opinion/19thu2.html?ex=1334635200&en=3f412665d4cc9b5f&ei=5088&partner=rssnyt&emc=rss.

The Nobel Foundation. "Kofi Annan—Biography." 2001. http://www.nobel.se/peace/laureates/2001/annan-bio.html.

"Nobel Winner Yunus: Microcredit Missionary." *Business Week,* December 26, 2005. http://www.businessweek.com/magazine/content/05_52/b3965024.htm.

Norman, Richard. *Ethics, Killing, and War.* New York: Cambridge University Press, 1995.

"Novel Menu Promotions Throughout the Years…(Since 1993)." McDonald's. *http://www.mcdonalds.com/countries/singapore/food/foodpromo/foodpromo.html*; *http://www.mcdonalds.com/countries/india/index.html.*

"Now We Are 300,000,000." *The Economist,* October 12, 2006. http://www.economist.com/world/na/Printerfriendly.cfm?story_id=8031359.

"Number of Cell Phones Worldwide Hits 4.6B." CBS News. February 15, 2010. http://www.cbsnews.com/stories/2010/02/15/business/main6209772.shtml.

Nurske, Ragnar. *Problems of Capital Formation in Underdeveloped Countries.* New York: Blackwell, 1953.

Nye, Joseph S., Jr. "The Decline of America's Soft Power." *Foreign Affairs* 83 (2004): 16–20.

———. "Soft Power." *Foreign Policy* 80 (Autumn 1990): 153–171.

Oakeshott, Michael, ed. *Thomas Hobbes, Leviathan.* New York: Collier, 1962.

Oberdorfer, Don. "Missed Signals in the Middle East." *Washington Post Magazine,* March 17, 1991, 19–41.

O'Byrne, Darren J. *Human Rights.* New York: Longman, 2003.

Odell, John. *U.S. International Monetary Policy.* Princeton, NJ: Princeton University Press, 1982.

O'Donnell, Guillermo. *Modernization and Bureaucratic-Authoritarianism.* Berkeley: University of California Press, 1979.

Oezcan, Veysel. "Germany: Immigration in Transition." Migration Information Source. July 2004. http://www.migrationinformation.org/Profiles/display.cfm?ID=235.

O'Hanlon, Michael, et al. *Defending America: The Case for Limited National Missile Defense.* Washington, DC: Brookings, 2001.

Olson, Robert. "Turkey–Syria Relations Since the Gulf War: Kurds and Water." *Middle East Policy* 5 (1997): 168–193.

Onyango, Oloka. "Women, War, and Rape." *Human Rights Quarterly* 17 (1995): 650–690.

Oots, Kent Layne. *A Political Organization Approach to International Terrorism.* Westport, CT: Greenwood, 1986.

Organization for Economic Cooperation and Development. *International Trade and Core Labour Standards.* Paris: OECD Publishing, 2000. http://www.oecdbookshop.org/oecd/display.asp?lang=EN&sf1=identifiers&st1=222000041p1.

Organization on Economic Cooperation and Development. *Trends in International Migration 1996.* Paris: OECD, 1996.

Oxfam, "History of Oxfam." http://www.oxfam.org.uk/about_us/history/index.htm.

———. "One Programme: One Goal." http://www.oxfam.org.uk/about_us/history/history8.htm.

———. "Tsunami Crisis." http://www.oxfam.org.uk/oxfam_in_action/emergencies/tsunami.html.

Pape, Robert A. "The Strategic Logic of Suicide Terrorism." *American Political Science Review* 97 (2003): 343–361.

Parker, Geoffrey. *The Military Revolution.* Cambridge, UK: Cambridge University Press, 1988.

Parry, J. H. *The Spanish Seaborne Empire.* London: Hutchinson, 1966.

———. *Trade and Dominion: The European Overseas Empire in the Eighteenth Century.* London: Weidenfeld & Nicolson, 1971.

Paskins, Barrie, and Michael Dockrill. *The Ethics of War.* Minneapolis: University of Minnesota Press, 1979.

Pasquier, André. "Humanitarian Action: Is Its Legitimacy in Question?" In *Making the Voice of Humanity Heard: Essays on Humanitarian Assistance and International Humanitarian Law,* edited by Liesbeth Lijnzaad, Johanna van Sambeek, Bahia Tahzib-Lie, Corinne A A Packer, and Margriet, Princess daughter of Juliana Queen of the Netherlands, 465–472. Herndon, VA: Nijhoff, 2004.

Patel, Freny. "Manufacturers Prefer India to US in FDI Stakes." Rediff.com. http://inhome.rediff.com/money/2005/aug/16fdi.htm.

Paterson, Thomas G., and Robert J. McMahon, eds. *The Origins of the Cold War,* 3rd ed. Lexington, MA: D. C. Heath, 1991.

Paul, John. "Microfinance: Fighting World's Poverty Through Investment." Next billion.net, June 9, 2006. http://www.nextbillion.net/newsroom/2006/06/09/microfinance-fighting-worlds-poverty-through-investment.

Paul, T. V., Richard J. Harknett, and James J. Wirtz, eds. *The Absolute Weapon Revisited: Nuclear Arms and the Emerging International Order.* Ann Arbor: University of Michigan Press, 2000.

Payne, Keith B. *The Fallacies of Cold War Deterrence and a New Direction.* New York: University Press of Kentucky, 2001.

Payne, Keith B., and Colin S. Grey. *Deterrence in the Second Nuclear Age.* New York: University Press of Kentucky, 1996.

Peterson, V. Spike, and Anne Sisson Runyan. *Global Gender Issues.* Boulder, CO: Westview Press, 1993.

Petrovic, Drazen. "Ethnic Cleansing—An Attempt at Methodology." *European Journal of International Law* 5.1 (1994): 342–359.

Pew Global Attitudes Project. "Global Warming Seen as a Major Problem Around the World: Less Concern in the U.S., China, and Russia." *Pew Research Center Publications* (2009). http://pewresearch.org/pubs/1427/global-warming-major-problem-around-world-americans-less-concerned.

Pflanze, Otto. *Bismarck and Development of Germany: The Period of Unification, 1815–1871.* Princeton, NJ: Princeton University Press, 1973.

Pirages, Dennis, and Paul Runci. "Ecological Interdependence and the Spread of Infectious Disease." In *Beyond Sovereignty: Issues for a Global Agenda,* 3rd ed., edited by Maryann Cusimano Love, 233–250. Belmont, CA: Thomson Wadsworth, 2007.

Pitt, William Rivers, and Scott Ritter. *War on Iraq: What Team Bush Doesn't Want You to Know.* New York: Context, 2002.

"Plundering Politicians and Bribing Multinationals Undermine Economic Development, Says TI." Transparency International. March 25, 2004.

Polachek, Solomon W., John Robst, and Yuan-Ching Chang. "Liberalism and Interdependence: Extending the Trade-Conflict Model." *Journal of Peace Research* 36 4 (1999): 405–422.

Pollack, Kenneth M. "Next Stop Baghdad?" *Foreign Affairs* 81 (March–April 2002): 32–47.

Pollard, Sidney. *Peaceful Conquest: The Industrialization of Europe, 1760–1970.* New York: Oxford University Press, 1981.

"Poor Relations: Are Third-World Commodity Producers Condemned to Eternal Poverty?" *The Economist*, April 16, 1994, 15–25, 76.

Popkin, Samuel. *The Rational Peasant: The Political Economy of Rural Society in Vietnam.* Berkeley: University of California Press, 1979.

Population Reference Bureau. *Unsafe Abortions: Facts and Figures.* Washington, DC: Population Reference Bureau, 2006.

———. "2008 World Population Data Sheet." August 19, 2008. http://www.prb.org/Publications/Datasheets/2008/2008wpds.aspx?p=1.

Population Resource Center. "Executive Summary: The Middle East." 2004. http://www.prcdc.org/summaries/middleeast/middleeast.html.

Porter, Bernard. *The Lion's Share: A Short History of British Imperialism 1850–1970.* London: Longman, 1976.

Postel, Sandra L., and Aaron T. Wolf. "Dehydrating Conflict." *Foreign Policy* 126 (September–October 2001): 60–67.

"Poverty Rate Rises by a Third in Russia." *The Times of India*, August 28, 2009. http://timesofindia.indiatimes.com/NEWS/World/Europe/Poverty-rate-rises-by-a-third-in-Russia/articleshow/4945939.cms.

Power, Samantha. "Bystanders to Genocide." *Atlantic Monthly*, September 2001.

Prebisch, Raul. "Commercial Policy in the Underdeveloped Countries." *American Economic Review* 49 (1959): 251–273.

Putnam, Robert, with Robert Leonardi and Raffaella Y. Nanetti. *Making Democracy Work: Civic Traditions in Modern Italy.* Princeton, NJ: Princeton University Press, 1994.

Pye, Lucian. *Communications and Political Development.* Princeton, NJ: Princeton University Press, 1963.

Quiring, Steven M. "Science and Hollywood: A Discussion of the Scientific Accuracy of *An Inconvenient Truth*." *GeoJournal* 70 (2007): 1–3. http://www.springerlink.com/content/e135182138xl0412/?p=4be8836dc4ad49ca92083a09356fa72b&pi=0.

Rahman, Waliur. "Bangladesh–India Water Talks Fear." BBC News. September 19, 2005. http://news.bbc.co.uk/go/pr/fr/_/1/hi/world/south_asia/4261320.stm.

Ramet, Sabrina Petra. *Balkan Babel.* Boulder, CO: Westview, 1996.

Ramsbotham, Oliver, and Tom Woodhouse. *Humanitarian Intervention in Contemporary Conflict.* Cambridge, UK: Polity, 1996.

Ray, David. "The Dependency Model of Latin American Underdevelopment: Three Basic Fallacies." *Journal of Interamerican Studies and World Affairs* 15 (1973): 4–20.

Reimann, Kim D. "A View from the Top: International Politics, Norms and the Worldwide Growth of NGOs." *International Studies Quarterly* 50 (2006): 45–67.

The Responsibility to Protect. Ottawa, Canada: International Commission on Intervention and State Sovereignty, 2001.

Reynolds, C. G. *Command of the Sea: The History and Strategy of Maritime Powers.* New York: Morrow, 1974.

Rhodes, Richard. *The Making of the Atomic Bomb.* New York: Simon & Schuster, 1988.

Riasanovsky, Nicholas V. *A History of Russia.* 4th ed. New York: Oxford University Press, 1984.

Ricardo, David. *The Works and Correspondence of David Ricardo,* edited by Piero Sraffa. Cambridge, UK: University Press for the Royal Economic Society, 1951.

Ricks, Thomas E. *Fiasco: The American Military Adventure in Iraq.* New York: Penguin, 2007.

Rigby, Andrew. *Justice and Reconciliation: After the Violence.* London: Lynne Rienner, 2001.

Rioux, Jean-Pierre. *The Fourth Republic, 1944–1958.* Translated by Godfrey Rogers. Cambridge, UK: Cambridge University Press, 1989.

"River Ganges." The Water Page. 2000–2001. http://www.africanwater.org/ganges.htm.

Robinson, Joan. "Trade in Primary Commodities." In *International Political Economy: Perspectives on Global Power and Wealth,* 2nd ed., edited by Jeffry A. Frieden and David Lake, 376–385. New York: St. Martin's, 1991.

Robinson, Ronald. "The Non-European Foundations of European Imperialism: Sketch for a Theory of Collaboration." In *Studies in the Theory of Imperialism,* edited by E. R. J. Owen and R. Sutcliffe, 117–140. London: Longman, 1972.

———, and John Gallagher. "The Imperialism of Free Trade." *The Economic History Review* (New series) 6 (1953): 1–15.

Rodrik, Dani. *Has Globalization Gone Too Far?* New York, Institute for International Economics, 1997.

Rogoff, Kenneth. "The IMF Strikes Back." *Foreign Policy* 134 (January/February 2003): 38–46.

"Role of Microcredit in the Eradication of Poverty." Secretary General's Report, A/53/223, August 10, 1998. http://www.un.org/documents/ga/docs/53/plenary/a53-223.htm.

"Romanian Mine Re-opens after Environmental Disaster." BBC News. June 14, 2000. http://news.bbc.co.uk/1/hi/world/europe/790547.stm

Rose, Gideon. "Neoclassical Realism and Theories of Foreign Policy." *World Politics* 51 (1998): 144–172.

Rosecrance, Richard N. *The Rise of the Trading State: Commerce and Conquest in the Modern World.* New York: Basic Books, 1986.

Rostow, Dankwort. *A World of Nations: Problems of Political Modernization.* Washington, DC: Brookings, 1967.

Rostow, W. W. *Stages of Economic Growth: A Non-Communist Manifesto.* Cambridge, UK: Cambridge University Press, 1960.

Rothstein, Robert L. *After the Peace: Resistance and Reconciliation.* Boulder, CO: Lynne Rienner, 1999.

Roudi-Fahimi, Farzaneh, Liz Creel, and Roger-Mark De Souza. *Finding the Balance: Population and Water Scarcity in the Middle East and North Africa.* Washington, DC: Population Reference Bureau, 2002. http://wwww.prb.org/pdf/FindingTheBalance_Eng.pdf.

Roudi-Fahimi, Farzaneh, and Mary Mederios Kent. "Challenges and Opportunities—The Population of the Middle East and North Africa." Population Reference Bureau. 2007. http://www.prb.org/Publications/PopulationBulletins/2007/ChallengesOpportunitiesinMENA.aspx.

Roul, Avilash. "Beyond Tradition: Securitization of Climate Change." Society for the Study of Peace and Conflict. May 1, 2007. http://sspconline.org/article_details.asp?artid=art124.

Rubin, Andrew. "We Are No Longer Able to See the Sun Set." *Al-Ahram.* July 7, 2005. http://www.globalpolicy.org/intljustice/icj/2005/0707israel.htm.

Rude, George. *Revolutionary Europe 1783–1815.* London: Collins, 1964.

Ruggie, John Gerard. "International Regimes, Transactions, and Change: Embedded Liberalism and the Postwar Economic Order." *International Organization* 36 (1982): 379–415.

———. "What Makes the World Hang Together? Neo-Utilitarianism and the Social Constructivist Challenge." *International Organization* 52 (1998): 855–885.

Russian News and Information Agency NOVOSTI, January 7, 2005. http://en.rian.ru/society/20050701/40827814.html.

Sachs, Jeffrey. "Proposals for Reform of the Global Financial Architecture." Paper prepared for the United Nations Development Programme Meeting on Reform of the Global Financial Architecture, New York, December 8, 1998. http://www.undp.org/rblac/documents/poverty/archit/harvard.pdf.

Sachs, Jeffrey, Aaron Tornell, and Andres Velasco. "The Collapse of the Mexican Peso: What Have We Learned?" Paper presented at National Bureau of Economic Research, Project on Exchange Rate Crises in Emerging Market Countries, *Currency Crises: Lessons from Mexico* conference, Cambridge, MA, May 6, 1999.

Sadik, Nafis. "The 1990s: The Decade of Decision." *Populi* 17 (1990): 4–22.

Sagan, Scott D., and Kenneth N. Waltz. *The Spread of Nuclear Weapons: A Debate Renewed.* New York: Norton, 2003.

Samuelson, Paul. "Illogic of Neo-Marxist Doctrine of Unequal Exchange." In *Inflation, Trade, and Taxes,* edited by David Belsey et al., 96–107. Columbus: Ohio State University Press, 1976.

Sanger, David E. "Dollar's Slide Adding to Tensions U.S. Faces Abroad." *The New York Times,* January 25, 2005.

Schelling, Thomas C. "The Retarded Science of International Strategy." *Midwest Journal of Political Science* 4 (May 1960): 107–137.

Scholte, Jan Aart. *Globalization: A Critical Introduction.* New York: St. Martin's Press, 2000.

Schwartau, Winn. *Information Warfare: Chaos on the Electronic Superhighway,* 3rd ed. New York: Thunders' Mouth Press, 1996.

Schwartzstein, Stuart J. D., ed. "The Information Revolution and National Security," *Significant Issues Series,* Vol. 18. Washington, DC: Center for Strategic and International Studies, 1997.

ScienceDaily. "Fossil Fuel Carbon Dioxide Emissions Up by 29 Percent Since 2000." November 17, 2009. http://www.sciencedaily.com/releases/2009/11/091117133504.htm.

"Scientific Facts on Forests." *Green Facts: Facts on Health and the Environment.* March 7, 2007. http://www.greenfacts.org/en/forests/index.htm#2.

Semmel, Bernard. *The Rise of Free Trade Imperialism.* Cambridge, UK: Cambridge University Press, 1970.

Schelling, Thomas C. "The Retarded Science of International Strategy." *Midwest Journal of Political Science* 4 (1960): 107–137.

Scheuer, Michael. *Through Our Enemies' Eyes: Osama bin Laden, Radical Islam, and the Future of America,* revised ed. Dulles, VA: Potomac Books, 2006.

Schweller, Randall L. "Bandwagoning for Profit: Bringing the Revisionist State Back In." *International Security* 19 (1994): 72–107.

——. *Deadly Imbalances: Tripolarity and Hitler's Strategy of World Conquest.* New York: Columbia University Press, 1998.

Seybolt, Taylor B. "Major Armed Conflicts." Chapter summary from the *SIPRI Yearbook 2001: Armaments, Disarmament, and International Security.* Oxford: Oxford University Press, 2001.

Sharma, D. P. *Countering Terrorism.* New Delhi: Lancers, 1992.

Sharp, Sonja. "Cell Phones Could Send Real-Time Safety Data." *The Daily Californian,* September 21, 2005. http://www.dailycal.org/sharticle.php?id=19586.

Shaw, Paul. "Population Growth: Is It Ruining the Environment?" *Populi* 16, (1989): 20–29.

Sherwin, Martin J. *A World Destroyed: The Atomic Bomb and the Grand Alliance.* New York: Random House, 1987.

Shriver, Donald W., Jr. "The Long Road to Reconciliation: Some Moral Stepping-Stones." In *After the Peace: Resistance and Reconciliation,* edited by Robert L. Rothstein, 207–222. Boulder, CO: Lynne Rienner, 1999.

Sieghart, Paul. *The International Law of Human Rights.* Oxford, UK: Clarendon, 1983.

Singer, J. David. "The Level-of-Analysis Problem in International Relations." *World Politics* 14 (1961): 77–92.

Small, Melvin, and David J. Singer. "The War Proneness of Democratic Regimes, 1816–1965." *Jerusalem Journal of International Relations* 1 (1976): 50–69.

Smil, Vaclav. "The Energy Question, Again." *Current History* 99 (2000): 408–12.

Smith, Dan. *The State of War and Peace Atlas,* 2nd ed. New York: Penguin, 1997.

Smith, David Bullard. "The Egyptian Military Elite: An Operational Code." Master's thesis, Naval Postgraduate School, 1977.

Smith, Tony. "The Underdevelopment of the Development Literature: The Case of Dependency Theory." *World Politics* 32 (1979): 247–288.

Snyder, Glenn H. *Deterrence and Defense: Toward a Theory of National Security.* Princeton, NJ: Princeton University Press, 1961.

Somalia, Operation Restore Hope: A Preliminary Assessment. London: African Rights, 1993.

Spero, Joan E. *The Politics of International Economic Relations.* New York: St. Martin's, 1985.

———. *The Politics of International Economic Relations,* 4th ed. New York: St. Martin's, 1990.

Srivastava, Anupam, and Seema Gahlaut. "Curbing Proliferation from Emerging Suppliers: Export Controls in India and Pakistan." *Arms Control Today* 33 (September 2003): 12–16.

Starr, Joyce R. "Water Wars." *Foreign Policy* 82 (1991): 17–36.

"Statement of John R. Bolton." In *Taking Sides: Clashing Views on Controversial Issues in World Politics,* 11th ed., edited by John T. Rourke, 295–301. Guilford, CT: McGraw-Hill/Dushkin, 2004.

Steele, Ian K. *The English Atlantic, 1675–1740.* New York: Oxford University Press, 1986.

Steinberg, Richard H., and Jonathan M. Zasloff. "Power and International Law." *The American Journal of International Law* 100 (2006): 64–87.

Stern, Jessica. *Terror in the Name of God: Why Religious Militants Kill.* New York: Harper Collins Publishers, 2003.

———. *The Ultimate Terrorist.* Cambridge, MA: Harvard University Press, 1999.

Stokesbury, James L. *A Short History of World War I.* New York: Morrow, 1981.

Strange, Susan. "Cave! Hic Dragones: A Critique of Regime Analysis." In *International Regimes,* edited by S. Krasner, 337–35. Ithaca, NY: Cornell University Press, 1983.

"Suddenly, the Old World Looks Younger." *The Economist,* June 14, 2007. http://www.economist.com/world/europe/displaystory.cfm?story_id=9334869.

Summy, Ralph, and Michael E. Salla, eds. *Why the Cold War Ended: A Range of Interpretations.* Westport, CT: Greenwood, 1995.

Sunkel, Osvaldo, and Pedro Paz. *El Subdesarrollo Latinoamericano y la Teoria del Desarollo.* Mexico City: Siglo Veintiuno, 1970.

Svoboda, Elizabeth. "The Global Warming Fix Stinks." *Wired.* August 21, 2006. http://www.wired.com/science/discoveries/news/2006/08/71613.

Swain, Ashok. "Displacing the Conflict: Environmental Destruction in Bangladesh and Ethnic Conflict in India." *Journal of Peace Research* 33 (1996): 189–204.

Talbott, Strobe. *The Russians and Reagan.* New York: Vintage, 1984.

Tanca, Antonia. *Foreign Armed Intervention in Internal Conflict.* Dordrecht, The Netherlands: Martinus Nijhoff, 1993.

Taylor, A. J. P. *The Struggle for Mastery in Europe.* (Oxford: Clarion, 1957).

Thakur, Ramesh, and Luk Van Langenhove. "Enhancing Global Governance Through Regional Integration." *Global Governance* 12 (2006): 233–241.

Thompson, J. M. *Napoleon Bonaparte: His Rise and Fall.* Cambridge, MA: Blackwell, 1990.

Tickner, Judith Ann. *Gender in International Relations: Feminist Perspectives on Achieving Global Security.* New York: Columbia University Press, 1993.

"To Give or Forgive." *The Economist,* June 16, 2005.

"Tobin Tax Motion Passes Canada's Parliament." http://www.ceedweb.org/iirp/canadames.htm.

Transparency International. "Plundering Politicians and Bribing Multinationals Undermine Economic Development, Says TI." Press release. Transparency International, March 25, 2004.

Tucker, Jonathan B., ed. *Toxic Terror: Assessing Terrorist Use of Chemical and Biological Weapons.* Cambridge, MA: MIT Press, 2000.

Udombana, Nsongurua J. "When Neutrality Is a Sin: The Darfur Crisis and the Crisis of Humanitarian Intervention in Sudan." *Human Rights Quarterly* 27 (2005): 1149–1199.

Ul-Haq, Mahbub. "The New Deal." *The Internationalist,* December 1994.

UNA-USA. "On the Lines: The UN Role in Preventing and Containing Conflict." United Nations Association of United States of America News, 1985.

———. "Status of US Financial Obligations to the United Nations." June 2002. http://www.globalpolicy.org/finance/unitedstates/2002/06status.htm.

UNAIDS. "Asia." 2009. http://www.unaids.org/en/CountryResponses/Regions/Asia.asp.
———. "Cosponsors." http://www.unaids.org/en/AboutUNAIDS/Cosponsors_about/default.asp.
———. "Eastern Europe and Central Asia." 2009. http://www.unaids.org/en/CountryResponses/Regions/EasternEuropeAndCentralAsia.asp.
———. "Global Facts and Figures: The Global AIDS Epidemic." 2009. http://data.unaids.org/pub/Factsheet/2009/20091124_FS_global_en.pdf.
———. "Tracking, Monitoring and Evaluation." http://www.unaids.org/en/Coordination/FocusAreas/track-monitor-evaluate.asp.
———. "UNAIDS 10-Year Anniversary." 2006. http://data.unaids.org/pub/FactSheet/2006/20060428_FS_UNAIDS10Years_en.pdf.
UNICEF. "Billions Still Lack Clean Water and Sanitation." *The Progress of Nations 2000.* http://www.unicef.org/pon00/billions.htm.
———. "Expanding Immunization Coverage." 2010. http://www.unicef.org/immunization/index_coverage.html.
Union of Concerned Scientists. "Each Country's Share of CO2 Emissions." May 13, 2009. http://www.ucsusa.org/global_warming/science_and_impacts/science/each-countrys-share-of-co2.html.
Union of International Associations. *Yearbook of International Organizations 2009/2010,* 46th ed. Munich: K. G. Saur Verlag, 2009. http://www.uia.be/ybvolall.
United Kingdom Government. "Terrorism Act 2000." http://www.opsi.gov.uk/Acts/acts2000/20000011.htm.
United Nations. "Africa and the Millennium Development Goals: 2007 Update." June 2007. http://www.un.org/millenniumgoals/docs/MDGafrica07.pdf.
———. "Background Information." http://www.un.org/ecosoc/about/.
———. "Biography of Kofi A. Annan" (2000–2002). http://www.un.org/News/ossg/sg/pages/sg_biography.html.
———. *The Blue Helmets: A Review of United Nations Peacekeeping,* 2nd ed. New York: United Nations, 1997.
———. "Convention on Migrant Worker Rights Adopted." *UN Chronicle* 28(1991): 80–81.
———. Department of Economic and Social Affairs, Population Division. "2010 Update for the MDG Database: Contraceptive Prevalence (POP/DB/CP/A/MDG2010)." 2010.
———. Department of Peacekeeping Operations. "United Nations Peacekeeping Fact Sheet." March 2010.
———. "Fatalities by Year: Up to June 2007." July 5, 2007. http://www.un.org/Depts/dpko/fatalities/StatsBy Year%201.pdf.
———. "General Assembly Message to World: Reduce Drug Demand." *UN Chronicle* 27 (1990): 53–60.
———. "General Assembly President Proposes Three options on Security Council reform." UN News Service. December 13, 2006. http://www.un.org/apps/news/story.asp?NewsID=20970&Cr=Security&CR1=Council#.
———. "Global Food Security Crisis. "Background." 2009. http://www.un-foodsecurity.org/background.
———. "International Day of Families 2010: 'The Impact of Migration on Families Around the World.'" May 15, 2010. http://www.un.org/esa/socdev/family/idf/2010/backgroundnote.pdf.
———. "Key Conference Outcomes on Population." http://www.un.org/esa/devagenda/population.html.
———. "Majority of World's Couples Are Using Contraception." May 2002. http://www.un.org/esa/population/publications/contraceptive2001/Wall Chart_CP2001_pressreleaseUN.html.
———. "Millennium Indicators." http://millenniumindicators.un.org/unsd/mifre/mi_series_results.asp?rowID=749&FID=r15&cgID=.
———. "Monthly Summary of Military and Police Contribution to United Nations Operations." April 2010. http://www.un.org/Depts/dpko/dpki/contributors/index.htm.

———. "New Peacebuilding Fund Reflects Commitment to Sustained Engagement in Countries Emerging from Conflict, says Secretary-General at Fund's Launch." General Assembly PBC/4. October 11, 2006. http://www.un.org/News/Press/docs/2006/pbc4.doc.htm.

———. "Progress Towards Development Targets is Mixed, UN Finds." The Millennium Development Goals Report 2007. July 2007. http://www.un.org/millenniumgoals/pdf/mdg2007-globalpr.pdf.

———. "Reform at the United Nations: UN Reform Highlights Since 1997." (2006). http://www.un.org/reform/highlights/shtml.

———. "Report to the President of the General Assembly on the Consultations Regarding Revitalizing the Role and Authority of the General Assembly." August 2, 2007. http://www.un.org/ga/president/61/follow-up/revitalization/Facilitators-Report-GARev.pdf.

———. "Rome Statute of the International Criminal Court: Overview." *United Nations*, 1998–1999. http://www.un.org/law/icc/general/overview.htm.

———. "Secretariat." 2004. http://www.un.org/documents/st.htm.

———. "Secretary-General Addresses International Peace Academy Seminar on 'The Responsibility to Protect.'" February 2, 2002. http://www.un.org/News/Press/docs/2002/sgsm8125.doc.htm.

———. *UN Chronicle*, June 1993.

———. "UN Diplomatic Conference Concludes in Rome with Decision to Establish Permanent International Criminal Court." UN press release L/ROM/22. July 1998. http://www.un.org/icc/pressrel/lrom22.htm.

———. "United Nations Population Fund: Report on Contributions by Member States and Others to UNFPA and Revenue Projections for 2010 and Future Years." April 30, 2010.

———. "UN Reform Dossier: 1997–2000." http://www.un.org/reform/dossier.htm.

———. "Violence Against Women." *UN Chronicle*, June 1995.

———. "Water: It's Attitude that Counts." Statement from the World Water Assessment Programme on the occasion of World Water Day. March 22, 2005. http://www.unesco.org/water/wwap/news/wwap_wwd_05.shtml.

———. "World Population Prospects: The 2008 Revision Population Database (births per year both sexes combined)." March 11, 2009. http://esa.un.org/unpp/p2k0data.asp.

———. "World Population Prospects: The 2008 Revision Population Database." March 11, 2009. http://esa.un.org/unpp/p2k0data.asp.

———. *World Urbanization Prospects: the 2007 Revision (Executive Summary)*. February 26, 2008. http://www.un.org/esa/population/publications/wup2007/2007WUP_ExecSum_web.pdf.

United Nations Children's Fund. *The State of the World's Children 2009*. December 2008.

United Nations Development Fund for Women (UNIFEM). "Women Migrant Workers." 2006. http://www.unifem.org/gender_issues/women_poverty_economics/women_migrant_workers.php.

United Nations Development Programme. *Human Development Report 2006—Beyond Scarcity: Power, Poverty and the Global Water Crisis*. New York: United Nations Development Programme, 2006.

United Nations Educational, Scientific and Cultural Organization (UNESCO). "Facts and Figures extracted from the 2nd United Nations World Water Development Report. 2006. http://www.unesco.org/water/wwap/wwdr2/facts_figures/index.shtml.

United Nations Environment Programme. "China Closes Ozone Depleting Chemical Plants: A Contribution to Avert a Global Health Catastrophe." July 1, 2007. http://www.unep.org/Documents.Multilingual/Default.Print.asp?DocumentID=514&ArticleID=5624&l=en.

———. "Key Facts About Cities: Issues for the Urban Millennium." 2005. http://www.unep.org/wed/2005/english/Information_Material/facts.asp.

———. "Workmanlike Plan Agreed to Fight Against Poverty and Fight for Sustainable Development Says Klaus Toepfer." September 4, 2002. http://www.unep.org/Documents.Multilingual/Default.asp?DocumentID=264&ArticleID=3120.

United Nations Environment Programme. "World Summit on Sustainable Development." http://www.rrcap.unep.org/wssd/Political%20declaration_4%20Sep%2002.pdf.

United Nations General Assembly. "Implementing the Responsibility to Protect: Report of the Secretary-General," A/63/677. January 12, 2009.

United Nations High Commissioner for Refugees (UNHCR). "A New Beginning in a Third Country." http://www.unhcr.org/pages/4a16b1676.html.

———. "Chad-Darfur Emergency." http://www.unhcr.org/cgi-bin/texis/vtx-chad?page=intro.

———. "Convention on Protection of Rights of Migrant Workers to Enter into Force Next July." March 19, 2003. http://www.unhchr.ch/huricane/huricane.nsf/view01/B87E9E85C7147498C1256CEF00385E50?opendocument.

———. "Global Appeal 2007: Mission Statement." http://www.unhcr.org/publ/PUBL/4565a5742.pdf.

———. "Refugees by Numbers (2004 Edition)." 2004. http://www.unhcr.ch/cgi-bin/texis/vtx/basics.

———. "Refugees by Numbers (2006 Edition)." September 1, 2006. http://www.unhcr.org/basics/BASICS/3b028097c.html.

———. "UNHCR Global Appeal 2007: Mission Statement." http://www.unhcr.org/pub/PUBL/4565a5742.pdf.

———. *2008 Global Trends: Refugees, Asylum-seekers, Returnees, Internally Displaced and Stateless Persons.* June 16, 2009.

———. "2010 UNHCR Country Operations Profile—Chad." 2010. http://www.unhcr.org/cgi-bin/texis/vtx/page?page=49e45c226.

———. "Returnees: Going Back Home." 2010. http://www.unhcr.org/pages/49c3646c1ca.html.

United Nations Human Development Programme. "International Cooperation at a Crossroads: Aid, Trade, and Security in an Unequal World." In *Human Development Report 2005.* New York: United Nations Development Programme, 2005. http://hdr.undp.org/reports/global/2005/.

United Nations Millennium Development Goals. http://www.un.org/millenniumgoals/.

United Nations Office on Drugs and Crime. *World Drug Report.* http://www.unodc.org/documents/wdr/WDR_2009/Executive_summary_LO-RES.pdf.

United Nations Population Division. "Future World Population Growth to Be Concentrated in Urban Areas of the World According to New Report Issued by United Nations Population Division." 2002. http://www.un.org/esa/population/publications/wup2001/WUP2001-pressrelease.pdf.

———. "Levels and Trends of Contraceptive Use as Assessed in 1998: Key Findings." May 2002. www.un.org/esa/population/pubsarchive/contraceptives1998/contraceptives1998.htm.

———. "Number of World's Migrants Reaches 175 Million Mark." UN press release POP/844. 2002. http://www.un.org/esa/population/publications/ittmig2002/press-release-eng.htm.

———. "World Urbanization Prospects: The 2001 Revision." 2002. http://www.un.org/esa/population/publications/wup2001/WUP2001report.htm.

United Nations Population Fund. "Contraceptives Save Lives." http://www.unfpa.org/webdav/site/global/shared/safemotherhood/docs/contraceptives_factsheet_en.pdf. 2009.

———. "The Day of 6 Billion—Fast Facts." October 12, 1999. http://www.unfpa.org/6billion/facts.htm.

———. "Family Planning Essentials." http://www.unfpa.org/supplies/family.htm.

———. "International Conference on Population and Development." September 1994. http://www.unfpa.org/icpd/icpd.htm.

———. "Investing in Sexual and Reproductive Health Key to Global Health Security, UNFPA Head Tells World Health Assembly." May 15, 2007. http://www.unfpa.org/news/news.cfm?ID=976&Language=1.

———. "Make Women and Young People Your Top Priority, UNFPA Chief Urges World Leaders." September 14, 2005. http://www.unfpa.org/news/news.cfm?ID=677.

———. "The Need for Steady Funding." http://www.unfpa.org/supplies/funding.htm.

———. "New Population Projections Underline Urgency of Family Planning Needs in Developing Nations." March 13, 2007. http://www.unfpa.org/.

———. "New Push to Promote Women's Health in Africa: Health Ministers Adopt Measures to Curb Maternal Death." September 22, 2006. http://www.unfpa.org/news/news.cfm?ID=8702language=1.

———. "The Power of Two Women, One Idea and 34 Million Friends." http://www.unfpa.org/support/friends/34million.htm.

———. "Quotes on Human Rights." http://www.unfpa.org/rights/quotes.htm.

———. "Record Number of Countries Contribute Record Amount to UNFPA in 2006." January 15, 2007. http://www.unfpa.org/news/news.cfm?ID=925.

———. "Reproductive Health Commodity Security—Challenges." October 19, 2006. http://www.unfpa.org/news/news.cfm?ID=887.

———. "State of World Population 2004: The Cairo Consensus at Ten: Population, Reproductive Health and the Global Effort to End Poverty." 2004. http://www.unfpa.org/swp/2004/pdf/en_swp04.pdf.

———. "State of World Population 2004." Press summary. 2004. http://www.unfpa.org/swp/2004/pdf/summary.pdf.

———. "State of World Population 2006: A Passage to Hope: Women and International Migration." 2006. http://www.unfpa.org/swp/2006/english/chapter_1/index.html.

———. "State of World Population 2006." Press summary. 2006. http://www.unfpa.org/swp/2006/pdf/press-summary-en.pdf.

———. "State of World Population 2007: Unleashing the Potential of Urban Growth." June 27, 2007. http://www.unfpa.org/swp/swpmain.html.

———. "UNFPA's Contribution to Meeting the MDGs: Findings from the United Nations Millennium Project." September 2005. http://www.unfpa.org/icpd/gender.htm.

———. "UNFPA-2008 Annual Report" (2008). http://www.unfpa.org/about/report/2008/en/ch4.html.

———. "UNFPA Welcomes Restoration of U.S. Funding." January 23, 2009. http://www.unfpa.org/public/site/global/lang/en/pid/1562.

———. "World Population to Exceed 9 Billion by 2050: Developing Countries to Add 2.3 Billion Inhabitants with 1.1 Billion Aged over 60 and 1.2 Billion of Working Age." March 11, 2009.

United Nations Relief and Work Agency (UNRWA). "About UNRWA: Frequently Asked Questions." 2010. http://www.unrwa.org/etemplate.php?id=87.

———. "Finances." http:/www.un.org/unrwa/finances/index.html.

———. "U.S. Intends to Donate $40 Million to UNFWA's Emergency Appeal." June 21, 2007. http://www.un.org/unrwa/news/releases/pr-2007/jer_21Jun07.pdf.

United States Air Force. "New World Vistas." In *Air and Space Power for the 21st Century, Summary Findings Volume*. December 15, 1995. http://www.fas.org/spp/military/docops/usaf/vistas/vistas.html.

"Urban Population (Percent of Total Population Living in Urban Areas) 2009." U.S. Global Health Policy. http://www.globalhealthfacts.org/topic.jsp?i=85&srt=1#table.

"Urbanization and Global Change." University of Michigan. April 3, 2005. http://www.globalchange.umich.edu/globalchange2/current/lectures/urban_gc/.

Urdal, Henrik. "A Clash of Generations? Youth Bulges and Political Violence." *International Studies Quarterly* 50 (2006): 607–629.

Urquhart, Gerald, Walter Chomentowski, David Skole, and Chris Barber. "Tropical Deforestation." http://www.earthobservatory.nasa.gov/Library/Deforestation.

U.S. Army's Area Handbook for Colombia. Washington, DC: American University, 1961.

U.S. Committee for Refugees and Immigrants. *Refugee Reports*. December 31, 1992.

———. "Country Reports: United States 2006." http://www.refugees.org/countryreports.aspx?subm=&ssm=&cid=1607.

———. "World Refugee Survey 2004: Returns and Expulsions." http://www.refugees.org/data/wrs/04/pdf/involuntary.pdf.

———. "World Refugee Survey 2009: Best and Worst Places for Refugees." http://www.refugees.org/FTP/WRS09PDFS/BestandWorst.pdf.

U.S. Council on Environmental Quality and Department of State. *The Global 2000 Report to the President*, vol. 2. Washington, DC: U.S. Council on Environmental Quality and Department of State, 2000.

U.S. Department of Commerce, Bureau of the Census. "An Aging World: 2001." November 2001. http://www.census.gov/prod/2001pubs/p95-01-1.pdf.

———. "Global Population at a Glance: 2002 and Beyond." March 2004. http://www.census.gov/ipc/prod/wp02/wp02-1.pdf.

———. "Total Midyear Population for the World: 1950–2050." http://www.census.gov/ipc/www/idb/worldpop.html.

———. "World Population Profile 1996." http://www.census.gov/ipc/www/wp96.html.

———. "World Population Profile: 1998—Highlights." http://www.census.gov/ipc/www/wp98001.html.

U.S. Department of Defense, Office of the Secretary of Defense. *Proliferation: Threat and Response*. Washington, DC: DOD, 2001.

U.S. Department of Energy, Energy Information Administration. *Annual Energy Outlook 2003 with Projections to 2025*, Report #DOE/EIA-0383. Washington, DC: U.S. Department of Energy, Energy Information Administration, 2003. http://www.eia.doe.gov/oiaf/aeo/index.html.

———. "Electricity—A Secondary Energy Source." Washington, DC: U.S. Department of Energy, Energy Information Administration, 2006. http://www.eia.doe.gov/kids/energyfacts/sources/electricity.html.

———. "International Energy Annual (2000–2004), International Petroleum Monthly (2005–2006)." http://www.eia.doe.gov/emeu/cabs/topworldtables1_2.htm.

———. *International Energy Outlook 2002: Coal*. Report #DOE/EIA-0484. Washington, DC: U.S. Department of Energy, Energy Information Administration, 2002. http://www.eia.doe.gov/oiaf/archive/ieo02/index.html.

———. *International Energy Outlook 2007*. Washington, DC: U.S. Department of Energy, Energy Information Administration, 2007. http://www.ei.doe.gov/oiaf/ieo/index.html.

———. *International Energy Outlook 2007: Natural Gas*. Washington, DC: U.S. Department of Energy, Energy Information Administration, 2007. http://www.eia.doe.gov/oiaf/ieo/pdf/nat_gas.pdf.

———. *International Energy Outlook 2009: Chapter 1—World Energy Demand and Economic Outlook*. Washington, DC: Energy Information Administration, 2009. http://www.eia.doe.gov/oiaf/archive/ieo09/world.html.

———. *International Energy Outlook 2009: Coal*. Washington, DC: U.S. Department of Energy, Energy Information Administration, 2007. http://www.eia.doe.gov/oiaf/archive/ieo09/coal.html.

———. *International Energy Outlook 2009—Electricity*. Washington, DC: U.S. Department of Energy, Energy Information Administration, May 27, 2009. http://www.eia.doe.gov/oiaf/archive/ieo09/electricity.html.

———. *International Energy Outlook 2009: Chapter 8—Energy-Related Carbon Dioxide Emissions*. Washington, DC: U.S. Department of Energy, Energy Information Administration, May 27, 2009. http://www.eia.doe.gov/oiaf/archive/ieo09/emissions.html.

———. "International Energy Outlook 2010: Highlights." http://www.eia.doe.gov/oiaf/ieo/highlights.html.

———. "Short-Term Energy Outlook." May 11, 2010. http://www.eia.doe.gov/emeu/steo/pub/.

———. *South Korea: Environmental Issues*. Washington, DC: U.S. Department of Energy, Environmental Information Administration, 2003. http://www.eia.gov/emeu/cabs/skoren.html.

———. "Table 2.1—World Oil Balance, 2005–2009." *International Petroleum Monthly* (April 2010). May 11, 2010. http://www.eia.doe.gov/emeu/ipsr/t21.xls.

———. "Table 2.4, World Oil Demand, 1998–2002." *International Petroleum Monthly* (December 2002). http://www.eia.doe.gov/emeu/ipsr/t24.xls.

———. "Table 3. International Petroleum Supply and Demand: Base Case." July 2007. http://www.eia.doe.gov/emeu/steo/pub/3tab.html.

———. "Table 4.2, OPEC Crude Oil Production (Excluding Lease Condensate), 1980–2006." *International Petroleum Monthly* (June 2007). http://www.eia.doe.gov/emeu/ipsr/supply.html.

———. "Table A4. World Oil Consumption by Region, Reference Case, 1990–2030." *International Energy Outlook 2006.* http://www.eia.doe.gov/oaif/ieo/pdf/ieoreftab_4.pdf.

———. "Table A6. World Coal Consumption by Region, Reference Case, 1990–2030." *International Energy Outlook 2006.* http://www.eia.doe.gov/emeu/international/coalconsumption.html.

———. "Table E1, World Primary Energy Consumption (Btu), 1992–2001." 2003. http://www.eia.doe.gov/ emeu/iea/tablee1.html.

———. "World Carbon Dioxide Emissions from the Consumption and Flaring of Fossil Fuels, 1992–2001." *International Energy Annual 2001.* http://www.eia.doe.gov/emeu/iea/tablehI.html.

U.S. Department of State. "America's Principles and Multilateral Commitment." August 2003. http://usinfo.state.gov/products/pubs/unesco/.

———. "Foreign Terrorist Organizations." Office of the Coordinator of Counterterrorism, January 19, 2010, http://www.state.gov/s/ct/rls/other/des/123085.htm.

———. "Patterns of Global Terrorism, 2003." http://www.state.gov/s/ct/rls/crt/2003/cl2153.htm.

———. "State Sponsors of Terrorism." Office of the Coordinator of Counterterrorism. http://www.state.gov/s/ct/c14151.htm

———. "United States Rejoins UNESCO: President Bush Announced This September 12." September 12, 2002. http://usinfo.state.gov.

———. "U.S. Supports Japan as Permanent Member of U.N. Security Council." September 13, 2006. http://usinfo.state.gov/xarchives/display.html? p=washfile-english&y=2006&m=September&x=20060913180611esnamfuak. 3.509158e-02.

U.S. Drug Enforcement Administration. "Drug Trafficking in the United States." DEA Briefs & Background. http://www.usdoj.gov/dea/concern/drug_traffickingp.html.

U.S. Treasury. "Major Foreign Holders of Treasury Securities, 2007." United States Treasury. http://www.treas.gov/tic/mfh.txt.

Van Evera, Stephen. "The Cult of the Offensive and the Origins of the First World War." *International Security* 9 (1984): 58–107.

Voice of America. "Another Cholera Death Reported in Midlands, Zimbabwe." January 11, 2010. http://www1.voanews.com/zimbabwe/news/health/Zimbabwe-Another-Cholera-Death-Reported-in-Midlands-11Jan10-81153597.html.

Volgy, Thomas J., Elizabeth Fausett, Keith Grant, and Stuart Rodgers. "Ergo FIGO: Identifying Formal Intergovernmental Organizations." Working Paper Series in International Politics. Department of Political Science, University of Arizona (December 2006).

Von Clauswitz, Carl. *On War*, rev. ed. Translated by Michael Howard and Peter Paret. Princeton, NJ: Princeton University Press, 1984.

Van Creveld, Martin. *Technology and War from 2000 BC to the Present*, rev. ed. New York: Free Press, 1991.

———. *The Transformation of War.* New York: Free Press, 1991.

Waever, Ole. "All Dressed Up and Nowhere to Go? Securitization of Climate Change." Paper presented at the annual meeting of the International Studies Association's 50th annual convention, "Exploring the Past, Anticipating the Future," New York, NY. February15, 2009. http://www.allacademic.com/meta/p311899_index.html.

Wainaina, Binyavanga. "Generation Kenya." *Vanity Fair*, July 2007. http://www.vanityfair.com/culture/features/2007/07/wainaina200707?currentPage=1.

Walker, Martin. *The Cold War: A History.* New York: Holt, 1995.

Walker, Stephen G. "The Evolution of Operational Code Analysis." *Political Psychology* 11 (1990): 403–418.

Wallerstein, Immanuel. *The Modern World-System, Part I: Capitalist Agriculture and the Origins of the European World-Economy in the Sixteenth Century.* Orlando, FL: Academic, 1974.

———. *The Modern World-System: Capitalist Agriculture and the Origins of the European World-Economy in the Sixteenth Century.* New York: Academic, 1976.

———. "The Rise and Future Demise of World Systems Analysis." Paper delivered at the 91st annual meeting of the American Sociological Association, New York, August 16, 1996. http://fbc.binghamton.edu/iwwsa-r&.htm.

Waltz, Kenneth N. *Man, the State, and War.* New York: Columbia University Press, 2001.

———. *Theory of International Politics.* Cambridge, UK: McGraw-Hill, 1979.

Walzer, Michael. *Just and Unjust Wars: A Moral Argument with Historical Illustrations.* New York: Basic Books, 1977.

"War." Mongabay.com. http://rainforests.mongabay.com/0810.htm.

Ward, Chris. "Environmental Degradation and Political Instability: Lessons from Sudan." World Resources Institute. July 6, 2007. http://www.earthtrends.wri.org/updates/node/217.

"Water Facts." Water.org. http://water.org/learn-about-the-water-crisis/facts/.

Water Partners International. "Thirsty Planet: Coping with Water Scarcity." March 21, 2007. http://water.org/news/releases/PDF/NR_2007_03_21_WWD.pdf.

Web Genocide Documentation Centre. "Charter of the International Military Tribunal." http://www.ess.uwe.ac.uk/documents/chtrimt.htm.

———. "Resolution on German War Crimes by Representatives of Nine Occupied Countries, January 12, 1942." http://www.ess.uwe.ac.uk/genocide/trials.htm.

Weish, James. "The Partnership to Remember." *Time*, March 11, 1991.

Weiss, Thomas G. "Halting Genocide: Rhetoric vs. Reality." *Genocide Studies and Prevention* 2 (2007): 7–30.

Weller, Christian. "Currency Speculation: How Great a Danger?" *Dollars & Sense* 217 (May–June 1998). http://www.dollarsandsense.org/archives/1998/0598weller.html.

Wendt, Alexander. "Constructing International Politics." *International Security* 20 (1995): 71–81.

"Where to Start." *Economist*, September 7, 2006. http://www.economist.com/surveys/PrinterFriendly.cfm?story_id=7852974.

White House, G-8 Summit 2007. "Growth and Responsibility in the World Economy." June 7, 2007. http://www.whitehouse.gov/g8/2007/g8agenda.pdf.

Wiarda, Howard. "Toward a Nonethnocentric Theory of Development: Alternative Conceptions from the Third World." *Journal of Developing Areas* 17 (1983): 443–452.

Wijesiri, Lionel. "NGOs or New Gods Overseas?," *Sunday Observer* (2005). http://www.sunday-observer.lk/2005/05/08/fea29.html.

Williams, Michael C. "Words, Images, Enemies: Securitization and International Politics." International Studies Quarterly 47.4 (December 2003): 511–531.

Williams, William A. *The Tragedy of American Diplomacy*, rev. ed. New York: Delta, 1962.

———. *The Roots of the Modern American Empire.* New York: Random House, 1969.

Williamson, John. "What Washington Means by Policy Reform." In *Latin American Adjustment: How Much Has Happened?* edited by John Williamson, 7–38. Washington, DC: Institute for International Economics, 1990.

Wind, Rebecca. "Abortion and Unintended Pregnancy Decline Worldwide as Contraceptive Use Increases." Guttmacher Institute (2009), http://www.guttmacher.org/media/nr/2009/10/13/index.html.

Winik, Jay. *On the Brink: The Dramatic, Behind-the-Scenes Saga of the Reagan Era and the Men and Women Who Won the Cold War.* New York: Simon & Schuster, 1996.

Wolfstahl, Jon Brook, Cristina-Astrid Chuen, and Emily Ewell Daughtry, eds. *Nuclear Status Report: Nuclear Weapons, Fissile Material, and Export Controls in the Former Soviet Union.* Washington, DC: Carnegie Endowment for International Peace and Center for Nonproliferation Studies, 2001.

Wood, Rachel Godfrey. "Banking on Coal in the Global South?" International Institute for Environment and Development. April 28, 2010. http://www.iied.org/sustainable-markets/blog/banking-coal-global-south.

Woodruff, William. *Impact of Western Man: A Study of Europe's Role in the World Economy, 1750–1960.* New York: St. Martin's, 1967.

Woodward, Susan. *Balkan Tragedy.* Washington, DC: Brookings, 1995.

World Bank. *World Development Report 1991: The Challenge of Development.* Washington, DC: The World Bank, 1991.

World Bank Group. 2005. http://web.worldbank.org/WBSITE/EXTERNAL/PROJECTS/STRATEGIES/CDF/0,,pagePK:60447~theSitePK:140576,00.html.

———. "World Bank Group Fiscal Year Highlights, 2009."

———. "2010 Spring Meetings Endorse $86 Billion Capital Increase, Voting Reform." April 25, 2010. http://web.worldbank.org/WBSITE/EXTERNAL/NEWS/0,,contentMDK:22556192~menuPK:34457~pagePK:34370~piPK:34424~theSitePK:4607,00.html.

World Food Program. "Facts & Figures: Hunger Facts." 2007. http://www.wfp.org/aboutwfp/facts/hunger_facts.asp?section=1&sub_section=5.

———. "Fighting Hunger Worldwide." February 4, 2010. http://documents.wfp.org/stellent/groups/public/documents/communications/wfp215812.pdf.

———. "Hunger, Humanity's Oldest Enemy." 2007. http://www.wfp.org/about wfp/introduction/hunger_what.asp?section=1&sub_section=1.

———. "Overview." 2010. http://www.wfp.org/our-work.

———. "Why Does Hunger Exist?" 2007. http://www.wfp.org/aboutwfp/introduction/hunger_causes.asp?section=1&sub_section=1.

"The World Goes to Town." *The Economist,* May 3, 2007. http://www.economist.com/surveys/PrinterFriendly.cfm?story_id=9070726.

World Health Organization. "Air Quality and Health." August 2008. http://www.who.int/mediacentre/factsheets/fs313/en/index.html.

———. "Communicable Diseases and Severe Food Shortage Situations." August 25, 2005. http://www.who.int/hac/crises/ner/sitreps/CDs_severe%20 food%20shortages_FINAL_25082005.pdf.

———. "Control of Neglected Tropical Diseases." June 2010. http://www.who.int/neglected_diseases/en/.

———. "Global Immunization Data." October 2009. http://www.who.int/immunization/newsroom/GID_english.pdf.

———. "Global Outbreak Alert and Response: Report of a WHO Meeting." 2000. http://who.int/csr/resources/publications/surveillance/WHO_CDS_CSR_2000_3/en/.

———. "Initiative for Vaccine Research (IVR): Cholera." February 2009. http://www.who.int/vaccine_research/diseases/diarrhoeal/en/index3.html.

———. "MDG 4: Reduce Child Mortality." 2007. http://www.who.int/topics/millennium_development_goals/child_mortality/en/index.html.

———. "Malaria: Key Facts." 2010. http://www.who.int/mediacentre/factsheets/fs094/en/index.html.

———. "Reducing Mortality from Major Killers of Children." WHO Fact Sheet no. 178. 1998. http://www.who.int/inf-fs/en/fact178.html.

———. "State of the Art of New Vaccines Research & Development: Initiative for Vaccine Research." 2003. http://www.who.int/vaccine_research/documents/new_vaccines/en/index1.html.

———. "Statue Commemorates Smallpox Eradication." May 17, 2010. http://www.who.int/mediacentre/news/notes/2010/smallpox_20100517/en/index.html.

———. "10 Facts on Neglected Tropical Diseases." April 17, 2007. http://www.who.int/features/factfiles/neglected_tropical_diseases/en/index.html.

———. "Update 62—More Than 8000 Cases Reported Globally, Situation in Taiwan, Data on In-Flight Transmission, Report on Henan Province, China." May 22, 2003. http://www.who.int.csr/don/2003_05_22/en/print.html.

———. "Weekly Epidemiological Record," 31 (August 4, 2006). http://www.who.int/wer/2006/wer8131.pdf.

———. *Women's Health: Across Age and Frontier.* New York: United Nations Press, 1992.

World Health Organization. "The World Health Report 2000: Health Systems: Improving Performance." 2000. http://www.who.int/whr/2000/en/whr00_en.pdf.

———. "WHO Marks Turning Point for 1 Billion People: Partners Commit to Global Action Against Forgotten Diseases." April 19, 2007. http://www.who.int/mediacentre/news/releases/2007/pr19/en/index.html.

World Resources Institute. "Demographics: Life Expectancy 2005–2010." http://www.earthtrends.wri.org.

———. "Earth Trends: Agriculture and Food." http://earth trends.wri.org/features/view_feature.php?theme=8&fid=24.

———. "Earth Trends: The Environmental Information Portal: Agriculture and Food (Nutrition: Calorie Supply per Capita)." http://earthtrends.wri.org/.

———. "Live Earth: The Concerts for a Climate in Crisis." 2007. http://earth trends.wri.org/updates/node/219.

———. "Population, Health and Human Well-Being—Public Health: Contraceptive Prevalence Rate." http://earthtrends.wri.org.

———. World Resources 1996–1997. New York: Oxford University Press, 1996.

World Trade Organization (WTO). "What Is the WTO?" http://www.wto.org/english/thewto_e/whatis_e/tif_e/fact4_e.htm.

Worldwatch Institute. "Global Fossil Fuel Consumption Surges." May 9, 2005. http://www.worldwatch.org/node/1811.

"World Water Day 2005." http://www.worldwaterday.org/page/130.

World Wildlife Fund. "How Is WWF Organized." http://www.panda.org/about_wwf/who_we_are/offices/organization.cfm.

———. "Preserving Fresh Water—WWF's Work and What You Can Do to Help." 2006. http://worldwildlife.org/earthday/freshwater-work.cfm.

———. "WWF—The Global Conservation Organization." http://www.panda.org/about_wwf/who_we_are/index.cfm.

Yergin, Daniel. Shattered Peace: The Origins of the Cold War, 2nd ed. New York: Penguin, 1990.

———. The Prize: The Epic Quest for Oil, Money & Power. New York: Simon & Schuster, 1991.

Ye, Zhang. "Hope for China's Migrant Women Workers." The China Business Review (2002). http//www.chinabusinessreview.com/public/0205.ye.html.

Young, Crawford. The Politics of Cultural Pluralism. Madison: University of Wisconsin Press, 1976.

Young, Oran R. International Cooperation: Building Regimes for Natural Resources and the Environment. Ithaca. NY: Cornell University Press, 1989.

———. "Regime Dynamics: The Rise and Fall of International Regimes." International Organization 36 (1982): 277–297.

———. "Review: International Regimes: Toward a New Theory of Institutions." World Politics 39 (1986): 104–122.

Zakaria, Fareed. From Wealth to Power: The Unusual Origins of America's World Role. Princeton, NJ: Princeton University Press, 1998.

Sources of Illustrations

Chapter 1

PHOTO 1.1   AP Photo/Hassan Amini
PHOTO 1.2   Thomas CoexAFP/Getty Images
MAP 1.2   Korean Culture and Information Service (KOCIS)
PAGE 2   Lasse Kristensen/shutterstock images
PAGE 15   9 Chickweed Lane reprinted by permission of the United Feature Syndicate

Chapter 2

FIGURE 2.1   Climate Change 2007: Synthesis Report. Contribution of Working Groups I, II and III to the Fourth Assessment Report of the Intergovernmental Panel on Climate Change, Figure I.1. IPCC, Geneva, Switzerland.
PHOTO 2.1   AP Photo/Color China Photo
PHOTO 2.2   AP Photo
PHOTO 2.3   Culver Pictures
PHOTO 2.5   AP Photo/Susan Walsh
PAGE 18   Imaginechina via AP Images
PAGE 27   Copyright © 1996 United Feature Syndicate, Inc.

Chapter 3

MAP 3.1   From Spiegel/Taw/Wehling/Williams. World Politics in a New Era (with CD-ROM and InfoTrac®), 3E. © 2004 Wadsworth, a part of Cengage Learning, Inc. Reproduced by permission. www.cengage.com/permissions.
MAP 3.2   From Spiegel/ Taw/ Wehling/ Williams. World Politics in a New Era (with CD-ROM and InfoTrac®), 3E. © 2004 Wadsworth, a part of Cengage Learning, Inc. Reproduced by permission. www.cengage.com/permissions
PHOTO 3.1   Réunion des Musées Nationaux / Art Resource, NY
MAP 3.3   From Spiegel/ Taw/ Wehling/ Williams. World Politics in a New Era (with CD-ROM and InfoTrac®), 3E. © 2004 Wadsworth, a part of Cengage Learning, Inc. Reproduced by permission. www.cengage.com/permissions
MAP 3.4   From Spiegel/ Taw/ Wehling/ Williams. World Politics in a New Era (with CD-ROM and InfoTrac®), 3E. © 2004 Wadsworth, a part of Cengage Learning, Inc. Reproduced by permission. www.cengage.com/permissions
PHOTO 3.2   Adoc-photos / Art Resource, NY
MAP 3.5   From Spiegel/ Taw / Wehling/ Williams. World Politics in a New Era (with CD-ROM and InfoTrac®), 3E. © 2004 Wadsworth, a part of Cengage Learning, Inc. Reproduced by permission. www.cengage.com/permissions
PHOTO 3.3   Hulton Archive/Getty Images
PHOTO 3.4   Culver Pictures

MAP 3.6	From Spiegel/Taw/Wehling/Williams. World Politics in a New Era (with CD-ROM and InfoTrac®), 3E. © 2004 Wadsworth, a part of Cengage Learning, Inc. Reproduced by permission. www.cengage.com/permissions
MAP 3.7	From Spiegel/Taw/Wehling/Williams. World Politics in a New Era (with CD-ROM and InfoTrac®), 3E. © 2004 Wadsworth, a part of Cengage Learning, Inc. Reproduced by permission. www.cengage.com/permissions
PHOTO 3.6	AP/Str
PAGE 58	Hulton Archive/Getty Images

Chapter 4

MAP 4.1	From Spiegel/Taw/Wehling/Williams. World Politics in a New Era (with CD-ROM and InfoTrac®), 3E. © 2004 Wadsworth, a part of Cengage Learning, Inc. Reproduced by permission. www.cengage.com/permissions
PHOTO 4.1	AP Photo
MAP 4.2	From Spiegel/Taw/Wehling/Williams. World Politics in a New Era (with CD-ROM and InfoTrac®), 3E. © 2004 Wadsworth, a part of Cengage Learning, Inc. Reproduced by permission. www.cengage.com/permissions
PHOTO 4.2	AP Photo/U.S. Department of Defense
PHOTO 4.3	AP Photo
PHOTO 4.4	AFP/Getty Images
PHOTO 4.6	AP Photo/U.S. White House
PAGE 110	(AP-Photo) 25.10.1961
PAGE 143	Ranan Lurie, 1970 by permission of Cartoonews International Syndicate

Chapter 5

PHOTO 5.2	Culver Pictures
PHOTO 5.3	AP Photo
PHOTO 5.4	Culver Pictures
PHOTO 5.5	AP Photo/Peter DeJong
PAGE 156	SSPL/Getty Images

Chapter 6

PHOTO 6.1	The European Convention: http://european-convention.eu.int/images/gallery/conv47co.jpg
PHOTO 6.2	AP Photo/Charles Dharapak
PHOTO 6.3	Andrews/Reuters/Corbis
PHOTO 6.4	Gianluigi Guercia/AFP/Getty Images
PHOTO 6.5	Mirrorpix/Getty Images
PHOTO 6.7	Indranil Mukherjee/AFP/Getty Images
PAGE 200	AP Photo/Amy Sancetta

Chapter 7

PHOTO 7.1	Bildarchiv Preussischer Kulturbesitz / Art Resource, NY
PHOTO 7.2	AP Photo/Daily Record/Tony Nicoletti/Pool
PHOTO 7.3	Israeli Aircraft Industries via Getty Images

PHOTO 7.4	AP Photo/Alex Brandon
PHOTO 7.5	AP Photo/Hasan Jamali
PAGE 238	AP Photo/Gurinder Osan
PAGE 272	© 2007 Cam Cardow, The Ottawa Citizen, and PoliticalCartoons.com

Chapter 8

PHOTO 8.1	AP Photo, File
PHOTO 8.3	AP Photo
PHOTO 8.4	Chris Rainier/Getty Images
PAGE 292	© Shaul Schwarz/Corbis
PAGE 301	© 2006 Florida Today
PAGE 323	www.CartoonStock.com

Chapter 9

PHOTO 9.1	Robert Gilhooly/Bloomberg via Getty Images
FIG. 9.1	Danmarks Nationalbank
PHOTO 9.2	AP Photo/Richard Drew
PHOTO 9.3	Jovan Nikolic/Shutterstock images
FIG. 9.2	Global Policy Forum: http://www.globalpolicy.org/tables-and-charts-ql/ social-and-economic-policy-tcql/foreign-direct-investment-tcql.html
PHOTO 9.4	Toussaint Kluiters/AFP/Getty Images
PHOTO 9.5	Jaafar Ashtiyeh/AFP/Getty Images
PHOTO 9.7	AP Photo/David Longstreath
PAGE 336	AP Photo/The Canadian Press,Adrian Wyld
PAGE 353	Cartoon by Jeff Danziger, New York Times Syndicate

Chapter 10

PHOTO 10.1	Peter Jordan//Time Life Pictures/Getty Images
PHOTO 10.2	AP Photo/David Longstreath
PHOTO 10.3	Paula Bronstein/Getty Images
PHOTO 10.4	AP Photo/Ajit Solanki
FIG. 10.1	© Freedom House, Inc.
PHOTO 10.5	Fethi Belaid/AFP/Getty Images
PAGE 378	© Jan S. / Shutterstock Images

Chapter 11

FIG. 11.1	United Nations, World Population Prospects: The 1994 Revision; U.S. Census Bureau, International Programs Center, International Data Base and unpublished tables
PHOTO 11.1	AP Photo/Ed Wray
PHOTO 11.2	AP Photo/Shabbir Hussain Imam
PAGE 426	© Carlos Barria/Reuters/Corbis
PAGE 443	By permission of John Sherffius and Creators Syndicate, Inc

Chapter 12

Chapter 13

Chapter 14

Index